ENCYCLOPEDIA OF COMPUTER SCIENCE AND TECHNOLOGY

VOLUME 41

ENCYCLOPEDIA OF COMPUTER SCIENCE AND TECHNOLOGY

EXECUTIVE EDITORS

Allen Kent   James G. Williams

UNIVERSITY OF PITTSBURGH
PITTSBURGH, PENNSYLVANIA

ADMINISTRATIVE EDITOR

Carolyn M. Hall

ARLINGTON, TEXAS

VOLUME 41
SUPPLEMENT 26

 **CRC Press**
Taylor & Francis Group
Boca Raton London New York

CRC Press is an imprint of the
Taylor & Francis Group, an **informa** business

First published 1999 by Marcel Dekker, Inc.

Published 2021 by CRC Press
Taylor & Francis Group
6000 Broken Sound Parkway NW, Suite 300
Boca Raton, FL 33487-2742

© 1999 by Taylor & Francis Group, LLC
CRC Press is an imprint of Taylor & Francis Group,
an Informa business

No claim to original U.S. Government works

ISBN 13: 978-0-8247-2294-4 (hbk)

**Visit the Taylor & Francis Web site at
http://www.taylorandfrancis.com**

**and the CRC Press Web site at
http://www.crcpress.com**

LIBRARY OF CONGRESS CATALOG CARD NUMBER; 74-29436

CONTENTS OF VOLUME 41

CONTENTS OF VOLUME 41

CONTRIBUTORS TO VOLUME 41

CARLA E. BRODLEY, Ph.D.   Assistant Professor, School of Electrical and Computer Engineering, Purdue University, West Lafayette, Indiana: *Machine Learning*

JEFF A. CLOUSE, Ph.D.   CAP Consulting Services, Jamestown, North Carolina: *Machine Learning*

KOFI KISSI DOMPERE   Associate Professor, Department of Economics, Howard University, Washington, D.C.: *Cost–Benefit Analysis of Information Technology*

JACK DONGARRA   Department of Computer Science, University of Tennessee, Knoxville, Tennessee and Computer Science and Mathematics Division, Oak Ridge National Laboratory, Oak Ridge, Tennessee: *Numerical Linear Algebra*

VICTOR EIJKHOUT   Department of Computer Science, University of Tennessee, Knoxville, Tennessee: *Numerical Linear Algebra*

ROBERT J. HAMMELL II, Ph.D.   Senior Computer Scientist, United States Army Research Laboratory, Aberdeen Proving Ground, Maryland: *Learning, Adaptivity, and Complexity in a Hierarchical Fuzzy Model*

CHRIS HANKIN   Professor of Computing Science, Department of Computing, The Imperial College of Science, Technology and Medicine, London, England: *Models of Computation*

C. M. KRISHNA   Department of Electrical and Computer Engineering, College of Engineering, University of Massachusetts, Amherst, Massachusetts: *Cache Memory*

JAMES T. LUXHOJ, Ph.D.   Associate Professor, Department of Industrial Engineering, Rutgers University, Piscataway, New Jersey: *Application of Bayesian Belief Networks to Highway Construction*

NADIA MAGNENAT-THALMANN   Professor, MIRALab, University of Geneva, Geneva, Switzerland: *Virtual Reality Software and Technology*

INDERJEET MANI, Ph.D.   The MITRE Corporation, Reston, Virginia: *Intelligent Scalable Text Summarization*

MARK-JAN NEDERHOF, Ph.D.   German Research Center for Artificial Intelligence GmbH, Saarbrucken, Germany: *Efficient Generation of Random Sentences*

JAMES A. REGGIA   Department of Computer Science and Neurology, University of Maryland, College Park, Maryland: *Neural Network Modeling of Brain and Cognitive Disorders*

PANOS RONDOGIANNIS, Ph.D.   Department of Computer Science, University of Ioannina, Ioannina, Greece: *Intensional Programming Languages*

EYTAN RUPPIN   Department of Computer Science and Physiology, Tel-Aviv University, Tel-Aviv, Israel: *Neural Network Modeling of Brain and Cognitive Disorders*

COSTEL SÂRBU, Ph.D.   Associate Professor, Department of Analytical Chemistry, Faculty of Chemistry and Chemical Engineering, Babeş-Bolyai University, Cluj-Napoca, Romania: *Information Energy and Its Applications*

SANJAY SINGH   University of Waterloo, Waterloo, Ontario, Canada: *User Documentation*

THOMAS A. SUDKAMP, Ph.D.   Professor, Department of Computer Science, Wright State University, Dayton, Ohio: *Learning, Adaptivity, and Complexity in a Hierarchical Fuzzy Model*

DANIEL THALMANN   Professor, Computer Graphics Laboratory, Swiss Federal Institute of Technology, Lausanne, Switzerland: *Virtual Reality Software and Technology*

RICHARD A. THOMPSON   Telecommunications Program, University of Pittsburgh, Pittsburgh, Pennsylvania: *Optical Fiber Communications*

W. W. WADGE   Department of Computer Science, University of Victoria, Victoria, British Columbia, Canada: *Intensional Programming Languages*

TREFOR P. WILLIAMS, Ph.D.   Associate Professor, Department of Civil and Environmental Engineering, Rutgers University, Piscataway, New Jersey: *Application of Bayesian Belief Networks to Highway Construction*

PHILIP A. WILSEY   Computer Architecture Design Laboratory, Department of ECECS, University of Cincinnati, Cincinnati, Ohio: *Modeling, Analysis, and Simulation of Computer and Telecommunication Systems*

ENCYCLOPEDIA OF COMPUTER SCIENCE AND TECHNOLOGY

VOLUME 41

APPLICATION OF BAYESIAN BELIEF NETWORKS TO HIGHWAY CONSTRUCTION

INTRODUCTION

Construction projects are becoming increasingly complex. The construction of highways is a dynamic process that requires the use of complex equipment in an uncontrolled environment. When new highways are constructed, or old highways reconstructed, it is important to provide the highest possible construction quality. Deficient quality can lead to a highway that will not provide the maximum service life possible before reconstruction is necessary. A poorly constructed highway will also be more expensive to maintain, because it will require more frequent maintenance.

Because of monetary constraints, construction contractors and owner agencies, such as state departments of transportation, may not be able to provide construction experts to monitor the quality of highway construction on a full-time basis. Often, inexperienced engineers and inspectors are required to make decisions about the quality and acceptability of new construction. Construction mistakes can have a profound effect on the quality of the constructed roadway. Therefore, there has been considerable interest in providing computerized decision support systems at the construction site to support engineers with improved decision-making information. Potentially, the expert knowledge about construction processes can be made available to less experienced engineers, and improve highway construction quality.

Bayesian belief networks are an emerging area for the development of diagnostic systems. In particular, they hold considerable promise for application to highway construction problems because they do not require as extensive a knowledge acquisition phase as rule-based expert systems.

Problems with Rule-Based Systems

There has been considerable study of the use of rule-based expert systems of Civil Engineering problems. Several prototype rule-based systems have been developed in the area of highway construction (1,2). However, the limitations of rule-based expert systems did not allow for the full development and use of many of these systems. It was found that much of an expert's reasoning could not be easily incorporated in the format of rules or example tables.

For many experts, it is difficult to verbalize rules. Johnson (3) has postulated that there are three stages in which humans acquire cognitive skills. These stages are cognitive, associative, and autonomous. A construction expert's knowledge is in the autonomous stage. At this level of cognition, the expert compiles the relationship from repeated practice stages to the point where the expert can perform them without conscious awareness. At this stage, the knowledge has become tacit. This knowledge is difficult to obtain because tacit knowledge is not accessible to conscious awareness and introspection. Consequently, the Bayesian belief network technique offers a method that does not force experts to answer questions they cannot reliably answer.

It was found that experts are not often available for extensive knowledge-acquisition sessions. In developing a rule-based system for asphalt paving, it was found that paving experts could not devote sufficient time to developing rules (4). The primary asphalt paving expert was responsible for approximately 70 projects covering a wide geographic area. The expert was not available to delve deeply into the rules pertaining to paving. It was also found that uncertainty was difficult to incorporate into the expert system, and the final rule-based system developed did not use uncertainty factors.

Bayesian Belief Networks

Recently, artificial intelligence researchers have focused on the development of expert systems based on a probabilistic scheme in which the structure of domain knowledge is represented in a directed graph. This approach makes the domain structure explicit and utilizes the topology of the graph. A Bayesian belief network is a graph where the nodes represent domain objects and the links between nodes represent casual relationships between the objects. The relationships expressed by the links are represented by conditional probabilities. Together with methods derived from Bayesian decision theory, this formalism offers a consistent means of handling uncertainty inherent in the expert systems (5). Details of this method are given by Pearl (6).

ASPHALT PAVING EXAMPLE

Asphalt paving was selected as an example of a Bayesian belief network application in highway construction. This topic was selected because it is complex and poorly understood by many construction field personnel. Many factors affect the quality of asphalt paving during construction. Variations can occur in the quality of the material and the operation of the asphalt paver. Complex interactions can occur among the various mechanical components of the paving machine that cause a reduction in the quality of the completed pavement. If a severe paving problem is allowed to persist, the service life of the pavement can be seriously reduced.

The construction of modern asphalt concrete highway pavements is accomplished using a bituminous paver that spreads the asphalt mixture in a uniform layer of the desired thickness and finishes the layer to the required elevation and cross section. During construction, the asphalt mixture, prepared at a batch plant, is dumped into the receiving hopper of the paver by trucks. Material is fed from the hopper toward the finishing section of the machine, where it is agitated by an auger to ensure that the mix is uniform and spreads evenly. The spread material is then struck off at the required elevation by a screed (7).

The construction of asphalt pavements is fast-moving and requires inspectors to quickly interpret the quality of the construction. Often, inexperienced inspectors cannot correctly identify or interpret a construction deficiency as it is occurring. Traditional sources of information, such as standard specifications and reference manuals, are difficult to use during the dynamic paving construction operation. Additionally, paving experts are scarce and may not be available when a problem is occurring. Therefore, a decision support system to provide rapid diagnosis of paving problems in the field could significantly increase the quality of construction and reduce future maintenance costs.

Asphalt Paving Construction Problems

There are many problems that can occur during the construction of an asphalt concrete pavement. Very often during paving, several interrelated paving problems can be observed. These problems are well documented (8,9). The most common asphalt paving problems during construction of the pavement mat are as follows:

- Tearing of the pavement mat
- Wavy surface
- Screed marks
- Nonuniform mix texture
- Screed responsiveness

All of these construction problems can have significant effects on the rideability, serviceability, and life of a pavement. If not corrected, these problems can result in a paving project that provides motorists with a low quality ride, and a pavement that will require more frequent maintenance.

There are three types of mat tearing: full-width tearing, center streaks, and outside streaks. Tearing of the pavement mat causes changes in mixture density. Areas of tearing are susceptible to premature raveling caused by the rough texture of the mat adjacent to the tear.

Typically, there are two types of surface waves that occur during construction. There are short waves or ripples, and long waves. These waves affect paving performance by reducing the smoothness of the pavement.

Screed marks are longitudinal and transverse indentations in the pavement. Screed marks affect the quality of ride by creating a bump wherever visible. Nonuniform mat texture can be described as a difference of appearance of the asphalt mixture as it is placed. This nonuniform texture can have significant effects on the fatigue life and serviceability of the pavement.

Screed responsiveness refers to the ability of the screed to react to changes in paver thickness control settings. An unresponsive screed causes a rough asphalt concrete mat. The rideability of the pavement can be significantly reduced.

Problem Diagnoses

There are nine basic diagnoses: the asphalt mix temperature is too cold; the screed of the paving machine is too cold; the speed of the paver is too fast; the screed needs to be replaced; the flow gates of the paving machine need to be adjusted; the screed extensions need to be adjusted; the screed needs to be repaired; the paver is stopped between loads of asphalt; and the improper use of paver thickness controls. In many situations, multiple diagnoses may be applicable.

There is an optimum placement temperature for asphalt mixtures. If a truck is delayed enroute from the batch plant, it may be too cold. All paving inspectors carry thermometers to check the temperature. If the mix is too cold, the truck should be rejected. The paving machine is self-propelled and produces the best quality pavement at a speed of 5 miles per hour. The operator can easily reduce the speed if it is going too fast.

The screed is intended to float automatically over depressions or irregularities during paving. Often, inexperienced operators attempt to adjust the screed height too often by using the manual thickness control crank. Adjustments should be made sparingly.

The flow from the paver hopper to the auger is adjusted by a control on the paver. These gates should be adjusted when there is too much or little asphalt mix at the auger. Ideally, the level of material should be half of the auger height. The screed of the paving machine can become worn out, and it may need to be replaced. The screed can also become warped, or mechanical connections in the screed can become worn out. In this case, the screed will need to be repaired. The paver should never be stopped between truckloads of asphalt material. Trucks should be scheduled so there is a constant supply of material.

Table 1 shows a matrix of the common paving deficiencies and the related problem diagnosis. Some of the diagnoses are very simple. For example, if longitudinal screed marks are observed, it means that the screed extensions need to be adjusted. However, other relationships are more subtle. The diagnosis of a wavy surface problem depends on the length of the wave, the condition of the paver screed, the use of paver settings, and whether trucks approach the paver without bumping it.

Network Development

The Bayesian belief network was developed using an expert system shell called HUGIN. This program provides tools to create a Bayesian belief network. The software allows the developer to create a graphical interface to the domain structure of a problem. The software also provides tools for entering quantitative information about the state of the domain and for propagating this in the network (5). The Hugin program employs the Algebra of Bayesian Beliefs. This scheme is a simplification of the algorithm's developed by Lauritzen and Spiegelhalter (10).

The first step in developing the system is to formulate the problem in the form of a Bayesian belief network. Figure 1 shows the asphalt paving network. The network is composed of three layers. The top-layer nodes are the paving problems that can be observed during construction. These are the problems described earlier. The bottom layer

TABLE 1   Construction Problems and Possible Diagnoses

	Cold mix	Cold screed	Speed	Adjust screed	Replace screed	Adjust flow gates	Repair screed	Paver stops	Bumping	Adjust extensions	Use of controls
Center mat tearing				X		X					
Outside mat tearing				X		X					
Full mat tearing	X	X	X		X	X					
Texture	X	X				X	X				
Screed marks							X	X		X	
Wavy surface						X			X		
Screed not responsive			X				X				X

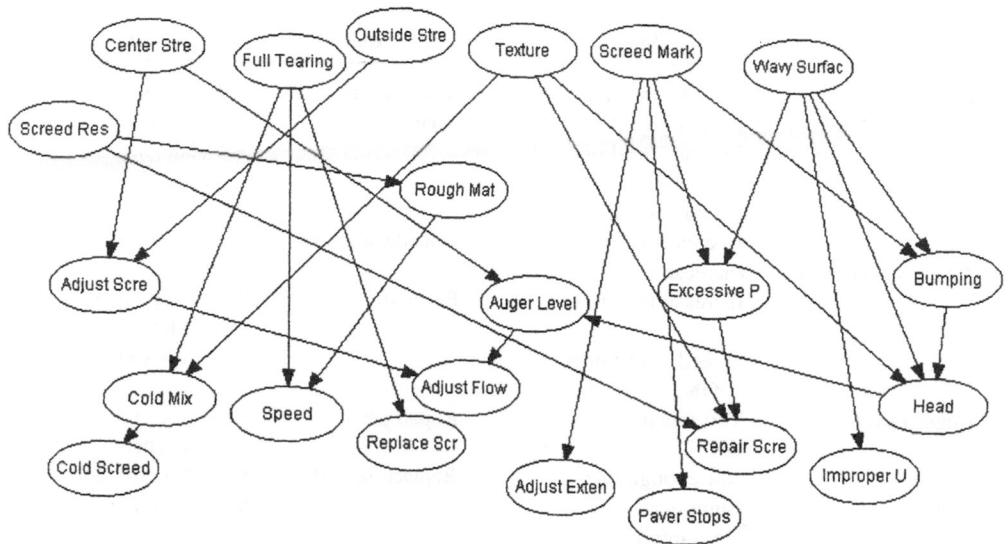

FIGURE 1   Asphalt paving belief network.

consists of diagnoses for the paving problems. The intermediate layer represents additional information necessary to make a specific diagnosis.

Nodal States

The second step in developing the system is to determine the possible states for each node in the Bayesian belief network. For example, the Auger level node has three possible states. There can be too little mix, the auger can have the right amount of mix, or the auger can be buried with too much material. Table 2 provides a list of the possible states of each node.

Defining Probabilities

The third phase in developing the model is to determine the numeric part of each link. This is accomplished through the use of conditional probability tables. For each node, we input a conditional probability for each node given the state of its parent nodes. The sum of the probabilities of the states of a node must equal 1. Figure 2 shows an example of the conditional probabilities entered for the "Repair Screed" node.

These probabilities were defined through the use of expert knowledge. Asphalt paving experts were shown an initial version of the probabilities and they suggested revisions based on their experience.

INTERACTIVE PROBLEM SOLVING

The Hugin program allows the model users to adjust the probabilities of states of nodes based on observed information. The software propagates this change through the network and updates the conditional probabilities at each node based on the new information.

TABLE 2   Node States

Node	State	Node	State
Adjust extensions	Adjust extensions	Improper use of	Changing manual
	Do not adjust	controls	thickness crank
Adjust flow gates	Increase head of		Not changing
	material		frequently
	No adjustment		
	Decrease head	Outside streaks	Yes
Adjust screed crown	Increase lead crown		No
	Increase tail crown	Paver stops	Paver stops between
			truckloads
	Screed adjustment		Paver does not stop
	OK		
Auger Level	Too much mix	Repair screed	Repair screed
	OK		Do not repair
	Not enough mix	Replace screed	Screed worn out
Bumping	Bumping		Screed warped
	No bumping		Screed OK
Center streaks	Yes	Rough mat	Mat OK
	No		Mat rough
Cold mix	Mix cold	Screed marks	Transverse
	Mix OK		Longitudinal
Cold screed	Cold screed		None
	Screed temperature	Screed responsive	Yes
	OK		No
Excessive play in	Screed OK	Speed	Fast
screed connections	Excessive play in		Normal
	screed connections	Texture	Uniform
			Nonuniform
		Wavy surface	Ripples
			Long waves
			No waves
Full tearing	Yes		
	No		
Head	Fluctuating head		
	Head normal		

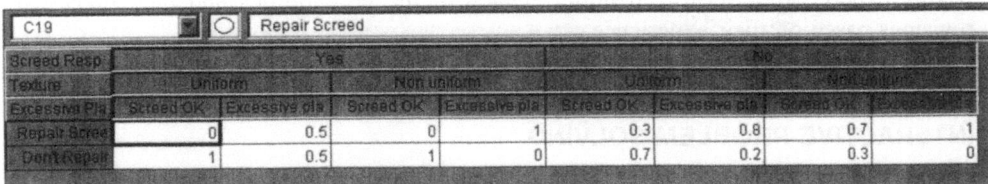

FIGURE 2   Conditional probabilities for the "Repair Screed" node.

Figure 3, a screen snapshot from the Hugin program, shows the unperturbed conditional probabilities. If we observe a paving problem, such as center streaks, and change its probability to 100% (i.e., we have found "evidence" of center streaks), the software can propagate the effects of this new knowledge through the network. Figure 4 shows the changes in conditional probabilities. Note that the probabilities for a diagnosis of not enough mix at the auger and opening the flow gates is greatly increased. An engineer monitoring asphalt paving could use this system in the field using a laptop computer. If a paving problem occurs, the engineer could receive a rapid diagnosis of the problem.

CONCLUSIONS

The asphalt paving Bayesian belief network illustrates several features that make the development of Bayesian belief networks attractive. The knowledge acquisition effort required is less than a rule-based expert system. The knowledge of the system is embodied in the structure of the network and the conditional probabilities assigned to each node. There is no need for experts to elucidate complex rules. The initial network devel-

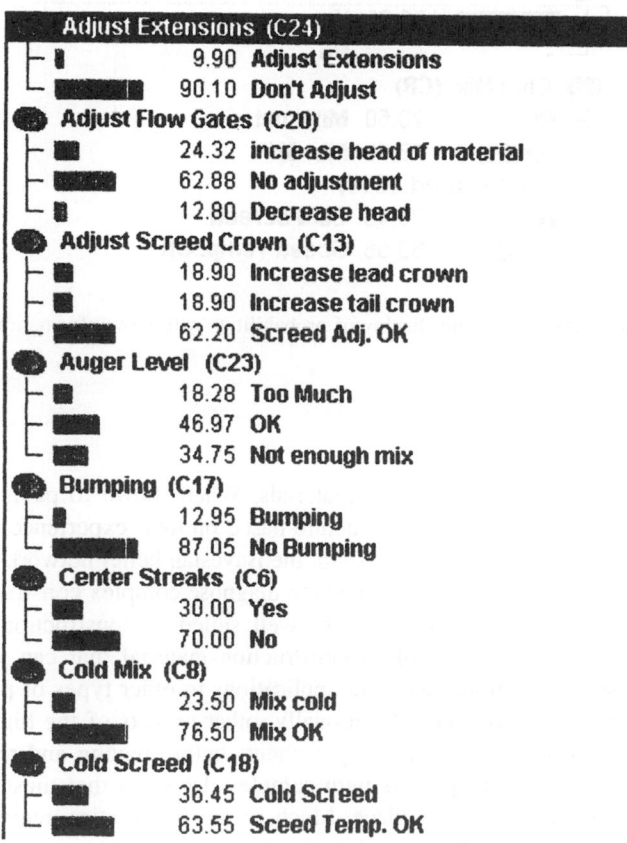

FIGURE 3 Hugin display of initial node probabilities.

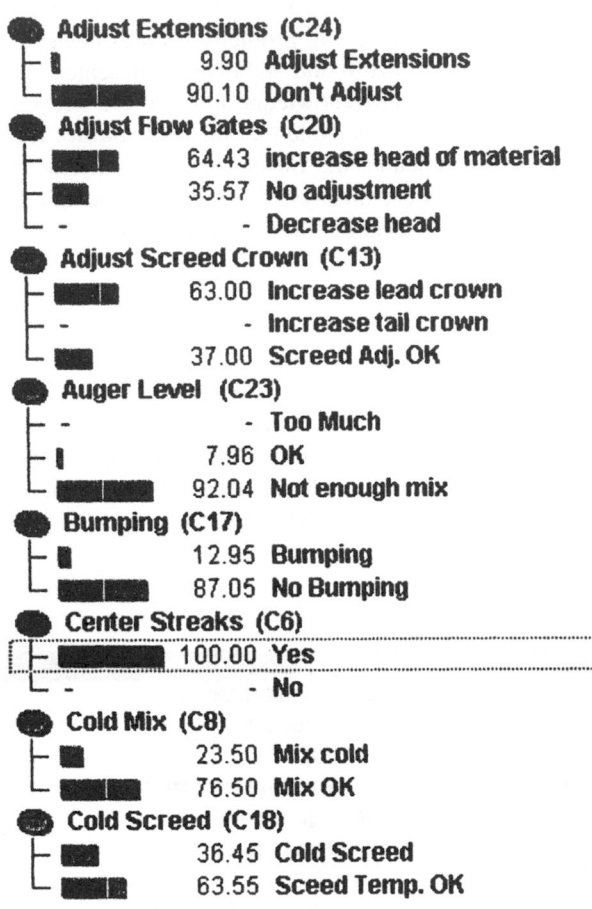

FIGURE 4   Hugin display of probabilities with new information.

oped was based on available reference materials. When shown to paving experts, they were able to suggest revisions to the structure based on their experience.

Based on the prototype asphalt system, the Bayesian belief network approach holds great promise for developing usable systems to diagnose complex construction problems. Specifically, this modeling approach seems well suited to construction processes that require complex machinery to apply a construction material that can vary in quality. Examples of possible additional uses are applications to other types of paving materials such as Portland cement concrete. Additionally, other aspects of the highway construction process such as milling of existing pavements before paving and reconstruction of drainage structures present inspectors with complex decisions that must be made while the construction process is taking place. Much of the information required is not well documented. Potentially, the Bayesian belief network approach can provide an efficient method for capturing the knowledge of construction experts.

REFERENCES

1. R. A. Harris, L. F. Cohn, and W. Bowlley, *J. Transport Eng.*, *113*, 127 (1987).
2. K. T. Hall, et al., *Roads Bridges*, *26*(4), 35 (1988).
3. P. E. Johnson, *J. Med. Phil.*, *7*, 77 (1983).
4. T. P. Williams, R. C. Parks, and J. J. LiMarzi, *J. Construct. Eng. Manag.*, *4*, 370 (1990).
5. S. K. Andersen, K. G. Andersen, F. V. Jensen, and F. Jensen, "Hugin—A Shell for Building Bayesian Belief Universes for Expert Systems," in Proceedings of the Eleventh International Joint Conference on Artificial Intelligence, 1989, pp. 1080–1085.
6. J. Pearl, *Probabilistic Reasoning in Intelligent Systems*: *Networks of Plausible Inference*, Morgan Kaufman, San Mateo, CA, 1988, p. 1.
7. P. Wright, *Highway Engineering*, John Wiley & Sons, New York, 1996, p. 545.
8. J. A. Scherocman and E. D. Martensen, *Placement and Compaction of Asphalt Mixtures* (F. T. Wagner (ed.), ASTM Special Technical Publication 829, ASTM, Philadelphia, PA, 1984, p. 3.
9. *Hot Mix Asphalt Paving Handbook*, AC 150/5370-14 Appendix 1, U.S. Army Corps of Engineers, Washington, DC, pp. 3–89.
10. S. L. Lauritzen and D. J. Spieglehalter, *J. Roy. Statist. Soc.*, *50*, 157 (1988).

TREFOR P. WILLIAMS

JAMES T. LUXHOJ

CACHE MEMORY

INTRODUCTION

A cache is a high-speed, and relatively small, memory which is used to hold the most frequently accessed contents of the main memory. The idea is that if most of the accesses made by a program are to a small subset of the main memory and if that subset can be brought into the cache, most of the program accesses will be done at cache speed. This allows one to mask the relative slowness of the main memory.

Caches are typically much smaller than the main memory. At the time of writing this article, a typical workstation would have a 16–32-KByte cache and a main memory of between 16 and 128 MBytes. Caches run at CPU speed,* whereas the main memory runs over an order of magnitude slower.

The usefulness of caches is motivated by the following factors:

F1. The speed of both CPUs and RAMs has increased greatly over the past several years. However, because high-speed memory is expensive, the computer's main memory consists of RAMs, which are much slower than the CPU they serve. As technology advances, this speed differential is expected to become worse, not better. Without some mechanism to compensate for this differential, the memory will become the performance bottleneck of a computer, vitiating any advances in processor speeds. A cache is such a compensatory mechanism.

F2. Communication between entities is much faster if they are both on the same VLSI chip than if they are on different chips. However, because the area of a chip is limited (mainly due to yield considerations: the larger a chip, the smaller the yield tends to be), one cannot place both the CPU and the entire main memory on the same chip. However, caches are often small enough to fit on the same chip as the processor. This greatly speeds up access to the cache.

F3. Software generally exhibits *locality* of addressing; that is, if one examines the sequence of addresses generated by a process, it does not wander randomly over the entire real address space, but is usually limited to a subset of that space. Successive accesses tend to be correlated; that is, if access i is to memory location m, access $i + 1$ is generally to some memory location close to m. This is, of course, not always the case: Branches in code or the accessing of sparse arrays will generally break such correlation. However, in most instances, this correlation tends to hold. Locality ensures that even a small cache can hold over 90% of the accesses made by a program.

---

*This is true only of first-level caches. We will describe multilevel caches later.

This article is organized as follows. First, we present a brief technical background, to acquaint users with the basics of cache organization. We then discuss variations of the basic cache organization, including virtually addressed caches, victim caches, and separate instruction and data caches. Next, we explain how to model or to efficiently simulate caches. Finally, we discuss algorithms to ensure *coherence* among the multiple caches of a multiprocessor system.

CACHE BASICS

Access Time

When a processor seeks to read or write a word in memory, it first checks the cache to see if that word is in the cache. If it is, a *hit* is said to take place. If it is not, and we have to access main memory, a *miss* is said to occur. The *miss rate*, m, of a cache is the fraction of accesses which encounter a miss. The *hit* rate is $h = 1 - m$.

Let us denote the cache access time by t_{cache} and the main memory access time by t_{main}. Ignore page faults. Then, the expected access time of the memory system is given by

$$t_{access} = ht_{cache} + mt_{main}$$

$$= \left[1 + m\left(\frac{t_{main}}{t_{cache}} - 1 \right) \right] t_{cache}. \qquad [1]$$

We can see from Eq. (1) that the impact of a cache miss is proportional to the ratio t_{main}/t_{cache}. The greater this ratio, the greater the need to keep the miss rate low. This is graphically shown in Figure 1.

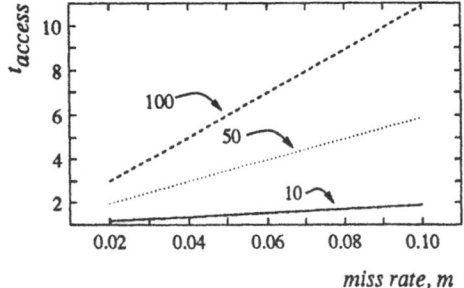

FIGURE 1   Impact of speed differential on expected access time. The line labels indicate main memory access time; the time unit is the cache access time.

Cache Organization

When a cache miss occurs, the missing item must be brought in from main memory. The unit of transfer is usually not a single byte, but rather a *line* (also called a *block*) containing the desired byte. If an L-byte line is used, line k consists of the contents of addresses $kL, kL + 1, \ldots, (k + 1)L - 1$. A byte whose address is $b_{m-1}b_{m-2} \ldots b_0$ belongs to a line whose line address is $b_{m-1}b_{m-2} \ldots b_l$, where $l = \log_2 L$.

Example 0: Suppose we have 4-byte lines. Then, line 0 consists of the contents of addresses 0, 1, 2, 3; line 1 of addresses 4, 5, 6, 7; and so on. If we have 24-bit addresses, then the line address of the line to which address 5 belongs is 0000 0000 0000 0000 01. (The gaps between the groups of bits are only to make the number easier to read; they have no technical significance.)

Most caches follow the set-associative organization. A cache is subdivided into S non-overlapping sets, $S_0, \ldots, S_{s-1}$. Set S_i is restricted to holding lines whose line address satisfies the equation

$$(\text{line address}) \bmod s = i.$$

Example 1: Suppose we have a cache with four sets, S_0, S_1, S_2, and S_3. Let the lines consist of 16 bytes each. Then, set S_i is restricted to holding lines whose line address satisfies the equation

$$(\text{line address}) \bmod 4 = i.$$

The address of a byte can be subdivided into fields as shown in Figure 2. The first $l = \log_2 L$ bits (starting from the right) specify the position of the byte in its line. The next $s = \log_2 S$ bits specify the set to which the byte belongs. In other words, if the byte is in the cache, it must be in the set specified by those bits. The remaining bits of the address form the *tag*. Associated with each line of the cache is a line in the cache directory, which contains the tag part of the address of the contents of that line.

When the processor generates an access request, the first thing to do is to check if the cache contains the requested byte(s). The set field of the address specifies the set of the cache in which the desired byte would be stored. The directory associated with that set is then checked to see if it contains the tag of the line to which reference has been made.

Example 2: Suppose we have a four-set cache. The address is 24 bits long and each line is 8 bytes long. The line address is $24 - \log_2 8 = 21$ bits long, and there are 2 bits to specify the set number. Suppose the CPU generates an access request 0010 0011 0111 0111 1111 1011. The line address corresponding to this is the byte address minus 3 (i.e., 0010 0011 0111 0111 1111 1). This address maps into set 11 of the cache and would

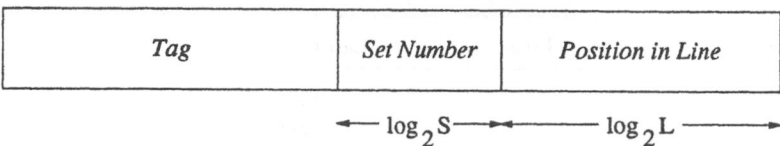

FIGURE 2   Fields of the address.

have a tag of 0010 0011 0111 0111 111. Therefore, when this request is generated, the system would check the cache directory associated with set 11 to see if it contained this tag. It so, we have a hit, and the desired byte is in the cache. If not, we have a miss, and the line containing this byte has to be brought into the cache.

A K-way cache is one that has K lines per set. If $K = 1$, the cache is said to be *direct mapped*. If the cache has only one set, it is said to be *fully associative*. The total size of a K-way cache whose line size is L and has S sets is

$$C = KLS \text{ bytes.} \qquad [2]$$

The size of the cache directory is a function of the cache organization. If the address length is α bits, then the tag has $\alpha - \log_2 S - \log_2 L$ bits. The number of lines in a cache of C bytes is given by C/L, so the total capacity of the cache directory is

$$\frac{C(\alpha - \log_2 S - \log_2 L)}{L} \text{ bits.} \qquad [3]$$

The ratio of the size of the cache directory to that of that of the cache is

$$\rho = \frac{\alpha - \log_2 S - \log_2 L}{L} \qquad [4]$$

Caches with short lines or few sets have relatively large cache directories.

Replacement Strategies

When a cache miss occurs, the line containing the referenced line has to be brought into the appropriate set of the cache. One of the lines currently in that set has to be replaced to make room for this new line. If the cache is direct-mapped, there is no choice to be made. If there is more than one line in the set, there are several ways in which the replaced line can be chosen.

The optimum strategy would be to replace the line, which will not be referenced again for the longest time into the future. This, however, is not realistic, because normally, the program has no prior intimation of which addresses will be accessed in the future.

Another strategy is Least Recently Used (LRU). When a miss occurs, we determine the set into which the new line will be brought. Of the lines in the set, we replace the one which has been least recently used.

Example 3: Table 1 indicates when the last reference happened to each line in set S_0 in a four-way cache. If a cache miss occurs which will require one of these lines to be

TABLE 1   Last Reference Times

Line	Last reference
0	1276
1	4218
2	1010
3	2333

replaced by a new line, we will replace the second line, as it was least recently referenced.

To support the LRU algorithm, we have to maintain information about the relative times at which each line was last accessed. This can prove expensive in terms of hardware.

A less expensive alternative is the random replacement algorithm. Here, we simply replace one line in the affected set at random. Caches with random replacement generally have miss rates 10 to 20% higher than those with LRU; the difference is most marked in fully associative configurations and is much smaller for two-way caches.*

Many variations exist on the above replacement strategies; for example, the Not Last Used algorithm keeps track of which line in each set was last used. The line to be replaced is chosen at random from all lines except the one which was last used in that set.

What do we do with a line that is replaced? In a *write-through* cache, the main memory is updated in parallel with the cache update. (To avoid stalling the CPU while the main memory write is in progress, we can write into a buffer and let the memory update complete at its own pace.) As a result, the main memory is always current, and the line being replaced can thus be simply discarded from the cache. In a *write-back* cache, the main memory is not updated in parallel with the cache. When a line is replaced, the system checks if it has been changed since it was read from the memory. If the answer is yes, the line is written back to the main memory; if not, then the main memory already has the current version, and the line can simply be discarded.

Split Caches

So far, we have implicitly assumed that a single cache contains both instructions and data. Instead, some machines have separate caches for each. Having separate caches allows one to double the number of cache ports: With a unified one-port cache, no data fetch can take place while an instruction fetch is in progress, and vice versa. Also, the optimum organization of the cache in terms of its line size and number of lines per set may be different for instruction and data caches.

Victim Cache

In addition to the cache, it is often useful to have a small (four to eight lines) fully associative memory that holds the last few lines which ejected from the cache. This is called the *victim cache*. A victim cache has the same access time as the cache itself. Upon a cache miss, the victim cache is checked to see if it can supply the referenced line. In experimental studies with a 4 KByte direct-mapped cache and a four-line victim cache,† it was found that between 20% and 95% of the misses on the cache were found in the victim cache. These misses can then avoid the delays in being accessed from the main memory.

A victim cache does not change the miss rate of the (main) cache. However, it does greatly reduce the miss penalty (i.e., the time taken to complete the access upon

---

*Note that there is a difference only for caches which are not direct-mapped.

†Meaning that the last four lines ejected from the cache are held in the victim cache.

a miss). Victim caches are the most useful in association with direct-mapped caches (why?).

Multilevel Caches

With the disparity between CPU and main-memory speeds set to increase over the next few years, multiple levels (most commonly two levels) of cache offer some advantages. In addition to the cache running at CPU speed (called the first-level cache), one can have a larger, second-level cache which is slower than the first-level cache but is still much faster than the main memory. Multilevel caches offer the designer another degree of freedom in the trade-off between cost and speed. Also, the designer has the freedom to place the first-level (L1) cache on the CPU chip while moving and the second-level (L2) cache to another chip.

Example 4: A first-level cache of size 32 KBytes is observed to have a miss rate of 0.04. A second-level cache of size 1 MByte is introduced which has a miss rate of 0.01. Access time of the caches and the memory are 5 ns, 25 ns, and 100 ns, respectively. The expected access time is then given by

$$0.96 \times 5 + 0.03 \times 25 + 0.01 \times 100 = 6.55 \text{ ns}.$$

Without the second-level cache, the expected access time would be

$$0.96 \times 5 + 0.04 \times 100 = 8.80 \text{ ns}.$$

Virtually Addressed Caches

Most cache directories hold the real address of their lines. This raises the need for a translation fom vitual to real addresses. One way of removing the need for such a translation is to use virtually addressed caches (i.e., have cache directories hold the virtual address of their lines).

To make a virtually addressed cache workable, we need to solve the aliasing problem; that is, it is possible for the same virtual address to represent two distinct real lines; conversely, it is possible for different virtual addresses from different processes to represent the same real line. This problem can be countered in two ways:

- Flush the cache whenever there is a context switch. This is done by simply invalidating the cache lines.
- Append the process ID (which generated the access that brought the line into cache) to the tag in the directory. Note that each process in the system has a unique tag.

Flushing the cache obviously worsens performance. Appending the process ID to the tag works well; however, it increases the size of the cache directory.

CACHE PERFORMANCE

The purpose of a cache is to reduce the average number of cycles per instruction (CPI). Cache performance is a function of the following:

- *Cache access time.* This includes the time to determine if the required item is in the cache, as well as the time taken in actually reading or writing. Determining if the access is a hit requires a parallel hardware search of the directory of the appropriate cache set. The greater the number of lines per set, the more complex is the logic associated with this search, and, hence, the longer it takes. All other things being equal, fully associative caches are therefore more time-consuming to access than direct-mapped caches.

- *Cache miss rate.* This is a function of the access pattern of the process and the cache size and organization. The miss rate tends to decrease as the locality of addressing exhibited by the process increases, or as the cache size increases. Cache organization also has an impact. For a fixed cache size, increasing the number of lines per set tends to decrease the miss rate. The reason is that the system is limited to placing a line to a set specified by the line address. If the individual sets are small, they are more likely to cause "thrashing." The difference in miss rates between fully associative and direct-mapped caches is greatest when the caches are small; it decreases as the cache size is increased.

  The advantage of having multibyte lines is that due to locality of addressing, a process access to a given address will very likely be followed by another access to either the next address in sequence or one close to it. It therefore makes sense to bring into the cache a cluster of bytes, rather than just 1 byte. However, as the line size is increased beyond a point, the risk increases that we are bringing into the cache bytes that will not be referenced by the program and that will displace bytes that might be needed in the future. As with the number of lines per set, the impact of very long line lengths is reduced as the cache size increases.

The computer designer is faced with the task of choosing the cache size and organization. This choice has a profound impact on the overall system performance and must be done extremely carefully. Too small a cache can result in a memory bottleneck. Too large a cache is a waste of money. Also, if the cache is to be placed on the same chip as the CPU, more area occupied by the cache leaves less for the CPU. In this section, we will outline simulation and analytical techniques to predict cache miss rates as a function of cache size and organization.

It is worth remarking at this point that probabilistic analysis and simulation are used differently. Because of the assumptions that must be made to render any analysis tractable, most analytical models are approximate. However, they are much cheaper to use (in terms of computer time) than simulations, and so are used to indicate a region of the parameter space that can then be investigated more accurately using simulation.

Cache Simulation

The first step in a cache simulation is to gather representative address traces. An *address trace* is the sequence of memory accesses made by the computer. It is very important that the address traces be representative of the workload that the computer is expected to run in real life. Traces are typically gathered by monitoring computers at representative consumer sites.

Once the traces have been gathered, they are used as inputs to a cache simulator. One data point on the miss rate can be obtained for each cache size and organization (number of sets, lines per set, bytes per line) that the designer wishes to consider. The caches being studied are called *target caches*.

Cache simulators are relatively easy to write, but because the traces can consist of hundreds of millions of references and the designer is interested in studying a large number of sizes and organizations, they can prove to be time-consuming to run. A clever way to reduce the simulation time when the LRU algorithm is used is called "trace stripping."

Define the set of misses that are generated when we run trace T on cache C as $M(C, T)$. Suppose we are able to construct a subtrace, $T' \subset T$, which has the property that $M(C, T) = M(C, T')$ for every cache C in some set of caches C. Then, to count the number of misses generated by T on C, it is sufficient to just run the subtrace T' through the simulator. Because the simulation time tends to be proportional to the length of the trace, the shorter the subtrace, the greater the improvement in simulation speed.

How can a suitable subtrace be obtained? Consider a direct-mapped cache of S sets and a line length of L bytes. Run the full trace T through this cache (called the "trace stripper") and record the references which result in misses. This list of references constitutes the "stripped trace," T'. It is relatively easy to show that $M(C, T') = M(C, T)$ for all caches C with S, $2S$, $4S$, $8S$, . . . sets and line lengths of L bytes. In fact, coming up with a proof of this is a useful test on one's understanding of set-associative cache organization; we invite the reader to produce such a proof. As a hint, we point out the following facts.

- The trace stripper is a direct-mapped cache (i.e., it has one line per set). Thus, if a reference is a hit (say to set S_i of the trace stripper), the previous reference to an address mapped into set S_i must also have the same tag.
- The family of caches under consideration has the same line size as the trace stripper, and σ times the number of sets as the trace stripper, where $\sigma \in \{1, 2, 4, 8, . . . \}$.

To simulate a family of cache organizations, all of the same line length L, and S, $2S$, $4S$, $8S$, . . . sets, all that is required is to run the full trace through a cache simulator representing an S-set direct-mapped cache of L bytes per line and to list the references that result in a miss. This is the stripped trace and is typically much smaller than the full trace. The stripped trace can be used to simulate the performance of the other caches in the family, thus significantly improving simulation speed.

Cache Analysis*

When all that is sought is a quick-and-approximate study of the miss rate, analysis is suitable. The analytical model that we present here sums up the miss rate due to various factors.

- *First-access miss rate:* Whatever the size of the cache, the first occasion on which a line is accessed results in a miss. This is also called a cold-start miss.
- *Intrinsic interference:* Intrinsic interference occurs when accesses by a single program interfere with one another.

---

*This section is meant for readers with some knowledge of probability theory and a measure of mathematical maturity.

Example 5: Consider a direct-mapped cache. Suppose a program has the access sequence *ABA*, where *A* and *B* are lines mapping into the same set. When *B* is brought into the cache, *A* has to be replaced. However, the program makes a subsequent access to *A*, which results in a miss (owing to the prior ejection of *A* by the program). This is intrinsic interference.

- *Extrinsic interference:* Extrinsic interference occurs when accesses by a single program interfere with one another. Extrinsic interference occurs largely due to the round-robin scheduling algorithm used by most general-purpose computers.

Example 6: Suppose we have a multiprogrammed computer. Job *A* finishes its current time-slice and goes to the back of the ready queue. Before its next turn at the CPU, a number of other jobs, say $B_1, B_2, \ldots, B_n$, will have had executed at the CPU. When *A* returns, it will find that some, or all, of the lines it had brought into the cache have been displaced by these other tasks. Many cache misses will result from *A* having to bring back these lines into its cache. These misses are due to extrinsic interference.

The first-access miss rate is easy to evaluate. If the program makes a total of N accesses during its lifetime and the total number of distinct lines accessed is l, the first-access miss rate is

$$m_{\text{first}} = \frac{l}{N}.$$
[5]

Now consider the intrinsic miss rate. It is reasonable to assume that the miss rate due to any one set in the cache is approximately equal to the miss rate due to any other set. Let us, therefore, focus on one set and multiply the intrinsic miss rate due to this set by the number of sets.

We start by computing the expected number of *potentially colliding lines* of a program. Two lines are potentially colliding if (1) they map into the same set and (2) the total number of such lines mapping into that set exceeds the number of lines in the set.

Let l be the number of distinct bytes accessed by the program during its lifetime. Let the cache have S sets and K lines per set. The probability of a random one of these lines being in a given set is therefore $1/S$. Thus, the mapping of lines onto sets can be regarded as a Bernoulli process and we can write the expression for the probability that a particular set has λ lines mapping into it:

$$P(\lambda, l, S) = \binom{l}{\lambda} \left(\frac{1}{S}\right)^{\lambda} \left(1 - \frac{1}{S}\right)^{l-\lambda}.$$
[6]

The expected number of non-potentially-colliding lines in the entire cache is then given by $S \sum_{\lambda=0}^{K} i P(\lambda, l, S)$. The expected number of potentially colliding lines in the cache is thus given by

$$n_{\text{coll}} = l - S \sum_{\lambda=0}^{K} i P(\lambda, l, S).$$
[7]

n_{coll} is a static quantity in that it indicates how many lines in all can be expected to be involved in interference with other lines belonging to the same program. If c is the collision ratio

$$c = \frac{\text{Average number of intrinsic collisions}}{\text{Average number of potentially colliding lines}},\qquad [8]$$

then the intrinsic miss rate is given by

$$m_{\text{intrins}} = \frac{cn_{\text{coll}}}{N}.\qquad [9]$$

From where do we get c? First, it has been observed experimentally that for direct-mapped caches, c is not a sensitive function of the cache size [so long as the cache is not unrealistically small (e.g., less than 1 Kbyte)]. So, if we obtain c for one direct-mapped cache configuration by simulation or experiment, we can use the same value in the analysis for direct-mapped caches of other sizes. What about when the number of lines per set is $K > 1$? This is also quite easy to deal with. In fact, we can write

$$R(K, d) = c_{\text{direct}}\left(1 - \frac{K-1}{d-1}\right),\qquad [10]$$

where $R(K, d)$ is the collision rate for an individual set of K lines if d potentially colliding lines of the working set are mapped onto that set, c_{direct} is the value of the collision ratio for a direct-mapped cache with the same number of sets, and d is the number of potentially colliding lines of the working set mapped onto that set.

The reasoning behind Eq. (10) is as follows. In a direct-mapped cache, any reference to a line that is not the last-referenced line in that set will cause a miss. The impact of accesses to the most recently used (MRU) line has already been taken account of in c_{direct}. Therefore, we have to correct for the possibility that some of the $K-1$ other lines in the set also result in hits. If there are $d-1$ potentially colliding lines mapping onto that set (besides the MRU line), the probability that one of these potentially colliding lines is already in the set is $(K-1)/(d-1)$. Accesses to such lines do not cause misses. This reasoning leads directly to Eq. (10).

The value of the collision ratio for a K-way cache can then be written as

$$c(K) = \frac{\sum_{d=K+1}^{l} R(K, d)\, dP(d)}{\sum_{d=K+1}^{l} dP(d)}.\qquad [11]$$

The intrinsic miss rate is then given by

$$m_{\text{intrins}} = \frac{c(K)n_{\text{coll}}}{N}.\qquad [12]$$

Let us now turn to the extrinsic miss rate. We will first compute the number of misses that are caused every time the process is switched out of the CPU and then switched back again.

As with intrinsic interference, we will concentrate on the miss rate due to an individual cache set (say, set S_0) and invoke symmetry to obtain the overall miss rate (by multiplying by the number of sets).

Suppose that at the moment a task is switched out, it has n_1 lines in set S_0.* Be-

*The probability of this occurring can be computed in a manner identical to the probability of there being d potentially colliding lines in a set.

tween the time this task is switched out and then switched back again, suppose that a total of m_1 lines are brought into set S_0. The number of such lines that will be in the set when the task is switched back in again will be $m_2 = \min(m_1, K)$. Then, the number of lines of its working set that the task will find in the cache when it is switched back in again is given by

$$n_2 = \min(n_1, K - m_2). \tag{13}$$

Assuming that when the task is switched back in, it will require all of the lines that it had in cache when it was switched out (this is a conservative assumption), then the number of misses as a result of the context switch is given by $n_1 - n_2$. The expected number of extrinsic misses due to all cache sets is thus

$$M_{\text{extrins}} = E[n_1 - n_2]S, \tag{14}$$

where $E[\cdot]$ denotes the expectation.

If the task suffers k context switches over its lifetime, the expected extrinsic miss rate is then given by

$$m_{\text{extrins}} = \frac{kM_{\text{extrins}}}{N}. \tag{15}$$

The overall miss rate of the program is then given by

$$m_{\text{first}} + m_{\text{intrins}} + m_{\text{extrins}}. \tag{16}$$

CACHE COHERENCE

So far, we have dealt with caches in uniprocessors. Multiprocessors in which each processor has its own cache pose an additional challenge. It is possible that the same line may be held by more than one cache. The danger now exists that a processor may use an outdated line.

Example 7: Suppose line A is in the cache of processors P_1 and P_2 by some time t_0. At time $t_1 > t_0$, P_1 writes into that line. At some later time t_2, P_2 reads its copy of that line from its cache. Because P_2's copy predates the update made by P_1, P_2 will read an incorrect (outdated) line.

It is therefore necessary to have some mechanism by which we can ensure coherence (i.e., that no processor gets an outdated value). The simplest way of ensuring this is to forbid the caching of shared data. The caches only contain lines not shared by multiple processors. However, this solution imposes a severe performance penalty on the shared lines and is often not acceptable.

In this section, we will present two cache coherence techniques.

Snoopy Cache Protocols

These algorithms assume a bus-based architecture. Communication between the processors and the main memory is through a bus that can be monitored by all the processors. As a result, every read and write operation on the bus by any processor can be seen by every other processor (i.e., the processors all snoop on the bus operations).

There are many snoopy cache protocols which are very similar to one another. Here, we will confine ourselves to the *write-invalidate* protocol.

Each line in the cache is in one of the following three states:

Invalid: The contents of the line are out of date and must not be used.

Valid: The contents of the line can be used. They are unchanged since they were imported into the cache. It is possible that more than one cache holds the same line.

Dirty: The contents of the line can be used. However, they have been changed since being imported into the cache. This cache is the only one which holds a copy of that line.

Whenever a line is in state valid or dirty of a processor, a reference to that line results in a cache hit by that processor. The difference is that if a processor wishes to write into a valid line, it has to take account of the possibility that other copies of the same line may be extant in other caches. The moment an update occurs into that line, these other copies will become out of date and must be invalidated. This is done by broadcasting an invalidation signal on the bus. When a processor observes such a signal, it checks to see if it has a copy of that valid line in its cache; if so, it invalidates the line. On the other hand, if the processor wishes to update a line which is in state dirty, it need not inform anyone else because no other cache has a usable copy of that line.

If a read miss occurs, the accessed line must be brought into the cache. If this line is not in any other cache, the main memory provides it. If another cache holds that line in state dirty, that cache (which snoops on the bus and is therefore aware of the read miss) provides the line to both the requesting cache and the memory. The state of the line is now valid.

The situation with a write miss is identical, with one important difference. If the line is being held by one or more other caches, these copies must be invalidated (because that line is to be updated by the processor which generated the write miss).

When a dirty line is to be replaced in the cache, it is written back into memory. Valid lines do not need to be written back because the corresponding line in memory is current.

The write-invalidate protocol can be described as a finite-state machine representing the contents of each line in the cache, with states valid, invalid, and dirty. As described earlier, transitions can be caused either by reads or writes generated by the processor owning the cache, or by reads or writes observed on the bus, and emanating from other processors. The latter are called bus reads or writes. Figure 3 is a representation of the finite-state machine.

The obvious performance bottleneck in a snoopy cache protocol is the bus. As the number of processors increases, contention for the bus increases and concomitant queueing delays also increase. This can increase the effective memory access time for the CPU. One way around this is to divide the main memory address space into multiple nonoverlapping subsets and use multiple buses, with a separate bus designated to carry the traffic associated with each subset.

Directory-Based Protocols

Directory-based protocols manage cache coherence from the main memory. Associated with each line in the main memory is an entry in the directory which indicates which processors have that line in the cache. This entry can be implemented in several ways:

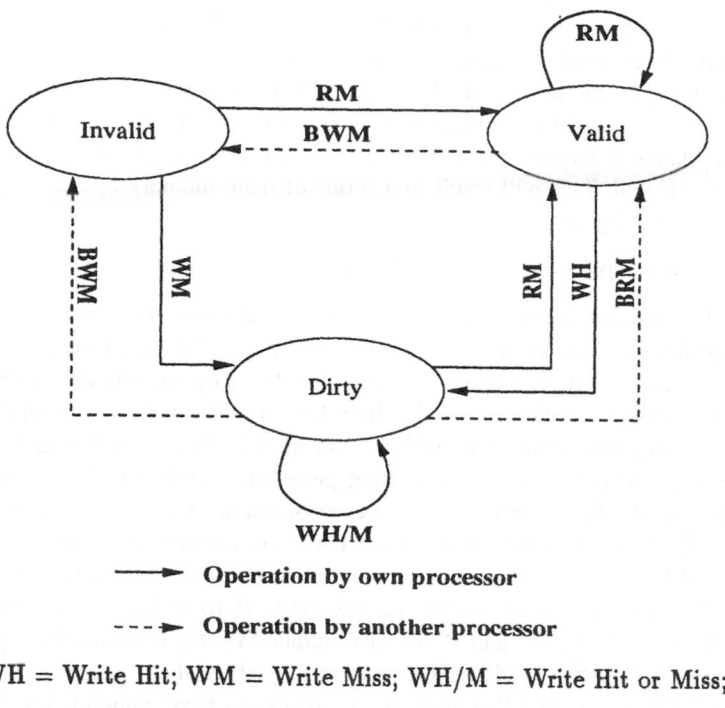

> Operation by own processor

> Operation by another processor

WH = Write Hit; WM = Write Miss; WH/M = Write Hit or Miss;

BWM = Bus Write Miss; BWH = Bus Write Hit.

FIGURE 3   Write-invalidate protocol. WH = write hit; WM = write miss; WH/M = write hit or miss; BWM = bus write miss; BWH = bus write hit.

- The entry consists of N bits, where N is the number of processors; one bit is associated with each processor. If the bit associated with processor P_i is 0, P_i does not have a copy of that line in cache; if it is 1, it does. The size of this directory is the number of lines in the main memory multiplied by the number of processors.
- The entry consists of a linked list of the IDs of the processors which hold a copy of the line. The space occupied by the directory is therefore not fixed, but varies with the extent of data possession among the processors. When N is large and the extent of data sharing is small, this directory tends to occupy less space (on the average) than the one-bit-per-processor approach. However, linked lists can be more time-consuming to update.
- The entry consists of a limited number (say, F) of fields per line. Each field can hold the ID of one processor. The number of bits per memory line is therefore given by $F\lceil \log_2 N \rceil$. The correct choice of F is crucial to the success of this approach. If F is too large, we are wasting directory space. If F is too small, it can lead to thrashing.

Example 8: Suppose $F = 3$ and processors A, B, and C all have copies of one line l_i. If processor D wishes to have a copy of the line, one of A, B, and C will have to give up its copy, as there is no space in the directory to store the fact that copies of the line are held in four processors. Let us suppose the system reacts by invalidating the copy held by processor A. Now, if in the next cycle, A makes a request for a copy of l_i, some other copy of l_i will have to be invalidated. This will result in a series of main memory operations, which can severely degrade the system performance.

The following example illustrates how the directory-based protocol works:

Example 9: Consider an eight-processor system and a one-bit-per-processor scheme. Focus on the directory entries associated with some particular line of memory. Processors P_0, P_2, and P_4 are holding a copy of that line. The directory entry is therefore 10101000. Now, suppose P_7 has a read miss for that line. It is provided with a copy of the line, and the directory entry now reads 10101001. Following this, P_0 wishes to update this line. It sends a message to the directory, requesting permission to do so. Two approaches can now be taken. In the first approach, the directory sends messages to P_2, P_4, and P_7, telling them to invalidate their copies of that line. The main memory copy of that line is also invalidated. When it receives a message from each of these processors confirming that the invalidation has been done, it gives permission to P_0 to update the line. In the second approach, the lines in P_2, P_4, and P_7 are also updated by P_0; P_0 sends this update to the directory, which can then send the information to each of these processors. The update is completed when P_0 is told that all of these processors have completed their updates.

FURTHER READING

There is a vast literature on caches. A good introduction can be found in Refs.1–3. In addition, there are two useful books devoted to cache memory (4,5): Ref. 4 is an introductory book, and Ref. 5 focuses more on performance studies. The article by Smith (6) is perhaps the best known general survey on caches. See Ref. 7 for a discussion of multilevel caches.

The material on trace stripping is from the doctoral dissertation of Puzak (8) and is also described in detail in Ref. 3. The analytical cache model presented here is due to Agrawal et al. (9).

Snoopy cache protocols are surveyed in detail by Archibald and Baer (10). See Refs. 11 and 12 for a description of directory-based cache coherence protocols.

REFERENCES

1   J. L. Hennessy and D. A. Patterson, *Computer Architecture: A Quantitative Approach*, Morgan Kaufmann, San Francisco, 1996.
2. M. J. Flynn, *Computer Architecture*, Jones and Bartlett, Boston, 1995.
3. H. S. Stone, *High-Performance Computer Architecture*, Addison-Wesley, Reading, MA, 1993.
4. J. Handy, *The Cache Memory Book*, Academic Press, San Diego, CA, 1993.
5. S. A. Przybylski, *Cache and Memory Hierarchy Design: A Performance-Directed Approach*, Morgan Kaufman, San Francisco, 1990.

6. A. J. Smith, "Cache Memories," *ACM Comput. Surveys*, *14*, 437–530 (1982).
7. S. A. Przybylski, M. Horowitz, and J. Hennessy, "Characteristics of Performance—Optimal Multi-Level Cache Hierarchies," in *Proceedings of the 16th Annual Symposium on Computer Architecture*, 1989, pp. 114–121.
8. T. R. Puzak, "Cache Memory Design," Ph.D. dissertation, University of Massachusetts (1985).
9. A. Agarwal, J. Hennessy, and M. Horowitz, "Cache Performance of Operating System and Multiprogramming Workloads," *ACM Trans. Computer Syst.*, *6*, 393–431 (1988).
10. J. Archibald and J.-L. Baer, "Cache Coherence Protocols," *ACM Trans. Computer Syst.*, *4*, 258–261 (1986).
11. A. Agarwal, J. L. Hennessy, R. Simoni, and M. A. Horowitz, "An Evaluation of Directory Schemes for Cache Coherence," in *Proc. 15th International Symposium on Computer Architecture*, 1988, pp. 280–289.
12. D. B. Glasco, B. A. Delagi, and M. J. Flynn, "Update-Based Cache Coherence Protocols for Scalable Shared-Memory Multiprocessors," in *Proc. 27th Annual Hawaii International Conference on Systems Sciences*, 1994, Vol. 1, pp. 534–545.

C. M. KRISHNA

COST–BENEFIT ANALYSIS OF INFORMATION TECHNOLOGY

INTRODUCTION

We present a cost–benefit framework in a general decision space for analyzing the choice process to invest in information technology (IT) either as an initial undertaking or as a modernization of existing facilities made obsolete by rapid technological progress. The method is preferred to all other analytical frameworks such as "decision analysis," "portfolio analysis," scoring model, and so on currently known. These frameworks can be subsumed under a cost–benefit analysis by a process of logical mapping irrespective of the epistemic positions held by their proponents. The objective of the cost–benefit analysis presented here is to develop a comprehensive accounting framework in which all relevant benefits and costs are identified so as to construct cost and benefit data as inputs to decision on information technology projects (ITP).

THE INFORMATION TECHNOLOGICAL SET

The development of the cost–benefit framework will begin by defining a set of conceptual blocks relevant to decisions on information technology projects. Let $\Omega(t, z)$ be a feasible information technological set with a generic element, $\omega(t, z)$. We consider a set, $\mathbb{A}$, of information technologies from which an organization may select some of its elements as its initial investments and a set, $\mathbb{M}$, composed of technologies available for potential modernization of existing facilities. The variable z captures the average rate of technological progress and other factors such as social acceptability, legal conditions, and so forth, and t is a time element.

Definition 1: The space of information technologies that an organization may undertake for its investment projects is a set of the form

$$\Delta = \{\delta \mid \delta \in (\mathbb{A} \cup \mathbb{M}), \mathbb{A} \subset \Omega \text{ and } \mathbb{M} \subset \Omega\}$$

called δ-technologies.

Each δ-technology brings with it technical benefit and cost characteristics in terms of what they either positively or negatively affect in the overall efficiency of the organizational operations and dynamics. The technical benefit and cost characteristics define the quality and operational limitations as well as the strengths of the δ-technology. The set of all possible real technological benefit characteristics is denoted by $\mathbb{B}$, whereas those of technological cost characteristics is represented as $\mathbb{C}$ with generic elements $b \in \mathbb{B}$ and $c \in \mathbb{C}$, respectively. Examples of technological benefit characteristics include increased speed of computation, larger memory, light-weightedness, small size, and so on. Similarly, examples of technological cost characteristics include boredom, eyesight deterioration, user-unfriendliness, increased risk to users, and so forth.

COST, BENEFIT, AND DECISION SPACES FOR INFORMATION TECHNOLOGIES

We shall now relate the δ-technologies to the technological costs and benefits relevant to IT decisions.

Definition 2: An organization's decision space, Θ, of investment projects in information technology is made up of a quadruplet of a set of organizational objectives, $\mathbb{H}$, a set of technologies, Δ, a set of technological cost characteristics, $\mathbb{C}$, and a set of technological benefit characteristics, $\mathbb{B}$, whose generic elements are $h \in \mathbb{H}$, $\delta \in \Delta$, $c \in \mathbb{C}$, $b \in \mathbb{B}$, and $\theta \in \Theta$. Thus,

$$\Theta = \mathbb{H} \otimes \Delta \otimes \mathbb{C} \otimes \mathbb{B}$$
$$= \{\theta = (h, \delta, c, b) \mid h \in \mathbb{H}, \delta \in \Delta, c \in \mathbb{C} \text{ and } b \in \mathbb{B}\},$$

where $\otimes$ is used as the Cartesan product.

To transform the technological benefit and cost characteristics into economic benefit and cost characteristics, we partition the decision space into subspaces of cost and benefit characteristics.

Definition 3: A technological benefit decision space, Φ with generic element $\varphi \in \Phi$ for IT projects is composed of a set of technological benefit characteristics, $\mathbb{B}$, a set of information technologies, Δ, and a set of organizational objectives, $\mathbb{H}$, that may be represented as

$$\Phi = \{\varphi = (b, h, \delta) \mid b \varepsilon \mathbb{B}, h \in \mathbb{H}, \text{ and } \delta \in \Delta\} = \mathbb{B} \otimes \Delta \otimes \mathbb{H}$$

Definition 4: A technological cost decision space, Γ, with a generic element $\gamma \in \Gamma$ for IT projects is composed of a set of technological cost characteristics, $\mathbb{C}$, a set of technologies, Δ, and a set of organizational objectives, $\mathbb{H}$, that may be written as

$$\Gamma = \{\gamma = (c, \gamma, h) \mid c \in \mathbb{C}, \delta \in \Delta, \text{ and } h \in \mathbb{H}\}$$
$$= \mathbb{C} \otimes \Delta \otimes \mathbb{H}$$

From the technological subspaces of cost and benefit characteristics, another partition is imposed on the organizational decision space in terms of economic costs and benefits. The economic partition is superimposed on the technological partition in a manner such that the set of technological cost (benefit) characteristics can be mapped into the space of economic cost (benefit) characteristics.

Definition 5: An economic benefit space, Π, of an organization's decision space, Θ, of IT projects is composed of a triplet of sets of information technologies, Δ, organizational objectives, $\mathbb{H}$, and economic benefit characteristics, $\mathbb{R}$, that may be written as

$$\Pi = \Delta \otimes \mathbb{H} \otimes \mathbb{R} = \{\pi = (\delta, h, \rho) \mid \delta \in \Delta, h \in \mathbb{H}, \text{ and } \rho \in \mathbb{R}\},$$

where $\pi \in \Pi$ is the generic element.

Definition 6: An economic cost space, $\mathbb{G}$, of an organization's decision space, Θ, of IT projects is composed of a triplet of sets of information technologies, Δ, organizational objectives, $\mathbb{H}$, and economic cost characteristics, $\mathbb{N}$, that may be represented as

$$\mathbb{G} = \Delta \otimes \mathbb{H} \otimes \mathbb{N} = \{g = (\delta, h, v) \mid \delta \in \Delta, h \in \mathbb{H}, \text{ and } v \in \mathbb{N}\},$$

where $g \in \mathbb{G}$ is a generic element.

Examples of economic benefit characteristics of the δ-technologies are (1) cost savings such as increases in productivity and lower operating expenses, (2) cost avoidance such as costs of professional staff and facilities, and (3) intangible organizational benefits that are value enhancing such as increased efficiency in asset utilization, resource management and control, overall planning, and structural flexibility in rapidly changing technological environment, organic decision making in addition to improvements in product quality and design, and so on. Examples of economic cost characteristics include the following:

1. Procurement costs such as equipment costs and equipment installation costs
2. Operational readiness costs such as software acquisition cost for the operating systems, costs of communication equipments and installation, workstations, including space and furniture, data conversion and/or collection costs
3. Implementation costs such as technical staff and usage
4. Ongoing costs such as maintenance costs for the system's operations (facility, hardware, software, etc.), supplies, staff and staff training, consultancy, and modernization,
5. Adjustment costs such as organizational disruption and operational restructuring
6. Intangible costs such as employees' eyesight deterioration and boredom due to operational routines on the use of IT equipments.

One may look at any δ-technology as a portfolio of operations in which the cost–benefit framework is developed under an analytical construct that there are technological benefit and cost characteristics that come with each portfolio of δ-technology. The sets of technological benefit characteristics, $\mathbb{B}$, and cost characteristics, $\mathbb{C}$, are transformed into sets of economic benefit characteristics, $\mathbb{R}$, and cost characteristics, $\mathbb{N}$, whose generic elements are $\rho \in \mathbb{R}$ and $v \in \mathbb{N}$, respectively.

MAPPING THE SETS OF TECHNOLOGICAL COST AND BENEFIT CHARACTERISTICS INTO THE SETS OF ECONOMIC BENEFIT AND COST CHARACTERISTICS

We now consider the relationships between the technological benefit space and economic benefit space on one hand, and the technological cost space and economic cost space on the other hand, and construct a functional transformation where technical benefit and cost spaces are mapped into economic benefit and cost spaces.

Definition 7: A benefit functional transformation, R_b, given the set of information technologies, Δ, is a mapping from the technological benefit space, $\mathbb{B}$, into the economic benefit space, $\mathbb{R}$, and is written as $R_b \mid_\Delta: \mathbb{B} \to \mathbb{R}$, where

$$R_b \mid_\Delta = \{(b, \rho) \mid \rho = R_b(b),\ b \in \mathbb{B},\ \text{and}\ \rho \in \mathbb{R}\}.$$

Definition 8: A cost-functional transformation, R_c, given the set of information technologies, Δ, is a mapping from the technological cost space, $\mathbb{C}$ into the economic cost space, $\mathbb{N}$, written as $R_c \mid_\Delta: \mathbb{C} \to \mathbb{N}$, where

$$R_c \mid_\Delta = \{(c, v) \mid v = R_c(c),\ c \in \mathbb{C},\ \text{and}\ v \in \mathbb{N}\}$$

The assumptions that underly the definitions of technological and economic benefit and cost characteristics are that their generic elements are identifiable and that the technological benefit and cost characteristics can be transformed into economic benefit and cost characteristics when the IT project is undertaken. To operationalize these definitions, we seek an analytical process where for each $\delta \in \Delta$, the elements $b \in \mathbb{B}$ and $c \in \mathbb{C}$ can be identified. Additionally, the elements of economic benefit and cost characteristics, $\rho \in \mathbb{R}$ and $v \in \mathbb{N}$, must be identifiable and/or measurable in some meaningful sense relative to $b \in \mathbb{B}$ and $c \in \mathbb{C}$, given $\delta \in \Delta$. All the identifiable and/or measurable characteristics must be related to the organizational decision space, Θ, regarding projects on information technologies.

Each information technology, $\delta \in \Delta$, may produce multiple benefit and cost characteristics that are identifiable but not necessarily measurable. Associated with each $\delta \in \Delta$, we develop two identifiable technological characteristic sets of the form

$$\{b_1, b_2, \ldots, b_i, \ldots\} = \mathbb{E} \subseteq \mathbb{B}, \tag{1}$$

$$\{c_1, c_2, \ldots, c_i, \ldots\} = \mathbb{Q} \subseteq \mathbb{C}. \tag{2}$$

Associated with each $b \in \mathbb{E}$ and $c \in \mathbb{Q}$, we identify two sets, $\mathbb{M}$ and $\mathbb{F}$, of economic benefit and cost characteristics, respectively, and specify them as

$$\{\rho_1, \rho_2, \ldots, \rho_i, \ldots\} = \mathbb{M} \subseteq \mathbb{R}, \tag{3}$$

$$\{v_1, v_2, \ldots, v_i, \ldots\} = \mathbb{F} \subseteq \mathbb{N} \tag{4}$$

The economic benefit and cost characteristics are identified in real units and therefore appear as heterogeneous entities. Therefore, we need cost and benefit aggregates in the choice analysis in the decision space, Θ, if the choice alternatives are to be compared. The existence of the needed aggregate values requires that the cost and benefit spaces must be equipped with measures that allow heterogenous real benefit and cost characteristics to be summable. Additionally, the organizational decision space must have some important properties of the separation of spaces and the comparability of IT projects, given the organizational set of objectives.

Definition 9: An organizational decision space, Θ, is said to be technologically and economically cost and benefit separable if there exist technological benefit and cost subspaces, Φ and Γ, respectively, and economic benefit and cost subspaces, Π and $\mathbb{G}$, respectively, such that

1. $\Phi, \Gamma \subset \Phi$
2. $\Phi \cap \Gamma = \Delta \otimes \mathbb{H} = \Pi \cap \mathbb{G}$
3. $\Phi \cup \Gamma = \Theta$
4. $\Phi \neq \phi$ and $\#\Gamma \geq 0$
5. $\mathbb{B} \cap \mathbb{C} = \phi$
6. $\mathbb{R} \cap \mathbb{N} = \phi$
7. $\exists R_b : \mathbb{B} \to \mathbb{R} \neq \phi$
8. $\exists R_c : \mathbb{C} \to \mathbb{N}, \ni \#\mathbb{N} \geq 0$.

Properties 5 and 6 mainly state that a characteristic cannot be both cost and benefit. Property 2 suggests that common among the economic and technological cost–benefit spaces are the spaces of organization's objectives and the IT projects.

COST AND BENEFIT IDENTIFICATION MATRICES

The framework presented so far requires us to develop a process of constructing the needed cost and benefit data for analyzing the elements of the information technology. To do this, we consider each $\delta \in \Delta$ defined in the decision space, Θ. The method of data construct begins with what we shall call *cost and benefit identification matrices*. We shall first consider the case of technological benefit and cost characteristics.

Identification Matrices for Technological Cost and Benefit Characteristics

We consider each δ-technology that is a candidate for choice as an investment project. We then develop a comprehensive accounting framework for identifying the associated technological benefit and cost characteristics, $b \in \mathbb{B}$ and $c \in \mathbb{C}$, respectively. A characteristic is defined to be a technological benefit if it has a potential to improve organizational operations or enhance revenues for any given cost or increase safety, broadly defined, and so forth. Similarly, a characteristic is defined to be a technical cost if it is a technical by-product that either reduces efficiency of organizational operations or increases risk to the organization and/or its employees or increases cost for any given revenue stream, and so forth.

Let us consider the set of size $n = \# \Delta$ of information technologies. Let the sizes of sets $\mathbb{B}$ and $\mathbb{C}$ equals m and k, respectively (i.e., $m = \#\mathbb{B}$ and $k = \#\mathbb{C}$). The manner in which the technological benefit and cost characteristics are distributed over the δ-technologies are portrayed in the benefit and cost identification matrices, which allow a comprehensive accounting of relevant benefit and cost characteristics. These matrices are shown in Tables 1 and 2, respectively (see also Refs. 1–3).

The identification of the technological benefit and cost characteristics may be developed with the help of experts, departmental heads, and selected members of the organization's workforce. The degree of relative importance of each characteristic may be ascertained through an information elicitation from the set of individuals that participate

TABLE 1   Technological Benefit Identification Matrix

δ	b					
	b_1	b_2	$\cdots$	b_j	$\cdots$	b_m
δ_1	b_{11}	b_{12}		b_{1j}		b_{1m}
δ_2	b_{21}	b_{22}		b_{2j}		b_{2m}
$\vdots$	$\cdot$					
δ_i	$\cdot$			b_{ij}		
$\vdots$	$\cdot$					
δ_n	b_{n1}	b_{n2}	$\cdots$	b_{nj}	$\cdots$	b_{nm}

Note: $b_{ij} = \begin{cases} 1 & \text{if } \delta_i \text{ produces the } b_j \text{ benefit characteristic} \\ 0 & \text{otherwise} \end{cases}$

TABLE 2   Technological Benefit Identification Matrix

δ	c_1	c_2	$\cdots$	c_j	$\cdots$	c_k
δ_1	c_{11}	c_{12}		c_{ij}		c_{1k}
δ_2	c_{21}	c_{22}		c_{2j}		c_{2k}
$\vdots$						
δ_i	c			c_{ij}		
$\vdots$						
δ_n	c_{n1}	c_{n2}	$\cdots$	c_{nj}	$\cdots$	c_{nk}

The column group heading above is c.

Note: $c_{ij} = \begin{cases} 1 & \text{if } \delta_i \text{ produces the } c_j \text{ type of cost characteristic} \\ 0 & \text{otherwise} \end{cases}$

in the characteristic identification. The elicitation of the relative importance may take the form of a score model, fuzzy membership function, or some form of differential weighting. The information obtained may then be processed by some method of combination of expert judgments or aggregate of information from differential sources (see also Refs. 4–11).

Economic Benefit and Cost Identification Matrices

The identification matrices for technological benefits and costs present data sets on the technological characteristics of the set of information technologies. They must be related to economic benefits and costs whose characteristics must be identified and processed. The process requires the construction of a second set of identification matrices directed toward developing a comprehensive accounting framework for economic cost and benefit characteristics in real values. In this identification process, a characteristic is viewed as an economic benefit if it has a potential to add economic value, broadly defined, to the organization's operational output. It is considered an economic cost if it has a potential of reducing the organization's net output flow, where output is measured in some form.

In developing the required identification matrices for economic benefit and cost characteristics, we select each technological benefit characteristic, $b_{ij} > 0$, from Table 1 or cost characteristic, $c_{ij} > 0$, from Table 2, for any given $\delta \in \Delta$ and develop a comprehensive accounting for the structure of associated real benefit and cost characteristics. The emphasis is on a comprehensive accounting and the observation is that each technological benefit characteristic, b_{ij}, and cost characteristic, c_{ij}, associated with any δ-technology may generate multiple economic benefit and cost characteristics. These economic cost and benefit characteristics may be differentially distributed over different departments or user groups in organization. A user group is defined in terms of either similar or approximately identical user needs.

As such, a partition of size, K, is imposed on the organization in terms of either departments or user groups. The size of K will vary from organization to organization. The criterion for partitioning the organization where there are no crisply established departments will depend on the nature of the organization and its structure. Given the crisp partitioning, let the sets of economic benefit characteristics associated with the b_{ij} technological benefit of size L, and the set of economic cost characteristics associated with the c_{ij} technological cost is of size Z and distributed over all the K departments or user groups of the organization. Given this conceptual structure, two identification matrices of economic cost and benefit characteristics may be developed. They are presented in Tables 3 and 4.

The values ρ_j^G and v_j^G in Tables 3 and 4 are composite aggregates, whereas the values of ρ_i^T and v_i^T may assume single aggregate values. For example, if characteristic ρ_1 is the reduction in the number of departmental employees, then ρ_1^T is the total number of reduction in the organizational workforce. Similarly, if v_1 is the number of personal computers, then v_j^G will constitute the total number of personal computers and so forth. The structure of the identification matrices for the economic benefit and cost characteristics is such that if $\rho_j^G = 0$ ($v_j^G = 0$), then $\rho_{ij} = 0$ ($v_{ij} = 0$) for all i and a fixed j. The implication here, for the benefit side of the accounting, is that the jth department does not experience any economic benefit resulting from a particular technological benefit characteristic. On the cost side of the accounting, $v_j^G = 0$ implies that the jth department is not affected by the presence of a particular technological cost characteristic. On the side of horizontal aggregation, if $\rho_i^T = 0$ ($v_i^T = 0$) for any fixed i, then the economic benefit (cost) characteristic is not realized from the technological benefit (cost) characteristic to any of

TABLE 3 Economic Benefit Identification Matrix

				g			
ρ	g_1	g_2	$\cdots$	g_j	$\cdots$	g_k	Total
ρ_1	ρ_{11}	ρ_{12}		ρ_{ij}		ρ_{1k}	ρ_1^T
ρ_2	ρ_{21}	ρ_{22}					
$\vdots$							$\vdots$
ρ_i	ρ_{i1}			ρ_{ij}			ρ_i^T
$\vdots$							$\vdots$
ρ_L	ρ_{L1}		$\cdots$		$\cdots$	ρ_{LK}	ρ_L^T
Total	ρ_1^G		$\cdots$	ρ_j^G	$\cdots$	ρ_K^G	

Note: g represents departments or user groups and ρ represents benefit characteristics such that

1. $\rho_{ij} \begin{cases} = 0 & \text{if the real benefit does not apply to the cohort} \\ = 1 & \text{if the real benefit is physically incommensurable} \\ \geq 1 & \text{if the real benefit is physically measurable} \end{cases}$
2. $\rho_j^G = \{\rho_{1j}, \rho_{2j}, \cdots, \rho_{Lj}\}, j = 1, 2, \ldots, K$
3. $\rho_i^T = \sum_{j=1}^{K} \rho_{ij}, i = 1, 2, \ldots, L$

and g_j identifies the jth organization's department or user group.

TABLE 4   Economic Cost Identification Matrix

			g			
v	g_1	g_2	$\cdots$	g_j	$\cdots$	g_k	Total
v_1	v_{11}	v_{12}		v_{ij}		v_{1k}	v_1^T
v_2	v_{21}	v_{22}		v_{2j}			
$\vdots$							$\vdots$
v_i	v_{i1}	$\cdots$		v_{ij}			v_i^T
$\vdots$							$\vdots$
v_z	v_{z1}		$\cdots$	v_{zj}	$\cdots$	v_{zk}	v_s^T
Total	v_1^G		$\cdots$	v_j^G	$\cdots$	v_z^G	

Note: v represents the cost characteristic such that

$$
1.\ v_{ij} = = \begin{cases} = 0 & \text{if the cost characteristic does not apply to the cohort} \\ 1 & \text{if the real cost characteristic is physically incommensurable} \\ \geq 1 & \text{if the real cost characteristic is physically measurable} \end{cases}
$$

$$2.\ v_j^G = \{\rho_{1j}, \rho_{2j}, \cdots, \rho_{Lj}\}, j = 1, 2, \ldots, K$$

$$3.\ v_i^T = \sum_{j=1}^{K} v_{ij}, i = 1, 2, \ldots, z$$

the identified departments or user groups in the organization and, hence, should be neglected in the computational process.

It is also possible to have a situation where $\rho_{ij} = 0$ ($v_{ij} = 0$) for some $i - j$ cohorts when $\rho_i^T \neq 0$ ($v_i^T \neq 0$). In this case, the jth department does not share (is not affected by) the ith economic benefit (cost) characteristic. The $\rho_{ij}s$ ($v_{ij}s$) are the identified and estimated real values of the economic benefit (cost) characteristics resulting from a given technological benefit (cost) characteristic for the $i - j$ cohorts. It must be kept in mind that each b_{ij} resulting from δ-technology of IT projects has as its economic benefit support those attributes that constitute the elements in the economic benefit identification matrix. Similarly, each c_{ij} resulting from a δ-technology has as its economic cost support those elements that define the economic cost identification matrix for any given value of the IT investment. There are, therefore, as many socioeconomic benefit and cost identification matrices as there are elements in the technological benefit and cost identification matrices. This is one important reason why cost–benefit analysis in a comprehensive manner is always challenging and time-consuming depending on the nature of the decision space.

In constructing the identification matrices for economic benefit and cost characteristics, the process of identification and estimation of the technological and economic real benefit and cost characteristics of an IT investment project may be designed with the help of experts, managers, and a well-structured survey set of workers who may utilize the conceived information technology when the investment project is undertaken. The identification process for accounting may be made through the method of revealed preference or through contingent variation or through fuzzy information elicitation (1,2,7,12–

16). An important advantage of the theoretical framework offered here is that it provides a decision flexibility where the technological set, Δ, considered as a portfolio, allows intrabenefit and interbenefit and cost complementability and substitutability to be simultaneously evaluated in the benefit–cost decision construct of the IT investment project. In this way, a flexibility is built into the decision-making process, where chief executive officers, executive officers, and departmental heads can embark on a feedback analytical process where IT investment strategies on acquisition and modernization can be evaluated for restructuring as we move through decision time while taking advantage of differential judgments (17).

Given that the departments or user groups of the organization will depend on the nature of its production activity, the combined interactions between the sets of technological benefit and cost characteristics on one hand and the space of the IT projects on the other hand induce crisp partitions on the spaces of benefit and cost imputations, where each cohort identifies either a real technological benefit, b_{ij}, or a real technological cost, c_{ij}, for the ith IT investment project and either jth technological benefit or cost. The mapping from the technological benefit and cost spaces onto the economic benefit and cost spaces, respectively, is such that the combined interactions between sets of benefit and cost characteristics and the organization's departments similarly induce crisp partitions on the spaces of economic benefit and cost imputations, where each department is assigned a value of either economic benefit or cost attribute. (For other helpful approaches that complement this framework, see Refs. 1,3,5,7, and 18–22).

BENEFIT AND COST AGGREGATES

From the identification matrices of economic benefit and cost characteristics we seek aggregate values B_T and C_T for each $\delta \in \Delta$. To obtain these aggregate values, we need to reduce all the heterogeneous benefit–cost characteristics into a common denominator for aggregation and comparison. The common economic denominator that allows aggregation is money in a specified unit, say dollars. To obtain the needed aggregate values requires finding prices, p_i, for each ith benefit characteristic and for each ith cost characteristic in the economic space in the case where there is no differential price distribution over the departments or user groups of the organization (e.g., when the same type of personal computers are purchased for different departments or user groups). If differential pricing over departments is required, then we must find p_{ij} for the identified cost and benefit characteristics. These prices may be imputations on the basis of market-revealed preferences (indirect method) (23–27) or they may be computed on the basis of contingent valuation (direct method) (16,18,28) or they may be computed as fuzzy prices (29) or they may be obtained by combination of all or some of these methods, depending on the real benefit and cost characteristics. The framework for the construction of these prices belongs to the logical construct of the theory of efficient prices (23,26,27,30).

The manner in which these prices are abstracted and the quality of information they may carry will depend on the distribution of economic benefit and cost characteristics over the departments or user groups and whether real measures exist for their accountability. To conceptualize these prices and compute their values, the real economic benefit and cost characteristics in the identification matrices are divided into two groups of tangibles and intangibles which, in turn, are subdivided into those that are pecuniary and nonpecuniary measurables. Objectively direct physical measures may not exist for intangibles (e.g., employees' job satisfaction). In some cases, monetary measures may not exist except, perhaps, through a creatively complicated construct of surrogate monetary measures.

The elemental differences in terms of characteristics, identifiability, and measurements induce important partitions on the spaces of economic benefit and cost attributes (characteristics). Let I_R and I_N be the index sets of benefit and cost attributes, respectively. We subdivide each index set into three mutually exclusive subsets of price measurables with index sets K_R and K_N, respectively; quantitatively but nonpecuniary measurables with index sets, Q_R and Q_N, respectively; and pecuniary and quantitative nonmeasurables with index sets, M_R and M_N, respectively. Structurally, $I_R = Q_R \cup K_R \cup M_R$ and $I_N = Q_N \cup K_N \cup M_N$ and they are mutually exclusive. The subscripts R and N identify benefit and cost index sets, respectively.

We now suppose that the sets of required prices for the cost and benefit characteristics have been obtained. The needed cost–benefit information support for a decision on the IT technologies (Δ) may be presented. Three different sets of benefit data and three different sets of cost data are available from the comprehensive benefit and cost accounting and for processing.

Benefit Data for IT Investment Projects

The three types of benefit data are available for decision on IT projects are (1) total monetary benefits, B_{ST}^{M}, (2) composite quantitative and nonpecuniary measurables, $B^{Q_{st}}$, and (3) nonmeasurable benefit data, $B_{st}*$.

1. The total nonweighted value of monetary benefit, B_{ST}^{M}, is represented as

$$B_{ST}^{M} = \sum_{i \in K_R} \sum_{j \in J_R} p_{ij}\rho_{ij}, \tag{5}$$

   where J_R is the index set of departments or user groups that share in the economic benefits flowing from a technological benefit which may be attributed to the selection and implementation a particular IT investment project.

   There are occasions where a particular economic benefit (cost) characteristic may generate multiple real economic benefit (cost) for a particular cohort. This situation tends to complicate the computational process for the aggregate benefit and cost. To account for this complication, we introduce into the analysis two index sets, L_R and L_N, of economic benefit and cost characteristic that may be associated with such joint benefit and cost output, respectively. In this case, Eq. (5) may be modified to $\hat{B}_{ST}^{M}$ as

$$\hat{B}_{ST}^{M} = \sum_{l \in L_R} \sum_{i \in K_R} \sum_{j \in J_R} p_{ijl}\rho_{ijl}. \tag{6}$$

2. The composite quantitatively and nonpecuniarily measurable benefit sum may be written as an information matrix in the form

$$B_{ST}^{Q} = \{\rho_{1jl}, \rho_{2jl}, \ldots, \rho_{ijl}, \ldots\}, \quad i \in Q_R, j \in J_R, l \in L_R. \tag{7}$$

3. The nonmeasurable benefit data may be represented as

$$B_{ST}^{*} = \{\rho_{1jl}, \rho_{2jl}, \ldots, \rho_{ijl}, \ldots\}, \quad i \in M_R, j \in J_R, l \in L_R \tag{8}$$

Cost Data for IT Investment Projects

Similar to the benefit data, there are three types of cost data. They are the total monetary aggregate of costs without and with multiple technological cost characteristics for each $\delta \in \Delta$. Divisionally, they are (1) total nonweighted monetary values of C_{ST}^M or $\hat{C}_{ST}^M$, (2) a quantitatively but nonpecuniarily measurable composite sum, C_{ST}^Q, and (3) nonmeasurable cost data, C_{ST}^*. The required data sets are presented in a sequence:

1. The total nonweighted value of monetary cost, C_{ST}^M or $\hat{C}_{ST}^M$, is

$$C_{ST}^M = \sum_{i \in K_N} \sum_{j \in J_N} p_{ij} v_{ij} \tag{9}$$

   or

$$\hat{C}_{ST}^M = \sum_{l \in L_N} \sum_{i \in K_N} \sum_{j \in J_N} p_{ijl} v_{ijl} \tag{10}$$

2. The quantitatively but nonpecuniarily measurable composite sum is

$$C_{ST}^Q = \{v_{1jl}, v_{2jl}, \ldots, v_{ijl}, \ldots \}, \quad i \in Q_N, j \in J_N, l \in L_N \tag{11}$$

3. The nonmeasurable cost data, C_{ST}^*, are

$$C_{ST}^* = \{v_{1jl}, v_{2jl}, \ldots, v_{ijl}, \ldots \}, \quad i \in M_N, j \in J_N, l \in L_N. \tag{12}$$

The cost and benefit data sets of Eqs. (5)–(12) are comprehensive. They are designed to assist decision makers in examining the economic impact of investment of different information technologies on the organization and in constructing a cost–benefit ranking index for ordering various IT technological projects that the organizational policy-makers may consider to invest the organization's resource.

EFFECTS OF DISTRIBUTIONAL WEIGHTS AND TIME

The three different types of benefit and cost data sets furnish us with raw data without the assessment of their relative intensities of economic impacts as the benefits and costs are distributed over the departments or user groups of the organization. In all economic decisions about the commitment of investible funds to improve organizational efficiency through the investment in the new information technologies that may have differential economic impacts on different departments or user groups of the organization weighting of benefits and costs are the norm rather than the exception. This is particularly the case when some benefit and cost characteristics may be considered more important by different departments or user groups as they examine their departmental needs and when the departmental or user-groups benefits (costs) are additionally and complementarily interlinked. For example, certain types of benefits of the $(i - j)_k$ cohort may be necessary to obtain the full economic benefit (cost) of the $(i - j)_l$ cohort. The weighting must reflect the organizational and departmental or user-group degree of importance and possible shifting of benefits and costs among departments or user groups and decision time points. In other words, secondary benefits and costs must reflect the weighting process while making sure to avoid double counting.

   If an assignment of weights is required, then the total benefit and cost imputations may be modified by introducing the appropriate benefit and cost intensity weights of α_{ijl} and β_{ijl}, respectively, into the aggregation process. The construction and the use of these weights may proceed under some form of decision rationality. (see Refs. 7–9, 31, and 32 for examples of rational construct and use of distributional weights). Given the optimal set of distributional weights, we may write the monetary value of benefit and cost data, respectively, as

$$\hat{\hat{B}}_{ST}^{M} = \sum_{l \in L_R} \sum_{i \in K_R} \sum_{j \in J_R} \alpha_{ijl} p_{ijl} \rho_{ijl}, \quad \alpha_{ijl} \geq 1, \tag{13}$$

and

$$\hat{\hat{C}}_{ST}^{M} = \sum_{l \in L_N} \sum_{i \in K_N} \sum_{j \in J_N} \beta_{ijl} p_{ijl} v_{ijl}, \quad \beta_{ijl} \geq 1. \tag{14}$$

The difference between the total monetary values of social benefits and costs with and without distributional weights respectively are

$$\Delta B_{ST} = \sum_{l \in L_R} \sum_{i \in K_R} \sum_{j \in J_R} (\alpha_{ijl} - 1) p_{ijl} \rho_{ijl} \tag{15}$$

and

$$\Delta C_{ST} = \sum_{l \in L_N} \sum_{i \in K_N} \sum_{j \in J_R} (\beta_{ijl} - 1) p_{ijl} v_{ijl} \tag{16}$$

So far, the benefit–cost accounting that we have presented for investment in information technology is only for one period. Because economic costs and benefits spread over time, the cost–benefit assessments are time dependent, yielding vectors of vectors of three important information sets for benefits and costs. To account for time, the benefit–cost data must be assessed or forecasted for all relevant decision time points (1,4,33). If T^* is a decision time set, then each assessed economic benefit characteristic will be a representation of the form ρ_{ijlt} with a corresponding weight α_{ijlt} and price, p_{ijlt}, while each assessed economic cost characteristic will be a representation of the form v_{ijlt} with corresponding distributional weights, β_{ijlt} and price p_{ijlt}. The time series of data in support of the decision to invest in IT project for $t \in T^*$ are

$$\hat{\hat{B}}_{ST_t}^{M} = \left[\sum_{l \in L_R} \sum_{i \in K_R} \sum_{j \in J_R} \alpha_{ijlt} p_{ijlt} \rho_{ijlt} \right]^{t \in T^*}, \tag{17}$$

$$B_{ST_t}^{Q_R} = [\rho_{1jlt}, \rho_{2jlt}, \ldots, \rho_{ijlt}, \ldots]^{t \in T^*}, \quad i \in Q_R, j \in J_R, l \in L_R, \tag{18}$$

$$B_{ST_t}^{*} = [\rho_{1jlt}, \rho_{2jlt}, \ldots, \rho_{ijlt}, \ldots]^{t \in T^*}, \quad i \in M_R, j \in J_R, l \in L_R. \tag{19}$$

The corresponding time-dependent cost data sets are

$$\hat{\hat{C}}_{ST_t}^{M} = \left[\sum_{l \in L_N} \sum_{i \in K_N} \sum_{j \in J_N} \beta_{ijlt} p_{ijlt} v_{ijlt} \right]^{t \in T^*}, \tag{20}$$

$$C_{ST_t}^{Q_N} = [v_{1jlt}, v_{2jlt}, \ldots, v_{ijlt}, \ldots]^{t \in T^*}, \quad i \in Q_N, j \in J_N, l \in L_N, \tag{21}$$

$$C_{ST_t}^{*} = [v_{1jlt}, v_{2jlt}, \ldots, v_{ijlt}, \ldots]^{t \in T^*}, \quad i \in Q_N, j \in J_N, l \in L_N. \tag{22}$$

The framework for analyzing the decision to invest in IT project is through cost and benefit *identification matrices* used to help answer some important questions such as the following:

1. What are the cost and benefit characteristics associated with each information technology?
2. What departments receive the benefits and incidental cost?
3. How are the cost and benefit characteristics valued and aggregated and in what units?
4. What are appropriate distributional weights of benefit and cost intensities?
5. What is the effect of time on cost and benefit imputations and how do all these questions and answers relate to the decision to invest in IT project?

The cost–benefit framework as presented seems to deal with the choice problem of alternative information technology when the decision to invest in IT has been made. This is not necessarily the case. The framework can be used to take account of the binary choice problem where the cost–benefit analysis must deal with the question as to whether the organization must invest or not invest in information technology and must modernize or not modernize its current information technology. This is the case of the "with and without" problem of assessment, where $\delta_1 \in \Delta$ represents "without" (current status) and all $\delta \in \Delta$ with $\delta \neq \delta_1$ represent IT project alternatives.

A NOTE ON DISTRIBUTIONAL WEIGHTS

The values α and β are the distributional weights. They reflect the value of the importance that the members of the organization collectively attach to the benefit and cost characteristics, respectively, as they affect each department or user group and simultaneously weigh in the general organizational welfare as measured in terms of some efficiency index. The α and β represent aggregate values. These values may be obtained from the logical framework of traditional applied welfare economics (4,31–33), scoring model (8,9), or fuzzy decision and aggregation (1,3,7).

All these frameworks require information elicitation through an acceptable instrument of aggregation of such information and tests of sensitivity and stability of the aggregates. The framework that produces the least sensitive and greatest stable aggregate in addition to being flexible should be used. Experience seems to suggest that fuzzy aggregation leading to fuzzy equilibrium weights meets all of the needed criteria (10,11, 34,35).

THE COST–BENEFIT CRITERION AND THE RANKING OF IT ALTERNATIVES

Given the time stream of cost and benefit data, a criterion is selected among a set of criteria and then constructed to be used in ranking the alternative IT projects. The criterion must connect the future to the present by a discounting process where decreasing weights are attached to monetary values of costs and benefits through the use of a discount rate as we move through future decision times (see also Refs. 4,22, and 33). The appropriate discount rates for the project must be selected to reflect, in a way, the conditions of interest-income and interest-cost preferences of the organization, all of which are adjusted to account for the dynamics of the organizational preferences.

The framework of the cost–benefit data construct allows for a number of criteria to be developed and used, depending on the organization's circumstances and conditions. Let the organization cost of IT project be divided into fixed cost, K, and variable cost, c_t. Similarly, let the total benefit be divided into fixed benefit, H, and variable benefit B_t. Fixed cost is easily conceptualized. The fixed benefit will depend on the nature of the organization. It may be a one-time rise in the market value of the organization through a rise in the goodwill of the enterprise. Given these fixed and variable values, the present values of costs and benefits of the IT project over time may be written as

$$C_{pv} = \sum_{t \in T} \frac{C_t}{(1 + r_1)^t} + K \tag{23}$$

and

$$B_{pv} = \sum_{t \in T} \frac{B_t}{(1 + r_2)^t} + H \tag{24}$$

where r_1 is the average interest rate on the liabilities of the firm (borrowed funds) and r_2 is the average interest rate obtainable on the organization's financial assets. At equilibrium, $r_1 = r_2$. Such an equilibrium rate of discount may be obtained by the method of fuzzy decision (36) or by the traditional method (37–39).

Equations (23) and (24) may be combined to develop five criteria: (1) net difference criterion, k_1, (2) present value of benefit over present value of cost, k_2, (3) present value of cost over the present value of benefit, k_3, (4) net present value benefit over present value of cost, k_4 and (5) present value of cost over net present values of benefit and cost, k_5;

$$k_1 = B_{pv} - C_{pv},$$

$$k_2 = \frac{B_{pv}}{C_{pv}},$$

$$k_3 = \frac{C_{pv}}{B_{pv}},$$

$$k_4 = \frac{B_{pv} - C_{pv}}{C_{pv}},$$

$$k_5 = \frac{C_{pv}}{B_{pv} - C_{pv}}.$$

Additionally and perhaps alternatively, we may use the present value of benefit–cost or cost–benefit ratios when $r_1 = r_2$ is equal to some conceived equilibrium rate of interest, r. Thus,

$$k_6 = \frac{H}{K} + \sum_{t \in T} \left(\frac{B_t}{C_t} \right) (1 + r)^{-t},$$

$$k_7 = \frac{K}{H} + \sum_{t \in T} \left(\frac{C_t}{B_t} \right) (1 + r)^{-t},$$

$$k_8 = (H - K) + \sum_{t \in T} \left(\frac{B_t - C_t}{C_t} \right) (1 + r)^{-t}.$$

The appropriate use of any of these criteria depends on the goals and objectives of the organization. These goals and objectives may lead to one of the following behaviors with the choice of appropriate ranking criteria:

1. Minimize present value of cost subject to a predetermined organization's benefit
2. Maximize the present value of the benefit stream at a given cost
3. Maximize the difference between present values of benefits and costs
4. Maximize (minimize) the ratio of present value of benefit (cost) to the present value of cost (benefit)
5. Maximize the difference between present value of benefits and that of costs subject to a minimum threshold value of net benefit, β^*.

Behavior 1 is consistent with benefit effective analysis, behavior 2 is consistent with cost-effective analysis, and behaviors 3–5 are consistent with the general cost and

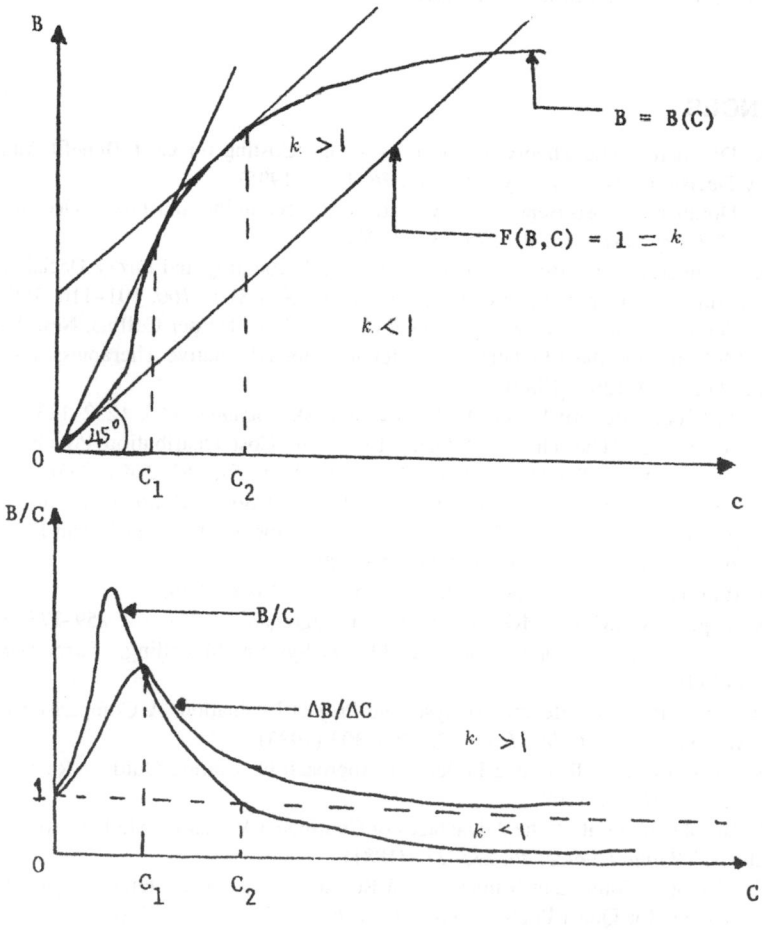

FIGURE 1   Relationships of some of the ranking criteria.

benefit analysis in decision. The relationships among some of the criteria are illustrated in Figure 1, where benefit is a function of cost $[B = B(c)]$ and $k_i = k_i(B, C) = B/C = B(C)/C$ is an example. The choice process is such that the IT projects are ranked according to a criterion that is consistent with the selected optimal behavior.

We may point out in conclusion that an important advantage of the comprehensive accounting framework is to make available to decision- and policy-makers all conceivable (measurable and nonmeasurable) cost and benefit information pertaining to any of the IT projects. In this way, all relevant costs and benefits that are likely to be omitted from the decision and policy processes because of measurement and weighting difficulties are made explicit and clear. Such explicit omissions of sensitive and perhaps costs and benefits will point to the directions of possible bias that may result from the use of truncated cost and benefit information and the effect it may exert on policy alternative and restructuring.

Finally, we are left with the question of uncertainty and risk. These can be partially dealt with in some manner by developing an appropriate measure of the success–failure-path analysis of the IT project. Alternatively, such riskiness conditions may be taken care of by increasing the dimension of the IT portfolio or by introducing a minimum benefit constraint on the choice behavior.

REFERENCES

1. K. K. Dompere, "The Theory of Social Costs and Costing for Cost–Benefit Analysis in a Fuzzy-Decision Space," *Fuzzy Sets Syst.*, *76*, 1–24 (1995).
2. K. K. Dompere, "Cost–Benefit Analysis, Benefit Accounting and Fuzzy Decisions: Part I: Theory," *Fuzzy Sets Syst.*, *92*, 275–287 (1996).
3. K. K. Dompere, "Cost–Benefit Analysis, Benefit Accounting and Fuzzy Decisions: Part II: Mental Illness in Hypothetical Community," *Fuzzy Sets Syst.*, *100*, 101–116 (1998).
4. R. O. Zerbe, Jr. and D. D. Dively, *Benefit Cost Analysis*, Harper Collins, New York, 1994.
5. B. J. McNeil, "On the Elicitation of Preferences for Alternative Therapies," *New Engl. J. Med.*, *306*, 1259–1262 (1982).
6. C. Starr, "Social Benefit Versus Technological Risk," *Science*, *165*, 1232–1238 (1969).
7. K. K. Dompere, "The Theory of Fuzzy Decisions, Cost Distribution Principle in Social Choice and Optimal Tax Distribution," *Fuzzy Sets Syst.*, *53*, 253–274 (1993).
8. K. Lehrer, "Consensus and Comparison: A Theory of Social Rationality," in *Foundations and Applications of Decision Theory, Vol. 1*, C. A. Hooker, J. J. Leach, and E. F. McClennen (eds.), D. Reidel, Boston, 1978, pp. 283–309.
9. B. Mirkin, *Group Choice*, John Wiley & Sons, New York, 1979.
10. R. R. Yager, "MAM and MOM Operators for Aggregation," *Sci.*, *69*, 259–273 (1983).
11. R. R. Yager, "Aggregation Operations and Fuzzy Systems Modelling," *Fuzzy Sets Syst.*, *69*, 125–145 (1994).
12. W. E. Diewert, "Cost–Benefit Analysis and Project Evaluation: A Comparison of Alternative Approaches," *J. Public Econ.*, *22*, 265–302 (1983).
13. B. J. McNeil et al., "Revealed Preference Approach to Valuing Outdoor Recreation," *Nat. Res. J.*, *23*, 607–618 (1983).
14. D. S. Brookshire et al., "The Advantages of Contingent Valuation Methods for Benefit Cost Analysis," *Public Choice*, *36*, 235–252 (1981).
15. R. T. Carson, "Contingent Valuation and Revealed Preference Methodologies: Comparing the Estimates for Quasi Public Goods," *Land Econ.*, *72*, 80–93 (1996).

16. R. G. Cummings, L. A. Cox., Jr., and A. M. Freeman, III, "General Methods for Benefit Assessment," in [18], 161–191 (1986).

16a. Green, E. J., "On the Difficulty of Eliciting Summary Information," *J. Econ. Theory*, *32*, 228–245 (1984).

17. B. A. Weisbrod, "A Guide to Benefit–Cost Analysis, As Seen Through a Controlled Experiment in Treating the Mentally Ill," Institute for Research on Poverty, Discussion Papers, DP #559-798, University of Wisconsin, Madison (1979).

18. J. D. Bentkover, V. T. Covello, and J. Mumpower (eds.), *Benefit Assessment: The State of the Art*, D. Reidel, Boston, 1986.

19. P. R. Portney, "The Contingent Valuation Debate: Why Economists Should Care," *J. Econ. Perspect.*, *8*, 3–17 (Fall 1994).

20. N. Ahituv, "A Systematic Approach Towards Assessing the Value of an Information System," *MIS Quart.*, *3*, 61–75 (1980).

21. K. Ewusi-Mensah, "Evaluating Information Systems Projects: A Perspective on Cost–Benefit Analysis," *Inform. Syst.*, *14*, 205–217 (1989).

22. J. L. King and E. L. Schrens, "Cost–Benefit Analysis in Information Systems Development and Operation," *Comput. Survey*, *10*, 19–34 (1978).

23. K. K. Dompere, "Technological Progress and Optimal Supply Price," *Int. J. Product. Econ.*, *32*, 365–381 (1993).

24. X. Freixas and J.-J. Laffont, "Average Cost Pricing Versus Marginal Cost Pricing Under Moral Hazard," *J. Public Econ.*, *26*, 135–146 (1985).

25. S. Mushkin (ed.), *Public Prices for Public Products*, The Urban Institute, Washington, DC, 1972.

26. J. R. Nelson (ed.), *Marginal Cost Pricing in Practice*, Prentice-Hall, Englewood Cliffs, NJ, 1964.

27. H. E. Scarf, "The Computation of Equilibrium Prices," in *Applied General Equilibrium Analysis*, H. E. Scarf and J. B. Shoven (eds.), Cambridge University Press, New York, 1984, pp. 4–49.

28. R. Gregory, "Interpreting Measures of Economic Loss: Evidence from Contingent Valuation and Experimental Studies," *J. Environ. Econ. Manag.*, *13*, 325–337 (1986).

29. K. K. Dompere, "The Theory of Approximate Prices: Analytical Foundations of Experimental Cost–Benefit Analysis in a Fuzzy-Decision Space," *Fuzzy Sets Syst.*, *87*, 1–26 (1997).

30. E. S. Paul, "Pricing Rules and Efficiency," in *Public Prices for Public Products*, The Urban Institute, Washington, DC, 1972, pp. 73–95.

31. A. C. Harberger, "On the Use of Distributional Weights in Social Cost Benefit Analysis," *J. Political Econ.*, *86*(2), S87–S120 (1978).

32. A. C. Harberger, "Basic Needs Versus Distributional Weights in Social Cost Benefit Analysis," *Econ. Dev. Cultural Change*, *32*, 455–474 (1984).

33. J. A. Maciariello, *Dynamic Benefit–Cost Analysis*, D. C. Heath and Co., Lexington, MA, 1975.

34. A. Billot, "Aggregation of Preferences: The Fuzzy Case," *Theory Decision*, *3*, 51–93 (1991).

35. A. Billot, *Economic Theory of Fuzzy Equilibria: An Axiomatic Analysis*, Springer-Verlag, New York, 1992.

36. K. K. Dompere, "A Fuzzy Decision Theory of Optimal Social Discount Rate: Collective-Choice-Theoretic," *Fuzzy Sets Syst.*, *58*, 269–301 (1993).

37. M. S. Felstein, "The Social Time Preference Discount Rate in Cost–Benefit Analysis," *Econ. J.*, *74*, 360–379 (1964).

38. M. S. Felstein, "The Derivation of Social Time Preference Rates," *Kyklos*, *18*, 277–287 (1965).

39. R. E. Mikesell, *The Rate of Discount for Evaluating Public Projects*, American Enterprise Institute for Public Policy Research, Washington, DC, 1977.

BIBLIOGRAPHY

A. C. Harberger et al. (eds.), *Benefit-Cost and Policy Analysis 1971*, Aldine Publ., Chicago.

R. H. Haveman et al. (eds.), *Benefit-Cost and Policy Analysis 1973*, Aldine Publ., Chicago, 1974.

R. Zeckhauser et al. (eds.), *Benefit-Cost and Policy Analysis 1974*, Aldine Publ., Chicago, 1975.

C. Blackorby et al., "Consumers' Surpluses and Consistent Cost–Benefit Tests," *Social Choice Welfare*, *1*, 251–262 (1985).

J. R. Facey, "Critical Technologies Investment Portfolio Development," Office of Aeronautics, National Aeronautics and Space Administration, Washington, DC (August 1992).

D. Freeburg and E. S. Mills, *Measuring Benefits of Water Pollution Abatement*, Academic Press, New York, 1980.

J. Lesourne, *Cost–Benefit Analysis and Economic Theory*, North-Holland, New York, 1975.

Z. Grihches, "Reflections on Social Project Evaluation," *Acad. Econ. Papers*, *16*(2), 1–38 (1988).

R. W. Judy, "Costs: Theoretical and Methodological Issues," in *Cost-Benefit Analysis of Manpower Policies*, *Proceedings of North American Conference May 14–15, 1969*, G. G. Somers and W. D. Wood (eds.), The University of Wisconsin Press, Madison, 1969, pp. 16–29.

H. Jurgenson, "Private and Social Costs," *German Econ. Rev.*, *2*(4), 273–288 (1964).

R. N. McKean, "The Use of Shadow Prices," in *Cost–Benefit Analysis*, R. Layard (ed.), Penquin, Harmondsworth, U.K., 1972.

L. A., Cox, Jr., "Theory of Regulatory Benefits Assessment: Econometric and Expressed Preference Approaches," in [18], 85–159 (1986).

E. A. Crouch et al., *Risk/Benefit Analysis*, Ballinger, Cambridge, MA, 1982.

E. J. Green, "On the Difficulty of Eliciting Summary Information," *J. Econ. Theory*, *32*, 228–245 (1984).

A. Randall, J. P. Hoehn, and D. S. Brookshire, "Contingent Valuation Survey for Evaluating Environmental Assets," *Nat. Res. J.*, *23*(3), 635–648 (1983).

K. K. Dompere, "The Theory of Fuzzy Decisions," in *Fuzzy Information and Decision Processes*, M. M. Gupta and E. Sanchez (eds.), North-Holland, New York, 1982, pp. 365–379.

A. Kaufmann and M. M. Gupta, *Fuzzy Mathematical Models in Engineering and Management Science*, North-Holland, New York, 1988.

G. J. Klir, and B. Yuan, *Fuzzy Sets and Fuzzy Logic*, Prentice-Hall, Englewood Cliffs, NJ, 1995.

J. Artis, "Quantifying the Costs and Benefits of Computer Projects," in *Economics of Information*, A. Fridink (ed.), North-Holland, New York, 1975, pp. 15–24.

P. J. Dixon, "Planning MIS Investment expense Levels," *Inform. Manag.*, *1*, 173–175 (1978).

A. Fridink (ed.), *Economics of Informatics*, North-Holland, New York, 1975.

M. J. Ginzberg, "Improving MIS Project Selection," *Omega*, *7*, 527–537 (1979).

W. R. King and B. J. Epstein, "Assessing the Value of Information," *Manag. Datamatr.*, *5*, 171–180 (1976).

J. P. C. Kleijnen, "Quantifying the Benefits of Information Systems," *Eur. J. Oper. Res.*, *15*, 38–45 (1984).

J. Marschak, "Economics of Information Systems," *J. Am. Statist. Assoc.*, *66*, 192–219 (1971).

P. B. Turney, "Transfer Pricing Management Information Systems," *MIS Quart.*, *1*, 27–35 (1977).

S. R. Watson, "Decision Analysis as a Replacement for Cost/Benefit Analysis," *Eur. J. Oper. Res.*, *7*, 242–248 (1981).

W. J. Baumal, "On the Social Rate of Discount," *Am. Econ. Rev.*, *58*(40) 788–802 (1968).

W. S. Vickrey, "Economic Efficiency and Pricing," in *Public Prices for Public Products*, The Urban Institute, Washington, DC, 1972.

KOFI KISSI DOMPERE

EFFICIENT GENERATION OF RANDOM SENTENCES

INTRODUCTION

Writing a grammar for a natural language is a difficult task. A number of tools have been devised to assist the author of a grammar. For example, detection of *undergeneration* (i.e., the grammar generates not all the sentences it should) can be accomplished by automatically parsing a large corpus, and then selecting those sentences for which there is no parse according to the current version of the grammar.

For the detection of the opposite of undergeneration (viz. *overgeneration*), corpus analysis is not useful. However, the detection of overgeneration may be achieved by the (mechanical) random generation of sentences.* The grammar writer can inspect these sentences to find constructs that are unjustly generated by his grammar, and then make the appropriate corrections.

Random generators of sentences and sentence fragments have been incorporated into a number of development environments for grammatical formalisms (1–6). See Ref. 7, Chap. 8 for a more playful use.

Apart from the detection of overgeneration, some other applications can be found. For example, some grammar developers use sentence generation for monitoring the consequences that alterations to a grammar have with respect to the generated language. This is done as follows. A set of sentences is generated from the grammar, once before and once after the alteration. The grammaticality of the sentences from one version of the grammar is then checked with regard to the other. This may reveal wanted or unwanted differences in the languages generated by the two versions. This is an example of *progressive evaluation* (8).

Random generation of sentences may not only be applied for testing grammars but also for testing parsers (9,10) and natural language processing (NLP) systems (8). In the area of programming languages, randomly generated programs may be used to test compilers (11–15).

Further use may be found in the area of natural language interfaces: A frequent complaint is that a system's linguistic capabilities are not obvious to the user (16, Sec. 3). Perhaps, automatically generated sentences may be used by the developer of the system to compose a sample list of sentences within the linguistic coverage. This list is then used to instruct users in the possibilities of the system.

This article treats some technical aspects of the random generation of sentences and sentence fragments. We concentrate on a formalism called AGFL, which is a type of context-free grammar extended with arguments. The arguments range over finite domains, which causes useful properties related to parsing and generating to be decidable.

Our first implementation of the generator made use of naive top-down backtracking

---

*By "random," we mean that the sentences are *not* generated from some semantic value.

techniques, with a limit on the depth of derivations in order to ensure termination in the presence of recursion. However, extensive experimentation convinced us that the time complexities of such algorithms were unacceptably high for practical grammars, even with some techniques of smart backtracking.

Additional problems were caused by informal requirements that the generated sentences should not be too short, in order to allow interesting constructs to occur, but not too long, in order to allow insight into the structure of the sentences.

We have solved the problem of efficiency by precomputing for each nonterminal those combinations of argument values with which derivations from that nonterminal are possible. Together with such a combination of values, we also compute the minimal depth of such derivations.

The actual generation algorithm does not use any backtracking, so that it has a very low time complexity. The problem of generating sentences of convenient lengths has been solved by applying appropriate heuristics.

Because nonterminals may have a very large number of agruments, an efficient representation for sets of tuples of argument values was required. (This representation can also be applied for *parsing*, which has been discussed in Ref. 17.)

The structure of this article is as follows. First, we give an introduction to the formalism AGFL and show that naive generation algorithms are inadequate. This is followed by a discussion of the analysis of AGFLs and the actual random generation of sentences, which uses the results of this analysis. Subsequently, an efficient representation for sets of tuples or, in other words, for subsets of Cartesian products is discussed. We conclude by outlining possible variants and extensions of the basic analysis and generation algorithms, in two sections. The first of these sections proposes simple variants and extensions for formalisms such as AGFL. The second discusses generalization to unification-based formalisms.

AFFIX GRAMMARS OVER FINITE LATTICES

Affix grammars over finite lattices (AGFLs) are a restricted form of affix grammars (18–20). An affix grammar can be seen as a context-free grammar for which the rules are extended with *affixes* (cf. parameters, attributes, or features) to express agreement between parts of the rule. The distinguishing property of AGFLs is that the domains of the affixes are given by a restricted form of context-free grammar, the *meta-grammar*, in which each right-hand side consists of one terminal.

Formally, an AGFL G is a 7-tuple $(A_n, A_t, A_p, G_n, G_t, G_p, S)$ with the following properties.

The disjoint sets A_n and A_t and the function A_p together form the *meta-grammar* of G, where the following hold:

- A_n is the finite set of *affix nonterminals*.
- A_t is the finite set of *affix terminals*.
- A_p is a function from elements in A_n to subsets of A_t. The fact that A_p maps some affix nonterminal A to some set of affix terminals $\{x_1, \ldots, x_m\}$ is written as

$$A :: x_1; \ldots; x_m.$$

We call the set $\{x_1, \ldots, x_m\}$ the *domain* of A.

The elements from A_n occur in the rules of G_p, which we will define shortly, in the so-called *displays*. A display is a list of elements from A_n, separated by "," and enclosed in brackets "(" and ")." Displays consisting of zero affix nonterminals are omitted.

The set of lists of zero or more elements from some set D is denoted by D^*. Thus, the set of all displays is formally described as A_n^*.

For the second part of an AGFL G, we have the following:

- G_n is the finite set of *nonterminals*. Each nonterminal has a fixed arity, which is a non-negative integer.
- G_t is the finite set of *terminals* ($G_n \cap G_t = \varnothing$).
- G_p is the finite set of *rules* $\subseteq (G_n \times A_n^*) \times ((G_n \times A_n^*) \cup G_t)^*$. Rules are written in the form

$$N(\vec{d}): N_1(\vec{d}_1), \ldots, N_m(\vec{d}_m),$$

where $m \geq 0$ and N is a nonterminal, which is followed by a display $(\vec{d})$, and each member N_i, $1 \leq i \leq m$, is a terminal or nonterminal, which is followed by a display $(\vec{d}_i)$. The number of affix nonterminals in a display should correspond to the arity of the symbol preceding it (we assume the arity of terminals to be zero).
- The start symbol $S \in G_n$ has arity 0.

Example 1: The small AGFL in Figure 1 illustrates some of the above definitions. This example incorporates a number of shorthand constructions, which are explained as follows.

The affix terminal sing in the first alternative of pers pron constitutes a so-called *affix expression*, which is to be seen as an anonymous affix nonterminal, the domain of which is the singleton set {sing}. In general, an affix expression consists of one or more affix terminals, separated by "|" and denotes an anonymous affix nonterminal, the domain of which is the set of all specified affix terminals (e.g., the affix expression 1 | 3 denotes an affix nonterminal with domain {1,3}).

Another example of shorthand is the *guard* in the second alternative of "to be", which specifies under what conditions a form of "to be" is "are". The comma is to be seen as "and" and the semicolon as "or." The operator = denotes unification.

The full syntax of AGFLs is defined in Ref. 21. □

We use the term *variable* to refer to an instance of an affix nonterminal in an instance of a rule in a derivation (during parsing or generating).

Because the domains are finite, all possible values that variables can be instantiated with may be computed simultaneously, which reduces the amount of nondeterminism during parsing (and generating). Now, the unification of variables is no longer a test on equality of values, but it causes an intersection of two sets of values, which should be nonempty for the unification to succeed. It should be noted that even some formal presentations of AGFLs consider variables to be set-valued.

For now, we will assume that variables are instantiated with single affix terminals. We define a *substitution* σ for a rule to be a mapping from the affix nonterminals in the rule to affix terminals from the domains of the nonterminals. If $(\vec{d})$ is some display in a rule and σ is a substitution for that rule, then $\sigma(\vec{d})$ is defined to be the tuple of affix terminals that the affix nonterminals in $(\vec{d})$ are mapped to by σ.

```
PER ::  1; 2; 3.



NUM ::  sing; plur.



simple sentence:  pers pron (PER, NUM),

                  to be (PER, NUM),

                  adjective.



pers pron (1, sing):  "I".

pers pron (1, plur):  "we".

pers pron (2, NUM ):  "you".

pers pron (3, sing):  "he".

pers pron (3, plur):  "they".



to be (1,   sing):  "am".

to be (PER, NUM ):  "are", [PER = 2;

                             PER = 1 | 3, NUM = plur].

to be (3,   sing):  "is".



adjective:  "supercalifragilisticexpialadocious".
```

FIGURE 1   An example AGFL (with thanks to Mary Poppins).

Later, we will return to the idea that variables may be instantiated with sets of affix terminals.

NAIVE RANDOM GENERATION

In this section, we present an algorithm for generating random sentences using a naive top-down strategy. This algorithm consists of a recursive procedure G, which is to be called with two arguments, the first being a terminal or nonterminal and the second a tuple of affix terminals, the length of which matches the arity of the terminal or nonterminal. If it terminates, it returns a string derived from that (non)terminal with that tuple of affix terminals.

The procedure $\mathcal{G}$ is given in Figure 2. If the first argument is a terminal, then that terminal is the return value of the procedure. If the first argument is a nonterminal, then an appropriate rule is selected and the procedure is called recursively on the members from the right-hand side, with appropriate tuples of affix terminals. The string formed by the concatenation of the strings yielded by the recursive calls is the result of the procedure. (We denote the concatenation of strings by the operator +.)

The nondeterminism involved in choosing a rule and an appropriate substitution can be implemented using a generator of random numbers. For example, assume that for a nonterminal N and a tuple t, the grammar contains n rules of the form $N(\vec{d})$: $N_1(\vec{d_1})$, $\ldots, N_m(\vec{d_m})$ such that a substitution σ can be found that satisfies $\sigma(\vec{d}) = t$. The procedure may then make its choice based on a random number between 1 and n. A further random number may dictate the choice of an appropriate substitution σ if more than one exists.

In order to handle cases when no rule at all can be found, a backtracking mechanism may be introduced.

Regrettably, this simple algorithm does not perform very well in practice. It may loop or require a long time to terminate. [Termination is related to consistency of probabilistic grammars (22).]

Example 2: Consider the following AGFL, which is also a context-free grammar due to the absence of affix nonterminals:

procedure $\mathcal{G}(N, t)$:

    if N *is a terminal*

    then return *the name of* N

    else **for some** *rule* $N(\vec{d}) : N_1(\vec{d_1}), \ldots, N_m(\vec{d_m})$.

            and substitution σ *for this rule*

            and tuples $t_1, \ldots, t_m$

      such that $\sigma(\vec{d}) = t$, *and*

            for $1 \leq j \leq m$ *we have* $t_j = \sigma(\vec{d_j})$

      do return $\mathcal{G}(N_1, t_1) + \mathcal{G}(N_2, t_2) + \ldots + \mathcal{G}(N_m, t_m)$

      end

    end

  endproc

FIGURE 2   The naive generation algorithm.

```
a:  b.
a:  "p", a.
a:  a, "q", a.
b:  a.
b:  "r".
```

An example of a string generated by a call $\mathcal{G}$(a,( )) is given in Figure 3.

Note that if the algorithm selects one of the three rules for a by a probability of 1/3 each, and similarly selects one of the two rules for b by a probability of 1/2 each, then, in general, the chances are against termination of the algorithm.

The above grammar also demonstrates that simple refinements that introduce a bias toward selecting rules that do not lead to recursive calls cannot by themselves ensure termination, because *each* of the three rules for a may lead to recursion.   □

Termination can be ensured by imposing a limit on the depths of derivations: An additional argument to the procedure is a counter which is increased for each level of recursion. If this counter reaches a certain threshold, the algorithm backtracks.

However, the generation process may still be very expensive, as exponentially many prospective derivations are considered within the threshold.

Example 3: Consider the following grammar.

```
a:   b, c.
b:   b, b.
b:   "p".
c:   c1.
c1:  c2.
. . .
c8:  c9.
c9:  "q".
```

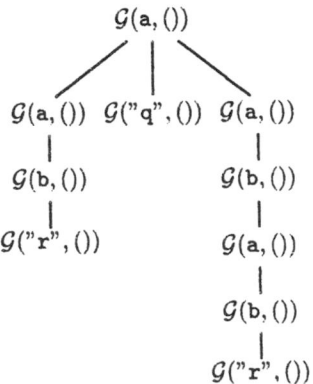

FIGURE 3   A call-graph for generation of "rqr".

For this grammar, no derivations exist of depth smaller than 11. If the threshold is set to 10, then eventually the algorithm will terminate (unsuccessfully), but many subderivations will have been computed for b; note that the number of subderivations for b is exponential in the threshold.   □

ANALYSIS OF AGFLs

For the generation of sentences to be possible using an algorithm which is guaranteed to return a result but does not use backtracking, we need to know in advance whether a derivation is possible from some nonterminal with some affix values within some restriction on the depths of derivations. The extra restriction on the depths of derivations pertains to our previously mentioned desire to generate sentences which are not too long. It also ensures termination of the generation process.

This information for each nonterminal and each tuple of affix values can be obtained by bottom-up analysis of the grammar. The result is a set of tuples for each nonterminal, such that derivations with those tuples of affix terminals exist. The tuples are partitioned according to the minimal depth of the possible derivations.

For our algorithm, we need the following variables. For each nonterminal N, we have the sets $D_i(N)$ of all tuples t such that with t a derivation of depth i has been found, but not of any depth $i' < i$; the maximum value for i that we need depends on the grammar. We also have the sets $D(N) = \cup_i D_i(N)$ of all tuples with which derivations of any depth have been found.

We compute the sets $D_i(N)$ for all nonterminals N, for $i = 1, 2, 3, \ldots$ in that order, based on the sets $D_{i'}(N')$ for other nonterminals N' and for $i' < i$, which have been computed earlier. We assume that initially $D_i(N) = \varnothing$ and $D(N) = \varnothing$ for all nonterminals N and indices i. For technical reasons, we also have constant values $D_0(T) = \{( )\}$ for all terminals T.

Figure 4 presents the algorithm in a naive way in order to enhance the simplicity of our presentation. The algorithm we actually implemented is more complicated and more efficient. In particular, we do not manipulate individual tuples but sets of tuples, as will be discussed later.

Note that we can correctly deal with rules with empty right-hand sides if we define *maximum*( ) = 0.

Example 4: Consider the following AGFL:

$$X :: 1;\ 2.$$
$$Y :: 1;\ 2;\ 3.$$
$$Z :: 1;\ 2.$$
$$W :: 2;\ 3.$$

$$a(X, Z): b(X, Y), c(Y, Z).$$
$$a(X, Z): a(X, Z), d(Z).$$

$$b(X, X): \text{``p''}.$$
$$c(W, Z): \text{``q''}.$$
$$d(W): \text{``r''}.$$

$i := 0;$

repeat $i := i + 1;$

    for each *rule* $N(\vec{d}) : N_1(\vec{d_1}), \ldots, N_m(\vec{d_m}).$

        and substitution σ *for this rule*

        and tuples $t_1, \ldots, t_m$

        and indices $i_1, \ldots, i_m$

    such that *for* $1 \le j \le m$ *we have*

$$t_j \in D_{i_j}(N_j) \text{ and}$$

$$t_j = \sigma(\vec{d_j}), \text{ and}$$

$$maximum(i_1, \ldots, i_m) = i - 1$$

    do $t := \sigma(\vec{d});$

      if $t \notin D(N)$

      then $D(N) := D(N) \cup \{t\};$

$$D_i(N) := D_i(N) \cup \{t\}$$

    end

  end

until $D_i(N) = \emptyset$ *for all* N

end.

FIGURE 4   The analysis algorithm.

The algorithm computes

$$D_0(\text{``p''}) = D_0(\text{``q''}) = D_0(\text{``r''}) = \{(\ )\},$$
$$D_1(\text{b}) = \{(1,1),(2,2)\},$$
$$D_1(\text{c}) = \{(2,1),(2,2),(3,1),(3,2)\},$$
$$D_1(\text{d}) = \{(2),(3)\},$$
$$D_2(\text{a}) = \{(2,1),(2,2)\}.$$

The $D_i(N)$ for all other combinations of i and N remain $\emptyset$. $\square$

RANDOM GENERATION OF SENTENCES

Relying on the sets $D_i(N)$ which have been computed by the algorithm from the previous section, we can generate sentences top-down without backtracking. We usually begin at the start symbol S, but we can also begin at any other nonterminal N. In the case where we begin at N, we take some tuple t from $D_i(N)$, for some i. We know that derivations within some maximum depth $k \geq i$ from N with t are possible.

We determine some value $k \geq i$ using some heuristics (the higher k is chosen, the deeper the computed derivation may be). We then call a procedure $\mathcal{G}$ with arguments N, t, and k. This procedure is to return a string generated by some derivation from N with t, of some depth $\leq k$. (For some applications, the derivation itself may be returned.)

The procedure $\mathcal{G}$ is a recursive function which selects some rule such that derivations from the members with appropriate affix values are possible, and of which the depths are within the limit dictated by the argument k. The procedure then calls itself recursively for each member in the chosen rule with an appropriate tuple of values and with the limit on the depths of derivations reduced by (at least) 1.

Formally, $\mathcal{G}$ is defined by Figure 5.

The nondeterminism in this algorithm may be resolved using random generators, possibly guided by some heuristics.

Example 5: For the running example, we may call, for example, $\mathcal{G}(\mathsf{a},(2,2),6)$, as $(2,2) \in D_2(\mathsf{a})$ and $6 \geq 2$. One of the sentences which may be generated by this call is "pqr", as shown by the call-graph in Figure 6. Due to the nondeterminism of the generation algorithm, other third components in calls of $\mathcal{G}$ might have been used. For example, instead of the call $\mathcal{G}(\mathsf{d},(2),4)$, we may have had any call $\mathcal{G}(\mathsf{d},(2),k)$ for k less than 6 (the third component of the mother node in the call-graph) but greater than or equal to 1 [the value i such that $(2) \in D_i(\mathsf{d})$].

Furthermore, other sentences, such as "pq" and "pqrr", would have been generated by $\mathcal{G}(\mathsf{a},(2,2),6)$ if other rules had been chosen in recursive incarnations of $\mathcal{G}$. □

EFFICIENT PROCESSING OF SETS OF TUPLES

Typically, nonterminals in AGFLs for natural languages have large arities—in some cases, more than eight. Furthermore, the domains sometimes contain more than 50 affix terminals. Consequently, processing and storage of all possible combinations of affix terminals is often not feasible.

Fortunately, the set of tuples of affix terminals with which derivations exist from a certain nonterminal is typically a Cartesian product of a number of domains. (For nonterminals where this does not hold, usually a mistake in the design of the grammar can be found.) Note that a Cartesian product of domains may be represented as a list of those domains, which requires $\mathcal{O}(m \times q)$ space although $\mathcal{O}(q^m)$ tuples may be represented, where m is the arity of the nonterminal and q is the size of the largest domain.

Also, for the intermediate results in our analysis and during random generation of sentences, this representation may be used. In those cases, however, we sometimes need a union of a number of Cartesian products to represent a set of tuples. This amounts to the representation of a set of tuples of affix terminals by a set of tuples of sets of affix terminals.

For example, the set of tuples

procedure $\mathcal{G}(N, t, k)$:

    if N *is a terminal*

    then return N

    else for some *rule* $N(\vec{d}) : N_1(\vec{d_1}), \ldots, N_m(\vec{d_m})$.

            and substitution σ for this rule

            and tuples $t_1, \ldots, t_m$

            and indices $i_1, \ldots, i_m$

      such that $\sigma(\vec{d}) = t$, *and*

          for $1 \leq j \leq m$ we have

               $t_j = \sigma(\vec{d_j})$ *and*

               $t_j \in D_{i_j}(N_j)$ *and*

               $i_j < k$

    do *choose some numbers $k_1, \ldots, k_m$ such that*

        $i_j \leq k_j < k$ *for* $1 \leq j \leq m$;

        return $\mathcal{G}(N_1, t_1, k_1) + \mathcal{G}(N_2, t_2, k_2) + \ldots + \mathcal{G}(N_m, t_m, k_m)$

    end

  end

endproc

FIGURE 5   The efficient generation algorithm.

$$\{(a,\ b,\ d),\ (a,\ b,\ e),$$
$$(a,\ c,\ d),\ (a,\ c,\ e),$$
$$(p,\ x,\ y),\ (q,\ x,\ y)\}$$

can be represented by the set of tuples of sets

$$\{(\{a\},\ \{b,\ c\},\ \{d,\ e\}),\ (\{p,\ q\},\ \{x\},\ \{y\})\}.$$

This form can be obtained by first taking the following set of tuples of singleton sets:

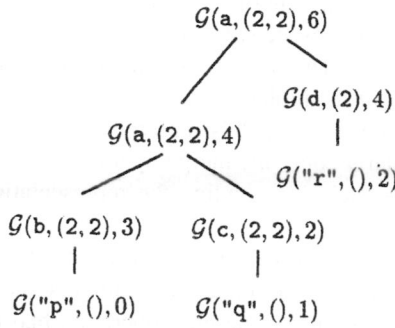

FIGURE 6   One possible call-graph for generation of "pqr".

$$\{(\{a\}, \quad \{b\}, \quad \{d\}), \quad (\{a\}, \quad \{b\}, \quad \{e\}),$$
$$(\{a\}, \quad \{c\}, \quad \{d\}), \quad (\{a\}, \quad \{c\}, \quad \{e\}),$$
$$(\{p\}, \quad \{x\}, \quad \{y\}), \quad (\{q\}, \quad \{x\}, \quad \{y\})\}$$

and by then merging pairs of tuples; for example, $(\{a\}, \{b\}, \{d\})$ and $(\{a\}, \{b\}, \{e\})$ can be merged into $(\{a\}, \{b\}, \{d, e\})$. Repeated application of merging leads to the desired form.

The union of two sets represented in this form is complicated by the fact that two tuples may overlap; for example, if we want to compute the union of $\{(X, Y, Z)\}$ and $\{(P, Q, R)\}$, where $X, Y, Z, P, Q,$ and R denote sets of affix terminals, we may have that $X \cap P \neq \varnothing$, $Y \cap Q \neq \varnothing$, and $Z \cap R \neq \varnothing$. A solution is to formulate, for example, $\{(P, Q, R)\}$ into a different form*:

$$\{(P \; - \; X, \quad Q, \qquad R),$$
$$(P \; \cap \; X, Q \; - \; Y, \; R),$$
$$(P \; \cap \; X, Q \; \cap \; Y, R \; - \; Z),$$
$$(P \; \cap \; X, Q \; \cap \; Y, R \; \cap \; Z)\}.$$

Possibly some of the tuples in this form may be discarded because one or more of their parts may be the empty set.

The union of the two sets is now represented by

$$\{(X, \qquad Y, \qquad Z),$$
$$(P \; - \; X, \quad Q, \qquad R),$$
$$(P \; \cap \; X, Q \; - \; Y, \; R),$$
$$(P \; \cap \; X, Q \; \cap \; Y, R \; - \; Z)\}.$$

This example demonstrates that this representation can become fragmented considerably because of the union operation (this also holds for subtraction of sets of tuples,

---

*Note a similarity to lifting disjunction in feature descriptions (23).

not shown here). To be exact, the union of k (nonoverlapping) tuples of sets with m (nonoverlapping) tuples of sets, respectively, may yield a set consisting of more than $k + m$ (again, nonoverlapping) tuples of sets, in general, less than or equal to $k + m \times t^k$ tuples, where t is the width of the tuples.

To prevent quick degeneration of this representation to sets of tuples of singleton sets, it is necessary to regularly apply the merge operation, which reduces the number of tuples (possibly after deliberately fragmenting the representation further to allow more extensive merging).

We have found that the costs of merging tuples of sets do not outweigh the high costs of operating on tuples of affix terminals. It required some experimenting, however, to determine how often the expensive merging operation had to be applied to improve instead of deteriorate the time complexity. In some cases, allowing temporary overlapping of tuples in a set proved to reduce the time costs of the analysis.

In the present implementation, overlapping is allowed during an iteration of the analysis algorithm (i.e., for one instance of counter i). At the end of each such iteration, the sets $D_i(N)$ and $D(N)$ are restructured by eliminating the overlapping of tuples and by applying the merging operation.

A representation of sets of tuples similar to ours is proposed in Ref. 24. This representation, called *sharing trees*, may be more compact than ours and has the advantage that a unique sharing tree exists for each set of tuples, which simplifies the test for equivalence. However, sharing trees were developed with a certain application in mind (analysis of synchronized automata) and it seems that, for our case, sharing trees would not behave any better than the above representation, using sets of tuples of sets. This is because the analysis of AGFLs requires different operations (such as subtraction), some of which are more complicated for sharing trees than for our representation.

SIMPLE VARIANTS AND EXTENSIONS

The analysis and the generation algorithm are based on the idea of computing, for each nonterminal and each tuple, the minimal depth of which derivations exist. An obvious variant results from using other quantities besides the minimal depths of derivations. We could, for instance, also take the minimal lengths of generated sentences from nonterminals with certain tuples. Other quantities, such as the number of nodes in derivations, are possible as well. For some grammars, such alternative quantities may give better results.

One may further consider the use of rule head information (25) to influence the generation process. For example, one may choose k_j to be $k - 1$ if $N_k(\vec{d_k})$ is the head of the rule $N(\vec{d}): N_1(\vec{d_1}), \ldots, N_m(\vec{d_m})$, and i_j otherwise. This results in deep but narrow derivations, with the depth in the direction of the heads.

Such assignments to k_j may also play a role when sentences of specific forms are desired: The user may want to find sentences exhibiting a certain linguistic phenomenon. For this, certain subderivations may need to be deep, whereas other subderivations should be short and simple because they do not directly pertain to the investigated phenomenon (8). This idea may be realized by marking certain grammar rules that should be contained in the constructed derivations, or by allowing the user instead of the automatic generator to select the appropriate grammar rules at some critical moments (5). After construction of a part of a derivation containing the required rules, where all k_j are chosen to be

$k - 1$, the remaining parts of the derivation are completed in the most simple way, by choosing all k_j to be i_j.

We have not considered the task of generating a set of sentences that is as small as possible, yet contains at least one occurrence of each rule. We refer to Refs. 9, 12, and 13 for such algorithms. We feel that these algorithms, devised for the testing of compilers for programming languages, are not very useful for the detection of overgeneration of natural language grammars, as overgeneration seems to be typically caused by the unforeseen interaction of several rules, instead of by individual rules. The requirement that each rule occurs at least once is therefore not sufficient. However, the general idea of increasing the coverage of a limited set of generated sentences by avoiding frequent repetition of language constructions may lead to interesting variants of our algorithm.

Other possible refinements include extension of the grammar with probabilities (11,14,15).

A last remark concerns an optimization of the analysis with regard to the subsequent generation. Our algorithm also allows generation from nonterminals other than from the start symbol S. Because, from a certain nonterminal N, not every other nonterminal M may be reachable, the execution of $\mathcal{G}(N,t,k)$ for some t and k may be performed without previous computation of $D(M)$ and $D_i(M)$ for many nonterminals M. In addition, the tuple t with which $\mathcal{G}$ is called may give rise to a further reduction of the search space, as not all tuples t' for a nonterminal M reachable from N may be relevant for derivations from N with t. Computing only the relevant tuples can, for example, be achieved by *magic transformations* (26).

UNIFICATION-BASED FORMALISMS

The formalism of AGFL we have considered up to this point has attractive properties from a computational point of view. In particular, we have seen that the minimal depth of derivations from a certain nonterminal with a certain tuple is effectively computable.

However, the grammatical formalisms that are used in practice for natural language processing are often more expressive than AGFL. An example are the unification-based formalisms, of which the definite clause grammars (DCGs) (27) are a well-known instance.

In DCGs, we have *terms* as arguments instead of affixes. A term can be one of the following:

- A constant, which is comparable to an affix terminal
- A variable, comparable to an affix nonterminal
- An expression of the form $f(\tau_1, \ldots, \tau_m)$, $m > 0$, where f is a *functor* and $\tau_1, \ldots, \tau_m$ are terms

There is no equivalent to the meta-grammars that we known from AGFLs, although a similar system can be derived, as shown later in this section. A nonterminal together with arguments will itself be seen as a term, by regarding the nonterminal as functor.

The language described by a grammar can be defined analogously to that in the case of AGFLs: The variables in instances of rules are instantiated with *ground* terms, which means that no variables occur within those terms. A *parse tree* formed by such a collection of the rule instances derives a string in the language (cf. the tree structure in

Fig. 6). Two rules are linked through the left-hand side of the one and a member in the right-hand side of the other, which is allowed if they are identical after the instantiation.

For efficiency reasons however, practical implementations do not instantiate arguments further than necessary, or more precisely, variables are instantiated with terms which may contain variables themselves, until additional rule instances in the parse tree under construction provide sufficient information to further guide such instantiations effectively (cf. computations with tuples of sets of affix terminals in the case of AGFLs).

An example of a substitution is $\sigma = \{X/g(a,Y),Z/b\}$, which means that all occurrences of X are to be replaced by the term $g(a,Y)$ and those of Z are to be replaced by b; for example, $\sigma(f(X,h(Z,Z))) = f(g(a,Y),h(b,b))$.

We say a term τ is *more general* than τ', denoted $\tau \sqsubseteq \tau'$, if there is a substitution σ such that $\sigma(\tau) = \tau'$.

A key notion for parsing and generation with DCGs is *unification* of terms. An example is unification of two terms $f(X,a)$ and $f(g(Y,Z),Y)$, which is given by $f(X,a) \sqcup f(g(Y,Z),Y) = f(g(a,Z),a)$. Informally, the term $f(g(a,Z),a)$ is the most general term that can be obtained from both $f(X,a)$ and $f(g(Y,Z),Y)$ by a substitution. If such a unification of terms τ and τ' exists, we say τ and τ' are *unifiable*.

The substitution that instantiates the variables from two terms such that the unified term results is called the *most general unifier*. The most general unifier for terms τ and τ', if it exists, is denoted by $mgu(\tau,\tau')$. In general, $\sigma = mgu(\tau,\tau')$ implies $\sigma(\tau) = \sigma(\tau') = \tau \sqcup \tau'$. For the running example, $mgu(f(X,a),f(g(Y,Z),Y)) = \{X/g(a,Z),Y/a\}$.

The definition of *mgu* can be generalized to pairs of tuples of equal lengths: $mgu((\tau_1, \ldots, \tau_m), (\tau_1', \ldots, \tau_m'))$ is the most general substitution σ such that $\sigma(\tau_1) = \sigma(\tau_1')$, $\ldots, \sigma(\tau_m) = \sigma(\tau_m')$.

The precise definition of unification is outside the scope of the present article; we refer to Ref. 28 for further explanation.

Analysis of DCGs

Because the number of (ground) terms that arguments can be instantiated to is, in general, infinite, we need to adapt the analysis that we have performed for AGFLs. Instead of computing the minimal depths of derivations for all possible ground instantiations, we compute those depths for a finite number of tuples of arguments that have been instantiated down to a certain depth, but no further. This is achieved by the notion of *restriction* (29). A *restrictor* is a function that truncates a term (i.e., that replaces subterms by fresh variables). A suitable restrictor for our purposes maps each term over a fixed set of functors and constants to a truncated one from a *finite* set of such terms.

A simple example of a restrictor is Φ_2, which truncates terms beyond the depth of two nested functors; for example, $\Phi_2(f(g(h(X,a),i(b)),c)) = f(g(Y,Z),c)$. We will discuss more refined types of restrictor later.

The objective of the analysis of DCGs is to compute the minimal depths of derivations from the finite set of truncated terms. As Figure 7 shows, existing terms from D_{i_j} are combined by unifying them with members in the right-hand side of a rule. The most general unifier is then applied to the left-hand side. The result is truncated according to some suitable restrictor Φ and matched against terms derived earlier. It is discarded if some existing term is more general; otherwise, it is added to the sets D and D_i.

We initialize $D_i = \varnothing$ for all indices $i > 0$, and $D_0 = \{T \mid T \text{ is a terminal}\}$.

$$i := 0;$$

repeat $i := i + 1;$

    for each *rule* $\tau : \tau_1, \ldots, \tau_m$.

        and substitution σ

        and terms $\tau_1', \ldots, \tau_m'$

        and indices $i_1, \ldots, i_m$

    such that *for* $1 \leq j \leq m$ *we have* $\tau_j' \in D_{i_j}$, *and*

$$\sigma = mgu((\tau_1, \ldots, \tau_m), (\tau_1', \ldots, \tau_m')), \; and$$

$$maximum(i_1, \ldots, i_m) = i - 1$$

    do $\tau' := \Phi(\sigma(\tau));$

        if $\neg \exists \tau'' \in D[\tau'' \sqsubseteq \tau']$

        then $D := D \cup \{\tau'\};$

            $D_i := D_i \cup \{\tau'\}$

    end

  end

until $D_i = \emptyset$

end.

FIGURE 7   The analysis algorithm for DCGs.

Generation for DCGs

The use of restrictors ensures termination of the analysis, but it no longer guarantees the existence of derivations of a certain depth: If $\tau \in D_i$ for some i, then a derivation from τ of depth i may exist, but it is not guaranteed to exist. The generation algorithm must, therefore, be able to deal with failure of the construction of a prospective derivation.

There are two obvious ways to deal with failure. First, if certain choices lead to failure, we may backtrack. This has the advantage that computation done before a "wrong" choice was made can still be used to successfully obtain a derivation. The disadvantage is that excessive (unsuccessful) computation may be needed before that choice is ever retracted. The other option is to restart the generation process from the beginning upon failure.

In our implementation, we have avoided the use of backtracking as long as possible, in order to avoid the disadvantage mentioned above. Only in the process of choosing the next rule is backtracking applied. Once a rule is chosen, the algorithm is committed to that choice. When the generation process arrives at a situation where no appropriate rules can be found, the current attempt is abandoned and the procedure is started afresh. (In our experiments, failure occurs for about two out of three attempts to generate a sentence.)

The procedure is given in Figure 8 in an abstract form. What is not given explicitly is the backtracking needed to find some rule, a substitution, terms, and indices with the required conditions. Also not shown is that all incarnations of the procedure are aborted when the above-mentioned objects cannot be found in one such incarnation.

The procedure is to be called with arguments τ' and k, where τ' is unifiable with some $\tau \in D_i$ and $k \geq i$, analogously to the generation algorithm for AGFLs that we have seen earlier.

In selecting the rule, we demand that the left-hand side τ unifies with the first parameter τ' and that the members in the right-hand side unify with terms in appropriate sets D_{i_j} (cf. Fig. 5). The most general unifier σ_0 is determined, and in the first recursive call for the first member τ_1 of the rule, this substitution is applied on that member τ_1. The motivation for instantiating variables in that member at an early stage is that it may help recursive incarnations of the procedure to select only those rules that are likely to lead to successful generation. Note that there is no need to take into account the unification of the first member τ_1 itself with some τ_1' for the purpose of computing σ_0, as the variables in τ_1 will be appropriately instantiated in the first recursive call in any case.*

The first recursive call results in a pair (τ_1'', w_1), where w_1 is a string derived from τ_1'' and $\sigma_0(\tau_1) \sqsubseteq \tau_1''$ due to possible further instantiation of variables from τ_1 in recursive incarnations. Now, a substitution σ_1 is computed, this time taking into account τ_1'' instead of τ_1', and the next recursive call is made.

This is repeated until, for each member in the right-hand side, a string w_i has been found that is generated from that member. The substitution σ^m accumulates the results from all unifications performed recursively and is applied on the left-hand side to form $\sigma_m(\tau)$, which is returned together with the concatenated string $w_1 + \cdots + w_m$.

We have performed experiments with HPSG-style grammars (30), which were compiled to DCGs. Such grammars contain many lexical entries, which are, in effect, rules of the form $\tau : T$, where T is a terminal and τ a term. In comparison to the lexical entries, the grammar contains few other rules. This means that if lexical entries and other rules are treated on an equal footing, then the generation procedure will choose lexical entries with a very high probability, which leads to very short sentences being generated.

Our solution is the following. We choose fixed numbers a and b, where $0 < b < a$. Appropriate values can be determined empirically. At the beginning of the procedure in Figure 8, a random number r between 0 and a is generated, and if $b < r$, then lexical entries will be tried first and only then the other rules; otherwise, lexical entries are tried last.

Among the rules that are not lexical entries, we further implemented a bias toward selection of rules that have not been selected very often before. Among lexical entries, a similar bias is implemented.

---

*For a rule with zero members or one member in the right-hand side, we have $m=0$ or $m=1$, respectively. In both cases, the expression $mgu((\tau, \tau_2, \ldots, \tau_m), (\tau', \tau_2', \ldots, \tau_m'))$ should be read as $mgu(\tau, \tau')$. For a rule with zero members, the condition "τ_1 and $\sigma_0(\tau_1')$ are unifiable" should be read as "true."

procedure $\mathcal{G}(\tau', k)$:

    if τ' *is a terminal*

    then return (τ', τ')

    else   **for some** *rule* $\tau : \tau_1, \ldots, \tau_m$.

                and substitution σ_0

                and terms $\tau'_1, \ldots, \tau'_m$

                and indices $i_1, \ldots, i_m$

      such that $\sigma_0 = mgu((\tau, \tau_2, \ldots, \tau_m), (\tau', \tau'_2, \ldots, \tau'_m))$,

              τ_1 *and* $\sigma_0(\tau'_1)$ *are unifiable, and*

              for $1 \le j \le m$ *we have*

              $\tau'_j \in D_{i_j}$ *and*

              $i_j < k$

    do *choose some numbers* $k_1, \ldots, k_m$ *such that*

        $i_j \le k_j < k$ *for* $1 \le j \le m$;

      for $j = 1, \ldots, m$

      do $(\tau''_j, w_j) := \mathcal{G}(\sigma_{j-1}(\tau_j), k_j)$;

        $\sigma_j := mgu((\tau, \tau_1, \tau_2, \ldots, \tau_m), (\tau', \tau''_1, \ldots, \tau''_j, \tau'_{j+1}, \ldots, \tau'_m))$

      end;

      return $(\sigma_m(\tau), w_1 + \ldots + w_m)$

    end

  end

endproc

FIGURE 8   Generation for DCGs.

It is important to note that the above ideas are merely heuristics. They work well for some grammars that we have developed, but for other grammars, the analysis and generation algorithms may require changes.

Appropriate Restrictors

The analysis applies a restrictor Φ to reduce the number of terms that need to be stored in the sets D_i. In order to ensure that the analysis terminates, only a finite number of such terms should be considered, and for this, it is sufficient that the restrictor maps each term to a truncated term from a *finite* set of such terms. A second requirement is that the restrictor does not truncate more than necessary, because the more is truncated, the worse the precision becomes and the larger is the chance that subsequent attempts to generate sentences will fail.

These requirements are satisfied by a restrictor that truncates subterms that are potentially unbounded in depth. What subterms possess this potential can be found by means of type inference. Not all kinds of type inference are equally precise. The algorithm we have implemented is relatively crude with respect to other published algorithms (31–33).

For each argument position, we introduce a *type*, not only for arguments to nonterminals but also for arguments to functors embedded in terms in the grammar. Such a type represents the set of terms that may occur at the argument position. We record how different types are related according to the way the corresponding terms and subterms are related by functor and argument position.

If in a rule two subterms are represented by the same variable, the corresponding types are unified. In contrast to more advanced kinds of type inference, described, for example, in Refs. 31–33, our type unification amounts to union only; no intersection is applied. This means that unification of types T_1 and T_2 results in a type T_3, which represents at least as many terms as those represented by T_1 and T_2 together.

If types are then found to be recursive, this indicates that corresponding subterms may be unboundedly deep and our restrictor will apply truncation of just those subterms.

Example 6: Consider the following grammar:

$$a(h(f(X)), Y): a(h(X), Y), b(g(Y)).$$

$$a(h(i), j): \text{"p"}.$$

$$b(g(j)): \text{"q"}.$$

The type system below can be inferred. Our notation stresses that the system is very similar to a meta-grammar for AGFLs:

$$S :: a(T1, T3); b(T4).$$

$$T1 :: h(T2).$$

$$T2 :: f(T2); i.$$

$$T3 :: j.$$

$$T4 :: g(T3).$$

The "supertype" S represents all nonterminals together with their arguments. For nonterminal a, the arguments are of type T1 and T3. A term of type T1 is composed of a functor h and an argument of type T2. Type T2 is recursive: It is a subtype of itself. This indicates that terms of that type may be unboundedly deep.

A restrictor Φ that truncates terms at recursive types will map a term such as $a(h(f(f(i)))), j)$ to $a(h(X), j)$. □

CONCLUSIONS

We have presented an algorithm for AGFLs which finds random derivations without resorting to backtracking. This algorithm relies on an analysis of the grammar. The reason the algorithm always terminates is that a non-negative value is kept which decreases each time we descend the derivation under construction. The reason the algorithm cannot fail is that the results of the analysis provide enough information to successfully guide the algorithm toward a complete derivation.

The feasibility of the analysis depends on the efficient processing of sets of tuples. Experience has shown that the analysis takes less time than finding a single derivation using a top-down backtrack algorithm.

Our technique allows much flexibility: Many variants are possible, and the under-specified parts of the generation algorithm can be made more precise so as to generate sentences according to certain syntactic requirements.

The technique has also been generalized to unification-based grammars. Because the analysis in this case cannot be exact without risking nontermination, the subsequent generation algorithm cannot rely on precise guidance of how to find a complete derivation and may consequently fail. However, because each attempt at constructing a derivation is inexpensive, it does not necessarily lead to excessive time consumption if a successful generation attempt is preceded by several unsuccessful attempts.

ACKNOWLEDGMENTS

Cambridge University Press has kindly granted permission for reprint of a number of sections from an article with the same name, published as *Natural Language Engineering*, 2(1), 1–13 (1996).

Much of the ideas in this paper were developed at the Computer Science Department of the University of Nijmegen and at the Department of Humanities Computing of the University of Groningen. The author is currently funded by the German Federal Ministry of Education, Science, Research and Technology (BMBF) in the framework of the VERBMOBIL Project under Grant 01 IV 701 V0.

REFERENCES

1. V. H. Yngve, "Computer Programs for Translation," *Sci. Am.*, 68–76 (June 1962).
2. V. H. Yngve, "Random Generation of English Sentences," in *1961 International Conference on Machine Translation of Languages and Applied Language Analysis*, Her Majesty's Stationery Office, London, 1962, Vol. 1, pp. 66–82.
3. O. Lecarme, "Usability and Portability of a Compiler Writing Systems," in *Methods of Algorithmic Language Implementation*, Lecture Notes in Computer Science Vol. 47, Springer-Verlag, Berlin, 1977, pp. 41–62.
4. L. Karttunen and M. Kay, "Parsing in a Free Word Order Language," in *Natural Language*

Parsing: Psychological, Computational, and Theoretical Perspectives, D. R. Dowty, L. Karttunen, and A. M. Zwicky (eds.), Cambridge University Press, Cambridge, 1985, pp. 279–306.

5. B. Boguraev, J. Carroll, T. Briscoe, and C. Grover, "Software Support for Practical Grammar Development," in *Proc. of the 12th International Conference on Computational Linguistics*, 1988, Vol. 1, pp. 54–58.

6. M.-J. Nederhof and K. Koster, "A Customized Grammar Workbench," in *English Language Corpora: Design, Analysis and Exploitation*, J. Aarts, P. de Haan, and N. Oostdijk (eds.), Rodopi, 1992, pp. 163–179.

7. D. R. Hofstadter, *Gödel, Escher, Bach: An Eternal Golden Braid*, Basic Books, New York, 1979.

8. L. Balkan, D. Arnold, and F. Fouvry, "Test Suites for Evaluation in Natural Language Engineering," in *Proceedings of the Second Language Engineering Convention*, 1995, pp. 203–210.

9. P. Purdom, "A Sentence Generator for Testing Parsers," *BIT*, *12*, 366–375 (1972).

10. C. S. Mellish, "Some Chart-Based Techniques for Parsing Ill-Formed Input," in *27th Annual Meeting of the Association for Computational Linguistics, Proceedings of the Conference*, 1989, pp. 102–109.

11. A. J. Payne, "A Formalised Technique for Expressing Compiler Exercisers," *SIGPLAN Notices*, *13*(1), 59–69 (1978).

12. A. Celentano, et al., "Compiler Testing Using a Sentence Generator," *Software—Practice Experience*, *10*, 897–918 (1980).

13. F. Bazzichi and I. Spadafora, "An Automatic Generator for Compiler Testing," *IEEE Trans. Software Eng.*, *8*(4), 343–353 (1982).

14. V. Murali and R. K. Shyamasundar, "A Sentence Generator for a Compiler for PT, a Pascal Subset," *Software—Practice Experience*, *13*, 857–869 (1983).

15. D. L. Bird and C. U. Munoz, "Automatic Generation of Random Self-Checking Test Cases," *IBM Syst. J.*, *22*(3), 229–245 (1983).

16. I. Androutsopoulos, G. D. Ritchie, and P. Thanisch, "Natural Language Interfaces to Databases—An Introduction," *Nat. Lang. Eng.*, *1*(1), 29–81 (1995).

17. M.-J. Nederhof and J. J. Sarbo, "Efficient Decoration of Parse Forests," in *Feature Formalisms and Linguistic Ambiguity*, H. Trost (ed.), Ellis Horwood, New York, 1993, pp. 53–78.

18. C. H. A. Koster, "Affix Grammars," in *ALGOL68 Implementation*, J. E. L. Peck (ed.), North-Holland, Amsterdam, 1971, pp. 95–109.

19. C. H. A. Koster, "Affix Grammars for Natural Languages," in *Attribute Grammars, Applications and Systems, International Summer School SAGA*, Lecture Notes in Computer Science Vol. 545, Springer-Verlag, New York, 1991, pp. 358–373.

20. M.-J. Nederhof, "On the Borderline Between Finite and Infinite Argument Domains," in *Proceedings of the First AGFL Workshop*, C. H. A. Koster and E. Oltmans (eds.), Technical Report CSI-R9604, Computing Science Institute (January 1996), pp. 17–43.

21. C. Dekkers, C. H. A. Koster, M.-J. Nederhof, and A. van Zwol, "Manual for the Grammar WorkBench Version 1.5," Technical Report 92-14, Department of Computer Science, University of Nijmegen (July 1992).

22. T. L. Booth and R. A. Thompson, "Applying Probabilistic Measures to Abstract Languages," *IEEE Trans. Computers*, *C-22*(5), 442–450 (1973).

23. A. Eisele and J. Dörre, "Unification of Disjunctive Feature Descriptions," in *26th Annual Meeting of the Association for Computational Linguistics, Proceedings of the Conference*, 1988, pp. 286–294.

24. D. Zampuniéris and B. Le Charlier, "A Yet More Efficient Algorithm to Compute the Synchronized Product," Research Report 94/5, Institute of Computer Science—FUNDP Namur, Belgium (1994).

25. G. van Noord, "Reversibility in Natural Language Processing," Ph.D. thesis, University of Utrecht (1993).

26. S. Debray and R. Ramakrishnan, "Abstract Interpretation of Logic Programs Using Magic Transformations," *J. Logic Program.*, *18*, 149–176 (1994).
27. F. C. N. Pereira and D. H. D. Warren, "Definite Clause Grammars for Language Analysis—A Survey of the Formalism and a Comparison with the Augmented Transition Networks," *Artif. Intell.*, *13*, 231–278 (1980).
28. J. W. Lloyd, *Foundations of Logic Programming*, Springer-Verlag, New York, 1984.
29. S. M. Shieber, "Using Restriction to Extend Parsing Algorithms for Complex-Feature-Based Formalisms," in *23rd Annual Meeting of the Association for Computational Linguistics, Proceedings of the Conference*, 1985, pp. 145–152.
30. C. Pollard and I. A. Sag, *Information-Based Syntax and Semantics*, Center for the Study of Language and Information, Leland Stanford Junior University, 1987.
31. P. Mishra, "Towards a Theory of Types in Prolog," in *International Symposium on Logic Programming*, 1984, pp. 289–298.
32. E. Yardeni and E. Shapiro, "A Type System for Logic Programs," *J. Logic Program.*, *10*, 125–153 (1991).
33. N. Heintze and J. Jaffar, "Set Constraints and Set-Based Analysis," in *Principles and Practice of Constraint Programming, Second International Workshop*, Lecture Notes in Computer Science Vol. 874, Springer-Verlag, New York, 1994, pp. 281–298.

MARK-JAN NEDERHOF

INFORMATION ENERGY AND ITS APPLICATIONS

INTRODUCTION

The concept of information appears as one of the most fundamental concepts in science and technical fields of our century, a concept of larger importance than that of matter and energy. According to Wiener (1), "information is neither matter, nor energy." Ashby (2) considers information as "a measure of the variety in a given system." Following Glushkov (3), "information is a measure of the non-homogeneity in the distribution of matter or energy in space and time." All the progress in this field has pointed out that besides their substantial and energetic aspect, the objects, phenomena, and systems in the universe also have an information character. Moreover, it becomes more and more evident that in the future scientific research will be focused on the information nature of the process and systems. This assertion is essentially based on the possibility to control and define the systems and processes by information as is stated in cybernetics.

The fundamentals of information theory was originated by Shannon in 1948 (4). The concept of information as a quantity related to entropy is, however, much older. In 1894, Boltzmann (5) stated that every piece of information obtained for a physical system is related to decreasing its number of possible states, therefore increasing its entropy, which means "loss of information." In 1929, Szillard (6) developed this idea for the general case of information in physics. Later, Brillouin (7,8) generalized the concept of entropy and information in his negentropy principle of information. The possible connection between information theory and thermodynamics and, in particular, between entropy and information continues to be a scientific and philosophical subjet of permanent interest (9,10).

Information theory, considered also "as a special theory of communications," among other interesting applications, has been used in different scientific and technical areas: physics, chemistry, biology, medicine, psychology, linguistics, aesthetics, and so forth.

The role of information was first recognized in biology. Some important problems of conservation, processing, and transmission of information in living creatures were solved, such as coding of genetic information (11–13), estimation of the possibility of spontaneous self-generation of life on Earth (14), formulation of the fundamental laws of biological thermodynamics (15), and analysis of the problems of bioenergetic (16). The information content of systems was used as a quantitative criteria of evolution (17,18). The information character of food-consuming processes was pointed out to be dominant over the stubstantial and energetic processes (19,20).

Information theory has found many applications in chemistry. Levine, Bernstein, and co-workers (21–25) developed an information approach to molecular dynamics which describes the behavior of molecular systems far from equilibrium, in vibrationally and rotationally excited states (26,27). Daudel et al. (28–30) used the minimization of the information function on the distribution of the molecular systems space into mutually exclusive spaces called loges, which contain localized groups of electrons. The sensitivity and catalytic activity of catalysts were connected to its information content by Kobozev et al. (31–33). An information analysis concerning the surface treatment with different chemical reagents was also realized (34–36). The formation and growth of crystals has also been treated as an information process (37). This approach has a wide application in the geochemistry of the distribution's characterization (38,39), the complexity determination (40), and the general classification of geochemical systems (41).

Information theory was extensively applied in analytical chemistry (42) for minimization of errors and time of analysis, improvement of selectivity and sensitivity, and estimation of the efficiency of analytical methods and procedures (42–50).

FUNDAMENTALS OF INFORMATION ENERGY

The information energy (IE) concept and its detailed theoretical study and as well as its implications in the field of mathematics called "Information Statistics" was introduced by Onicescu (51) and Onicescu and Ştefănescu (52).

It is well known by scientists from information theory that the Shannon entropy measure may be calculated as a function of probabilities, p_i (42,51–55):

$$H(A) = -\sum_{i=1}^{n} p_i \ \log_2 p_i. \tag{1}$$

Onicescu observed that $H(A)$ is the mean value of logarithm to base 2 of all the probabilities and he addressed the question of whether the mean value of probabilities

$$E = \sum_{i=1}^{n} p_i^2 \tag{2}$$

could not be a function "with similar characteristics of representation like Shannon entropy." Onicescu called it information energy (IE). Moreover, for a system having a continuous distribution function, one can write

$$E = \int_{-\infty}^{+\infty} \rho^2(x) \ dx, \tag{3}$$

where

$$\rho(x) = \frac{dF(x)}{dx}$$

is the derivative of the distribution function of information and, hence, a particular form of energy (56).

Information energy describes, with the same success, as Shannon's entropy the uniformity or diversity of a system, process, or phenomenon. IE is more sensitive in some ways than entropy to modification of a system. Moreover, this informational function permits the calculation of the informational correlation (IC) and the informational correlation coefficient (ICC), parameters of interest in science and technical areas.

Information Energy

The IE of a finite set of events or states $A_1, A_2, \ldots, A_n$, each having an associated probability $p_1, p_2, \ldots, p_n$ with $p_i \geq 0$ and $\Sigma_{i=1}^{n} p_i = 1$ is given by

$$E_{(p_1, p_2, \ldots, p_n)} = \sum_{i=1}^{n} p_i^2. \tag{4}$$

According to Mihoc's consideration (57) concerning the estimation of IE, if the probabilities p_i ($i = 1, 2, \ldots, n$) of a finite set of sates that are estimated by relative frequencies f_i of a real experiment, then the empirical IE may be calculated with the following expression:

$$E_{(f_1, f_2, \ldots, f_n)} = \sum_{i=1}^{n} f_i^2. \tag{5}$$

Equations (4) and (5) give information concerning the degree of organization of a system or the mode of partitioning of its elements. Defined in this way, IE reveals some remarkable properties. First, it reaches its minimum value when all the probabilities are equal ($p_1 = p_2 = \cdots = p_n$) (i.e., the case of a totally unorganized systems):

$$E_{(p_1, p_2, \ldots, p_n)} = \frac{1}{n}. \tag{6}$$

If $p_k = 1$ and $p_{i \neq k} = 0$ (i.e., the case with well-organized systems), then IE is

$$E_{(p_1, p_2, \ldots, p_n)} = 1. \tag{7}$$

Hence, it results that the possible values for IE are between $1/n$ and 1.

It is also interesting that Cresin (58), applying IE in biology, demonstrated that it is more useful to consider the normalized informational energy; that is,

$$E' = \frac{\sum_{i=1}^{n} f_i^2 - (1/n)}{1 - (1/n)}. \tag{8}$$

It is obvious that in this case, the possible values of E' are between 0 and 1 and do not depend on n.

In the particular case of a set of two finite systems of events $A_1, A_2, \ldots, A_n$ and $B_1, B_2, \ldots, B_m$, each with probability $p_1, p_2, \ldots, p_n$ and $q_{i1}, q_{i2}, \ldots, q_{im}$, respectively, q_{ij} is the conditional probability of the event B given event A; that is,

$$q_{ij} = P(B_j/A_i) \tag{9}$$

The IE of the system of events $B_1, B_2, \ldots, B_m$ conditioned by the occurrence of the integral system of events $A_1, A_2, \ldots, A_n$, the so-called "conditional information energy" (CIE) is defined as

$$E_{(B_1, B_2, \ldots, B_m/A_1, A_2, \ldots, A_n)} = \sum_{i=1}^{n} \sum_{j=1}^{m} p_i^2 \, q_{ij}^2. \tag{10}$$

When two systems are independent, the IE of the system of events (A_i, B_j) will be

$$E_{(A_i, B_j)} = E_{(A_1, A_2, \ldots, A_n)} E_{(B_1, B_2, \ldots, B_n)}. \tag{11}$$

This means that IE is multiplicative and not additive like Shannon's entropy.

The Informational Correlation

The informational correlation (IC) between two systems (probabilistic partitions) has the following equation:

$$C_{(p_1, p_2, \ldots, p_n : q_1, q_2, \ldots, q_n)} = \sum_{i=1}^{n} p_i q_i. \qquad [12]$$

The IC is always positive, but <1, being zero if and only if all $p_i q_i$ are zero (i.e., the two systems are "indifferent").

By the normation of correlation, similar to the statistical correlation coefficient, an informational correlation coefficient (ICC) may be obtained:

$$r_{(p_1, p_2, \ldots, p_n : q_1, q_2, \ldots, q_n)} = \frac{C_{(p_1, p_2, \ldots, p_n : q_1, q_2, \ldots, q_n)}}{E_{(p_1, p_2, \ldots, p_n)} E_{(q_1, q_2, \ldots, q_n)}} = \frac{\sum_{i=1}^{n} p_i q_i}{\sum_{i=1}^{n} p_i^2 \sum_{i=1}^{n} q_i^2}. \qquad [13]$$

It is obvious that the possible values for ICC are between 0 and 1, being unity if and only if the probability distributions of the two partitions are the same.

Informational Analysis of Variance

In any experiment, two or more measurement methods (laboratories) yield generally more or less different results because the measurement processes may be influenced by basic factors (qualitative or quantitative) that control the conditions of the experiment and also by random factors.

It is the objective of analysis of variance (ANOVA) to investigate the several kinds of factors, operating simultaneously, and to decide which are important and to estimate their effects. ANOVA assumes the additivity of variances of random variables due to the effects of independent factors. It is used to break down the total variance into its components (i.e., into a sum of several distinct components), each corresponding to a source of variance.

The F-tests that are subsequently made are determined from the ratios of these respective components. The F ratio can then be compared with tabulated F values using the degrees of freedom corresponding to the numerator and demoninator for each F ratio. If the observed F ratio exceeds the tabulated value at the chosen confidence level, then one would conclude statistical significance at this level of confidence. If, on the other hand, the calculated value of the F ratio is smaller than that given in tables, the factor in question does not affect the mean value.

When applying ANOVA, one assumes that the overall errors are normally distributed, statistically independent, and have the same variance. Often the homogeneity of variance is not respected, and in such instances, ANOVA could lead to erroneous conclusions if experiments (methods) with widely different precisions are compared. The analysis of variance can be applied in several distinct forms, according to the structure of the process being investigated. Excellent discussions of this topic were presented by Hirsch (59) and Massart and co-workers (54,55).

The majority of ANOVA methods refer to the testing of the null hypothesis H_0: $\mu_1 = \mu_2 = \cdots = \mu_q$, where $\mu_i > 0$ ($0 \leq i \leq q$) are means of q statistical populations. If the null hypothesis is true, it results that the q populations have the same mean. This homogeneity concerning the means may also be tested using the informational energy concept (60–63).

The One-Way Layout

Suppose some factor A which we consider as having some effect on a response variable of interest Y has q levels. An experiment is set up in which n measurements are made of the response y at all levels. The levels q are called treatments or controlled factors, there being q controlled factors in the experimental design. Each y_{ij} result can be written as a sum of a constant μ (the general mean), α_i, a term which measures the effect of the factor A at the ith level, and an error term e_{ij}, called the residual error or residual. The linear (or additive) model

$$y_{ij} = \mu + \alpha_i + e_{ij} \tag{14}$$

can be written for the one-way layout. It is necessary now to test the null hypothesis H_0: $\mu_1 = \mu_2 = \cdots = \mu_q$.

Let ξ be a new random variable with q values, each having an associated probability p_i:

$$p_i = \frac{\mu_i}{\sum\limits_{i=1}^{q} \mu_i} \quad, \quad i = 1, 2, \ldots, q. \tag{15}$$

Now, it is possible to observe that the null hypothesis H_0 is equivalent to the hypothesis H*: $p_1 = p_2 = \cdots = p_q = 1/q$. The H* hypothesis is true when $E_{(\xi)} = 1/q$ (i.e., when the information energy of the random variable ξ is minimal).

If we define μ_i as

$$\mu_i = \sum_{j=1}^{n} \frac{y_{ij}}{n} \quad, \quad i = 1, 2, \ldots, q \tag{16}$$

and substitute Eq. (16) into Eq. (15), we obtain

$$p_i = \left(\frac{1}{n} \sum_{j=1}^{n} y_{ij} \right)\left(\frac{1}{n} \sum_{i=1}^{q} \sum_{j=1}^{n} y_{ij} \right)^{-1} = \left(\sum_{j=1}^{n} y_{ij} \right)\left(\sum_{i=1}^{q} \sum_{j=1}^{n} y_{ij} \right)^{-1} \tag{17}$$

Substituting Eq. (17) into Eq. (4), the empirical information energy of random variable ξ is given by the following expression:

$$\tilde{E}_{(\xi)} = \sum_{i=1}^{q} p_i^2 = \sum_{i=1}^{q} \left[\left(\sum_{j=1}^{n} y_{ij} \right)^2 \left(\sum_{i=1}^{q} \sum_{j=1}^{n} y_{ij} \right)^{-2} \right]$$

or

$$\tilde{E}_{(\xi)} = \left[\sum_{i=1}^{q} \left(\sum_{j=1}^{n} y_{ij} \right)^2 \right]\left(\sum_{i=1}^{q} \sum_{j=1}^{n} y_{ij} \right)^{-2}. \tag{18}$$

As the numerator of the expression for $\tilde{E}_{(\xi)}$ contains a sum of squares of the random variables, it is possible using the theorems of classical partitions to construct a criterion for testing the hypothesis H*: $E_{(\xi)} = 1/q$.

If $E_{(\xi)} = \tilde{E}_{(\xi)}$, the null hypothesis is accepted; on the other hand, if $E_{(\xi)} \neq \tilde{E}_{(\xi)}$, the null hypothesis is rejected, hence the effect of factor A is taken as significant.

The Two-Way Layout

Let us consider the case in which an experiment must be set up to study the effects of two factors A and B on a response variable Y. Factor A has q levels, whereas factor B

has m levels. For each combination of levels, we measure the response y_{ij} by carrying out n observations. In cases with no replications and if we assume that there is no interaction between the two factors, one may adopt a linear model:

$$y_{ij} = \mu + \alpha_i + \beta_i + e_{ij}. \qquad [19]$$

The hypothesis H_0 ($\alpha_i = 0$) (i.e., the factor A has no significant effect) is equivalent to the hypothesis H^*: $p_1 = p_2 = \cdots = p_q$. This is equivalent to H_1^*: $E_{(\xi)} = 1/q$.

The estimated information energy, $\tilde{E}_{(\xi)}$, concerning the probabilities p_i is given by Eq. (18). The null hypothesis is then accepted when $E_{(\xi)} = \tilde{E}_{(\xi)}$. Hence, all α_i values are equal to zero; the effect of factor A is not significant.

The hypothesis $\beta_i = 0$ ($j = 1, 2, \ldots, m$) (i.e., the factor has no significant effect) is equivalent to the hypothesis H^*: $p_1' = p_2' = \cdots = p_n'$, where

$$p_j' = \frac{y_j}{\displaystyle\sum_{j=1}^{n} y_j} \qquad [20]$$

and which is equivalent to the hypothesis H_1^*: $E_{(\xi')} = 1/m$.

The estimated information energy concerning the probabilities p_j' is given by

$$\tilde{E}(\xi') = \sum_{i=1}^{m} p_j'^2 = \sum_{j=1}^{m} y_j^2 \left(\sum_{j=1}^{m} y_j^2 \right)^{-2}. \qquad [21]$$

If $E_{(\xi')} \neq \tilde{E}_{(\xi')}$, the null hypothesis is rejected; hence, the effect of factor B is significant.

APPLICATIONS OF INFORMATION ENERGY

Optimal Choice of Sets of Solvent Systems in Thin-Layer Chromatography

A rather common problem in chromatography is to find objective criteria for the evaluation of the most efficient chromatographic system and an optimal choice of combinations to identify a group of compounds.

Regardless of the kind of chromatography used for a sample analysis [e.g., thin-layer chromatography (TLC), gas chromatography (GC), paper chromatography (PC)], the optimal set of chromatographic systems includes those which differ very much in identification characteristics (e.g., hR_f values and/or colors in TLC).

The idea of using TLC in qualitative analysis has long been pursued due to the simplicity, low cost, rapidity and sensitivity of the analytical technique. Obviously a single retention factor, hR_f, is not always sufficient for the identification of any compound and it is evident that more measurements are needed. The hR_f values in different solvent systems reported either in graphical representations such as the "chromatographic spectrum" (64) and "chromatographic profile" (65), or in tables (66) have been considered to be suitable for identification purposes. In this order, the choice of the minimum number of solvent systems containing different information is of crucial importance for the identification of unknowns and has been the topic of several statistical studies.

For the choice of the most appropriate solvent system recommended in the literature for thin-layer chromatography of carotenoids, the information content (I) has been calculated using Shannon's entropy (67). In the same respect, the informational energy was also used (61–62).

The hR_f values for the 11 components and the 7 solvent systems presented in Table 1 were divided into 20 groups of hR_f values in the range 0–5, 6–10, and so on (68).

By comparing the IE obtained values for the seven solvent sytems with the information content (I) (see Table 1), it is easy to observe a high similarity. Considering the reversed slope of the IE values by comparing with *I*, it results that, for example, in the case of the VIIth solvent system, the greatest IE and the lowest *I* has been obtained, whereas for the IVth system, the lowest IE and the greatest *I* have been obtained.

As none of the seven solvent systems achieves a complete separation, two-dimensional chromatography has to be considered. In this order, we have computed the conditional information energy (CIE), informational correlation (IC), informational correlation coefficient (ICC), and the statistical correlation coefficient (*r*). The results obtained for different solvent combinations are presented in Table 2.

By careful examination of the data depicted in Table 2, it is difficult to find some relationships or trends between the CIE, ICC, and *r* computed in order to get the best possible combination between any two of the seven solvent systems for a bidimensional thin-layer chromatography. The choice of the two solvents has been done in such a way that the correlation should be minimum; that is, the two systems should not realize the separation of the same chemical compounds. In this case, any correlation parameter has to have the minimum value. Taking into account the values of CIE, the best combination appears to be between solvents III and IV (0.0016). Considering the values of *r*, the minimum (0.062) was obtained between solvents III and VII. The value of the CIE obtained for the same pair of solvents is rather high (0.0443) compared with any other combination of two solvents in Table 2.

The fact that CIE better reveals the (non)similarity between two solvent systems in the field of thin-layer chromatography is not surprising. We have to observe that only

TABLE 1 hR_f Values of 11 Carotenoids, Information Content (*I*), and Information Energy (*E*) of the Proposed Separation

Compound	Solvent*						
	I	II	III	IV	V	VI	VII
Cryptoxanthine	62	70	76	74	39	21	4
Rubixanthine	45	60	64	45	15	4	0
Lycoxanthine	29	37	40	32	8	0	0
Izozeaxanthine	34	56	92	91	36	36	10
Escholtzxanthine	12	22	25	22	8	1	0
Lycophyll	8	20	22	20	7	0	0
Euglenanone	62	68	81	80	54	34	9
Canthaxanthine	58	65	79	80	55	37	20
Rhodoxanthine	28	42	43	40	14	7	1
8-Apo-B-carotenic acid	28	38	30	15	5	0	0
Torularhodin	6	10	9	2	1	0	0
I	2.66	2.91	3.08	3.26	2.11	1.79	1.49
E	0.174	0.141	0.124	0.107	0.190	0.355	0.570

Source: Data from Ref. 69.

TABLE 2   Results Obtained for Conditional Information Energy (CIE), Informational Correlation (IC), Informational Correlation Coefficient (ICC), and Statistical Correlation Coefficient (r)

Pair of solvents	CIE	IC	ICC	r
III–IV	0.0016	0.0744	0.6445	0.9804
II–III	0.0020	0.0578	0.4384	0.9358
II–IV	0.0020	0.0413	0.3363	0.8862
I–III	0.0032	0.0661	0.4507	0.8630
I–IV	0.0032	0.0248	0.4095	0.8236
I–V	0.0036	0.0744	0.3540	0.7716
II–V	0.0036	0.0578	0.2691	0.8070
IV–V	0.0042	0.0413	0.2892	0.9673
III–V	0.0048	0.0331	0.2153	0.9261
I–II	0.0050	0.0575	0.3705	0.9708
IV–VI	0.0155	0.0826	0.4229	0.9384
II–VI	0.0204	0.0496	0.2219	0.7615
III–VI	0.0204	0.0413	0.1969	0.8886
I–VI	0.0253	0.0248	0.0998	0.7349
V–VI	0.0352	0.1405	0.5406	0.9933
IV–VII	0.0356	0.0744	0.3005	0.7800
II–VII	0.0443	0.0248	0.0876	0.6181
III–VII	0.0443	0.0165	0.0622	0.7219
I–VII	0.0706	0.0331	0.1051	0.6276
V–VII	0.0793	0.1818	0.5523	0.8730
VI–VII	0.1667	0.4132	0.9179	0.9039

this parameter is able to take into account the changes in the sequence of retention of the components from one system to another, in this way being more sensitive to the nature of the components separated by a solvent system as compared with another one.

The IC and ICC allow a comparison of the solvent only from the point of view of similarity in the distribution of hR_f values within the 20 groups, without taking into account the identity of the components.

It is also important to point out that ICC does not have the same trend of variation as the statistical correlation coefficient (i.e., the last one), but, occasionally, it can reveal the same situation. Moreover, the statistical correlation coefficient is incapable of finding the best combination of two solvent systems in thin-layer chromatography.

This algorithm may also be used in gas chromatography for optimal selection of two or multiple columns and, generally, for the optimal combination of two analytical methods.

Applications of Informational Analysis of Variance in Analytical Chemistry

Two relevant cases discussed by Massart and co-workers (54,55) using classical ANOVA methods are considered for comparing the advantages of informational analysis of variance.

The One-Way Layout

Seven laboratories were asked to determine aflatoxin M_1 in milk using the same method. A portion of a well-homogenized milk sample was given to each of the seven laboratories and each was asked to perform five independent determinations. The aim of the study was to investigate whether there is an effect of the laboratory (between laboratory precision) on the results. The results obtained (ng/g) are given in Table 3.

The null hypothesis $\alpha_i = 0$ ($i = 1, 2, \ldots, 7$) is equivalent to the hypothesis H*: $p_1 = p_2 = \cdots = p_7$. The probabilities p are calculated using Eq. (16). This is equivalent to the hypothesis H*: $E_{(\xi)} = 1/q$ or $E_{(\xi)} = 1/7 = 0.143$.

The empirical information energy associated with the probabilities p_i is given by

$$\tilde{E}_{(\xi)} = \sum_{i=1}^{7} p_i^2 = \frac{\displaystyle\sum_{i=1}^{7} y_{i.}^2}{\left(\displaystyle\sum_{i=1}^{7} y_{i.}\right)^2} = \frac{96.88}{615.04} = 0.158.$$

Because $E_{(\xi)} \neq \tilde{E}_{(\xi)}$, the difference between laboratories is significant and it is concluded that there is an important laboratory effect, which means that one or more laboratories show a bias. For identifying extreme values, one may perform pairwise comparisons of the group means using the same algorithm.

By applying classical ANOVA, one obtains the same results because the calculated F value (9.33) is higher than the tabulated value $F_{0.05; 6, 24}$ (2.45).

The Two-Way Layout

The work discussed by Amenta (70) was concerned with quality control in clinical laboratories and involved the analysis of 50 samples from the same pool, 2 per day at different places in the run of the routine determinations carried out during that day for 25 consecutive days. The following questions were asked: Is there a significant contribution to the total variance from day-to-day variations? Is there a significant effect due to the position in the run? (See Table 4.)

Using ANOVA at the 5% confidence level, both null hypotheses are rejected, which means that there is a significant contribution to the total variance due to the variation between days and between positions.

TABLE 3   Determination of Aflatoxin M (ng/g) in Seven Laboratories

	Laboratory						
	a	b	c	d	e	f	g
	1.6	4.6	1.2	1.5	6.0	6.2	3.3
	2.9	2.8	1.9	2.7	3.9	3.8	3.8
	3.5	3.0	2.9	3.4	4.3	5.5	5.5
	1.8	4.5	1.1	2.0	5.8	4.2	4.9
	2.2	3.1	2.9	3.4	4.0	5.3	4.5
Mean	2.4	3.6	2.0	2.6	4.8	5.0	4.4

TABLE 4   Two-Way Layout Table for the Clinical Laboratory Problem

	Day												
	1	2	3	4	5	6	7	8	9	10	11	12	13
Position 1	138	137	137	136	137	136	140	139	137	135	132	136	138
Position 2	140	137	136	139	138	137	139	138	139	135	136	137	142

	Day											
	14	15	16	17	18	19	20	21	22	23	24	25
Position 1	141	137	136	137	138	138	138	136	140	139	140	138
Position 2	139	137	139	137	138	138	138	139	140	141	141	139

At the 1% confidence level, the first null hypothesis is rejected because the calculated F value (3.72) is higher than the tabulated value $F_{0.01; 24, 24}$ (2.66), which means that there is a significant contribution to the total variance due to the variation between days. The second hypothesis is accepted because the calculated F value (6.12) is smaller than the tabulated value $F_{0.01; 1, 24}$ (7.82), which means that there is no significant contribution to the total variance due to variations between positions. However, this results in a paradox because $s_{day}^2 < s_{position}^2$ (5.36 < 8.82).

Considering the informational analysis of variance, the hypothesis $\alpha_i = 0$ ($i = 1, 2, \ldots, 25$) is equivalent to the hypothesis H*: $p_1 = p_2 = \cdots = p_{25}$. This is equivalent to H_1^*: $E_{(\xi)} = 1/25 = 0.040$.

The empirical information energy associated with the probabilities p_i is given by

$$E_{(\xi)} = \sum_{i=1}^{25} p_i^2 = \frac{\sum_{i=1}^{25} y_{i.}^2}{\left(\sum_{i=1}^{25} y_{i.} \right)^2} = \frac{475,198.75}{11,878,362} = 0.040.$$

Because $E_{(\xi)} = \tilde{E}_{(\xi)}$, there is not a significant contribution to the total variance from day-to-day variations.

The hypothesis $\beta_j = 0$ ($j = 1, 2$) is equivalent to the hypothesis H*: $p_1' = p_2'$. This is equivalent to H_1^*: $E_{(\xi')} = 1/2 = 0.500$.

The estimated information energy concerning probabilities p_j' is given by

$$E_{(\xi')} = \sum_{j=1}^{2} p_j'^2 = \frac{\sum_{j=1}^{2} y_{j}^2}{\left(\sum_{j=1}^{2} y_{j} \right)^2} = \frac{38,011.112}{76,021.518} = 0.500.$$

Because $E_{(\xi)} = \tilde{E}_{(\xi)}$, there is not a significant effect due to the position in the run. Hence, both null hypotheses are accepted. These results illustrate the efficiency of the informational analysis of variance in comparison with classical ANOVA.

Information Analysis of Variance Applied to Methods—Comparison

To illustrate the potential of information analysis of variance in the field of analytical chemistry, we refer to the data discussed in Ref. 71 concerning the effectiveness of traditional water-bath digestion used in U.S. EPA method 7471 and microwave digestion method 3051.

The results obtained in the determination of mercury (ppm) in solid wastes by AAS using the two preparation sample methods (see Table 5) were compared through statistical parametric and nonparametric tests. The conclusion according to these tests was that there is no significant difference between the two methods.

Applying information analysis of variance in that case (72), the null hypothesis is equivalent to the hypothesis H*: $p_1 = p_2 = \cdots = p_8$. The probabilities p are calculated as above using Eq. (16). This is equivalent to the hypothesis H*: $E_{(\xi)} = \tilde{E}_{(\xi)} = 1/q$ or $E_{(\xi)} = 1/8 = 0.125$.

The empirical information energy associated with probabilities p_i is given by

$$\tilde{E}_{(\xi)} = \sum_{i=1}^{8} p_i^2 = \frac{\displaystyle\sum_{i=1}^{8} D_i^2}{\left(\displaystyle\sum_{i=1}^{8} D_i\right)^2} = \frac{137}{604} = 0.227,$$

where D_i is the difference between pairs of the mean results in Table 5.

Because $E_{(\xi)} \neq \tilde{E}_{(\xi)}$, the difference between the two methods of sample preparation is significant and it is concluded that here is an important method effect, which means that one method shows a bias. This contradictory result in comparison with the other parametric and nonparametric tests is confirmed by using implicit linear regression and information analysis of variance.

Implicit Linear Function

When two analytical methods or two other measurement procedures are compared, because both, more and less, are affected by errors, practically it is not important which is X and which is Y. In other words, we may write $y = f(x)$ or $x = f(y)$ equally. In this

TABLE 5 Determination of Mercury (ppm) in Solid Wastes by ASS Using Two Standard Methods of Sample Preparation Discussed in Ref. 71

Sample	Method 3051				Method 7471				D_i
	a	b	c	Mean	a	b	c	Mean	
1	7.12	7.66	7.17	7.32	5.50	5.54	5.40	5.48	+1.84
2	16.1	15.7	15.6	15.8	13.1	12.8	13.0	13.0	+2.80
3	4.89	4.62	4.28	4.60	3.39	3.12	3.36	3.29	+1.31
4	9.64	9.03	8.44	9.04	6.59	6.52	7.43	6.84	+2.20
5	6.76	7.22	7.50	7.16	6.20	6.03	5.77	6.00	+1.16
6	6.19	6.61	7.61	6.80	6.25	5.65	5.61	5.84	+0.96
7	9.44	9.56	10.7	9.90	15.0	13.9	14.0	14.3	−4.40
8	30.8	29.0	26.2	28.7	20.4	16.11	20.0	18.8	+9.90

situation, a more illuminating and intuitive alternative is to consider the implicit form of a linear function (73,74). It is well-known from analytical geometry that the general linear function

$$Ax + By + C = 0 \qquad\qquad [22]$$

represents a straight line when the coefficients A and B are different from zero. Considering $B \neq 0$, then Eq. (22) can be formulated as follows:

$$y = -\frac{A}{B}\, x - \frac{C}{B} = mx + n. \qquad\qquad [23]$$

In this case, the distance of any point $(x_i,\, y_i)$ to the line (22) will have the following expression:

$$d_i^2 = \frac{(Ax_i + By_i + C)^2}{A^2 + B^2}. \qquad\qquad [24]$$

The resulting fitting problem will be defined by the condition

$$S = \frac{1}{A^2 + B^2} \sum_{i=1}^{n} (Ax_i + By_i + C)^2 = \min. \qquad\qquad [25]$$

The minimum of S follows as the derivative of S approaches zero with respect to A, B, and C. From the resulting system, considering $M(x) = 0$, $M(y) = 0$, and $C = 0$, we obtain

$$\frac{M(y^2) - M(x^2)}{M(xy)} = \frac{B^2 - A^2}{AB} = \frac{B}{A} - \frac{A}{B}. \qquad\qquad [26]$$

Now, it is easy to observe that $-A/B$ in Eq. (26) is the slope of the linear equation

$$y = mx + n \qquad\qquad [27]$$

resulting from Eq. (23). After substitution of m in Eq. (6) and taking $[M(y^2) - M(x^2)]/M(xy) = w$, we obtain a quadratic equation,

$$m^2 - wm - 1 = 0. \qquad\qquad [28]$$

Taking into account only the positive value of m and considering that the centroid of x and y must satisfy the equation of the straight line (27), we can calculate n from

$$y = mx + \bar{y} - m\bar{x}. \qquad\qquad [29]$$

By comparing Eqs. (2) and (7) and taking $C = 1$, we can immediately obtain A and B.

The ratio of A to B could indicate the (dis)similarity between the analytical methods compared. Thus, it is now possible to compare analytical methods, considering either the ration A/B or B/A (the equations are symmetrical) or, much more simply, their value. Considering the last possibility, we have to stress that in the ideal case, when the two methods produce practically equal results, A and B will have the same absolute value. To the contrary, in the other case, the higher the difference between A and B, the more different will be the two methods. However, at this moment, one problem remains: How to test objectively and rationally the significance of the difference between the absolute values of the two coefficients A and B. This can be done using, for example, informational analysis of variance, as demonstrated below.

The null hypothesis in this case is equivalent to the hypothesis H_0: $p_A = p_B$. The probabilities p are calculated using

$$p_A = \frac{A}{A + B} \quad \text{and} \quad p_B = \frac{B}{A + B}.$$

The H_0 hypothesis is true when $E_{(\xi)} = \frac{1}{2}$; that is, when the information energy is minimal and the two coefficients A and B are equal in their absolute values. As was shown earlier, the null hypothesis is accepted if $E_{(\xi)} = \tilde{E}_{(\xi)}$, where $E_{(\xi)} = \frac{1}{2}$ represents the theoretical information energy, and $\tilde{E}_{(\xi)} = (A^2 + B^2)/(A + B)^2$ represents empirical information energy. On the other hand, if $E_{(\xi)} \neq \tilde{E}_{(\xi)}$, the null hypothesis is rejected. Hence, the difference between the two compared methods is taken as significant.

To illustrate the characteristics of performance of the algorithm discussed earlier, taking into account the errors in both methods we refer also to the data in Table 5 concerning the effectiveness of traditional water-bath digestion used in U.S. EPA method 7471 and microwave digestion method 3051. The implicit linear equation obtained using the mean values of the two methods is $3.86x - 5.76y + 1 = 0$. The empirical information energy associated with the probabilities p_A and p_B is given by

$$\tilde{E} = \sum_{i=1}^{2} p_i^2 = \frac{A^2 + B^2}{(A + B)^2} = \frac{48.1}{92.5} = 0.520.$$

Because $E_{(\xi)} \neq \tilde{E}_{(\xi)}$ ($E_{(\xi)} = 0.500$ and $\tilde{E}_{(\xi)} = 0.520$), it is concluded that, also according to this test, there is a statistically significant difference between the results of the two methods, which means that one method shows a bias. This conclusion (i.e., the presence of proportional errors introduced by the microwave digestion method) concerning the analysis of mercury in waste samples was also demonstrated applying other statistical methods. This result and others (73) showed that the implicit linear function model (ILF) is an effective method for parameter estimation and methods comparison and can replace the least-squares method and other proposed approaches. For any given set of data, an evaluation based on an informational analysis of variance test allows a more reliable bias detection.

In closing, the information analysis of variance method (IANOVA) discussed earlier can be successfully used in analytical chemistry and other fields, being much simpler and rather fast. Also, we have to stress that IANOVA can be more efficient than the usual ANOVA methods because, like robust statistical techniques, it is resistant to uncertainties concerning the data, such as outliers or divergence from the Normal distribution. However, it should be noted that although the theory is conceptually simple, it has a very firm mathematical foundation and, in some instances, the mathematics can become complex.

REFERENCES

1. N. Wiener, *Cybernetics*, MIT Press, Cambridge, MA, 1948.
2. W. Ashby, *An Introduction to Cybernetics*, John Wiley & Sons, New York, 1956.
3. V. Glushkov, "On Cybernetics as a Science," in *Cybernetics, Thinking, Life*, Misl, Moscow, 1964, p. 53 (in Rusian).
4. C. Shannon and W. Weaver, *Mathematical Theory of Communication*, University of Illinois Press, Urbana, 1949.
5. L. Boltzmann, *Vorlesungen über Gastheorie*, Leipzig, 1896.
6. L. Szilard, *Z. Phys.*, *53*, 840 (1929).
7. L. Brillouin, *Science and Information Theory*, Academic Press, New York, 1956.
8. L. Brilouin, *Scientific Uncertainty and Information*, Academic Press, New York, 1964.

9. D. Bonchev and G. Lickomannov, *Math. Chem.*, *3*, 269 (1977).
10. N. I. Kobozev, *A Study on the Thermodinamics of Information and Thinking Processes*, Moscow University Press, Moscow, 1971 (in Russian).
11. H. Quastler (ed.), *Essays on the Use of Information Theory in Biology*, University of Illinois Press, Urbana, 1953.
12. P. G. Seybold, *Int. J. Quantum Chem.*, *3*, 39 (1976).
13. M. Hasegawa and T. A. Yano, *Origins Life*, *6*, 219 (1975).
14. C. Yockey and P. Hubert, *J. Theoret. Biol.*, *67*, 377 (1977).
15. K. S. Trincher, *Biology and Information*, Nauka, Moscow, 1964 (in Russian).
16. A. I. Bykhovskii, *Math. Biosci.*, *3*, 353 (1968).
17. A. D. Ursul, *Filossofskie Nauki*, *2*, 43 (1966) (in Russian).
18. D. Bonchev, *Biol. Chem. (Bulg.)*, *13*, 4 (1970).
19. E. Schroedinger, *What is Life*, Cambridge University Press, Cambridge, 1944.
20. I. I. Brekhman, *Man and Biological Active Substances*, Nauka, Moscow, 1976 (in Russian).
21. R. B. Bernstein and R. D. Levine, *J. Chem. Phys.*, *57*, 434 (1972).
22. A. Ben-Shaul, R. D. Levine, and R. B. Bernstein, *J. Chem. Phys.*, *57*, 5427 (1972).
23. R. D. Levine and R. B. Bernstein, *Acc. Chem. Res.*, *7*, 393 (1974).
24. R. B. Bernstein and R. D. Levine, *Adv. Atomic Mol. Phys.*, *11*, 215 (1975).
25. N. Agmon and R. D. Levine, *Chem. Phys. Lett.*, *52*, 197 (1977).
26. R. K. Huddleston and E. Weitz, *J. Chem. Phys.*, *66*, 1740 (1977).
27. E. Ludena and V. Amzel, *J. Chem. Phys.*, *52*, 5293 (1970).
28. C. Aslangul, R. Constanciel, R. Daudel, and P. Kottis, *Adv. Quant. Chem.*, *6*, 93 (1972).
29. R. Daudel, R. F. Bader, M. E. Stefens, and D. S. Borett, *Can. J. Chem.*, *52*, 1310 (1974).
30. R. Daudel, R. F. Bader, M. E. Stefens, and D. S. Borett, *Can. J. Chem.*, *52*, 3077 (1974).
31. N. I. Kobozev, B. V. Strakhov, and A. M. Rubashov, *Zh. Fiz. Khim.*, *45*, 86 (1971).
32. N. I. Kobozev, B. V. Strakhov, and A. M. Rubashov, *Zh. Fiz. Khim.*, *45*, 375 (1971).
33. N. I. Kobozev and B. V. Strakhov, in *Proc. Int. Congr. Catal, 4th, 1968*, Akid. Kiado, Budapest, 1971, p. 332.
34. B. Rackow, *Z. Chem.*, *7*, 399 (1967).
35. B. Rackow, *Z. Chem.*, *7*, 472 (1967).
36. B. Rackow, *Z. Chem.*, *9*, 318 (1969).
37. D. H. Andrews and M. L. Boss, *Yale Sci.*, *45*, 11 (1971).
38. B. V. Andrew, *Nature*, *202*, 1206 (1964).
39. G. A. Bulkin and K. B. Gatalin, *Geol. Zh.*, *36*, 76 (1976) (in Russian).
40. T. G. Petrov, *Dokl. Akad. Nauk SSSR*, *191*, 924 (1970).
41. T. G. Petrov, *Vest. Leningrad Univ. Geol. Geogr.*, *3*, 30 (1971).
42. K. Eckschlager and V. Stepanek, *Information Theory as Applied to Chemical Analysis*, John Wiley & Sons, Chichester, 1979.
43. K. Eckschlager and V. Stepanek, *Anal. Chem.*, *54*, 1115A (1982).
44. K. Doerffel, *Fresenius Z. Anal. Chem.*, *330*, 24 (1988).
45. K. Danzer, K. Eckschlager, and D. Wienke, *Fresenius Z. Anal. Chem.*, *327*, 312 (1987).
46. K. Danzer, K. Eckschlager, and M. Matherny, *Fresenius Z. Anal. Chem.*, *334*, 1 (1989).
47. P. Cleij and A. Dijkstra, *Fresenius Z. Anal. Chem.*, *298*, 97 (1979).
48. S. C. Rutan, D. D. Gerow, and G. Hartmann, *Chemom. Intell. Lab. Syst.*, *3*, 61 (1988).
49. D. E. Clegg and D. L. Massart, *J. Chem. Ed.*, *70*, 19 (1993).
50. C. Liteanu and I. Rîcă, *Statistical Theory and Methodology of Trace Analsyis*, Ellis Horwood, Chichester, 1980.
51. O. Onicescu, *C.R. Acad. Sci., Ser. A*, *263*, 841 (1966).
52. O. Onicescu and V. Ştefănescu, *Informational Statistics*, Editura Tehnică, Bucharest, 1979.
53. O. Onicescu, *Rev. Statist.*, *11*, 4 (1966).
54. D. L. Massart, A. Dijkstra, and L. Kaufman, *Evaluation and Optimization of Laboratory Methods and Analytical Proccedures*, Elsevier, Amsterdam, 1978.

55. D. L. Massart, B. G. M. Vandeginste, S. N. Deming, Y. Michotte, and L. Kaufman, *Chemometrics: A Textbook*, Elsevier, Amsterdam, 1988.
56. I. Petrică and V. Ştefănescu, *New Aspects of the Theory of Information*, Editura Academiei, Bucharest, 1982.
57. V. Ştefănescu, *Applications of Informational Energy and Correlation*, Editura Academiei, Bucharest, 1979.
58. R. Cresin, *Rev. Statist.*, *12*, 17 (1966).
59. R. F. Hirch, *Anal. Chem.*, *49*, 691A (1977).
60. C. Sârbu and H. Naşcu, *Rev. Chim. (Bucharest)*, *41*, 276 (1990).
61. C. Sârbu and H. Naşcu, *Rev. Roum. Chim.*, *37*, 945 (1992).
62. C. Sârbu and I. Haiduc, *Studia Babeş-Bolyai, Seria Chemia*, *38*, 49 (1993).
63. C. Sârbu, *Anal. Chim. Acta*, *271*, 269 (1993).
64. J. Franc and Z. Stransky, *Collect. Czech. Chem. Commun.*, *24*, 3611 (1959).
65. V. Milan, G. Romano, and G. Scaralata, *Minerva Medicoleg.*, *99*, 15 (1979).
66. A. H. Stead, R. Gill, T. Wright, J. P. Gibbs, and A. C. Moffat, *Analyst*, *107*, 1106 (1982).
67. D. L. Massart, *J Chromatogr.*, *79*, 157 (1973).
68. I. Simon and M. Lederer, *J. Chromatogr.*, *63*, 448 (1971).
69. K. Egger and H. Veight, *Z. Pflanzenphysiol.*, *53*, 64 (1965).
70. J. S. A. Amenta, *Am. J. Clin. Pathol.*, *49*, 842 (1968).
71. R. Maw, L. Witry, and T. Emond, *9*, 39 (1994).
72. C. Sârbu, *Anal. Lett.*, *30*, 1051 (1997).
73. C. Sârbu and J. Lorentz, *Rev. Chim. (Bucharest)*, *49*, 19 (1998).
74. H. Zwanziger and C. Sârbu, *Anal. Chem.*, *70*, 1277 (1998).

COSTEL SÂRBU

INTELLIGENT SCALABLE TEXT SUMMARIZATION

INTRODUCTION

The goal of automatic text summarization is to take a partially structured source text, extract information content from it, and present the most important content to the user in a condensed form and in a manner sensitive to the user's or application's needs. This goal has been pursued in research and development activities since the 1950s. A wide variety of techniques, both application-specific and application independent, have been developed, some of which have made their way into commercial practice. With the rapid growth of on-line information and services in the 1990s, research and development in this field has grown considerably in scope and importance. In addition, there has been renewed interest in scalable techniques, namely application-independent techniques which scale up when dealing with large volumes and varieties of unrestricted text. There is also some consensus that for such techniques to be effective, they need to be fairly sophisticated, exploiting a variety of different sources of knowledge in a flexible manner—in short, the summaries generated would exhibit a degree of intelligence. Intelligent scalable text summarization, therefore, represents a growing trend of research and development in intelligent scalable techniques aimed at meeting the special challenges posed by both the growth of information and the growing varieties of methods for exploiting this information.

This article gives an overview of the main challenges in intelligent scalable text summarization, the methodologies currently available to deal with these challenges, and prospects for the future, given current trends.

Varieties of Summarization Tasks

The uses of text summarization vary with different applications. Summaries can be used to indicate what topics are addressed in the source text and, thus, can be used to alert the user as to the source content (the "indicative" function). Summaries can also be used to cover the concepts in the source text to the extent possible, given the compression requirements for the summary (the "informative" function). Informative summaries are viewed as standing in place of the source. They can even offer a critique of the source (the "evaluative" function) (1). Present technical capabilities are limited to indicative and informative summaries. The information in the summary can differ widely across these cases. In some applications, such as abstracting services for technical texts (2), it is useful to have summaries which consist of fluent, well-connected text, whereas in other applications where a mere gist is desired, the summaries may be more fragmentary in nature, consisting of words and phrases. Summaries can be tailored to a reader's interests and expertise, yielding user-focused summaries, or they can be aimed at a particular—usually broad—readership community, as in the case of "generic" summaries. Traditionally, generic summaries written by authors or professional abstractors serve as surrogates for full text. However, as our computing environments have continued to accommodate full-text searching, browsing, and personalized information filtering, user-focused abstracts have assumed increasing importance.

Summaries do not, of course, have to consist of extracts of source material, although many domain-independent systems provide exactly that; summaries can include abstracts, where information in the summary is not necessarily in the source. Furthermore, a summary could be in a different language from the source, although, at present, such a capability is not extensively developed. A summary may stand for a single source or it may stand for a whole collection. The source or sources need not, in fact, be text; while text summarization deals with cases in which the input is text, this text input, in turn, may represent information represented in some other media such as imagery, audio, or video.

It is worth distinguishing text summarization from the related fields of information extraction and information retrieval. In the typical use of information extraction (3,4), occurrences of proper names in the input text are tagged as being the name of a person, organization, or place, and associated with each other (e.g., a mention of "President Clinton" can be associated with a mention of "Mr. Clinton"). Also, an information extraction system can fill out information about the time and place of certain prespecified types of events, such as terrorist incidents or corporate takeovers, along with information about the participants in the event. While information extraction is used in text summarization, summarization aims at going beyond information extraction: First, rather than filling out prespecified types of information, text summarization tries to determine what is salient in the text. Second, whereas the information extraction ends with the filling out of templates, text summarization aims at producing text as output. Of course, this output text may be presented in various ways, and may take advantage of various kinds of structuring, hyperlinking, and visualization. Finally, text summarization is fundamentally concerned with *condensing* the information in the text for generic or user-focused, indicative or informative summaries, rather than simply extracting information.

Summarization is also closely related to the field of information retrieval. Summarizers are, of course, used quite widely in information-retrieval applications. For example, commercial tools can apply summarization at the stage of building an index to a text collection, which can then be searched using a search engine. Further, a number of World Wide Web search engines use summarization as a postfilter to characterize the content of retrieved documents. In addition, information-retrieval techniques are used quite widely in summarization. For example, the process of producing user-focused summaries can be viewed as one of ranking passages in a source or sources for their relevance to a query. Information-retrieval techniques may be used to characterize document content, whether in the form of words, phrases, or clusters thereof. However, whereas the notion of salience in summarization is related to the notion of relevance (to a query or a user's interest), in summarization, the notion of novelty (i.e., what is new in the summary, relative to what I know already?) is also important. Further, text summarization, as pointed out earlier, is not limited to extracts of source material, whereas information retrieval is not concerned with synthesis of new text. Overall, though, there is a similar concern with scalability in both fields.

SOME FUNDAMENTAL CONCEPTS

Abstract Architecture

Text summarization can be viewed as consisting of three phases: analysis, refinement, and synthesis. The analysis phase builds a representation of the source text. The refinement phase transforms this representation into a summary representation, condensing text content by selecting relevant information. In this phase, information may also be aggregated and generalized. The synthesis phase takes the summary representation and renders it in natural language using appropriate presentation strategies. Most of the work in scalable text summarization has focused on the analysis and refinement phase, and relatively little on the synthesis phase. The reason for this is that techniques for synthesis have explored the use of natural language generation (5); however, generation approaches, although of considerable interest, require a considerable amount of handcrafting for each domain. As a result, most of the scalable techniques have limited themselves to extracting salient parts of the source text and then arranging and presenting them in some effective manner. This may be accompanied by a degree of smoothing based on some degree of syntactic analysis; for example, material explicitly marked in parentheses, or subordinate clauses, or various modifiers of nouns might be excluded, as indicated below.

It is also worth pointing out that in the ideal case, the summary representation built in the analysis phase would encode the meaning of the text's sentences using some abstract formal representation of meaning, usually thought of in terms of a logical language, such as the predicate calculus. Such a representation would include representing the predicates in the sentence together with their arguments, capturing the scope of various quantifiers, and so forth. However, progress in natural language understanding has not reached a point where constructing such a meaning representation in an accurate manner for unrestricted texts is feasible (although fragmentary representations can be constructed). As a result, most of the scalable approaches use "shallow semantics," where the demands for deeper meaning representations are sidestepped.

Extraction and Coherence

When extracting sentences from a source, an obvious problem is preserving context. Picking sentences out of context can result in incoherent summaries. For example, if an anaphor (e.g., a pronoun such as "they") is present in a summary extract, the extract may not be entirely intelligible if a description of the entity referred to by the anaphor (called the "referent") is not included as well. Unfortunately, identifying which of the referring expressions in the text corresponds to the referent is difficult in the general case, requiring both linguistic knowledge and knowledge of the domain. Further, when sentences are extracted with missing sentences in between, some of the missing sentences may be reintroduced to preserve continuity (6).

Most systems which attempt to deal with this problem of *dangling anaphors* include some window (usually size 1) of previous sentences for readability (leaving less text for the rest of the summary) or they exclude all sentences containing specific anaphors. There are also systems such as in Ref. 7 which use simple within-sentence position to guess where the anaphor's referent might be located; for example, "he" might be considered as requiring at least the previous sentence as context if there is no other occurrence of "he," "his," or "him" earlier in the sentence and if it occurs within the first

10 words of the sentence. Finally, in systems that attempt to resolve anaphora in the large, it is possible to present the referent alongside the resolved anaphor, reducing the need for the introduction of referent-containing sentences.

It is worth noting that a certain degree of incoherence in the summary may be tolerated by the end user, especially in applications where the user just needs to skim through the text, where polished summaries are not required. In such cases, summaries which are quite fragmentary (e.g., expressed in terms of lists of words and phrases) may be quite acceptable.

Approaches to Salience

Fundamental Feature Model

A basic model used in text summarization is what may be called the fundamental feature model. This model characterizes a family of approaches to scalable text summarization. It uses a set of features that have been explored by numerous researchers and found to be useful. The overall idea is to weight text units for salience based on the weight of features in that unit. Of the features discussed in the literature, location features (7,8) are among the most prominent. The leading sentences of an article, the first sentence of a paragraph, information in the title, in the abstract, in section headings, in the introduction, or in the conclusion have been suggested as being important in certain genres of text. Also, the length of the sentence or paragraph, based on some ad hoc limits, is often used. A variety of term-weighting schemes have been explored in information retrieval (9–11), all of them based on the frequency of terms in a document combined with other factors, including maximum frequency of any term in the document, number of documents in which the term occurs, frequency of the term in a large text corpus, and so forth. It is worth noting that although such term-weighting methods have been explored for a variety of information-retrieval tasks, use of these measures in text summarization remains some-what ad hoc and unmotivated; however, they are widely used (6,12) in both research and commercial systems as a means of filtering terms (and thus sentences) for salience. In addition, syntactic features, such as whether the subject of the sentence is in the initial position in the sentence, are often used to establish whether the sentence is salient.

Additional features (13,14) include the presence of proper names as well as fixed phrases. There are phrases that cue the presence of in-text summaries, phrases such as "in conclusion," "in summary," "our investigation," and so forth. In addition, there are phrases which indicate special emphasis by the writer (e.g., "important," "in particular," etc.). There are also phrases used to exclude sentences (e.g., "perhaps" suggests the information is less definitive).

An implicit assumption behind the fundamental feature model is that it is possible to define salience of information in the text as a linear combination of feature values. The attractiveness of the fundamental feature model lies in its simplicity. Many sentence extraction techniques in use today are based on this model. However, determining what the total set of features to be considered is, as well as what particular weight each feature should have, is an important issue. This determination is likely to be very genre dependent; for example, material at the end of the text may be important in scientific articles (e.g., in the conclusion), whereas that location may not be important in a news story. Approaches that are trainable, in particular, those which learn feature weights and key phrases based on a corpus of texts in the genre for which summaries are desired, are therefore of considerable interest. These are discussed later.

An example of a summarization system based on the fundamental feature model is found in the ADAMS system (2). This is a summarization system developed by Chemical Abstracts Service, focused on generating short abstracts (20% of the original) of chemistry articles. Developed at a time when not that much full-text material was on-line, the summarizer uses a fixed term list of words and phrases as positive and negative tests for sentences to be included in the summary. Because a text which has lots of positive terms could end up having a longer summary, some control over compression is achieved by making positive terms which occur frequently in the text have less positive weight, and having negative terms which occur frequently in the text contribute less negative weight. The frequency criteria also helps tune the impact of the word list for each chemistry subdomain. For example, in articles on photographic chemistry, "negative" would have less of a negative impact.

The terms in the list also have part-of-speech information (noun, verb, etc., umabiguously specified), used mainly in contextual tests to classify commas in the text, in order to identify clause boundaries. Introductory and parenthetical clauses, as well as phrases ending in "that" (likely to be followed by a conclusion) or beginning with "in" ("in conclusion") are deleted from the final summary, resulting in some "text smoothing" in the synthesis stage. The authors conclude that although the overall quality of the abstracts is lower than that of good manual abstracts, they believe the automatically generated ones to be "functionally adequate." It is interesting to note that Chemical Abstracts has since discontinued this line of research; they are currently more oriented toward an environment for machine-assisted human summarization.

As another example of the fundamental feature model, consider the ANES system (6), developed at General Electric in the early 1990s. Term-weighting (term frequency combined with the number of documents in which the term occurs) is used to extract "signature" words, with words below a particular weight threshold being excluded. Sentences are weighted based on weights of signature words. To address the dangling anaphor problem, sentences beginning with certain anaphors are excluded. For continuity, sentences without signature words that lie in between two sentences containing signature words are selected; also, the first (or second) sentence of a paragraph is added to the summary if the second (or third) sentence of a paragraph contains signature words. The system is highly robust, using patterns to flag various kinds of formats found in newswire source, such as embedded lists, tables, speeches, op-ed pieces, multitopic documents, and so forth.

More Complex Models

In addition to the Fundamental Feature Model, there are more complex models that have been investigated, some in combination with the fundamental feature model. One set of these (15–17) is based on *relationships* between text units, often represented as some sort of graph structure. These relational models can be viewed as extending the fundamental feature model with binary relations. The basic idea here is that the more strongly connected a text unit is to other units, the more salient it is. Examples of relations between text units include proximity, coreference (that two text units are referring to the same entity), synonymy, hypernymy (e.g., "dog" and "animal"), and similarity between text units. In Ref. 15, paragraphs from one or more documents are compared in terms of similarity, using a measure based on similarity of vocabulary. Those paragraphs above a particular similarity threshold are linked to form a "text relationship" graph. Paragraphs connected to many other paragraphs (i.e., "bushy nodes" in the graph) are considered salient. Summaries can then be generated by traversing a path along links and extracting text from each paragraph along the path. More recent uses of relational models (17,18) have exploited thesauri and proper name extraction to compute measures of connectivity among text units.

Yet another set of models being explored is based on more global models of discourse structure. These fall into two classes: models of rhetorical structure (19–22) and models of topic structure (23,24). These models are still evolving. Here, we discuss rhetorical structure; topic structure is discussed later. The overall idea is that in certain contexts (e.g., scientific texts, expository texts), it may be possible to determine a fairly fine-grained overall structure for the document (beyond the coarser formatting structure of a document into sections, subsections, and paragraphs). This can help influence what is to be selected in a summary, as well as provide a scaffolding for use in the synthesis phase of summarization. The role of relations based on *coherence* is of particular interest: In Refs. 19, 25, and 26, the structure of a multisentence text is represented in terms of macrolevel relations between sentences or clauses (although, in some accounts, the elements being related may be smaller than clauses). For example, the cue phrase "in order to," one could argue, expresses some sort of purpose relation between clauses; likewise, clauses linked by "although" together express some sort of contrast relation. These relations determine the overall argumentative structure of the expository text, represented in the form of a tree diagram. An example of such a tree is shown in Figure 1. Each node in the tree is either a nucleus node (foregrounded at some level) or a satellite node.

In recent work, Ref. 20 has provided an algorithm which ranks the nodes in the tree for salience. In essence, each parent node identifies its nuclear children as salient, and this identification is continued recursively down the tree. A partial ordering is defined on these salient clauses, based on depth from the root of the tree, so that salient clauses identified with a parent are higher in the ordering than salient clauses identified with the children. The extent to which such trees can be constructed automatically, and the extent to which they are correlated with human judgments of salience, are the subject of current investigations (20–22,27).

Machine Learning Approaches

As mentioned earlier, approaches which are trainable are of considerable interest. The work in Ref. 13 represents a major advance in this area. It uses the fundamental feature model, but with weights being derived from a corpus. The corpus here is a collection of 188 full-text/summary pairs, drawn from 21 different scientific collections. Each summary was written by a professional abstractor and was three sentences long on average. The algorithm takes each test sentence and computes a probability that it should be included in a summary, based on the frequency of features in the full-text and in the corresponding summary.

The features used in these experiments are sentence length, presence of fixed-cue phrases ("in summary," etc.), whether a sentence is paragraph-initial, paragraph-medial, or paragraph-final, the presence of high-frequency content words, and the presence of proper names. Of course, the summaries do not necessarily lift sentences from the full text. In addressing this, Ref. 13 describes various categories of matches, including a direct match, where the summary sentence and source sentence are identical or can be considered to have the same content. Indirect join matches occur when two or more sentences from the source text (called joins) appear to have the same content as a single

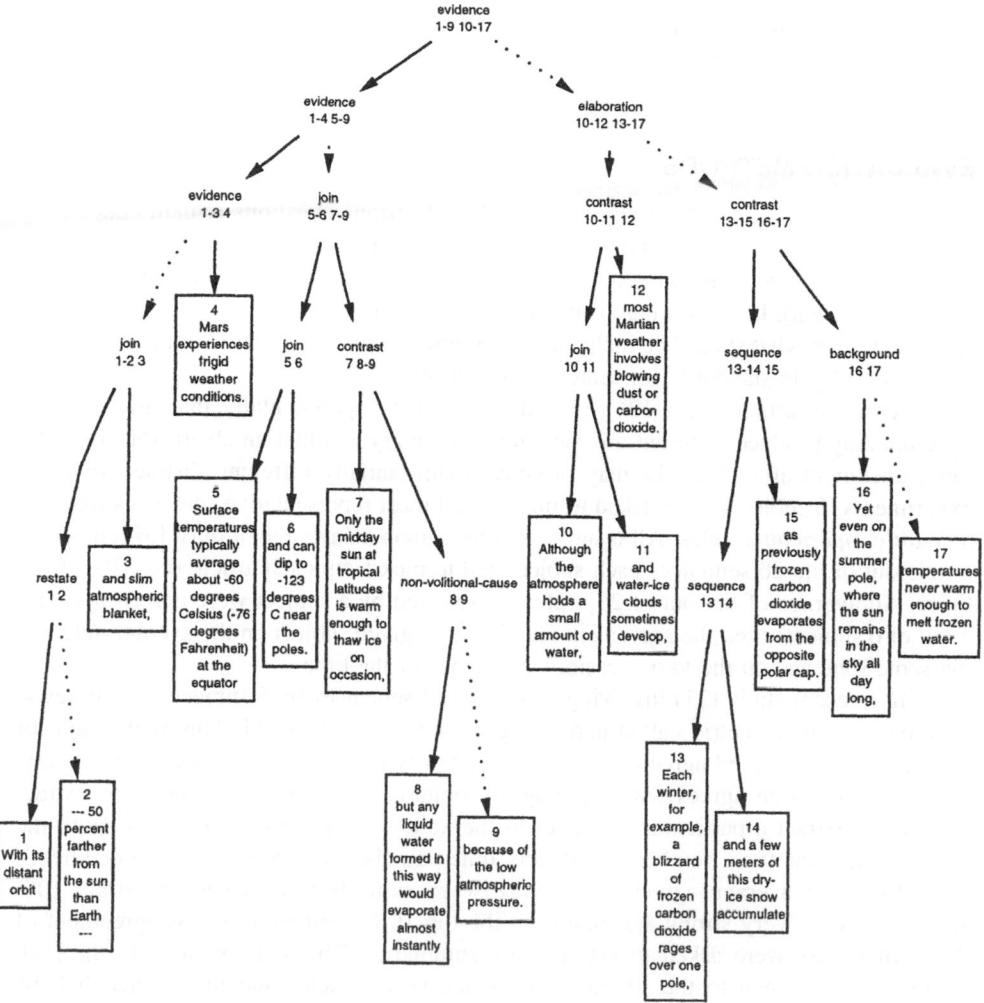

FIGURE 1   Coherence structure for an encyclopedia article. Dotted arcs lead to satellite nodes.

summary sentence. An incomplete match occurs when a source sentence only partially covers a summary sentence, or if a direct match is not clear.

The overall performance on test documents using a strict measure was 201 direct sentence matches and direct joins out of 568 sentences; that is, 35% of the sentences were recalled using this method. Looking at just the direct matches and direct joins, 211 out of 498 were correctly identified (i.e., 42% sentence recall). As the summaries were lengthened, performance improved, peaking at 25% of the full-text length. Although these results are encouraging, it should be remembered that the fixed phrases themselves are genre-specific. Also, the sentence overlap measures are somewhat problematic. Of course, without further evaluation, this method does not tell us how effective the summaries were. Reference 28 has extended this model to user-focused summaries, generating summarization rules for a particular genre (articles on computational linguistics), and others (21,29) have also extended this approach.

EVALUATION METHODS

Text summarization is still an emerging field, and serious questions remain concerning the appropriate methods and types of evaluation. There is little consensus as to what basis is best for comparison (e.g., summary of source, machine to human-generated, system to system). In comparing against human summaries, reports of low interannotator agreement over what should be included in a summary raise questions about the appropriateness of a "gold standard" for sentence extraction.

A classic article from 1961 (30) demonstrated experimentally that different abstractors may produce different abstracts for a summary and that an abstractor given the same document after 8 weeks may produce a substantially different abstract. In these experiments, 6 subjects were asked to pick the 20 most representative sentences from 10 *Scientific American* articles. All 6 subjects agreed upon an average of only 1.6 sentences/ article out of the 20 sentences each subject had to pick from each article (i.e., 8% of the time). An average of 6.4 out of 20 sentences selected by a subject were agreed upon by 5 out of 6 subjects (i.e., the agreement was 32%). A given subject on the average selected the same sentence on the two occasions only 55% of the time.

In a recent study (31) involving extraction of sentences by 5 subjects for 40 newswire documents, a metric called percent agreement was calculated. This is the ratio of the number of observed agreements with the majority opinion (i.e., number of times that a subject's decision agrees with the majority opinion—including agreements to extract and not to extract a particular sentence) to the number of possible agreements with the majority opinion (i.e., number of subjects times number of sentences in a document). They found an average agreement of 96% when subjects were asked to extract 10% summaries (i.e., very strong agreement on the top 10%), and slightly less agreement of 90% when they were asked to extract 20% summaries. The authors attribute the high levels of consistency to the similar style of the news articles and to the fact that the authors were asked to extract summaries of a given length.

In general, methods for evaluating text summarization approaches can be broadly classified into two categories. The first is an *extrinsic* evaluation, in which the quality of a summary is judged based on how it affects the completion of some other task. The second approach, an *intrinsic* evaluation, judges the quality of the summarization directly based on user judgments of informativeness, coverage of stipulated "key/essential ideas," fluency of the summary (32), and so forth.

ANES, the GE system described earlier, was evaluated in an intrinsic evaluation. Judges were asked to assess how "acceptable" short extracts of new stories were, given the full source of the article. These extracts were 50, 150, and 250 words long. ANES was deemed acceptable 68–78% of the time (the percentages vary for different lengths of abstracts). Now, one of the simplest approaches to scalable summarization is to pick out the *leading text*, that is, the first *n* characters or sentences, possibly completing to the nearest word or end of sentence mark. This technique, quite ubiquitous in its use, is useful in genres where the most salient information is right at the beginning, such as headline news stories. In comparison against Searchable Lead, a leading-text system from Mead Data Central, the latter was deemed acceptable 87–96% of the time, outperforming

ANES. The few cases where leading-text abstracts were unacceptable could be attributed to anecdotal, human-interest style lead-ins, or multitopic documents. Whereas the effect of the leading text baseline might serve as a cautionary tale for sentence extraction methods used on news-wire texts, it is unclear whether leading text serves a useful function in other genres, or in user-focused summaries of documents where the query-relevant information is not at the beginning.

The TIPSTER evaluation (33) is the first large-scale developer-independent evaluation of text summarization systems. TIPSTER is an extrinsic evaluation. A dry-run evaluation (33) was conducted in October 1997 with 6 systems, and a formal evaluation was completed in May 1998 with 16 systems. The experimental hypothesis is that use of summarization saves time in relevance assessment in certain tasks, without impacting accuracy. In each task, summaries were of two types: fixed length (10% of source) and variable length (where there was no restriction on summary length). In the first "ad hoc query" task, subjects are asked to judge whether a text (which could be a user-focused indicative summary or a full text—the subject is not told which) is relevant or irrelevant to a query. In the second "categorization" task, a text (which could be a "generic" indicative summary or a full text) is judged as to whether it belongs in one of five mutually exclusive subject categories, or "none of the above." As a leading text baseline to compare against, the first 10% of the document was used. The accuracy of the subject in determining relevance of a document to a query or category is scored in terms of the "ground-truth" relevance judgments used in the TREC (9) conferences, which are standard evaluations of information retrieval systems conducted by the U.S. government. The texts were 2000–15,000 characters in length and were all news-wire texts.

The results of the dry-run experiment were rather interesting (the formal results are forthcoming). The 10% fixed-length user-focused and generic summaries performed no better than the leading text method in terms of accuracy and time in these tasks. They confirm the trend observed earlier in the evaluation carried out in Ref. 6 on generic summaries. Variable-length summaries, on the other hand, were always significantly faster than full text; they were also more accurate than the fixed-length summaries. They were more effective on shorter full texts (less than median length), where presumably less of the information is being thrown away by the summary. The time taken by subjects to make their relevance decisions was proportional to the length of the summary, but not to the length of the original source, suggesting that the time taken is reading time. The other striking effect was a sizable disagreement among subjects in terms of their judgments of the relevance of the full text: Subjects agreed with each other pairwise on the average only about 70% of the time.

MULTIDOCUMENT AND MULTIMEDIA SUMMARIZATION

Multidocument Summarization

In summarizing a collection rather than just an individual document, a variety of techniques can be applied. It should be noted that techniques that do not necessarily involve text summarization can clearly be used to characterize the content of a collection. This includes enumerating entities (such as people, organizations, and places) extracted using information-extraction methods (3) from the collection. Another such technique is the clustering of documents, with particular key terms associated with each cluster, or grouping text passages in the collection in terms of subject areas from a thesaurus (34,35). A very simple approach to multidocument summarization is to extend the single-document sentence filtering to multiple documents, in effect treating the entire collection as a big document; the problem with this is that it ignores redundancy among passages.

Earlier, we discussed the use of text maps based on paragraph similarity. These can be used to extract paragraphs across documents. Another approach is called "Maximal Marginal Relevance" (36). Here, multiple texts (which can be individual documents or passages from multiple documents) can be ranked in terms of relevance to a query. Once the user has scanned some of these, the remaining texts can then be reranked so as to maximize the dissimilarity of the remaining ones from the ones already seen.

A recent approach (17) uses a weighting method to activate different locations in a text related to a query, then compares these locations across texts to find out commonalities and differences. When the documents are ordered, the differences are presented in terms of what's new in relation to the rest of the documents. Similar passages in multiple documents can also be highlighted, as shown in Figure 2, where the first paragraphs in the body of each text are marked as most similar to each other, as well as the passages in each text discussing the "book deal." In cases where there are multiple stories about a similar event, near-duplicates can be identified based on similarity computations, removing some of the redundancy across documents.

A final approach is based on information extraction. As mentioned earlier, systems can be used to fill templates for prespecified kinds of information, such as terrorist incidents (3). In the method used in Ref. 5, a number of different operators can be applied to these templates. When applied to texts describing terrorist incidents, the contradiction operator compares two templates which have the same incident location but which originate from different sources, and identifies slots that have different values in each template. The summarizer then uses text generation techniques to express the contradiction; for example, *On the afternoon of February 26, 1993 Reuters reported that a bomb killed at least 5 people. However, Associated Press later announced that exactly 5 people were killed.* Other operators include agreement—*UPI reported that three people were killed. Later, this was confirmed by Reuters*—and the superset operator, which fuses summaries together—*A total of 5 criminals were arrested in Colombia last week: Reuters reported that two drug traffickers were arrested in Bogota, and according to UPI three terrorists were arrested in Medellin.* Although such examples are extremely promising, it is worth noting that these techniques only apply to documents for which such templates can be reliably filled. Further, the generation system uses rules which specify the mapping between the operators and output English text, and many of these rules have to be instantiated by hand for each application. As a result, the techniques do not scale up to arbitrary text.

Multimedia Summarization

As mentioned earlier, the input text to be summarized may represent information represented in some other media, such as imagery, audio, or video. In particular, the text might be produced as a result of automatic speech recognition applied to audio. Also, the output text might be supplemented by (and coordinated with) presentation of information in different media. The work in Ref. 24 combines the result of processing closed-captioned Japanese text with representative images extracted from the video stream b to produce multimedia summaries for skimming by the user. A coherence structure for the text is extracted based on tracking cue phrases. These include Japanese phrases such as

SIMPSON JURY HEARS FROM GOLDMAN'S DAD

EMOTIONAL TESTIMONY ENDS PLAINTIFFS' CASE

By Vincent J. Schodolski, Tribune Staff Writer Web-posted Tuesday, December 10, 1996; 6:02 a.m. CST

Dateline: SANTA MONICA, Calif.

Weeping at times and throwing angry glances at O.J. Simpson, sitting a few feet away, the father of slaying victim Ron Goldman told Simpson's civil trial jury Monday the loss of his son left a hole in his life that could never be filled.

"There isn't a day ... I don't think of Ron," said Fred Goldman, who along with the family of Nicole Brown Simpson, brought a wrongful-death suit against the former football star......

Petrocelli's questioning ended with a video made at Laura's bat mitzvah in 1993.

A closing shot showed Ron Goldman holding a microphone and speaking into the camera: "I'm very glad I was able to be here and spend this time with you because God knows where I'll be in a year."

He was murdered seven months later.

Simpson's attorney, Robert Baker, questioned Goldman briefly and gently, establishing that the family had a $450,000 book deal.

After the plaintiffs rested, Baker called retired Los Angeles police detective Philip Vannatter, who was in charge of the murder investigation.

....

1996 Chicago Tribune

TEARFUL FATHER IS FINAL WITNESS FOR PLAINTIFFS

SIMPSON'S DEFENSE STARTS WITH FORMER L.A. COP

Associated Press Web-posted Tuesday, December 10, 1996; 6:02 a.m. CST

Dateline: SANTA MONICA, Calif.

Plaintiffs finished up their side of the wrongful death case against O.J. Simpson Monday with Fred Goldman, who told tearfully how he loved his slain son "more than you can imagine."

Taking the stand as the final plaintiffs' witness, Goldman shot Simpson angry glances as he testified about his son's life and dreams.

After a gentle cross-examination of Goldman in which he acknowledged he had a $450,000 book deal Simpson attorney Robert Baker began presenting Simpson's defense.

Baker immediately ran into problems with the judge, who disallowed many questions.

....

1996 Chicago Tribune

FIGURE 2   Multidocument summarization: passage alignment.

mazu ("first") and *tsugi ni* ("next"), which indicate topic nesting, *kore wa* ("this is") and *kono kekka* ("as a result"), which are supposedly indicative of topic continuation, and *ni tsuite* ("with regard to"), *ga* (subject marker), and *wa* ("as for"), which are explicit topic markers in Japanese. Noun phrases are then extracted as potential topic labels and given weights based on a variety of heuristics. The text is then synchronized with the video based on time spans associated with the captions (somewhat inaccurate, given that the closed-caption time stamps are often slightly out of synch with the video soundtrack). Based on this synchronization, a topic is associated with the first image in any images synchronized with the sentence's time span, if such images exist, or with an image within a 5-second delta of the sentence's time span. Images within the same topic are grouped, and the topic is chosen as a label for the group. Using these methods, the system is able to create effective multimedia summaries.

Reference 37 investigates the effectiveness of different types of multimedia summarization strategies in answering questions related to TV news broadcasts. An example of a multimedia summary is shown in Figure 3. The questions asked were identification questions (e.g., Which stories are about the United Nations?) and comprehension questions (e.g., What disease has been detected in Europe again?). They found that in the identification task, subjects who viewed "generic" summaries which used combinations of strategies (e.g., a key frame extracted from the video, extracted topics from the closed-captioned text, all the proper names extracted from the text, and a one-line summary) were just as accurate in their answers as when viewing the full video, but took no more than a third of the time. These results indicate that multimedia presentation strategies are often more effective than single-media ones. For the comprehension task however, the summarization methods "did not include sufficient factual details required to answer the comprehension questions."

CHALLENGES FOR THE FUTURE

Text summarization is still a growing research field. There is some improved consensus on evaluation metrics, largely as a result of recent evaluations reported on in the literature (17,20,31,33,38,39). There is also growing interest in developing standard methods for evaluating multidocument summarization techniques.

Of course, evaluation is not the only focus. The effectiveness of different summari-

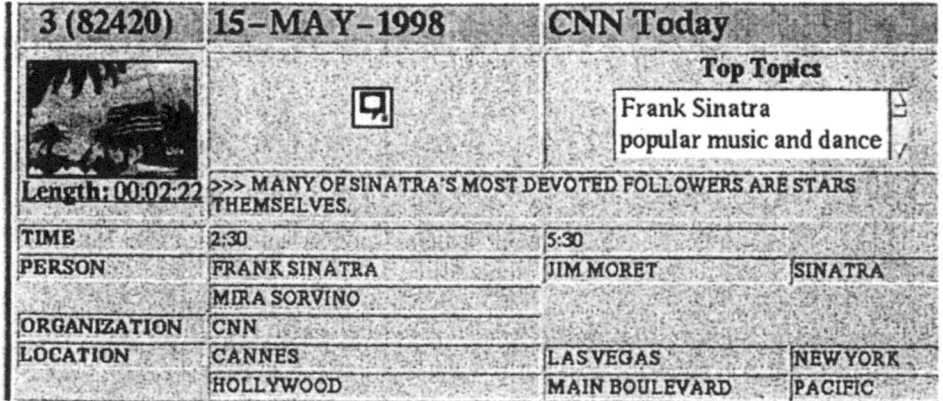

FIGURE 3   Multimedia summarization: an example. Topics, a one-line summary, and key proper names are shown.

zation techniques can vary greatly across tasks and genres. The highly task- and genre-dependent nature of summarization makes it especially crucial to be able to automatically adapt summarization techniques to different genres. Research on discourse structure continues to be very active for use in determining salience, resolving anaphora, and structuring summaries. The ability to generate abstracts instead of extracts in a scalable fashion is of considerable interest; researchers have begun exploring the use of thesauri in this area (38). In multidocument summarization, it would be useful for a system to be able to recommend not just which documents are relevant to a particular query but how they differ in the way they are relevant. For example, in comparing medical literature about cases against a patient's record (40), a user-focused summarizer can indicate information like "3 papers weakly support Treatment A, while 9 papers strongly support Treatment B."

Despite the many outstanding problems, many of the summarization technologies can be useful today. For example, the ability to smooth text in various ways makes possible a number of applications that can be of tremendous use. Gisting of retrieved information from World Wide Web searches (which can result in large numbers of hits) are an obvious example. Also, the contents of large collections could also be summarized and stored as surrogates for indexing and retrieval. Summarization for word processing is another example (e.g., Microsoft Word 97's AutoSummarize). Reference 41 reports on the use of smoothing techniques to construct a telegraphic reduction of the text to different levels (e.g., just proper names, or just subjects, objects, and main verbs) to be read aloud using speech synthesis for use in a reading machine for the blind. A challenge here is to find good trade-offs between compaction and intelligibility. We can also expect increased use of summaries for specialized domains (e.g., where structured representations are already available). Finally, the ability to combine summarization with machine translation is of considerable interest for searching and retrieving foreign-language information. These are only a few examples of what is possible; the precise ecological niches for summarization for human and machine remain to be explored.

REFERENCES

1. K. Sparck-Jones, "Summarizing: Where Are We Now? Where Should We Go?" in *Proceedings of the ACL/EACL'97 Workshop on Intelligent Scalable Text Summarization*, I. Mani and M. Maybury (eds.), 1997.
2. J. J. Pollock and A. Zamora, "Automatic Abstracting Research at Chemical Abstracts Service," *J. Chem. Inform. Computer Sci.*, *15*, 4 (1975).
3. *Proceedings of the Sixth Message Understanding Conference (MUC-6)*, 1995.
4. I. Mani and T. MacMillan, "Identifying Unknown Proper Names in Newswire Text," in *Corpus Processing for Lexical Acquisition*, B. Boguraev and J. Pustejovsky (eds.), MIT Press, Cambridge, MA, 1995.
5. K. McKeown and D. Radev, "Generating Summaries of Multiple News Articles," in *Proceedings of ACM–SIGIR '95*, 1995.
6. R. Brandow, K. Mitze, and L. Rau, "Automatic Condensation of Electronic Publications by Sentence Selection," *Inform. Process. Manag.*, *31*(5), 675–685 (1994).
7. C. Paice, "Constructing Literature Abstracts by Computer: Techniques and Prospects," *Inform. Process. Manag.*, *26*(1), 171–186 (1990).
8. H. P. Edmundson, "New Methods in Automatic Abstracting," *J. Assoc. Comput. Machin.*, *16*(2), 264–285 (1969).

9. D. K. Harman and E. M. Voorhees (eds.), "The Fifth Text Retrieval Conference (TREC-5)," *National Institute of Standards and Technology*, Gaithersburg, MD, 1996.

10. K. Sparck-Jones, "A Statistical Interpretation of Term Specificity and Its Application in Retrieval," *J. Document.*, *28*(1), 11–20 (1972).

11. J. D. Cohen, "Highlights: Language- and Domain-Independent Automatic Indexing Terms for Abstracting," *J. Am. Soc. Inform. Sci.*, *46*(3), 162–174 (1995); erratum: *47*(3), 260 (1996).

12. H. P. Luhn, "The Automatic Creation of Literature Abstracts," *IBM J. Res. Develop.*, *2*, 159–165 (1959).

13. J. Kupiec, J. Pedersen, and F. Chen, "A Trainable Document Summarizer," in *Proceedings of the 18th ACM SIGIR Conference (SIGIR'95)*, 1995, pp. 68–73.

14. C. Paice and P. Jones, "The Identification of Important Concepts in Highly Structured Technical Papers," in *Proceedings of the 16th ACM SIGIR Conference (SIGIR'93)*, 1993, pp. 69–78.

15. G. Salton, J. Allan, C. Buckley, and A. Singhal, "Automatic Analysis, Theme Generation, and Summarization of Machine-Readable Texts," *Science*, *264*, 1421–1426 (1994).

16. E. F. Skorokhodko, "Adaptive Method of Automatic Abstracting and Indexing," *IFIP Congress*, 1972, pp. 1179–1182.

17. I. Mani and E. Bloedorn, "Multi-document Summarization by Graph Search and Merging," in *Proceedings of the Fourteenth National Conference on Artificial Intelligence (AAAI-97)*, 1997, pp. 622–628.

18. R. Barzilay and M. Elhadad, "Using Lexical Chains for Text Summarization," in *Proceedings of the ACL/EACL '97 Workshop on Intelligent Scalable Text Summarization*, I. Mani and M. Maybury (eds.), 1997, pp. 10–17.

19. E. R. Liddy, "The Discourse-Level Structure of Empirical Abstracts: An Exploratory Study," *Inform. Process. Manag.*, *27*(1), 55–81 (1991).

20. D. Marcu, "From Discourse Structures to Text Summaries," in *Proceedings of the ACL/EACL'97 Workshop on Intelligent Scalable Text Summarization*, I. Mani and M. Maybury, 1997, pp. 82–88.

21. S. Teufel and M. Moens, "Sentence Extraction and Rhetorical Classification for Flexible Abstracts," in *Working Notes of the AAAI Spring Symposium on Intelligent Text Summarization, Spring 1998, Technical Report*, AAAI, 1998, pp. 16–25.

22. S. Corston-Oliver, "Beyond String Matching and Cue Phrases: Improving Efficiency and Coverage in Discourse Analysis," in *Working Notes of the AAAI Spring Symposium on Intelligent Text Summarization, Spring 1998, Technical Report*, AAAI, 1998, pp. 9–15.

23. M. Hearst, "TextTiling: Segmenting Text into Multi-Paragraph Subtopic Passages," *Comput. Linguist.*, *23*(1), 33–64 (1997).

24. A. Takeshita, T. Inoue, and K. Tanaka, "Topic-based Multimedia Structuring," in *Intelligent Multimedia Information Retrieval*, M. Maybury (ed.), AAAI/MIT Press, Cambridge, MA, 1997.

25. W. C. Mann and S. A. Thompson, "Rhetorical Structure Theory: Towards a Functional Theory of Text Organization," *Text*, *8*(3), 243–281 (1988).

26. T. A. vanDijk, *News as Discourse*, Lawrence Erlbaum, Hillsdale, NJ, 1988.

27. I. Mani, E. Bloedorn, and B. L. Gates, "Using Cohesion and Coherence Models for Text Summarization," in *Working Notes of the AAAI Spring Symposium on Intelligent Text Summarization, Spring 1998, Technical Report*, AAAI, 1998, pp. 69–76.

28. I. Mani and E. Bloedorn, "Machine Learning of Generic and User-Focused Summarization," in *Proceedings of AAAI'98*, 1998.

29. C. Aone, M. E. Okurowski, J. Gorlinsky, and B. Larsen, "A Scalable Summarization System Using Robust NLP," in *Proceedings of the ACL/EACL'97 Workshop on Intelligent Scalable Text Summarization*, I. Mani and M. Maybury (eds.), 1997, pp. 66–73.

30. G. J. Rath, A. Resnick, and T. R. Savage, "The Formation of Abstracts by the Selection of Sentences," *Am. Document.*, *12*(2), 139–143 (1961).

31. H. Jing, R. Barzilay, K. McKeown, and M. Elhadad, "Summarization Evaluation Methods:

Experiments and Analysis," in *Working Notes of the AAAI Spring Symposium on Intelligent Text Summarization, Spring 1998, Technical Report*, AAAI, 1998, pp. 60–68.

32. J-L. Minel, S. Nugier, and G. Piat, "How to Appreciate the Quality of Automatic Text Summarization," in *Proceedings of the ACL/EACL'97 Workshop on Intelligent Scalable Text Summarization*, I. Mani and M. Maybury (eds.), 1997, pp. 25–30.

33. T. F. Hand and M. J. Chrzanowski, "An Evaluation of Automatic Text Summarization Systems," in *Advances in Automatic Text Summarization*, I. Mani and M. Maybury (eds.), MIT Press, Cambridge, MA, 1999.

34. E. R. Liddy and W. Paik, "Statistically Guided Word-Sense Disambiguation," in *Working Notes of the AAAI Fall Symposium on Probablistic Approaches to Natural Language, Fall 1992, Technical Report*, AAAI, 1992, pp. 98–107.

35. E. R. Liddy and S. Myaeng, "DR-LINK's Linguistic–Conceptual Approach to Document Detection," in *Proceedings of the First TREC Retrieval Conference (TREC-1)*, D. Harman (ed.), National Institute of Standards and Technology, Gaithersburg, MD, 1992.

36. J. Carbonell, Y. Geng, and J. Goldstein, "Automated Query-Relevant Summarization and Diversity-Based Reranking," in *Proceedings of the IJ–CAI'97 Workshop on AI in Digital Libraries—Moving from Chaos to (More) Order, Fifteenth National Conference on Artificial Intelligence (IJCAI'97)*, 1997.

37. A. Merlino and M. Maybury, "An Empirical Study of the Optimal Presentation of Multimedia Summaries of Broadcast News," in *Advances in Automatic Text Summarization*, I. Mani and M. Maybury (eds.), MIT Press, Cambridge, MA, 1999.

38. E. Hovy and C.-Y. Lin, "Automated Text Summarization in SUMMARIST," in *Proceedings of the ACL/EACL'97 Workshop on Intelligent Scalable Text Summarization*, I. Mani and M. Maybury (eds.), 1997, pp. 18–24.

39. A. Tombros, M. Sanderson, and P. Gray, "Advantages of Query Biased Summaries in Information Retrieval," in *Working Notes of the AAAI Spring Symposium on Intelligent Text Summarization, Spring 1998, Technical Report*, AAAI, 1998, pp. 44–52.

40. K. McKeown, D. Jordan, and V. Hatzivassloglou, "Generating Patient-Specific Summaries of Online Literature," in *Working Notes of the AAAI Spring Symposium on Intelligent Text Summarization, Spring 1998, Technical Report*, AAAI, 1998, pp. 34–43.

41. G. Grefenstette, "Producing Intelligent Telegraphic Text Reduction to Provide an Audio Scanning Service for the Blind," in *Working Notes of the AAAI Spring Symposium on Intelligent Text Summarization, Spring 1998, Technical Report*, AAAI, 1998, pp. 111–117.

INDERJEET MANI

LEARNING, ADAPTIVITY, AND COMPLEXITY IN A HIERARCHICAL FUZZY MODEL

INTRODUCTION

Fuzzy set theory provides a formal system for modeling complex systems. A system model attempts to capture the relationships between the input and the resulting output. In classical modeling, these relationships are expressed as mathematical functions. As the systems being modeled have become more complex, it is increasingly difficult to develop mathematical models directly from knowledge of the system. This is due to the complexity of interactions within the system as well as an incomplete knowledge of the system operations.

Fuzzy models have been used to model complex systems for which an imprecise or approximate specification is all that is available. A fuzzy model is defined by a set of fuzzy rules that specify a relationship between the input domain(s) and the output domain(s). The earliest applications were pioneered by the research of Mamdani (1) in the area of automatic control theory. Although the most well-known achievements for fuzzy modeling have been in controls theory, fuzzy models have been successfully applied to many other fields including pattern recognition, decision support, approximate reasoning, robotics, natural language and image understanding, and machine learning (2–4).

In the classical development of fuzzy inference systems, fuzzy rules have been obtained by knowledge acquisition from experts. Recently, learning algorithms have been used to analyze a set of training examples and build the rule base(s) of a fuzzy model. Techniques for building fuzzy models from training data were presented by Wang and Mendel (5), and Kosko (6), and examined by Sudkamp and Hammell (7). The accuracy of the resulting model is affected by the inference technique employed, the domain decompositions, and the size and precision of the training set.

Learning rules from training examples admits the possibility that the resulting rule base may be incomplete; that is, there may be a possible input for which no action is specified. This problem is overcome by the incorporation of completion algorithms into the rule construction process. Completing a rule base uses the existing rules and interpolation to produce rules for the undefined configurations (8).

A hierarchical architecture was developed to enhance the performance of fuzzy models constructed using supervised learning from training data (9). The knowledge base of the model consists of two fuzzy associative memories (FAMs). When constructed, one FAM provides a rough approximation of the underlying system and the other refines the model. Originally designed for constructing models with supervised learning, the hierarchical architecture has been modified for modeling adaptive systems. The adaptive capability has been incorporated using rule modification based on system performance feedback. Analysis of the system feedback determines when adaptation is necessary, selects the rules to modify, and appropriately adjusts either or both of the FAMs.

The adaptive algorithm for the hierarchical model has been utilized in three types of adaptive behavior: continued learning, gradual change, and drastic change. In continued learning, the underlying system does not change and the adaptive algorithm utilizes the real-time data and associated feedback to improve the performance of the existing model. Gradual and drastic change represent fundamental alterations to the system being modeled. In the latter two cases, the adaptation process is augmented with rule base completion to expand the influence of the most recent information in the model construction process.

The majority of successful applications of fuzzy systems have a small number of input domains. As more sophisticated systems are modeled, the complexity of the FAM grows in two aspects. The *granularity* of a system is determined by the scope of applicability of the rules. The granularity is increased by using more fuzzy sets in the decomposition of the input domain. The *dimensionality* of a model reflects the number of inputs processed by the model. The dimensionality is increased by using more input variables. Higher degrees of granularity or dimensionality affect the rule-generation process as well as the run-time performance of the resulting fuzzy system.

This article presents an examination of the process of and problems associated with learning fuzzy rules from data. We begin by discussing fuzzy models and rule-learning algorithms in general. The hierarchical architecture for constructing fuzzy models is then introduced, followed by a description of the adaptive algorithm. Experimental results are provided that demonstrate the ability of the algorithm to modify the model based on changes in the underlying system. Finally, the problems within fuzzy learning algorithms caused by increased granularity and dimensionality are presented along with techniques that may be useful for minimizing the impacts of these problems.

FUZZY MODELS

The input to a fuzzy model consists of the values of a set of variables that describe the state or configuration of the system being modeled. Figure 1 is a diagram of the components of a two-input, one-output fuzzy model with inputs from the domains U and V and output in W. Fuzzification transforms the input based on the noise in the source of the data or the degree of precision required for the analysis. Defuzzification converts the output from the fuzzy set C produced by the inference system to a singleton c in W. In this section, we will introduce fuzzy sets and rules and illustrate their role in the development of fuzzy models.

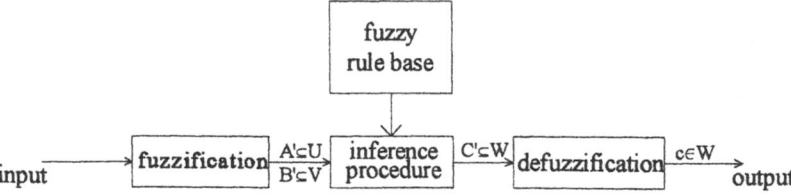

FIGURE 1   Components of a fuzzy model. (Reprinted from *Expert Systems with Applications*, Vol. 11, No. 2, Hammell and Sudkamp, "An Adaptive Hierarchical Fuzzy Model," pp. 125–136, Copyright 1996, with permission from Elsevier Science.)

A fuzzy set represents approximate or vague information over a domain. The membership function μ for a fuzzy set assigns a grade of membership ranging from 0 to 1 for all elements in the domain. For domain U, a fuzzy set A over U is defined by a membership function $\mu_A: U \to [0, 1]$, where $\mu_A(x)$ denotes the membership grade of x in A. The membership grade $\mu_A(x)$ indicates the degree to which x satisfies the predicate A.

The *height* of a fuzzy set A is the supremum of the membership grades of the elements in A. A normal fuzzy set has a height of 1; otherwise, the set is subnormal. The *support* of a fuzzy set A is the crisp set containing all elements of the domain that have nonzero membership in A. The *core* of a fuzzy set consists of all elements with a membership grade equal to 1.

The first step in the design of a fuzzy model consists of defining the terms to be used in the antecedents and consequents of the rules. This specifies the language of the rule base and is accomplished by decomposing the input and output domains into families of fuzzy sets. A decomposition of a domain U is a set of fuzzy sets $A_1, \ldots, A_n$ over U wherein the union of the supports of the fuzzy sets completely covers U. Figure 2 shows the domain $[-1, 1]$ decomposed into five triangular fuzzy sets A_1 through A_5; fuzzy set A_3 is highlighted to illustrate the core, support, and height characteristics. In triangular fuzzy sets, the core is a unique element and is referred to as the midpoint. The decomposition of a domain U is assumed to form a fuzzy partition of U. A fuzzy partition satisfies

$$\sum_{i=1}^{n} \mu_{A_i}(u) = 1$$

for every u in U.

The combination of triangular membership functions and the fuzzy partition requirement ensures that any input will have nonzero membership in at most two fuzzy sets and that the input will have membership of ≥ 0.5 in at least one fuzzy set. In this article, all domains are assumed to be normalized to take values from the interval $[-1, 1]$ and the domain decompositions consist of a partition by triangular fuzzy sets.

The domain knowledge of a fuzzy model is encapsulated by its set of fuzzy rules. A fuzzy rule with two antecedents has the form "if X is A and Y is B, then Z is C,"

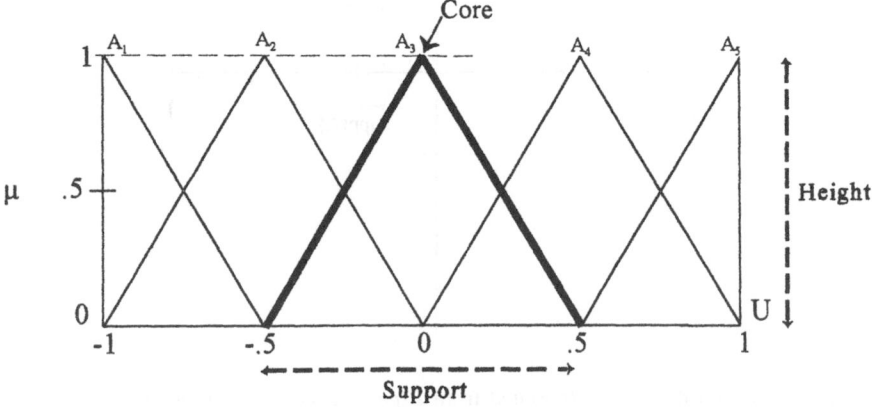

FIGURE 2   Triangular decomposition of $[-1, 1]$.

where A and B are fuzzy sets over the input domains U and V, respectively, and C is a fuzzy set over the output domain W. Thus, a fuzzy rule is used to linguistically represent relationships between domains. For example, "if speed is *fast* and distance is *medium*, then apply brake *medium*" is a fuzzy rule that might be used in a brake pressure control system, where *fast* is a fuzzy set describing speed, *medium* a fuzzy set over distance, and *medium* in the consequent a fuzzy set over pressure. The linguistic variables are used to approximately characterize the values of variables as well as their relationships. The combination of linguistic variables and fuzzy set theory provides a formal system for representing and manipulating imprecise or approximate quantities.

The region in which a rule provides information for inference is defined by the supports of the fuzzy sets. Figure 3 illustrates the region of influence for the rule "if X is A, then Z is C." The supports of A and C describe a fuzzy relation patch which bounds the area covered by the rule. This is called the *locality principle* of fuzzy approximation. As more fuzzy sets are used, the region covered by each rule decreases. Thus, the domain decompositions define the granularity of the approximations.

A fuzzy associative memory (FAM) is an l-dimensional table where each dimension corresponds to one of the input universes. The ith dimension of the table is indexed by the fuzzy sets that constitute the decomposition of the ith input domain. Consider a fuzzy model with input domains U and V and output domain W, as depicted in Figure 1. Let $A_1, \ldots, A_m$ be a partition of U and $B_1, \ldots, B_n$ be a partition of V. A fuzzy rule base for such a system consists of rules of the form "if X is A_i and Y is B_j, then Z is $C_{k_{ij}}$," where $C_{k_{ij}}$ is a fuzzy set over the output domain W. The FAM representing this rule base has the form

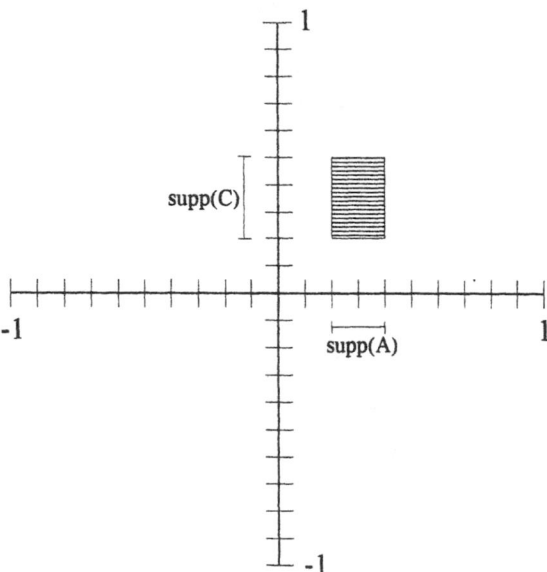

FIGURE 3   Fuzzy rule patch. (Reprinted from *Expert Systems with Applications*, Vol. 11, No. 2, Hammell and Sudkamp, "An Adaptive Hierarchical Fuzzy Model," pp. 125–136, Copyright 1996, with permission from Elsevier Science.)

	A_1	A_2	$\cdots$	A_{m-1}	A_m
B_1	$C_{k_{11}}$	$C_{k_{21}}$	$\cdots$	$C_{k_{(m-1)1}}$	$C_{k_{m1}}$
$\vdots$	$\vdots$	$\vdots$		$\vdots$	$\vdots$
B_n	$C_{k_{1n}}$	$C_{k_{2n}}$	$\cdots$	$C_{k_{(m-1)n}}$	$C_{k_{mn}}$

where the consequent of a rule with antecedent "if X is A_i and Y is B_j," is entered in the (i, j)th position.

A fuzzy rule base consists of a series of rules that trace a fuzzy function from the input domain to the output domain. A one-input one-output system with input domain decomposition $A_1, \ldots, A_7$ and output domain decomposition $C_1, \ldots, C_7$ is used to show the interpretation of a fuzzy rule base as a function approximation. A rule base is defined by the one-dimensional FAM

A_1	A_2	A_3	A_4	A_5	A_6	A_7
C_1	C_2	C_3	C_4	C_3	C_2	C_1

Figure 4 shows the supports of the fuzzy sets in the domain decompositions along the horizontal and vertical axes. The boxed areas indicate the regions in the space that are influenced by each rule. The parabolic shape of the overlapping regions suggests that this may be a fuzzy approximation of the function $f(x) = -(x^2)$.

Inference in a fuzzy model compares the input with the antecedent of a rule to produce the response indicated by that particular rule. The output is obtained by summarizing the responses indicated by each individual rule. As mentioned earlier, a fuzzy rule "if X is A, then Z is C" represents a functional relationship between input A and output

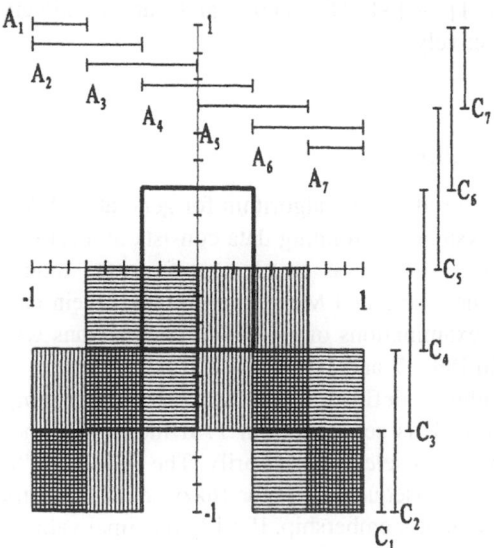

FIGURE 4   Rule base as function approximation.

C. The area covered by such a rule is bounded by the supports of *A* and *C*. For example, the shaded lower right-hand rectangle in Figure 4 is the region associated with the rule "if *X* is A_7, then *Z* is C_1."

The role of a fuzzy model is to determine an appropriate output based on the input to the system. The inference technique determines the degree to which each rule affects the outcome. For the experimental results given in this article, Mamdani-style inference and weighted-averaging defuzzification are used to produce the output; this algorithm will be described using a one-input one-output inference system where the domain decompositions are triangular with evenly spaced midpoints. The input universe is subdivided into triangular regions $A_1, \ldots, A_n$ and the output domain is decomposed by the fuzzy partition $C_1, \ldots, C_m$ with associated midpoints $c_1, \ldots, c_m$. The restrictions on the decomposition make inference in such a system very straightforward and efficient. Assume that A_i and A_{i+1} are the two fuzzy sets providing nonzero membership for an input value *x* with associated FAM entries C_r and C_s, respectively (there will only be two for a one-input system). Using weighted-averaging defuzzification, the result *z* specified by input *x* is given by

$$z = \frac{\mu_{A_i}(x)c_r + \mu_{A_{i+1}}(x)c_s}{\mu_{A_i}(x) + \mu_{A_{i+1}}(x)} \qquad [1]$$

Rewriting Eq. (1) in terms of the midpoints produces

$$z = \frac{x(c_s - c_r) + a_{i+1}c_r - a_i c_s}{a_{i+1} - a_i} \qquad [2]$$

where c_r and c_s are as defined earlier and a_i and a_{i+1} denote the midpoints of A_i and A_{i+1}, respectively. Equation (2) shows that the result is completely determined by the rule base and the midpoints of the triangular decomposition of the domains. As mentioned earlier, each of the input and output domains are assumed to be the interval $I = [-1, 1]$. When the input is precise, a fuzzy model and weighted-averaging defuzzification defines a real-valued function $\hat{f}: [-1, 1]^k \to [-1, 1]^t$, where *k* and *t* are the dimensions of the input and output domains, respectively.

LEARNING FUZZY RULES

Wang and Mendel (5) introduced an algorithm for generating FAM entries from training data. For a one-input system, the training data consists of a set of input–output pairs $T = \{(x_i, z_i) \mid I = 1, \ldots, k\}$, where x_i is an element from the input domain and z_i is the associated response. The Wang and Mendel algorithm, herein called FLM, is described below. More detailed examinations of FLM and comparisons with other learning algorithms can be found in Refs. 7 and 10.

The FLM algorithm is defined as follows: A training example (x_i, z_i) that has the maximal membership in A_j is selected from *T*. If more than one example assumes the maximal membership, one is selected arbitrarily. The fuzzy rule "if *X* is A_j, then *Z* is C_r" is constructed where the consequent C_r is the fuzzy set in the output domain decomposition in which z_i has maximal membership. If z_i has maximal value in two adjacent regions $[\mu_{C_r}(z_i) = \mu_{C_{r+1}}(z_i) = 0.5]$, then the consequent C_r is selected.

The generation of a rule with antecedent "if *X* is A_j" requires at least one training example with membership 0.5 or greater in the set A_j. Learning a large number of rules may require a large set of training data, especially with multidimensional input. An inference system with five input domains, with each decomposed into five regions, produces a FAM with 3125 rules. If the training set is obtained by sampling an operational system, a suitable training example may not be encountered for all FAM entries. Entries left undefined by FLM are filled using rule base completion (7,8), which is discussed in Example 1.

To enhance the performance of models constructed using supervised learning from training data, a two-level architecture was designed by modifying the FLM algorithm (11). The FLM algorithm is extended to utilize an analysis of the error between the approximating function $\hat{f}$ and the training data. The first step of the FLE (Fuzzy Learning with Error analysis) algorithm is to construct the initial approximation $\hat{f}$ with FLM. The second step then reuses the training data to refine the approximation. This is done by producing a second FAM that defines a function $\hat{f}_e$ which is used to approximate the error between the training data and $\hat{f}$.

The training set T_e used to learn $\hat{f}_e$ is obtained from the training data T and the initial approximation $\hat{f}$. An element in T_e represents the difference between an original training example and the approximation produced by $\hat{f}$; the training set is $T_e = \{(x_i, z_i - \hat{f}(x_i) \mid (x_i, z_i) \in T\}$.

To define the fuzzy associative memory to approximate the error function, called the EFAM to distinguish it from the original FAM, it is necessary to identify the input and output domains of the error function. The input domain is $[-1, 1]$, the same as the approximating function $\hat{f}$. The output of the error function, however, takes values from a smaller interval than the domain of the original FAM. To allow for the largest possible error, the EFAM size is set to one-half of the length of the support of the largest fuzzy set in the FAM output domain decomposition. For an output domain decomposition of five equally spaced triangular fuzzy sets, the support of each such fuzzy set is an interval of length 0.5; thus, the associated EFAM output domain is the interval of $[-0.25, 0.25]$.

Once the domain decompositions have been selected, learning the function $\hat{f}_e$ follows the FLM algorithm using T_e as the training set. The last step in the creation of the EFAM is to use completion to fill in any missing entries.

The approximation produced by the FLE algorithm uses the two FAMs, as illustrated in Figure 5. An input x is processed by each of the FAMs. The resulting values

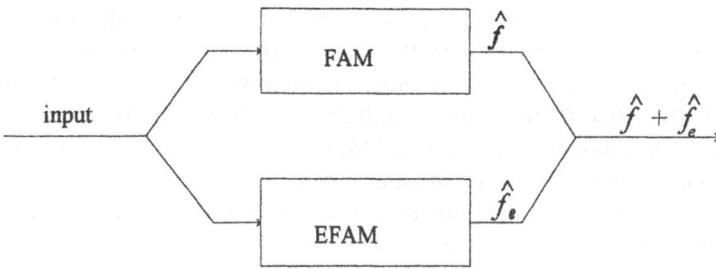

FIGURE 5   Two-level architecture. (Reprinted from *Expert Systems with Applications*, Vol. 11, No. 2, Hammell and Sudkamp, "An Adaptive Hierarchical Fuzzy Model," pp. 125–136, Copyright 1996, with permission from Elsevier Science.)

$\hat{f}(x)$ and $\hat{f}_e(x)$ are added to produce the single overall system output. The following example details the steps in the process of constructing a two-level system.

Example 1: This example illustrates constructing a two-level system to approximate the function $f(x) = x^2$ from training data $T = \{(-1, 1), (-0.4, 0.16), (0, 0), (0.5, 0.25), (0.7, 0.49), (1, 1)\}$. The function $f(x)$ from which the training data is obtained is called the target function. Note that the training set consists of precise data; each pair has the form $(x, f(x))$ with no noise introduced into the function value.

The first step is to construct the approximation $\hat{f}$ from T. In this example, the input and output universes for the FAM are decomposed into the five equally spaced triangular fuzzy regions with midpoints -1, -0.5, 0, 0.5, and 1 as shown in Figure 2. The FLM algorithm produces the FAM

A_1	A_2	A_3	A_4	A_5
C_5	C_3	C_3	C_3	C_5

which provides the approximation $\hat{f}$.

Observe that the x values in both training pairs $(0.5, 0.25)$ and $(0.7, 0.49)$ belong to region A_4 the most. However, because 0.5 has a higher membership value in this region than 0.7, the corresponding z value of 0.25 is used to determine the consequent for the rule "if X is $A_4 \ldots$". Also, note that training set T completely covers the input regions so no rule base completion is necessary.

If the process were to stop here, the result would be that of the original Wang and Mendel algorithm. To illustrate how the addition of the EFAM increases the accuracy of the approximation, the table below shows the approximations $\hat{f}(x)$ provided by the FAM for the input values from the training set. The second line of the table gives the values of x^2 for the corresponding input; the third line of the table is the approximation provided by the FAM; the last line of the table provides the error in the approximation.

	x					
	-1	-0.4	0	0.5	0.7	1
$f(x) = x^2$	1	0.16	0	0.25	0.49	1
$\hat{f}(x)$	1	0	0	0	0.4	1
$f(x) - \hat{f}(x)$	0	0.16	0	0.25	0.09	0

The FLE algorithm continues by augmenting the FAM with an EFAM. The next step is to build the training set T_e for the construction of the EFAM. From above, the $(x, \hat{f}(x))$ pairs are $(-1, 1)$, $(-0.4, 0)$, $(0, 0)$, $(0.5, 0)$, $(0.7, 0.4)$, and $(1, 1)$. Combining a training example $(x, z) \in T$ with $\hat{f}$ produces the example $(x, z - \hat{f}(x))$. The error training set $T_e = \{(-1, 0), (-0.4, 0.16), (0, 0), (0.5, 0.25), (0.7, 0.09), (1, 0)\}$.

To begin the construction of the EFAM, it is necessary to define the output domain and the decompositions. Let the input domain $[-1, 1]$ be decomposed into seven regions, as shown in Figure 6. The output domain, however, will not be the interval $[-1, 1]$; it is determined by using one-half of the length of the support of the largest fuzzy set in the FAM output domain decomposition. For the input domain decomposition of five equally spaced triangular fuzzy sets as used earlier, the EFAM output domain is the interval $[-0.25, 0.25]$. Let this interval also be decomposed into seven regions as illustrated in Figure 7.

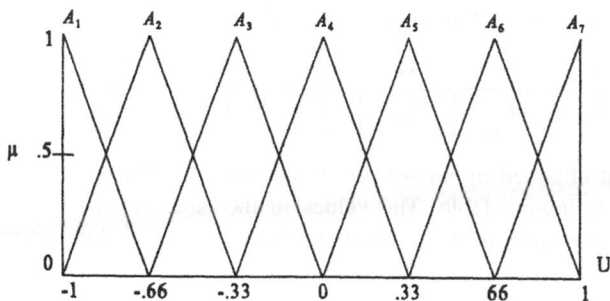

FIGURE 6   EFAM input decomposition. (Reprinted from *Expert Systems with Applications*, Vol. 11, No. 2, Hammell and Sudkamp, "An Adaptive Hierarchical Fuzzy Model," pp. 125–136, Copyright 1996, with permission from Elsevier Science.)

The EFAM constructed using T_e is

A_1	A_2	A_3	A_4	A_5	A_6	A_7
E_4		E_6	E_4		E_5	E_4

Note that two entries in the EFAM are unfilled; each represents an input for which no action is specified. Overcoming this problem motivates the use of completion algorithms. Completing the EFAM uses the existing rules and interpolation to produce rules for the undefined configurations.

The completion algorithm used in this research is a region growing technique often used in image segmentation (12). Empty cells in the EFAM that border nonempty cells are filled by extending the values in the neighboring cells. Because the "growing" only occurs on the boundaries of filled regions, the procedure must be repeated until the entire table is filled. Region growing is the most local of a family of completion algorithms examined in Ref. 7.

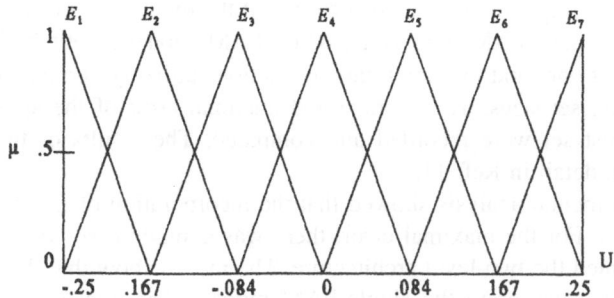

FIGURE 7   EFAM output decomposition. (Reprinted from *Expert Systems with Applications*, Vol. 11, No. 2, Hammell and Sudkamp, "An Adaptive Hierarchical Fuzzy Model," pp. 125–136, Copyright 1996, with permission from Elsevier Science.)

Using region growing, the completed EFAM is

A_1	A_2	A_3	A_4	A_5	A_6	A_7
E_4	E_5	E_6	E_4	E_4	E_5	E_4

The improvement obtained by incorporating the error function $\hat{f}_e$ into the approximation is shown in the following table. The values in the table are the error, at the training points, in the approximation of the function $f(x) = x^2$ using $\hat{f}$ alone compared with that of $\hat{f} + \hat{f}_e$.

	x					
	-1	-0.4	0	0.5	0.7	1
$f(x) - \hat{f}(x)$	0	0.16	0	0.25	0.09	0
$f(x) - \hat{f}(x) + \hat{f}_e(x))$	0	0.01	0	0.25	0.02	0

The region growing technique allowed the rule base to be completed so that a reasonable output could be produced for all possible inputs. The completion process for region A_5 was limited to arbitrarily choosing either E_4 or E_5; if E_5 had been picked, then the error for $x = 0.5$ would have decreased to 0.17, with all other results remaining the same. Also, it should be observed that for input $x = -0.4$, the approximation used the "grown" consequent of region A_2, producing a significant decrease in error over the original FAM-only system.

In addition to illustrating the algorithmic steps, the above example shows other aspects of the FLE algorithm as well. One point is the increase in accuracy provided by using the error analysis to construct the EFAM. Another very important detail is the use of completion, especially within the EFAM. More detail about the theory, implementation, and examples of completion can be found in Refs. 7 and 8. Specifically, Ref. 7 compares two completion techniques, outlines the general notion of approximation with similarity relations, and introduces a general completion algorithm. This information is carried further by presenting two applications of rule base completion in Ref. 8.

Experimental Analysis

Example 1 illustrates how adding the EFAM to incorporate the error function $\hat{f}_e$ into the approximation can improve the overall accuracy of the model. Experimental analysis was conducted to compare FAM-only and FAM–EFAM models, both built from training data, over a set of one- and two-input target functions utilizing various model configurations and training set sizes. The average and maximal error of the approximations obtained from a test set were recorded and compared. The results of these experiments were reported in detail in Ref. 11.

The experimental analysis showed that the incorporation of $\hat{f}_e$ reduced the average error in all cases. For the maximal error, there was a single case where the FLM algorithm outperformed the two-level architecture. The results show that the two-level architecture is clearly superior to the single-FAM models. The construction of the FAM–EFAM model requires only one additional pass through the training data, maintaining the efficiency of the FAM learning approach.

The experiments also indicated that the selection of the number of regions in the

EFAM should be influenced by the number of training examples. With a small training set, the construction of the EFAM results in many unoccupied cells. The accuracy of the completion algorithm decreases as the proportion of cells it must fill grows. Consequently, it is preferable to use fewer regions in the EFAM when only a small number of training instances is available.

Although the experiments showed the improvement that can be obtained by using an EFAM with the FAM learning algorithm, the improvement did not come for free. The reduction in error was achieved by adding a second rule base. This begs the question of whether it would be better to simply use more regions in the FAM of a single-FAM model. On a strictly theoretical level, free of resource limitations, the answer is yes. The single FAM model with an unlimited number of regions in the domain decompositions produces a universal approximator of real-valued functions (7); that is, for any real-valued function f, there is a FAM that will approximate f to within any predetermined degree of accuracy. Using a learning algorithm to build such a FAM, however, may require an inordinate or unobtainable amount of training data.

The experiments reported in Ref. 11 illustrated that with a limited amount of training data, the two-level architecture can outperform the single FAM models in several important ways. First, the FAM–EFAM model requires fewer training examples than a single FAM model to reach a desired level of accuracy. Both types of models are universal approximators, but the FLE algorithm generally produces comparable performance with a smaller training set.

As noted above, the increase in performance for the FLE algorithm is obtained at the expense of adding the rules of the EFAM. The experiments also showed, however, that the two-level architecture generally outperforms single FAM models, even when the same total number of rules is used; that is, the two-level models produce more accurate approximations, even when the total rules (FAM rules + EFAM rules) is equal to or less than the total rules in a single FAM model.

Finally, with a fixed number of training examples, a two-level model can outperform a FAM-only model regardless of the number of regions used in the FAM of the single-level model. Increasing the number of regions in the FAM requires a corresponding increase in the size of the training set needed for the FLM algorithm to learn the function. Because completion becomes less useful as the proportion of empty FAM entries increases, there will come a point when a fixed size training set will no longer support larger FAMs. The experiments showed that with a fixed amount of training data, a simple FLE model is able to outperform a single-FAM model of any size.

ADAPTIVITY

The FAM-based fuzzy models presented so far are static; that is, the design of the model, including the rule generation and domain decomposition, is done off-line and is not changed once the system is put into operation. This produces the obvious disadvantage of prohibiting a fuzzy model from adapting to changes in its environment.

Consider a fuzzy controller as part of a braking system. Suppose the fuzzy rules have been learned off-line, based on the performance of new parts and the system begins operation. Initially, a brake pressure of *medium* may be sufficient to stop within a certain distance at a particular speed. As the braking components wear, the same amount of pressure in the same situation may be inadequate to meet the required stopping parameters. A nonadaptive model is unable to adjust its performance to rectify this problem. An adaptive model, however, has the capability to adjust one or more of its design components based on system performance feedback. As performance moves outside of some acceptable range, the feedback causes on-line "tuning" to occur. Although this adaptive capability might be desirable in some systems, it may be absolutely necessary in others.

As pointed out in Ref. 13, there are basically three sets of parameters that can be manipulated to allow adaptivity: (1) the input and output scaling factors, (2) the membership functions, and (3) the fuzzy rules. The adaptive fuzzy systems developed here use the strategy of modifying the fuzzy rules. Details of this decision are discussed in Ref. 10, but three basic reasons prevail. First, this technique is intuitive to humans. Second, rule base modification allows changes in system performance to be directly reflected and understood by changes that occur in the linguistically interpretable rules provided by the FAM. Finally, the FLE algorithm provides an excellent platform for allowing rule base adaptivity. Fine-grain adaptivity can be achieved by modifying the error estimation rule base (EFAM). Only when system performance differs greatly from the desired result will the "original" rule base (FAM) require modification. Thus, the model can make small changes to improve the quality of the approximations without changing an original rule, thereby diminishing the possibility of improving in a single narrowly defined region at the expense of overall system performance. Only when the model needs to change its "basic knowledge" will the FAM rule base be modified.

Adaptive fuzzy models using the two-level architecture modify the FAMs based on system performance feedback. The structure of the adaptive fuzzy model constructed here is shown in Figure 8. This adaptive structure, presented in Ref. 14, uses a reference model to calculate the desired configuration of the system based on the input that was supplied. The difference between the desired configuration and the actual system configuration provides the error that drives the adaptation. The module labeled supervisor analyzes the error and makes the appropriate FAM or EFAM modifications.

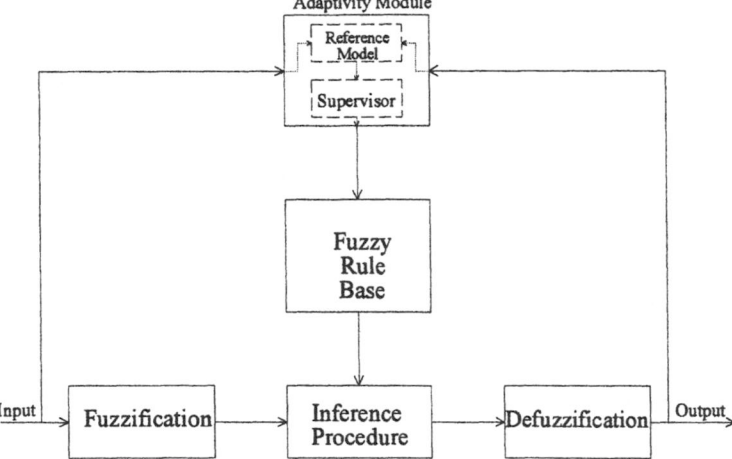

FIGURE 8 Adaptive fuzzy model structure. (Reprinted from *Expert Systems with Applications*, Vol. 11, No. 2, Hammell and Sudkamp, "An Adaptive Hierarchical Fuzzy Model," pp. 125–136, Copyright 1996, with permission from Elsevier Science.)

The initial rule bases may be learned from training examples or by knowledge acquisition from domain experts. Three basic types of operational system behavior can be identified. One type is when the system does not change at all; in this case, there is *continued learning*. Continued learning uses the system feedback as additional training data which will decrease the model error. In the two-level architecture, the majority of the adaptation should be accomplished by modifying the EFAM.

Another type of operational behavior is the *drastic change*. In this case, the underlying model changes significantly. An adaptive system must be able to quickly modify all or a good portion of its rules to represent a very different underlying model.

The third type of operational system behavior is a *gradual change* in the system spread over a period of time. This type of behavior is the most common for many real systems, such as in the gradual wear of the components in a braking system. For the two-level system, the initial small changes would be reflected in EFAM modifications, with FAM rule changes only when the cumulative change is too large for the EFAM structure to accommodate.

The adaptive process begins after the original FAM and EFAM are constructed and the system is put into operation. The objective was to develop a general algorithm that will modify the rule bases in response to changes in the underlying system's performance. The adaptive FLE (AFLE) algorithm described in this section makes no assumption of the type change, if any, that will occur.

The design decisions required in producing an adaptive algorithm for the two-level architecture include establishing the following:

1. The criteria for adaptation
2. The order of the rule base modifications
3. The rule modification strategy
4. The completion strategy

Each of these components employed in the AFLE algorithm will be briefly discussed.

Criteria for Adaptation

Once the system becomes operational and the error feedback is provided, an adaptation threshold determines when adaptation should occur. The decision could be based on the size of the error, the size of the average error accumulated over several input–output steps, the number of errors in a particular input region since the last update of the appropriate rule, or some combination. If information about the probable operating environment was known, the criteria could be tailored for that environment. For example, adapting too quickly in an environment with occasional noisy inputs might inappropriately modify desirable rules. On the other hand, adapting too slowly when the rules no longer apply is also unwanted.

The AFLE implementation utilizes a simple counter and accumulator to initiate adaptation. Whenever an error reading is received from the reference model, the counter of the rule corresponding to the input region in which the input had maximal membership is incremented. The amount of error for that particular rule is added to the associated accumulator. Whenever a rule's counter reaches the predefined threshold, adaptation is begun for the rules that contributed to this last error feedback. The amount of error to correct is calculated as (accumulated error/counter) × learning rate, where the learning rate governs how much of the reported error is to be used in the adaptation process.

Order of Rule Base Modifications

The output of the two-level model is the sum of the outputs of the FAM and the EFAM. The rules in both rule bases influence system performance, and both rule bases contribute to the error between actual output and desired output. A strategy for which rule base to modify first, and by how much, is a major design decision for an implementation of the AFLE algorithm.

If the error reported by the reference model is large enough that an adjustment to the FAM would reduce the error, the FAM is adjusted first and then any remaining error is addressed by an adjustment to the EFAM. Only if the FAM adjustment would not be beneficial is the EFAM adjusted alone. This order was chosen for two reasons. First, adjusting the FAM allows the system to more quickly adapt to drastic changes. Second, adjusting the EFAM as much as possible first and then considering an adjustment to the FAM is unintuitive, given that the premise of the two-level architecture is to use the EFAM to remove small errors left by the FAM approximations.

Rule Modification Strategy

For an n-input system, a precise input causes 2^n rules in each of the FAMs to fire. A decision must be made whether to modify all rules that contributed to the output or to modify a subset of these rules. The combination that provided the best experimental results and is reflected in the AFLE implementation is as follows. The total error to be corrected is allocated to the rule whose antecedent matches the input to the maximal degree. For the remaining rules that match the input to some degree, the total error scaled by the minimal degree to which the input matches any antecedent in this set of rules is assigned to each rule. Thus, for the one-input case, the total error is assigned to the rule in which the input has maximal membership. The error assigned to the other rule is scaled by the degree to which the input matches its antecedent. Once an error value has been assigned to a rule, a new consequent is selected using the input value and the center point of the current consequent plus the error as the training instance.

Whereas this strategy allocates more than the total error to rules, the output from the modified rule bases will remove less than the sum of the allocations. To see this, a closer look must be taken at how an individual rule is changed. Consider the modification to the rule with maximal membership when error e occurs. The consequent of the rule is then modified so that when it is fired, the result will be approximately e greater. However, defuzzification will scale this increase by the membership degree associated with the input when the output is produced. Thus, this rule will not remove the total error but only its share; the other rules will only have a portion of their share of the error adjusted because the amount of the error assigned to them was the total error scaled by the minimum membership degree for each rule.

Example 2: This example illustrates how the total error is allocated among rules. For simplicity, a one-input, one-output FAM-only system is used. In a two-level system, changes to the EFAM are done in the same manner as the FAM changes shown here. Assume the function to be learned is $f(x) = x$ and the input and output domain decompositions are as shown in Figure 2.

Let the current input to the system be $x = 0.2$ and the two associated rules be

R1: If X is A_3, then Y is C_1.
R2: If X is A_4, then Y is C_3.

The membership value of 0.2 in A_3, written $\mu_{A_3}(0.2)$, is 0.6 and $\mu_{A_4}(0.2) = 0.4$. Using weighted-averaging defuzzification, the output for the system is

$$\frac{[\mu_{A_3}(0.2)](\text{midpoint of } C_1) + [\mu_{A_4}(0.2)](\text{midpoint of } C_3)}{\mu_{A_3}(0.2) + \mu_{A_4}(0.2)} = \frac{(0.6)(-1) + (0.4)(0)}{1} = -0.6$$

Because the desired output of $f(0.2) = 0.2$, there is an error of 0.8. The new training instance for modifying R1 is (x, midpoint of C_1 + total error), giving (0.2, −0.2). Because −0.2 has maximal membership in output region C_3, R1 now becomes "if X is A_3, then Y is C_3."

For R2, the total error is scaled by the minimum membership value of both rules, giving an allocated error of $(0.8)(0.4) = 0.32$. The new training instance for R2 is (x, midpoint of C_3 + scaled error) = (0.2, 0.32), causing R2 to change to "if X is A_4, then Y is C_4."

The output for the modified rule base with input 0.2 is $[(0.6)(0) + (0.4)(0.5)]/1 = 0.2$.

Using the strategy described above, the rule in which the input has maximal membership, called the maximal rule, is adjusted significantly and the remaining rules are given a push in the probable right direction. As the error becomes smaller, the error scaled by the minimal membership degree for the nonmaximal rules will eventually become so small that no adjustment is made. Thus, large errors cause all involved rules to be adjusted to some degree, thereby providing the capability for quick convergence. Small errors cause only the maximally matching rule to be adjusted by any significant degree, which tends to prevent already accurate rules from being mistakenly modified. Assuming that each rule requiring adjustment becomes maximal one or more times, the rules will eventually converge to approximate the new system.

Completion Strategy

If the operational system undergoes a drastic change, the majority of the rules become obsolete. In this case, the new underlying system must be learned from scratch. To accurately rebuild both rule bases would take many inputs. This is especially true for a large EFAM because as the FAM changed, the EFAM would have to reconfigure for that particular portion of the input domain. The idea behind using completion within the adaptation process is to replace many old, inaccurate rules and complete the rule base using the most recent rule modifications. Even in the case of a slowly but continuously changing system, only the last few rule adjustments would accurately reflect the current configuration.

A major part of the adaptation step is to determine if rule base completion should be used on the EFAM. The completion process must be carefully controlled, because deleting useful rules is undesirable. If the error feedback is small or perhaps decreasing, signaling small changes or accurate adaptation, then the completion algorithm will not be used. If the error feedback suddenly becomes very large or continually increases, indicating that a significant change to the system has occurred, the most recent EFAM corrections are used to reconfigure the EFAM. A more thorough discussion of the benefit of completion in adaptation can be found in Ref. 8.

Experimental Results

To test the effectiveness of the AFLE algorithm to adapt to changes in the underlying system, the FLE algorithm was used to build a model to approximate a target function $f: [-1, 1] \rightarrow [-1, 1]$. The system was then put into simulated operation, whereupon the target function either underwent no change, a drastic change, or a gradual change, producing a new function f': $[-1, 1] \rightarrow [-1, 1]$.

The operation phase consisted of a number of loops through the adaptation process with randomly selected input on each loop. After the given number of inputs were processed and used for adaptation, the model was tested to see how well it approximated the "new" target function. The test consisted of comparing the approximating function $\hat{f}$ + $\hat{f_e}$ with the modified target function f' on a sample of points evenly distributed over the input domain. For one-dimensional functions, the error $|f'(x) - (\hat{f}(x) + \hat{f_e}(x))|$ is obtained at 0.05 intervals. The average and maximum errors that occur on this set are recorded.

All the experiments discussed in this article consider one-input systems. Additional experiments with different target functions and multiple input tests were run and the results were similar to those reported below. In the experiments, adaptation was performed after every input from the operational system. Experiments were also run with adaptation occurring after several inputs. Intuitively it was thought that this strategy would produce smoother adaptation by accumulating error readings and then adjusting based on the average error. However, these experiments had a slower adaptation time without any benefit of increased accuracy in approximations and did not reach the same level of performance as models that adapted with every input. The learning rate, which governs how much of the actual error gets reported to the adaptation process, was set at 1 for all experiments; this corresponds to reporting all the error.

Continued Learning

The experiments in this section demonstrate the ability of the AFLE algorithm to continue to learn and improve its performance as additional inputs are received. To provide the continued learning environment, the "new" function is identical to the initial function; that is, there is no change in the system once it becomes operational.

Table 1 provides the results by "adapting" $f(x) = x^3$ to $f'(x) = x^3$ in models with 15

TABLE 1   Continued Learning: $x^3 \rightarrow x^3$

Built for x^3 with FLE (15/51 system)		
Examples	Avg. error	Max. error
100	0.005	0.043
200	0.003	0.017

Continued learning		
On-line inputs	Avg. error	Max. error
50	0.009	0.103
100	0.008	0.060
200	0.002	0.009
1000	0.002	0.009

Source: Reprinted from *Expert Systems with Applications*, Vol. 11, No. 2, Hammell and Sudkamp, "An Adaptive Hierarchical Fuzzy Model," pp. 125–136, Copyright 1996, with permission from Elsevier Science.

FAM and 51 EFAM regions. This FAM–EFAM configuration was selected because it shows that the average and maximal errors may increase slightly at the beginning of the operation. The FAM–EFAM model used for adaptation was constructed using the FLE algorithm with 100 randomly selected training examples, and then additional inputs were provided during operation to observe the ability for continued learning. The average and maximal errors initially increased slightly, but by 200 on-line inputs, the continued learning process improved the overall system accuracy. This type of behavior is present in many of the results; a momentary increase in error seems to be caused by an ongoing internal settling of the FAM and/or EFAM rules.

The results from systems with other numbers of EFAM regions and other target functions were similar. The experimental results indicate that the AFLE algorithm can continue to learn and improve performance during on-line operation. Note that no completion occurs in the adaptation process because the error feedback from the reference model is below the threshold needed to trigger this process. Completion during continued learning is not desirable, as many of the relevant rules in the EFAM would be discarded.

Drastic Change

To test the adaptive capability of the fuzzy inference system in the drastic change scenario, a model was constructed based on one target function and then put into operation based on another; that is, the FAM and EFAM were trained with input–output pairs representing a particular function, but after training ended and on-line operation began, the error for a specific input was computed based on a different target function. This simulated a drastic change in the system's environment, thereby testing the ability of the model to adapt to the extent of basically relearning a major portion, if not all, of the rule base.

For example, consider $f(x) = x^2$ "drastically changed" to $f(x) = x^3$. This means that the model was originally built from training data reflecting $f(x) = x^2$, but as soon as the system went operational, the desired output was changed to $f(x) = x^3$. With the system operational and no adaptation, an input of -1 would result in an error of -2 assuming that the model learned x^2 accurately. Thus, the adaptation procedure would be based on an error of -2. After the given number of inputs is processed, $f(x) = x^3$ is used to obtain the average and maximal errors for the resulting adapted system.

The results from a 15 FAM and 51 EFAM model adapting from an initial approximation of $f(x) = x^2$ to $f(x) = x^3$ are shown in Table 2. This demonstrates the ability of the AFLE algorithm to adapt to a drastic change. Results based on 200, 400, and 600 input values are given. After only 600 inputs, the average and maximal error produced by the adapted model were lower than that of the system directly built for x^3 with 100 or 200 training examples.

The results from the drastic-change experiments show that the AFLE algorithm is able to adapt quickly from one function to another. Employing completion on the EFAM is a significant factor in this success. Table 3 provides results for the same experiment as Table 2 but without using completion in the adaptation process. The results after 1000 on-line inputs and no completion are comparable to results after only 600 on-line inputs with completion.

Gradual Change

Gradual change is the third type of potential change in an operational system. In this scenario, the system behavior gradually changes from one function to another over time.

TABLE 2   Drastic Change: $x^2 \rightarrow x^3$

Built for x^3 with FLE (15/51 system)

Examples	Avg. error	Max. error
100	0.005	0.043
200	0.003	0.017

Drastic change: $x^2 \rightarrow x^3$

On-line inputs	Avg. error	Max. error
200	0.012	0.054
400	0.003	0.027
600	0.003	0.007

Source: Reprinted from *Expert Systems with Applications*, Vol. 11, No. 2, Hammell and Sudkamp, "An Adaptive Hierarchical Fuzzy Model," pp. 125–136, Copyright 1996, with permission from Elsevier Science.

The classic example of this is the braking system, where the components wear and increased pressure is needed to stop within a certain distance for a certain speed. This type of change is perhaps the most realistic for many systems.

Table 4 provides results from using a 5 FAM and 15 EFAM region model to follow the change of the one-input function $f(x) = x$ to the one-input function $f'(x) = x^3$ over

TABLE 3   Drastic Change: $x^2 \rightarrow x^3$, No Completion

Built for x^3 with FLE (15/51 system)

Examples	Avg. error	Max. error
100	0.005	0.043
200	0.003	0.017

Drastic change: $x^2 \rightarrow x^3$ (no completion)

On-line inputs	Avg. error	Max. error
200	0.136	0.419
400	0.031	0.139
600	0.003	0.017
1000	0.002	0.009

Source: Reprinted from *Expert Systems with Applications*, Vol. 11, No. 2, Hammell and Sudkamp, "An Adaptive Hierarchical Fuzzy Model," pp. 125–136, Copyright 1996, with permission from Elsevier Science.

TABLE 4   Gradual Change: $x \rightarrow x^3$

Built for x^3 with FLE (15/51 system)		
Examples	Avg. error	Max. error
100	0.014	0.089

Gradual change: 10,000 steps		
Inputs per step	Avg. error	Max. error
1	0.021	0.125
5	0.020	0.125
10	0.017	0.071
13	0.014	0.089

Source: Reprinted from *Expert Systems with Applications*, Vol. 11, No. 2, Hammell and Sudkamp, "An Adaptive Hierarchical Fuzzy Model," pp. 125–136, Copyright 1996, with permission from Elsevier Science.

10,000 time steps. The total number of on-line inputs processed in the gradual change situation is the number of time steps multiplied by the number of inputs per step. Thus, 1 input per step utilizes 10,000 on-line inputs 2 inputs per step use 20,000, and so on. Note that in the gradual change, only the last few inputs correctly represent the final system.

Even at one input per step, the difference between the average error in the adapted model and the corresponding "built for" average error is 0.007; the maximum error is not as close, however. By 13 inputs per step, the average and maximal "built for" error is matched by the AFLE results. As in the drastic-change scenario, results without completion were significantly worse.

The results for systems with 25, 51, and 75 EFAM regions were similar. The error at any given number of inputs per step was generally smaller as the number of EFAM regions grew. However, because a gradually changing system represents a "moving target," the updated approximations were always somewhat behind the current system configuration. The objective of gradual change adaptivity is to reduce the difference between the current system and the model.

GRANULARITY AND DIMENSIONALITY

The majority of successful applications of fuzzy systems have a limited number of input domains. In particular, systems built for control applications generally have two or three input variables. As increasingly sophisticated systems are modeled, the complexity of the FAM will grow accordingly.

The complexity of a FAM can be affected in two different ways. One way is by increasing the number of fuzzy sets in the decomposition of an input domain; this determines the *granularity* of the system, which thereby defines the space of approximating functions that may be realized (7). Granularity increases as the fuzzy sets are made smaller, thus growing in number. The second way to increase the complexity of a FAM is to add additional input variables. The number of input domains for the system determines the *dimensionality* of the system.

As seen in the previous discussions regarding EFAM construction, increasing the granularity usually causes a corresponding need for an increase in the amount of training data. Increasing the dimensionality of a system will also cause a need for a larger training set. In addition to possibly requiring more training data, increases in dimensionality or granularity also affect the off-line learning of the rules and the run-time performance of the resulting system. These two aspects are examined below, followed by a presentation of potential methods for reducing the impact of dimensionality.

Run-Time Considerations

The execution cycle of a fuzzy model consists of the acquisition of input, determination of the appropriate set of rules, the evaluation of the rules, and the aggregation of the results. The final value, either fuzzy or precise depending on the application, is then returned as the appropriate response or action.

During operation, the input is received and the set of rules applicable for the input is selected. For well-defined domain decompositions, especially the triangular decompositions with the fuzzy partition constraint, hash functions may be used to make this determination independent of the number of terms in the decomposition (15). Thus, the granularity of the system has little effect on the run-time. For multidimensional FAMs, the work required for determining the applicable rules increases linearly with the number of dimensions; the overall set of indices is the Cartesian product of the indices of the individual dimensions.

The introduction of additional input dimensions, however, may have an exponential affect on the time needed to evaluate the rules. For a precise input value and a triangular domain decomposition, there are typically two fuzzy sets in which the input has a non-zero support; the sole exception to this is when the input has membership value of 1 in a single fuzzy set. For an n-dimensional system, there are 2^n applicable rules. If the input is fuzzy, the set of applicable indices in each domain increases, exacerbating the growth in the number of rule evaluations required.

Finally, the amount of work required in the aggregation of the results of the individual rules is determined by the number of rules that were evaluated. Thus, the impact of increasing the number of rules in each dimension can be limited by the use of hash functions, but increased dimensionality will adversely affect the performance of the system.

Although increased granularity does not affect the run-time performance of the system, it has important consequences on the modeling capabilities. Because the number of fuzzy sets determines the family of realizable approximating functions, increasing the granularity presents the possibility of overfitting the training data. Overfitting occurs when a learning algorithm attempts to match minute variations within the training data rather than producing a generalization from the data. Intuitively, one may consider the ability to generalize from the training data to vary inversely with the granularity of the input domains.

Rule-Generation Considerations

The primary effect on the rule-generation process caused by increased dimensionality or granularity is the corresponding need for a larger training set. A larger training set will, of course, impact the amount of computer memory required to execute the learning algorithm as well as increase the time required to construct the rule set. These drawbacks are minimal, however, especially given the processing speed and available memory of modern computers and the fact that the rules will be learned off-line. The main drawback is simply the need for more training data and the negative impacts on system accuracy if the required amount of data is not available.

The generation of a rule by the learning algorithm requires at least one training example in the region defined by the supports of the fuzzy sets in the antecedent of the rule. If the training set is small or the rule base is large, there may be regions in the rule base that are not represented by a suitable training example. As discussed in Example 1, completion can be used to interpolate over the rule base and fill in missing rules. The ability of the completion process to accurately build the missing rules depends on the density of the rules that are learned, which, in turn, depends on the density of the training data. Completion can be used to minimize the effect of a moderate increase in granularity.

Even with completion, increases in granularity can impact the performance of the resulting system. In theory, an increase in granularity permits a more precise model to be constructed. This is only true, however, if there is sufficient training data to exploit the precision afforded by the model. Table 5 illustrates the impact of increased granularity on the performance of the hierarchical learning algorithm. The model configuration n/m indicates the number of fuzzy sets in the decomposition of the FAM and EFAM, respectively. The target function is a three-input function; thus, a 5/9 system has 125 FAM rules ($5 \times 5 \times 5$) and 729 EFAM rules ($9 \times 9 \times 9$).

The first set of data in Table 5 indicates that when the number of EFAM regions is increased, with a fixed training set size, the precision of the model decreases slightly. Other experiments have demonstrated that the point at which the precision of the model declines is dependent on the amount of available training data. The effectiveness of completion depends on the proportion of regions that are filled compared to those that

TABLE 5   Increasing EFAM Granularity

Model	No. of examples	Max. error	Avg. error
Fixed number of examples			
5/9	5,000	0.250	0.016
5/13	5,000	0.290	0.017
5/17	5,000	0.350	0.019
5/21	5,000	0.201	0.019
5/25	5,000	0.209	0.221
Fixed configuration			
5/9	5,000	0.250	0.016
5/9	7,500	0.189	0.015
5/9	10,000	0.189	0.013
5/9	20,000	0.127	0.009

must be filled by the completion algorithm. Increasing the number of EFAM regions while maintaining a fixed size training set alters this ratio.

The second set of data in Table 5 illustrates that increasing the number of training examples for a fixed configuration produces a more accurate model. This reflects the dependence of the learning algorithm on the data rather than on the interpolation technique.

Increased dimensionality also leads to a larger FAM rule base, which, in turns, drives the need for more training data as well. A 5/25 model for a two-input function has 25 FAM and 625 EFAM rules; the same model for a three-input function has 125 FAM rules and 15,625 EFAM rules.

The easiest way to demonstrate the effect of dimensionality on the hierarchical learning algorithm is to add a redundant dimension to the model; that is, choose a two-dimensional target function $f(x, y)$ and, from f, construct the three-dimensional target $f'(x, y, z) = f(x, y)$. Under these conditions, the difference in the effectiveness of the learning algorithm with targets f and f' can be attributed directly to the additional dimension.

Table 6 provides the results of approximating $f(x, y) = (x + y)/2$ and $f'(x, y, z) = (x + y)/2$. For the 5/25 model configuration, the three-dimensional model generated with 50,000 training examples was less accurate than the two-dimensional approximation produced with 5000 examples. This same pattern is exhibited by the 9/25 and 13/25 models. Similar results were found in the experiments on models of one- and two-input dimensions (7); an order-of-magnitude increase in the number of training examples was required to produce models of approximately equal precision.

Active Regions and Dimension Reduction

The effects of multiple input dimensions on FAM systems were clearly illustrated by the results in Table 6. Consequently, strategies need to be developed that reduce the effects of increasing dimensionality on the efficiency and data requirements of the learning algorithms. In this section, two such techniques are presented.

TABLE 6   Two- and Three-Dimensional Results

Model	No. of examples	Max. error	Avg. error
Approximation: $f(x, y, z) = (x + y)/2$			
5/25	5,000	0.209	0.221
	10,000	0.209	0.012
	20,000	0.106	0.009
	50,000	0.073	0.007
9/25	20,000	0.081	0.009
	50,000	0.052	0.007
13/25	50,000	0.076	0.007
Approximation: $f(x, y) = (x + y)/2$			
5/25	500	0.132	0.015
	1,000	0.088	0.009
	5,000	0.043	0.005
9/25	5,000	0.027	0.005
13/25	5,000	0.049	0.006

In complex systems, there may be combinations of potential inputs that do not represent feasible system configurations. When this occurs, the corresponding regions of the input space need not be covered by a model. Moreover, there may be distinct and identifiable regions of the input space in which the system is constrained to operate. These disjoint areas in the input space will be referred to as the *active regions*.

The above conditions, which occur for some but not all problems, were encountered in the development of a fuzzy model to predict the propagation loss of a signal (16). The model used five characteristics of the topography, the signal, and the relationship between the transmitter and the receiver to produce an estimate of the signal loss. A rule base was generated from a set of 100 training examples.

The training data for this model were concentrated in several distinct regions of the input space. The particular region could be determined by the value of a single input variable. Due to the properties of this application, a large model covering the entire five-dimensional input space was not required; a set of four-dimensional FAMs was sufficient to cover the active regions of the input space.

Because of the small number of training data, the identification of the active regions was straightforward for the propagation loss model. In more complex problem domains and with larger training sets, the dependencies may not be easily discernable. For this reason, the following approach for the location of active regions and dimension reduction is proposed.

The first step is to use the training set to identify areas of high activity in the input space. If the training set is obtained from sampling an operating system, then the selections should provide a representative distribution of the input processed by the system. Clustering is then used to group the training data and define regions of the input space. If the analysis produces compact and separable clusters, these are identified as the active regions of the system. The criteria for the degree of compactness and separability required to identify a distinct active region depends on the application and the dimensions of the input space.

When the active subregions of the input space have been identified, a FAM will be generated to cover each such region from the training data in that region. The entire model will then consist of a supervisor that receives the input and a set of localized FAMs. The action of the supervisor is to direct the input to the appropriate FAM for evaluation. By only generating rules to cover the active regions in the input space, the requirement for training data should be reduced.

The second technique is to identify and eliminate unnecessary dimensions. As in the case of the propagation model, the localized FAMs may not require all of the dimensions of the input space to produce an appropriate response. In fact, the target function and experimental data shown in Table 6 is an example of this type of behavior.

The test for the contribution of the *i*th input dimension begins by constructing the n-dimensional FAM for the region. This FAM defines an n-dimensional function $\hat{f}$. The $n-1$ dimensional FAM is then built by deleting the *i*th dimension from the training set, creating an approximation function $\hat{f}_i$. The values of the two approximations are compared on the training set. The maximal difference between the approximations

$$er_i = \max\{ |\hat{f}(x_1, \ldots, x_n) - \hat{f}_i(x_1, \ldots, x_{i-1}, x_{i+1}, \ldots, x_n)| \}$$

is recorded. Following a "leaving-one-out" strategy, this process is repeated for each input dimension. The dimension with minimal difference, call it *I*, is considered for removal. If er_i is less than a predetermined threshold, the reduced FAM obtained by omitting the ith dimension will be used. The threshold for removal of a dimension is based on the degree of precision in the training data and the precision required from the system. This process can be iteratively repeated with the potential of removing additional dimensions from the domain.

The strategy underlying the dimension deletion procedure is similar to the selection of attributes for testing in the construction of decision trees and the removal of features in the derivation of classification rules (17). The hierarchical system consisting of a supervisor and localized FAMs of smaller dimension than the input space combine to reduce the effect in the growth of the number of rules that must be considered in high-dimensional systems.

CONCLUSIONS

Fuzzy learning algorithms provide an efficient method for producing approximating functions from training data. Fuzzy algorithms are local: The decomposition of the input domains into a fuzzy partition produces a set of overlapping regions such that the approximation over a region is determined solely by the examples within that region. Restricting the influence of a training example to a local region focuses the information contained in the example. Locality, however, introduces the possibility that all regions within a domain may not be covered by a training example. Completion algorithms can be used to extend the training information to the entire rule base.

The two-level architecture increases the accuracy over the traditional methods of learning fuzzy rules from data. When restricted to a fixed set of training examples, the FAM–EFAM system produces better approximations than those obtainable from a single FAM system, regardless of the number of rules in the single FAM. The two-level architecture requires only one additional pass through the training data, maintaining the efficiency of the FAM learning approach. The improved approximations are obtained without additional training instances, making this technique particularly suitable for problem domains in which training data are unavailable or expensive to obtain.

The combination of the two-level architecture and the AFLE algorithm provides an excellent platform for adaptation. The use of the EFAM provides a rule base that can be modified for small changes in the system's behavior without reconfiguring the main FAM rule base. The experimental analysis, especially for gradual change, generally supported the intuition that a smaller number of rules permits faster adaptation. The experimental analysis demonstrated the need for completion in both the drastic change and gradual scenarios. The management of the completion process is a complex issue and small perturbations in starting or stopping the process produce significant variations in experimental results.

The granularity and dimensionality of the system being modeled has a direct impact on the complexity of the resulting fuzzy rule base. The creation of robust learning algorithms will ultimately require a combination of techniques. These techniques will be dependent on the available training data, the basic properties of the system being modeled, and the degree of accuracy required from the model.

Fuzzy models are currently constructed using information provided by domain experts or generated using learning algorithms, but not by both. Being data driven, the algorithms construct precise rules with each rule having a limited range of applicability over the input space. Experts, however, decompose the problem into subdomains determined by the similarity of the input conditions. Thus, the granularity and precision of rules provided by domain experts differ considerably from those of rules generated from training data. Techniques to allow the combination of domain expertise and fuzzy learning must be developed to further the capability for modeling complex systems. Such techniques might also assist in providing the needed ability to combine rule bases of various degrees of granularity.

REFERENCES

1. E. H. Mamdani, "Applications of Fuzzy Algorithms for Simple Dynamic Plant," *Fuzzy Sets Syst.*, *51*(3), 1585–1588 (1974).
2. H. J. Zimmerman, *Fuzzy Set Theory and its Applications*, Kluwer-Nijhoff, Boston, MA, 1985.
3. J. C. Bezdek, "Fuzzy Models—What Are They, and Why?" *IEEE Trans. Fuzzy Syst.*, *FS-1*(1), 1–6 (1993).
4. D. G. Schwartz and G. J. Klir, "Fuzzy Logic: Concepts to Constructs," *AI Expert*, 26–33 (November 1993).
5. L. Wang and J. M. Mendel, "Generating Fuzzy Rules from Numerical Data, with Applications," Technical Report USC-SIPI-169, Signal and Image Processing Institute, University of Southern California, Los Angeles (1991).
6. B. Kosko, *Neural Networks and Fuzzy Systems*: *A Dynamical Systems Approach to Machine Intelligence*, Prentice-Hall, Englewood Cliffs, NJ, 1992.
7. T. Sudkamp and R. J. Hammell II, "Interpolation, Completion, and Learning Fuzzy Rules," *IEEE Trans. Syst., Man, Cybern.*, *SMC-24*(2), 332–342 (1994).
8. T. Sudkamp and R. J. Hammell II, "Rule Base Completion in Fuzzy Models," in *Fuzzy Modeling*: *Paradigms and Practice*, W. Pedrycz (ed.), Kluwer Academic Publishers, Boston, 1996, pp. 313–330.
9. R. J. Hammell II and T. Sudkamp, "An Adaptive Hierarchical Fuzzy Model," *Expert Syst. Applic.*, *11*(2), 125–136 (1996).
10. R. J. Hammell II, "A Fuzzy Associative Memory Architecture for Fuzzy Inference and Adaptivity," Ph.D. dissertation, Wright State University, Dayton, OH (1995).
11. R. J. Hammell II and T. Sudkamp, "A Two-Level Architecture for Fuzzy Learning," *J. Intell. Fuzzy Syst.*, *3*(4), 273–286 (1995).
12. R. M. Haralick and L. G. Shapiro, "Image Segmentation Techniques," *Computer Vision, Graphics Image Process.*, *29*, 100–132 (1985).
13. P. Isomursu and T. Tauma, "A Self-Tuning Fuzzy Logic Controller for Temperature Control of Superheated Steam," in *Proceedings of the Third IEEE International Conference on Fuzzy Systems*, 1994, pp. 1560–1563.
14. J. R. Layne and K. M. Passino, "Fuzzy Model Reference Learning Control for Cargo Ship Steering," *IEEE Control Syst.*, *13*(6), 23–34 (1993).
15. T. Sudkamp and R. J. Hammell II, "Scalability in Fuzzy Rule-Based Learning," *Inform. Syst. J.*, *109*, 135–147 (1998).
16. M. Hayes, "The Development of the Fuzzy Propagation Loss Model, Version 2," Technical Report, CSC Corporation (1986).
17. S. Chiu, "An Efficient Method for Extracting Fuzzy Classification Rules from High Dimensional Data and Its Aerospace Applications," in *Proceedings of the International Workshop on Breakthrough Opportunities for Fuzzy Logic*, 1996, pp. 18–23.

BIBLIOGRAPHY

Klir, G. J., and B. Yuan, *Fuzzy Sets and Fuzzy Logic*: *Theory and Applications*, Prentice-Hall, Englewood Cliffs, NJ, 1995.

Kosko, B., *Neural Networks and Fuzzy Systems*: *A Dynamical Approach to Machine Intelligence*, Prentice-Hall, Englewood Cliffs, NJ, 1992.

Langari, R., and L. Wang, "Fuzzy Models, Modular Networks, and Hybrid Learning," *Fuzzy Sets Syst.*, *79*(2), 141–150 (1996).

Yager, R., and D. P. Filev, *Essentials of Fuzzy Modeling and Control*, John Wiley & Sons, New York, 1994.

Zadeh, L. A., *Fuzzy Sets and Applications*: *Selected Papers by L. A. Zadeh*, R. Yager, S. Ouchinnikov, R. M. Tong, and H. T. Nguyen (eds.), John Wiley & Sons, New York, 1987.

Zimmerman, H. J., *Fuzzy Set Theory and its Applications*, 2nd ed., Kluwer Academic Publishers, Boston, 1991.

ROBERT J. HAMMELL II

THOMAS A. SUDKAMP

INTENSIONAL PROGRAMMING LANGUAGES

INTRODUCTION

One of the major challenges of computer science is the design of programming language paradigms that would free the programmers from low-level, machine-related tasks. Such paradigms are usually based on sound mathematical foundations and they allow for a cleaner and more declarative way of programming. The *intensional* programming paradigm is a relatively recent one and has its foundations in the area of *intensional logic* (1).

Although it is not easy to give a brief and nontechnical explanation of what an intensional language really is, we could say that one of the main characteristics of the paradigm is that it deals with infinite entities of ordinary data values. Such entities could be a stream of numbers, a two-dimensional table of characters, a tree of strings, and so on. These entities are treated as first-class objects by intensional languages: two streams of numbers can be added together as if they were ordinary data values, functions can be applied on infinite tables and trees, and so on. Because of the above characteristic, intensional languages are especially appropriate for describing the behavior of systems that change with time or physical phenomena that depend on more than one parameter (such as time, space, temperature, etc.). Moreover, because intensional languages are based on solid mathematical foundations (i.e., intensional logic), they promote a purer and more declarative way of programming than traditional imperative programming languages.

In this article, we introduce the basic principles underlying intensional languages. The next section presents at an intuitive level, the area of mathematical logic known as *intensional logic*. The third section introduces Lucid, an intensional language based on the notion of stream, and GLU, an extension of Lucid which supports multidimensional entities. The fourth section discusses the main issues in implementing intensional languages. The fifth section surveys existing intensional programming systems and their applications. The article concludes with a case study on how an intensional language can be used in order to efficiently implement a first-order functional language.

INTENSIONAL LOGIC

Intensional logic (1–3) is a branch of mathematical logic that has been used to describe concisely context-dependent entities. The initial motivation for the development of intensional logic was the formal description of the meaning of natural languages. Many sentences of the languages we use in everyday life are often ambiguous (i.e., they can be interpreted in different ways under different situations or from different people). This has led many scientists to believe that natural languages are not formal from a mathematical point of view, and it is, therefore, impossible to analyze and study them systematically.

However, Montague (the father of intensional logic) firmly believed that natural languages have a mathematical basis analogous to that of artificial languages (e.g., computer languages). Montague's work is extremely technical and is, therefore, difficult to present in detail (a very good introduction to the subject can be found in Ref. 2). Intuitively speaking, we can say that Montague developed a formal system for effectively describing entities whose value depends on implicit contexts. The meaning of natural language expressions often depends on such hidden parameters. Consider, for example, the expression:

Athens is the capital of Greece.

The truth value of this sentence depends on the time at which it was uttered. Today, it is certainly true, but there existed time periods in the past when Greece had a different capital. In other words, the truth value of the above sentence is time dependent; formally, the meaning of the sentence is a function from the set of time points to the set of boolean values.

One can easily think of sentences or expressions that depend on more than one hidden context, such as *time*, *space*, *audience*, and so on. For example, the meaning of the expression

The value of the temperature

can be thought of as a two-dimensional table of the form

	London	Paris	Rome	⋯
1/1/98	−3	2	7	
2/1/98	−2	2	6	
3/1/98	0	3	4	
⋮	⋮	⋮	⋮	⋮

In other words, the meaning of the above expression is a function in $(T \times S) \to D$, where T is the set of time points, S is the set of space points, and D is a set of values the temperature can have.

Generalizing the above discussion, we can say that in many cases, the meaning of a natural language expression is a function from contexts (also called *possible worlds*) to values. Such a function is called the *intension* of the expression. The value of the intension at a particular context is called the *extension* of the expression at that particular context. Thus, in the temperature example, the intension of the expression is the whole table; the extension of the expression in the time point 1/1/98 and at the space coordinate of Rome is 7.

This context-dependent character of natural languages is possibly due to practical reasons: when we talk to each other, it would be completely impractical if we had to explain explicitly the context under which our sentences are true. So, for example, when we say "the prime minister," we most probably mean the prime minister at the time we are speaking and in the place where we talk (although we do not usually have to specify explicitly these two parameters) .

Another characteristic of natural languages is that they use *context-manipulation operators* to alter the present context. For example, we say "yesterday's temperature" in order to refer to the value of the temperature the previous day. Words such as *north*, *tomorrow*, and *next* are often used to change the context. Again, using these operators, we avoid referring to the new context explicitly, but we specify it as a function of the present context.

Concluding this brief and unavoidably informal introduction to the intricacies of natural language, the reader should keep in mind that most of the expressions used in everyday talk are context dependent. Intensional logic is a branch of mathematical logic that captures the context-dependent characteristics of natural languages. However, if intensional logic is so close to real languages, why not use it in order to design new, more powerful and expressive programming languages? This topic is further discussed in the coming sections of this article.

INTENSIONAL LANGUAGES

Most existing programming languages are machine oriented: the programmer is often required to know many aspects of the architecture of the underlying machine in order to be able to write even the simplest programs. Consider, for example, the notions of *variable* and *assignment* in an imperative language. Programmers usually think of *variables* as memory locations and *assignments* as commands that alter the contents of such locations. Another example is *arrays*: Programmers usually think of them as consecutive memory locations which they can access and alter at will.

Therefore, many aspects of traditional programming languages, although widely used, are usually understood operationally. In other words, traditional programming languages have the architecture of the underlying machine very *explicit* in their design. We are interested in a programming paradigm that would hid unnecessary operational concepts from the programmer, in the same way that a natural language helps people hide many unnecessary context details during everyday talk. One approach is to develop programming languages based on intensional logic. Before describing in detail the philosophy behind such a language, we present a simple intensional program that computes the infinite sequence of all natural numbers:

```
result = nat;
nat    = 0 fby (nat+1);
```

Note the use of the operator fby (read *followed by*) in the above program. The semantics of the operator will be defined precisely later. For the time being, we provide the intuitive reading of the program:

> The result of the program is the sequence of natural numbers. The first value of the natural number sequence is 0. The next value in the sequence can be produced by adding 1 to the previous value of the sequence.

Note that the usual mathematical definition of the sequence of natural numbers involves the use of a *time index*:

$$nat_0 = 0$$

$$nat_{t+1} = nat_t + 1$$

The intensional program avoids the explicit use of the time index. The sequence of natural numbers is defined using the temporal operator fby rather than using subscripts (i.e., indices).

The above example is actually a program of the intensional language Lucid (4) (which was probably the first such language). The value of a Lucid expression depends on a hidden time parameter. In other words, the meanings of entities in Lucid programs are not ordinary data values but infinite sequences of ordinary values.

The statements of a Lucid program are equations defining individual and function variables required to be true at every context (time point). Ordinary data operations (such as +, *, and if–then–else) are referentially transparent. This means, for example, that the value of $x + y$ at time point t is the sum of the values of x and y at the same time point t.

The basic Lucid context-switching operators are first, next, and fby. The operator first switches us to time point 0, next takes us from t to $t+1$. The operator fby takes us back from $t+1$ to t (giving us the value of its second operand at that point) or from 0 to 0, giving us the value of its first operand.

Let x and y be sequences. Then, the above ideas are formalized by the following semantic equations:

$$(x + y)_t = x_t + y_t,$$

$$first(x)_t = x_0,$$

$$next(x)_t = x_{t+1},$$

$$(x \text{ fby } y)_t = \begin{cases} x_0 & \text{if } t = 0 \\ y_{t-1} & \text{if } t > 0. \end{cases}$$

These equations constitute what we call the *indexical semantics* of the operations; they define the extensions of the result of an operation in terms of the extensions of the operands.

A Lucid intension x can be thought of as a value varying over time; for example, a loop variable in an iterative computation. Thus, x_0 is the initial value of x, x_1 is the value after the first iteration step, and x_2, x_3, x_4, and so on are the values after subsequent steps.

The fby operator allows us to express many iterative algorithms concisely; the first operand of the fby gives the initial value, and the second operand specifies the way in which each succeeding value is determined by the current value. For example, the following program computes the stream $\langle 1, 1, 2, 3, 5, \dots \rangle$ of all Fibonacci numbers:

```
result = fib
fib    = 1 fby (fib+g)
g      = 0 fby fib
```

The Lucid language also supports user-defined functions that operate on sequences and return sequences as results. For example, consider the following program:

```
result = fact(nat);
nat    = 0 fby (nat+1);
fact(x) = if (x<2) then 1 else x*fact(x-1) fi;
```

The output of the program is the infinite stream of the factorials of the natural numbers (i.e., the sequence $\langle 0!, 1!, 2!, \dots \rangle$).

The language Lucid presents so far obviously differs in many aspects from the usual imperative programming languages. For example, the notion of variables that change values using assignment commands in imperative programming is modeled in Lucid by sequences that possess different values at different time points. Similarly, the notion of an infinite sequence that Lucid supports can be used to model one-dimensional arrays of traditional programming languages. But what about two, or three or generally n-dimensional arrays? Lucid, as described above, is a one-dimensional intensional language. For many applications, such a language might be enough. However, there exist many natural problems that can be better thought of and solved if viewed from a multidimensional perspective.

Lucid has recently been extended to support more than one-dimensional entities (5,6). This new extended language was named GLU and its first implementation was developed at SRI. GLU allows the user to declare new dimensions and to define multidimensional entities that vary across these dimensions. Thus, a two-dimensional entity can be thought of as an infinite table, a three-dimensional one as a cube extending infinitely across the three dimensions, and so on. One can perform various operations with arguments such that higher-dimensional entities or even define functions take them as parameters and return new entities as results. Moreover, the new language supports intensional operators that work along each dimension.

As an illustration of the expressive power of GLU, we consider a simple program which first appeared in Ref. 7 and which models the problem of heat transfer in a solid. Suppose that we have a long thin metal rod which initially has temperature 0 and whose left-hand end touches a heat source with temperature 100. As the heat is transferred, the temperature at the various points of the rod changes. In other words, the temperature can be thought of as a two-dimensional entity because it depends on the spatial position on the rod that we are interested in as well as on the time point (the temperature increases as time passes). It can be shown that the temperature of the rod as a function of time and space is given by the following recurrence relations (where k is a small constant related to the physical properties of the rod):

$$Temp_{t+1,s+1} = \text{k} * Temp_{t,s} - (1 - 2 * k) * Temp_{t,s+1} + k * Temp_{t,s+2},$$
$$Temp_{t,0} = 100$$
$$Temp_{0,s+1} = 0$$

The GLU program that models the above equation is the following*:

```
dimension   time, space;
result      = temp;
temp        = 100.0 fby.space (0.0 fby.time (k * temp -
              (1.0- 2.0 * k) * (next.space temp) + k * (next.space next.
              space temp)));
k           = 0.3;
```

The first line in the above example declares that the program uses two dimensions, namely time and space. Note the new operators that appear in the definition of temp: fby.space, fby.time, and next.space. These operators are straightforward generalizations of the corresponding Lucid operators. For example, if x and y are entities varying across the time and space dimensions, the semantics of fby.time is

---

*The syntax we use is slightly different than the actual GLU syntax.

$$(x\ fby.time\ y)_{t,s} = \begin{cases} x_{0,s} & \text{if } t = 0 \\ y_{t-1,s} & \text{if } t > 0, \end{cases}$$

whereas the semantics of fby.space is

$$(x\ fby.space\ y)_{t,s} = \begin{cases} x_{t,0} & \text{if } s = 0 \\ y_{t,s-1} & \text{if } s > 0. \end{cases}$$

It should be noted here that the temperature example described above is expressed very compactly and naturally in the GLU formalism. The solution for such a problem in a traditional imperative language would most probably require the use of a two-dimensional array together with the use of for loops in order to fill the entries of the array.

With the above example, we conclude our brief introduction to the syntax and the (informal) semantics of intensional languages. Clearly, one can easily propose alternative intensional languages in which the underlying context space is more complicated and which can be used in different application domains. One such approach and its implications will be presented in the sixth section.

IMPLEMENTATION OF INTENSIONAL LANGUAGES

The infinite nature of intensional programming languages suggests that their implementation might be problematic. For example, we know that the output of a Lucid program is an infinite sequence of ordinary data values. How can such a sequence be computed and delivered to the user? This is obviously not possible, as it would require an infinite amount of time. However, we can always expect to be able to compute larger and larger parts of the desired output of the program. An implementation can start by computing the first value of the output sequence, then the second, and so on.

The traditional implementation of Lucid programs is based on a computational model known as *education* (4). We illustrate the main idea of eduction using an example. Suppose we want to calculate the first three Fibonacci numbers. Moreover, assume that we have implemented a simple interpreter *EV AL*, which computes the output of Lucid programs at successive time points. The interpreter uses the definitions in a program as well as the semantics of the Lucid operators in order to calculate the output sequence. Thus, the output of the Fibonacci program of the previous section at time 0 can be calculated as follows:

$EVAL(\text{fib}, 0) =$
$\qquad = EVAL((1\ \text{fby}\ (\text{fib+g})), 0)$
$\qquad = 1$

The time 1 output of the program is calculated as follows:

$EVAL(\text{fib}, 1) =$
$\qquad = EVAL((1\ \text{fby}\ (\text{fib+g})), 1)$
$\qquad = EVAL(\text{fib+g}, 0)$
$\qquad = EVAL(\text{fib}, 0) + EVAL(\text{g}, 0)$
$\qquad = EVAL((1\ \text{fby}\ (\text{fib+g})), 0) + EVAL(0\ \text{fby}\ \text{fib}, 0)$
$\qquad = 1 + 0$
$\qquad = 1$

Finally, the time 2 output is computed in the following way:

$$EVAL(\text{fib}, 2) = EVAL((1 \text{ fby } (\text{fib}+g)), 2)$$
$$= EVAL((\text{fib}+g), 1)$$
$$= EVAL(\text{fib}, 1) + EVAL(g, 1)$$
$$= EVAL((1 \text{ fby } (\text{fib}+g)), 1) + EVAL((0 \text{ fby fib}), 1)$$
$$= EVAL((\text{fig}+g), 0) + EVAL(\text{fib}, 0)$$
$$= EVAL(\text{fib}, 0) + EVAL(g, 0) + EVAL((1 \text{ fby } (\text{fib}+g)), 0)$$
$$= EVAL((1 \text{ fby } (\text{fib}+g)), 0) + EVAL((0 \text{ fby fib}), 0) + 1$$
$$= 1 + 0 + 1$$
$$= 2$$

A careful examination of the above steps reveals that many computations take place on more than one occasion. For example, the value of fib at time 0 is demanded in many cases. This suggests that an efficient implementation of an intensional language should store values of variables that have been computed under specific contexts, so that these results will be available if demanded later during evaluation. The process of storing intermediate results is known as *warehousing* and the data structure that is used for this purpose (usually a hash-table) is known as the *warehouse*. Maintaining the warehouse during execution is not always a simple task: Garbage collection is often required as the table tends to get full with old entries (which may be useless for future calculations). Many techniques have been devised for managing the warehouse component of the implementation and the interested reader is referred to Refs. 4 and 8.

When one considers the multidimensional version of Lucid (i.e., GLU), things become more complicated in terms of implementation. The evaluator has to compute the values of variables on more than one dimensions. Moreover, the warehouse has to be more complicated as it now stores the values of variables under more complicated contexts. A new problem that appears now is the so-called *dimensionality* of variables; that is, knowing in advance on exactly which dimensions a variable depends. Knowing the exact dimensionality of program variables is important because it helps in reducing the cost associated with the warehouse operations. A promising dimensionality algorithm is reported in Ref. 9.

Note that the main characteristic of education is that it computes the value of expressions with respect to contexts. There exists a class of hardware architectures [namely the *dataflow* ones (10,11)] that efficiently supports such execution with respect to context. In other words, dataflow machines are ideal candidates on which education can be implemented. This suggests the following three aspects to which an intensional language is related:

- Intensional Logic provides the theoretical framework on which intensional languages are based.
- Eduction provides the conceptual execution model for implementing the intensional programs.
- Dataflow architectures provide the appropriate hardware on which education can be executed in an efficient way.

Concluding this section, we should mention that although dataflow architectures are probably the most appropriate hardware platforms on which an intensional language can be executed, it is easy to implement eduction efficiently on traditional architectures (see, for example, Refs. 12 and 13).

EXISTING INTENSIONAL SYSTEMS AND THEIR APPLICATIONS

As we have already seen in previous sections, Lucid (4,14,15) was the first (to our knowledge) intensional language developed. Lucid is actually a *functional–intensional* language, in the sense that it supports (first-order) user-defined functions which operate on streams. The most comprehensive description of the language, its semantics, its applications, and its potential extensions is described in Ref. 4 (the *Lucid book*). From the programs in the Lucid book, it becomes obvious that the language is especially appropriate for dataflowlike computations. Moreover, due to its temporal nature, the language appears to be appropriate for developing interactive software and potentially real-time applications. The appendix of the Lucid book describes the implementation of an interactive vi-like screen editor in Lucid (note that at the time the book was written, most existing functional programming languages were not capable of efficiently executing applications of this type).

Since its inception, Lucid has been extended in several ways. Its variants have been used to specify three-dimensional spreadsheets (16,17), parallel computation models such as systolic arrays (18), attribute grammars (19,20), real-time systems (21,22), database systems (23), and so on. The most vital extension to the language was the addition of multiple dimensions, which resulted in the language GLU (Granular Lucid) (5,6). A GLU program consists of a declarative part (which is, in fact, a program in multidimensional Lucid) and an imperative part. The declarative part "glues" together sequential functions that are specified in an imperative language. GLU has been used for the development of real-world applications (6, Chap. 7; 24; 25).

Logic programming (26–29) is another programming paradigm which has benefitted from its interaction with intensional logic. Many intensional logic programming languages have been proposed (30). A temporal logic programming language influenced by the style of Lucid is Chronolog (31). For example, the following is a Chronolog (31) program that simulates the operation of the traffic lights:

```
first light(green).
next light(amber) ← light(green).
next light(red) ← light(amber).
next light(green) ← light(red).
```

The theory behind Chronolog is very well understood and developed (32,33). Many extensions of basic Chronolog have been proposed [to handle integer time (34), to provide multiple dimensions in the style of GLU (35,36), to use *choice-predicates* that support a dataflow style of computations (37), to provide branching time (38), to allow uncertainty to be expressed using rules with disjunction in the heads (39), etc.]. However, despite its theoretical advances, Chronolog has not been evaluated in practical applications of significant size that would help reveal its potential as well as its deficiencies.

Another area in which intensional programming appears to offer significant benefits is the area of *version control* (40). The intensional versioning approach described in Ref. 40 has recently found applications in the evolving area of *Internet computing*. One example application in this domain is development of the language IHTML (Intensional HTML) (41), a high-level Web authoring language. The advantage of IHTML over conventional HTML is that it allows practical specification of Web pages that can exist in many different versions. Web sites created by IHTML are easier to maintain and require significantly less space when compared to the sites created by cloning conventional HTML files.

RELATIONSHIP TO FUNCTIONAL LANGUAGES

As mentioned in previous sections, the intensional language Lucid is also functional in nature, as it supports functions that operate on infinite sequences and return infinite sequences as results. However, Lucid is certainly not a conventional functional language: Its basic data type is the infinite sequence, it supports several operators that can be applied on sequences, and it possesses many other features that are not available in traditional functional programming.

Of course, it would be possible to translate every Lucid program to a program of a more mainstream functional language, but this would, in general, be a nonstraightforward task and the resulting program would be much more complicated (42). In this section, we examine the opposite problem: Given a first-order functional program, can we transform it into a simpler intensional one? Can this transformation be used to efficiently compute the output of the initial functional program? The transformation that we present below was initially proposed in Yaghi's Ph.D. dissertation (43) and was later formalized and proven correct in Ref. 44.

We will demonstrate the transformation through an example. The interested reader can consult Ref. 44 for a formal exposition to the corresponding algorithm. Consider the following recursively defined functional program, which computes the fourth Fibonacci number*:

```
result = fib(4)
fib(n) = if (n<2) then 1 else fib(n-1)+fib(n-2)
```

In order to compute fib(4), we need to know fib(3) and fib(2). Similarly, fib(3) requires fib(2) and fib(1), and so on. Therefore, one can actually think of the formal parameter n as being a labeled tree with root 4. The left child of 4 is 3 and the right one is 2. The left child of 3 is 2 and the right is 1, and so on.

Similarly, the function fib can be thought of as a labeled tree that has been created by "consulting" the tree for n. The bottom labels of the tree for fib are all equal to 1, because this is the value that fib takes when the corresponding value of n is less than 2. As we move up the tree for fib, the label on each node is formed by adding the values of the right and left children of the node. The initial program can be transformed into a new one that reflects the above ideas:

```
result = first(fib)
fib    = if (n<2) then 1 else next₁(fib)+next₂(fib)
n      = 4 fby (n-1,n-2)
```

Note that the above program is a Lucid-like one, the only difference being that it is manipulating tree intensions and not just stream ones. The definition of n in terms of the generalized fby operator expresses the fact that n is a tree with root labeled 4; the root of the left subtree is equal to the current root minus 1, and the root of the right subtree is the current root minus 2. The operators $next_l$ are used in order to create the tree for fib. The definition of fib can be read as follows:

> The value of a node of the tree for fib, is equal to 1 if the value of the corresponding node of the tree for n is less than 2; otherwise, it is equal to the sum of the values found at the roots of the left and right subtrees of the node.

---

*The syntax adopted is valid for many well-known functional languages.

Note the main difference between the initial and the resulting programs. The source functional program contains a used defined function (namely fib), whereas the target intensional program is *zero order*, i.e., it contains only nullary definitions. It can be shown that every functional program can be so transformed into an intensional zero-order one and that the transformation is semantics preserving (i.e., the initial and final programs are semantically equivalent) (44). Moreover, as the outcome of the transformation is an (extended) Lucid program, eduction can be used in order to compute its output. As a result, the above technique provides a promising implementation approach for first-order functional languages.

The transformation presented above has been extended to also apply to a significant class of higher-order functional programs (12,45–47). However, the existence of a transformation that could handle a fully higher-order functional language is still an interesting research problem (47).

CONCLUSIONS

In this article, we have presented the basic principles of intensional programming languages. The distinguishing characteristic of intensional languages is that the basic entities they manipulate are *intensions* (i.e., functions from a context space to a set of data values). Depending on the context space, one can obtain different languages that can serve different types of applications. In this article, two such examples are given: the language Lucid whose context space is a set of time points and the language GLU which allows for other dimensions except for time. In the previous section, we saw that we can also have intensional languages in which intentions are trees.

The area of intensional programming is continuously evolving and new interesting problems are posed. Some of the most important ones are techniques for efficient implementations of intensional languages, relationship to WEB programming, application domains that would benefit from the interaction with intensional programming, and relationships with the more traditional programming paradigms. Answers to the above problems would result in a better understanding of the field and would reveal its real potential.

REFERENCES

1. R. Thomason, ed., *Formal Philosophy, Selected Papers of R. Montague*, Yale University Press, New Haven, CT, 1974.
2. D. Dowty, R. Wall, and S. Peters, *Introduction to Montague Semantics*, Reidel, 1981.
3. J. van Benthem, *A Manual of Intensional Logic*, CSLI Lecture Notes, 1988.
4. W. W. Wadge and E. A. Ashcroft, *Lucid, the Dataflow Programming Language*, Academic Press, New York, 1985.
5. E. A. Ashcroft, A. A. Faustini, and R. Jagannathan, "An Intensional Language for Parallel Applications Programming," in *Parallel Functional Languages and Compilers*, B. K. Szymanski, ed., ACM Press, New York, 1991, pp. 11–49.
6. E. A. Ashcroft, A. A. Faustini, R. Jagannathan, and W. W. Wadge, *Multidimensional Programming*, Oxford University Press, Oxford, 1995.
7. A. A. Faustini and W. W. Wadge, "Intensional Programming," Technical Report DCS-55-IR, Department of Computer Science, University of Victoria (1986).
8. R. Bagai, "Compilation of the Dataflow Language Lucid," master's thesis, Department of Computer Science, University of Victoria (1986).

9.   C. Dodd, "Rank Analysis in the GLU Compiler," in *Intensional Programming I*, M. Orgun and E. Ashcroft, eds., World Scientific, Singapore, 1996, pp. 76–82.

10. C. Kirkham, J. Gurd, and I. Watson, "The Manchester Prototype Dataflow Computer," *Commun. ACM*, 34–52 (January 1985).

11. Arvind and R. S. Nikhil, " Executing a Program on the MIT Tagged-Token Dataflow Architecture," *IEEE Trans. Computers*, *39*(3), 300–318 (1990).

12. P. Rondogiannis and W. Wadge, "Higher-Order Dataflow and its Implementation on Stock Hardware," in *Proceedings of the ACM Symposium on Applied Computing*, ACM Press, New York, 1994, pp. 431–435.

13. P. Rondogiannis and W. Wadge, "A Dataflow Implementation Technique for Lazy Typed Functional Languages," in *Proceedings of the Sixth International Symposium on Lucid and Intensional Programming*, 1993, pp. 23–42.

14. E. Ashcroft and W. Wadge, "Lucid—A Formal System for Writing and Proving Programs," *SIAM J. Computing*, *5*(3), 336–354 (1976).

15. E. Ashcroft and W. Wadge, "Lucid, a Nonprocedural Language with Iteration," *Commun. ACM*, *20*(7), 519–526 (1977).

16. W. Du and W. W. Wadge, "A 3D Spreadsheet Based on Intensional Logic," *IEEE Software*, 78–89 (July 1990).

17. W. Du and W. W. Wadge, "The Eductive Implementation of a Three-dimensional Spreadsheet," *Software—Pract. Exper.*, *20*(11), 1097–1114 (1990).

18. W. Du, "Indexical Parallel Programming," Ph.D. thesis, Department of Computer Science, University of Victoria, Canada, (1991).

19. S. Tao, "Indexical Attribute Grammars," Ph.D. thesis, Department of Computer Science, University of Victoria, Canada (1994).

20. S. Tao, "TLucid and Intensional Attribute Grammars," in *Proceedings of the Sixth International Symposium on Lucid and Intensional Programming*, 1993, pp. 94–106.

21. A. A. Faustini and E. Lewis, "Toward a Real-Time Dataflow Language," in *Hard Real-Time Systems*, J. Stankovic and K. Ramamrithan, eds., IEEE, New York, 1989, pp. 139–145.

22. R. Khedri, J. Plaice, and R. Lalement, "From Abstract Time to Real Time," in *Proceedings of the Sixth International Symposium on Lucid and Intensional Programming*, 1993, pp. 83–93.

23. J. Paquet and J. Plaice, "On the Design of an Indexical Query Language," in *Proceedings of the Seventh International Symposium on Lucid and Intensional Programming*, 1994, pp. 28–36.

24. I. Agi, "GLU for Multidimensional Signal Processing," in *Intensional Programming I*, M. Orgun and E. Ashcroft, World Scientific, Singapore, 1996, pp. 135–148.

25. P. Rao and R. Jagannathan, "Developing Scientific Applications in GLU," in *Proceedings of the Seventh International Symposium on Lucid and Intensional Programming*, 1994, pp. 45–52.

26. L. Sterling and E. Shapiro, *The Art of PROLOG*, MIT Press, Cambridge, MA, 1986.

27. J. Lloyd, *Foundations of Logic Programming*, Springer-Verlag, New York, 1987.

28. K. Apt, "Logic Programming," in *Handbook of Theoretical Computer Science*, J. van Leeuwen, ed., Elsevier Science, New York, 1990, pp. 494–574.

29. M. H. vanEmden and R. A. Kowalski, "The Semantics of Predicate Logic as a Programming Language," *J. ACM*, *23*(4), 733–742 (1976).

30. M. Orgun, "Temporal and Modal Logic Programming," *SIGART Bull.*, *5*(3) (1994).

31. W. W. Wadge, "Tense Logic Programming: A Respectable Alternative, in *Proc. of the 1988 International Symposium on Lucid and Intensional Programming*, 1988, pp. 26–32.

32. M. A. Orgun, "Intensional Logic Programming," Ph.D. thesis, Department of Computer Science, University of Victoria, Canada (1991).

33. M. A. Orgun and W. W. Wadge, "Towards a Unified Theory of Intensional Logic Programming," *J. Logic Program.*, *13*(4), 113–145 (1992).

34. M. A. Orgun, W. W. Wadge, and W. Du, Chronolog (*Z*): "Linear-Time Logic Programming," in *Proc. of the Fifth International Conference on Computing and Information*,

   O. Abou-Rabia, C. K. Chang, and W. W. Koczkodaj, eds., IEEE Computer Society Press, Los Alamitos, CA, 1993, pp. 545–549.

35. M. A. Orgun and W. Du, "Multi-dimensional Logic Programming," *J. Comput. Inform.*, *1*(1), 1501–1520 (1994).

36. M. A. Orgun and W. Du, "Multi-dimensional Logic Programming: Theoretical Foundations," *Theoret. Computer Sci.*, *158*(2), 319–345 (1997).

37. M. A. Orgun and W. W. Wadge, "Extending Temporal Logic Programming with Choice Predicates Non-determinism," *J. Logic Computat.*, *4*(6), 877–903 (1994).

38. P. Rondogiannis, M. Gergatsoulis, and T. Panayiotopoulos, "Cactus: A Branching-Time Logic Programming Language," in *Proc. of the First International Joint Conference on Qualitative and Quantitative Practical Reasoning, ECSQARU-FAPR'97, Bad Honnef, Germany*, Lecture Notes in Artificial Intelligence Vol. 1244, Springer-Verlag, New York, 1997, pp. 511–524.

39. M. Gergatsoulis, P. Rondogiannis, and T. Panayiotopoulos, "Disjunctive Chronolog," in *Proceedings of the JICSLP'96 Post-Conference Workshop "Multi-Paradigm Logic Programming,"* M. Chacravarty, Y. Guo, and T. Ida, eds., 1996, pp. 129–136.

40. J. Plaice and W. Wadge, "A New Approach to Version Control," *IEEE Tran. Software Eng.*, *SE-19*(3), 268–276 (1993).

41. T. Yildirim, "Intensional HTML," master's thesis, Department of Computer Science, University of Victoria (1997).

42. A. A. Faustini, E. A. Ashcroft, and R. Jagannathan, An Intensional Language for Parallel Applications Programming, in *Parallel Functional Languages and Compilers*, B. K. Szymanski, ed., ACM Press, New York, 1991, pp. 11–49.

43. A. A. Yaghi, "The Intensional Implementation Technique for Functional Languages," Ph.D. thesis, Department of Computer Science, University of Warwick, Coventry, UK (1984).

44. P. Rondogiannis and W. W. Wadge, "First-Order Functional Languages and Intensional Logic," *J. Functional Program.*, *7*(1), 73–101 (1997).

45. W. W. Wadge, "Higher-Order Lucid," in *Proceedings of the Fourth International Symposium on Lucid and Intensional Programming*, 1991.

46. P. Rondogiannis and W. Wadge, "Compiling Higher-Order Functions for Tagged-Dataflow," in *Proceedings of the IFIP International Conference on Parallel Architectures and Compilation Techniques*, North-Holland, Amsterdam, 1994, pp. 269–278.

47. P. Rondogiannis, "Higher-Order Functional Languages and Intensional Logic," Ph.D. thesis, Department of Computer Science, University of Victoria, Canada (December 1994).

BASIC READINGS

E. A. Ashcroft, A. A. Faustini, R. Jagannathan, and W. W. Wadge, *Multidimensional Programming*, Oxford University Press, Oxford, 1995.

D. Dowty, R. Wall, and S. Peters, *Introduction to Montague Semantics*, Reidel, 1981.

W. Du and W. W. Wadge, "A 3D Spreadsheet Based on Intensional Logic," *IEEE Software*, 78–89 (1990).

A. A. Faustini, E. A. Ashcroft, and R. Jagannathan, "An Intensional Language for Parallel Applications Programming," in *Parallel Functional Languages and Compilers*, B. K. Szymanski, ed., ACM Press, New York, 1991, pp. 11–49.

W. W. Wadge and E. A. Ashcroft, *Lucid, the Dataflow Programming Language*, Academic Press, New York, 1985.

PANOS RONDOGIANNIS

W. W. WADGE

MACHINE LEARNING

INTRODUCTION

A fundamental part of intelligence is the ability to learn based on previous experience. For example, driving a car, solving a differential equation, playing chess, and tying one's shoes are all tasks at which humans improve by learning from past experiences. *Machine learning* is concerned with the problem of how a computer can learn to improve its performance at a particular task through experience. Research in machine learning addresses practical algorithm development and fundamental questions such as what is and what is not learnable. In the past decade, applications of machine learning in a wide variety of domains (such as detecting cellular phone fraud, diagnosing equine colic, and performing elevator scheduling) have illustrated the utility of machine learning.

There are many approaches to machine learning, each differing in several aspects: the type of feedback used to train the learner (or agent), when training is performed, and whether an existing model of the concept to be learned can be used to aid in training. Perhaps the problem that has received the most attention historically is learning from examples, which is also referred to as *supervised learning*. In this scenario, the learner is given a set of training examples (or instances), each described by a set of attributes and labeled with one of a discrete number of labels. The computer's task is to form a generalization of the instances that can be used to predict the class of new objects. For example, using patient data, the computer can learn to diagnose whether a patient does or does not have a specific type of pathology. A second problem area is learning from instances that do not have a class label. Here, an *unsupervised learner* must form generalizations of the data typically by first clustering the data into similar groups and then forming a generalization using the cluster structure. A third learning situation, which sits between these two extremes of supervised and unsupervised learning, is learning from feedback received after performing a sequence of steps or actions. For example, in the game of chess, it is not feasible to provide feedback about each separate move, but at the end of the game one knows the result and can use that information to train the learner. The objective of the learner is to develop a policy—a mapping from states to actions—that allows it to select actions that optimize a measure of its performance on the task; for example, reducing the number of steps necessary to complete the task successfully, or, as in chess, allowing the learner to win the game. This type of learning is called *reinforcement learning*.

In addition to differing in the type of feedback, machine learning methods differ in whether they are on-line or off-line algorithms. Off-line algorithms look at the training data all at once and form a generalization. Whereas on-line (or incremental) learning algorithms continually learn as new information comes along. A third dimension in which machine learning algorithms differ is in whether they are based on Bayesian probability theory, which states how to combine different forms of probabilistic evidence in order to make principled statements about the probability of certain events.

In the past two decades, there has been considerable research in the area of computational learning theory, which is the theoretical analysis of what is learnable. In the early 1980s, Valiant developed a framework for judging the correctness of learning algorithms that allowed a significant body of work to be done on determining what types of tasks are learnable. His framework introduced the idea that a learned fact is permitted to be only approximately correct and that with some (low) probability, the learning system will form an incorrect fact.

LEARNING FROM EXAMPLES

The ability to classify objects with respect to various class definitions is a fundamental property of intelligence. A question of great interest is how such definitions are acquired and how the acquisition process can be automated—one would like a machine to be able to find and use such definitions. The question of how to learn to classify instances has been studied by researchers in statistics, pattern recognition, control theory, psychology, neuroscience, philosophy, and computer science. In machine learning, the problem is defined as follows: given a set of examples, each described by a set of features and labeled with a class name, the goal of the learning algorithm is to form a generalization of the examples that can be used to classify previously unobserved objects with a high degree of accuracy. For example, given the results of several blood tests of a particular patient and a hepatitis B classifier formed from previous patient data, one can classify the new patient's data as indicative or not indicative of hepatitis B. In this section, we focus on four well-known approaches to learning from examples: decision trees, neural networks, lazy learning, and inductive logic programming.

Decision Trees

Decision trees are perhaps the most widely applied learning method. They have been put to use successfully on problems such as detecting credit card fraud, classifying sky objects in image data, and predicting whether conditions are ripe for a bush fire. A decision tree is a classification procedure that partitions the training instances recursively into smaller subdivisions based on a set of tests defined at each branch (or node) in the tree. The tree is composed of a root node (formed from all of the data), a set of internal nodes (splits), and a set of terminal nodes (leaves). Each node in a decision tree has only one parent node, and two or more descendant nodes. In this framework, a data set is classified by subdividing it sequentially according to the decision framework defined by the tree, and a class label is assigned to each observation according to the leaf node into which the observation falls. Perhaps the main reason for its widespread use is that decision trees have significant intuitive appeal because the classification structure is explicit and, therefore, easily interpretable.

Decision trees require that the quantity to be predicted be categorical, such as predicting whether a patient is or is not susceptible to breast cancer based on medical records and family history. There is no restriction on the input features; they can be categorical (nominal), Boolean, or numeric. For a test node based on a categorical feature, one creates a branch for each value of the feature. For example, given the task of predicting the political party of an elected official based on their voting history, a test would be their vote on a particular issue and have three branches: one for each of "yes," "no," and "abstain." For numeric features, one constructs a test by creating a Boolean range test of the form $F_i < v$, where v is a value in the observed range of feature F_i.

Numerous tree construction approaches have been developed over the past 30 or so years. To form a decision tree, the splits defined at each internal node of a decision tree are estimated from training data using a statistical procedure. A classic example of this approach is the classification and regression tree (CART) model described by Breiman et al. (1). In CART, a tree-structured decision space is estimated by recursively splitting the data at each node based on a statistical test that increases the homogeneity of the training data in the resulting descendant nodes.

Finally, a key step in any decision tree estimation problem is to correct the tree for overfitting by pruning the tree back. Conventionally, a tree is grown such that all training observations are correctly classified (i.e., training classification accuracy = 100%). If the training data contain errors in the class labels or noise in the measurements of the features, then overfitting the tree to the data in this manner can lead to poor performance on unseen data. Therefore, the tree must be pruned back to reduce classification errors when data outside of the training set are to be classified. For a comprehensive introduction to decision trees, see Refs. 1 or 2.

Artificial Neural Networks

Artificial neural networks are based loosely on actual, biological neural systems, such as the human brain. Like biological systems, artificial neural networks are made up of many simple processing units interconnected in possibly complex ways. Although the individual units are quite simple, often computing their output with only addition, subtraction, multiplication, and division, networks of these units can represent complex functions and produce complex classifiers. Artificial neural networks range in complexity from the very simple, involving only one unit, to the vastly elaborate, being made up of millions of units.

The simplest artificial neural network, which was first described in 1960, is the Widrow–Hoff unit. This unit takes as input a real-valued vector (a list of real numbers) that describe an example and produces a single real-valued output. One can think of the unit as a function with many inputs and one output. For every input parameter, there is an associated real-valued *weight*. For example, a unit that has five input parameters has five weights. The output of the unit is simply the sum of the products of each individual input value with its associated weight.

Like other learning architectures, training the Widrow–Hoff unit involves the presentation of training examples to the unit. Each example is composed of an input vector and the value that the unit should produce when presented with the input vector. During training, the values of the weights are adjusted to reduce the difference between the output value specified in the training example and the output value actually produced by the unit. There are several algorithms (or learning rules) for changing the values of the weights, including the least means squared rule, and the absolute difference rule.

A more complex artificial neural network is the multilayer, feed-forward network. This type of network can be thought of as a function with many inputs and many outputs and is composed of layers of interconnected units that are only slightly more complex than the Widrow–Hoff unit. There are three classes of units in this type of network. The units whose values are set directly by the input vector are in the input layer. The units whose values produce the output of the network are in the output layer. Between the input and output layers are one or more hidden layers. Each of the units in one layer is connected to every unit in the next layer; that is, the output value of every unit in one layer serves as input to every unit in the next layer. Producing the output of the network involves the iterative process of calculating the output of every unit in each layer, starting with the input layer, and passing those values to the units in the next layer. This process continues until the output values are produced.

Training a multilayer, feed-forward network works similarly to training a Widrow–Hoff unit and begins by producing the actual output of the network based on the input vector in the training example. Then, every weight of every unit is adjusted to minimize the difference between the outputs produced by the network and the outputs given in the training example. One of the most popular training algorithms for this type of network is *back-propagation*, which starts adjusting weights in the units in the output layer and progresses backward through the network, changing the weights in the units of each successive hidden layer next. The goal of back-propagation is to minimize the square of the differences between the actual outputs and the training example outputs. One reason for back-propagation's popularity is that it is based on sound mathematics.

Artificial neural networks have been applied to many areas, including function approximation, classification, such as face recognition and handwriting recognition, and control tasks, such as game-playing and robotics. An example of a successful use of these networks is ALVINN (autonomous land vehicle in a neural network) (3), which controls the steering of a vehicle on the road at highway speeds. ALVINN acquires its training examples by observing a human driving the vehicle. Another success is TD-Gammon (4), which is considered the best computerized backgammon player in the world and is often compared to the top human players.

For more details on artificial neural networks, see Ref. 5 or one of the many textbooks on the subject.

Lazy Learning

Lazy learning algorithms differ from traditional classification algorithms (such as decision trees and neural networks) in that they retain all training instances and defer processing of them until asked to classify a new instance. An example of a lazy algorithm is an algorithm that has its roots in the statistical pattern recognition community—the k nearest-neighbor algorithm. During training, all instances are stored. When asked to classify a new instance, the algorithm finds the instance's k nearest neighbors and returns the class held by the majority of the k neighbors. This method can also be used to do numeric prediction by taking the mean value predicted by the k neighbors. There have been many variations of this basic approach developed in the machine learning community. These approaches are designed to attack the issues that some instances may be noisy (mislabeled) and that not all features are equally predictive. The extensions to the basic algorithm include weighting instances by their importance/reliability, discarding irrelevant and noisy features, and weighting features by their importance to classification. Reference 6 provides a good overview of these methods.

Inductive Logic Programming

The three methods discussed previously all have in common the assumption that one is learning a mapping from a feature vector to a set of classes. In some cases, one would like a more expressive representation. When the variables contain first-order Horn clauses, one can express relations among the baseline features. A common approach to learning with such a representation is to form if–then rules. This form of learning is called inductive logic programming (ILP), because a set of first-order Horn clauses can be interpreted as programs in Prolog, a logic programming language. ILP is a research area formed at the intersection of machine learning and logic programming. ILP systems develop predicate descriptions from examples and background knowledge. The examples, background knowledge, and final descriptions are all described as logic programs. This representation allows one to specify recursive relations, which are difficult to specify in the propositional language used by learning algorithms such as decision trees.

The typical approach is to form the set of learned rules from a training set by learning one rule at a time. An example of this approach is FOIL (7), which searches incrementally for the rule that best covers all of the positive instances and none of the negative instances of the concept to be learned. During the search for each rule, it searches from general to specific by adding a single new literal to the rule's preconditions. To select the literal for addition, FOIL uses a metric based on entropy. Inductive logic programming is an active research area and more details can be found in Refs. 8 and 9.

REINFORCEMENT LEARNING

Reinforcement learning is designed to allow autonomous learners to learn to perform tasks that can only be solved via a sequence of decisions, such as robotics navigation and grasping problems, classic problem-solving, and game-playing. The objective of the learner is to develop a policy—a mapping from states to actions—that allows it to select actions that optimize a measure of its performance on the task (e.g., reducing the number of steps necessary to complete the task successfully). In order to achieve this goal, the learner adapts its policy based on the consequences of its own actions.

There are three components in the reinforcement learning scenario: the *learner*, the *task* (or *environment*), and the *critic* (a type of *trainer*). The learner and task interact through *actions*, by which the learner manipulates its environment, and through *states*, which represent the current task configuration. The learner and critic interact only via *rewards*, which are the training signals that the critic gives to the learner after each of the learner's actions. These rewards are simply scalar values that indicate to the learner how well it is performing on the task. Negative-valued rewards are assigned to undesirable actions, positive values to desirable actions, and the value zero to all other actions.

At each time step, the learner selects an action based on its developing policy and the current state. After the learner performs the action, which changes the state of the task, it receives a reward from the critic. This evaluative feedback is only weakly informative, simply revealing the short-term performance level of the learner and not giving specific information about the applicability of any of the previous actions. Even so, receipt of these scalar rewards allows the learner to develop a policy that optimizes an additive measure of those rewards. As an example of one step of the learning process, consider a mobile robot that is facing a wall. After examining its options, the robot chooses to move forward, only to receive a negative reward for having run into the wall. The robot can then update its policy to make moving into the wall less likely to be chosen as the preferred action when in a similar situation in the future.

The learner in a reinforcement learning scenario is faced with two inherent challenges. The first is the problem of *temporal credit assignment*, which deals with assigning credit or blame to previously chosen actions based on the current reward. This issue is particularly difficult when nonzero rewards are sparse. Without addressing this issue, the learner would not be able to learn a policy at all. The other difficulty, called the *explore/exploit trade-off*, arises because the agent must choose between picking the action that its policy suggests—exploiting the knowledge that is gathered so far—versus experimenting with its options—exploring its environment—in order to learn more about the task. Although the learner can develop a working policy without explicitly exploring its environment, simply exploiting the knowledge gathered so far may limit the utility of the policy found. Each of the reinforcement learning algorithms that have been developed are designed to deal with these two complications.

There are two main classes of reinforcement learning methods: model free and model based. A model is a representation of the current task that contains information about the rewards that an agent may receive and about the state transitions. The model-free methods, which include the Adaptive Heuristic Critic and Q-Learning, allow the learner to develop a good policy without the benefit of any information about the task except the direct results of performing actions in the task. Model-based methods, such as Dyna, Prioritized Sweeping, and Queue-Dyna, learn models of the task that indicate how state transitions and rewards are related to actions and use those models to help develop the policy. Model-based methods tend to require more computation, but they need much less exposure to the real environment than model-free methods.

Reinforcement learning has received the attention of theorists and, thus, there exist many proofs that the application of certain reinforcement learning approaches will lead to optimal solutions, due mostly to the links reinforcement learning has with the classic control engineering solution method called dynamic programming. Given that the policy is stored in a particular representation and assuming that every action and every state is experienced an infinite number of times, there are several reinforcement learning techniques that allow the policy to converge to optimality. Although the assumptions of the proofs are rather restrictive, the learning techniques allow optimal policies to be found.

Reinforcement learning has found success in several areas, including game-playing, robotics, control, and maze tasks. Tesauro's TD-Gammon (4), is considered the best computerized backgammon player in the world and is often compared to the top human players. Crites and Barto's Elevator Control System (10) performs better at certain types of elevator scheduling problems than the solutions that people have developed in the many decades of elevator use.

For an in-depth look at reinforcement learning, see Ref. 11 or 12.

UNSUPERVISED LEARNING

Unsupervised learning refers to a learning situation in which the task is not to predict a particular feature, but rather to understand the relationships among the data points. For example, one might seek to find associations among the features, or group points in the example space together in terms of a measure of their similarity. A fundamental goal of unsupervised learning is discovery of new concepts. Indeed a whole area of research has focused on scientific discovery, the process of applying unsupervised methods to scientific data. This area of machine learning is closely linked to the emergent field of *data mining*, which refers to the process extracting patterns from data.

An area first developed in statistical pattern recognition is clustering, which finds natural groupings in the data based on the chosen similarity metric. To cluster the data, one must first choose a clustering criterion, which ideally maximizes intracluster homogeneity while maximizing intercluster heterogeneity. In addition, one must specify k, the number of clusters to find in the data. A focus of recent research is what to do when k is not known. One use of clustering is *deviation detection*, which seeks to identify points in the data that deviate or are outliers from the general trends in the data. These methods try to explain whether each such point is noise or should be examined in more detail and is often the source of true discovery because outliers express deviation from expected norms. An example of deviation detection is trying to find intrusions in computer audit trail data.

Another area that falls under the rubric of unsupervised learning is link analysis (often called market basket analysis), which seeks to establish relations among the features (fields in a database). For example, link analysis is used to determine which items sell well with one another based on consumer data. Given a collection of items and a set of records, each of which contain some number of items from the given collection, an association discovery function is an operation against this set of records that returns associations that exist among the collection of items. The goal is to discover rules of the form: When X and Y occur, Z will occur ($P = 0.93$). The specific percentage of occurrences (in this case, 93) is called the confidence factor of the association.

BAYESIAN LEARNING

Bayesian learning is based on a powerful result from probability theory known as Bayes' theorem, which states how to combine different forms of probabilistic evidence together in order to make principled statements about the probability of certain events. In machine learning, the event of interest is the choice of hypothesis, and the evidence is in the form of training examples and prior knowledge about the problem being studied. Thus, one can choose the hypothesis that is the most probable given the prior knowledge and the training examples. Bayes' theorem also makes it possible to produce probabilistic hypotheses; that is, hypotheses that make probabilistics classifications, such as classifying a flower as 95% dandelion.

With respect to machine learning, Bayes' theorem relates mathematically the probabilities associated with the hypotheses and the training examples. One piece of evidence is the probability of the training examples will be observed given that one has no other information. This is written as $P(E)$ and is called the prior probability of the training examples ("prior" because it assumes no other evidence is available). Another form of evidence is the prior probability of each hypothesis, $P(h)$, which indicates how probable each hypothesis is, given that one does not have any other knowledge. The final piece of prior knowledge is the conditional probability that the training examples are observed, given that a particular hypothesis holds. This quantity is written as $P(E|h)$ (the probability of the examples given the hypothesis) and must be available for each of the possible hypotheses. Bayes' theorem indicates how each of these three forms of evidence can be combined to produce the posterior probability of h, $P(h|E)$, which is the probability of the hypothesis, given that the training examples are observed. According to Bayes' theorem, $P(h|E)$ is simply $P(E|h)P(h)/P(E)$.

One of the simplest uses of Bayes' theorem is to identify the *maximum a posterior*, or MAP, hypothesis. One simply calculates the posterior probability for each of the candidate hypotheses using Bayes' theorem and then chooses the hypothesis with the highest probability. A simplification of the mathematics allows one to choose the hypothesis whose value of the product $P(E|h)P(h)$ (the numerator in Bayes' theorem) is the largest. One does not need to divide this product by the $P(E)$ term to get the actual posterior probability because doing so simply divides the product for each hypothesis by a constant factor. The hypothesis with the highest posterior probability will also have the highest value for this product. Not only does this simplification reduce the amount of calculations necessary, it also means that one does not need to gather the knowledge about the prior probability of the training examples. If one is willing to assume that all of the hypotheses have the same prior probability (which is easy to do when there are thousands or millions of possible hypotheses), then the calculations become even simpler. However, with this assumption, one is no longer able to identify the MAP hypothesis; instead, one identifies what is called the *maximum likelihood*, or ML, hypothesis. Because $P(h)$ is the same for every hypothesis, one simply needs to choose the hypothesis whose value of $P(E|h)$ is the highest. Once one identifies either the MAP or ML hypothesis, one can use that hypothesis to classify new examples.

In addition to choosing the hypothesis with the highest probability given the evidence, one can also find the best classification for a new example, given the evidence. This classification is called the maximum *a posterior* classification and involves the posterior probability of the classification, given the values of each of the attributes in the new example. Similar to the MAP hypothesis, the MAP classification can be calculated via Bayes' theorem, but with different probabilities. One needs the prior probabilities of the classification $P(c)$ and the conditional probabilities of the values of the attributes of the example, given that the classification is observed, written as $P(a_1, a_2, \dots |c)$. $P(c)$ can be calculated easily simply by counting the occurrences of the classification in the training examples and dividing by the total number of training examples. Unfortunately, calculating the conditional probability is complicated and often impossible. However, by making an assumption, one can approximate the value. One simply assumes that $P(a_1, a_2, \dots |c)$ can be approximated by the product of the individual terms $P(a_1|c)$, $P(a_2|c)$, . … In statistical parlance, one assumes that the values $a_1, a_2, \dots$ are conditionally independent, given c. Determining the values for each of the $P(a_i|c)$'s is simply a matter of counting occurrences of a_i in the training examples when c is the classification for the example, and dividing by the total number of examples that have classification c. Thus, every value needed to estimate the probability of a particular classification can be determined easily from the training data. The name of this method, which makes the simplifying assumptions discussed above, is the naive Bayes' classifier. Not only is the naive Bayes' classifier easy to use, but it has been shown to outperform such methods as artificial neural networks and decision trees in particular problems.

Each of the methods discussed combines prior evidence to produce either a hypothesis or a classification based on Bayes' theorem. Bayes' theorem also serves as the foundation for the Bayesian belief network, which is a framework used for reasoning about many forms of evidence to arrive at probable conclusions. Each node of the network represents an attribute; links between nodes represent conditional probabilities between the attributes linked. Given a belief network, one can use Bayes' theorem to estimate the probable values of certain attributes, given the value of other attributes. An area of active research is concerned with using a set of training data to learn a belief network. One needs to learn the architecture of the network: What are the pertinent attributes? How are they linked together? What are the values of the conditional probabilities? Bayesian belief networks are a richer representation than the naive Bayes classifier and, thus, have the ability to make more accurate estimates about posterior probabilities.

For more information on these topics, see Ref. 13.

COMPUTATIONAL LEARNING THEORY

A large body of research in maching learning is devoted to the theoretical characterization of machine learning problems and the analysis of different learning algorithms. The goal is to understand what is and what is not "learnable." There are several different frameworks. Here, we consider two of the most widely used: the *probably approximately correct* (PAC) *learning* framework, which analyzes what is and what is not learnable from a polynomial number of training instances, and the *mistake-bounded* framework, which focuses on the analysis of how many errors will be made by an incremental learning algorithm before it converges to the correct hypothesis.

The PAC model has been used to answer the following question: Given a random sample drawn from a population and a target error rate, how many instances must be in the sample to guarantee that the error rate on new cases will be approximately the same as the target rate? This question is posed independently of any particular population distribution, so one does not know the characteristics of the samples. Many different classification algorithms have been analyzed in this manner. This is a worst-case analysis because it applies to *any* distribution. The goal is to characterize classes of target concepts that can be learned reliably from a polynomial number of randomly drawn training samples in a computationally feasible (polynomial) amount of time. A typical use is to specify a class of concepts (e.g., all Boolean linear discriminant functions), require that the error be bounded by some constant ε and that the estimate of the error be bounded by some small constant δ, and then try to determine how many training instances are required to meet these conditions.

In a *mistake-bounded model*, the learner receives a sequence of training samples, and must predict its class after each. The measure of interest is how many errors it makes before the learner converges to the correct concept. This situation differs from the previous model, in that, here, learning is assumed to be incremental—the learner must actually do prediction before it has seen enough training examples to focus in on the target concept.

APPLYING MACHINE LEARNING

We conclude with a discussion of the issues that must be considered when applying machine learning to practice. For a more comprehensive discussion of these issues, see Ref. 14. Solving a learning problem requires that one first formulate the learning task and then select a model and algorithm. The next step is to test the model to determine whether it meets the specified performance requirements. If it does not, then the practitioner tries to understand why not and how to reformulate the problem such that a satisfactory model can be constructed. Poor performance can be due to a variety of causes which include inadequate features, error in the training data, or a poor choice of algorithm and model. Once the problem is diagnosed, the model can be refit to the data.

The myriad of successful applications of machine learning and the dramatic evolution of the related field of data mining make machine learning an exciting field of research. Machine learning has been applied successfully to fields such as medicine, computer vision, computer security, planetary science, credit card fraud, assembly plant automation, game playing, and many more.

REFERENCES

1. L. Breiman, J. H. Friedman, R. A. Olshen, and C. J. Stone, *Classification and Regression Trees*, Wadsworth International Group, Belmont, CA, 1984.
2. J. R. Quinlan, *C4.5: Programs for Machine Learning*, Morgan Kaufmann, San Mateo, CA, 1993.
3. D. A. Pomerleau, "Rapidly Adapting Artificial Neural Networks for Autonomous Navigation," in *Advances in Neural Information Processing Systems*, Lippman, Moody, and Touretzky, Eds., Morgan Kaufmann, San Mateo, CA, 1991.
4. G. Tesauro, "Temporal Difference Learning and TD-Gammon," *Commun. ACM*, *38*, 58–68 (1995).
5. D. Rumelhart, B. Widrow, and M. Lehr, "The Basic Ideas in Neural Networks," *Commun. ACM*, *37*(3), 87–92, 1994.
6. *Artifi. Intell. Rev.*, *11* (1997), Special issue on lazy learning.
7. J. R. Quinlan, "Determinate Literals in Inductive Logic Programming," *Machine Learning: Proceedings of the Eighth International Workshop*, Morgan Kaufmann, Evanston, IL, 1991, pp. 442–446.
8. N. Lavrac and S. Dzeroski, *Inductive Logic Programming: Techniques and Applications*. Ellis Horwood, London, 1994.
9. S. Muggleton, *Foundations of Inductive Logic Programming*, Prentice-Hall, Englewood Cliffs, NJ, 1995.
10. R. H. Crites and A. G. Barto, "Improving Elevator Performance Using Reinforcement Learning," in *Advances in Neural Information Processing Systems*, MIT Press, Cambridge, MA, 1996.
11. L. P. Kaelbling, M. L. Littman, and A. W. Moore, "Reinforcement Learning: A Survey," *J. Artif. Intell. Res.*, *4*, 237–285 (1996).
12. R. S. Sutton and A. G. Barto, *Reinforcement Learning: An Introduction*, MIT Press/Bradford Books, Cambridge, MA, 1998.
13. D. Heckerman, D. Geiger, and D. Chickering, "Learning Bayesian Networks: The Combination of Knowledge and Statistical Data," *Machine Learning*, *20*, 197 (1995).
14. C. E. Brodley and P. J. Smyth, "Applying Classification Algorithms in Practice," *Statist. Comput.*, *7*, 45–56 (1997).

CARLA E. BRODLEY

JEFF A. CLOUSE

MODELING, ANALYSIS, AND SIMULATION OF COMPUTER AND TELECOMMUNICATION SYSTEMS

INTRODUCTION

Computer and telecommunication systems play a central role in everyday life. The complexity of these systems has experienced an exponential growth with the ever-increasing demands on performance, efficiency, compactness, cost, functionality, operability in harsh environments, fault tolerance, and even aesthetic appeal. In turn, this growth has been reflected in the complexity of designing and manufacturing these systems. Accordingly, there is an increased interest in the efficient use of modeling and simulation tools to increase the reliability and allow design space exploration in all phases of the design cycle. In addition, the increased complexity of the systems challenges the capabilities of present-day modeling and analysis techniques. This article overviews the current status of modeling, analysis, and simulation techniques that have emerged to support the design and analysis of today's complex systems.

Modeling is an invaluable tool that is heavily used in all engineering disciplines. Webster's dictionary defines a *model* to be a tentative description of a theory or system that accounts for all its known properties. *Modeling* is the process of translating a real system into a model. Compared to the system, a model may be (i) a more tractable representation (1), (ii) less expensive to construct, (iii) more observable, and (iv) more adaptable. Once a model is constructed, it must be *verified* against the model specification and *validated* to match the real system it represents. Verification not only confirms the validity of the model as a boolean property, but is also useful in establishing the boundaries of this validity and the confidence in the model. The verified model is then *analyzed* and the observed behavior is used to draw inferences about the original system. Note that both verification and analysis require that the model be exercised (or "executed"). During analysis, the observability of the model is useful in gaining insight into the parameters of the system that are difficult to observe on the real system (e.g., the temperature at the core of a nuclear plant). The adaptability allows controlled study of the design parameters to fine-tune performance and compare trade-offs.

The remainder of this article is organized as follows. The next section describes the process of modeling a system, and the life cycle of the model. The third section reviews the various modeling strategies available. With the advent of computers, computer-based simulation has become an important analysis methodology for design and analysis of computers and telecommunication systems. The fourth section deals exclusively with computer-based simulation. Some conclusions and a discussion on future trends is presented in the fifth section. The final section presents a glossary of terms used in this document.

THE LIFE CYCLE OF THE MODEL

Building a model is an engineering design process—the model itself is a design that must satisfy a set of functional requirements. The model is the enabling transitional step between the physical system and the analyses applied to it. Thus, it inherits functional requirements from both the system and the desired analyses. System requirements ensure that the model must be faithful to the original system it models. These requirements specify functional and accuracy specifications that must be satisfied within accepted tolerances. Analysis-derived requirements are followed from the desired analyses; the model must be sufficient for achieving the analysis goals. A model is a specific abstraction of the system that might not be suitable for all types of analyses. For example, a functional model of a computer system does not include information sufficient for a power dissipation analysis. Alternatively, an axiomatic model of the system is not suitable for a functional simulation of the system.

The relationship between the system and the model is illustrated in Figure 1. Usually, an iterative process is used to refine the model in order to satisfy the functional requirements. This model is verified to meet the functional requirements (usually the system-derived requirements). Failure in the verification stage suggests that the model does not represent the system accurately; the model is refined and the verification repeated. The analysis-derived requirements are often impossible to satisfy within a single model. Thus, different facets (models) of the system are maintained and used in a complementary manner to satisfy the analysis requirements [*multifaceted modeling* (2)].

The relationship between the model and the system has been described under the assumption of a static system design. However, one of the most important uses for modeling is the evaluation of systems under design. When the system changes, the functional requirements placed on the model also change; the model must be modified to conform with the new state of the system.

Once the model has been successfully verified, it is ready for analysis. During analysis, the model is studied to acquire information about the original system. Recall that the required analyses form part of the functional requirements for each model; there is a fundamental relationship between the model and the types of analyses for which it

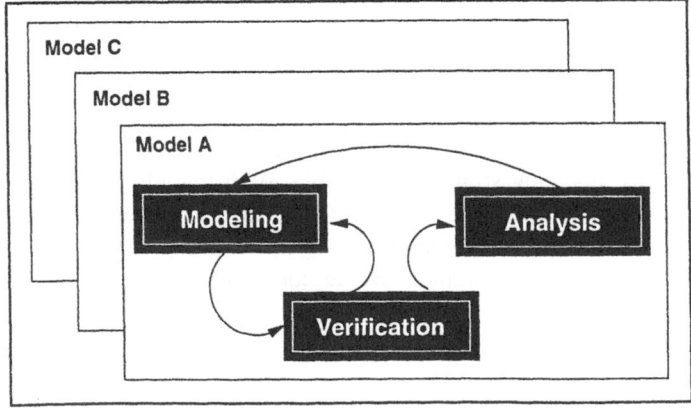

FIGURE 1   Life cycle of a model.

is suitable. Thus, the choice of the modeling strategy must take into account not only the type of system under consideration, but also the analysis targets. The remainder of this article will overview the prevalent modeling strategies and discuss the types of analyses for which each is suitable.

MODELING STRATEGIES

There are no well-defined rules for modeling a system. However, the type of the system under study and the desired targets of the analysis often suggests a modeling methodology. There are four broad modeling strategies that sometimes overlap. The remainder of this article discusses and compares these strategies and provides guidelines to when and how to use each of them.

Prototyping

In this approach, a real system representative of the system under design is constructed. The use of prototypes is usually restricted to the latter parts of the design process when the design is mature because (1) building a prototype is costly, (2) for the prototype to be studied, it has to be operational (a full system or a subsystem that can be tested within an available apparatus is required), and (3) building the prototype may require a long time (building the prototype while the design is still evolving will likely mean that the prototype is obsolete by the time it is ready).

Prototyping is usually employed when reliability of the final system is of high importance, as the results of analysis of prototypes is proven to provide a good understanding of the system. A prototype proves to be a convenient tool to study the interaction of complex time-dependent factors of a system (a simple example would be behavior of an inductive–capacitative network). Simulation studies of such analog systems has proven to be extremely complex.

Verification of prototypes usually involves subjecting the prototypes to a studied sample of the stimuli the actual system would experience and observing the behavior of the prototype. The range of inputs to a system is usually large, and in many cases, it is not feasible to exhaustively test a prototype. Hence, only a small subset of the inputs are used to test the model. Therefore, care must be taken to select the sample stimuli. The instruments used to measure some of the parameters of the system could also introduce errors. Care should be taken to ensure that the final output of the system is not dramatically affected.

Care must be taken while prototyping because some of the behaviors of the prototype may be different from those of the actual system. Scaling issues significantly deviate the behavior of the final system from that of the prototype. Some of the transient behaviors of the system may be absent in the prototype but present in the final system, and vice versa. This could dramatically affect the behavior of the final system compared to that of the prototype. The working of the system may also deviate from normal if the environment of the final system changes. Hence, prototypes are not only rigorously tested in different environments but are often subjected to failure tests that determine the failure point of a system by stressing the system until failure occurs.

Prototyping is prevalently used to verify and analyze newer technologies in microprocessor fabrication, communication media, and areas that are less understood.

Constraint Models

Constraint modeling is one of the well-understood and developed methods of modeling. In constraint modeling, the constraints or boundaries of the system are defined and the analysis of the system are performed within these boundaries. These models are most useful for representing systems that can be modeled using mathematical equations and are most applicable to simulation, as they involve time as an independent variable.

Linear programming is commonly used to solve such problems. A linear programming problem is a mathematical program in which the objective function is linear in the unknowns and the constraints consist of linear equalities and linear inequalities (3). The goal is usually to determine optimal (usually a minimum or a maximum value) value(s) for the objective function. Linear programming is often used to determine trade-offs through *what-if* analysis.

A good example of such a model would be determining the *grade of service* of a telephone network (4). The grade of service of a telephone network is defined as the probability that a telephone system can establish a called-for interconnection. In a community of N subscribers, it is extremely unlikely that all N will use the phone system at the same time. Also, although the usage of a telephone system is not deterministic, it is still predictable. Hence, a set of linear inequalities are formulated involving all the parameters of the system and the objective is usually to minimize the setup cost of the system.

Simulation proves to be a strong tool for verification and analysis of such models. The model (usually in the form of equations) is implemented on a computer using an appropriate language or package. A set of observed data is fed and the results are cross-verified with the observed set of results. Once the model has been verified, the metrics of the system can be further analyzed with a new set of data.

Computers are valuable tools for performing *what-if* analysis on such models. In such an analysis, certain parameters of the system are fixed and the variation of the objective with change in other parameters is studied. Computers are also used to interpolate and produce graphical representation of the results.

The major drawback of this modeling strategy is in formulating the set of equations representing the system. Abstracting the system into a set of simultaneous equations can prove to be a tedious task. Determining the constants in the set of equations may involve performing tests. Using empirical constants may introduce errors into the model. However, the ease, reliability, and accuracy of the results obtained from the analysis of the model offset the modeling effort.

Functional Modeling

In this approach, the system under consideration is modeled as a black box with a set of inputs and outputs. The modeler is concerned only with its working and not with the nitty gritty details of its internals. The catch phrase here is, "Given this input, what is the output of the system?"

The main advantage of this methodology is its simplicity and its ability to combine smaller models to obtain a model of a larger system. Functional models are not appropriate when the objects are tightly interconnected in a nondirectional way, as with analog electrical networks. Digital logic networks are not a problem because directionality is built into the design; integrated circuits and other chip-based devices update their output,

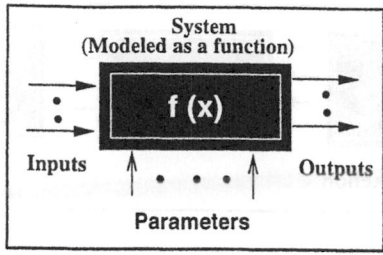

FIGURE 2 Functional modeling.

given the current input signal when a clock signal triggers the device. The main key words suggesting functional model use are *distinct components* and *directionality*.

Functional modeling can be further classified into two approaches: *function-based approach* and *variable-based approach*.

Function-Based Approach

Function-based modeling relies on functional elements as the building blocks upon which a model is constructed. Functions, along with inputs and outputs, are often depicted in a "block" form, where each block basically represents the most atomic (depending on the level of abstraction required) subsystem. Such functions are often called *transfer functions*. The system is represented by connecting a number of such blocks together, usually with arrows indicating the direction of data flow. An example of such a system at different levels of abstraction is shown in Figures 3 and 4.

Function-based models may optionally include a state along with the function. The state can be visualized as an internal parameter whose values are changed by the function depending on the inputs.

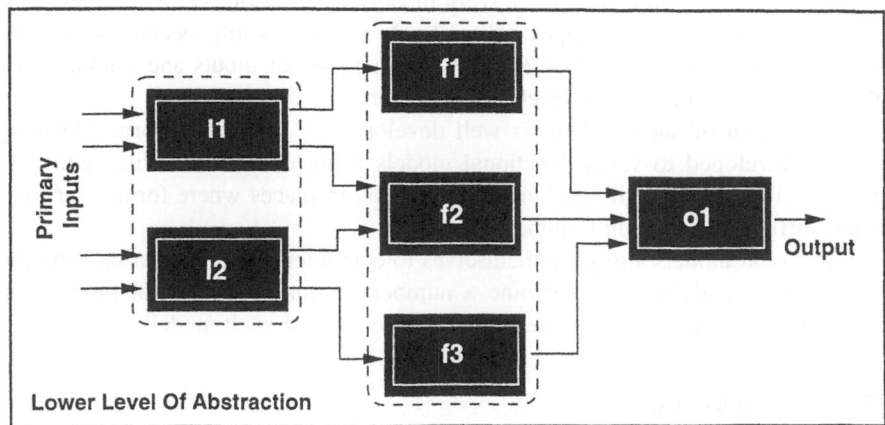

FIGURE 3 A function-based model.

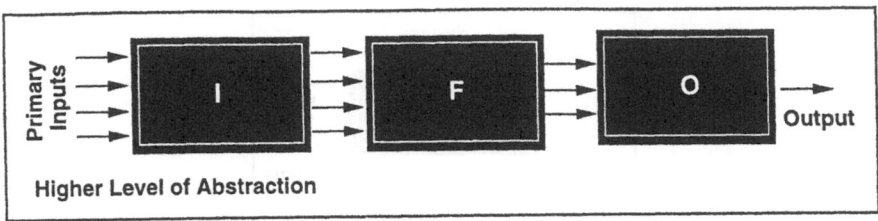

FIGURE 4   A function-based model.

Variable-Based Approach

Functional modeling can also focus on the variables that are affected by the functions rather than the functions themselves. In this modeling approach, the variables serve as the focal points of the modeling. The functional aspect is deemphasized to the point that a particular functional structure is often presupposed. For instance, a well-known structure such as a linear system is assumed and the modeler specifies only the variable dependencies and parameters.

Functional modeling is widely used in modeling computer and communication systems because it insulates the designer from the intricate details of the hardware needed to implement them. The designer is given the functionality of the various components available to him (usually in the form of input–output pairs), which he puts together to build and analyze larger systems. Functional modeling techniques are extremely attractive because they are easy to translate to computer-usable form. Introducing timing information into a functional model is usually simple and can be used to model circuits (digital in particular) effectively. The output of such models is usually a time-dependent graph.

Functional modeling enables a number of views of the system to coexist, but it wraps appropriate subsystems to form a more abstract and larger system. When a more abstract view of the system is needed, the predefined set of subsystems are combined together into a larger subsystem with the same set of inputs and outputs. This process is often referred to as *folding*. This effectively models the behavior of the interacting subsystems. This process can be repeated iteratively and the whole system can be represented as a single functional block (with the primary set of inputs and outputs), which would then serve as the highest level of abstraction.

Verification of such systems is well developed. A number of formal techniques have been developed to verify functional models using computers, which adds to the ease of developing and verifying functional models. In places where formal verification becomes difficult, simulation becomes effective.

Functional models also yield themselves to computer-based simulation. Computers have been effectively used to combine a number of smaller functional models into a larger model and simulation has been employed to analyze such models.

Declarative Modeling

In this approach, the system is modeled by a series of assertions on the inputs, outputs, or state changes. Declarative modeling is good for modeling problem domains that decompose into discrete steps or phases. This modeling strategy is not the best when the system is seen as a collection of objects or when state changes are continuous in nature.

The simplest forms of declarative models are where we specify points in a multidimensional state space with transitions between point pairs. Although this provides a very simple method of modeling, there remains the deficiency of having to denote explicitly every state-space element and its associated transitions to other elements. A classic way around this difficulty is to allow a mapping of patterns rather than a mapping of point elements. In other words, the model becomes more abstract as the size of the patterns used becomes larger.

The two approaches commonly employed in declarative modeling are *state-based* and *event-based* approaches.

State-Based Approaches

A *state* of a system describes a "snapshot" of the system at a specific point in time. In practice, the state usually consists of variables and constants of a system at a given point of time. More formally, the state of a system summarizes the information concerning past inputs that is needed to determine the behavior of the system on subsequent inputs (5). A state may stay in effect for some interval of time, or state-to-state changes may be instantaneous. In a state-based approach, the system is modeled as a set of state changes. The changes in state are called *transitions*. State transitions occur in response to inputs, which are often called *events*. Such models are also termed *finite automatons*. Traditionally, a finite automaton consists of a finite set of states and a set of transitions from state to state that occur on input symbols chosen from an alphabet set σ. Such models are represented using simple directed graphs, with the vertices of the graph representing the states and directed arcs (with optional labels to indicate when the transitions occur) to different vertices representing transitions, an example of which is shown in Figure 5. Such directed graphs are usually given specific names, depending on context such as *transition diagrams*, *PERT charts*, and *flow diagrams*.

The finite automatons are classified into two broad categories:

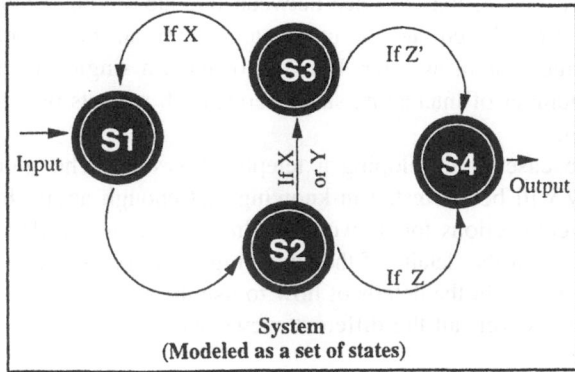

FIGURE 5 State-based model.

- **Deterministic automata:** Finite automata that have unique transitions from one state to the next for an input are termed as deterministic automata (6). As the name suggests, the behavior of the model is deterministic; that is, the system produces the same set of outputs for a given set of inputs and parameters. Most of the declarative models fall under this category. They are simple to model and understand. They are commonly used to model digital circuits.
- **Nondeterministic automata:** Finite automata that have nonunique transitions from one state to the next for an input are termed nondeterministic automata. The behavior of the model is not deterministic; that is, the system may not produce the same set of outputs for a given set of inputs and parameters. These models are useful to model actions that are not controllable in systems.

State-based approaches are predominantly used to model control systems, network protocols, and so forth. Verification of such models is well established. Automated theorem provers have been developed to verify such models (7).

Event-Based Approach

In an event-based approach, the emphasis is more on the events rather than on the states. Event-based models are often used to represent time-triggered systems. In simple terms, because events are just what happens between states, the finite automaton can be exploited to represent such models. Here, the vertices are used to represent the occurrence of events in the system and the transitions indicate the sequence in which various events occur in the system.

Levels of Abstraction

Depending on the type of analysis and verification needed, different models are developed with different levels of abstraction or detail. Usually different views of a system are developed to suit the needs of the various individuals involved in the system. Most of the medium and large-scale systems are scaled down to smaller, well defined subsystems interacting between each other. Each of these subsystems usually needs a specialized set of people working on it. In such a scenario, each of the small groups will be interested in knowing just enough about the other subsystems with which it interacts and not the intricate details. Each subsystem may have its own modeling strategy and the interacting subsystems are modeled at a much higher level of abstraction with respect to the subsystem in concern. Of course, the interface between the subsystems should be maintained so that they can be combined and the complete system can be modeled, verified, and analyzed. Hence, the system as a whole may not have a single modeling strategy but may consist of a number of interacting subsystems, each with its own modeling strategy and levels of detail.

Consider the case of developing a telephone system. The group designing the switching circuitry will be interested in knowing just enough about the phones, the cables, and satellite connections for its working. In turn, the group designing the phones will not be interested in the details of the switching circuitry. Similarly, the users of the system will be interested in the details of how to use the system but not the exact details of how it works. However, all the different views should fit together to yield the final system as a whole.

Sometimes, the same functionality and the same system is represented at different levels of detail, often referred to as *granularity*. This is often done when the system is modeled as layers, one layer working on top of another. Consider the example of developing a microprocessor. The fabrication group looks at the microprocessor in terms of the transistors and the functions involved. The routing and placement group looks at the microprocessor at the gate level. The architecture designers have a higher-level perspective in terms of subcomponents. Functional and declarative models inherently provide this feature.

Categories of Models

Models can be placed into some fundamental categories depending on their design strategies and methodologies used to verify and simulate them. Perhaps the most basic categorization relates to the *time base* on which model events occur (8). A model is a *continuous-time* model if time is specified to flow continuously—the model clock advances smoothly in real numbers toward ever-increasing values. A model is a *discrete-time* model if, in contrast, time flows in jumps—the model clock advances periodically, jumping from one integer to the next (the integer represents multiples of some specified time unit).

A second category relates to the range sets of a model's descriptive variables. The model is a *discrete-state* model if its variables assume a discrete set of values; it is *continuous state* if their ranges can be represented by the real numbers (or intervals thereof) and it is *mixed-state* if both kinds of variables are present.

Continuous-time models can be further divided into *discrete event* and *differential equation* classes. A differential equation specified model is a continuous time–continuous state model in which state changes are continuous. In a discrete-event model, even though time flows continuously, state changes can only occur in discontinuous jumps. A jump can be thought of as triggered by an event and (because time is continuous) these events can occur arbitrarily separated from each other. No more than a finite number can occur in a finite time interval.

A third category incorporates random variables in the model description. In a *deter-*

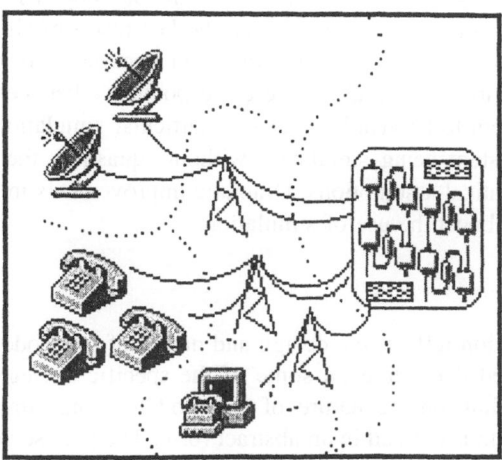

FIGURE 6   Levels of abstraction.

ministic model, no such random variables appear. A. *probabilistic* or *stochastic* model contains at least one such variable.

A fourth way of categorizing the models relates to the manner in which the model considers the real system to interact with its environment. If the real system is assumed by the model to be cut off from all influences of its environment, the model is said to be *autonomous*. A *nonautonomous* model, then, allows for influence of the environment.

A fifth category relates to whether the rules of interaction of a model explicitly depend on time. A model is *time invariant* if the rules of interaction are stated entirely in terms of the values that the descriptive variables can assume. On the other hand, in a *time-varying* model, time may enter explicitly as an argument of the rules of interaction, which may thus appear to be different at different times.

A sixth category of models relates to whether their responses are or are not influenced by past history. Actually, time variance and memory are related concepts. A time-varying model can be expressed without time dependence by incorporating time as a descriptive variable. Models may also be classified depending on the level of abstraction. *Behavioral models* just define the inputs and outputs of a system. The model as such is a "black box." *Structural models* define the structure of the model and illustrate how the output is obtained from the inputs.

COMPUTER SIMULATION

What Is Computer Simulation?

Simulation is the imitative representation of the functioning of one system or process by means of the functioning of another. Computer-based simulation or, in short, computer simulation is a discipline of implementing a model on a digital computer and verifying and analyzing it. In other words, "an experiment is the process of extracting data from a system by exerting it through its inputs" and "a simulation is an experiment performed on a model" (9). Simulation embodies the principle of "learning by doing." It is a highly interdisciplinary field and is widely used.

As a technique, it is attractive for two reasons. First, it is possible to simulate many complicated systems. "When all else fails" is a suitable slogan for many such simulations. However, it is surprising just how often the last resort of simulation is necessary. Second, the technique itself is straightforward and does not rely on a great degree of mathematical abstraction but can allow the correspondence between a simulation model and some "real" system to be visible; that is, a particular simulation can be very closely tailored to fit the system being simulated, without squashing the system into any ill-fitting set of mathematical assumptions. Dramatic improvements in hardware technology has served to further boost the use of simulation.

Classifications

The nature of simulation reflects the design and nature of the models simulated. Simulators are also classified depending on some of the specific strategies used. Simulations are classified depending on the nature of the models being simulated. In *behavioral* simulations, the system is defined in an abstract form. The precise details and the constituents of the system are not specified in detail. *Structural* simulations, on the other hand, define precisely how the outputs are obtained from the inputs. All necessary intermediate steps are specified. For example, consider a simple full-adder. A full-adder is a device whose inputs are two binary digits and its outputs, the sum and carry bits, are the result of adding the two binary digits together. A simple full-adder circuit in a behavioral simulation would be modeled as a "black box" and would be implemented by using standard arithmetic operations provided by the simulation language (the language that is supported or provided by the simulator). In a structural simulation, the full-adder circuit would be implemented in the form of logic gates (exclusive-or gate for sum and and gate for carry).

Behavioral simulations are very useful for studying the system from a higher perspective. They are useful for modeling entities with which the system needs to interact, but the details are not needed. Functional models yield themselves to behavioral simulations. Structural simulations are useful to study the working and interaction of the various components in the system. Usually, the development and study of structural simulations are complex and, hence, smaller modules are built for structural simulations. They are abstracted to behavioral simulation components when they are used as subsystems to build larger systems to reduce the overall complexity of the simulation. Behavioral simulations usually proceed faster in real time (the actual wall clock time) than structural simulations and, in general, behavioral models are easier to develop as compared to structural models.

Simulations are classified into *continuous-time simulations*, *discrete-time simulations*, and *mixed-time simulations*, depending on how the state of the system changes over time. In continuous-time simulations, the system changes state is a smooth continuous pattern with respect to time. The simulation time* increases smoothly throughout the real numbers. When the system changes state in discrete steps (i.e., the change is not continuous and smooth but occurs abruptly at specific points in simulation time), they are termed discrete-time simulations. A sample trajectory behaviors of a continuous-time and a discrete-time simulation are shown in Figure 7. Mixed-mode simulations combine the two techniques as and when necessary.

Depending on whether the simulation is run as one single process or program on a single computer, a single processor to be more precise, or as multiple processes on multiple processors, they are classified into *sequential simulations* and *parallel simulations*. Sequential simulators perform the operations of the model in a serial manner (one after another) in real time. Parallel simulations proceed simultaneously on different processors (they proceed serially on one processor); that is, the different operations of the model (if so modeled) proceed simultaneously.

Simulations are classified into *compiled simulations* and *interpreted simulations*. In compiled simulations, a compiled version of the model is run and simulation results are obtained. Sometimes the simulation engine interprets the model and performs the necessary operations. Such simulations are termed interpreted simulations.

Parallel Simulation

Parallel simulation involves breaking a given simulation into two or more components and simulating each component as independent processes (not necessarily on independent processors) and synchronizing the distributed components in the system. Advancements

---

*It is important to understand and distinguish between real time and simulation time, which is best illustrated by an example. We might simulate an logic circuit and the simulation time may range from 0 to 10ns. The real or actual time needed to simulate the model can be tens of seconds.

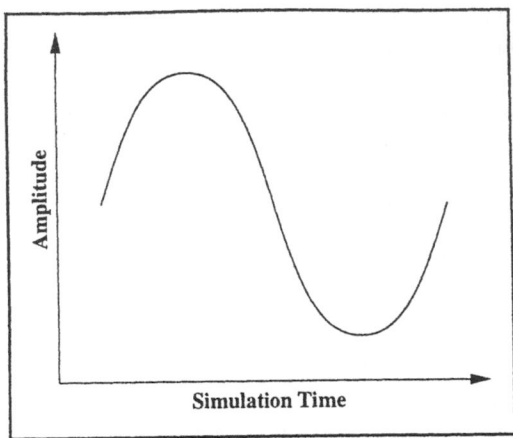

Output Of Continuous Time Simulation

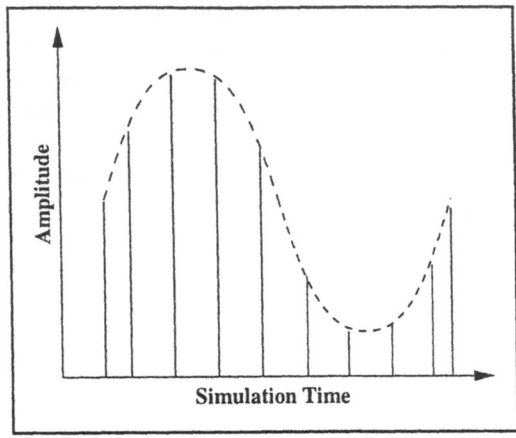

Output Of Discrete Time Simulation

FIGURE 7   Outputs from continuous- and discrete-time simulations.

in microprocessor and communication technology have made parallel simulation an effective solution. With ever-increasing complexity of simulations, parallel simulation has
attained tremendous importance.

Synchronization is an important activity in parallel simulations. Synchronization
involves sequencing the activities of the various components in a simulation so that the
"causality" of the various events in the system are maintained. Sequencing of activities
in a simulation is achieved using an artificial clock that generates simulation time. All
activities in the system are sequenced based on this simulation time. For example, if
some activity *A* has to occur before activity *B*, then *A* should be performed before *B*, in
simulation time.

Parallel simulations can be classified depending on the type of synchronization
used. *Synchronous* parallel simulations proceed in a "lock-step" fashion. In such simulations, each of the components' progress is fixed-time increments in lock-step with each
other. In synchronous simulations, "causality" is never broken. In *asynchronous* parallel
simulations, the different components are allowed to proceed asynchronously to each
other. In such simulations, "causality," if broken, is restored using a number of synchronization techniques.

Discrete-Event Simulation

The class of simulation where changes in the state of various components in the system
(and hence the overall system) are brought about by exchanging events at discrete-time
steps are termed *discrete-event simulations*. As the term suggests, the inputs and outputs
to and from the various components and subcomponents of the model are in the form of
events. An "event" is a message that is exchanged between the various components t hat
contains, apart from user data, a time stamp, indicating when this event is to be processed
by the recipient. The time stamp is in simulation time units. The term "virtual time,"
synonymous to simulation time, is commonly used. Virtual time is used to synchronize
the various components of the simulation. For example, if an event A should be pro-

cessed before B, then event A has a lower virtual time stamp compared to that of event B. In other words, event B is said to be causally dependent on event A. Discrete-event simulation may be sequential or parallel.

Synchronization between different components, or processes, in the system is maintained by enforcing the causal ordering between the various events in the system. When discrete-event simulation proceeds in parallel, depending on the strategy used to maintain causal ordering of various events in a simulation, simulations are classified into *conservative simulations* and *optimistic simulations*.

Conservative simulations (10–14) proceed in strict concordance with the time at which events occur in the entire system. Here, causality is never violated; that is, the chronology or ordered occurrence of events in the system is always maintained. Conservative simulations are simple to visualize. For example, if task a has to be done before another task b, then task a will be done before task b. The most widely used conservative algorithm is by Chandy, Misra, and Bryant.

Optimistic simulations (15,16), on the other hand, do not adhere to strict causality and each component of the system may deviate away from the mean path. The causality of the system is maintained by restoring the state when causal constraints are violated. For example, in optimistic simulations, if event a has to be processed before some other event b, event b could occur before event a. When event a is eventually processed, the erroneous processing of event b is realized and that processing is undone. The state of the system is saved, usually every time the state changes, to undo erroneous computation. "Time warp" (16) is a classic example of an optimistic synchronization strategy.

Each of the above methodologies have their own advantages and disadvantages. One proves to be a better strategy than the other in different domains. In spite of the great deal of research that has gone into them, there are still many open questions.

CONCLUDING REMARKS AND FUTURE TRENDS

Although modeling and verification have been well developed, care must be taken to understand the limitations and boundaries of the model. Certain models may be useful only in certain domains. The model developed may be applicable only with a given set of parameters and may fail with others. Scalability is an important issue that must be carefully studied before extrapolating the results of a model. Transient phenomena absent in the model but present in the final system and vice versa could dramatically affect the results of analysis.

With the advancement in semiconductor technology, computers and networking systems have seen tremendous advances in recent times. Along with hardware, more powerful software techniques have also evolved for modeling, verification analysis, and simulation. Extensive studies are being done to completely automate the process of computer verification using formal methods. Parallel simulation is reaching newer horizons. Discrete-event simulation has helped in breaking barriers, especially in the field of hardware simulation. Parallel simulation, with all its open questions, holds great promises for the future.

GLOSSARY

Analysis: The separation of a whole into constituents with a view to its examination and interpretation

Asynchronous: Not simultaneous; not concurrent in time

Automaton: One that behaves in an automatic or mechanical fashion

Causality: The relationship between causes and effects

Compiler: A program that decodes instructions written in a higher-order language and produces a machine language program

Granularity: The quality of being composed of relatively large particles

Model: A tentative description of a theory or system that accounts for all of its known properties

Modeling: Process of translating a real system into a model

Simulate: To experiment on a model

Synchronization: The relation that exists when things occur at the same time

Synchronous: Happening at the same time; simultaneous

REFERENCES

1. P. A. Fishwick, *Simulation Model Design and Execution: Building Digital Worlds*, Prentice-Hall, Englewood Cliffs, NJ, 1995.
2. B. P. Zeigler, *Multifacetted Modelling and Discrete Event Simulation*, Academic Press, London, 1984.
3. D. G. Luenberger, *Linear and Nonlinear Programming*, Addison-Wesley, Reading, MA, 1989.
4. D. L. S. H. Taub, *Principles of Communication Systems*, McGraw-Hill, New York, 1986.
5. J. E. Hopcroft, *Introduction to Automata Theory, Languages and Computation*, Addison-Wesley, Reading, MA, 1979.
6. P. Linz, *Introduction to Formal Languages and Automata*, D.C. Heath and Company, Lexington, KY, 1990.
7. C. Hoare, *Communicating Sequential Processes*, Prentice-Hall International, Herfordshire, U.K., 1985.
8. B. P. Zeigler, *Theory of Modelling and Simulation*, John Wiley & Sons, New York, 1976.
9. F. E. Cellier, *Continuous System Modeling*, Springer-Verlag, New York, 1991.
10. R. E. Bryant, "Simulation on a Distributed System," in *Proc. of the 16th Design Automation Conference*, 1979, pp. 544–552.
11. K. M. Chandy and J. Misra, "Distributed Simulation: A Case Study in Design and Verification of Distributed Programs," *IEEE Trans. Software Eng.*, 5, 5 (September 1979).
12. K. M. Chandy and J. Misra, "Asynchronous Distributed Simulation via a Sequence of Parallel Computations," *Commun. ACM*, 24(11), 198–206 (1981).
13. Y.-B. Lin, E. D. Lazowski, and J.-L. Baer, "Conservative Parallel Simulation for Systems with no Lookahead Prediction," in *Distributed Simulation*, Society for Computer Simulation, 1990, pp. 144–149.
14. J. Misra, "Distributed Discrete-Event Simulation," *Comput. Surveys*, 18, 1, 39–65 (1986).
15. R. Fujimoto, "Parallel Discrete Event Simulation," *Commun. ACM*, 33(10), 30–53 (1990).
16. D. Jefferson, "Virtual Time," *ACM Trans. Program. Lang. Syst.*, 7(3), 405–425 (1985).

PHILIP A. WILSEY

MODELS OF COMPUTATION

INTRODUCTION

What is a model of computation? When we use the term *computation*, we refer to sequence of "states," which starts with some initial state and either ends with some final state or does not end. The notion of computation implies a *computer* (human or machine). The kind of computer is reflected in the states. For example, if the computer is human, the states might be mental states; if an electronic calculator, the states might be intermediate results in an arithmetic calculation; and if a digital computer, the states might be snapshots of the store. A model of computation should formalize this notion of computation (at some level of abstraction). For the rest of this article, we will focus on computations where the computer is a digital computer.

Why do we need models of computation? The act of computation involves the computer following a script. The script can be described at various levels of abstraction (e.g., high-level language program, assembler program, or machine code). A compiler translates programs at one level to programs at a lower level and is necessary because the computer can only execute scripts that are written in machine code. If we have the appropriate models of computation, we can *verify* that the original and translated programs define the same computation. Programming is the end stage of the software engineering process; models of computation also allow the program to be verified against specifications produced at an earlier stage of the process. This talk of verification might seem to be remote from most programmers' experience; however, as computers become more pervasive, the need for verification is becoming more widespread (particularly in safety-critical or high-availability settings).

How do we define a model of computation? We will take a programming-language-based approach. We identify the computations that a program defines from the *semantics* of the program. We will look at three main ways of defining the semantics of a programming language:

1. **Operational Semantics:** This is the least abstract approach. We will base our presentation on Plotkin's *Structural Operational Semantics* (1–3). A computation is represented by a derivation sequence: Each element of the sequence is a *configuration* that might include some "code" and a snapshot of the store.
2. **Denotational Semantics:** This is the most abstract approach that we will present. Computations are represented by their end points (nontermination is treated in a special way). The focus is on what is computed (not how it is computed) (1–5).
3. **Axiomatic Semantics:** The states are abstracted by properties (predicates). The semantics defines how the properties of the state change as the result of the execution of statement (1,2).

Operational semantics provide a yardstick against which implementations can be measured. Denotational semantics form a good basis for reasoning about properties of programs. Axiomatic semantics may be used for program verification. The next three sections consider these different approaches in detail. The final section contains some concluding remarks. Before embarking on our tour, we introduce two tiny programming languages which will be used to illustrate the approaches.

Two Small Programming Languages

The language W is a very simple imperative language; for statements, it just has assignments, a skip, sequences of statements, conditionals, and while loops. The syntax of W is shown in Figure 1.

An example program is

```
y := 1;
while not (n = 0) do
  y := y * x;
  n := n - 1;
```

which, given positive n, computes the nth power of the value of x, leaving the result in y.

The language F is a functional programming language. We assume that parameters are passed by value. The syntax is shown in Figure 2. The following example introduces a power function (equivalent to the W example) and uses it to compute the square of 3.

```
let power(x,n) = if n = 0 then 1 else x * power(x,n-1)
in power(3,2)
```

OPERATIONAL SEMANTICS

The Operational Semantics of W

The operational semantics of W is shown in Figure 3. The figure defines a relation $\Rightarrow$ between *configurations*. Configurations are either a pair consisting of a statement and a state, or a state. The latter are terminal; if the sequence reaches a terminal configuration,

$$a \in AExp$$
$$x \in Var$$
$$n \in Num$$
$$a \quad ::= \quad x \mid n \mid a_1{+}a_2 \mid a_1{-}a_2 \mid a_1{*}a_2$$

$$b \in BExp$$
$$b \quad ::= \quad a_1{=}a_2 \mid \texttt{not } b \mid b_1 \ \& \ b_2$$

$$S \in Stmt$$
$$S \quad ::= \quad x := a \mid \texttt{skip} \mid S_1; S_2 \mid$$
$$\qquad \texttt{if } b \texttt{ then } S_1 \texttt{ else } S_2 \mid$$
$$\qquad \texttt{while } b \texttt{ do } S$$

FIGURE 1   The syntax of W.

$$x \in Var$$
$$n \in Num$$
$$e \in Exp$$

$$
\begin{aligned}
e \quad ::= \quad & x \mid \\
& n \mid e_1 + e_2 \mid e_1 - e_2 \mid e_1 * e_2 \mid \\
& e_1 = e_2 \mid \\
& \texttt{if } e \texttt{ then } e_1 \texttt{ else } e_2 \mid \\
& e(e_1, \ldots, e_n) \\
& \texttt{let } f(x_1, \ldots, x_n) = e_1 \texttt{ in } e_2
\end{aligned}
$$

FIGURE 2   The syntax of F.

the sequence stops: The state is the answer. A state is just a function which maps variables to values: $\sigma \in$ State $= Var \rightarrow Z$. The relation is defined *inductively* by axioms, such as the (assign) axiom, and rules, such as (seq)$_1$. In the latter case, the premise of the rule (above the horizontal line) must be true in order for the conclusion (below the line) to be true.

We assume the existence of functions:

$$\mathcal{A}: AExp \rightarrow State \rightarrow Z$$

and

$$\mathcal{B}: BExp \rightarrow State \rightarrow T$$

which evaluate arithmetic and boolean expressions, respectively; Z is the set of integers and T is the truth values (true and false).

(assign)	$\langle x := a, \sigma \rangle \Rightarrow \sigma[x \mapsto \mathcal{A}[\![a]\!]\sigma]$
(skip)	$\langle \texttt{skip}, \sigma \rangle \Rightarrow \sigma$
(seq$_1$)	$\dfrac{\langle S_1, \sigma \rangle \Rightarrow \langle S_1', \sigma' \rangle}{\langle S_1; S_2, \sigma \rangle \Rightarrow \langle S_1'; S_2, \sigma' \rangle}$
(seq$_2$)	$\dfrac{\langle S_1, \sigma \rangle \Rightarrow \sigma'}{\langle S_1; S_2, \sigma \rangle \Rightarrow \langle S_2, \sigma' \rangle}$
(if$_{\text{true}}$)	$\langle \texttt{if } b \texttt{ then } S_1 \texttt{ else } S_2, \sigma \rangle \Rightarrow \langle S_1, \sigma \rangle \qquad$ if $\mathcal{B}[\![b]\!]\sigma = \text{true}$
(if$_{\text{false}}$)	$\langle \texttt{if } b \texttt{ then } S_1 \texttt{ else } S_2, \sigma \rangle \Rightarrow \langle S_2, \sigma \rangle \qquad$ if $\mathcal{B}[\![b]\!]\sigma = \text{false}$
(while$_{\text{true}}$)	$\langle \texttt{while } b \texttt{ do } S, \sigma \rangle \Rightarrow \langle S; \texttt{while } b \texttt{ do } S, \sigma \rangle \quad$ if $\mathcal{B}[\![b]\!]\sigma = \text{true}$
(while$_{\text{false}}$)	$\langle \texttt{while } b \texttt{ do } S, \sigma \rangle \Rightarrow \sigma \qquad$ if $\mathcal{B}[\![b]\!]\sigma = \text{false}$

FIGURE 3   The operational semantics of W.

We illustrate the use of the semantics to evaluate the power program starting with a state, σ, that has x set to 3 and n set to 2:

$\langle y := 1;$ while not(n=0) do (y := y * x; n := n-1;),$\sigma \rangle \Rightarrow$
$\langle$while not(n=0) do (y := y * x; n := n-1), $\sigma[y \mapsto 1]\rangle \Rightarrow$
$\langle y := y * x; n := n-1;$ while not(n=0) do (y := y * x; n := n-1),
    $\sigma[y \mapsto 1]\rangle \Rightarrow$
$\langle n := n-1;$ while not(n=0) do (y := y * x; n := n-1;), $\sigma[y \mapsto 3]\rangle \Rightarrow$
$\langle$while not(n=0) do (y := y * x; n := n-1;), $\sigma[y \mapsto 3, n \mapsto 1]\rangle \Rightarrow$
$\langle y := y * x; n := n-1;$ while not(n=0) do (y := y * x; n := n-1;),
    $\sigma[y \mapsto 3, n \mapsto 1]\rangle \Rightarrow$
$\langle n := n-1;$ while not(n=0) do (y := y * x; n := n-1;),
    $\sigma[y \mapsto 9, n \mapsto 1]\rangle \Rightarrow$
$\langle$while not(n=0) do (y := y * x; n := n-1;), $\sigma[y \mapsto 9, n \mapsto 0]\rangle \Rightarrow$
    $\sigma[y \mapsto 9, n \mapsto 0]\rangle$

The Operational Semantics of F

The operational semantics of F is shown in Figure 4. Configurations are just expressions, with values being terminal. The semantics is defined as a relation $\rightarrow$ between configurations. The value of an expression is defined relative to an *environment* which defines the current values of variables appearing in the expression:

$\rho \in Env = Var \rightarrow Val$,
$v \in Val = Z + T + Clos$,

$cl \in Clos$
$cl ::= \text{close}(x_1, \ldots, x_n)e \text{ in } \rho$

The set *Clos* is the set of *closures*; closures are the values of functions; they are denoted by the function text and the environment that was extent at the point that the function was defined. The environment is shown to the left of the $\vdash$ symbol in the rules of Figure 4.

The semantics also uses (intermediate) expressions of the form

bind ρ in e

which create appropriate environments for the evaluation of function bodies.

The rules app_1, and app_2 enforce call-by-value parameter passing. We have assumed the existence of semantic operators δ_+, δ_-, δ_* and $\delta_=$ which interpret the basic operators of the language.

We close by illustrating the derivation sequence for the power program. For presentation purposes, at the two steps marked by (*), we have dropped the bind because the expression no longer has any free variables in it. We use γ to abbreviate

close(power,x,n)if n=0 then 1 else x*power(x,n-1) in [ ]

The derivation is much longer than the corresponding derivation for W; this is partly because the semantics of F includes the evaluation of arithmetic and boolean expressions.

(var) $\quad \rho \vdash x \;\rightarrow\; \rho(x)$

(op$_1$) $\quad \dfrac{\rho \vdash e_1 \;\rightarrow\; e_1'}{\rho \vdash e_1 \text{ op } e_2 \;\rightarrow\; e_1' \text{ op } e_2}$

(op$_2$) $\quad \dfrac{\rho \vdash e_2 \;\rightarrow\; e_2'}{\rho \vdash v_1 \text{ op } e_2 \;\rightarrow\; v_1 \text{ op } e_2'}$

(op) $\quad \rho \vdash v_1 \text{ op } v_2 \;\rightarrow\; \delta_{op}(v_1, v_2)$

(if$_1$) $\quad \dfrac{\rho \vdash e \;\rightarrow\; e'}{\rho \vdash \text{ if } e \text{ then } e_1 \text{ else } e_2 \;\rightarrow\; \text{ if } e' \text{ then } e_1 \text{ else } e_2}$

(if$_2$) $\quad \rho \vdash \text{ if true then } e_1 \text{ else } e_2 \;\rightarrow\; e_1$

(if$_3$) $\quad \rho \vdash \text{ if false then } e_1 \text{ else } e_2 \;\rightarrow\; e_2$

(app$_1$) $\quad \dfrac{\rho \vdash e \;\rightarrow\; e'}{\rho \vdash e(e_1,\ldots,e_n) \;\rightarrow\; e'(e_1,\ldots,e_n)}$

(app$_2$) $\quad \dfrac{\rho \vdash e_i \;\rightarrow\; v_i}{\rho \vdash v(v_1,\ldots,v_{i-1},e_i,\ldots,e_n) \;\rightarrow\; v(v_1,\ldots,v_{i-1},v_i,\ldots,e_n)}$
$$1 \leq i \leq n$$

(app$_3$) $\quad \rho \vdash (\text{close}(f,x_1,\ldots,x_n)e \text{ in } \rho')(v_1,\ldots,v_n) \;\rightarrow\;$
$\qquad\qquad \text{bind } \rho'[f \mapsto (\text{close}(f,x_1,\ldots,x_n)e \text{ in } \rho')][x_i \mapsto v_i \mid_{i=1}^{n}]$
$\qquad\qquad \text{in } e$

(let) $\quad \rho \vdash \text{let } f(x_1,\ldots,x_n) = e_1 \text{ in } e_2 \;\rightarrow\;$
$\qquad\qquad \text{bind } [f \mapsto (close(f,x_1,\ldots,x_n)e_1 \text{ in } \rho)] \text{ in } e_2$

(bind$_1$) $\quad \dfrac{\rho[\rho'] \vdash e \;\rightarrow\; e'}{\rho \vdash (\text{bind } \rho' \text{ in } e) \;\rightarrow\; (\text{bind } \rho' \text{ in } e')}$

(bind$_2$) $\quad \rho \vdash (\text{bind } \rho' \text{ in } v) \;\rightarrow\; v$

FIGURE 4   The operational semantics of F.

```
⊢ let power(x,n) = if n=0 then 1 else x*power(x,n-1) in
power(3,2) →
bind [power ↦ γ] in power(3,2)  →
γ(3,2)  →
bind [power ↦ γ, x ↦ 3, n ↦ 2] in
if n=0 then 1 else x*power(x,n-1)  →
bind [power ↦ γ, x ↦ 3, n ↦ 2] in
if 2=0 then 1 else x*power(x,n-1)  →
bind [power ↦ γ, x ↦ 3, n ↦ 2] in
if false then 1 else x*power(x,n-1)  →
```

```
bind [power ↦ γ, x ↦ 3, n ↦ 2] in x*power(x,n-1)  →
bind [power ↦ γ, x ↦ 3, n ↦ 2] in 3*power(x,n-1)  →
bind [power ↦ γ, x ↦ 3, n ↦ 2] in 3*γ(x,n-1)  →
bind [power ↦ γ, x ↦ 3, n ↦ 2] in 3*γ(3,n-1)  →
bind [power ↦ γ, x ↦ 3, n ↦ 2] in 3*γ(3,2-1)  →
bind [power ↦ γ, x ↦ 3, n ↦ 2] in 3*γ(3,1)  →
3*(bind [power ↦ γ, x ↦ 3, n ↦ 1] in                              (*)
if n=0 then 1 else x*power(x,n-1))  →
3*(bind [power ↦ γ, x ↦ 3, n ↦ 1] in
if 1=0 then 1 else x*power(x,n-1))  →
3*(bind [power ↦ γ, x ↦ 3, n ↦ 1] in
if false then 1 else x*power(x,n-1))  →
3*(bind [power ↦ γ, x ↦ 3, n ↦ 1] in x*power(x,n-1))  →
3*(bind [power ↦ γ, x ↦ 3, n ↦ 1] in 3*power(x,n-1))  →
3*(bind [power ↦ γ, x ↦ 3, n ↦ 1] in 3*γ(x,n-1))  →
3*(bind [power ↦ γ, x ↦ 3, n ↦ 1] in 3*γ(3,n-1))  →
3*(bind [power ↦ γ, x ↦ 3, n ↦ 1] in 3*γ(3,1-1))  →
3*(bind [power ↦ γ, x ↦ 3, n ↦ 1] in 3*γ(3,0))  →
3*(3*(bind [power ↦ γ, x ↦ 3, n ↦ 0] in                          (*)
if n=0 then 1 else x*power(x,n-1)))  →
3*(3*(bind [power ↦ γ, x ↦ 3, n ↦ 0] in
if 0=0 then 1 else x*power(x,n-1)))  →
3*(3*(bind [power ↦ γ, x ↦ 3, n ↦ 0] in
if true then 1 else x*power(x,n-1)))  →
3*(3*(bind [power ↦ γ, x ↦ 3, n ↦ 0] in 1))  →
3*(3*1)  → 3*3  →  9
```

DENOTATIONAL SEMANTICS

As stated earlier, in denotational semantics, we are interested in *what* the result of the computation is, not how it is computed. The meaning of a piece of program is represented by a function; in the case of W, the semantics of a statement is a function from states to states and in the case of F, the semantics of an expression is a function from environments (giving meanings to the free variables) to values. One problem we have to solve is how to give a meaning to loops in W (or recursively defined functions in F). Consider the following example from F (extended with the not operator and boolean literals):

let f(x) = not f(x) in f(true)

What is the meaning of f? If we model booleans by the set {true, false}, then f must map booleans to booleans and there is no function that satisfies the definition. Thus, our semantics would say nothing about the meaning of the above program—this is unsatisfactory. To overcome this, we work with domains rather than sets.

A Brief Detour into Domain Theory

$(D, \sqsubseteq)$ is a *partially ordered set* if and only if

- D is a set and $\sqsubseteq$ is a binary relation on D.
- *Reflexivity:* $\forall d \in D.d \sqsubseteq d$.

- *Antisymmetry:* $\forall d_1, d_2 \in D.d_1 \sqsubseteq d_2 \; \& \; d_2 \sqsubseteq d_1 \Rightarrow d_1 = d_2$
- *Transitivity:* $\forall d_1, d_2, d_3 \in D.d_1 \sqsubseteq d_2 \; \& \; d_2 \sqsubseteq d_3 \Rightarrow d_1 \sqsubseteq d_3$.

Given a partial order, $(D, \sqsubseteq)$, and a subset, X, of D, $d \in D$ is an *upper bound* of X if and only if

$$\forall x \in X.x \sqsubseteq d$$

and is the *least upper bound* if and only if

$$\forall d' \in \mathrm{UB}(X).d \sqsubseteq d',$$

where $\mathrm{UB}(X)$ is the set of upper bounds of X. We write $\sqcup X$ to denote the least upper bound of X. A *chain*, X, is a set in which every element is related to every other via the approximation ordering

$$\forall x_1, x_2 \in X.x_1 \sqsubseteq x_2 \text{ or } x_2 \sqsubseteq x_1$$

Finally, $(D, \sqsubseteq)$ is a *complete partial order* (cpo) if and only if every chain in D has a least upper bound. Notice that every cpo $(D, \sqsubseteq)$ has a least element, $\sqcup \emptyset$, which we write as $\bot_D$ and which satisfies

$$\forall d \in D. \bot_D \sqsubseteq d.$$

For the purposes of this section, we will work with *domains* and functions on domains which satisfy the following:

- A *domain* is a complete partial order.
- *Monotonicity:* Every computable function, $f\colon D \to E$, between domains is monotonic:

$$\forall d_1, d_2 \in D.d_1 \sqsubseteq d_2 \Rightarrow f(d_1) \sqsubseteq f(d_2).$$

- *Continuity:* Every computable function, $f\colon D \to E$, between domains is continuous:

$$\forall \text{ chains } X \subseteq D.f(\sqcup X) = \sqcup \{ f(x) \,|\, x \in X \}.$$

The payoff from respecting these requirements is that we have the following:

THEOREM 1. *If $f\colon D \to D$ is a continuous function on a domain D, it has a least fixed point $d \in D$, satisfying:*

1. $f(d) = d$.
2. $\forall e \in D.f(e) = e \Rightarrow d \sqsubseteq e$.

Moreover, d is defined by

$$d = \sqcup f^n(\bot_D),$$

where $f^0(x) = x$ and $f^{n+1}(x) = f(f^n(x))$.

We write $fix(f)$ to represent the least fixed point of f. The theorem guarantees the existence of fixed points and also gives a construction for the least fixed point. Referring back to our example, the standard domain of booleans is $\{\bot, \text{true}, \text{false}\}$. The function f is the fixed point of a higher-order function $\mathbf{F}$.

$$\mathbf{F}(g,x) = \text{not } g(x)$$

and we can compute the least fixed point to be $fix(F)(x) = \bot$. This function does satisfy the equation, since not $\bot = \bot$.

Given some domains, there are some standard ways of constructing new domains which we will require in the following.

1. *Lifting:* Given a set S, the lift of S, which is written $S_\bot$, is $S \cup \bot$ ordered by

    $$x \sqsubseteq y \quad \text{iff } x = \bot \lor x = y.$$

    The standard domain of booleans is the lifting of the set of booleans mentioned earlier.

2. *Product:* Given domains D and E, $D \times E$ is the domain

    $$\{\langle d, e \rangle \mid d \in D \land e \in E\}$$

    ordered by

    $$\langle d_1, e_1 \rangle \sqsubseteq \langle d_2, e_2 \rangle \quad \text{iff } d_1 \sqsubseteq d_2 \land e_1 \sqsubseteq e_2.$$

    The bottom element is $\langle \bot, \bot \rangle$.

3. *Sum:* Given domains D and E, $D + E$ is the domain

    $$\{\langle 0, d \rangle \mid d \in D, d \neq \bot\} \cup \{\langle 1, e \rangle \mid e \in E, e \neq \bot\} \cup \{\bot\}$$

    ordered by

    $$\forall de \in D + E. \bot \sqsubseteq de,$$
    $$\langle 0, d_1 \rangle \sqsubseteq \langle 0, d_2 \rangle \quad \text{iff } d_1 \sqsubseteq d_2,$$
    $$\langle 1, e_1 \rangle \sqsubseteq \langle 1, e_2 \rangle \quad \text{iff } e_1 \sqsubseteq e_2.$$

4. *Functions:* Given domains D and E, $D \to E$ is the domain of continuous functions from D to E. The domain is ordered pointwise:

    $$f \sqsubseteq g \quad \text{iff } \forall d \in D. f(d) \sqsubseteq g(d).$$

The least element is the function that maps everything to $\bot$.

The Denotational Semantics of W

The denotational semantics of W is shown in Figure 5. The figure defines a function

$$S: Stmt \to State \to State,$$

where *State* is the cpo $Var \to Z_\bot$ ordered pointwise:

$$
\begin{aligned}
\mathcal{S}[\![x := a]\!]\sigma &= \sigma[x \mapsto \mathcal{A}[\![a]\!]\sigma] \\
\mathcal{S}[\![\text{skip}]\!]\sigma &= \sigma \\
\mathcal{S}[\![S_1; S_2]\!]\sigma &= (\mathcal{S}[\![S_2]\!] \circ \mathcal{S}[\![S_1]\!])\sigma \\
\mathcal{S}[\![\text{if } b \text{ then } S_1 \text{ else } S_2]\!]\sigma &= \text{cond}(\mathcal{B}[\![b]\!]\sigma, \mathcal{S}[\![S_1]\!]\sigma, \mathcal{S}[\![S_2]\!]\sigma) \\
\mathcal{S}[\![\text{while } b \text{ do } S]\!]\sigma &= (\text{fix } F)\sigma \\
&\text{where} \quad F \, g \, \sigma = \text{cond}(\mathcal{B}[\![b]\!]\sigma, g(\mathcal{S}[\![S]\!]\sigma), \sigma)
\end{aligned}
$$

FIGURE 5   The denotational semantics of W.

$\sigma_1 \sqsubseteq \sigma_2 \quad$ iff $\forall x \in Var.\sigma_1(x) \sqsubseteq \sigma_2(x).$

The bottom element is the state which maps every variable to $\perp$.

The semantics uses two operations, $\circ$ and cond, which are defined as follows:

$\circ: ((State \rightarrow State) \times (State \rightarrow State)) \rightarrow (State \rightarrow State),$

$$(f \circ g)(\sigma) = \begin{cases} \perp & \text{if } g(\sigma) = \perp \\ f(g(\sigma)) & \text{otherwise,} \end{cases}$$

cond: $(T \times State \times State) \rightarrow State,$

cond(true, $\sigma_1, \sigma_2) = \sigma_1,$

cond(false, $\sigma_1, \sigma_2) = \sigma_2.$

Considering the example program, we calculate

$S[[y := 1; \text{while not}(n=0) \text{ do } (y := y * x; n := n-1)]]\sigma \quad =$
$(S[[\text{while not}(n=0) \text{ do } (y := y * x; n := n-1;)]] \circ S[[y := 1]])(\sigma) =$
$S[[\text{while not}(n=0) \text{ do } (y := y * x; n := n-1;)]]\sigma[y \mapsto 1] \quad =$
$(\text{fix } F)\sigma[y \mapsto 1]$

where

$$Fg\sigma = \begin{cases} g(\sigma[y \mapsto \sigma(y) * \sigma(x), n \mapsto \sigma(n) - 1]) & \text{if } \sigma(n) \neq 0 \\ \sigma & \text{otherwise.} \end{cases}$$

We can use the construction in the fixed point theorem to compute the least fixed point of F:

$F^0(\perp)\sigma = \perp,$

$$F^1(\perp)\sigma = \begin{cases} \perp & \text{if } \sigma(n) \neq 0 \\ \sigma & \text{otherwise,} \end{cases}$$

$$F^2(\perp)\sigma = \begin{cases} \perp & \text{if } \sigma(n) \geq 2 \vee \sigma(n) < 0 \\ \sigma[y \mapsto \sigma(y) * \sigma(x), n \mapsto 0] & \text{if } \sigma(n) = 1 \\ \sigma & \text{otherwise,} \end{cases}$$

$$F^3(\perp)\sigma = \begin{cases} \perp & \text{if } \sigma(n) \geq 3 \vee \sigma(n) < 0 \\ \sigma[y \mapsto \sigma(y) * (\sigma(x) * \sigma(x), n \mapsto 0] & \text{if } \sigma(n) = 2 \\ \sigma[y \mapsto \sigma(y) * \sigma(x), n \mapsto 0] & \text{if } \sigma(n) = 1 \\ \sigma & \text{otherwise,} \end{cases}$$

$\vdots$

$$F^m(\perp)\sigma = \begin{cases} \perp & \text{if } \sigma(n) \geq m \vee \sigma(n) < 0 \\ \sigma[y \mapsto \sigma(y) * \sigma(x)^{\sigma(n)}, n \mapsto 0] & \text{otherwise,} \end{cases}$$

from which we get

$$(\text{fix } F)\sigma = \begin{cases} \perp & \text{if } \sigma(n) < 0 \\ \sigma[y \mapsto \sigma(y) * \sigma(x)^{\sigma(n)}, n \mapsto 0] & \text{otherwise.} \end{cases}$$

Thus, if we "run" the program with an initial store, σ, which sets n to 2 and x to 3, we terminate with

$$\sigma[y \mapsto 9, n \mapsto 0]$$

The Denotational Semantics of F

The denotational semantics of F is shown in Figure 6, where we define a function:

$$\mathcal{E}: Exp \rightarrow Env \rightarrow Val$$

where

$$Env: Var \rightarrow Val$$

and

$$Val = Z_\perp + T_\perp + (Val \rightarrow Val).$$

For the power program, we calculate

$\mathcal{E}[[\text{let power(x,n)} = \text{if n=0 then 1 else x*power(x,n−1) in}$
$\text{power (3,2)}]]\rho =$
$\mathcal{E}[[\text{power (3,2)}]]\rho[\text{power} \mapsto \text{fix } F]$

where

$$Fg(z_1, z_2) = \begin{cases} 1 & \text{if } z_2 = 0 \\ z_1 * g(z_1, z_2 - 1) & \text{otherwise.} \end{cases}$$

We can use the fixed-point theorem to find the fixed point of F:

$$F^0(\perp)(z_1, z_2) = \perp,$$

$$F^1(\perp)(z_1, z_2) = \begin{cases} 1 & \text{if } z_2 = 0 \\ \perp & \text{otherwise,} \end{cases}$$

$$F^2(\perp)(z_1, z_2) = \begin{cases} 1 & \text{if } z_2 = 0 \\ z_1 & \text{if } z_2 = 1 \\ \perp & \text{otherwise,} \end{cases}$$

$$
\begin{aligned}
\mathcal{E}[x]\rho &= \rho(x) \\
\mathcal{E}[n]\rho &= n \\
\mathcal{E}[e_1 \text{ op } e_2]\rho &= \delta_{op}(\mathcal{E}[e_1]\rho, \mathcal{E}[e_2]\rho) \\
\mathcal{E}[\text{if } e \text{ then } e_1 \text{ else } e_2]\rho &= \text{cond}(\mathcal{E}[e]\rho, \mathcal{E}[e_1]\rho, \mathcal{E}[e_2]\rho) \\
\mathcal{E}[e(e_1, \ldots, e_n)]\rho &= \begin{cases} \perp & \text{if } \mathcal{E}[e]\rho = \perp \text{ or} \\ & \quad \mathcal{E}[e_i]\rho = \perp \text{ for any i} \\ \mathcal{E}[e]\rho(\mathcal{E}[e_1]\rho, \ldots, \mathcal{E}[e_n]\rho) \\ & \text{otherwise} \end{cases} \\
\mathcal{E}[\text{let } f(x_1, \ldots, x_n) = e_1 \text{ in } e_2]\rho &= \mathcal{E}[e_2]\rho[f \mapsto \text{fix } F] \\
\text{where } F \, g \, (z_1, \ldots, z_n) &= \mathcal{E}[e_1]\rho[f \mapsto g, x_i \mapsto z_i \mid_{i=1}^n]
\end{aligned}
$$

FIGURE 6   The denotational semantics of F.

$$F^3(\perp)(z_1, z_2) = \begin{cases} 1 & \text{if } z_2 = 0 \\ z_1 & \text{if } z_2 = 1 \\ z_1 * z_1 & \text{if } z_2 = 2 \\ \perp & \text{otherwise,} \end{cases}$$

$$\vdots$$

$$F^m(\perp)(z_1, z_2) = \begin{cases} z_1^{z_2} & \text{if } z_2 \geq 0 \wedge z_2 \leq m \\ \perp & \text{otherwise,} \end{cases}$$

from which we get

$$(\text{fix } F)(z_1, z_2) = \begin{cases} z_1^{z_2} & \text{if } z_2 \geq 0 \\ \perp & \text{otherwise} \end{cases}$$

and so

$$\mathcal{E}[[\text{power } (3,2)]]\rho[\text{power} \mapsto \text{fix F}] = (\text{fix F})(3, 2) = 9.$$

PROGRAM LOGICS

The main use of axiomatic semantics has been in the verification of imperative programs. We follow this trend by concentrating on a program logic for W; the logic is shown in Figure 7. The logic is shown as an inference system (compare with the operational semantics rules). The individual judgments are written as triples $\{P\}S\{Q\}$; such triples are sometimes called *Hoare triples*, where P and Q are predicates (*State* $\rightarrow$ *T*). P is called the *precondition* and Q is called the *postcondition*. The triple specifies that if P is true for the state before the execution of the statement, then Q is true afterward. The logic is a *partial correctness* logic—the triple holds only if the statement executioin terminates.

(assign) $\quad \{P[x \mapsto \mathcal{A}[a]]\}x := a\{P\}$

(skip) $\quad \{P\}\texttt{skip}\{P\}$

(seq) $\quad \dfrac{\{P\}S_1\{Q\}, \quad \{Q\}S_2\{R\}}{\{P\}S_1; S_2\{R\}}$

(if) $\quad \dfrac{\{\mathcal{B}[b] \wedge P\}S_1\{Q\}, \quad \{\neg\mathcal{B}[b] \wedge P\}S_2\{Q\}}{\{P\}\texttt{if } b \texttt{ then } S_1 \texttt{ else } S_2\{Q\}}$

(while) $\quad \dfrac{\{\mathcal{B}[b] \wedge P\}S\{P\}}{\{P\}\texttt{while } b \texttt{ do } S\{\neg\mathcal{B}[b] \wedge P\}}$

(cons) $\quad \dfrac{\{P'\}S\{Q'\}}{\{P\}S\{Q\}}$
$\quad\quad\quad$ if $P \Rightarrow P'$ and $Q' \Rightarrow Q$

FIGURE 7 Axiomatic semantics of W.

The language of predicates is more formally defined as follows:

$(P_1 \vee P_2)(\sigma) = P_1(\sigma) \vee P_2(\sigma),$

$(P_1 \wedge P_2)(\sigma) = P_1(\sigma) \wedge P_2(\sigma),$

$(\neg P)(\sigma) = \neg(P(\sigma)),$

$(P[x \mapsto \mathcal{A}[[a]]])(\sigma) = P(\sigma[x \mapsto \mathcal{A}[[a]]\sigma]).$

We write $P_1 \Rightarrow P_2$ to mean

$\forall \sigma \in State.P_1(\sigma) \Rightarrow P_2(\sigma).$

The predicate P used in the rule for while is called the *invariant* of the loop. It is true before and after the execution of every iteration of the loop. The rule (cons) is sometimes called the rule of consequence; it enables us to strengthen the precondition and weaken the postcondition.

We apply the logic to verify the power program. We want to prove that the following triple is valid:

$\{\sigma(x) = z_1 \wedge \sigma(n) = z_2\}$
$y := 1; \text{while not } (n = 0) \text{ do } (y := y*n; n := n-1;)$
$\{\sigma(y) = z_1^{z_2} \wedge \sigma(x) = z_1 \wedge \sigma(n) = 0\}$

The (seq) rule shows that we have to prove something about the assignment to y and the while loop. So we must define an invariant, inv, for the loop; we take

$$inv = (\sigma(n) \geq 0) \Rightarrow ((\sigma(y) * \sigma(x)^{\sigma(n)} = \sigma(x)^{z_2}) \wedge (\sigma(x) = z_1) \wedge (\sigma(n) \leq z_2)).$$

Using the (assign) rule twice and the (seq) rule, we have

$\{inv[n \mapsto n - 1][y \mapsto y*x]\}y := y*x; n := n-1;\{inv\}$

and because it can be verified that

$((\sigma(n) \neq 0 \wedge inv) \Rightarrow inv[n \mapsto n - 1][y \mapsto y * x]$

by (cons), we have

$\{(\sigma(n) \neq 0 \wedge inv\}y := y * x, n := n - 1;\{inv\}.$

Thus from (while), we get

$\{inv\}\text{while not } (n=0) \text{ do } (y := y*x; n := n-1;)\{(\sigma(n) = 0) \wedge inv\}$

Using (assign), we get

$\{inv[y \mapsto 1]\}y := 1\{inv\}$

and because

$((\sigma(x) = z_1) \wedge (\sigma(n) = z_2)) \Rightarrow inv[y \mapsto 1]$

(cons) gives

$\{(\sigma(x) = z_1) \wedge (\sigma(n) = z_2)\}y := 1\{inv\}.$

We can now use (seq) to get

$$\{\sigma(x) = z_1 \wedge \sigma(n) = z_2\},$$
$$y := 1; \text{ while not } (n=0) \text{ do } (y := y*x; n := n-1;),$$
$$\{(\sigma(n) = 0) \wedge inv\}$$

Finally, observe that

$$((\sigma(n) = 0) \wedge inv) \Rightarrow (\sigma(y) = z_1^{z_2} \wedge \sigma(x) = z_1 \wedge \sigma(n) = 0)$$

and we can use (cons) to get the desired result.

CONCLUSIONS

By focusing on two simple languages, we have only managed to cover a small part of this important topic. However, the focus has enabled us to be quite concrete about the concepts that we have introduced. Of course, some other programming paradigms employ radically different models of computation; for example, some models of logic programming are based on resolution theorem proving (6) and concurrency also introduces new methods and problems (4,7).

REFERENCES

1. H. R. Nielson and F. Nielson, *Semantics with Applications: A Formal Introduction*, John Wiley and Sons, Chichester, 1992.
2. R. D. Tennent, *Semantics of Programming Languages*, Prentice-Hall International, Hemel Hempstead, U.K., 1991.
3. G. Winskel, *The Formal Semantics of Programming Languages*, MIT Press, Cambridge, MA, 1993.
4. D. Schmidt, *Denotational Semantics: A Methodology for Language Development*, Allyn & Bacon, New York, 1986.
5. J. E. Stoy, *Denotational Semantics: The Scott–Strachey Approach to Programming Language Theory*, MIT Press, Cambridge, MA, 1977.
6. R. A. Kowalski, *Logic for Problem Solving*, North-Holland, Amsterdam, 1979.
7. G. Agha, *Actors: A Model of Concurrent Computation in Distributed System*, MIT Press, Cambridge, MA, 1986.

CHRIS HANKIN

NEURAL NETWORK MODELING OF BRAIN AND COGNITIVE DISORDERS

INTRODUCTION

Neural modeling is currently a very active scientific field involving substantial multidisciplinary research. While much work in this area has focused on applications in industry, business, and related areas, other work has considered using neural models to study brain and cognitive functions. Most of this latter research has been based on the investigation of intact neural networks. However, a new direction has recently emerged, that of using "lesioned" neural models to study various brain and cognitive disorders from a computational point of view (1). The term "lesioned" is interpreted broadly here to mean that an intact model's structural or functional mechanisms are disrupted in some fashion. The goals of this research have been to construct computational models that can explain how specific neuroanatomical and neurophysiological abnormalities can result in various clinical manifestations, and to investigate the functional organization of the symptoms that result from specific brain disruptions.

Neural models necessarily simplify the biological phenomena occurring in the nervous system and are generally constrained in size. The simulated lesions (damage) in such models are also substantial simplifications of abnormal events occurring within the brain and/or in cognitive processes. Nevertheless, such computer-based models complement traditional methods of studying brain disorders in substantial and important ways. The size and location of simulated brain damage can be controlled precisely and can be systematically varied over arbitrarily large numbers of experimental "subjects" and information processing tasks. Furthermore, computational experiments are open to detailed inspection in ways that biological systems are not, permitting one to determine the underlying mechanisms and trace the behavioral changes following network damage or lesioning.

In this article, we give a broad overview of representative past efforts to model brain and cognitive disorders computationally. We divide this past work into four categories:

- Memory disorders
- Language disorders
- Neurological disorders
- Psychiatric disorders

This division is somewhat arbitrary in that some studies fall into more than one of these categories. For example, simulations of memory impairments in Alzheimer's disease might be grouped with neurological disorders or models of memory impairment. Nevertheless, it provides a useful starting orientation for someone previously unfamiliar with this work. We assume that the reader already has a basic familiarity with neural modeling and its terminology.

MEMORY DISORDERS

Simulating various aspects of memory has been of central importance in neural modeling. Because of this, it is not surprising that substantial efforts have also gone into developing models of memory disorders and that some of the earliest modeling of disorders was in this area. Representative examples are listed in Table 1.

Early Associative Memories

Some of the earliest neural models systematically studied and analyzed were simple linear associative memories. Some of this early work is summarized in Refs. 3 and 12. Lesion studies with these models can be viewed as precursors of both the contemporary models of Alzheimer's disease, to be discussed in this section, and the focal cortical lesions, described later in this article. In a neural model of this kind, there is typically a set of input neurons and a set of output neurons. Each input neuron sends a one-way connection to every output neuron, so this is a fully connected, feedforward architecture. Output neurons compute their activation level as a linear sum of their inputs, where the coefficients in this sum are the weights on the respective connections. It is this linearity that makes such models readily analyzable and thus encouraged their early development. These models typically used a distributed representation of information and learned using Hebb's rule. They are generally said to be associative memories because they are trained to produce a specific associated output pattern in response to each input pattern they are given.

Perhaps the earliest systematic lesioning study of brain models was done with linear associative memories (2). In this study, there were only eight input neurons and eight output neurons, and the model was trained with four pairs of input–output patterns. A very large number of simulations were run in which a set of cells and all of their connections were deleted from the network. All possible lesions involving combinations of 1–7 input neurons, 1–7 output neurons, and 1–14 input and output neurons were tested. Performance of each lesioned model was measured based on how well it generated the correct output pattern for each of the input patterns it was given.

The lesioned models in this study exhibited a number of interesting properties.

TABLE 1   Example Neural Models of Memory Disorders

Abnormality	Investigators	Year (Ref.)
Random network lesions	Wood	1978 (2)
	Anderson	1983 (3)
Disconnection syndromes	Gordon	1982 (4)
Amnesia	McClelland and Rumelhart	1986 (5)
Alzheimer's disease	Hasselmo	1994 (6)
	Ruppin and Reggia	1995 (7)
Agnosia	Farah and McClelland	1991 (8)
Consolidation and forgetting	McClelland et al.	1995 (9)
Semantic memory impairments	Small et al.	1995 (10)
Structural versus functional damage	Ruppin and Reggia	1995 (11)

They were fault tolerant in that small lesions tended to have little effect. As lesion size increased, performance decreased. On the other hand, removal of any neuron produced a deficit roughly similar to removal of any other neuron in terms of its effect on performance. These results led to the conclusion that lesioning of associative networks of linear neurons produced effects resembling Lashley's "mass action" and "equipotentiality" (2). Although this is true, the situation is more complex than such statistical measures might suggest (e.g., removing some neurons may be more harmful for specific associations than for others). (See Refs. 13 and 14 for further discussion.)

Subsequent work with similar but more sophisticated networks of neurons largely confirmed the above results and demonstrated new phenomena. One well-known related model that has been lesioned is the autoassociative memory, sometimes called the "brain-state-in-a-box" (3). This model consists of a single set of neurons fully connected to one another. It is "autoassociative" in that activity patterns became associated with themselves during Hebbian learning. The network thus serves as an associative memory: Complete patterns "stored" in the network are retrieved by presenting the network with part of the pattern or noisy version of the pattern.

A 50-neuron autoassociative memory trained on images representing the 26 letters of the alphabet was systematically lesioned, and its degradation in performance was assessed as a function of lesion size (3). Lesions consisted of randomly removing a specific percentage of the synapses (connections) rather than neurons as was done in Ref. 2. In spite of this difference and the different network structures, the same pattern of results was obtained. In addition, it was observed that if lesions were made incrementally rather than all at once while synaptic modifiability was allowed to continue, then there was much less deterioration in performance for a given lesion size. This latter result is intriguing because it is consistent with observations that slow damage is less harmful than rapid damage in animal ablation studies (3) and in clinical experience (15–17).

A more complex architecture has been used to simulate various syndromes manifested by deficits in naming objects after brain damage (4). The network in this study was composed of 4 sets of 32 neurons, each set combining features of the simple associative and autoassociative memories described above. The four sets of neurons represented visual input, tactile input, "semantics," and motor-output brain regions. Lesions were induced by partially or completely removing the connections among these sets. The resulting degraded performance in the network was interpreted as being consistent with optic aphasia, tactile aphasia, and other clinical syndromes.

These early lesioning studies of neural models were intended, at least loosely, as models of cerebral cortex and its connections. They showed how lesions of highly parallel information processing systems could account for various neuropsychological phenomena. However, their small size and abstract nature make it difficult to relate them directly to real biophysical neural circuitry. For example, the neurons in these models generally do not have a spatial relationship to one another as occurs in the brain. All neurons in a set of neurons in these models are "equidistant" from one another so that there cannot be a concept of "focal lesion" (spatially localized damage) in the physical sense that a neuropsychologist or neurologist would mean.

Alzheimer's Disease

Alzheimer's disease is the most common dementing illness. Because of its medical importance, we focus on this topic in the rest of this section. The essential feature of Alzheimer's is broad-based intellectual decline from previous levels of functioning. Although Alzheimer's disease is characterized by the development of multiple cognitive deficits manifested by disturbances in language, motor, and executive functions, a major clinical hallmark of the disease is memory impairment, which manifests itself as an inability both to recall previously learned knowledge and to learn new information.

The clinical course of Alzheimer's disease is usually characterized by gradual deterioration, although both slow and rapidly progressive forms have been reported, exhibiting a large variation in the rate of progression. The diagnosis of Alzheimer's disease is traditionally based on the presence of specific microscopic structural abnormalities, such as neurofibrillary tangles and senile plaques, in brain tissue (which, in small numbers, are found also in the normal aging brain). A confirmed diagnosis of Alzheimer's disease is usually made only after autopsy or, less frequently, after brain biopsy. Although considerable progress has been made recently in understanding some neurobiological features of Alzheimer's disease, its causes and pathogenesis are still generally unknown (the interested reader is referred to Ref. 18 for a review of Alzheimer's disease).

In the following, we summarize two previous neural models of the pathogenesis of Alzheimer's disease. The first concentrates on studying the possible role of synaptic deletion and compensation; the second investigates the role of synaptic runaway.

Synaptic Deletion and Compensation

Recent neuroanatomical investigations have repeatedly demonstrated that the progress of Alzheimer's disease is accompanied by considerable synaptic changes, including synaptic deletion and compensation. Whereas *synaptic deletion* is manifested in a reduction of the number of synapses per unit of cortical volume, a concomitant increase in the size of the remaining synapses has also been observed and is referred to as *synaptic compensation*.

In light of the major place that memory impairment occupies among the clinical manifestations of Alzheimer's disease, the neuronal and synaptic degenerative changes that occur as the disease progresses are an ideal candidate for neural modeling. This approach was taken by Horn et al. (19) in studying how the interplay between synaptic deletion and compensation determines the observed patterns of memory deterioration and what strategies of increased synaptic efficacy could best maintain memory capacities in the face of synaptic deletion.

Investigating these synaptic changes in an attractor neural network model of association memory, it has been shown that the deterioration of memory retrieval due to synaptic deletion can be much delayed by strengthening the remaining synaptic weights by a uniform compensatory factor (19). Variations of the rate and exact functional form of synaptic compensation were used to define various compensation strategies, leading to different dependencies of the network's memory performance on its connectivity (see Figure 1, for example). These different compensation strategies could account for the observed variation in the severity and progression rate of Alzheimer's disease. These results explain the specific patterns of cognitive decline observed in various subgroups of patients with Alzheimer's disease and have led to the formulation of a new hypothesis accounting for the appearance of parkinsonian symptoms in Alzheimer's disease patients (20). However, this work was limited in two important ways. First, because a prescribed synaptic memory matrix was used, only memory retrieval, not storage, could be addressed. Second, the synaptic compensation dependencies employed were realized in a "global" manner, which is biologically unrealistic.

The first limitation was addressed in Ref. 7, using a simple, activity-dependent

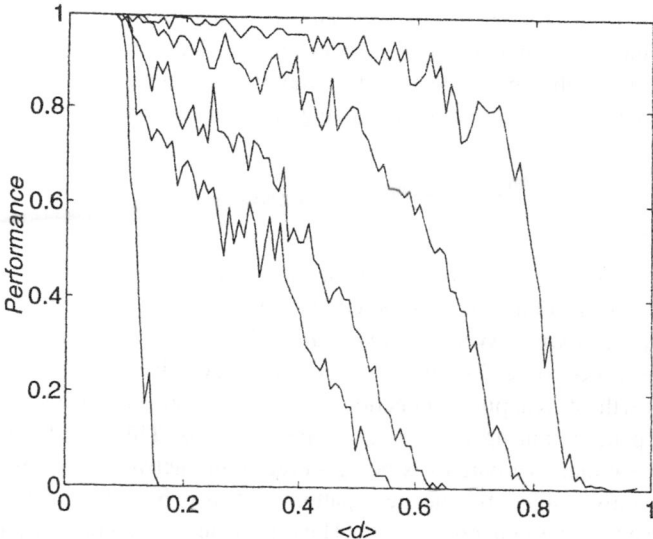

FIGURE 1 Synapses are gradually eliminated in an attractor neural network model of associative memory, and recall performance (vertical axis) is plotted versus fraction d of synapses deleted. The loss of synapses is counteracted by synaptic compensatory mechanisms which act to maintain each neuron's input by strengthening the remaining synapses. The different plotted lines correspond to different rates of compensation being used by the remaining synaptic connections. With no compensation by remaining synapses (leftmost curve), memory retrieval is dramatically impaired before even 20% of the synapses are gone. In contrast, with rapid compensation (rightmost curve), memory deterioration is substantially delayed. Simulations like this let one explore in theory how assumptions about brain responses to injury can influence the course of a patient's neurological deficit.

Hebbian synaptic storage scheme to simulate memory acquisition in the framework of an attractor neural network model. This work countered a recent claim that neural models cannot account for more detailed aspects of memory impairment, such as the relative sparing of remote versus recent memories observed in Alzheimer's patients (21). The model exhibits differential sparing of remote versus recent memories, accounts for the experimentally observed temporal gradient of memory decline, and shows that neural models can account for a large variety of experimental phenomena characterizing memory degradation in Alzheimer patients. Specific testable predictions were generated concerning the relation between the neuroanatomical degenerative findings and the clinical manifestations of Alzheimer's disease.

The biological appeal of the uniform synaptic compensatory regimes studied by Horn et al. (19) hinges on the ability to show that they can actually be realized in a "local" manner, where each neuron readjusts its synaptic weights only as a function of local information such as its postsynaptic potential. A recent study of such local compensatory mechanisms demonstrates that this is a nontrivial but feasible task (7). This study has revealed a new dependency between the extent of synaptic changes and the retrieval properties of the network. In contradistinction to the case of global compensatory strategies, the network's performance not only depends on the current magnitudes of deletion and compensation but also on the precise rates at which these processes progress; that is, the performance of the network is history dependent. This dependency provides a new explanation for the rather puzzling broad variability in structural indicators of damage observed in Alzheimer's disease patients having approximately similar levels of cognitive function.

Synaptic Runaway

Whereas the studies reviewed above have sought to explain memory degradation in Alzheimer's disease as a failure of synaptic compensatory responses to synaptic deletion, a different approach, *runaway synaptic modification*, has been studied in both attractor and feedforward networks (6,22–24). Runaway synaptic modification denotes an abnormal exponential growth of synaptic connections that may occur due to interference by previously stored patterns during the storage of new patterns. This interference occurs because when a new memory pattern is being stored in the network, the resulting network activity is not only guided by the new pattern but also by all the previous memory patterns engraved in the synaptic matrix. Thus, previously memorized patterns tend to bias the activation in "their direction" during new storage. This inherent reinforcement may lead to exponential synaptic growth and to a pathological increase in the number of synapses.

One possible way to prevent synaptic runaway is to assume that the strength of the external projections by which new patterns are stored in the network is sufficiently strong to overcome the interference of other memories. Another alternative is that runaway synaptic modification can be inhibited by suppression of internal synaptic connections (synapses between neurons belonging to the same cortical module) during learning.

What is the hypothesized role of synaptic runaway in the pathogenesis of Alzheimer's disease? Analysis shows that there is a critical storage capacity beyond which interference during learning cannot be prevented and synaptic runaway is unavoidable (6,22–24). Several factors can lead to the initiation of synaptic runaway, such as a decrease in the level of cortical inhibition, reduced synaptic decay, and excess memory storage. Once synaptic runaway occurs, it is claimed that its increased metabolic demands or excitotoxic effects could cause neuronal degeneration, parallel to that found in Alzheimer's disease. Furthermore, this work provides a theoretical framework for describing the specific distribution of neuronal degeneration observed in Alzheimer's disease, where certain regions lacking suppression of internal synaptic transmission are more markedly damaged than other cortical regions.

The synaptic runaway theory has been inspired by experimental work (22,23) that provides evidence that acetylcholine selectively suppresses excitatory synaptic transmission at the internal synapses while allowing external afferent synaptic transmission (i.e., projections from neurons belonging to other modules) to operate at full strength. Accordingly, it is claimed that the loss of cholinergic innervation in Alzheimer's disease may underlie the initiation of runaway synaptic modification, and that sprouting of cholinergic innervation observed in the dentate gyrus during Alzheimer's disease reflects attempts to arrest the progress of synaptic runaway.

This work on synaptic runaway is an excellent example of research that combines experimental physiological studies with computational modeling. It demonstrates how a computational model can raise a quandary (How are patterns actually stored without being accompanied by synaptic runaway?) that motivates an experimental study (the differential effects of acetylcholine on internal and external synapses). Moreover, the theoretical solution to this question gives rise to further hypotheses concerning the possible consequences of a disruption of the newly revealed computational mechanism (i.e., the role of synaptic runaway in the pathogenesis of Alzheimer's disease).

LANGUAGE DISORDERS

Many different types of brain damage can have devastating effects on the human cognitive system. Neurologists and neuropsychologists have identified a wide variety of cognitive and language disorders associated with both focal and diffuse brain lesions. Connectionist models have been developed to simulate normal cognitive function and the ways in which normal cognition is affected by brain injury. Although these cognitively oriented connectionist models often use a neuronlike processing structure, they are *not* brain models in that they do not directly model neuroanatomic and neurophysiological function. They are best viewed as simulations of cognitive functions and related phenomena that emanate from brain function, in contrast to the neural models described elsewhere in this survey that attempt to simulate specific aspects of brain anatomy and physiology.

Networks in cognitive connectionist models often represent concepts and associations—entities in the cognitive domain rather than biological structures. Such models often adopt a *local representation* of information, with nodes representing a complex psychological construct (e.g., words or morphemes) and connections representing associations between such constructs. Figure 2 gives an example. Models with this local representation of information are sometimes referred to as "symbolic" models and they may assume the existence of relatively complex cognitive units as parts of the normal cognitive architecture. Many of these models use a neuronlike activation rule borrowed from the neural modeling literature, although others do not. In either case, these spreading activation networks can be regarded as viable models of mental functional processes independent of the extent to which they are intended as models of brain activity.

Other connectionist models studied in cognitive science use a *distributed representation* of information. In these "subsymbolic" models, cognitive constructs are typically represented as patterns of activity across a population of primitive nodes that develop from repeated pairings of information from different sources. Such models may represent symbolic cognitive constructs as patterns of activity that develop over time.

Fully distributed connectionist models simulating cognitive mechanisms, just as models with local representations of information, must be distinguished from neural models of brain function. However, because biologically based neural models generally use distributed representations of information that appear to be very similar to the distributed representations of the cognitive models, there is a tendency to blur this distinction and to regard distributed cognitive models as direct representations of some level of brain activity. In fact, the details of how connectionist cognitive models map onto a neural substrate is an open research question. Table 2 presents a selective list of some connectionist models of neurogenic language dysfunction.

Structural Versus Emergent Cognitive Components

The distinction between completely distributed connectionist models and those employing a local representation is more than a minor detail of the model's implementation and can imply quite different views of the principles underlying cognitive processing. Several

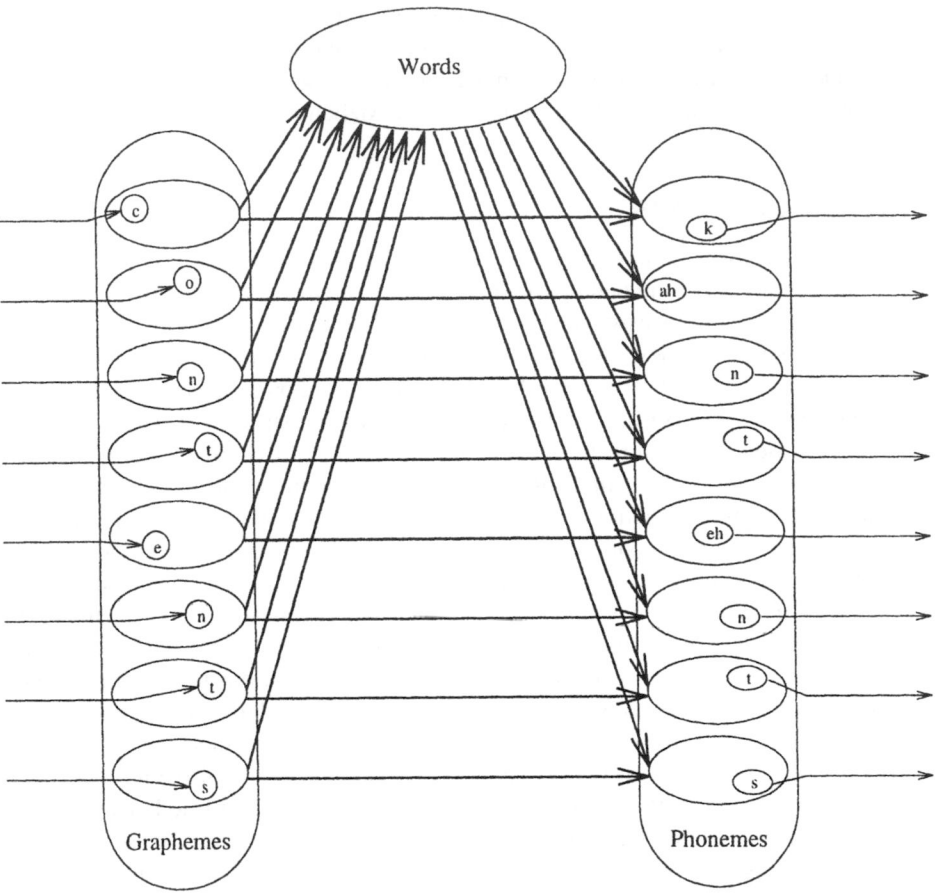

FIGURE 2   The print-to-sound network, used in a model of reading aloud, illustrates a local representation of information (29). The network transforms printed words given as a sequence of graphemes (characters), such as the characters of the word "contents" as shown here, into their spoken form as a sequence of phonemes (/k ah n t eh n t s/). Typically, nodes in a connectionist model like this do not represent neurons, but represent higher-level entities such as graphemes, phonemes, words, and concepts. The large ovals in this picture represent sets of nodes.

investigations of the behavior of lesioned distributed connectionist models question the necessity of components within symbolic cognitive models that are assumed to be necessary structural requirements of the normal cognitive architecture. Their goal is to demonstrate that, in principle, specific symptoms can arise from very general degradations of activation across fully distributed representations. For example, some symptoms of Alzheimer's disease that have been interpreted as evidence that multiple cognitive deficits may be explained by degradation of information flow within a single, putatively semantic information layer that mediates between visual and lexical information (e.g., between pictures of objects and their names) (39). Others have argued that category knowledge (which is frequently retained in Alzheimer's disease) and knowledge about

TABLE 2   Example Neural Models of Language Disorders

Abnormality	Investigators	Year (Ref.)
Aphasia symptoms	Gigley	1983 (25)
	Cottrell	1985 (26)
	Martin et al.	1994 (27)
	Harley	1995 (28)
Acquired dyslexia symptoms	Reggia et al.	1988 (29)
	Patterson et al.	1989 (30)
	Mozer and Behrmann	1990 (31)
	Hinton and Shallice	1991 (32)
	Plaut and Shallice	1993 (33)
	Coltheart et al.	1993 (34)
	Plaut	1996 (35)
	Plaut et al.	1996 (36)
Acquired dysgraphia symptoms	Olson and Caramazza	1994 (37)
	Shallice et al.	1995 (38)

the identity of category examples (which is subject to earlier deterioration) emerges naturally from frequency-sensitive graded processing of distributed representations of example attributes (40). This finding is used as a basis to account for cases of selective semantic category impairment that have been reported in patients with a variety of brain disorders. Still others have considered the topic of "covert recognition" following brain damage (the finding that patients may have information that they are not aware of about characteristics of stimuli). For example, Mayall and Humphreys describe a simple, distributed word recognition system that, when damaged in a variety of ways, simulates performance found among patients with a specific type of acquired dyslexia (41). As in the examples described above, it is argued that dissociations of symptoms (conscious versus unconscious "recognition") do not necessarily signal the selective disruption of discrete components in a complex, symbolic architecture. The contrast between completely distributed cognitive models and those with local representation of symbolic information is most evident in studies of language disorders involving focal brain injury, where both types of models have found some support.

Focal Language Disorders: Aphasia

Aphasia is impaired understanding/generation of language due to brain damage. Although some of the earliest attempts to model aphasic disturbances focused on disturbances of sentence processing (25,26), recent connectionist studies of language have been concerned not with sentence processing but with simple transcoding of information at the single-word level. Many of these efforts have been concerned with the issue of how information of different types (e.g., phonological, semantic) serves to trigger word responses under different conditions of stimulation: picture naming, word repetition, or written word naming.

As an example, a single-word model with local representation of information has been used to simulate the performance of individual patients with impaired picture naming and word repetition. Martin and colleagues used Dell's interactive activation model of sentence production (42) to simulate the performance of a patient with "deep dysphasia" (43). This type of aphasia is defined by a high rate of semantic substitutions ("semantic paraphasias") in repetition tasks and an inability to repeat nonsense words. The model used for the simulations combined three levels of linguistic representation (semantic, lexical, and phonological) with a spreading activation retrieval mechanism with feedforward and feedback connections that carry priming activation to target and related nodes in a small lexical network (42). In naming tasks, a target lexical node is activated by semantic processes (as if stimulated by the presence of a picture) and successively activates its corresponding phonemes. Feedback from all activated nodes reinforces activation of the target node but also activates phonologically related nodes. If this feedback raises activation of a nontarget node to a level higher than that of the target, a phonological error (formal paraphasia) will occur. In repetition tasks, the order of information flow is altered, with phonological activation occurring before semantic activation (as if from an aural stimulus presented for repetition).

Two parameters of the model, connection strength and decay rate, regulate the flow of information through the network, and these parameters were manipulated in the "lesion" simulations. Increasing the decay rate produced the specific effects that were found in the patient's data: a higher percentage of formal paraphasias in naming and of semantic errors in repetition. Furthermore, reduction of the decay rate "impairment" toward normal successfully reproduced the patient's error patterns as he recovered. These results suggest that a single impairment in a dynamic processing parameter within the language system can produce a variety of error patterns across different tasks.

In recent simulations of aphasic naming errors using this approach, Dell and colleagues simulated the individual error type distributions of 21 fluent aphasic patients by altering the model's parameters of connection weight and/or decay rate (43). Once the model was individually fitted to each aphasic patient's data, predictions were made about a number of other aspects of patient performance. The work described in this article contrasts markedly with the studies of completely distributed networks in the specificity of what the computational "lesion" represents. For Dell and colleagues, the nature and extent of information degradation is critical to interpreting the outcome; for many simulations with completely distributed models lesion, severity is the only lesion parameter of interest.

Single and Multiple "Routes" to Reading: Acquired Alexia

Many connectionist models of cognitive dysfunction are concerned with disorders of the ability to transcode between print and pronunciation—to read aloud and to write to dictation (see Table 2). Symptoms involving reading disorders (dyslexia or alexia) and writing disorders have been a favored research topic among cognitive neuropsychologists and have generated considerable interest among connectionists. This attention has, in large measure, been engendered by the interesting and distinct patterns of impairment that can occur in these disorders.

Several distinct types of acquired dyslexia have been simulated using connectionist models. Two of these types are characterized by special difficulty reading unfamiliar or "made-up" words; when such "nonwords" are misread, patients frequently produce a visually similar real word that looks similar to the target word. Among these patients with nonword reading impairment, *deep dyslexics* also demonstrate a variety of problems reading aloud real words, particularly abstract words, and they often produce errors that are either semantically or visually related to the target (44). *Phonological dyslexics*, who are also impaired in nonword reading, do not produce semantic errors when reading words and, in fact, may read real words very well (45,46). In contrast to these patterns of reading symptoms, *surface dyslexic* patients can read aloud nonwords and many real words but have difficulty reading words with irregular spelling/sound correspondences (47).

The occurrence of the dissociation between the ability to read words and nonwords has been used as a primary piece of data supporting the necessity of a distinction between lexical and nonlexical reading procedures or *routes* from print to sound (e.g., Ref. 48). The *dual-route model* postulates different procedures for achieving a pronunciation for a letter string when reading words and nonwords; thus, this view easily accommodates the occurrence of these different patient types by postulating selective impairments to one of the two routes. Challenges to the dual-route model have mounted numerous types of argument that the operation of a single route can explain the relevant data (e.g., Refs. 49–51), but those models have had difficulty accounting for the distinct patterns found in patients with acquired dyslexia.

Several of the characteristics of deep dyslexia have been simulated in a connectionist model that links orthography (word form) and meaning (semantic features) (32,33). In the initial implementation, a "direct" pathway generated initial semantic activity from visual input and a "clean-up" pathway refined this activity into the appropriate semantic activation for the target word. Although the model uses two pathways, it does not constitute a dual-route model because both pathways must be considered to support lexical reading only; it did not attempt to simulate nonword reading (or its impairment), but it did perform lesion simulations that succeeded in producing errors that were semantically related to the targets (32). The lesioned model also produced other interpretable error patterns that have been argued to occur in deep dyslexia, including errors visually related to the target and a higher proportion of "mixed" (semantic/visual) errors than would be expected by chance.

Another model of normal word recognition and pronunciation was developed to simulate a variety of empirical findings from normal subjects (52). It was also claimed that the model could be lesioned to simulate some of the characteristics of surface dyslexia (30). The fact that the model contained no explicit representations of morphemic or lexical information, or of specific rules for conversion of orthography to phonology, lent considerable theoretical interest to the model's performance. If a model with this completely "subsymbolic" architecture could successfully reproduce phenomena such as normal subjects' ability to pronounce unfamiliar letter strings and, at the same time, could succeed in pronouncing words with exceptional spelling/sound correspondences, dual-route reading models would face a formidable challenge. These theoretical implications fueled interest in the model's performance and led to serious challenges of the strong claims that have been made for this and related models with completely distributed architectures (e.g., Refs. 53 and 54). Some of the specific critiques that were leveled at the initial version of the model led to revision of how information was represented in the model. For example, the model's ability to pronounce nonwords and to perform lexical decisions was challenged (55). Changes were made to the way orthographic input and phonological output were represented, and the model's ability to "pronounce" nonwords improved markedly (56). A particularly detailed critique of the model's potential to achieve a reasonable simulation of acquired reading disorders without the provision of separate mechanisms for the reading of words and nonwords was offered by Coltheart et al. (34). Strong arguments were also advanced by Coltheart et al. (34) that the basic architecture required for any model of written word pronunciation to simulate patterns of acquired dyslexia must incorporate separate mechanisms for reading words and nonwords. These authors outlined the elements of a dual-route model that would be likely to perform better than the fully distributed model in a wide range of oral reading tasks. The nonlexical pathway of their model translates input letter strings into strings of phonemes using explicit grapheme-to-phoneme translation rules. The system learns these rules through recurrent pairings of spellings and phonetic transcriptions. This implemented nonlexical portion of the Coltheart et al. model is fully computational, although not connectionist, in its design. The lexical pathway is a local connectionist model with separate architectures for input [essentially reproducing the interactive activation model of word recognition (57)] and for output. This approach to connectionist modeling of cognitive function stands in sharp contrast to that of proponents of completely distributed systems, in which the structure of the system emerges from recurrent association of input and output.

A different approach to a dual-route reading model was taken by Reggia et al. (29,58). This model takes input in the form of presegmented "grapheme" units—one or more printed characters that serve as the written representation of a single phoneme (as illustrated in Fig. 2). The nonlexical route provides for the mapping of graphemes onto their corresponding phonemes by weighted links based on the probability of association between specific graphemes and phonemes (lower part of Fig. 2). These probabilities were not derived by rules or from linguistic principles (59) but are based on empirical observation of correspondences in a large corpus of English words (60). This representation of how pronunciations are derived from print nonlexically carves out a middle ground between the completely distributed models (e.g., Ref. 52, in which association strength is derived through learning from repeated pairings of written and spoken words) and the rule-based approach. The lexical route in this model consists of connections from the same grapheme nodes to a set of word nodes, and connections from the word nodes to phoneme nodes (Fig. 2, upper part, where a single oval labeled "words" represents over 1000 word nodes). The early implementations of this network succeeded in simulating several important characteristics of normal word pronunciation, including the frequency-by-regularity interaction in reading words; the model also achieved a high degree of success in pronouncing nonwords. Most importantly, performance patterns characteristic of both surface and phonological dyslexia were produced when the lexical and nonlexical routes, respectively, were degraded. This model has undergone a number of modifications, including the provision of competition between the two routes to allow for the simulation of behaviors that appear to reflect route interactions. The most recent version of the model has also been used to simulate distinct performance patterns produced by individual patients with phonological dyslexia (61).

NEUROLOGICAL DISORDERS

We now turn to models of neurological disorders such as stroke, epilepsy, migraine, and parkinsonism. In contrast to the more abstract "cognitive models" of the preceding section, this class of models is more closely related to anatomical structures and physiological processes occurring in the brain. Typically, each node represents a neuron or population of neurons, and its connections represent synapses or groups of synapses with other neurons. A weight on a connection represents a measure of synaptic strength or effectiveness (positive = excitatory; negative = inhibitory). The input to a node often represents the corresponding neuron's membrane potential, and the node's activation level or output often represents its firing rate. Although there are numerous models that fit this description, relatively few of these models have been used to study the effects of brain damage or dysfunction. Representative examples of these latter models are summarized in Table 3.

Memory and language disorders are, of course, of great importance in clinical neurology. They have already been described in the preceding sections of this article. In this section, we review simulations related to cortical effects of peripheral nerve lesions, stroke, epilepsy, extrapyramidal disorders, and migraine.

Focal Deafferentation of Cortical Maps

During the last several years, there have been numerous efforts to develop computational models of cortex that, unlike many earlier models (e.g., simple associative memories), incorporate more realistic spatial relationships (62,63,65,77–80). Typically these models are concerned with simulating map formation in the primary sensory cortex. It has long been known that each primary sensory region of the cerebral cortex has a "map" of relevant aspects of the external world (e.g., the homunculus in somatosensory cortex) (81,82). Here, the term "map" refers to the fact that stimuli in the sensory space (e.g., tactile stimuli on the surface of the hand) are projected in an order-preserving fashion onto the cortex so that similar stimuli generally excite cortical elements close to one another (e.g., adjacent points on the hand's surface are represented close to one another in the cortex). Perhaps most intriguing has been the repeated experimental demonstration

TABLE 3   Example Neural Models of Neurological Disorders

Abnormality	Investigators	Year (Ref.)
Focal cortical deafferentation	Pearson et al.	1987 (62)
	Sklar	1990 (63)
	Spitzer et al.	1995 (64)
Focal cortical lesions/stroke	Grajski and Merzenich	1990 (65)
	Sutton et al.	1993 (66)
	Weinrich et al.	1993 (67)
	Armentrout et al.	1994 (68)
	Ruppin and Reggia	1995 (11)
	Xing and Gerstein	1996 (69)
Seizures/epilepsy	Wong et al.	1986 (70)
	Zepka and Sabbatini	1991 (71)
	Mehta et al.	1993 (72)
	Traub	1995 (73)
Movement disorders	Borrett et al.	1993 (74)
	Contreras-Vidal and Stelmach	1995 (75)
Migraine aura	Reggia and Montgomery	1996 (76)

that such maps are highly plastic in adult animals: they undergo a reorganization in response to deafferentation (83–85), deefferentation (86), localized repetitive stimuli (87), and focal cortical lesions (88). For example, following a peripheral nerve lesion that deprives part of the somatosensory cortex of its input, the somatosensory map reorganizes to reuse the area of cortex that has lost its primary input. The map shifts so that the deafferented part of the cortex comes to represent other parts of the body surface. Recent noninvasive studies have suggested that such plasticity is also found in human cortical maps (89).

Models of normal cortical map formation typically take the form of a two- or three-layer network and use an unsupervised learning method (often a variant of Hebbian learning called competitive learning). For example, computational models of the hand region of the primary somatosensory cortex have demonstrated map refinement and reorganization in response to localized repetitive stimulation (62,63,65). These models have been partially deafferented by removing a portion of their input connections to cortex (e.g., by removing input from the palm surface of the first two fingers to simulate a median nerve lesion). When such deafferentation is done, the cortical map spontaneously reorganizes in a fashion reminiscent of experimental studies (62,63); the map shifts so that the part of the cortex originally representing the deafferented region of the sensory surface is reused to represent other nearby sensory surface areas. Receptive field changes consistent with an inverse magnification rule have been demonstrated (65).

Similar models of cortical deafferentation have been used more recently to support a theory of phantom limb experiences (64). *Phantom limbs* are the sensation that an extremity is still present after it has been lost (e.g., by traumatic amputation). Spitzer and colleagues combine a model of focal cortical deafferentation with input noise to account for various observations related to phantom limbs (64).

Focal Cortical Lesions and Stroke

The above computational studies of cortical maps provide an impressive demonstration that fairly simple assumptions about network architecture and synaptic modifiability can qualitatively account for several fundamental facts about map self-organization and reorganization following deafferentation. However, they have been less successful in accounting for some other effects. For example, it is known from limited animal experiments that focal cortical lesions also produce spontaneous map reorganization (88). In the first computational map model we know of that simulated a focal cortical lesion, map reorganization would not occur unless implausible steps were taken (complete rerandomization of weights) (65). Map reorganization following a cortical lesion is fundamentally different from that involving deafferentation or focal repetitive stimulation as described earlier. In both of the latter situations, there is a change in the probability distribution of input patterns seen by the cortex. Such a change has long been recognized to result in map alterations (12). In contrast, with a focal cortical lesion, there is no change in the probability distribution of input patterns, so some other factor must be responsible for map reorganization.

Motivated primarily by a desire to better understand the events occurring in stroke, recent work has developed successful computational models of acute focal lesions in cortex. A *stroke* is acute, focal brain damage due to altered blood supply to the brain. When there is sudden loss of blood flow to an area of the brain due to occlusion of an artery, the resultant brain damage is referred to as an *ischemic stroke*. Stroke is a common neurological disease; for example, it is the third leading cause of death in the United States. Because it often causes partial paralysis and/or language and memory problems, it is also a major cause of chronic disability. The complexity of brain changes during a stroke suggests that computational models can be powerful tools for its investigation. However, the same complexity and the limitations of current neural modeling technology and neuroscientific knowledge make it impractical to create immediately a detailed, large-scale model of the brain and all of the effects of a major stroke. The computational models done so far have involved simulating the effects of small ischemic cortical strokes.

Several modeling studies of acute focal cortical lesions have focused primarily on topographic somatosensory maps (66,68). In such maps, points close to one another on the body surface are represented close to each other in the cortical map. This work again involved the region of somatosensory maps representing the surface of the hand. When a focal lesion was introduced into the topographic map, the model reorganized such that the sensory surface originally represented by the lesioned area spontaneously reappeared in adjacent cortical areas, as has been seen experimentally in animal studies (88) (see Fig. 3). Perilesion receptive field sizes increased too, consistent with an inverse magnification rule. A more recently developed model of somatosensory cortex differing substantially in details (e.g., use of spiking neurons) has essentially duplicated these postlesion findings (69). Two key hypotheses emerged from this modeling work. First, postlesion map reorganization is a two-phase process, consisting of a rapid phase due to the dynamics of neural activity and a longer-term phase due to synaptic plasticity. Second, increased perilesion excitability is necessary for useful map reorganization to occur. Recent experimental work has confirmed some of these predictions and extended these modeling concepts to make them more biologically realistic (90).

Work in this area has subsequently evolved in a number of different ways. The initial cortical lesion studies, as well as other work with more abstract computational models of cortex not involving map organization, indicated the important role of intracortical interactions in postlesion brain reorganization. Specifically, following a *structural lesion* that simulates a region of damage and neuronal death, a secondary *functional lesion* can arise in a nearby cortex due to loss of synaptic connections from the damaged area to surrounding intact cortex (we use the term "functional lesion" in this limited sense and not to indicate the ischemic penumbra). This issue is considered in detail in Ref. 11.

Recent work has also examined the effects of focal damage in a computational model of primary sensorimotor cortex that controls the positioning of a simulated arm in three-dimensional space (91). This model involves both proprioceptive input as well as motor output in a "closed-loop" network. Maps initially form in the two cortical regions represented in the model: proprioceptive sensory cortex and primary motor cortex (MI). Unlike the previous computational models of the cortex described earlier that were subjected to simulated focal lesions, the maps involved here are nontopographic feature maps and involve motor output as well as sensory input information. In simulations with this model, both perilesion excitability and cortical map reorganization have been examined immediately after a lesion and over the long term. As described in Ref. 92, the results obtained are consistent with the two hypotheses given earlier. Most recently, various biochemical and biophysical factors have added more realism to computational models of stroke (93).

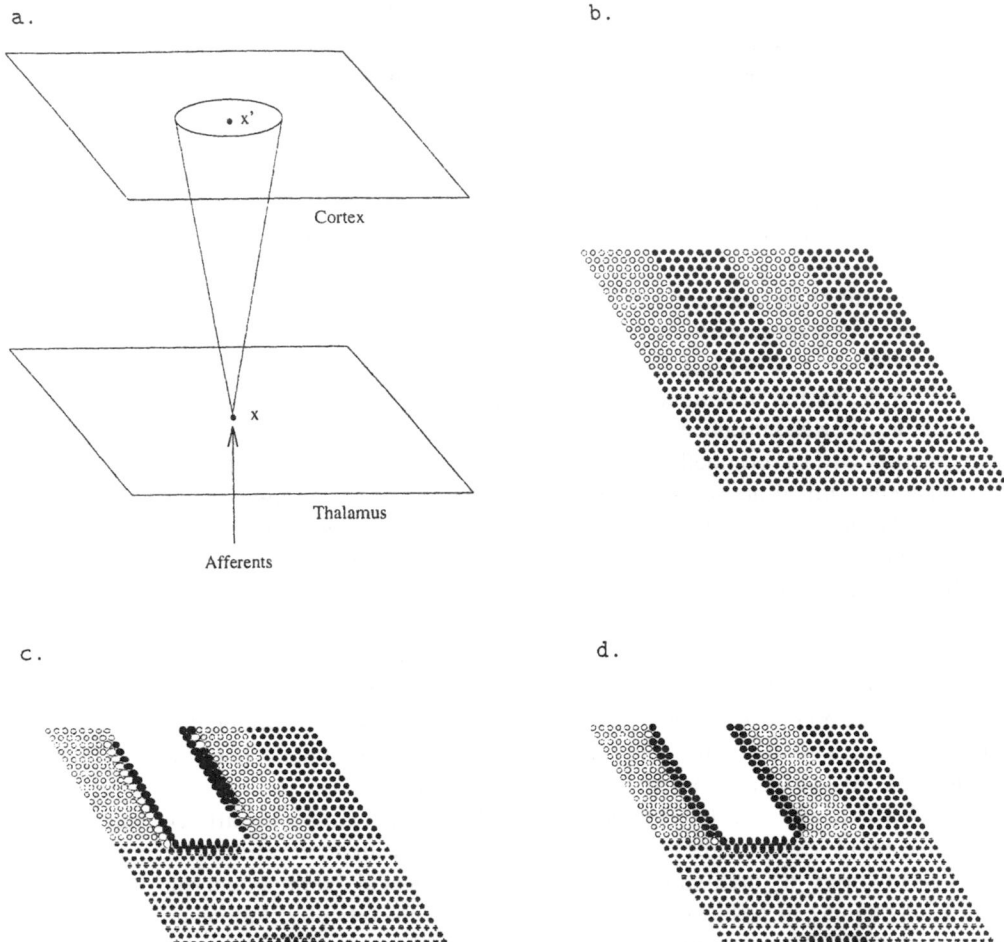

FIGURE 3   A model of a small stroke in the cerebral cortex: (a) network architecture; (b) cortical map of hand surface after training; (c) immediately postlesion; (d) after further training. In (a), sensory fibers from the hand surface (afferents) connect to intermediate neurons (thalamus) which then send diverging connections to the cerebral cortex. Following repeated stimuli to the hand surface, Hebbian synaptic changes on the connections lead to formation of a map of the hand over the cortical surface, as shown in (b). Shading indicates four fingers (b, top) and a palmar surface (b, bottom). A cortical lesion (simulated stroke) is simulated by clamping the cortical elements representing the second finger from the left to off or zero. In (c), immediately after the lesion, the representation of the second finger has reappeared in surrounding cortex (black ovals). Later, after further training, the second finger's representation has increased, as pictured in (d).

Epilepsy

Epilepsy is another very common and important disorder in clinical neurology. It is characterized by sudden, excessive electrical discharges in the cerebral cortex. Patients with epilepsy typically have recurrent convulsions, loss of consciousness, disturbances of sensation, impaired mentation, and related symptoms. These episodes are caused by paroxysmal high-frequency or synchronous low-frequency, high-voltage electrical disturbances observable in the electroencephalogram (EEG). Although many biochemical and physiological abnormalities have been described in epileptic brain tissue, the precise pathophysiology of these abnormalities is only partially understood at present. Contemporary research on the mechanisms underlying seizures and on pharmacological treatments is very active, involving both humans and animal models.

Some of the most detailed and well-known neural models of epileptic abnormalities have been developed by Traub and colleagues over a period of several years (70,73). They have primarily investigated a complex, multicompartmental model of area CA3 of the hippocampus, a brain region in which highly synchronized electrical activity and EEG spikes and sharp waves occur with certain types of epileptiform activity. By manipulating their models in ways corresponding to experimental procedures (e.g., simulating blockage of the inhibitory neurotransmitter $GABA_A$ caused by picrotoxin), they were able to gain insight into the mechanisms underlying abnormal neuronal bursting and after-discharges. More recently, it has been shown that a much simplified model of hippocampal pyramidal neurons is still able to account for many of the same sorts of abnormal neuronal firing (94).

Another very interesting phenomenon related to epilepsy is *kindling*. Kindling occurs when repeated electrical or chemical stimulation of a cortical region leads to the generation of a new focus of abnormal, epileptogenic activity. Mehta and colleagues have developed and studied a neural model in which repeated simulated electrical stimuli produce kindling due to synaptic changes (72). Their results are consistent with the hypothesis that kindling is due to the formation of a large number of excitatory synapses arising in the context of operation of Hebb's rule.

Other Neurological Disorders

A number of neural models of movement disorders associated with basal ganglia dysfunction have recently been developed. Most attention has been given to *Parkinson's disease*. Patient's have rigidity, tremor, slow movements, and poor balance. It has been possible to simulate the emergence of tremor as an oscillatory state in a recurrent neural network (74). More recently, a neural model of the opponent processes occurring in basal ganglia and thalamocortical circuitry has been developed and used to simulate movement abnormalities in both parkinsonism and Huntington's disease (75).

Migraine is another common neurological disorder that has recently been studied computationally. Migraine is an inherited disorder characterized by recurrent, usually unilateral throbbing headaches. In the "classic" form of migraine, pain is often preceded by sudden, bright visual hallucinations in a crescent-shaped region which moves across the visual field. The specific visual patterns that occur have never been definitively explained, although they are generally accepted to have a cortical origin. For many years, it has been hypothesized that they arise due to a wave of cortical spreading depression, but this is difficult to test in humans or animals. For this reason, a neural model of visual cortex incorporating spreading depression was developed and examined (76). It was found that during the wave of cortical spreading depression, the spatial pattern of neural activity broke up into irregular patterns of lines and small patches of highly activated elements. The corresponding visual disturbances that would be produced by these patterns of neural activity resemble the hallucinations reported during migraine, providing support for the cortical spreading depression hypothesis of migraine.

PSYCHIATRIC DISORDERS

Neural models have also been created for a wide range of psychiatric disorders. Representative examples are given in Table 4.

Schizophrenia

Schizophrenia is a clinically heterogeneous disorder with a broad spectrum of manifestations. Its symptoms are diverse and include both "positive symptoms," such as hallucinations, delusions, and disorganized speech and behavior, and "negative symptoms," such as loss of fluency of thought and speech, impaired attention, abnormalities in the expression and observation of emotion, and loss of volition and drive. Most schizophrenic patients stabilize at moderate levels of cognitive impairment and the disease does not have a progressive downhill course leading eventually to death. The interested reader is referred to Refs. 108–111 for recent reviews of schizophrenia.

The pathogenesis of schizophrenia is unknown. A few theories have been raised, based on neuropathological observations, the actions of antipsychotic medications, and ideas about the relation between brain and behavior. Perhaps the most enduring biochemical explanation of the pathophysiology of schizophrenia is the dopamine hypothesis, which postulates the coexistence of decreased dopaminergic activity in the mesocortical system, resulting in negative symptoms, and increased dopaminergic activity in the mesolimbic system, resulting in positive symptoms. Structural and functional imaging and neuroanatomical postmortem studies are providing converging evidence of the involve-

TABLE 4   Example Neural Models of Psychiatric Disorders

Abnormality	Investigators	Year (Ref.)
Schizophrenic, manic thought	Hoffman	1987 (95)
Schizophrenia (negative symptoms)	Cohen and Servan-Schreiber	1992 (96,97)
Schizophrenia (positive symptoms)	Hoffman and Dobscha	1989 (98)
	Hoffman	1992 (99)
	Horn and Ruppin	1995 (100)
	Ruppin et al.	1996 (101)
Depression	Webster et al.	1988 (102)
	Leven et al.	1992 (103)
	Luciano et al.	1994 (104)
Paranoid disorder	Vinograd et al.	1992 (105)
Delirium	Avni et al.	1998 (106)
Drug effects	Callaway et al.	1994 (107)

ment of specific brain regions in schizophrenia, such as the prefrontal areas, temporal lobes and the temporo-limbic circuitry, and subcortical and midline circuitry. At present, no single explanatory mechanism has prevailed (a few of the most prominent of these theories were presented in Refs. 112–115).

Neural modeling of schizophrenia has taken two main paths, perhaps reflecting the view of schizophrenia as composed of positive symptoms that arise due to temporo-frontal pathology and negative symptoms that are a result of prefrontal abnormalities. This is true both with regard to the symptoms modeled and to the models employed. The first avenue, pioneered by Hoffman, has concentrated on modeling schizophrenic positive symptoms in the framework of an associative memory attractor network (95,98). This work has pointed to a possible link between the appearance of specific neurodegenerative changes and the emergence of "parasitic foci," states in which a neural network's normal processing is disrupted and locked in dysfunctional patterns of activity. In another framework, that of feedforward layered networks employing back-propagation learning, Cohen and colleagues have provided a detailed computational account of how schizophrenic functional deficits can arise from neuromodulatory effects of dopamine (96,97,116,117).

Modeling Positive Symptoms of Schizophrenia with Attractor Networks

Although a few formal models of information processing breakdown were presented earlier (e.g., Refs. 118–120), the publication of Hoffman's 1987 article probably marks the beginning of "the era of neural modeling" of schizophrenia (95). In that article, Hoffman describes how pathological alterations in a Hopfield attractor neural network can lead to the formation of *parasitic attractors*, whose cognitive and perceptual manifestations may play an important role in the emergence of schizophrenic delusions and hallucinations. These parasitic states are spurious states generated when the network becomes "overloaded" [i.e., its memory capacity is exceeded and catastrophic breakdown occurs (121)]. Such memory overload presumably occurs in the brain of schizophrenics as a result of neurodegenerative changes or as a result of selective attention deficits.

Delusions (false beliefs) are common abnormalities of thought among schizophrenics. The inescapability of delusions and their being spontaneously invoked at times by seemingly irrelevant experiences led Hoffman to the idea that they can be conceived as parasitic attractor states that have broad and "deep" basins of attraction. Hoffman also proposed that hallucinations have a similar linkage to parasitic states. Building on the basic linkage between parasitic states and positive symptoms, a detailed simulation study examined the hypothesis that the onset of schizophrenia (usually marked by positive symptoms) is triggered by progressive elimination of synapses in the prefrontal cortex (98). In accordance with this hypothesis, the pathological excess of synaptic pruning reflects a normal developmental synaptic elimination process that fails to arrest in time and proceeds too far. Studying this hypothesis in an attractor neural network, prefrontal synaptic pruning is modeled as a process of random synaptic deletion that tends to damage weak and distal synaptic connections more than strong and proximal ones. This type of spatial-selective damage was found to lead to two kinds of behavior in the network that may have interesting parallels in schizophrenic symptomatology: "functional fragmentation" (denoting patches of convergence to different memories in distinct regions of the network) and spatially organized "parasitic foci" (denoting patches of the network that tend to lock into some nonmemory activation patterns regardless of initial input cues applied to the network).

In addition to the intuitive notion that schizophrenic delusions and hallucinations typically arise in a spontaneous and repetitive manner, what other characteristics of ill-formed attractor states can be thought of as linked to the pathogenesis and manifestations of schizophrenic positive symptoms? A detailed account of the possible role of parasitic foci in the formation of schizophrenic positive symptoms has recently been provided (122), suggesting that parasitic foci produce their effects by altering speech perception and production processes. For example, suppose that cortical speech production regions become dominated by a parasitic attractor. This may result in an experience of inner speech, which, because of the parasitic focus, is stereotyped in nature. Due to the possible detachment of such inner mental events from corresponding motor actions, these events may be experienced as unintended. This, combined with their stereotypical nature, may induce a patient to conclude that a particular alien force is inserting thoughts into his head. In a closely related spirit, it has recently been proposed that due to pathological changes the brain tends to settle in certain attractors which obtain a psychotic "attunement" (123).

A more recent study has examined a theory of Stevens (115) in the framework of an attractor neural network model (100). As summarized in Ref. 115, the wealth of data gathered concerning the pathophysiology of schizophrenia suggests that there are atrophic changes in temporal lobe regions in the brains of a significant number of schizophrenic patients, including neuronal loss and gliosis. On the other hand, neurochemical and morphometric studies testify to an expansion of various receptor binding sites and increased dendritic branching in the projection sites of temporal lobe neurons, including the frontal cortex. These findings have led Stevens to hypothesize that the onset of schizophrenia is associated with reactive anomalous sprouting and synaptic reorganization taking place in the projection sites of degenerating temporal neurons.

To study the functional implications of Steven's hypothesis, a frontal module was modeled as an associative memory neural network receiving its inputs from degenerating temporal projections and undergoing reactive synaptic regeneration (100). In this model, it is shown that while preserving memory performance, compensatory synaptic regenerative changes modeling those proposed by Stevens may lead to adverse, spontaneous activation of stored patterns. When *spontaneous retrieval* emerges, the incorporation of Hebbian activity-dependent synaptic changes leads to a *biased* retrieval distribution that is strongly dominated by a single memory pattern (101), as shown in Figure 4. The formation of biased, spontaneous retrieval is shown to require the concomitant occurrence of both degenerative changes in the external input (temporal) fibers and regenerative activity-dependent Hebbian changes in the intramodular (frontal) synaptic connections.

A few important characteristics of positive symptoms are reflected in the behavior of the network:

1. The emergence of spontaneous, nonhomogeneous retrieval is a self-limiting phenomenon; eventually, a global, spurious attractor is formed. The formation of such a cognitively meaningless spurious attractor, accompanied by a decrease in the size of basins of attraction of the memory patterns, may lead to the emergence of deficit, negative symptoms. This parallels the clinical observation that as schizophrenia progresses, positive symptoms tend to wane, whereas negative symptoms are enhanced.

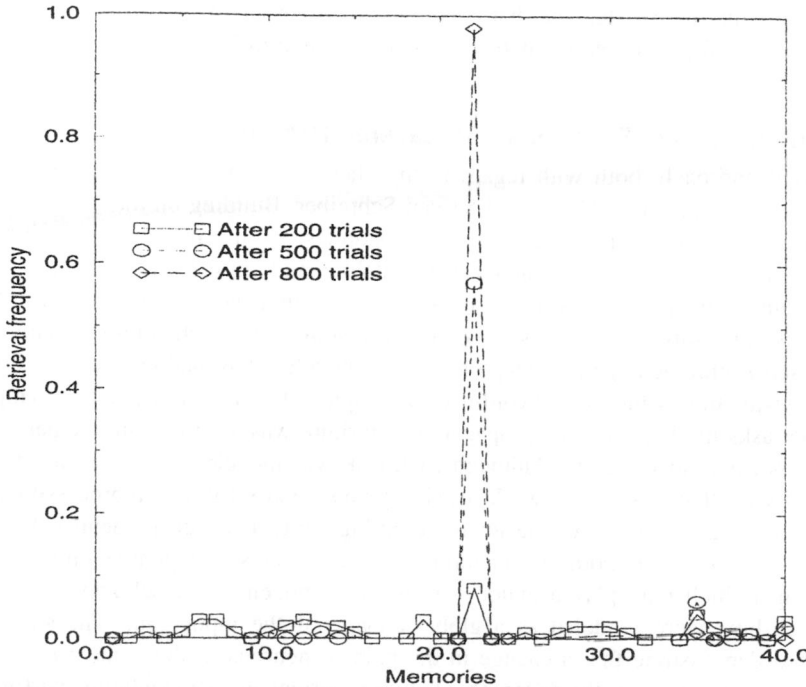

FIGURE 4   The distribution of memory patterns spontaneously retrieved in an attractor neural network model of schizophrenia. The horizontal axis enumerates the stored memories in arbitrary order; the vertical axis denotes the retrieval frequency of each memory. Note that as learning continues over time, the network pathologically retrieves one specific memory pattern (#22) more and more, analogous to a fixed delusion in schizophrenia.

2. When the network converges to a memory pattern that dominates the output in the spontaneous-retrieval scenario, it has an increased tendency to remain in this state for a much longer time than in its normal functioning state, in accordance with the persistence of positive symptoms.

3. The model points to the possibility that maintenance therapy may have an important role not only in preventing the recurrence of positive symptoms but also in slowing down the progression of the disease, by arresting the pathological evolution of the synaptic memory matrix.

4. In its spontaneous retrieval mode, the network may also converge to mixed retrieval states, which have some similarity to a few patterns concomitantly. Such retrieval of mixed patterns may play a part in explaining the generation of more complex forms of schizophrenic delusions and hallucinations, involving abnormal condensation of thoughts and imaginings. Interestingly, this account provides a neural "correlate" of the widely held notion that delusions and hallucinations are adaptive responses to preexisting disorganization as part of a compensatory "defense" mechanism. The model can be tested by quantitatively examining the correlation between a recent history of florid psychotic symptoms and postmortem neuropathological findings of synaptic compensation in schizophrenic subjects. The generation of spontaneous pattern activation fol-

lowing neural damage that alters the input/internal synaptic balance is a quite general phenomenon, as recently demonstrated in Ref. 124.

Modeling Cognitive Functions with Layered Networks

A different approach, both with regard to the phenomena studied and the models employed, has been taken by Cohen and Servan-Schreiber. Building on their work on modeling the neuromodulatory effects of catecholamines on information processing (116, 125), they have presented a comprehensive modeling study of the performance of normal subjects and schizophrenics in three attentional and language processing tasks (96,97). These tasks are important indices of cognitive dysfunction in schizophrenia and are related to schizophrenic negative symptoms. Their modeling has enabled a detailed quantitative investigation, which is not confined to the qualitative realm of positive symptoms. In all the tasks modeled, a back-propagation algorithm was used to train the networks to simulate normal performance. Although each task was modeled by a network designed specifically for that task, the networks used rely on similar information processing principles and share a common module for representing context, which is identified with the prefrontal cortex. The hypothesized neuromodulatory effects of dopamine on information processing (which may play a major role in the pathogenesis of schizophrenia, as described earlier) were modeled as a global change of the input gain. The simulations performed demonstrate that a change in the gain of neurons in the context module can quantitatively account for the differences between normal and schizophrenic performance in the tasks examined.

This work on modeling dopamine effects and schizophrenic deficits leaves many questions open, which has led to a vigorous discussion of their theory and its implications in the psychiatric literature (126,127). Based on the work of Servan-Schreiber et al. (116) on simulating human performance in a choice–reaction time task (Eriksen task), data from a similar task performed by subjects under the influence of various drugs was reanalyzed (107). The authors maintain that patterns of performance observed in the data are in accordance with those predicted by the model, when considering possible drug neuromodulatory effects on the gain and bias of units in different layers. They claim that "neural network models offer a better chance of rescuing the study of human psychologic responses to drugs than anything else currently available" (107).

Although the model presented in Refs. 96 and 97 has not addressed schizophrenic positive symptoms, the authors have pointed out that these may be studied in a similar modeling framework. This issue is precisely the goal of a recent study (128). Aiming to provide a quantitative description of the pathogenesis of auditory hallucinations, the authors have studied the hypothesis that hallucinated "voices" arise from altered verbal working memory. The model consists of a recurrent layered neural network and uses back-propagation to learn a speech perception task. In this task, sequences of randomly coded input words are translated into sequences of outputs in a semantic feature space. In parallel to the simulation studies, an experimental study of speech perception in schizophrenics and normal controls was conducted. The network's architectural and dynamical parameters were first tuned to model the performance of normal subjects. Thereafter, various alterations of network connectivity and dynamics were systematically studied and compared with the experimental findings. Several interesting insights and predictions have been generated: (1) Schizophrenics with auditory hallucinations should have significantly more severe speech perception abnormalities relative to nonhallucinating patients. (2) Several types of alterations can lead to auditory hallucinations, but the combined anatomical/modulatory model is the most likely one. (3) Drugs altering the response profile of neurons may be effective even when the primary pathology is neuro-anatomical rather than neuromodulatory. (4) With severe neuroanatomical damage, perceptual function must be sacrificed in order to reduce hallucinations.

Other Psychiatric Disorders

Paranoia is a tendency to develop suspicions and ambitions that gradually progress to "systematized" delusions of persecution and grandeur. A model of paranoid processes was recently developed within the framework of spreading activation networks (105). Motivated by high-level psychological models of semantic memory and associations, each computational unit represents a distinct cognitive item, and the links between units represent associations. The authors propose that paranoia gradually forms in a process where initial suspicions consolidate into a delusional system. In this process, associations are constructed among temporally contiguous perceptions in an excessive manner and are assigned an idiosyncratic meaning of malevolent motives or persecution by others. The authors suggest that this process can be modeled by a spreading activation network whose connectivity and dynamical parameters are altered, reflecting a 'hyperassociative' state.

Attractor neural networks have also been considered as a framework for modeling a few cognitive manifestations of manic–depressive disorder. Manic–depressive disorder is an affective disorder which includes patients with mania and/or depression. The manic bouts are characterized by a distinctly elevated, expansive, or irritable mood, accompanied by "hyperactivity" symptoms such as decreased need for sleep, pressure to keep talking, "racing" of thoughts, and inflated self-esteem. Hoffman has proposed that in contradistinction to schizophrenic positive symptoms, manic "hyperactivity" arises not as a result of structural damage leading to the formation of pathological attractors, but due to an increase in the noise levels resulting in enhanced rate of transition between attractors (95). Hoffman's views were inspired by the lack of evidence for widespread neuroanatomic damage in manic–depressive disorder, by the success of lithium drugs which alter neural metabolic pathways and, possibly, their firing dynamics, and by discourse studies showing that the basic structure of manic discourse is intact.

The possible role of threshold variation in the pathogenesis of delirium has been recently explored in a neural modeling study by Avni et al. (106). Delirium is characterized by a transient impairment of a wide range of cognitive functions due to a diffuse derangement in cerebral metabolism. Impairment of consciousness and reduced awareness of the environment are hallmarks of the disorder, together with cognitive dysfunction. Almost any process that causes a diffuse disruption of brain homeostasis may cause delirium. Avni et al. (1998) have examined the hypothesis that variations in the neural threshold underlie some memory-related cognitive disturbances in delirium (106). The attractor neural network model used incorporates two sets of connections: Hebbian connections storing memory patterns and randomly weighted connections. Depending on the values of the neuronal threshold and synaptic connectivity parameters, the network may either converge to a stable state or wander through its state space in a seemingly chaotic manner. The transition from the region of single stable states with near-perfect retrieval to unstable end states is sharp and is accompanied by a "syndrome" of poor memory retrieval, slower retrieval time, instability and inconsistency of end states, and storage disturbances, all of which are typical characteristics of memory and cognitive functioning in delirium.

Major depression has also been the focus of recent modeling work. Major depression, the most prevalent affective disorder, is characterized by depressed mood and symptoms like loss of interest, psychomotor retardation, fatigue, sleeplessness, impaired concentration, and suicidal ideation. The difficulty of representing the above symptoms in neural network models has restricted current modeling attempts to some cognitive aspects of major depression. Past work related to major depression has concentrated primarily on modeling learned helplessness, an experimental psychological model of depression, in an adaptive resonance network (129). A similar modeling framework has been used by Hestenes to model the selection and execution of behavioral plans in manic–depressive patients (130). A new approach to studying major depression is described in Ref. 131. The goal of their investigation is to develop a neural model examining the possible role of the limbic system in depressive disorders, creating "linking hypotheses" between model variables for brain regional activities and data describing the temporal progression of clinical symptoms.

PROSPECTS

As the previous sections have illustrated, the last several years have witnessed the development of a wide variety of interesting computational models of neurological, neuropsychological and psychiatric disorders. We now consider the general limitations of these models and what future developments may be anticipated.

Limitations

The use of neural models to study brain and cognitive disorders currently appears to be very promising. These models have already demonstrated that a small set of fairly simple assumptions can account for phenomena seen in recovery from brain damage and impaired cognitive information processing. However, most previous neural models greatly simplify the true psychological/biological phenomena being studied. For example, many of the models of cognitive disorders that have been discussed characterize patients' symptoms in only general terms, relying on syndrome classification labels such as "agrammatic aphasia," "deep dyslexia," and so forth. The point has been made repeatedly in the neuropsychological literature that there syndrome labels frequently present an erroneous picture of symptom homogeneity among patients. Modeling based on such syndrome labels will be subject to the same criticisms that are leveled against other uses of syndrome labels.

Another limitation of neural models relates to their size. Many of the models discussed here are quite small in scope. Even with this simplification, many are computationally very expensive to run on conventional computer architectures (e.g., they require very large amounts of processing time). Furthermore, past work in this area has only attempted to model a very small fraction of the clinical problems that are potentially amenable to study with neural networks.

With all of these limitations of current neural modeling technology, why has there been such a rapidly growing interest in using neural models to study brain and cognitive disorders? Traditional medical investigative techniques (clinical trials, animal experiments, etc.) are expensive and face substantial barriers in terms of what can be practically or ethically studied. Computational models, on the other hand, are relatively inexpensive and provide for large numbers of "subjects" without ethical concerns. They allow one, in theory, to vary any aspect of a system to assess its effects and to record virtually any variable from a system without interfering with the system's behavior. Ultimately, computational models may prove to be the most effective way of understanding the underlying mechanisms of brain and cognitive disorders. They may become important factors in suggesting new treatments or in their preliminary assessment. To a great extent, it is this hope of a deeper understanding of pathophysiology and of potential therapeutic guidance that motivates much of current modeling work in this area.

Future Expectations

It can be anticipated that the technological base supporting the development and use of neural models of cognitive and brain disorders will continue to grow, both in terms of hardware and software. Computer hardware suitable for supporting "massive" explicit parallelism of the sort used in neural models already exists and should be increasingly available in the future. Computer chips that mimic nervous system structure and functionality are also a very active research area and should greatly reduce the cost of access to such technology. Research is under way to understand better the parallel hardware architectures needed for neural models and should produce future systems that are especially suited for neural computations (132). In addition to these hardware implementations, investigation of more radical concepts is under way that could have a dramatic impact if successful. Examples of these latter endeavors include the development of "wetware" [biological neurons grown in culture on a chip and interfaced to electrical circuitry (133)], optical computing (134), connectionist control of prostheses (135), and "nanotechnology" (technology on a nanometer scale). It can be anticipated that progressively more powerful parallel processing computers will become available, allowing the development of larger, more realistic applications.

Software developments can also be anticipated, not only in terms of new methods for controlling network functionality but also in terms of more widespread availability of general-purpose software environments for implementing and using neural networks. Many general connectionist software environments now exist (136–138). Software like this can greatly expedite development of neural models.

Another important issue is the acceptance of computational modeling efforts as potentially useful by more traditional investigators. Physicians and neuroscientists have readily embraced mathematical formulations of single cell behavior in the past, but have been relatively reluctant to accept mathematical and computational neural modeling at the network level as "good science." As we have noted, these reservations have been appropriate in the sense that most neural modeling efforts greatly simplify the biological phenomena being studied. On the other hand, this criticism misses the point that even fairly simple neural network models can exhibit interesting behaviors and can generate hypotheses about important neurophysiological phenomena, suggesting that some emergent behaviors are quite robust in the context of simplified simulations. There has been growing acceptance of neural computation as an important research tool in biomedicine during recent years.

With regard to the modeling of cognitive disorders specifically, connectionist models provide a means for evaluating a number of hypotheses about the functional impairments that underlie neuropsychological deficits that are not easily investigated using other means. These models have already suggested that alteration of a single parameter can have some nonobvious effects on the operation of other cognitive functions. Future efforts can be expected to focus on manipulation of dynamic aspects of information processing and on interactions among relatively independent cognitive components, both of which are elements of cognition that are difficult to address using behavioral testing.

ACKNOWLEDGMENT

Preparation of this article was supported in part by NIH grants NS35460 and NS29414.

REFERENCES

1. J. Reggia, E. Ruppin, and R. Berndt, *Neural Modeling of Brain and Cognitive Disorders*, World Scientific, Singapore, 1996.
2. C. Wood, "Lesion Experiments on the Neural Model of Anderson, Silverstein, Ritz and Jones," *Psychol. Rev.*, *85*, 582–691 (1978).
3. J. Anderson, "Cognitive and Psychological Computation with Neural Models," *IEEE Trans. Syst., Man, Cybernet.*, *13*, 799–815 (1983).
4. B. Gordon, "Confrontation Naming: Computational Model and Disconnection Syndrome," in *Neural Models of Language Processes*, M. Arbib, D. Caplan, and J. Marshall, eds., Academic Press, New York, 1982, pp. 511–530.
5. J. McClelland and D. Rumelhart, "Amnesia and Distributed Memory," in *Parallel Distributed Processing*, J. McClelland, D. Rumelhart, et al., eds., 1986, Vol. 2, pp. 503–527.
6. M. E. Hasselmo, "Runaway Synaptic Modification in Models of the Cortex," *Neural Networks*, *7*, 13–40 (1994).
7. E. Ruppin and J. Reggia, "A Neural Model of Memory Impairment in Diffuse Cerebral Atrophy," *Br. J. Psychiatry*, *166*, 19–28 (1995).
8. M. Farah and J. McClelland, "A Computational Model of Semantic Memory Impairment," *J. Exp. Psychol.*, *120*, 339–357 (1991).
9. J. L. McClelland, B. L. McNaughton, and R. C. O'Reilly, "Why There Are Complementary Learning Systems in the Hippocampus and Neocortex," *Psychol. Rev.*, *102*, 419–437 (1995).
10. S. Small, J. Hart, T. Nguyen, and B. Gordon, "Distributed Representations of Semantic Knowledge in the Brain," *Brain*, *118*, 441–453 (1995).
11. E. Ruppin and J. Reggia, "Patterns of Damage in Neural Networks of Associative Memory," *Neural Computat.*, *7*, 1105–1127 (1995).
12. T. Kohonen, *Self-Organization and Associative Memory*, Springer-Verlag, New York, 1989.
13. P. Dean, "Recapitulation of a Theme by Lashley?" *Psychol. Rev.*, *87*, 470–473 (1980).
14. C. Wood, "Interpretation of Real and Simulated Lesion Experiments," *Psychol. Rev.*, *87*, 474–476 (1980).
15. W. Brain and J. Walton, *Brain's Diseases of Nervous System*, Oxford University Press, Oxford, 1969.
16. K. Walsh, *Neuropsychology*, Churchill Livingston, New York, 1978, p. 284.
17. K. Heilman and E. Valenstein, *Clinical Neuropsychology*, Oxford University Press, Oxford, 1979.
18. R. Katzman, "Alzheimer's Disease," *N. Engl. J. Med.*, *314*, 964–973 (1986).
19. D. Horn, E. Ruppin, M. Usher, and M. Herrmann, "Neural Network Modeling of Memory Deterioration in Alzheimer's Disease," *Neural Computat.*, *5*, 736–749 (1993).

20. D. Horn and E. Ruppin, "Extra-pyramidal Symptoms in Alzheimer's Disease," *Med. Hypothesis*, *39*, 316–318 (1992).

21. J. R. Carrie, "Evaluation of a Neural Network Model of Amnesia in Diffuse Cerebral Atrophy," *Br. J. Psychiatry*, *163*, 217–222 (1993).

22. M. E. Hasselmo and J. M. Bower, "Cholinergic Suppression Specific to Intrinsic Fiber Synapses in the Rat Piriform Cortex," *J. Neurophysiol.*, *67*(5), 1222–1229 (1992).

23. M. E. Hasselmo, B. P. Anderson, and J. M. Bower, "Cholinergic Modulation of Cortical Associative Memory Function," *J. Neurophysiol.*, *67*(5), 1230–1246 (1992).

24. M. E. Hasselmo, "Acetylcholine and Learning in a Cortical Associative Memory," *Neural Computat.*, *5*, 32 (1993).

25. H. Gigley, "HOPE-AI and the Dynamic Process of Language Behavior," *Cogn. Brain Theory*, *6*, 39–88 (1983).

26. G. Cottrell, "Implications of Connectionist Parsing for Aphasia," in *Proc. Ninth Symp. Comp. Applic. Med. Care*, M. Ackerman, ed., 1985, pp. 237–241.

27. N. Martin, E. Saffran, and G. Dell, "Recovery in Deep Dysphasia," *Brain Lang.*, *52*, 83–113 (1996).

28. T. A. Harley, "Connectionist Models of Anomia," *Lang. Cogn. Processes*, *10*, 47–58 (1995).

29. J. Reggia, P. Marsland, and R. Berndt, "Competitive Dynamics in a Dual-Route Connectionist Model of Print-to-Sound Transformation," *Complex Syst.*, *2*, 509–547 (1988).

30. K. Patterson, M. Seidenberg, and J. McClelland, "Acquired Dyslexia in a Computational Model of Reading Processes," in *Connectionism: The Oxford Symposium*, P. Morris, ed., Cambridge University Press, New York, 1989.

31. M. Mozer and M. Behrmann, "On the Interaction of Selective Attention and Lexical Knowledge: A Connectionist Account of Neglect," *Cogn. Neurosci.*, *2*, 96–123 (1990).

32. G. Hinton and T. Shallice, "Lesioning an Attractor Network: Investigations of Acquired Dyslexia," *Psychol. Rev.*, *98*, 74–95 (1991).

33. D. C. Plaut and T. Shallice, "Deep Dyslexia: A Case Study of Connectionist Neuropsychology," *Cogn. Neuropsychol.*, *10*, 377–500 (1993).

34. M. Coltheart, B. Curtis, and P. Atkins, "Models of Reading Aloud," *Psychol. Rev.*, *100*, 589–608 (1993).

35. D. C. Plaut, "Relearning After Damage in Connectionist Networks," *Brain Lang.*, *52*, 25–82 (1996).

36. D. C. Plaut, J. McClelland, M. S. Seidenberg, and K. Patterson, "Understanding Normal and Impaired Word Reading: Computational Principles," *Psychol. Rev.*, *103*, 56–115 (1996).

37. A. Olson and A. Caramazza, in *Handbook of Spelling: Theory, Process and Intervention*, G. Brown and N. Ellis, eds., John Wiley & Sons, New York, 1994.

38. T. Shallice, D. W. Glasspool, and G. Houghton, "Can Neuropsychological Evidence Inform Connectionist Modeling?" *Lang. Cogn. Processes*, *10*, 195–225 (1995).

39. M. Farah and L. Tippett, "Semantic Knowledge Impairments in Alzheimer's Disease," in *Neural Modeling of Brain and Cognitive Disorders*, J. Reggia, E. Ruppin, and R. Berndt, eds., World Scientific, Singapore, 1996, pp. 89–108.

40. S. Small, J. Hart, T. Nguyen, and B. Gordan, "Distributed Representations of Semantic Knowledge," *Brain*, *118*, 441–453 (1995).

41. K. Mayall and G. Humphreys, "Covert Recognition in a Connectionist Model of Pure Alexia," in *Neural Modeling of Brain and Cognitive Disorders*, J. Reggia, E. Ruppin, and R. Berndt, eds., World Scientific, Singapore, 1996, pp. 229–250.

42. G. Dell, "A Spreading Activation Theory of Retrieval and Sentence Production," *Psychol. Rev.*, *93*, 283–321 (1986).

43. G. Dell, M. Schwartz, N. Martin, E. Saffran, and D. Gagnon, "A Connectionist Model of Naming Errors in Aphasia," in *Neural Modeling of Brain and Cognitive Disorders*, J. Reggia, E. Ruppin, and R. Berndt, eds., World Scientific, Singapore, 1996, pp. 135–156.

44. M. Coltheart, K. Patterson, and J. Marshall, eds., *Deep Dyslexia*, Lawrence Erlbaum Assoc., London, 1980.

45. M. Beauvious and J. Derouesne, "Phonological Alexia," *J. Neurol., Neurosurg., Psychol.*, *42*, 1115–1124 (1979).

46. E. Funnel, "Phonological Processes in Reading," *Br. J. Psychol.*, *74*, 159–180 (1983).

47. K. Patterson, J. Marshall, and M. Coltheart, eds., *Surface Dyslexia*, Lawrence Erlbaum Assoc., London, 1985.

48. M. Coltheart, "Cognitive Neuropsychology and the Study of Reading," in *Attention and Performance XI*, M. I. Posner and O. S. M. Marin, eds., Lawrence Erlbaum Assoc., London, 1985, pp. 3–37.

49. R. Glushko, "Organization and Activation of Orthographic Knowledge in Reading Aloud," *J. Exp. Psychol.: Human Percept. Perform.*, *6*, 674–691 (1979).

50. J. Kay and A. Marcel, "One Process, Not Two, in Reading Aloud," *Quart. J. Exp. Psychol.*, *33A*, 397–413 (1981).

51. T. Shallice and R. McCarthy, "Phonological Reading," in *Surface Dyslexia*, K. Patterson, J. Marshall and M. Coltheart, eds., Lawrence Erlbaum Assoc., London, 1985, pp. 361–397.

52. M. Seidenberg and J. McClelland, "A Distributed Developmental Model of Word Recognition and Naming," *Psychol. Rev.*, *96*, 523–568 (1989).

53. J. Fodor and Z. Pylyshyn, "Connectionism and Cognitive Architecture," *Cognition*, *28*, 3–71 (1988).

54. S. Pinker and A. Prince, "On Language and Connectionism: Analysis of a Parallel Distributed Processing Model of Language Acquisition," *Cognition*, *28*, 73–184 (1988).

55. D. Besner, L. Twilley, R. McCann, and K. Seergobin, "On the Association Between Connectionism and Data," *Psychol. Rev.*, *97*, 432 (1990).

56. M. S. Seidenberg, D. C. Plaut, A. S. Petersen, J. L. McClelland, and K. McRae, "Nonword Pronunciation and Models of Word Recognition," *J. Exp. Psychol.: Human Percept. Perform.*, *20*, 1177–1196 (1994).

57. J. McClelland and D. Rumelhart, "An Interactive Activation Model of Context Effects," *Psychol. Rev.*, *88*, 375–407 (1981).

58. S. Goodall, J. Reggia, Y. Peng, and R. Berndt, "A Model of Oral Reading and Acquired Dyslexia," in *Proc. 14th Symp. Comp. Applic. Med. Care*, IEEE, New York, 1990, pp. 294–298.

59. R. L. Venezky, *The Structure of English Orthography*, Mouton, The Hague, 1970.

60. R. Berndt, J. Reggia, and C. Mitchum, "Empirically-Derived Probabilities for Grapheme-to-Phoneme Correspondences," *Behav. Res. Methods, Instrum. Computers*, *19*, 1–9 (1987).

61. C. Whitney, R. Berndt, and J. Reggia, "Simulations of Neurogenic Reading Disorders with a Dual-Route Connectionist Model," in *Neural Modeling of Brain and Cognitive Disorders*, J. Reggia, E. Ruppin, and R. Berndt, eds., World Scientific, Singapore, 1996, pp. 201–228.

62. J. Pearson, L. Finkel, and B. Edelman, "Plasticity in the Organization of Adult Cerebral Cortical Maps," *J. Neurosci.*, *7*, 4209–4233 (1987).

63. E. Sklar, "A Simulation of Somatosensory Cortical Map Plasticity," in *Proc. Int. Joint Conf. Neural Networks*, 1990, Vol. III, pp. 727–732.

64. M. Spitzer, P. Bohler, et al., "A Neural Network Model of Phantom Limbs," *Biol. Cybernet.*, *72*, 197–206 (1995).

65. K. Grajski and M. Merzenich, "Hebb-Type Dynamics and Inverse Magnification Rule in Cortical Somatotopy," *Neural Computat.*, *2*, 71–84 (1990).

66. G. Sutton, J. Reggia, S. Armentrout, and L. D'Autrechy, "Cortical Map Reorganization as a Competitive Process," *Neural Computat.*, *6*, 1–13 (1993).

67. M. Weinrich, G. Sutton, J. Reggia, and C. D'Autrechy, "Adaptation of Non-Competitive Neural Networks to Focal Lesions," *J. Artif. Neural Networks*, 51–60 (1993).

68. S. Armentrout, J. Reggia, and M. Weinrich, "A Neural Model of Cortical Map Reorganization Following a Focal Lesion," *Artif. Intell. Med.*, *6*, 383–400 (1994).

69. J. Xing and G. Gerstein, "Networks with Lateral Connectivity," *J. Neurophysiol.*, *75*, 184–232 (1996).

70. R. Wong, R. Traub, and R. Miles, "Cellular Basis of Neuronal Synchrony," *Adv. Neurol.*, *44*, 583–592 (1986).

71. R. Zepka and R. Sabbatini, "A Computer Program for Simulation of a Quantitative Model for Reflex Epilepsy," *Mathematical Approaches to Brain Functioning Diagnostics*, I. Dvorak and A. Holden, eds., Manchester University Press, Manchester, U.K., 1991, p. 249.

72. M. Mehta, C. Dasgupta, and G. Ullal, "A Neural Network Model for Kindling of Focal Epilepsy," *Biol. Cybernet.*, *68*, 335–340 (1993).

73. R. Traub, "Models of Synchronized Population Bursts in Electrically Coupled Interneurons," *J. Comp. Neurosci.*, *2*, 283–289 (1995).

74. D. Borrett, T. Yeap, and H. Kwan, "Neural Networks and Parkinson's Disease," *Can. J. Neurol. Sci.*, *20*, 107–113 (1993).

75. J. Contreras-Vidal and G. Stelmach, "Neural Model of Basal Ganglia—Thalomocortical Relations in Normal and Parkinsonian Movement," *Biol. Cybernet.*, *73*, 467–476 (1995).

76. J. Reggia and D. Montgomery, "A Computational Model of Visual Hallucinations in Migraine," *Comp. Biol. Med.*, *26*, 133–141 (1996).

77. T. Kohonen, "Self-Organized Formation of Topologically Correct Feature Maps," *Biol. Cybernet.*, *43*, 59–69 (1982).

78. K. Obermayer, H. Ritter, and K. Schulten, "A Neural Network Model For the Formation of Topographic Maps in the CNS, in *Proceedings of International Joint Conference on Neural Networks*, 1990, Vol. II, pp. 423–429.

79. H. Ritter, T. Martinetz, and K. Schulten, "Topology—Conserving Maps for Learning Visuo-Motor Coordination," *Neural Networks*, *2*, 159–168 (1989).

80. J. Reggia, C. D'Autrechy, G. Sutton, and M. Weinrich, "A Competitive Distribution Theory of Neocortical Dynamics," *Neural Computat.*, *4*, 287–317 (1992).

81. E. Knudsen, S. du Lac, and S. Esterly, "Computational Maps in the Brain," *Annu. Rev. Neurosci.*, *10*, 41–65 (1987).

82. S. Udin and J. Fawcett, "Formation of Topographic Maps," *Annu. Rev. Neurosci.*, *11*, 289–327 (1988).

83. M. Merzenich, J. Kaas, et al., "Topographic Reorganization of Somatosensory Cortical Areas 3b and 1 in Monkeys Following Restricted Deafferentation," *Neuroscience*, *8*, 33–55 (1983).

84. T. Pons, P. Garraghty, and M. Mishkim, "Lesion-Induced Plasticity in the Second Somotosensory Cortex of Adult Macaques," *Proc. Nat. Acad. Sci.*, *USA*, *85*, 5279–5281 (1988).

85. J. Kaas, "Plasticity of Sensory and Motor Maps," *Annu. Rev. Neurosci.*, *14*, 137–167 (1991).

86. J. Sanes, S. Suner, J. Lando, and J. Donoghue, "Rapid Reorganization of Adult Rat Motor Cortex Somatic Representation Patterns After Motor Nerve Injury," *Proc. Natl. Acad. Sci. USA*, *85*, 2003–2007 (1988).

87. W. Jenkins, M. Merzenich, T. Allard, and E. Guic-Robels, "Functional Reorganization of Primary Somatosensory Cortex," *J. Neurophys.*, *63*, 82–104 (1990).

88. W. Jenkins and M. Merzenich, "Reorganization of Neocortical Representations After Brain Injury," *Progress in Brain Research*, *Volume 71*, F. Seil, E. Herbert, and B. Carlson, eds., Elsevier, Amsterdam, 1987, pp. 249–266.

89. A. Pascual-Leone, E. Wassermann, N. Sadato, and M. Hallett, "The Role of Reading Activity on the Modulation of Motor Cortical Outputs," *Ann. Neurol.*, *38*, 910–915 (1995).

90. S. Sober, J. Stark, D. Yamasaki, and W. Lytton, "Receptive Field Changes After Strokelike Cortical Ablation: A Role for Activation Dynamics," *J. Neurophys.*, *78*, 3438–3443 (1997).

91. Y. Chen and J. Reggia, "Alignment of Coexisting Cortical Maps in a Motor Control Model," *Neural Computat.*, *8*, 731–755 (1996).

92. S. Goodall, J. Reggia, Y. Chen, E. Ruppin, and C. Whitney, "A Computational Model of Acute Focal Cortical Lesions," *Stroke*, *28*, 101–109 (1997).

93. K. Revett, E. Ruppin, S. Goodall, and J. Reggia, "Spreading Depression in Focal Ischemia: A Computational Study," *J. Cerebral Blood Flow Metab.*, 1998.

94. P. Pinsky and J. Rinzel, "Intrinsic and Network Rhythmogenesis in a Reduced Traub Model for CA3 Neurons," *J. Comp. Neurosci.*, *1*, 39–60 (1994).

95. R. Hoffman, "Computer Simulations of Neural Information Processing and the Schizophrenia-Mania Dichotomy," *Arch. Gen. Psychiatry*, *44*, 178–188 (1987).

96. J. Cohen and D. Servan-Schreiber, "A Neural Network Model of Disturbances in Schizophrenia," *Psychiatr. Annals*, *22*, 131–136 (1992).

97. J. Cohen and D. Servan-Schreiber, "A Connectionist Approach to Behavior and Biology in Schizophrenia," *Psychol. Rev.*, *99*, 45–77 (1992).

98. R. Hoffman and S. Dobscha, "Cortical Pruning and the Development of Schizophrenia: A Computer Model," *Schizophrenia Bull.*, *15*, 477 (1989).

99. R. Hoffman, "Attractor Neural Networks and Psychotic Disorders," *Psychiatr. Annals*, *22*, 119–124 (1992).

100. D. Horn and E. Ruppin, "Compensatory Mechanism in Attractor Neural Network Model of Schizophrenia," *Neural Computat.*, *7*, 182–205 (1995).

101. E. Ruppin, J. Reggia, and D. Horn, "Pathogenesis of Schizophrenic Delusions and Hallucinations: A Neural Model," *Schizophrenia Bull.*, *22*, 105–123 (1996).

102. C. Webster, R. Glass, and G. Banks, "A Depression Emulation Program," in *Proc. Twelfth Symp. on Comp. Applic. in Med. Care*, R. Greenes, ed., IEEE, New York, 1988, pp. 287–291.

103. S. J. Leven, "Learned Helplessness, Memory, and the Dynamics of Hope," in *Motivation, Emotion and Goal Direction in Neural Networks*, D. S. Levine and S. J. Leven, eds., Lawrence Erlbaum Assoc., London, 1992.

104. J. S. Luciano, M. A. Cohen, J. A. Samson, and P. G. Hagan, "A Neural Model of Unipolar Depression," in *Irish Neural Network Conference*, September 12–13, 1994.

105. S. Vinogradov, R. J. King, and B. A. Huberman, "An Associationist Model of the Paranoid Process," *Psychiatry*, *55*, 79–94 (1992).

106. A. Avni, E. Ruppin, and M. Stern, "Cognitive Function in Delerium: A Neural Model," 1998, submitted.

107. E. Callaway, R. Halliday, H. Naylor, et al. "Drugs and Human Information Processing," *Neuropsychopharmacology*, *10*, 9–19 (1994).

108. G. Roberts, "Schizophrenia: The Cellular Biology of a Functional Psychosis," *Trends Neurosci.*, *13*, 207–211 (1990).

109. J. L. Waddington, "Neurodynamics of Abnormalities in Cerebral Metabolism and Structure in Schizophrenia," *Schizophrenia Bull.*, *19*, 55–69 (1993).

110. W. T. Carpenter and R. W. Buchanan, "Schizophrenia," *N. Engl. J. Med.*, *330*, 681–690 (1994).

111. N. Andreasen, "The Mechanisms of Schizophrenia," *Curr. Opin. Neurobiol.*, *4*, 245–251 (1994).

112. J. R. Stevens, "An Anatomy of Schizophrenia?" *Arch. Gen. Psychol.*, *29*, 177–189 (1973).

113. D. R. Weinberger, "Implications of Normal Brain Development for the Pathogenesis of Schizophrenia," *Arch. Gen. Psychol.*, *44*, 660–669 (1987).

114. M. Carlsson and A. Carlsson, "Interactions Between Glutamatergic and Monoaminergic Systems within the Basal Ganglia," *Trends Neurosci.*, *13*, 272–276 (1990).

115. J. R. Stevens, "Abnormal Reinnervation as a Basis for Schizophrenia," *Arch. Gen. Psychiatry*, *49*, 238–243 (1992).

116. D. Servan-Schreiber, H. Printz, and J. D. Cohen, "A Network Model of Catecholamine Effects," *Science*, *249*, 892–895 (1990).

117. J. D. Cohen, D. Servan-Schreiber, and J. L. McClelland, "A PDP Approach to Automaticity," *Am. J. Psychol.*, *105*, 239–269 (1992).

118. E. Callaway, "Schizophrenia and Interference: An Analogy with a Malfunctioning Computer," *Arch. Gen. Psychol.*, *22*, 193–208 (1970).

119. D. E. Broadbent, *Decision and Stress.* Academic Press, New York, 1971.
120. M. H. Joseph, C. D. Frith, and J. L. Waddington, "Dopaminergic Mechanisms and Cognitive Deficits in Schizophrenia," *Psychopharmacology, 63,* 273–280 (1979).
121. D. J. Amit, *Modeling Brain Function: The World of Attractor Neural Networks*, Cambridge University Press, Cambridge, 1989.
122. R. E. Hoffman and T. H. McGlashan, "Parallel Distributed Processing and the Emergence of Schizophrenic Symptoms," *Schizophrenia Bull., 19,* 119–140 (1993).
123. G. G. Globus and J. P. Arpia, "Psychiatry and the New Dynamics," *Biol. Psychiatry, 35,* 352–364 (1994).
124. S. L. Thaler, "Virtual Input Phenomena Within the Death of a Simple Pattern Associator," *Neural Networks, 8,* 55–65 (1995).
125. D. Servan-Schreiber and J. C. Cohen, "A Neural Network Model of Catecholamine Modulation of Behavior," *Psychiatr. Ann., 22,* 125–130 (1992).
126. T. H. Jobe, M. Harrow, E. M. Martin, J. J. Whitfield, and J. R. Sands, "Schizophrenia Deficits—Neuroleptics and the Prefrontal Cortex," *Schizophrenia Bull., 20,* 413–416 (1994).
127. J. D. Cohen, R. D. Romero, D. Servan-Schreiber, and M. J. Farah, "Disengaging from the Disengage Function: The Relation of Macrostructure to Microstructure in Pareital Attentional Deficits," *J. Cogn. Neurosci., 6,* 377–387 (1994).
128. R. E. Hoffman, J. Rapaport, R. Ameli, et al., "The Pathophysiology of Hallucinated Voices and Associated Speech Perception Impairment in Schizophrenia," preprint, 1994.
129. D. S. Levine and P. S. Prueitt, "Modeling Some Effects of Frontal Lobe Damage," *Neural Networks, 2,* 103–116 (1989).
130. D. Hestenes, in *Motivation, Emotion and Goal Direction in Neural Networks*, D. S. Levine and S. J. Leven, eds., Lawrence Erlbaum Assoc., London, 1992.
131. J. S. Luciano, M. A. Cohen, and J. A. Samson, "A Neural Model of Unipolar Depression," in *Irish Neural Network Conference*, September 12–13, 1994.
132. T. Nordstrom and B. Svensson, "Using and Designing Massively Parallel Computers for Artificial Neural Networks," *J. Par. Distrib. Comp., 14,* 260–285 (1992).
133. G. Gross, W. Wen, and L. Jacob, "Indium–Tin Electrodes for Extracellular Recording in Neuronal Circuits," *J. Neurosci. Methods, 15,* 243–252 (1985).
134. D. Psaltis and N. Farhat, "Networks, Optical Information Processing Based on an Associative Memory Model of Neural Networks," *Optics Lett., 10,* 98–100 (1985).
135. E. Wan, G. Kovacs, J. Rosen, and B. Widrow, "Development of Neural Network Interfaces for Direct Control of Neuro Prostheses," in *Proc. Intl. Joint Conf. on Neural Networks*, Lawrence Erlbaum Assoc., London, 1990, Vol. II, pp. 3–21.
136. T. Schwartz, "Neural Networks," *AI Expert*, 73–85 (August 1988).
137. K. Reid and A. Zeichick, "Neural Network Resource Guide," *AI Expert*, 5–56 (June 1992).
138. M. Wilson, U. Bhalla, J. Uhley, and J. Bower, "GENESIS: A System for Simulating Neural Networks," *Advances in Neural Network Information Processing Systems*, D. Touretzky, ed., Morgan Kaufman, San Mateo, CA, 1989, pp. 485–492.

JAMES A. REGGIA

EYTAN RUPPIN

NUMERICAL LINEAR ALGEBRA

INTRODUCTION

The increasing availability of advanced-architecture computers has a significant effect on all spheres of scientific computation, including algorithm research and software development in numerical linear algebra. Linear algebra—in particular, the solution of linear systems of equations—lies at the heart of most calculations in scientific computing. This article discusses some of the recent developments in linear algebra designed to exploit these advanced-architecture computers. We discuss two broad classes of algorithms: those for dense and those for sparse matrices. A matrix is called sparse if it has a substantial number of zero elements, making specialized storage and algorithms necessary.

Much of the work in developing linear algebra software for advanced-architecture computers is motivated by the need to solve large problems on the fastest computers available. In this article, we focus on four basic issues: (1) the motivation for the work; (2) the development of standards for use in linear algebra and the building blocks for libraries; (3) aspects of algorithm design and parallel implementation; and (4) future directions for research.

As representative examples of dense matrix routines, we will consider the Cholesky and LU factorizations, and these will be used to highlight the most important factors that must be considered in designing linear algebra software for advanced-architecture computers. We use these factorization routines for illustrative purposes, not only because they are relatively simple but also because of their importance in several scientific and engineering applications that make use of boundary element methods. These applications include electromagnetic scattering and computational fluid dynamics problems, as discussed in more detail in the subsection Uses of LU Factorization in Science and Engineering.

For the past 15 years or so, there has been a great deal of activity in the area of algorithms and software for solving linear algebra problems. The goal of achieving high performance on codes that are portable across platforms has largely been realized by the identification of linear algebra kernels, the Basic Linear Algebra Subprograms (BLAS). We will discuss the Eispack, Linpack, Lapack, and Scalapack libraries, which are expressed in successive levels of the BLAS.

The key insight of our approach to designing linear algebra algorithms for advanced-architecture computers is that the frequency with which data are moved between different levels of the memory hierarchy must be minimized in order to attain high performance. Thus, our main algorithmic approach for exploiting both vectorization and parallelism in our implementations is the use of block-partitioned algorithms, particularly in conjunction with highly tuned kernels for performing matrix–vector and matrix–matrix operations (the Level 2 and 3 BLAS).

DENSE LINEAR ALGEBRA ALGORITHMS

Overview of Dense Algorithms

Common operations involving dense matrices are the solution of linear systems

$$Ax = b,$$

the least squares solution of over determined or underdetermined systems

$$\min_{x} \| Ax - b \|,$$

and the computation of eigenvalues and eigenvectors

$$Ax = \lambda x.$$

Although these problems are formulated as matrix–vector equations, their solution involves a definite matrix–matrix component. For instance, in order to solve a linear system, the coefficient matrix is first factored as

$$A = LU$$

(or $A = U^t U$ in the case of symmetry), where L and U are lower and upper triangular matrices, respectively. It is a common feature of these matrix–matrix operations that they take, on a matrix of size $n \times n$, a number of operations proportional to n^3, a factor n more than the number of data elements involved.

Thus, we are led to identify three levels of linear algebra operations:

- Level 1: Vector–vector operations such as the update $\bar{y} \leftarrow \bar{y} + \alpha \bar{x}$ and the inner product $d = \bar{x}^t \bar{y}$. These operations involve (for vectors of length n) $O(n)$ data and $O(n)$ operations.
- Level 2: Matrix–vector operations such as the matrix–vector product $y = Ax$. These involve $O(n^2)$ operations on $O(n^2)$ data.
- Level 3: Matrix–matrix operations such as the matrix–matrix product $C = AB$. These involve $O(n^3)$ operations on $O(n^2)$ data.

These three levels of operations have been realized in a software standard known as the Basic Linear Algebra Subprograms (BLAS) (1–3). Although BLAS routines are freely available on the net, many computer vendors supply a tuned, often assembly-coded, BLAS library optimized for their particular architecture. See also the subsection The BLAS as the Key to Portability.

The relation between the number of operations and the amount of data is crucial for the performance of the algorithm. We discuss this in detail in the subsection Discussion of Architectural Features.

Loop Rearranging

The operations of BLAS Levels 2 and 3 can be implemented using doubly and triply nested loops, respectively. With simple modifications, this means that for Level 2, each algorithm has two and for Level 3 six different implementations. For instance, solving a lower triangular system $Lx = y$ is mostly written

for $i = 1, \ldots, n,$
    $t = 0,$

$$\text{for } j = 1, \ldots, \ i - 1,$$
$$t \leftarrow t + \ell_{ij} x_j,$$
$$x = \ell_{ii}^{-1} (y_i - t),$$

but it can also be written as

$$\text{for } j = 1, \ldots, n,$$
$$x_j = \ell_{jj}^{-1} y_j,$$
$$\text{for } i = j + 1, \ldots, n,$$
$$y_i \leftarrow y_i - \ell_{ij} x_j.$$

(The latter implementation overwrites the right-hand side vector *y*, but this can be eliminated.)

Although the two implementations are equivalent in terms of numbers of operations, there may be substantial differences in performance due to architectural considerations. We note, for instance, that the inner loop in the first implementation uses a row of *L*, whereas the inner loop in the second traverses a column. Because matrices are usually stored with either rows or columns in contiguous locations, column storage the historical default inherited from the FORTRAN programming language, the performance of the two can be radically different. We discuss this point further in the subsection Discussion of Architectural Features.

Uses of LU Factorization in Science and Engineering

A major source of large dense linear systems is problems involving the solution of boundary integral equations. These are integral equations defined on the boundary of a region of interest. All examples of practical interest compute some intermediate quantity on a two-dimensional boundary and then use this information to compute the final desired quantity in three-dimensional space. The price one pays for replacing three dimensions with two is that what started as a sparse problem in $O(n^3)$ variables is replaced by a dense problem in $O(n^2)$.

Dense systems of linear equations are found in numerous applications, including the following:

* Airplane wing design
* Radar cross-section studies
* Flow around ships and other off-shore constructions
* Diffusion of solid bodies in a liquid
* Noise reduction
* Diffusion of light through small particles

The electromagnetics community is a major user of dense linear systems solvers. Of particular interest to this community is the solution of the so-called radar cross-section problem. In this problem, a single of fixed frequency bounces off an object; the goal is to determine the intensity of the reflected signal in all possible directions. The underlying differential equation may vary, depending on the specific problem. In the design of stealth aircraft, the principal equation is the Helmholtz equation. To solve this equation, researchers use the *method of moments* (4,5). In the case of fluid flow, the problem often involves solving the Laplace or Poisson equation. Here, the boundary integral solution is known as the *panel method* (6,7), so named from the quadrilaterals that discretize and approximate a structure such as an airplane. Generally, these methods are called *boundary element methods*.

Use of these methods produces a dense linear system of size $O(N)$ by $O(N)$, where N is the number of boundary points (or panels) being used. It is not unusual to see size $3N \times 3N$, because of three physical quantities of interest at every boundary element.

A typical approach to solving such systems is to use LU factorization. Each entry of the matrix is computed as an interaction of two boundary elements. Often, many integrals must be computed. In many instances, the time required to compute the matrix is considerably larger than the time for solution.

The builders of stealth technology who are interested in radar cross sections are using direct Gaussian elimination methods for solving dense linear systems. These systems are always symmetric and complex, but not Hermitian.

For further information on various methods for solving large dense linear algebra problems that arise in computational fluid dynamics, see the report by Edelman (8).

Block Algorithms and Their Derivation

It is comparatively straightforward to recode many of the dense linear algebra algorithms so that they use Level 2 BLAS. Indeed, in the simplest cases, the same floating-point operations are done, possibly even in the same order; it is just a matter of reorganizing the software. To illustrate this point, we consider the Cholesky factorization algorithm, which factors a symmetric positive definite matrix as $A = U^T U$. We consider Cholesky factorization because the algorithm is simple, and no pivoting is required on a positive definite matrix.

Suppose that after $j - 1$ steps, the block A_{00} in the upper left-hand corner of A has been factored as $A_{00} = U_{00}^T U_{00}$. The next row and column of the factorization can then be computed by writing $A = U^T U$ as

$$\begin{pmatrix} A_{00} & b_j & A_{02} \\ \cdot & a_{jj} & c_j^T \\ \cdot & \cdot & A_{22} \end{pmatrix} = \begin{pmatrix} U_{00}^T & 0 & 0 \\ v_j^T & u_{jj} & 0 \\ U_{02}^T & w_j & U_{22}^T \end{pmatrix} \begin{pmatrix} U_{00} & v_j & U_{02} \\ 0 & u_{jj} & w_j^T \\ 0 & 0 & U_{22} \end{pmatrix},$$

where b_j, c_j, v_j, and w_j are column vectors of length $j - 1$ and a_{jj} and u_{jj} are scalars. Equating coefficients of the jth column, we obtain

$$b_j = U_{00}^T v_j,$$
$$a_{jj} = v_j^T v_j + u_{jj}^2.$$

Because U_{00} has already been computed, we can compute v_j and u_{jj} from the equations

$$U_{00}^T v_j = b_j,$$
$$u_{jj}^2 = a_{jj} - v_j^T v_j.$$

The computation of v_j is a triangular system solution, a BLAS Level 2 operation. Thus, a code using this will have a single call replacing a loop of Level 1 calls or a doubly nested loop of scalar operations.

This change, by itself, is sufficient to result in large gains in performance on a number of machines; for example, from 72 to 251 megaflops for a matrix of order 500 on a processor of a CRAY Y-MP. Because this is 81% of the peak speed of matrix–matrix multiplication on this processor, we cannot hope to do very much better by using Level 3 BLAS.

We can, however, restructure the algorithm at a deeper level to exploit the faster speed of the Level 3 BLAS. This restructuring involves recasting the algorithm as a *block algorithm*; that is, an algorithm that operates on *blocks* or submatrices of the original matrix.

Deriving a Block Algorithm

To derive a block form of Cholesky factorization, we partition the matrices as shown in Figure 1, in which the diagonal blocks of A and U are square but of differing sizes. We assume that the first block has already been factored as $A_{00} = U_{00}^T U_{00}$ and that we now want to determine the second block column of U consisting of the blocks U_{01} and U_{11}. Equating submatrices in the second block of columns, we obtain

$$A_{01} = U_{00}^T U_{01},$$
$$A_{11} = U_{01}^T U_{01} + U_{11}^T U_{11}.$$

Hence, because U_{00} has already been computed, we can compute U_{01} as the solution to the equation

$$U_{00}^T U_{01} = A_{01}$$

by a call to the Level 3 BLAS routine STRSM; we can then compute U_{11} from

$$U_{11}^T U_{11} = A_{11} - U_{01}^T U_{01}.$$

This involves first updating the symmetric submatrix A_{11} by a call to the Level 3 BLAS routine SSYRK, and then computing its Cholesky factorization. Because FORTRAN does not allow recursion, a separate routine must be called, using Level 2 BLAS rather than Level 3. In this way, successive blocks of columns of U are computed.

However, that is not the end of the story, and the code given above is not the code actually used in the LAPACK routine SPOTRF. We mentioned earlier that for many linear algebra computations, there are several algorithmic variants, often referred to as i, j, and k variants, according to a convention introduced in Refs. 9 and 10 and explored further in Refs. 11 and 12. The same is true of the corresponding block algorithms.

It turns out that the j variant chosen for LINPACK and used in the above examples is not the fastest on many machines because it performs most of the work in solving triangular systems of equations, which can be significantly slower than matrix–matrix

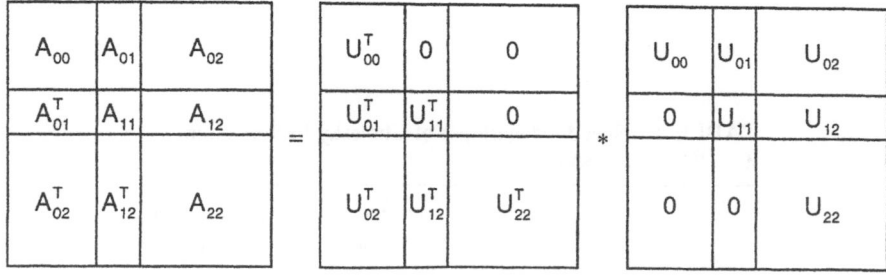

FIGURE 1 Partitioning of A, U^T, and U into blocks. It is assumed that the first block has already been factored as $A_{00} = U_{00}^T U_{00}$, and we next want to determine the block column consisting of U_{01} and U_{11}. Note that the diagonal blocks of A and U are square matrices.

multiplication. The variant actually used in LAPACK is the *i* variant, which relies on matrix–matrix multiplication for most of the work.

Table 1 summarizes the results.

THE INFLUENCE OF COMPUTER ARCHITECTURE ON PERFORMANCE

Discussion of Architectural Features

In the subsection Loop Rearranging, we noted that for BLAS Levels 2 and 3 several equivalent implementations of the operations exist. These differ, for instance, in whether they access a matrix operand by rows or columns in the inner loop. In FORTRAN, matrices are stored by columns, so accessing a column corresponds to accessing consecutive memory elements. On the other hand, as one proceeds across a row, the memory references jump across memory, the length of the jump being proportional to the length of a column.

We will now give a simplified discussion on the various architectural issues that influence the choice of algorithm. The following is, of necessity, a simplified account of the state of affairs for any particular architecture.

At first, we concentrate only on "nonblocked" algorithms. In blocked methods, discussed in more detail later, every algorithm has two levels on which we can consider loop arranging: the block level and the scalar level. Often, the best arrangement on one level is not the best on the other. The next two subsections concern themselves with the scalar level.

Using Consecutive Elements

The decision of how to traverse matrix elements should usually be taken so as to use elements that are consecutive in storage. There are at least three architectural reasons for this:

Page swapping: By using consecutive memory elements instead of ones at some stride distance of each other, the amount of memory page swapping is minimized.

Memory banks: If the processor cycle is faster than the memory cycle, and memory consists of interleaved banks, consecutive elements will be in different banks. By contrast, taking elements separated a distance equal to the number of

TABLE 1   Speed (Megaflops) of Cholesky Factorization $A = U^T U$ for $n = 500$

	CRAY T-90, 1 proc.	CRAY T-90, 4 proc.
j Variant: LINPACK	376	392
j Variant: using Level 3 BLAS	1222	2306
i Variant: using Level 3 BLAS	1297	3279

banks, all elements will come from the same bank. This will reduce the effective performance of the algorithm to the memory speed instead of the processor speed.

Cache lines: Processors with a memory cache typically do not bring in single elements from memory to cache, but move them one "cache line" at a time. A cache line consists of a small number of consecutive memory elements. Thus, using consecutive memory storage elements means that a next element will already be in cache and does not have to be brought into cache. This cuts down on memory traffic.

Whether consecutive elements correspond to rows or columns in a matrix depends on the programming language used. In FORTRAN, columns are stored consecutively, whereas C has row elements contiguous in memory.

The effects of column orientation are quite dramatic: On systems with virtual or cache memories, the LINPACK library codes (subsection LINPACK), which are written in FORTRAN and which are column oriented, will significantly outperform FORTRAN codes that are not column oriented. In C language, however, algorithms should be formulated with row orientation. We note that textbook examples of matrix algorithms are usually given in a row-oriented manner.

Cache Reuse

In many contemporary architectures, memory bandwidth is not enough to keep the processor working at its peak rate. Therefore, the architecture incorporates some cache memory, a relatively small store of faster memory. The memory bandwidth problem is now shifted to bringing the elements into cache, and this problem can be obviated almost entirely if the algorithm can reuse cache elements.

Consider, for instance, a matrix–vector product $y = Ax$. The doubly nested loop has an inner statement

$$y_i \leftarrow y_i + a_{ij}a_j,$$

implying three reads and one write from memory for two operations. If we write the algorithm as

$$y_* = x_1 a_{1*} + x_2 a_{2*} + \cdots,$$

we see that keeping y in cache* and reusing the elements of x, we only need to load the column of A, making the asymptotic demand on memory one element load, once x and y have been brought into cache.

Blocking for Cache Reuse

Earlier, we saw in the Cholesky example how algorithms can naturally be written in terms of Level 2 operations. In order to use Level 3 operations, a more drastic rewrite is needed.

Suppose we want to perform the matrix–matrix multiplication $C = AB$, where all matrices are of size $n \times n$. We divide all matrices in subblocks of size $k \times k$ and let, for

---

*Because many level-1 caches are write-through, we would not actually keep y in cache, but rather keep a number of elements of it in register, and reuse these registers by unrolling the "$*$" loop.

simplicity's sake, k divide n: $n = km$. Then, the triply nested scalar loop becomes, in one possible rearrangement,

$$
\begin{aligned}
&\text{for } i = 1 \ldots m \\
&\quad \text{for } k = 1 \ldots m \\
&\qquad \text{for } j = 1 \ldots m \\
&\qquad\quad C_{ij} \leftarrow C_{ij} + A_{ik}B_{kj},
\end{aligned}
$$

where the inner statement is now a size k matrix–matrix multiplication.

If the cache is now large enough, three of these smaller matrices, we can keep C_{ij} and A_{ik} in cache* while successive blocks B_{kj} are being brought in. The ratio of memory loads to operations is then (ignoring the loads of the elements of C and A, which are amortized) k^2/k^3 (i.e., $1/k$).

Thus, by blocking the algorithm and arranging the loops so that blocks are reused in cache, we can achieve high performance in spite of a low-memory bandwidth.

Target Architectures

The EISPACK and LINPACK software libraries were designed for supercomputers used in the 1970s and early 1980s, such as the CDC-7600, Cyber 205, and Cray-1. These machines featured multiple functional units pipelined for good performance (13). The CDC-7600 was basically a high-performance scalar computer, whereas the Cyber 205 and Cray-1 were early vector computers.

The development of LAPACK in the late 1980s was intended to make the EISPACK and LINPACK libraries run efficiently on shared-memory, vector supercomputers. The ScaLAPACK software library will extend the use of LAPACK to distributed-memory concurrent supercomputers. The development of ScaLAPACK began in 1991.

The underlying concept of both the LAPACK and ScaLAPACK libraries is the use of block-partitioned algorithms to minimize data movement between different levels in hierarchical memory. Thus, the ideas discussed in this article for developing a library for dense linear algebra computations are applicable to any computer with a hierarchical memory that (1) imposes a sufficiently large start-up cost on the movement of data between different levels in the hierarchy and for which (2) the cost of a context switch is too great to make fine-grain-size multithreading worthwhile. Our target machines are, therefore, medium- and large-grain-size advanced-architecture computers. These include "traditional" shared-memory vector supercomputers, such as the Cray C-90 and T-90, and MIMD distributed-memory concurrent supercomputers, such as the SGI Origin 2000, IBM SP, Cray T3E, and HP/Convex Exemplar concurrent systems.

Future advances in compiler and hardware technologies are expected to make multithreading a viable approach for masking communication costs. Because the blocks in a block-partitioned algorithm can be regarded as separate threads, our approach will still be applicable on machines that exploit medium- and coarse-grain-size multi-threading.

---

*Again, with a write-through level-1 cache, one would try to keep C_{ij} in registers.

DENSE LINEAR ALGEBRA LIBRARIES

Requirements on High-Quality, Reusable, Mathematical Software

In developing a library of high-quality subroutines for dense linear algebra computations, the design goals fall into three broad classes:

- Performance
- Ease of use
- Range of use

Performance

Two important performance metrics are *concurrent efficiency* and *scalability*. We seek good performance characteristics in our algorithms by eliminating, as much as possible, overhead due to load imbalance, data movement, and algorithm restructuring. The way the data are distributed (or decomposed) over the memory hierarchy of a computer is of fundamental importance to these factors. Concurrent efficiency, ε, is defined as the concurrent speedup per processor (14), where the concurrent speedup is the execution time, T_{seq}, for the best sequential algorithm running on one processor of the concurrent computer, divided by the execution time, T, of the parallel algorithm running on N_p processors. When direct methods are used, as in LU factorization, the concurrent efficiency depends on the problem size and the number of processors; therefore, on a given parallel computer and for a fixed number of processors, the running time should not vary greatly for problems of the same size. Thus, we may write

$$\varepsilon(N,N_p) = \frac{1}{N_p} \frac{T_{seq}(N)}{T(N,N_p)}, \tag{1}$$

where N represents the problem size. In dense linear algebra computations, the execution time is usually dominated by the floating-point operation count, so the concurrent efficiency is related to the performance, G, measured in floating-point operations per second by

$$G(N,N_p) = \frac{N_p}{t_{calc}} \varepsilon(N,N_p), \tag{2}$$

where t_{calc} is the time for one floating-point operation. For iterative routines, such as eigensolvers, the number of iterations, hence the execution time, depends not only on the problem size but also on other characteristics of the input data, such as condition number. A parallel algorithm is said to be scalable (15) if the concurrent efficiency depends on the problem size and number of processors only through their ratio. This ratio is simply the problem size per processor, often referred to as the granularity. Thus, for a scalable algorithm, the concurrent efficiency is constant as the number of processors increases while keeping the granularity fixed. Alternatively, Eq. (2) shows that this is equivalent to saying that, for a scalable algorithm, the performance depends linearly on the number of processors for fixed granularity.

Ease of Use

Ease of use is concerned with factors such as portability and the user interface to the library. Portability, in its most inclusive sense, means that the code is written in a standard language, such as FORTRAN or C, and that the source code can be compiled on an arbitrary machine to produce a program that will run correctly. We call this the "mail-order software" model of portability, because it reflects the model used by software servers such as *netlib* (16). This notion of portability is quite demanding. It requires that all relevant properties of the computer's arithmetic and architecture be discovered at runtime within the confines of a compilable FORTRAN code. For example, if it is important to know the overflow threshold for scaling purposes, it must be determined at runtime *without overflowing*, as overflow is generally fatal. Such demands have resulted in quite large and sophisticated programs (17,18), which must be modified frequently to deal with new architectures and software releases. This "mail-order" notion of software portability also means that codes generally must be written for the worst possible machine expected to be used, thereby often degrading performance on all others. Ease of use is also enhanced if implementation details are largely hidden from the user, for example, through the use of an object-based interface to the library (19).

Range of Use

Range of use may be gauged by how numerically stable the algorithms are over a range of input problems and the range of data structures the library will support. For example, LINPACK and EISPACK deal with dense matrices stored in a rectangular array, packed matrices, where only the upper or lower half of a symmetric matrix is stored, and banded matrices, where only the nonzero bands are stored. In addition, some special formats such as Householder vectors are used internally to represent orthogonal matrices. In the second half of this article, we will focus on sparse matrices; that is, matrices with many zero elements, which may be stored in many different ways.

Portability, Scalability, and Standards

Portability of programs has always been an important consideration. Portability was easy to achieve when there was a single architectural paradigm (the serial von Neumann machine) and a single programming language for scientific programming (FORTRAN) embodying that common model of computation. Architectural and linguistic diversity have made portability much more difficult, but no less important, to attain. Users simply do not wish to invest significant amounts of time to create large-scale application codes for each new machine. Our answer is to develop portable software libraries that hide machine-specific details.

In order to be truly portable, parallel software libraries must be *standardized*. In a parallel computing environment in which the higher-level routines and/or abstractions are build upon lower-level computation and message-passing routines, the benefits of standardization are particularly apparent. Furthermore, the definition of computational and message-passing standards provides vendors with a clearly defined base set of routines that they can implement efficiently.

From the user's point of view, portability means that as new machines are developed, they are simply added to the network, supplying cycles where they are most appropriate.

From the mathematical software developer's point of view, portability may require significant effort. Economy in development and maintenance of mathematical software demands that such development effort be leveraged over as many different computer systems as possible. Given the great diversity of parallel architectures, this type of portability is attainable to only a limited degree, but machine dependences can at least be isolated.

LAPACK is an example of a mathematical software package whose highest-level components are portable, whereas machine dependences are hidden in lower-level modules. Such a hierarchical approach is probably the closest one can come to software portability across diverse parallel architectures. Also, the BLAS that are used so heavily in LAPACK provide a portable, efficient, and flexible standard for applications programmers.

Like portability, *scalability* demands that a program be reasonably effective over a wide range of number of processors. Maintaining scalability of parallel algorithms and the software libraries implementing them over a wide range of architectural designs and numbers of processors will likely require that the fundamental granularity of computation be adjustable to suit the particular circumstances in which the software may happen to execute. Our approach to this problem is block algorithms with adjustable block size. In many cases, however, polyalgorithms* may be required to deal with the full range of architectures and processor multiplicity likely to be available in the future.

Scalable parallel architectures of the future are likely to be based on a distributed-memory architectural paradigm. In the longer term, progress in hardware development, operating systems, languages, compilers, and communications may make it possible for users to view such distributed architectures (without significant loss of efficiency) as having a shared memory with a global address space. For the near term, however, the distributed nature of the underlying hardware will continue to be visible at the programming level; therefore, efficient procedures for explicit communication will continue to be necessary. Given this fact, standards for basic message passing (send/receive), as well as higher-level communication constructs (global summation, broadcast, etc.), become essential to the development of scalable libraries that have any degree of portability. In addition to standardizing general communication primitives, it may also be advantageous to establish standards for problem-specific constructs in commonly occurring areas such as linear algebra.

The BLACS (Basic Linear Algebra Communication Subprograms) (20,21) is a package that provides the same ease of use and portability for MIMD message-passing linear algebra communication that the BLAS (1–3) provide for linear algebra computation. Therefore, we recommend that future software for dense linear algebra on MIMD platforms consist of calls to the BLAS for computation and calls to the BLACS for communication. Because both packages will have been optimized for a particular platform, good performance should be achieved with relatively little effort. Also, because both packages will be available on a wide variety of machines, code modifications required to change platforms should be minimal.

The BLAS as the Key to Portability

At least three factors affect the performance of compilable code:

1. **Vectorization/cache reuse.** Designing vectorizable algorithms is linear algebra is usually straightforward. Indeed, for many computations, there are several

---

*In a polyalgorithm, the actual algorithm used depends on the computing environment and the input data. The optimal algorithm in a particular instance is automatically selected at run time.

variants, all vectorizable but with different characteristics in performance (see, for example, Ref. 9). Linear algebra algorithms can approach the peak performance of many machines—principally because peak performance depends on some form of chaining of vector addition and multiplication operations or cache reuse, and this is just what the algorithms require. However, when the algorithms are realized in straightforward FORTRAN77 or C code, the performance may fall well short of the expected level, usually because FORTRAN compilers fail to minimize the number of memory references (i.e., the number of vector load and store operations or effectively reuse cache).

2. **Data movement.** What often limits the actual performance of a vector, or scalar, floating-point unit is the rate of transfer of data between different levels of memory in the machine. Examples include the transfer of vector operands in and out of vector registers, the transfer of scalar operands in and out of a high-speed cache, the movement of data between main memory and a high-speed cache or local memory, paging between actual memory and disk storage in a virtual memory system, and interprocessor communication on a distributed-memory concurrent computer.

3. **Parallelism.** The nested loop structure of most linear algebra algorithms offers considerable scope for loop-based parallelism. This is the principal type of parallelism that LAPACK and ScaLAPACK presently aim to exploit. On shared-memory concurrent computers, this type of parallelism can sometimes be generated automatically by a compiler, but it often requires the insertion of compiler directives. On distributed-memory concurrent computers, data must be moved between processors. This is usually done by explicit calls to message-passing routines, although parallel language extensions such as Coherent Parallel C (65) and Split-C (22) do the message passing implicitly.

These issues can be controlled while obtaining the levels of performance that machines can offer, through use of the BLAS, introduced in the subsection Overviews of Dense Algorithms.

The Level 1 BLAS are used in LAPACK, but for convenience rather than for performance: They perform an insignificant fraction of the computation and they cannot achieve high efficiency on most modern supercomputers. Also, the overhead entailed in calling the BLAS reduces the efficiency of the code. This reduction is negligible for large matrices, but it can be quite significant for small matrices. Fortunately, the Level 1 BLAS can be removed from the smaller, more frequently used LAPACK codes in a short editing session.

The Level 2 BLAS can achieve near-peak performance on many vector processors, such as a single processor of a CRAY X-MP or Y-MP, or Convex C-2 machine. However, on other vector processors such as a CRAY-2 or an IBM 3090 VF, the performance of the Level 2 BLAS is limited by the rate of data movement between different levels of memory.

The Level 3 BLAS overcome this limitation. This third level of BLAS performs $O(n^3)$ floating-point operations on $O(n^2)$ data, whereas the Level 2 BLAS perform only $O(n^2)$ operations on $O(n^2)$ data. The Level 3 BLAS also allow us to exploit parallelism in a way that is transparent to the software that calls them. Whereas the Level 2 BLAS offer some scope for exploiting parallelism, greater scope is provided by the Level 3 BLAS, as Table 2 illustrates.

TABLE 2   Speed in Mflop/s of Level 2 and Level 3 BLAS Operations on a CRAY

	\multicolumn{5}{c}{Number of processors}
	1	2	4	8	16
Level 2: $y \leftarrow \alpha Ax + \beta y$	899	1,780	3,491	6,783	11,207
Level 3: $C \leftarrow \alpha AB + \beta C$	900	1,800	3,600	7,199	14,282
Level 2: $x \leftarrow Ux$	852	1,620	3,063	5,554	6,953
Level 3: $B \leftarrow UB$	900	1,800	3,574	7,147	13,281
Level 2: $x \leftarrow U^{-1}x$	802	1,065	1,452	1,697	1,558
Level 3: $B \leftarrow U^{-1}B$	896	1,792	3,578	7,155	14,009

Note: All matrices are of order 1000; U is upper triangular.

The BLAS can provide portable high performance through being a standard that is available on many platforms. Ideally, the computer manufacturer has provided an assembly-coded BLAS tuned for that particular architecture, but there is a standard implementation available that can simply be compiled and linked. Using this standard BLAS may improve the efficiency of programs when they are run on nonoptimizing compilers. This is because doubly subscripted array references in the inner loop of the algorithm are replaced by singly subscripted array references in the appropriate BLAS. The effect can be seen for matrices of quite small order, and for large orders, the savings are quite significant.

Overview of Dense Linear Algebra Libraries

Over the past 25 years, we have has been directly involved in the development of several important packages of dense linear algebra software: EISPACK, LINPACK, LAPACK, and the BLAS. In addition, we are currently involved in the development of Sca-LAPACK, a scalable version of LAPACK for distributed-memory concurrent computers. In this section, we give a brief review of these packages—their history, their advantages, and their limitations on high-performance computers.

EISPACK

EISPACK is a collection of FORTRAN subroutines that compute the eigenvalues and eigenvectors of nine classes of matrices: complex general, complex Hermitian, real general, real symmetric, real symmetric banded, real symmetric tridiagonal, special real tridiagonal, generalized real, and generalized real symmetric matrices. In addition, two routines are included that use singular value decomposition to solve certain least-squares problems.

EISPACK is primarily based on a collection of Algol procedures developed in the 1960s and collected by Wilkinson and Reinsch in a volume entitled *Linear Algebra* in the *Handbook for Automatic Computation* (23) series. This volume was not designed to cover every possible method of solution; rather, algorithms were chosen on the basis of their generality, elegance, accuracy, speed, or economy of storage.

Since the release of EISPACK in 1972, over 10 thousand copies of the collection have been distributed worldwide.

LINPACK

LINPACK is a collection of FORTRAN subroutines that analyze and solve linear equations and linear least-squares problems. The package solves linear systems whose matrices are general, banded, symmetric indefinite, symmetric positive definite, triangular, and tridiagonal square. In addition, the package computes the QR and singular value decompositions of rectangular matrices and applies them to least-squares problems.

LINPACK is organized around four matrix factorizations: LU factorization, pivoted Cholesky factorization, QR factorization, and singular value decomposition. The term LU factorization is used here in a very general sense to mean the factorization of a square matrix into a lower triangular part and an upper triangular part, perhaps with pivoting. These factorizations will be treated at greater length later, when the actual LINPACK subroutines are discussed. However, first a digression on organization and factors influencing LINPACK's efficiency is necessary.

LINPACK uses column-oriented algorithms to increase efficiency by preserving locality of reference. By column orientation we mean that the LINPACK codes always reference arrays down columns, not across rows. This works because FORTRAN stores arrays in column major order. This means that as one proceeds down a column of an array, the memory references proceed sequentially in memory. Thus, if a program references an item in a particular block, the next reference is likely to be in the same block. See the subsection Using Consecutive Elements.

LINPACK uses the Level 1 BLAS; see the subsection The BLAS as a Key to Portability.

LAPACK

LAPACK (24) provides routines for solving systems of simultaneous linear equations, least-squares solutions of linear systems of equations, eigenvalue problems, and singular value problems. The associated matrix factorizations (LU, Cholesky, QR, SVD, Schur, generalized Schur) are also provided, as are related computations such as reordering of the Schur factorizations and estimating condition numbers. Dense and banded matrices are handled, but not general sparse matrices. In all areas, similar functionality is provided for real and complex matrices in both single and double precision.

The original goal of the LAPACK project was to make the widely used EISPACK and LINPACK libraries run efficiently on shared-memory vector and parallel processors. On these machines, LINPACK and EISPACK are inefficient because their memory-access patterns disregard the multilayered memory hierarchies of the machines, thereby spending too much time moving data instead of doing useful floating-point operations. LAPACK addresses this problem by reorganizing the algorithms to use block matrix operations, such as matrix multiplication, in the innermost loops (24,25). These block operations can be optimized for each architecture to account for the memory hierarchy (26) and so provide a transportable way to achieve high efficiency on diverse modern machines. Here, we use the term "transportable" instead of "portable" because for fastest possible performance, LAPACK requires that highly optimized block matrix operations be already implemented on each machine. In other words, the correctness of the code is portable, but high performance is not—if we limit ourselves to a single FORTRAN source code.

LAPACK can be regarded as a successor to LINPACK and EISPACK. It has virtually all the capabilities of these two packages and much more. LAPACK improves on LINPACK and EISPACK in four main respects: speed, accuracy, robustness, and functionality. Whereas LINPACK and EISPACK are based on the vector operation kernels of the Level 1 BLAS, LAPACK was designed at the outset to exploit the Level 3 BLAS—a set of specifications for FORTRAN subprograms that do various types of matrix multiplication and the solution of triangular systems with multiple right-hand sides. Because of the coarse granularity of the Level 3 BLAS operations, their use tends to promote high efficiency on many high-performance computers, particularly if specially coded implementations are provided by the manufacturer.

LAPACK is designed to give high efficiency on vector processors, high-performance "superscalar" workstations, and shared-memory multiprocessors. LAPACK in its present form is less likely to give good performance on other types of parallel architectures (e.g., massively parallel SIMD machines or MIMD distributed-memory machines), but the ScaLAPACK product, described in the following subsection, is intended to adapt LAPACK to these new architectures. LAPACK can also be used satisfactorily on all types of scalar machines (PCs, workstations, mainframes).

LAPACK, like LINPACK, provides LU and Cholesky factorizations of band matrices. The LINPACK algorithms can easily be restructured to use Level 2 BLAS, although restructuring has little effect on performance for matrices of very narrow bandwidth. It is also possible to use Level 3 BLAS, at the price of doing some extra work with zero elements outside the band (27). This process becomes worthwhile for large matrices and semibandwidth greater than 100 or so.

ScaLAPACK

The ScaLAPACK software library extends the LAPACK library to run scalably on MIMD, distributed-memory, concurrent computers (28,29). For such machines, the memory hierarchy includes the off-processor memory of other processors, in addition to the hierarchy of registers, cache, and local memory on each processor. Like LAPACK, the ScaLAPACK routines are based on block-partitioned algorithms in order to minimize the frequency of data movement between different levels of the memory hierarchy. The fundamental building blocks of the ScaLAPACK library are distributed-memory versions of the Level 2 and Level 3 BLAS, and a set of Basic Linear Algebra Communication Subprograms (BLACS) (20,21) for communication tasks that arise frequently in parallel linear algebra computations. In the ScaLAPACK routines, all interprocessor communication occurs within the distributed BLAS and the BLACS, so the source code of the top software layer of ScaLAPACK looks very similar to that of LAPACK.

We envisage a number of user interfaces to ScaLAPACK. Initially, the interface will be similar to that of LAPACK, with some additional arguments passed to each routine to specify the data layout. Once this is in place, we intend to modify the interface so the arguments to each ScaLAPACK routine are the same as in LAPACK. This will require information about the data distribution of each matrix and vector to be hidden from the user. This may be done by means of a ScaLAPACK initialization routine. This interface will be fully compatible with LAPACK. Provided "dummy" versions of the ScaLAPACK initialization routine and the BLACS are added to LAPACK, there will be no distinction between LAPACK and ScaLAPACK at the application level, although each will link to different versions of the BLAS and BLACS. Following on from this, we will experiment with object-based interfaces for LAPACK and ScaLAPACK, with the goal of developing interfaces compatible with FORTRAN90 (28), and C++ (19).

FUTURE RESEARCH DIRECTIONS IN DENSE ALGORITHMS

Traditionally, large, general-purpose mathematical software libraries have required users to write their own programs that call library routines to solve specific subproblems that arise during a computation. Adapted to a shared-memory parallel environment, this conventional interface still offers some potential for hiding underlying complexity. For example, the LAPACK project incorporates parallelism in the Level 3 BLAS, where it is not directly visible to the user.

However, when going from shared-memory systems to the more readily scalable distributed-memory systems, the complexity of the distributed data structures required is more difficult to hide from the user. Not only must the problem decomposition and data layout be specified, but different phases of the user's problem may require transformation between different distributed-data structures.

These deficiencies in the conventional user interface have prompted extensive discussion of alternative approaches for scalable parallel software libraries of the future. Possibilities include the following:

1. Traditional function library (i.e., minimum possible change to the status quo in going from serial to parallel environment). This will allow one to protect the programming investment that has been made.
2. Reactive servers on the network. A user would be able to send a computational problem to a server that was specialized in dealing with the problem. This fits well with the concepts of a networked, heterogeneous computing environment with various specialized hardware resources (or even heterogeneous partitioning of a single homogeneous parallel machine).
3. General interactive environments like Matlab or Mathematica, perhaps with "expert" drivers (i.e., knowledge-based systems). With the growing popularity of the many integrated packages based on this idea, this approach would provide an interactive, graphical interface for specifying and solving scientific problems. Both the algorithms and data structures are hidden from the user, because the package itself is responsible for storing and retrieving the problem data in an efficient, distributed manner. In a heterogeneous networked environment, such interfaces could provide seamless access to computational engines that would be invoked selectively for different parts of the user's computation according to which machine is most appropriate for a particular subproblem.
4. Domain-specific problem-solving environments, such as those for structural analysis. Environments like Matlab and Mathematica have proven to be especially attractive for rapid prototyping of new algorithms and systems that may subsequently be implemented in a more customized manner for higher performance.
5. Reusable templates (i.e., users adapt "source code" to their particular applications). A template is a description of a general algorithm rather than the execut-

able object code or the source code more commonly found in a conventional software library. Nevertheless, although templates are general descriptions of key data structures, they offer whatever degree of customization the user may desire.

Novel user interfaces that hide the complexity of scalable parallelism will require new concepts and mechanisms for representing scientific computational problems and for specifying how those problems relate to each other. Very high-level languages and systems, perhaps graphically based, not only would facilitate the use of mathematical software from the user's point of view but also would help to automate the determination of effective partitioning, mapping, granularity, data structures, and so forth. However, new concepts in problem specification and representation may also require new mathematical research on the analytic, algebraic, and topological properties of problems (e.g., existence and uniqueness).

We have already begun work on developing such templates for sparse matrix computations. Future work will focus on extending the use of templates to dense matrix computations.

We hope the insight we gained from our work will influence future developers of hardware, compilers, and systems software so that they provide tools to facilitate development of high-quality portable numerical software.

The EISPACK, LINPACK, and LAPACK linear algebra libraries are in the public domain and are available from *netlib*. For example, for more information on how to obtain LAPACK, send the following one-line e-mail message to

netlib@ornl.gov:
    send index from lapack

or visit the web site at *http://www.netlib.org/lapack/*. Information for EISPACK, LINPACK, and ScaLAPACK can be similarly obtained.

SPARSE LINEAR ALGEBRA METHODS

Origin of Sparse Linear Systems

The most common source of sparse linear systems is the numerical solution of partial differential equations. Many physical problems, such as fluid flow or elasticity, can be described by partial differential equations. These are implicit descriptions of a physical model describing some internal relation such as stress forces. In order to arrive at an explicit description of the shape of the object or the temperature distribution, we need to solve the partial differential equation (PDE), and for this we need numerical methods.

Discretized Partial Differential Equations

Several methods for the numerical solution of PDEs exist, the most common ones being the methods of finite elements, finite differences, and finite volumes. A common feature of these is that they identity discrete points in the physical object and give a set of equations relating these points.

Typically, only points that are physically close together are related to each other in this way. This gives a matrix structure with very few nonzero elements per row, and the nonzeros are often confined to a "band" in the matrix.

Sparse Matrix Structure

Matrices from discretized partial differential equations contain so many zero elements that it pays to find a storage structure that avoids storing these zeros. The resulting memory savings, however, are offset by an increase in programming complexity and by decreased efficiency of even simple operations such as the matrix–vector product.

More complicated operations, such as solving a linear system, with such a sparse matrix present a next level of complication, as both the inverse and the LU factorization of a sparse matrix are not as sparse, thus needing considerably more storage. Specifically, the inverse of the type of sparse matrix we are considering is a full matrix, and factoring such a sparse matrix fills in the band completely.

Example: Central differences in d dimensions, n points per line, matrix size $N = n^d$, bandwidth $q = n^{d-1}$ in natural ordering, number of nonzero $\sim n^d$, number of matrix elements $N^2 = n^{2d}$, number of elements in factorization $N^{1+(d-1)/d}$.

Basic Elements in Sparse Linear Algebra Methods

Methods for sparse systems use, like those for dense systems, vector–vector, matrix–vector, and matrix–matrix operations. However, there are some important differences.

For iterative methods, discussed in the section Iterative Solution Methods, there are almost no matrix–matrix operations. See Ref. 30 for an exception. Because most modern architectures prefer these Level 3 operations, the performance of iterative methods will be limited from the outset.

An even more serious objection is that the sparsity of the matrix implies that indirect addressing is used for retrieving elements. For example, in the popular row-compressed matrix storage format, the matrix–vector multiplication looks like

for $i = 1 \ldots n$
    $p \leftarrow$ pointer to row i
    for $j = 1, n_i$
        $y_i \leftarrow y_i + a(p + j)x(c(p + j))$,

where n_i is the number of nonzeros in row i, and $p(\cdot)$ is an array of column indices. A number of such algorithms for several sparse data formats are given in Ref. 31.

Direct methods can have a BLAS 3 component if they are a type of dissection method. However, in a given sparse problem, the denser the matrices are, the smaller they are on average. They are also not general full matrices but only banded. Thus, we do not expect a very high performance on such methods either.

DIRECT SOLUTION METHODS

For the solution of a linear system, one needs to factor the coefficient matrix. Any direct method is a variant of Gaussian elimination. As remarked earlier, for a sparse matrix, this fills in the band in which the nonzero elements are contained. In order to minimize the storage needed for the factorization, research has focused on finding suitable orderings of the matrix. Reordering the equations by a symmetric permutation of the matrix does not change the numerical properties of the system in many cases, and it can potentially give large savings in storage. In general, direct methods do not make use of the numerical properties of the linear system; thus, their execution time is affected only by the structural properties of the input matrix.

Matrix Graph Theory

The most convenient way of talking about matrix orderings or permutations is to consider the matrix "graph" (32). We introduce a node for every physical variable, and nodes i and j are connected in the graph if the (i, j) element of the matrix is nonzero. A symmetric permutation of the matrix then corresponds to a numbering of the nodes while the connections stay the same. With these permutations, one hopes to reduce the "bandwidth" of the matrix, and thereby the amount of fill generated by the factorization.

Cuthill–McKee Ordering

A popular ordering strategy is the Cuthill–McKee ordering, which finds levels or wavefronts in the matrix graph. This algorithm is easily described:

1. Take any node as starting point, and call that "level 0."
2. Now, successively take all nodes connected to the previous level and group them into the next level.
3. Iterate this until all nodes are grouped into some level; the numbering inside each level is of secondary importance.

This ordering strategy often gives a smaller bandwidth than the natural ordering, and there are further advantages to having a level structure (e.g., for out-of-core solution or for parallel processing). Often, one uses the "reverse Cuthill–McKee" orderings (33).

Minimum Degree

An explicit reduction of bandwidth is effected by the minimum degree ordering, which at any point in the factorization chooses the variable with the smallest number of connections. Considering the size of the resulting fill-in is used as a tie breaker.

Nested Dissection

Instead of trying to minimize fill-in by reducing the bandwidth, one could try a direct approach. The "nested dissection" ordering recursively splits the matrix graph in two, thus separating it into disjoint subgraphs. Somewhat more precisely, given a graph, this algorithm relies on the existence of a "separator": a set of nodes such that the nodes fall into two mutually unconnected subgraphs. The fill from first factoring these subgraphs, followed by a factorization of the separator, is likely to be lower than for other orderings.

It can be shown that for PDEs in two space dimensions, this method has a storage requirement that is within a log-factor of that for the matrix itself (i.e., very close to optimal) (34). This proof is easy for PDEs on rectangular grids, but with enough graph theory, it can be generalized (35,36). However, for problems in three space dimensions, the nested dissection method is no longer optimal.

An advantage of dissection-type methods is that they lead to large numbers of uncoupled matrix problems. Thus, to an extent, parallelization of such methods is easy. However, the higher levels in the tree quickly have fewer nodes than the number of available processors. In addition to this, they are also the larger subproblems in the algorithm, thereby complicating the parallelization of the method.

Another practical issue is the choice of the separator set. In a model case, this is trivial, but in practice, and in particular in parallel, this is a serious problem, as the balancing of the two resulting subgraphs depends on this choice. Recently, so-called "2nd eigenvector methods" have become popular for this (37).

ITERATIVE SOLUTION METHODS

Direct methods, as sketched above, have some pleasant properties. Foremost is the fact that their time to solution is predictable, either *a priori* or after determining the matrix ordering. This is due to the fact that the method does not rely on numerical properties of the coefficient matrix but only on its structure. On the other hand, the amount of fill can be substantial, and with it, the execution time. For large-scale applications, the storage requirements for a realistic size problem can simply be prohibitive.

Iterative methods have far lower storage demands. Typically, the storage and the cost per iteration with it are of the order of the matrix storage. However, the number of iterations strongly depends on properties of the linear system, and is at best known up to an order estimate; for difficult problems, the methods may not even converge because of accumulated round-off errors.

Basic Iteration Procedure

In its most informal sense, an iterative method in each iteration locates an approximation to the solution of the problem, measures the error between the approximation and the true solution, and, based on the error measurement, improves on the approximation by constructing a next iterate. This process repeats until the error measurement is deemed small enough.

Stationary Iterative Methods

The simplest iterative methods are the "stationary iterative methods." They are based on finding a matrix M that is, in some sense, "close" to the coefficient matrix A. Instead of solving $Ax = b$, which is deemed computationally infeasible, we solve $Mx_1 = b$. The true measure of how well x_1 approximates x is the error $e_1 = x_1 - x$, but because we do not know the true solution x, this quantity is not computable. Instead, we look at the "residual": $r_1 = Ae_1 = Ax_1 - b$, which is a computable quantity. One easily sees that the true solution satisfies $x = A^{-1}b = x_1 - A^{-1}r_1$, so replacing A^{-1} with M^{-1} in this relation, we define $x_2 = x_1 - M^{-1}r_1$.

Stationary methods are easily analyzed: We find that $r_i \to 0$ if all eigenvalues $\lambda = \lambda(I - AM^{-1})$ satisfy $|\lambda| < 1$. For certain classes of A and M, this inequality is automatically satisfied (38,39).

Krylov Space Methods

The most popular class of iterative methods nowadays of "Krylov space methods." The basic idea there is to construct the residuals such that the nth residual r_n is obtained from the first by multiplication by some polynomial in the coefficient matrix A; that is,

$$r_n = P_{n-1}(A)r_1.$$

The properties of the method then follow from the properties of the actual polynomial (40–42).

Most often, these iteration polynomials are chosen such that the residuals are orthogonal under some inner product. From this, one usually obtains some minimization property, although not necessarily a minimization of the *error*.

Because the iteration polynomials are of increasing degree, it is easy to see that the main operation in each iteration is one matrix–vector multiplication. Additionally, some vector operations, including inner products in the orthogonalization step, are needed.

The Issue of Symmetry

Krylov method residuals can be shown to satisfy the equation

$$r_n \in \text{span}\{Ar_{n-1}, r_{n-1}, \ldots, r_1\}.$$

This brings up the question of whether all $r_{n-1}, \ldots, r_1$ need to be stored in order to compute r_n. The answer is that this depends on the symmetry of the coefficient matrix. For a symmetric problem, the r_n vectors satisfy a three-term recurrence. This was the original conjugate gradient method (43).

For nonsymmetric problems on the other hand, no short recurrences can exist (44), and, therefore, all previous residuals need to be stored. Some of these methods are OrthoDir and OrthoRes (45).

If the requirement of orthogonality is relaxed, one can derive short-recurrence methods for nonsymmetric problems (46). In the biconjugate gradient method, two sequences $\{r_n\}$ and $\{s_n\}$ are derived that are mutually orthogonal and that satisfy three-term recurrences.

A disadvantage of this latter method is that it needs application of the transpose of the coefficient matrix. In environments where the matrix is only operatively defined, this may exclude this method from consideration. Recently developed methods, mostly based on the work in Refs. 47 and 48, obviate this consideration.

True Minimization

The methods mentioned so far minimize the error (over the subspace generated) in some matrix-related norm, but not in the Euclidean norm. We can effect a true minimization by collecting the residuals generated so far and finding a minimizing convex combination. This leads to one of the most popular methods nowadays: GMRES (49). It will always generate the optimal iterate, but for this, it requires storage of all previous residuals. In practice, truncated or restarted version of GMRES are popular.

Preconditioners

The matrix M that appeared in the section on stationary iterative methods can play a role in Krylov space methods too. There, it is called a "preconditioner" and it acts to improve spectral properties of the coefficient matrix that determine the convergence speed of the method. In a slight simplification, one might say that we replace the system $Ax = b$ by

$$(AM^{-1})(Mx) = b.$$

(Additionally, the inner product is typically changed.) It is generally recognized that a good preconditioner is crucial to the performance of an iterative method.

The requirements on a preconditioner are that it should be easy to construct, a system $Mx = b$ should be simple to solve, and, in some sense, M should be an approximation to A. These requirements need to be balanced: A more accurate preconditioner is usually harder to construct and more costly to apply, so any decrease in the number of iterations has to be set against a longer time per iteration, plus an increased setup phase.

The Holy Grail of preconditioners is finding an "optimal" preconditioner: one for which the number of operations for applying it is of the order of the number of variables, whereas the resulting number of iterations is bounded in the problem size. There are very few optimal preconditioners.

Simple Preconditioners

Some preconditioners need no construction at all. For instance, the Jacobi preconditioner consists of simply the matrix diagonal D_A. Because in PDE applications the largest elements are on the diagonal, one expects some degree of accuracy from this. Using not just the diagonal but the whole lower triangular part $D_A + L_A$ of the coefficient matrix, an even more accurate method results. As this triangular matrix is nonsymmetric, it is usually balanced with the upper triangular part as $(D_A + L_A)D_A^{-1}(D_A + U_A)$.

Incomplete Factorizations

A successful strategy for preconditioners results from mimicking direct methods, but applying some approximation process to them. Thus, the so-called "incomplete factorization" methods ignore fill elements in the course of the Gaussian elimination process. Two strategies are to ignore elements in fixed positions and to drop elements that are deemed small enough to be negligible. The aim is to preserve at least some of the sparsity of the coefficient matrix in the factorization while giving something that is close enough to the full factorization.

Incomplete factorizations can be very effective, but there are a few practical problems. For the class of M-matrices, these methods are well defined (50), but for other, even fairly common classes of matrices, there is a possibility that the algorithm breaks down (51–53).

Also, factorizations are inherently recursive, and coupled with the sparseness of the incomplete factorization, this gives very limited parallelism in the algorithm using a natural ordering of the unknowns. Different orderings may be more parallel, but take more iterations (30,54,55).

Analytically Inspired Preconditioners

In recent years, a number of preconditioners have gained in popularity that are more directly inspired by the continuous problem. First, for a matrix from an elliptic PDE, one can use a so-called "fast solver" as a preconditioner (56–58).

A particularly popular class of preconditioners based on the continuous problem is that of "domain decomposition" methods. If the continuous problem was elliptic, then decomposing the domain into simply connected pieces leads to elliptic problems on these subdomains, tied together by internal boundary conditions of some sort.

For instance, in the Schur complement domain decomposition method (59), thin strips of variables are assigned a function as the interface region and the original problem reduces to fully independent problems on the subdomains, connected by a system on the interface that is both smaller and better conditioned, but more dense, than the original one. Whereas the subdomains can trivially be executed in parallel, the interface system poses considerable problems.

Choosing overlapping instead of separated subdomains leads to the class of Schwarz methods (60). The original Schwarz method on two domains proposed solving one subdomain, deriving interface conditions from it for the other subdomain, and solving the system there. Repetition of this process can be shown to converge. In a more parallel variant of this method, all subdomains solve their system simultaneously, and the solutions on the overlap regions are added together.

Multilevel methods do not operate by decomposing the domain. Rather, they work on a sequence of nested discretization, solving the coarser ones as a starting point for solving the finer levels. Under certain conditions, such methods can be shown to be close to optimal (61,62). However, they require explicit knowledge of the operator and boundary conditions. For this reason, people have investigated algebraic variants (63,64). In both cases, these methods can be parallelised by distributing each level over the processors, but this may not be trivial.

LIBRARIES AND STANDARDS IN SPARSE METHODS

Unlike in dense methods, there are few standards for iterative methods. Most of this is due to the fact that sparse storage is more complicated, admitting of more variation, and therefore less standardized. Whereas the (dense) BLAS has been accepted for a long time, sparse BLAS is not more than a proposal under research.

Storage Formats

As is apparent from the matrix–vector example in the subsection Basic Elements in Sparse Linear Algebra Methods, storage formats for sparse matrices include not just the matrix elements but also pointer information describing where the nonzero elements are placed in the matrix. A few storage formats are in common use (for more details, see Ref. 31):

> **Aij format.** In the Aij format, three arrays of the same length are allocated: one containing the matrix elements and the other two containing the i and j coordinates of these elements. No particular ordering of the elements is implied.
>
> **Row/column compressed.** In the row-compressed format, one array of integers is allocated in addition to the matrix element, giving the column indices of the nonzero elements. Because all elements in the same row are stored contiguously, a second, smaller, array is needed giving the start points of the rows in the two larger arrays.
>
> **Compressed diagonal.** If the nonzero elements of the matrix are located, roughly or exactly, along subdiagonals, one could use contiguous storage for these diagonals. There are several diagonal storage formats. In the simplest, describing a contiguous block of subdiagonals, only the array of matrix elements is needed; two integers are sufficient to describe which diagonals have been stored.

There exist blocked versions of these formats for matrices that can be partitioned into small square subblocks.

Sparse Libraries

Because sparse formats are more complicated than dense matrix storage, sparse libraries have an added level of complexity. This holds even more so in the parallel case, where additional indexing information is needed to specify which matrix elements are on which processor.

There are two fundamentally different approaches for handling this complexity. Some sparse libraries require the user to set up the matrix and supply it to the library, and all handling is performed by the library. This requires the user to store data in a format dictated by the library, which might involve considerable work.

On the other hand, the library might do even the matrix setup internally, hiding all data from the user. This gives total freedom to the user, but it requires the library to supply sufficient access functions so that the user can perform certain matrix operations, even while not having access to the object itself.

CONCLUSION

The sparse linear systems that result from partial differential equations need very different techniques from those used for dense matrices. Although direct methods have the virtue of reliability, they also take copious amounts of space and time. Iterative methods, of one type or another, are considerably more frugal in their space demands, but on difficult problems, their convergence may be slow and is not even guaranteed.

ACKNOWLEDGMENTS

This research was performed in part using the Intel Touchstone Delta System operated by the California Institute of Technology on behalf of the Concurrent Supercomputing Consortium. Access to this facility was provided through the Center for Research on Parallel Computing.

REFERENCES

1. J. J. Dongarra, J. Du Croz, S. Hammarling, and I. Duff, "A Set of Level 3 Basic Linear Algebra Subprograms," *ACM Trans. Math. Software*, *16*(1), 1–17 (1990).
2. J. J. Dongarra, J. Du Croz, S. Hammarling, and R. Hanson, "An Extended Set of Fortran Basic Linear Algebra Subroutines," *ACM Trans. Math. Software*, *14*(1), 1–17 (1988).
3. C. Lawson, R. Hanson, D. Kincaid, and F. Krogh, "Basic Linear Algebra Subprograms for Fortran Usage," *ACM Trans. Math. Software*, *5*, 308–323 (1979).
4. W. Croswell, "Origin and Development of the Method of Moments for Field Computation," *IEEE Antennas Propagation Mag.*, *32*(3), 31–34 (June 1990).
5. J. J. H. Wang, *Generalized Moment Methods in Electromagnetics*. John Wiley & Sons, New York, 1991.
6. J. L. Hess, "Panel Methods in Computational Fluid Dynamics," *Annu. Rev. Fluid Mech.*, 22, 255–274 (1990).
7. J. L. Hess and M. O. Smith, "Calculation of Potential Flows about Arbitrary Bodies," in

Progress in Aeronautical Sciences, Volume 8, D. Küchemann, ed., Pergamon Press, Elmsford, NY, 1967.

8. A. Edelman, "Large Dense Numerical Linear Algebra in 1993: The Parallel Computing Influence," *Int. J. Supercomputer Applic.*, *7*, 113–128 (1993).

9. J. J. Dongarra, "Increasing the Performance of Mathematical Software Through High-Level Modularity," in *Proc. Sixth Int. Symp. Comp. Methods in Eng. and Applied Sciences, Versailles, France*, North-Holland, Amsterdam, 1984, pp. 239–248.

10. J. J. Dongarra, F. C. Gustavson, and A. Karp, "Implementing Linear Algebra Algorithms for Dense Matrices on a Vector Pipeline Machine," *SIAM Rev.*, *26*, 91–112 (1984).

11. J. M. Ortega, "The *ijk* Forms of Factorization Methods I. Vector Computers," *Parallel Comput.*, *7*, 135–147 (1988).

12. J. M. Ortega and C. H. Romine, "The *ijk* Forms of Factorization Methods II. Parallel Systems," *Parallel Comput.*, *7*, 149–162 (1988).

13. R. W. Hockney and C. R. Jesshope, *Parallel Computers*, Adam Hilger Ltd., Bristol, U.K., 1981.

14. G. C. Fox, M. A. Johnson, G. A. Lyzenga, S. W. Otto, J. K. Salmon, and D. W. Walker, *Solving Problems on Concurrent Processors*, Prentice-Hall, Englewood Cliffs, NJ, 1988, Vol. 1.

15. A. Gupta and V. Kumar, "On the Scalability of FFT on Parallel Computers," in *Proceedings of the Frontiers 90 Conference on Massively Parallel Computation*. IEEE Computer Society Press, Los Alamitos, CA, 1990; also available as technical report TR 90-20 from the Computer Science Department, University of Minnesota, Minneapolis.

16. J. J. Dongarra and E. Grosse, "Distribution of Mathematical Software via Electronic Mail," *Commun. ACM*, *30*(5), 403–407 (1987).

17. J. Du Croz and M. Pont, "The Development of a Floating-Point Validation Package," in *Proceedings of the 8th Symposium on Computer Arithmetic, Como, Italy, May 19–21, 1987*, M. J. Irwin and R. Stefanelli, eds., IEEE Computer Society Press, Los Alamitos, CA, 1987.

18. W. Kahan, "Paranoia," available from netlib (16): *http://www.netlib.org/paranoia*.

19. J. J. Dongarra, R. Pozo, and D. W. Walker, "An Object Oriented Design for High Performance Linear Algebra on Distributed Memory Architectures," in *Proceedings of the Object Oriented Numerics Conference*, 1993.

20. J. J. Dongarra, "LAPACK Working Note 34: Workshop on the BLACS," Computer Science Dept. Technical Report CS-91-134, University of Tennessee, Knoxville (May 1991); *http://www.netlib.org/lapack/lawns/lawn34.ps*.

21. J. J. Dongarra and R. A. van de Geijn, "Two-Dimensional Basic Linear Algebra Communication Subprograms," Technical Report LAPACK Working Note 37, Computer Science Department, University of Tennessee, Knoxville (October 1991); *http://www.netlib.org/lapack/lawns/lawn37.ps*.

22. D. E. Culler, A. Dusseau, S. C. Goldstein, A. Krishnamurthy, S. Lumetta, T. von Eicken, and K. Yelick, "Introduction to Split-C: Version 0.9," Technical Report, Computer Science Division—EECS, University of California, Berkeley (February 1993).

23. J. Wilkinson and C. Reinsch, *Handbook for Automatic Computation: Volume II—Linear Algebra*, Springer-Verlag, New York, 1971.

24. J. Demmel, "LAPACK: A Portable Linear Algebra Library for Supercomputers," in *Proceedings of the 1989 IEEE Control Systems Society Workshop on Computer-Aided Control System Design*, December 1989.

25. E. Anderson and J. Dongarra, "Evaluating Block Algorithm Variants in LAPACK," Technical Report LAPACK Working Note 19, Computer Science Department, University of Tennessee, Knoxville (1990); *http://www.netlib.org/lapack/lawns/lawn19.ps*.

26. E. Anderson and J. Dongarra, "Results from the Initial Release of LAPACK," Technical Report LAPACK Working Note 16, Computer Science Department, University of Tennessee, Knoxville (1989); *http://www.netlib.org/lapack/lawns/lawn16.ps*.

27. J. J. Dongarra, P. Mayes, and G. Radicati di Brozolo, "The IBM RISC System/600 and Linear Algebra Operations," *Supercomputer*, *44*(VIII-4), 15–30 (1991).

28. J. Choi, J. J. Dongarra, R. Pozo, and D. W. Walker, "ScaLAPACK: A Scalable Linear Algebra Library for Distributed Memory Concurrent Computers," in *Proceedings of the Fourth Symposium on the Frontiers of Massively Parallel Computation*, IEEE Computer Society Press, Los Alamitos, CA, 1992, pp. 120–127.

29. J. Choi, J. J. Dongarra, and D. W. Walker, "The Design of Scalable Software Libraries for Distributed Memory Concurrent Computers," in *Environments and Tools for Parallel Scientific Computing*, J. J. Dongarra and B. Tourancheau, eds. Elsevier Science Publishers, New York, 1993.

30. M. T. Jones and P. E. Plassmann, "Parallel Solution of Unstructed, Sparse Systems of Linear Equations," in *Proceedings of the Sixth SIAM Conference on Parallel Processing for Scientific Computing*, R. F. Sincovec, D. E. Keyes, M. R.. Leuze, L. R. Petzold, and D. A. Reed, eds., SIAM, Philadelphia, 1993, pp. 471–475.

31. R. Barrett, M. Berry, T. F. Chan, J. Demmel, J. Donato, J. Dongarra, V. Eijkhout, R. Pozo, C. Romine, and H. van der Vorst, *Templates for the Solution of Linear Systems: Building Blocks for Iterative Methods*, SIAM, Philadelphia, 1994. *http://www.netlib.org/templates/templates.ps*.

32. S. V. Parter, "The Use of Linear Graphs in Gaussian Elimination," *SIAM Rev.*, *3*, 119–130 (1961).

33. J. W-H. Liu and A. H. Sherman, "Comparative Analysis of the Cuthill–McKee and the Reverse Cuthill–McKee Ordering Algorithms for Sparse Matrices," *SIAM J. Numer. Anal.*, *13*, 198–213 (1973).

34. A. George and J. H-W. Liu, *Computer Solution of Large Sparse Positive Definite Systems*. Prentice-Hall, Englewood Cliffs, NJ, 1981.

35. R. J. Lipton, D. J. Rose, and R. Endre Tarjan, "Generalized Nested Dissection," *SIAM J. Numer. Anal.*, *16*, 346–358 (1979).

36. R. J. Lipton and R. Endre Tarjan, "A Separator Theorem for Planar Graphs," *SIAM J. Appl. Math.*, *36*, 177–189 (1979).

37. A. Pothen, H. D. Simon, and K. P. Liou, "Partitioning Sparse Matrices with Eigenvectors of Graphs," *SIAM J. Matrix Anal. Applic.*, *11*(3), 430–452 (1990).

38. L. A. Hageman and D. M. Young, *Applied Iterative Methods*, Academic Press, New York, 1981.

39. R. S. Varga, *Matrix Iterative Analysis*, Prentice-Hall, Englewood Cliffs, NJ, 1962.

40. O. Axelsson and A. V. Barker, *Finite Element Solution of Boundary Value Problems. Theory and Computation*, Academic Press, Orlando, FL, 1984.

41. G. Birkhoff and R. E. Lynch, *Numerical Solution of Elliptic Problems*, SIAM, Philadelphia, 1984.

42. T. Chan and H. van der Vorst, "Linear System Solvers: Sparse Iterative Methods, in *Parallel Numerical Algorithms, Proc. of the ICASW/LaRC Workshop on Parallel Numerical Algorithms, May 23–25, 1994*, H. van der Vorst et al., eds., Kluwer, Dordrecht, 1997, pp. 91–118.

43. M. R. Hestenes and E. Stiefel, "Methods of Conjugate Gradients for Solving Linear Systems," *Nat. Bur. Stand. J. Res.*, *49*, 409–436 (1952).

44. V. Faber and T. Manteuffel, "Orthogonal Error Methods," *SIAM J. Numer. Anal.*, *24*, 170–187 (1987).

45. D. M. Young and K. C. Jea, "Generalized Conjugate-Gradient Acceleration of Nonsymmetrizable Iterative Methods," *Linear Alg. Applic.*, *34*, 159–194 (1980).

46. R. Fletcher, "Conjugate Gradient Methods for Indefinite Systems," in *Numerical Analysis Dundee 1975*, G. A. Watson, ed., Springer-Verlag, New York, 1976, pp. 73–89.

47. P. Sonneveld, "CGS, a Fast Lanczos-Type Solver for Nonsymmetric Linear Systems," *SIAM J. Sci. Statist. Comput.*, *10*, 36–52 (1989).

48. H. van der Vorst, "Bi-CGSTAB: A Fast and Smoothly Converging Variant of BI-CG for

the Solution of Nonsymmetric Linear Systems," *SIAM J. Sci. Statist. Comput.*, *13*, 631–644 (1992).

49. Y. Saad and M. H. Schultz, "GMRes: A Generalized Minimal Residual Algorithm for Solving Nonsymmetric Linear Systems," *SIAM J. Sci. Statist. Comput.*, *7*, 856–869 (1986).

50. J. A. Meijerink and H. A. van der Vorst, "An Iterative Solution Method for Linear Systems of Which the Coefficient Matrix is a Symmetric m-Matrix," *Math Comput.*, *31*, 148–162 (1977).

51. A. Jennings and G. M. Malik, "Partial Elimination," *J. Inst. Math. Applic.*, *20*, 307–316 (1977).

52. D. S. Kershaw, "The Incomplete Cholesky-Conjugate Gradient Method for the Iterative Solution of Systems of Linear Equations," *J. Comput. Phys.*, *26*, 43–65 (1978).

53. T. A. Manteuffel, "An Incomplete Factorization Technique for Positive Definite Linear Systems," *Math. Comput.*, *34*, 473–497 (1980).

54. I. S. Duff and G. A. Meurant, "The Effect of Ordering on Preconditioned Conjugate Gradients," *BIT*, *29*, 635–657 (1989).

55. V. Eijkhout, "Analysis of Parallel Incomplete Point Factorizations," *Linear Alg. Appl.*, *154–156*, 723–740 (1991).

56. P. Concus and G. H. Golub, "Use of Fast Direct Methods for the Efficient Numerical Solution of Nonseparable Elliptic Equations," *SIAM J. Numer. Anal.*, *10*, 1103–1120 (1973).

57. H. C. Elman and M. H. Schultz, "Preconditioning by Fast Direct Methods for Non-Self-Adjoint Nonseparable Elliptic Equations," *SIAM J. Numer. Anal.*, *23*, 44–57 (1986).

58. O. Widlund, "On the Use of Fast Methods for Separable Finite Difference Equations for the Solution of General Elliptic Problems," in *Sparse Matrices and Their Applications*, D. J. Rose and R. A. Willoughby, eds., Plenum Press, New York, 1972, pp. 121–134.

59. P. Bjørstad and O. Widlund, "Iterative Methods for the Solution of Elliptic Problems on Regions Partitioned into Substructures," *SIAM J. Numer. Anal.*, *23*, 1097–1120 (1986).

60. P. L. Lions, "On the Schwarz Alternating Method," in *Domain Decomposition Methods for Partial Differential Equations*, *Proceedings of the First Internation Symposium, Paris, January 7–9, 1987*, SIAM, Philadelphia, 1988, pp. 1–42.

61. O. Axelsson and P. Vassileyski, "Algebraic Multilevel Preconditioning Methods, I." *Numer. Math.*, *56*, 157–177 (1989).

62. W. Hackbusch, *Multi-Grid Methods and Applications*, Springer-Verlag, New York, 1985.

63. O. Axelsson and V. Eijkhout, "The Nested Recursive Two-Level Factorization Method for Nine-Point Difference Matrices," *SIAM J. Sci. Statist. Comput.*, *12*, 1373–1400 (1991).

64. J. W. Ruge and K. Stüben, "Algebraic Multigrid," in *Multigrid Methods*, S. F. McCormick, ed., SIAM, Philadelphia, 1987, Chap. 4.

65. E. W. Felten and S. W. Otto, "Coherent Parallel C," in *Proceedings of the Third Conference on Hypercube Concurrent Computers and Applications*, G. C. Fox, ed., ACM Press, New York, 1998, pp. 440–450.

JACK DONGARRA

VICTOR EIJKHOUT

OPTICAL FIBER COMMUNICATIONS

INTRODUCTION

Optical fiber was patented by Corning Glass in the 1970s. Its potential for telecommunications was immediately recognized and a worldwide effort followed, which developed improved fiber manufacturing techniques, necessary related electronics, connectors and splicing technology, practicality, applications, and education. During the 1980s, research laboratories—most notably NTT Labs in Japan and Bell Labs in the United States—competed vigorously to break one another's world record for the optical fiber transmission "rate × distance product." Demand was so great and competition was so intense that the research state of the art was typically getting to the marketplace in only about 3 years. It is remarkable that within 10 years of its invention, optical fiber was practical enough that it was being deployed by many telephone and CATV companies and many users. Now, 20 years later, optical fiber has become the transmission medium of choice, worldwide. The real potential of optical fiber and the justification for investing in its deployment is its enormous and, as of yet, relatively unused bandwidth. Although we are pushing the limits of the bandwidth of moving electrons along copper, it seems hard to imagine running out of information-carrying capacity over optical fiber.

Here, we compare information moving along several different transmission media to water flowing through a pipe. The basis for these calculations is shown later in this article. Because a pipe with a larger diameter allows more water to flow, pipe diameter is analogous to bandwidth in the transmission channel. If a conventional analog telephone channel is analogous to conventional household 3/8-in. copper tubing (0.25 in. inner diameter), then coaxial cable carrying 70 television signals is analogous to a 6 ft-diameter sewer pipe. (This is not a comment about the content.) Admittedly, there is a bit of an apple/orange comparison, but the ratio of areas is equal to the ratio of the capacities of a 4-kHz telephone channel to 70 television channels at 4-MHz each. On this same scale, optical fiber's ultimate capacity is larger than the Grand Canyon—not just the Colorado River at the bottom, but the entire canyon, filled to the brim with moving water.

Although we are not even close to being able to use all this capacity, the capacity we can use is higher than the competing media; we are progressing toward using more and more of it every year, and the end is not in sight (like it is with copper). We can argue that the optical fiber currently in the ground is "future-proof."

Communications by optical fiber and its related technologies are described in this article in the following order. Some basic principles from the physics of optics that are discussed include the dual "wave/particle" nature of light and enough about optical refraction to explain "total internal reflection." Optical fiber is described: its mechanical and chemical construction, optical modes and the difference between multimode and single-mode fiber, and how optical signals are attenuated and distorted. The electronic-to-optic transducers in the transmitters and receivers are described by extending semiconductor diode operation to the photodiode, light-emitting diode, and semiconductor diode laser. A discussion of optical coupling not only includes descriptions of connectors, splices, and splitters, but extends to their architectural impact on bus and star network topologies. After appreciating the low level of noise in optical fiber, a sample power budget calculation relates bit-error rate and link length. Three photonic technology families are recommended, each optimized differently: for cost, maximum link length, and maximum data rate. Conventional transmission practices described include digital data formats, time-multiplexing and Sonet, and wavelength multiplexing (including the limitations imposed by fiber's nonlinearities). Related photonic devices—amplifiers and switches—are described and a discussion of the future includes solitons, optical computing, and photonic switching.

OPTICS

Optics is the "physics of light." Physicists have developed mathematical models for optics and have equations that are consistent with observed optical phenomena. However, our cognitive understanding of "how optics works and why" is so poor that we need to use two different models.

The "Wave" Model

In the first model, light is an "electromagnetic (EM) wave." As a periodic signal, this EM wave is characterized by its shape (think about it as a sine curve that moves), its frequency, and its amplitude. The "brightness" of the light, its *optical power*, corresponds to the amplitude or "height" of the signal, just like electrical power corresponds to AC voltage. Any "traveling wave," like a wave in the ocean or an EM wave, can be measured by its frequency (the number of wave cycles that pass a given point in a second) or by its wavelength (the distance between corresponding points in consecutive cycles). Simple algebra on the dimensions of frequency (cycles per second) and of wavelength (meters per cycle) shows that

$$fw = v,$$

where v is the wave's velocity through the particular medium. For EM waves, v, is the speed of light in the particular medium. In free space, $v = c = 3 \times 10^8$ m/s.

The phenomenon we call "light" is just a special kind of electromagnetic radiation that occupies a region on the electromagnetic spectrum between microwaves and x-rays. The region on this spectrum that we call "visible light" is defined by the sensitivity of nerve endings in the back of the human eye. EM radiation with a wavelength of 0.40 μm ($1\mu m = 10^{-6}$ m) has a frequency of 750 THz (one Tera-Hertz is 10^{12} cycles per second) and is perceived by humans as the color "violet." EM radiation with a wavelength of 0.66 μm has a frequency of 450 THz and is perceived by humans as the color "red." EM radiation with intermediate wavelengths is perceived by humans as the intermediate "rainbow" colors in the visible spectrum. EM radiation with wavelength a little smaller than 0.40 μm is called "ultraviolet light." EM radiation with wavelength a little greater than 0.66 μm is called "infrared light." Transmission of optical signals over optical fiber uses infrared light in three different narrow regions of the spectrum: at wavelengths 0.8, 1.3, and 1.5 μm.

The "Particle" Model

In the second model, light is a burst of moving particles, called *photons*, that travel in a straight line, called a *ray*. Although a photon has no mass, it does have energy, given by

$$e = hf,$$

where $h = 6.6 \times 10^{-34}$ is Planck's constant. For example, because infrared light with a 1-μm wavelength has frequency = 333 THz, each photon has energy = 2×10^{-20} Js. Then, a ray that carries 5×10^{16} photons per second comprises a light beam carrying 10^{-3} Js/s, which is equivalent to 1 mW of optical power. We see, in this model, that *optical power* is determined by the density of the photons in the ray and the energy in each photon. Although the *ray model's* "buck shot" representation seems to have no intuitive relationship to the *wave model's* "AC amplitude," each characterizes optical power in its respective model of what light is.

We know that light has a different velocity in different media. Light travels fastest in a vacuum and practically as fast in air. This maximum velocity is $c = 3 \times 10^8$ m/s. In any other medium, like water or silicon, light travels slower than it does in free space, at a rate given by

$$\frac{c}{n} \text{ m/s,}$$

where $n \geq 1$ is the medium's *index of refraction* (IoR). In the "glass" used in optical fiber, $n \approx 1.5$ and we see that optical signals travel along optical fibers at about two-thirds of the speed of light in free space. Because of the wire's inductance and capacitance, electrical signals travel slower than the speed of light along copper wires also.

Light "bends" at the boundary between two media. Although this phenomenon is not intuitive, it is easily observed and it is familiar. Figure 1 shows a schematic of a rod that is half immersed in water. Because the light rays bend when they cross the water–air

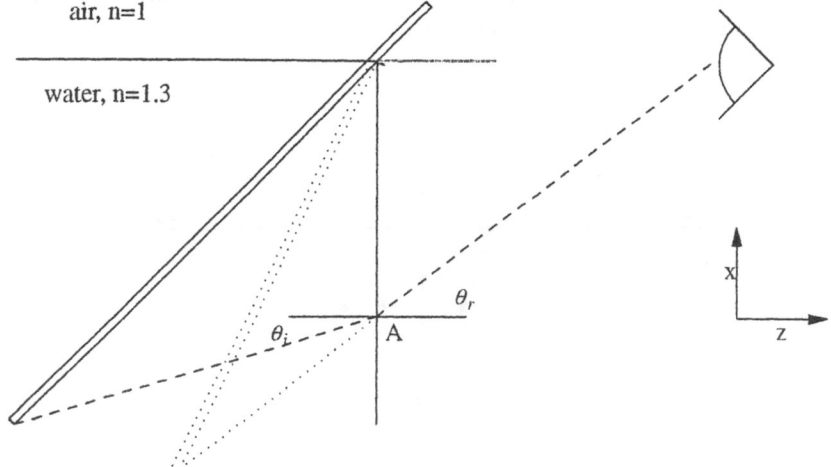

FIGURE 1   Bent rod, illustrating Snell's law.

boundary as they travel to the eye from the immersed part of the rod, the eye perceives the rod to be bent. The geometry of this "bend" is based on Snell's law.

Assume that the water–air boundary is a plane in x and y (y goes into the paper), seen along its x edge in Figure 1. The figure shows a light ray that travels from the end of the rod, through the water–air plane at point A, and on to the eye. The figure also shows the "normal line," in z, which is perpendicular to the boundary plane in x and y and intersects it at A. The angle, in three dimensions, between the ray in the water and the normal line in the water is θ_i, the *angle of incidence*. The angle, in three dimensions, between the ray in the air and the normal line in the air is θ_r, the *angle of refraction*. Snell's law states that

$$n_i \sin \theta_i = n_r \sin \theta_r.$$

By this same phenonemenon, lenses focus light onto the film in a camera, onto the retina in the eye, or into the end of an optical fiber. In optics, almost everything works identically in reverse. Suppose the eye in Figure 1 is replaced by a light source, capable of emitting a ray of light in a fine line. For this source to illuminate the tip of the rod, it cannot be aimed directly toward this tip, instead it must be aimed at point A, where refraction will cause the ray to "bend" toward the tip.

Total Internal Reflection

Referring back to Figure 1, imagine that the rod grows longer somehow. As the rod becomes longer, consider the ray that travels from the bottom of the rod to the eye. As its angle of incidence in the "slow medium" (the water) increases, its angle of refraction in the " fast medium" (the air) increases even more. When the rod is so long that the angle of refraction = 90°, the corresponding angle of incidence, θ_i, equals what is called the *critical angle*, θ_c. At this angle, the refracted ray lies in the surface of the water–air boundary and the end of the rod cannot be seen from outside the water.

The reverse situation, with the eye in the water, is more familiar. If you are submerged in dark water and look up into lit air above, the light appears to come down through a "manhole" in the surface. The geometry of this "manhole" can be seen in Figure 2. The rays at the extreme left and right form the critical angle with respect to a line orthogonal to the surface. By Snell's law,

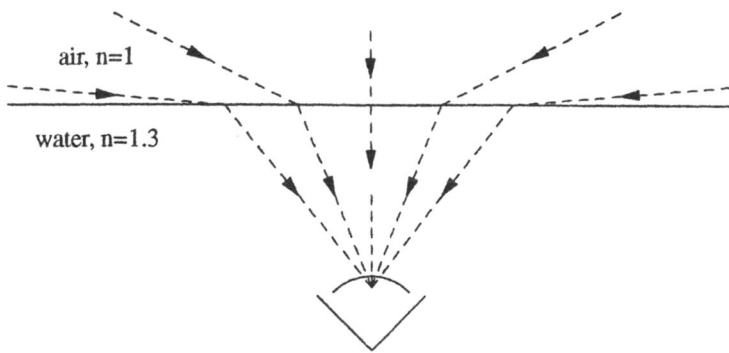

FIGURE 2   The underwater "manhole" effect.

$$\sin \theta_c = \frac{n_r}{n_i} .$$

Back to the lengthening rod in Figure 2, if the incident ray reaches the surface at θ_c, then the eye must lie directly in the water–air boundary if it is to see the refracted ray. If the incident ray reaches the surface at $\theta_i > \theta_c$, then the ray reflects off the surface back into the water again and the eye must be in the water if it is to see this reflected ray. The angle between the reflected ray and the normal is called the angle of reflection and it always equals θ_i. If we could make an air–water–air "sandwich" somehow or could somehow surround a "slow medium" by a "fast medium," then any ray of light that was inside the "slow medium" (the water) and that traveled such that its $\theta_i > \theta_c$ would travel along trapped inside this "slow medium," reflecting (ricocheting) off its upper and lower surfaces. This phenomenon is called "total internal reflection" and it is the fundamental physics of optical fiber communications.

Prisms

When the index of refraction was described earlier, we gave the false impression that the IoR was a constant, strictly a property of the material. It is not. IoR is a complicated nonlinear function of the material, the wavelength, and even the light intensity. Although the nonconstant nature of IoR has a detrimental effect on optical transmission through *chromatic dispersion* and other nonlinearities to be described later, it also has a beneficial effect.

Because the IoR depends on wavelength, light with a different wavelength must have a different angle of refraction. Let light with wavelength w_1 have an angle of incidence θ_i on one side of a material boundary and angle of refraction θ_{r1} in the second material. Then, light with wavelength w_2, but the same angle of incidence θ_i on one side of the same material boundary, has an angle of refraction θ_{r2} in the same second material. Because the IoR is different in each case, $\theta_{r1} \neq \theta_{r2}$. The effect is easiest to see when light is passed through a block of glass with nonparallel sides, called a *prism*.

If the incident light is *white*, the uniform superposition of all visible wavelength, refraction at the boundary causes all the component colors to physically separate in the second material, and we see the familiar "rainbow" pattern. Rainbows occur naturally when sunlight is "prismed" by raindrops in the atmosphere. If the incident light is the superposition of the two optical beams, each with a different wavelength, refraction at the boundary causes the two beams to physically separate when they get into the second material. This physical separation is the principle that underlies wavelength demultiplexing. Like most other passive optical devices, a prism is bidirectional. So, spatially separated optical signals at different wavelengths can be combined (wavelength multiplexed) by using the prism in reverse.

OPTICAL FIBER

This section describes the physical structure of optical fiber and how it is manufactured.

Structure

You rarely see a bare single fiber because, in the real world, they are usually covered by a protective plastic jacket, giving them the same appearance as insulated wires. Further-

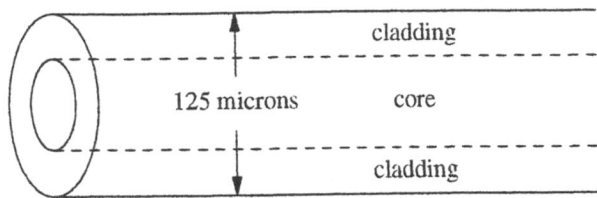

FIGURE 3   Optical fiber structure.

more, optical fibers are frequently bundled together into flat ribbons or into cables. However, a bare single optical fiber looks like a long coarse straight white hair, typically 125 μm (about 1/200 of an inch) in diameter.

Optical fiber is solid and made from silica—not crystalline silicon like a transistor, but closer to the chemistry of common glass. Just as different regions in a transistor's silicon are deliberately doped with certain chemicals to change their electrical properties, different regions in an optical fiber's silica are deliberately doped with certain chemicals to change their optical properties. Although it is a single solid material, the fiber acts optically as if it had an optical inner pipe deep in the center of the overall fiber. The internal smaller pipe, called the fiber's "core," is doped differently from the fiber's outer layer, called the "cladding." The two common types of optical fiber (multimode fiber and single-mode fiber) are physically distinguished by the difference in their core diameters. The core in multimode fiber typically has half the diameter of the overall fiber. The core in single-mode fiber is very thin, typically 8 μm.

The manufacturing process begins with a large hollow cylinder (called a "boule") of pure silica that is suspended as shown in Figure 4. The dopant for the core is injected

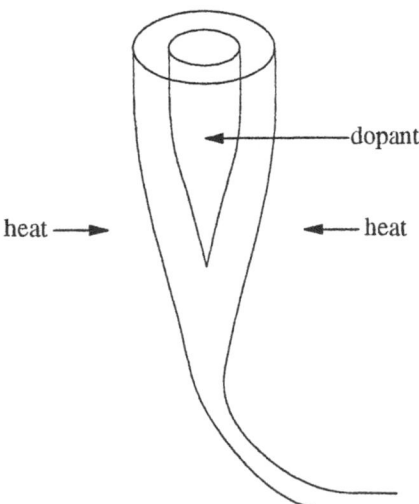

FIGURE 4   Manufacturing optical fiber.

as a gas into the hollow center. Heating the boule causes the core dopant to diffuse into the boule's inner surface and also causes the bottom of the boule to "melt" into a viscous fluid. By gravity, the fluid "oozes" and "necks down" into a thin continuous stream. The doped silica from the inner surface of the boule melts into the center of the stream and becomes the fiber's core. The stream cools into a solid fiber and is rolled onto a spool.

The core's index of refraction is slightly higher than the index of refraction in the cladding. Although the difference—typically less than 1%—seems small, it is large enough that this core-and-cladding structure comprises a "slower" material completely surrounded by a "faster" material. Thus, light injected into the core at a high enough angle of incidence experiences total internal reflection and stays inside the core, ricocheting off the core–cladding wall as it travels along the fiber.

Attenuation

Figure 5 shows the *attenuation spectrum* of modern optical fiber. It shows how different wavelengths of light suffer varying degrees of attenuation in optical fiber. Infrared wavelengths between 0.6 and 1.6 μm are shown on the horizontal axis. The vertical axis shows the degree of optical loss, or *attenuation*, in decibels (dB).

Although the logarithmic "dB" scale is initially confusing, it is used extensively in communications and we will use it here. Let P_1 and P_2 be the power intensities (in W), of two different optical signals, such as the input and output power of an optical transmission link. If P_1 is R times greater than P_2 on the real scale, then P_1 is $10 \log_{10} R$ incrementally larger than P_2 on the logarithmic dB scale. Each doubling of power corresponds to a 3-dB increment (because $\log_{10} 2 = 0.3$) and each 10-fold multiplication of power corresponds to a 10-dB increment. Decibel measurements are relative; they compare two powers and conveniently measure the gain of an amplifier or the loss in a link. The dB scale can also measure an absolute power by comparing it against a standard value. If the standard, $P_2 = 1$ mW, then the measurement is in dBm. For example, 3 mW → +2 dBm and 0.01 mW → 20 dBm.

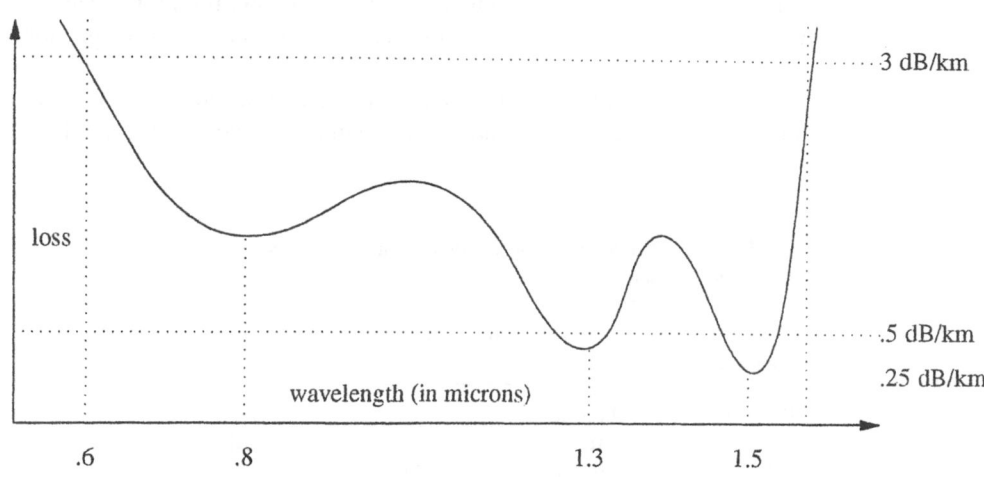

FIGURE 5   Attenuation spectrum of optical fiber.

Early optical fibers had a simple attenuation spectrum, with an attenuation minimum around 0.8 μm. Corresponding to the leftmost "valley" in Figure 5, optical attenuation at this global minimum was around 2 dB/km, which translates into the signal attenuating by one-half for every 1.5 km (0.9 miles). During the 1980s, along with the development of single-mode fiber, improved manufacturing techniques uncovered the two even lower-loss local minima in the attenuation spectrum of Figure 5. If an attenuation of 3 dB/km or better is acceptable, then the "broad attenuation spectrum" of modern conventional optical fiber has a bandpass window for optical signals with wavelengths between 0.6 and 1.6 μm, corresponding to frequencies between 500 and 180 THz.

Table 1 shows the calculations for a remarkable illustration of fiber's ultimate capacity. Let one voice-grade telephone channel, with a 4-kHz analog bandwidth, be analogous to standard household 3/8-in. copper tubing (inner diameter = 0.25 in.). On this same scale, one CATV coax carrying 70, 4-MHz channels corresponds to a "sewer pipe" with a diameter about 6 ft. And, continuing on this scale, the "broad spectrum" of one optical fiber corresponds to a "pipe" greater than a mile in diameter. Later, we will see that this full bandwidth is not readily accessible.

This "broad spectrum" capacity applies only to a small network, like a local area network (LAN), where the 3-dB attenuation is acceptable. However, because the optical fiber's cost is not very relevant in a LAN (because the link lengths are short), the cost of gaining access to all this bandwidth is probably less than the cost of extra fiber. So, it is in large networks, where the fiber costs more (because the links are longer), where bandwidth utilization is important. In a large network, the 3-dB attenuation is probably unacceptable.

Within this 0.06–1.6-μm window, the detailed attenuation spectrum of modern conventional optical fiber is typically characterized by three local minima: at wavelengths around 0.8, 1.3, and 1.5 μm. The two newer higher-wavelength minima are even less lossy than the original 0.8-μm minimum. Although optical transmitters at 1.3 μm and, especially at 1.5 μm, are more complex and costly than those at 0.8 μm, the spectral match between new fibers and transmitters means that optical signals are even less attenuated than in the old fibers. Typically, attenuation is less than 0.5 dB/km in a 60-nm window (1 nm = 10^{-9} m = 10^{-3} μm) around 1.3 μm and in a 90-nm window around 1.5 μm. There is about 15 THz of frequency bandwidth in each window, for a total "narrow spectrum" bandwidth of 30 THz, about one-tenth the bandwidth of the higher-attenuation window.

Allowing as much as 10 cycles/bit for a simple line coding scheme and for guard bands in time and frequency, even this low-attenuation window could provide a 3-Tbps

TABLE 1   Calculation for an Illustration of Fiber's Ultimate Capacity

"Pipe" diameter	Cross-section area	Area in ft.^{2}	Scaled by 11.8×10^6
0.25 in	0.05 in.^{2}	0.00034	4K
5.7 ft	26 ft.^{2}	26	280M
1.14 miles	1.025 miles^2	28.6M	320T
0.35 mile	0.096 mile^2	2.68M	30T

digital channel if we could figure out how to fully use it. A channel this large could carry over 1000 Sonet OC-48 streams at 2.4 Gbps each, or perhaps as many as 50 million DS0 voice channels. One optical fiber could carry all of the telephone traffic in the United States simultaneously.

Fiber's Modes

The word *mode* is confusing because it is used different ways. Optical fibers come in "multimode" and "single-mode" varieties and diode lasers also come in "multimode" and "single-mode" varieties. Although one is tempted to conclude that multimode lasers are used with multimode fiber and that single-mode lasers are used with single-mode fibers, this pairing is not necessary or even natural because the mode that is used to classify fibers is different from the mode that is used to classify lasers. It is natural to use multimode or single-mode lasers with single-mode fiber and it is rare to use any kind of laser with multimode fiber.

Although we will avoid the mathematics of guided traveling waves, the equation for the intensity of optical energy at any point in a fiber's core is a function of x, y, z, t, and w. Mathematically, a mode is a one of the integer number of functions that act as solutions to some differential equation. The concept of mode that distinguishes multimode from single-mode fiber is called "transverse mode." When light travels along a fiber (in z), optical power is distributed over the fiber's x–y cross section in certain consistent patterns. For a given wavelength and core diameter, only a certain integer number of energy distribution patterns are stable in the cross section of the fiber's core and the signals that correspond to these patterns are the only ones that can successfully propogate in z and t down the length of the fiber. Figure 6 shows three of these patterns, corresponding to the first-, second-, and third-order *transverse modes*. The thicker the core, the more modes are supported. The longer the wavelength, the more modes are supported.

Although the "mode distributions" in Figure 6 suggest that all the optical energy remains in the core, it actually does not. As optical energy travels along a fiber, it distributes itself across the fiber's cross-sectional area. Although most of the energy lies inside the core, a small percentage (called the *evanescent wave*) resides in the cladding. The evanescent wave is not lost in the cladding, but travels along the cladding, bound to the energy inside the core.

Multimode fiber has a core diameter that is large enough that many optical modes are transmitted along its length. Single-mode fiber has a core diameter that is so small that only one optical mode can be transmitted along its length—the mode that travels

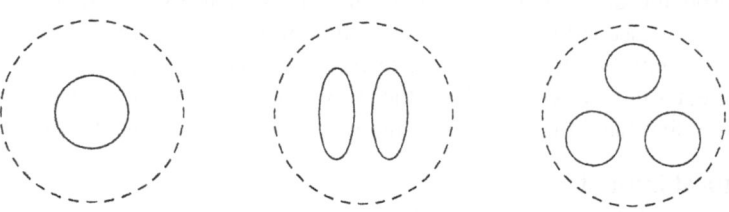

FIGURE 6   First-, second-, and third-order transverse modes.

straight down the center of the core. Because the core in single-mode fiber is so small, we can conclude the following:

- Single-mode fiber would be more difficult to manufacture (and hence, costs more) than multimode fiber.
- When trying to direct external light into the core at the end of a fiber, less light would get into the core of a single-mode fiber than into a multimode fiber.
- Because the cores must be aligned when trying to attach two fibers together to make one continuous fiber, single-mode splicing would be more difficult and single-mode connectors would have to be more carefully machined (and, hence, more expensive).

Distortion

In any waveguide, including optical fiber, every *transverse mode* has a different effective velocity of propogation. Suppose a logical ONE is implemented physically as a multi-mode pulse of light traveling down a multimode fiber. If this optical pulse is followed too closely by a "nonpulse" (a logical ZERO), the slow modes in the first bit could still be arriving at the receiver as optical energy when the receiver is making a 0/1 decision on the second bit. This effect is called *modal dispersion*. If the end-to-end data rate is limited by the fiber's modal dispersion, the problem may be solved by using singlemode fiber.

Single-mode optical fibers have core diameters of around 8 µm; so small that the core can only support the *fundamental mode*, that first-order transverse mode shown in Figure 6. Because the high-order modes do not transmit down the fiber, modal dispersion is completely eliminated and data rates can be much higher in single mode fiber (SMF) than in multimode fiber (MMF). The penalty, of course, is that SMF is more expensive, is more difficult to work with, and couples less light from the transmitter. However, removing modal dispersion by using single-mode fibers only means that data rates can be raised to values that are now limited by another characteristic of optical fiber.

When we discussed prisms earlier, we saw that glass' index of refraction (IoR) is not constant with respect to wavelength. Thus, if an optical signal has several component wavelengths (colors), besides having a different angle of refraction, each one has a differ-ent velocity of propogation along the fiber. This effect is called *chromatic dispersion*. If an optical pulse (a logical ONE) is followed too closely by a "nonpulse" (a logical ZERO), the slow colors in the first bit could still be arriving at the receiver as optical energy when the receiver is making a 0/1 decision on the second bit. Thus, a fiber's end-to-end data rate may be limited by the fiber's chromatic dispersion. Although we cannot eliminate chromatic dispersion (like we can eliminate modal dispersion), we have two ways to reduce its effect. One way to reduce chromatic dispersion is to use a wavelength where the effect is minimized. In one of those coincidences that nature seldom seems to give us, chromatic dispersion is minimum in conventional SMF around 1.3 µm, which happens to be the second best attenuation minimum. *Dispersion shifted fiber* is specially manufactured, with additional dopants, to have a different *dispersion minimum* wave-length, at greater cost, of course. The other way to reduce chromatic dispersion is to use a light source that has little variation in the wavelength (see the next section).

Architectural Impact

In this section and the sections Opto-Electronics, Passive Optics, and Optical Multiplex-ing that follow, the sections conclude with a discussion of how the section's particular subject impacts network architecture. Here, we discuss some analogies to how other technologies have had impact on other kinds of architectures. The distinction between *incremental application* and *architectural impact*, which is developed next, will be continued in the corresponding subsections later.

As primitive humans developed better construction components, they were able to build higher walls. Using a "brick-and-mortar" architecture, the height of a wall is limited by the ability of the lowest bricks to resist being crumbled by the weight of the upper bricks. As "brick technology" evolved—from simple adobe, to clay-and-straw, to cinder block—we were able to build higher and higher walls. When we developed steel, we could have made high walls with "steel bricks," but the significant breakthrough that allows us to build skyscrapers comes from also changing the architecture. If we use steel to build a framework that supports the wall, rather than pile up steel bricks, we can build very high walls. Although steel would have some *incremental* value as a material for making bricks that would be used in a conventional wall architecture, the really significant breakthrough occurred because steel was different enough to make us rethink the architecture.

The semiconductor transistor is another similar example. Initially, the transistor was conceived to be a miniature and low-power substitute for the vacuum tube in conventional electronic circuits; and, it was significant as such. However, the real breakthrough occurred when we rethought the architecture. If transistors had only been applied *incrementally*, we would have never developed *integrated circuits* and we could not possibly have the personal computer.

Optical fiber, and its related technologies, is similar. We can use fiber technology incrementally and we do. A long length of optical fiber, with a transmitter and receiver on each end, is a good point-to-point link. It is better than a twisted pair or coaxial cable and there is significant benefit in using a fiber link instead of these traditional links in conventional network architectures. However, this application is incremental, like making steel bricks. Fiber-optic technology is different enough that we should rethink the network architecture. We have only begun to do this. Optical fiber will affect the human species to the same extent that steel girders and transistors have affected the human species. This has not happened yet, because the devices are more advanced than the architectures.

OPTO-ELECTRONICS

In this section, we discuss the semiconductor devices that are used with optical fiber. These *opto-electronic* devices are partly optical and partly electronic. Passive "all-optical" devices are described in the next section. Newer "mostly optical" active *photonic* devices are described in the section Phototonic Technology for the Future. First, we briefly discuss the modulation and detection techniques that are used in optical fiber communications. Then, we describe in greater detail the *photodetectors* that perform optical-to-electronic conversion in optical receivers and the *light-emitting diodes* and *semiconductor diode lasers* that perform electronic-to-optical conversion in optical transmitters. We conclude with a discussion of *optical digital communications* and *synchronization*.

Optical Modulation and Detection

Because light is just a special case of electromagnetic radiation, all the modulation techniques employed in radio communications could be applied to optical communications—at least, in theory. Although most radio and modem techniques such as hetero-dyne, homodyne, phase modulation, QPSK, and CDMA have been tried in optical communications (at least in the lab), one modulation technique is most commonly found in practice. This most practical technique is called *direct detection* in optics, but it is identical to *amplitude modulation* (AM), the most basic technique for modulating a radio wave.

In AM, information is carried by the amplitude of a "carrier wave." However, recalling from the *wave model of light* that optical power corresponds to wave amplitude, carrying information as the amplitude of an (optical) EM wave is the same thing as carrying information as the power of the corresponding optical signal. However, from the *particle model of light*, carrying information as the power of an optical signal corresponds to a photon stream where information is carried by the photon density. This is *direct detection* and the capability requires opto-electronic devices that translate *directly* between electronic voltage and optical power. We require a transmitter that delivers into the fiber an optical power that is proportional to the voltage of its electronic input signal. The light-emitting diode and its cousin, the semiconductor diode laser, provide this capability. We require a receiver whose output electronic voltage is proportional to the optical power it receives from the fiber. The various types of photodiode provide this capability.

Optical-to-Electrical Conversion

This subsection describes the operation of the opto-electronic devices that are used as the optical-to-electronic converters in receivers. The operation of the semiconductor diode is reviewed and then extended to explain the operation of the basic photodiode and its two more powerful cousins, the PIN photodiode and the avalanche photodiode.

The basic semiconductor diode is a small crystal of silicon. In the crystalline structure, each "valence-4" silicon atom forms a covalent bond with four other atoms. The silicon crystal is manufactured with two "sides"; each side is "doped" with a different impurity whose atoms replace random silicon atoms in the crystalline structure. Although pure crystalline silicon is a mediocre conductor of electricity (giving us the term "semi-conductor"), the doped sides are good conductors because the dopant atoms contribute extra mobile charge carriers. In the "N side," the "valence-5" dopant contributes extra electrons and current flows because some negatively charged electrons are mobile and move in the opposite direction as the positive current. In the P side, the "valence-3" dopant contributes "holes" (the absence of an electron in the crystal's covalent bonds) and current flows because some bonded electrons "hop" into neighboring holes (leaving a "hole" behind), giving the effect that the positively charged holes move in the same direction as the current.

Consider connecting an external voltage source to the diode so that the P side is positive and the N side is negative, as in Figure 7A. Repelled by the positive voltage and attracted to the negative voltage, holes in the P side flow toward the P–N junction. Repelled by the negative voltage and attracted to the positive voltage, electrons in the N side flow toward the P–N junction. Holes from the P side and electrons from the N side meet at the P–N junction and combine there. The external effect is that net current flows through the diode, from P side to N side. Now, instead, consider connecting the external voltage to the diode so that the P side is negative and the N side is positive, as in Figure 7B. Attracted to the negative voltage and repelled by the positive voltage, holes in the P side flow away from the P–N junction. Attracted to the positive voltage and repelled by

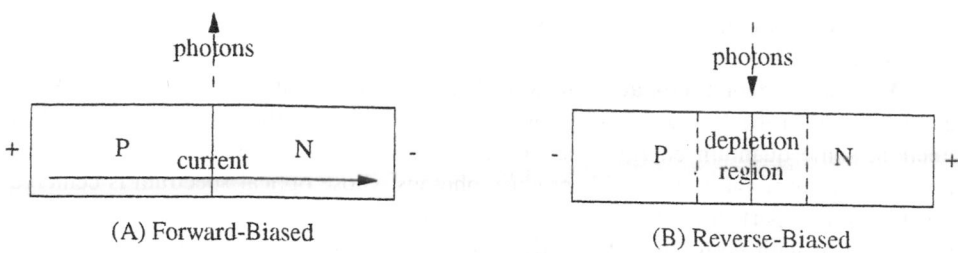

photons

| + | P   current   N | - |

(A) Forward-Biased

photons

| - | P | depletion region | N | + |

(B) Reverse-Biased

FIGURE 7   Light-emitting diode and photodiode.

the negative voltage, electrons in the N side flow away from the P–N junction. With no mobile charge carriers near the P–N junction, a nonconducting "depletion region" forms there. The external effect is that no net current flows through the diode. Electronic diodes are used in circuit applications, such as power supplies, where electrical current must flow in one direction but not the reverse direction.

We take a second look at the reverse-biased electronic diode in Figure 7B. Current cannot flow because the region near the P–N junction is depleted of mobile charge carriers. However, consider manufacturing the diode with a "window" so incident light can fall on the P–N junction. It turns out that when a photon with high enough energy (especially with the right wavelength), "crashes into" a bonded electron, it can "knock it" out of its covalent bond, creating a mobile hole and a mobile electron. It turns out that optical energy in the wavelengths of interest is just right for breaking covalent bonds in silicon—and we are very experienced at working with silicon. If a stream of photons were to bombard the depletion region in the vicinity of the P–N junction, a stream of holes would carry charge into the P side and a stream of electrons would carry charge into the N side. Current would flow, even though the diode is reverse biased, but only as long as the photons continue to hit the P–N junction: photons → current and no photons → no current. This is the basic silicon photodiode.

If a diode is manufactured with a layer of undoped "intrinsic" silicon between the P side and the N side, it will have a permanent enlarged depletion region. Although these PIN diodes perform poorly as electronic diodes, especially when forward biased, they are better photodiodes than conventional PN diodes because more of the incident photons are likely to hit the diode in the depletion region. Thus, PIN diodes provide more electrical current per optical watt than conventional PN diodes, but they cost a little more because they are a little harder to make. If a PIN diode is specially manufactured to be able to withstand a high-reverse voltage, then the holes and electrons created by photon bombardment attain greater momentum as they are attracted to their respective ends of the diode structure. These "high-energy" mobile carriers "crash into" other covalent bonds and create more carriers, in a process called an "avalanche." Thus, avalanche photodiodes (APDs) provide even more electrical current per optical watt than PIN diodes, but they are even more expensive because they are even harder to make.

Electrical-to-Optical Conversion

This subsection describes the operation of the opto-electronic devices that are used as the electronic-to-optical converters in transmitters. The operation of the semiconductor diode is extended to explain the operation of the basic light-emitting diode (LED) and its more powerful cousin, the diode laser. Multimode and single-mode diode lasers are distinguished.

We take a second look at the forward-biased electronic diode in Figure 7A. When an electron from the N side meets a hole from the P side and they combine at the P–N junction, some quantum energy is left over in the form of a photon. It turns out that diodes made from gallium arsenide produce photons whose optical spectrum is centered around 800 nm, perfect for that first attenuation minimum. Next to silicon, we have a lot of experience with GaAs also. If the diode is manufactured with a "window" near the P–N junction, then the diode will produce a photon stream, whose optical power is proportional to the forward-bias current: current → photons and no current → no photons. This is the basic LED. The LED and the photodiode are essentially the same device, except the LED is forward biased and made from GaAs and the photodiode is reverse biased and made from Si.

The GaAs LED produces an optical beam typically in the 0.8–0.85-μm range. Its relatively broad spectral content makes optical communications with LEDs susceptible to chromatic dispersion. However, because early optical systems used LEDs with multimode fiber anyway, the data rate was limited initially by modal dispersion.

Using a complicated (hence, high-cost) manufacturing process, an optical channel can be embedded laterally across the diode, in the plane of the P–N junction, as depicted in Figure 8. The channel is doped to have a higher index of refraction than the surrounding diode, is small enough in x and y that only the fundamental transverse mode can propogate in z, and its end faces (at the diode's edges) are polished to "partial-mirror" quality. Just like in a LED, when forward-bias current flows through the diode, electrons from the N side combine with holes from the P side and produce photons at the P–N junction. But, with this structure, many of the photons produced by this "spontaneous emission" get inside the optical channel and traverse it in z, trapped inside by its total internal reflection.

Now, it turns out if a photon gets near a high-energy electron, it can "induce" the electron to drop to a lower quantum level and, in so doing, cause it to emit a photon similar to the original photon. As there are many of these high-energy electrons near the junction, the photons in the channel multiply by this "stimulated emission." Although it is not exactly like avalanching, it is optical amplification. These are all the ingredients of a "laser." The term "laser" has become such a part of our vocabulary that most people do not know that the term is an acronym for Light Amplification by Stimulated Emission

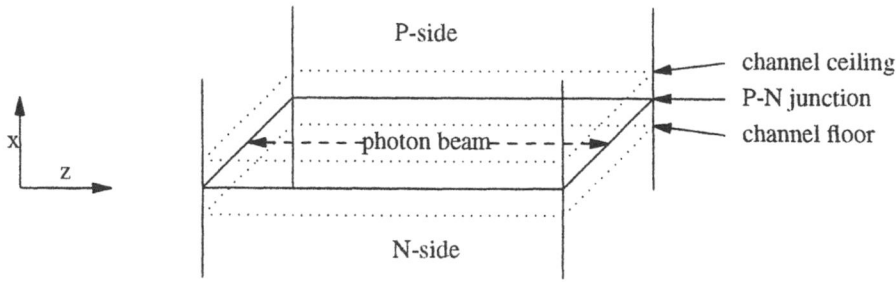

FIGURE 8   Semiconductor diode laser.

of Radiation. The amplified optical energy emerges from both ends of the channel on both edges of the diode. Because "stimulated emission" occurs over a narrow optical spectrum, the laser's optical bandwidth is much narrower than the LED's, and communications by lasers is less affected by chromatic dispersion. Whereas these miniature "semiconductor diode lasers" cannot cut steel, they can produce several milliwatts of optical power.

Although a semiconductor diode laser (SDL) is a better optical transmitter than a conventional light emitting diode, SDLs are much more expensive than LEDs because they are so much more difficult to manufacture, even at the LEDs conventional 800 nm center wavelength. If the basic CaAs diode is doped with indium and/or phosphorous, the center wavelength of the optical spectrum can be shifted to 1300 nm or even to 1500 nm. Because the fabrication complexity increases with the wavelength, we get the following cost inequalities:

$$\$LED(800) \ll \$SDL(800) \ll \$SDL(1300) \ll \$SDL(1500).$$

Because of the half-mirrored end faces, much of the optical energy in the channel reflects backward and is amplified even more. The highest optical energy occurs at those wavelengths that are within the optical bandwidth for *stimulated emission* and are such that the channel's length (the diode's thickness) equals an exact integer number of wavelengths. Each of these "peak" wavelengths, which are exact integer divisors of the channel's length, is called a longitudinal mode and the SDL is a "multimode laser." Figure 9 shows a typical optical spectrum of a multimode SDL. The modes are typically several nanometers apart. Confusing the laity, an SDL's longitudinal modes bear no relationship to an MMF's spatial modes.

Although the optical signal from an SDL has a much narrower optical spectrum than that from an LED, it may still be broad enough that the data rate can be limited by chromatic dispersion, even at the dispersion minimum wavelength of 1300 nm. SDLs can be constructed, at considerable additional expense, so that only one of these longitudinal modes is produced. These are called single-mode lasers. Today's extremely high data rates of 2.4 Gbps are obtained by using an SM with a SMF in the 1300-nm region.

Architectural Impact

Summarizing, we have gradually chipped away at those physical characteristics of optical transmission that limit data rate. First, modal dispersion was completely solved by switching to a single-mode fiber. More recently, chromatic dispersion has been eroded by using the dispersion minimum wavelength of 1300 nm and/or by using single-mode lasers. However, every step of the way—from MMF to SMF, from LEDs to SDLs, from

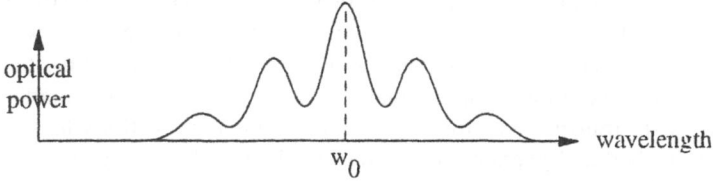

FIGURE 9   Longitudinal modes in a laser's spectrum.

MMLs to SMLs—has been accomplished by dramatically increased cost, not just more expensive fiber, but a much higher cost at the endpoints of the optical transmission system.

Communications of analog signals requires a linear medium. Although the light-emitting diode and the photodiode are relatively linear analog devices, the semiconductor diode laser and, especially, the optical fiber itself are annoyingly nonlinear. While analog signals are regularly transmitted over optical fibers, it is one of those incremental applications. It's not a misapplication of the technology, but optical analog communications is band limited, must be done carefully to avoid distortion caused by nonlinearity, and does not take advantage of all of fiber-optics characteristics.

When analog signals are multiplexed in practical optical systems, typically the various channels are modulated and multiplexed using conventional AM or FM and conventional electronic frequency division multiplexing. Then, the multiplexed signal, perceived as "broad band" when it is transmitted over coaxial cable, is the "narrow band" signal used to (analog) modulate an optical beam. Although only incremental, optical FM is still very practical and is commonly found in CATV "backbone" networks.

Digital Optical Signals

Partly because of the limited usefulness of optical FM, partly because digital signals do not require linearity, but mostly because the "world has gone digital anyway," most optical communications is digital—in fact, binary. However, the characteristics of the devices and of the fiber itself preclude the use of the modulation techniques used in modern modems, the use of the sophisticated digital pulse formats used with copper, and change the way we do bit synchronization in optics. Although we are not going to review digital transmission here, we will briefly discuss some of the differences in digital communications when the OSI physical layer is optical. For example, many of the highly multiplexed digital communications systems over copper use a binary pulse transmission format called *antipodal* or *alternate mark inversion* (AMI). (A mark is telegraphy terminology for a pulse that is transmitted as a logical ONE; a space is an unfilled pulse time slot that is transmitted as a logical ZERO.) In AMI, logical ZERO is transmitted as 0 V and logical ONE is transmitted alternately as $+A$ V and $-A$ V. This format guarantees that any binary signal has a net 0 DC, regardless of the distribution of ZEROs and ONEs in the signal. It turns out that this 0-DC property simplifies the design of the preamplifier and decision circuit in the electronic receiver. The corresponding property in an optical signal would be similarly beneficial, but we cannot do it because, even though engineers joke about needing "photons" and "darkons," there is no such thing as "negative light."

A modification of AMI for *binary k-zero substitution* (BkZS) is commonly used in "copper" digital communications to prevent the receiver's phase-locked loop from losing bit synchronization because of the presence of too many consecutive ZEROs in the binary signal. In digital optical communications, as we cannot use AMI, we cannot use BkZS, and bit synchronization is problematic. Fortunately, there are other techniques. In Manchester coding, we transmit space–mark for a logical ZERO and mark–space for a logical ONE. This transmission format provides enough transitions to keep a phase-locked loop refreshed and guarantees that the signal's net DC voltage is not 0 Vs, but at least a constant. However, at two transmitted bits for every logical bit, Manchester coding squanders bandwidth. In a LAN, this is typically not a problem. In a fiber wide area network (WAN), although we have not done it yet, we may need to use Manchester coding, or something similar, to provide synchronization as evolve toward 10-Gbps rates.

Fortunately, just in time to enable optical communication's high bit rates, major advances in the technology of phase-locked loops allows another solution for bit synchronization. The Synchronous Optical Network (SONet) is a standardized international digital transmission format for use over optical fiber. Synchronization in today's SONET WANs is accomplished by "plesiochronous transmission."

Essentially, we put an independent clock in every network node. If all the clocks could be manufactured to perfect tolerance, then all the network nodes would be perfectly synchronized (except for phase). If the clocks have slightly different frequencies, some receiver will eventually skip a bit (if the receiver's clock is slower than the transmitter's clock) or sample the same bit twice (if the receiver's clock is faster than the transmitter's clock). If this happens, we have an error; but if this error occurs even less often than a noise error, we will not even notice it and we can live with it. Our ability to make highly accurate clocks and the current standard bit error rate of 10^{-9} provides this architectural simplicity. As the data rates increase or as we strive for lower BER, we will have to abandon this scheme for something else.

PASSIVE OPTICS

The principal drawback to optical fiber is that it is difficult to physically connect up to. You cannot simply connect two optical components together using a wire-wrap tool or a soldering iron. Although this has ramifications on manual handling, the ramifications extend even to network topology.

We will need to attach fiber A to fiber B somehow so that an optical signal propagating down fiber A will continue past the point of attachment and continue to propagate down fiber B. The two principal means of fiber connection are connectors and splices. The trade-offs are simple and obvious: Splices have lower loss than connectors, but connectors are more easily disconnected and reconnected than splices.

Fiber Ends

Consider the problems of "coupling" the light emitted by an opto-electronic transmitter into the fiber's core at the transmit end of an optical fiber:

- When the light, emitted into the air by the device, tries to enter the fiber end, it partially reflects because of the change in IoR at the air–glass boundary. One effect is *attenuation* because all of the emitted light does not enter the fiber— there is not much we can do about this. Another effect, when the device is an SDL, is that this reflection can interfere with the laser's delicate cavity physics. If we cut the fiber on a slight slant, the reflected light will not go backward into the transmitter.
- If the fiber's end face is rough or even just scratched (across the opening into the core), light will scatter and cause additional attenuation. We must polish the fiber end and keep it clean.
- If the beam is not aimed correctly, some or all of the optical energy might miss the core. This is a much greater problem with single-mode fiber, where the core is such a smaller target.

- Even if the beam is aimed perfectly, if the beam diameter is greater than the core diameter, then much of the optical energy misses the core and hits the cladding. If we are willing to pay more to get increased optical power level, there are two standard solutions: a small lens installed between the device and the fiber end can focus more of the beam into the core or we can use SDLs instead of LEDs.

We discussed earlier that the optical energy emitted by an LED has a broader optical spectrum than the optical energy emitted by an SDL. It turns out that the optical energy emitted by an LED also has a broader physical beam than the optical energy emitted by an SDL. Although it seems foolish to use an SDL with MMF because of dispersion, we might do it if we need to increase the transmit power. And, although we might not need an SDL for some application that uses SMF, it is very difficult to couple a LED's beam into a SMF's core.

With all these difficulties, it is customary for the manufacturer of the opto-electronic transmitter to install a small length of fiber, called a *pig tail*, onto the device and encapsulate it. Because many of these same problems occur at the photodetector, the receivers are also typically pigtailed. Although many of these same difficulties also occur when trying to connect the ends of two fibers together (including connecting the pigtail to the main fiber), at least fiber-to-fiber coupling can be accomplished with connectors or splices.

Connectors

In their external appearance, many of the styles of connectors used for coaxial cable have been adapted for optical fiber. The general problem that connectors must solve is that, more then merely bringing the ends of the two different fibers into alignment and contact, the cores in these two ends must align and touch. If the cores are laterally misaligned, then light near the edge of the core in the fiber on one side of the connector might travel directly into the cladding in the fiber on the other side of the connector. If the two fiber ends do not lie in a straight line, then light from one fiber can enter the other one at less than the critical angle. Most of the other problems, like reflection and rough edges, can be alleviated by using index-matching gel. If this sticky gelatinous substance is applied to the two fiber ends before connecting them, most of the photons will traverse the connection because the gel has the same IoR as the fiber's "glass."

Figure 10 shows a typical connector, called *biconic*. The two fiber ends, labeled a and b, are shown perfectly aligned and butted against each other inside the connector's cross section. First, a conical plug is installed on the fiber end: Conical plug c is installed on fiber end a and conical plug d is installed on fiber end b. Then, the conical plugs are inserted into the conical jacks in connector housing e, and screwed tightly into place. If the core is perfectly centered inside the fiber, if the fiber is perfectly round, if the holes drilled in each conical plug are perfectly centered, if each fiber fits perfectly snugly in its respective drilled hole, and if the plugs and jacks are all perfectly machined, then the fiber cores will be perfectly aligned inside the connector. This is difficult enough for a multimode fiber with its relatively large core, but it is extremely difficult for a single-mode fiber, and SMF connectors are very expensive.

Connectors for multiple parallel fibers have been very successful. A small block of silicon, the size of a thick postage stamp, can have eight parallel V-grooves micromachined by photolithography. Eight fibers can be laid in parallel, one resting in each

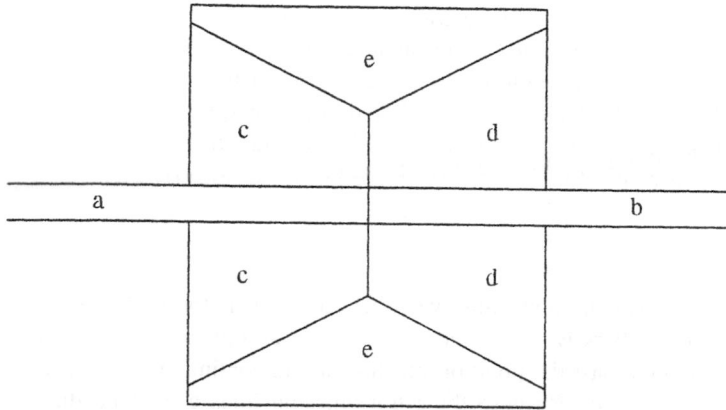

FIGURE 10   The biconic connector.

V-groove. A similar block on top "sandwiches" all eight fibers firmly in place. One face is polished so the fiber ends are polished and align with the end face of the silicon V-groove connector. When two such structures are butt-coupled and epoxied together, a handy eight-way fiber connection results. The technology for integrating fiber connectors onto the edge connectors on printed wiring boards would also be handy, but it has proven to be hard to do. The pigtails for PWB-mounted optical components typically stick out the front edge of equipment racks. However, of all connector types, the type that is most noticeable by its absence in optical systems is the "tap." The very reasons that make optical fiber immune to external noise and secure from external eavesdropping also, unfortunately, make it very difficult to "tap" in the manner of coaxial cable.

Splices

Two fibers can be attached permanently by a process called the *fusion splice*. The two steps in forming a splice are *alignment* and *fusion*.

In the alignment step, each fiber end is mechanically stabilized into a V-groove that is machined along the length of a small metal pad. Each fiber end is clamped into position in its V-groove and, in some splicers, it is even "sucked" into position by a vacuum applied through small holes drilled through the bottom of the V-groove. The extreme tip of each fiber protrudes over the end of its pad. The splicer mechanisms allow each pad to be positioned in the x, y, and z directions so that the two fiber ends can be mechanically aligned and positioned to just barely touch each other. Manual alignment can be performed visually through a microscope, or by optical test, if possible. If the technician has access to the "other end" of the two fibers, a transmitter can be attached to one end, a receiver attached to the other end, and the "joint" can be positioned to maximize the received signal. In modern splicers, fibers are aligned automatically by sophisticated imaging software. Although these "self-aligning" splicers are expensive, they are small enough to be carried manually up a utility pole and they allow a technician to perform the splicing operation very quickly.

After the two fiber ends are aligned and touching, the splice is *fused*. In many fusion splicers, the two fiber ends are positioned between two high-voltage electrodes and the ends are fused when an electric arc passes through the joint. The intensity and duration of the arc is determined experimentally. Typically, because the splice is visible only to the trained eye, it would be "painted" so that if the two ends ever needed to be disconnected again, the technician would "cut" out the splice. Considering that splices have lower loss than connectors, splices can be cost-justified in many applications that used to require a connector.

Splitters

Even more difficult than connecting two fibers together is the problem of *splitting*—attaching fiber A to fibers B and C somehow so that an optical signal propogating down fiber A will continue past the point of attachment and continue to propagate down fibers B and C simultaneously. Because three transmission lines cannot be directly attached, like three simple wires can, a three-port intermediate splitter is required. With coaxial cable and other transmission lines, a splitter is an "impedance matching" transformer that prevents the signal in A from reflecting from the point of attachment back to the source of the signal. An optical splitter serves a similar function.

The fundamental device is called a passive optical coupler. Physically, it consists of two parallel optical channels that are extremely close together over a certain distance, L_d. If the parallel channels are close enough, the evanescent wave of the optical energy in one channel extends through the intermediate cladding and reaches the other channel. If this happens, the optical energy in the first channel gradually transfers into the other channel, and still propagates in the same direction. The percentage of energy that couples from one channel to the other increases in z within L_d, where the channels are close. At $z = L_c$, the "coupling length," 100% of the energy has coupled across and now begins to couple back to the original channel. Channel coupling is symmetric and the device is reversible. Obviously, a multimode splitter is easier to build, and hence less expensive, than a single-mode splitter.

The typical application for passive optical couplers is as optical splitters (and combiners). If the segment where the channels are close has length $L_d = L_c/2$, then only 50% of the optical energy in each channel couples into the other channel. Although 50–50 splitters are most useful, other ratios are possible and even variable splitters have been manufactured (and are quite expensive). Although the underlying device has four terminals, frequently only three are actually used. In a typical 1-to-2 splitter, one of the input channels is unused. Notice that, in a perfect device, if the optical input power is 1 mW, then each output branch carries 0.5 mW after splitting. Thus, every 1-to-2 split causes a −3-dB loss from input to output.

A 1-to-4 split can be constructed using three 1-to-2 splitters, arranged in a tree topology. The signal on each of the four outputs is −6 dB attenuated from the optical power of the input signal because this input signal must pass through two splitters in series to reach each output and it suffers a −3-dB loss in each splitter. This concept generalizes to any power-of-2 optical split. Large tree structures of splitters have been integrated together into a device called a *star coupler*. These are effective in multimode environments. Because a 1-to-32 star coupler is physically a 32-by-32 device, it can be used effectively as a 32-way directional combiner in a small network with a "passive star" topology.

Frequently, optical signals on different fibers need to be "combined" and placed on one fiber. Applications include (1) time-multiplexing spatially separate optical signals that occupy different time slots or (2) wavelength-multiplexing spatially separate optical signals that use different wavelengths. Like splitting, optical signals cannot be combined directly and an intermediate 2-to-1 device is required. In fact, optical combining and splitting use the same device, a three-terminal *passive optical coupler*. Although the splitter has an unused input fiber, the combiner has an unused output fiber. The surprising result of this is that, like splitting, optical combining is accompanied by a −3-dB loss in the signal power. If each input to a combiner carries a 1-mW optical signal, the output fiber has a net signal power of 1 mW, with 0.5 mW contributed from each input. The easiest way to see this is to remember that there must be a similar combined signal on the unused output. In power budget calculations, it is easy to forget the −3-dB loss associated with optical combining.

A perfect prism, or similar device, could perform wavelength multiplexing and/or demultiplexing with no loss. Thus, although it would seem that a prism would be preferred over a passive optical coupler for wavelength multiplexing (because the coupler has an inherent −3-dB loss), prisms and related devices are so imperfect that they usually have about the same amount of loss anyway. Passive optical couplers are generally used for wavelength multiplexing because they are less expensive. Prisms are required for wavelength demultiplexing.

Architectural Impact

The three basic local area network (LAN) topologies are the *bus*, the *ring*, and the *star*. The very characteristics that make fiber so good for point-to-point communications make it a bad choice for a bus topology or for supporting broadcast communications. The principal drawback is that we just do not have an effective and practical way to "tap" an optical fiber. Although fiber buses have been proposed and even prototyped, typically using "90–10" passive optical couplers at each node, whether for a back-plane "mother board" or for a LAN, optics just is not as practical as copper and does not appear that it ever will be.

Although fiber is becoming commonplace in CATV networks, it is only used in the "backbone" network, the physical star "MAN" that connects the CATV "head end" to the bus LANs that serve each neighborhood. In these "hybrid fiber/coax" networks, the local distribution for a broadcast signal is logically performed best by a bus and the bus is physically implemented best by coaxial cable. Although fiber is also becoming commonplace in ethernet LANs, whenever ethernet is implemented in fiber, the classical ethernet topology must be changed. The ethernet "bus" is collapsed to a short bus at the hub of a physical star and the star's arms are implemented in optical fiber.

Fiber is more sensible for a ring topology, like FDDI, but even this international standard is an incremental application. FDDI is not a true optical ring. FDDI has electronic nodes whose interconnecting links happen to be optical. Although optical fiber, particularly multimode fiber, can be a smart choice to use as a physical link in a ring or bus topology, such applications do not take significant advantage of optical fiber's characteristics and will not evolve as this technology evolves.

If we need to move data from point A only to point B only, then optical fiber is a logical choice for the medium. Because optical fiber is such a natural medium for point-to-point communications, the star topology is most enhanced by fiber's strengths and least compromised by fiber's weaknesses. Optical fiber is, in fact, the medium of choice in virtually every telecommunications environment that has a star topology and that supports point-to-point communications.

POWER BUDGET

For any digital transmission medium, we can calculate its maximum unrepeated link length as a complicated function of transmitted signal power, line loss, line noise, receiver noise, transducer efficiency, and the required bit error rate. In optical fiber, line noise is so low that it is insignificant, and this greatly simplifies the link power budget computation.

Noise

In any material, its free electrons vibrate randomly with an intensity that is temperature dependent. However, moving electrons constitute an electric current and a random current inside a resistor produces a random voltage. Although this might seem that it would be an insignificant effect, optical communications is so relatively free of noise that this *thermal noise* in the photodiode's "load resistor" is the single most significant source of noise in the system.

Although thermal noise is neither "white" nor "Gaussian," we can use the classical mathematics of white Gaussian noise to show that to achieve a bit error rate (BER) = 10^{-9}, we require a signal-to-noise ratio (SNR) = 21.6 dB. Although a crude approximation, the result is consistent with practice. Thus, the received signal power must be 21.6 dB higher than, or 140 times greater than, the accumulated noise power at the receiver. Receiver sensitivity is the minimum signal power at the receiver that guarantees meeting the required BER in the presence of net accumulated noise.

Link Budget Calculation

Link power budget is the difference between signal power at the transmitter and the receiver sensitivity. Because a receiver sensitivity of −30 dBm (1 μW) and transmitter power of 0 dBm (1 mW) are easily attained in conventional electro-optic receivers and transmitters, a link power budget of 30 dB is not unreasonable in optical communications systems. The significance of this figure is lost in the "dB" log scale. It tells us, remarkably, that only one error is expected in every billion bits transmitted, even though for every thousand photons transmitted, only one arrives at the receiver.

The typical optical link has several splices and connectors and their loss must be accounted for in the power budget. The power budget must also account for −3 dB of loss in every passive splitter and combiner in the link. Even allowing for −10 dB of loss due to each passive devices, the typical link budget still has 20 dB left over for fiber loss. At −0.3 dB/km, a 10-km (6 mile) link contributes only −3 dB of loss (half the input power is lost). An optical link that is 60 km long contributes −18 dB of loss and is still within the power budget.

Figure 11 illustrates a simple fiber link and its power budget calculation. Assume that the laser transmitter has an internal optical power of +2 dBm, but because of coupling loss at the fiber pigtail of −3.5 dB, the optical power in the fiber on the transmit side of the link is −1.5 dBm. Assume that the thermal noise "floor" in the photodetector circuit is −50 dBm (10^{-5} mW = 10 nW). For BER = 10^{-9}, we need SNR = 21.6 dB; thus, the (internal) receiver sensitivity must be −28.4 dBm. However, because of coupling loss at the fiber pigtail of −2.5 dB, the minimum optical power in the fiber on the receiver side of the link is −25.9 dBm. Assume that the link consists of a single optical fiber and that it is attached by a connector to the transmitter's and receiver's pigtails. If connector

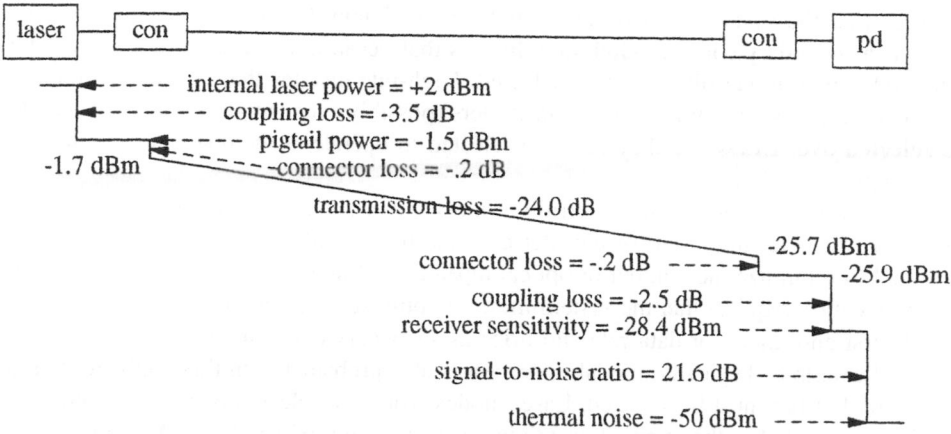

FIGURE 11   Example link power budget calculation.

loss is −0.2 dB on each end, the optical power entering the link is −1.7 dBm and the minimum optical power that can exit the link is −25.7 dBm. This leaves (−1.7) − (−25.7) = 24.0 dB for link loss. If fiber attenuation is −0.3 dB/km, then the link can be 80 km long.

As remarkable as this is, we can even do better. More expensive photodetectors (like APDs) have even better receiver sensitivity, and lower fiber loss can be attained by transmitting at the loss minimum wavelength of 1500 nm.

Technology Families

With multimode and single-mode fiber, with fiber attenuation minima at 800, 1300, and 1500 nm, and with LED or SDL transmitters, there might appear to be many different logical combinations. In reality, however, there are only three combinations that make any practical sense. Depending on your application, you pick one of these three "families."

First, let *price* be the overriding, most important issue. Suppose you have to implement the minimum-price system and, then, operate within its parameters, whatever they are. Price alone dictates that you must select multimode fiber, and not single-mode fiber. Price alone dictates that you must use LEDs, not lasers. Price alone dictates that you must use the 800-nm wavelength. Obviously, if your rate × distance requirements are modest and can be satisfied by this family, then this is your first choice. Although it is very tempting to use this technology in a LAN, where distance is short and rate can be moderate, be warned that this family is a near-term solution and it does not evolve well. Whereas the telephone and cable providers maintain relatively small user networks, they are using single-mode fiber in the "fiber to the home" and "hybrid fiber-coax" networks because of its potential for long-term growth.

Second, let *data rate* be the overriding, most important issue. Suppose you have an extremely broad-band application, that has the potential to evolve into even higher rates, or you are an "interexchange carrier" whose national network is "muxed to the max" (at least, that is the plan). Although cost is always important, this application

requires that the system must be optimized for maximum data rate first and, then, for price as a secondary concern. High rate dictates that because modal distortion cannot be tolerated, single-mode fiber must be selected. High-rate dictates that because chromatic dispersion must be minimized, laser transmitters (possibly even, single-mode lasers) must be selected over LEDs and they must be selected to operate at the dispersion minimum wavelength of 1300 nm.

Third, let *distance* be the overriding, most important issue. Suppose you have an extremely large territory and for repeater cost and the cost of repeater maintenance, it is essential to minimize the number of optical repeaters. Although cost is always important, this application requires that the system must be optimized for maximum unrepeated link length first and, then, for data rate and price as secondary concerns. Undersea fiber is a classical example. Typically, modal distortion is also problematic in this application and single-mode fiber must be selected. Laser diodes would be selected over LEDs and they would be operated at the attenuation minimum wavelength of 1500 nm. Although chromatic dispersion cannot be controlled by selecting the dispersion minimum wavelength, it can be controlled by using single-mode lasers or dispersion-shifted fiber (if you can afford either one).

OPTICAL MULTIPLEXING

Although FM is a viable incremental multiplexing technique, the two practical "truly optical" multiplexing techniques are *time multiplexing* and *wavelength multiplexing*. The vast usable bandwidth of optical fiber is shown to be only slightly accessible by using time-division multiplexing alone, or by using wavelength-division multiplexing alone. Only the combination of these two multiplexing techniques allows optimal utilization of this vast resource with reasonable data rates, reasonable channel separation, and consistency with the bizarre characteristics of optical fiber.

Time-Division Multiplexing

Even while the carriers were only first installing single-mode optical fiber, they knew that they were utilizing only a very small portion of the fibers' bandwidth. The promise that there would be so much room for growth was one of the reasons for selecting fiber over more conventional media and even has motivated replacement by fiber. The first attempt to increase the utilization of this bandwidth was by deploying time-division multiplexing (TDM).

If N "tributary" channels, each at R bps, are TDM'ed together, then the multiplexed stream must run at $N \times R$ bps. Typically, the "mainstream" rate is even higher because it also carries control and synchronization information. Different time multiplexing "granularities" are possible:

- The most obvious approach is to *bit interleave* the "tributary data" onto the "mainstream," as is done in the DS2 layer and above, of the so-called "Asynchronous Digital Hierarchy (ADH)." One problem with this technique is that the control processor in the multiplexor and in the demultiplexor must operate at least as quickly as the main stream's data rate. Thus, this simplest technique is problematic at rates above 200 Mbps and impossible at rates above 2 Gbps.
- In *byte interleave*, each tributary contributes eight consecutive bits to the mainstream, instead of only one. Whereas the electronics close to the mainstream's

transmitter and receiver must operate at the mainstream's data rate, the control processor operates on "eight-bit parallel" data at one-eighth of the main stream's data rate. This scheme that was used in DS1, the first digital time-multiplexing system, was readopted for the OC-1 through OC-48 layers of So-net, also called the "Synchronous Digital Hierarchy (SDH)." Because the "So-net integer" represents multiples of 50 Mbps, an OC-48 stream runs at 2.4 Gbps and its control processor must operate at 300 MHz, approaching the limit of processor speed, without going to a "supercomputer."

- Although optical fiber will allow much higher data rates, the transmitter and receiver electronics, whose architecture is specified by the data format, is seen to be the bottleneck. As the solution appears to be to use bigger "chunks" of data in the time-multiplexing format, the next obvious step is to use *cell inter-leave*, in which each tributary contributes 55 consecutive bytes to the mainstream, instead of only one. Typically in such systems, the cell's destination address is included as part of the cell and "packet switching" is employed. Packet switching is problematic if done directly off the mainstream data, because the processors that read the address and steer the cell must operate so quickly. Although incremental architectures are possible, photonics does not lend itself naturally to packet switching (as discussed in the next section). Although cell interleave could still be used in a "circuit-switched" system, it may be simpler to allocate "chunks" as a fixed duration of time instead of as a fixed number of bits.

- In *block multiplexing*, the mainstream's repetition interval, called a "frame," is divided into a fixed number of time slots at every layer of multiplexing, regardless of the number of bits in a frame. For example, in a block-multiplexing format with 8000 frames/s and 250 time slots/frame, each time slot has a duration of 500 ns. Then, if each time slot carries one cell, the net data rate is

$$8 \frac{\text{bits}}{\text{byte}} \times 55 \frac{\text{bytes}}{\text{cell}} \times 250 \frac{\text{cells}}{\text{frame}} = 8000 \frac{\text{frame}}{s} = 880 \text{ Mbps}.$$

If three such streams are multiplexed together, instead of having 750 time slots in the resulting frame, the multiplexed frame still has 250 time slots, but each time slots carries three cells instead of only one. If the line's actual data rate is a little faster than the nominal required rate, the data in each time slot can be "bunched" a little tighter inside each time slot, and time gaps can be inserted between successive time slots. As discussed in the next section, this "guard band" can be used for delay compensation and to allow time for switching operations. Although block-multiplexing has not been used yet, it may be the format that allows time-multiplexed data rates to approach 10 Gbps and perhaps go a little beyond this.

Whereas currently practical and still having more potential, time multiplexing is limited by fiber characteristics that cause modal and chromatic dispersion and by practical data rate limitations in the transmitter and receiver. It is clear that TDM will not be the multiplexing format that leads to optimal bandwidth utilization.

Wavelength-Division Multiplexing

In the research community, attention has recently turned to network architectures that use wavelength multiplexing, instead of TDM, to try to increase the utilization of optical fibers' bandwidth. Over the past 5 years, several network architects have reported research designs for so-called "All-Optical Networks (AONs)." These AONs are LANs, MANs, and WANs in which data would be carried end-to-end over a passive network of optical fiber (so-called "dark fiber") by using hundreds, or thousands, or even tens of thousands of different optical wavelengths. However, as interesting and provocative as these architectures are, they are inconsistent with the *physics* of optical fiber. Like TDM, wavelength-division multiplexing (WDM) is also limited by the fiber's characteristics—four different nonlinearities in optical fiber that cause "cross-channel" interference among optical wavelengths. These nonlinearities limit the number of wavelengths that can be transmitted simultaneously over an optical fiber and that this number depends on the length of the fiber.

The first of the four nonlinearities is called Stimulated Raman scattering. The natural vibration of the fiber's molecules interacts with the optical signals in the fiber to cause a Doppler shift. Optical energy at short wavelengths shifts to a longer wavelength in the presence of any other optical signals at the longer wavelength. Although this effect is enhanced by erbium doping to provide a physical mechanism for optical amplification (a good thing), unfortunately it also causes cross-channel interference between two WDM signals in the same fiber (a bad thing). Even at an extremely low optical power per channel, this effect limits the practical number of WDM channels to the high 100s—maybe as many as 1000. At a higher channel power, which is more practical, the allowable number of channels drops even lower, but the other effects become even more constraining.

The second of the four nonlinearities is called Carrier-Induced Cross-Phase Modulation (CICPM). Because of CICPM, an optical signal travels faster in a "lit" fiber than it does in a "dark" fiber. Although this phenomenon is essential for sustaining "optical solitons" (a good thing), unfortunately it also causes an odd coupling among multiple WDM channels and cross-channel interference (a bad thing). Although the theory is not well developed, the empirical rule of thumb is that the product of the number of channels times the power per channel (in mW) must be less than 21. Thus, at 0.1 mW per channel, there can only be 210 channels, and at 1 mW per channel, there can only be 21 channels.

The third of the four nonlinearities is called Four-Wave Mixing. This nonlinearity causes two or more optical signals to intermodulate, producing new optical signals at a variety of unusual sum and difference frequencies. Although there is an interesting research opportunity to derive an optimal nonuniform spacing of the WDM channels, the practical implications limit per channel power to less than 1.5 mW when the number of channels is in the range of 5–20.

The fourth of the four nonlinearities is called Stimulated Brillioun Scattering. Naturally occurring acoustic waves in the optical fiber interact with the optical signals in the fiber to cause reflections and wavelength shifting (to higher wavelengths). This nonlinearity limits the power per channel to 2 or 3 mW, independent of the number of WDM channels. This nonlinearity is the practical limiting case when the number of channels is the range of 1–5.

The net result of these four nonlinearities is a physical limit on the number of WDM channels in a fiber and the allowable length of a fiber link (with amplification). For example, with a state-of-the-art repeater and a 60-mile repeater spacing, it turns out that

$$NL \le 12K$$

where N is the number of WDM channels and L is the link length in miles. For example, a fiber carrying 100 WDM channels can only be 120 miles long and a fiber that is 1200 miles long can only support 10 WDM channels.

Architectural Impact

Although many architectures were proposed in many publications and considerable corporate and government research funding was spent on this endeavor, most of it has been for naught. It is clear that WDM, also, will not be the multiplexing format that leads to optimal bandwidth utilization. The primary purpose of this section is to clarify these limitations in TDM and in WDM caused by the physical characteristics of optical fiber and to show that the combination of TDM and WDM is essential to optimally utilizing the fibers' bandwidth. The secondary purpose of this section is to encourage those who perform research on network architecture and those who support it to adopt the causality that architecture does not come first. Architecture is a design phase that should be dependent on the market, applications, technology, and the laws of physics. It is naive and professionally lazy to propose an architecture and just assume that the physicists will be able to make it work.

Consider three network sizes:

- These nonlinearities do not constrain an intraoffice LAN, where the links are short. But, in this environment, the cost of wavelength-agile lasers and/or receivers probably makes WDM AONs too expensive compared to other optical and electronic LAN architectures that ought to provide acceptable performance in such a small network.
- A typical fiber-to-the-home (FTTH) MAN is more interesting. With maximum loop lengths around 4 miles, a WDM AON architecture should support 3000 WDM channels. This may be enough for a typical Central Office serving area. As with the intraoffice LAN, the links are short enough that full bandwidth utilization is not required economically. Use of WDM AONs in an FTTH MAN is an economic issue, which, again, comes down to the cost of wavelength-agile end points.
- However, the WDM AON architecture just will not work in a U.S.-size WAN. For link lengths to be long enough to build a practical network, the nonlinearities would constrain the number of WDM channels. With long links, where the economics requires optimizing the bandwidth utilization, WDM is no better than TDM at filling the available spectrum.

It has been shown that neither TDM nor WDM alone will be successful at even barely approaching the utilization of the optical fiber's enormous channel capacity. However, the combination of TDM and WDM is quite promising. If we assume a basic OC-3 (150 Mbps) channel and wish to achieve 150 Gbps (only 5% of optical fiber's low-attenuation capacity) on a single fiber by the year 2000: TDM requires a single transmitter and receiver capable of 150 Gbps and WDM requires 1000 channels (for a 12-mile maximum link length). However, if the basic OC-3 channels are multiplexed up to OC-96, or to some other structure at about 5 Gbps, then only 30 of these channels are required to achieve 150 Gbps, and the WAN's links can be 400 miles long.

Hopefully, the reader can see the futility of the TDM-only and WDM-only approaches in attempting to utilize fiber's capacity. Hopefully, the reader ca see the necessity to use both types of multiplexing to achieve even 5% of the fiber's low-attenuation capacity, let alone 100% of it and let alone to begin to achieve more than 10% of its higher-attenuation capacity.

PHOTONIC TECHNOLOGY FOR THE FUTURE

This final section describes four photonic technologies that could have significant impact on the future of telecommunications and computing. These are optical solitons, optical and photonic amplifiers, optical computing, and photonic switching.

Optical Solitons

Solitons are pulses that last longer than conventional physics would suggest. They were first observed as water waves in a canal and have been observed and predicted in many media, including optics. The existence of solitons in optical fiber was predicted many years ago and described mathematically. Then, they were observed in the laboratory and, then, demonstrated in reproducible experiments. Initially, a physical phenomenon with only academic interest, optical solitons now appear to be not only potentially practical, but they may be the "physics" by which we may come to utilize more of fiber's capacity.

The second of those four nonlinearities described previously was carrier-induced cross-phase modulation. The effect of this nonlinearity on optical transmission, that it causes an optical signal to travel faster in a "lit" fiber than it does in a "dark" fiber, was presented above as detrimental to wavelength multiplexing and a hindrance to bandwidth utilization. But, this same nonlinearity can be a benefit in the time domain. It is possible to "tune" the wavelength, optical spectrum, optical power intensity, and temporal width of an optical pulse so that a fiber's CICPM nonlinearity exactly cancels the fiber's chromatic dispersion. Chromatic dispersion causes the "slower colors" in a pulse to lag behind the "faster colors" and the pulse spreads in time. However, CICPM causes these slower colors to speed up because the faster colors have illuminated the fiber ahead of them. Such pulses, called *optical solitons*, are the most likely way to approach 10-Gbps data rates and even higher.

Optical Amplifiers

In an incremental architecture, attenuated optical signals can be amplified with a repeater. A repeater has a photodetector, receiver circuit, transmitter circuit, and semiconductor diode laser. As the electronics in the receiver and transmitter circuits are designed for a specified data rate, in order to double the data rate you not only have to replace transmitter and receiver at each end of a fiber link, you have to also replace every intermediate repeater. Network planners would like a technology for amplifying optical signals that is independent of the signal's data rate so that the decision to double the data rate on some link only has to affect the transmitter and receiver on each end. There are two technologies that offer direct amplification of optical signals and both are relatively independent of data rate. These are the erbium-doped fiber amplifier and the semiconductor laser amplifier.

The first nonlinearity described earlier, called simulated Raman scattering, causes optical energy at a low wavelength to shift upward to a higher wavelength, but only if optical energy is already present at the higher wavelength. If both wavelengths are channels carrying data, this phenomenon causes interference at the higher wavelength. However, if the lower wavelength is just constant energy, it simply adds to the energy in the higher wavelength, whenever energy is present there. Optical pulses at the higher wavelength could be amplified by taking energy from the lower wavelength. An erbium-doped fiber amplifier (EDFA) is a length of fiber, doped with erbium to enhance the simulated Raman scattering, and with a continuous laser (called a "pump") providing energy at a wavelength slightly under the channel's wavelength.

In describing the semiconductor diode laser earlier, two significant characteristics are photons in the cavity are amplified by stimulated emission and reflections at the cavity edges cause modes. Placing an "antireflective" coating on the edges of an SDL eliminates this second characteristic while still retaining the first. The coating is similar to the "radar absorbing" coatings applied to "spy planes." The device acts more like an LED than an SDL when it is turned on "hard." However, if it is barely turned on, there is enough energy for stimulated emission, but not enough to produce a significant amount of spontaneous emission. However, any photons injected into the cavity at one end from the outside will be amplified, but in only a single pass. This is the semiconductor laser amplifier (SLA). SLAs are manufactured with two pigtails, one for the attenuated input signal and one for the amplified output signal. Like the EDFA and most optical components, SLAs are bidirectional. The typical optical bandwidth is about 50 nm, limited by the static nature of the antireflective coating.

Although SLAs were developed first, the EDFAs have become the optical amplifier technology of choice because they are simpler (even considering that the SLA does not require a "pump laser"). However, the SLA also has a bright future because it can be used as an electronically controlled "single-pole single-throw" switch for optical signals. Although the EDFA has an extremely slow switching time, the SLA is a good optical switch because it can be turned on and off as quickly as an SDL and it has an extremely good "extinction ratio." When the forward bias is removed, virtually none of the input photons reach the output fiber. When forward biased, the SLA not only allows a signal to pass but it amplifies that signal.

Optical Computing

In this subsection and the next, we will introduce some more devices and we will discuss some *photonic* systems and architectures. However, first we will provide some motivation and, in so doing, we will illustrate what appears to be a natural dichotomy. Optics has two potential advantages over electronics and, although we have not fully exploited either advantage yet, the pursuit to do so motivates our research in photonic systems. These two "Holy Grail" characteristics are extremely high *connectivity* and extremely high *throughput*.

- The inherent "three-dimensional" nature of light suggests that a "broad beam" of light, or many parallel information-bearing "rays," could be projected onto a two-dimensional plane of interconnected nanoprocessors, each with its own opto-electronics. One application is highly parallel picture processing for video generation, pattern recognition, and robotic vision. Three-dimensional systems have also been hypothesized that might provide interconnectivity for thousands of parallel optical signals.
- Because optical transmission avoids the detrimental "inertia" that parasitic inductors and capacitors cause in electronic transmission, optical channels have

extremely high theoretical bandwidth (as discussed in the sections Introduction and Optical Fiber, which gives these channels the potential to carry vast information throughput.

The ultimate goal would seem to be a system with both characteristics—a physically small system in which thousands of optical channels, each carrying 100 Gbps, could be quickly interconnected. However, without a device breakthrough, this "ultimate" system may elude us because the devices that have the potential for *high connectivity* tend to have *low potential throughput* and the devices that have the potential for *high throughput* tend to have *low potential connectivity*. Although the ability to integrate many devices onto a single chip is important for commercial practicality of the device, it is essential if we are to construct that "projection plane" required for the three-dimensional high-connectivity system. The devices that could support high throughput, like the photonic amplifiers discussed and the fiber itself, do not "integrate" very well. The devices that can be highly integrated, while they have been operated quickly as discrete components, cannot operate quickly in integrated form because they get too hot.

The *self-electro-optic effect device* (seed) is such a component. The seed is an optical threshold device that can be implemented as an optical two-input "nor gate." It can perform computer logic operations and it serves as a simple "switch" in communications applications. "Integrated circuits" have been built with thousands of seeds on a chip, but (as with electronics) the data rate must be prespecified. As a true "digital" device, the seed has most of the same advantages that electronic digital devices have, including that binary pulses are "regenerated" as they pass through. The subtle disadvantage to being "digital" is that because electrons move around deep inside a seed with every logic operation and each bit that passes through, they produce heat. If a seed expends 10 pJ with each bit of throughput, then a discrete device operating at 10 Gbps dissipates 0.1 W of thermal energy. If 10,000 seeds on a chip could all operate at this data rate, then the chip would dissipate 1 kW and would "melt." We see that discrete seeds will excel at throughput that "integrated seeds will excel at connectivity, and that there exists an interesting "design space" in which to try to get a little of both.

Although researchers have proposed (on paper) many *optical computer* architectures, an actual working prototype has been built using seeds and another one has been built using the switched directional couplers, described in the next subsection. Although both prototypes are "bit-serial" computers, built with discrete components in a "two-dimensional" architecture, they are still important demonstrations of "proof of concept." The "three-dimensional" architecture was also prototyped, but as an optical switching system and not as an optical computer. As the "projection plane" in this prototype was made from seed integrated circuits, net throughput was restricted, as discussed. However, this project is also an important "proof of concept" and it illustrates that more work on *imaging optics* is necessary if the "three-dimensional" architecture is ever to become practical. Whereas optical computing is important research, there is still a lot to be done and we will be executing programs on electronic computers for many years to come.

The *switched directional coupler* (SDC) is like the *passive optical coupler*, described in the section Power Budget, except that the "coupling ratio" can be changed under electronic control. Because the IoR in lithium niobate is very dependent on any applied electric field intensity, if an optical coupler structure is diffused into a $LiNbO_3$ crystal and appropriate electrodes are arranged, the SDC's throughput can be controlled by an external voltage, as shown in Figure 12. With V_1 V applied, the input signals cross

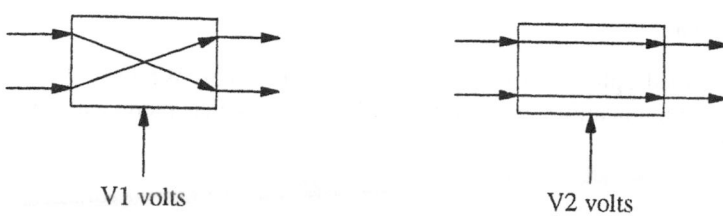

V1 volts   V2 volts

FIGURE 12   The LiNbO₃ switched directional coupler.

over 100% to the opposite channels. With V_2 V applied, the input signals remain in their respective optical channels. The SDC can be switched between the two states shown in Figure 12 in only several nanoseconds. Although SDCs can also be integrated, it would be difficult to get a hundred of them on a chip. As a true "analog gate," and SDC not only does not regenerate its binary pulses but it also introduces *loss* and *cross-talk* to them.

However, the subtle advantages of the SDC are that as follows: Because SDC fabrication is independent of data rate, any SDCs in a network do not have to be replaced whenever the network's data rate is increased, and because electrons do not move around whenever photons flow through an SDC, the flow of optical data produces no heat. If data are "switched by the bit," there is no advantage. However, if data are "packetized" or *block multiplexed*, then the only switching operations occur on the packet or time slot boundaries. If an SDC expends 10 pJ with each switching operation, then a discrete device operating on one time slot every 100 ns dissipates 0.1 mW of thermal energy, for any data rate. If 100 SDCs on a chip could all operate at this time slot rate, then the entire chip would dissipate only 10 mW. We see that SDCs will excel at throughput and are consistent with serial time-multiplexed optical data streams that are confined to separate channels; that is, the existing real world.

When an SLA is operated as a switch, it has the same "analog" properties as the SDC. The SLA's big advantage over the SDC is that the SLA amplifies the signals that flow through it. Although the SLA is a one-by-one switch and the SDC is a two-by-two, two-by-two structures can be fabricated using SLAs and passive optical couplers. New "integrated-circuit" structures similar to the SLA are getting a lot of attention in the research community.

Many network architectures for "photonic space switching" and for "photonic time slot interchange" have been proposed and scores of prototypes have demonstrated "proof of concept." Whereas much of the early work was based on classical space switching architectures, significant new architectures have been proposed for time, space/time, and even space/time/wavelength switching. Although optical "packet-switching" networks have been proposed, the technology is more easily applied to circuit switching.

Just when photonic switching was coming close to practicality, the worldwide research effort slowed down because so much of the available research funding was directed to asynchronous transport mode (ATM), a packet-switched electronic format. Now, that it is becoming clear that the ATM will not be all that its proponents have claimed, photonic switching should receive more attention (and funding) again, and practical products may well result.

CONCLUSION

We have described optical fiber and its related technologies. We have discussed its advantages in communications and we have tried to show that there will be many more still to come.

ADDITIONAL READING

Any good physics textbook should provide further background in optics. For much greater detail, there are any number of good textbooks that specialize in optics. A greater understanding of synchronization, signal-to-noise-ratio, link power budgets, and SoNET can be obtained from any good textbook on digital communications; for example, *Digital Telephony* by Bellamy. A recommended textbook on optical communications is *Fiber Optic Communications* by Palais. Greater depth can be found in *Optical Fiber Telecommunications*, edited by Miller and Chynoweth, or *Fiber Optic Networks* by Green. For more information on "switching," consult *Fundamentals of Digital Switching* by McDonald, or my own soon-to-be-published textbook, *Telecommunications Switching Systems*.

Many of the concepts from the sections Optical Multiplexing and Phototonic Technology for the Future are not recent enough or of enough general interest to have found their way into textbooks. Yet, most of these concepts represent group efforts and the life's work of some individuals. Rather than cite some individual papers, it is more appropriate to cite the researchers themselves. Anyone seeking further background on any of the topics from the last two sections should browse through the collected works of the following researchers, whom I acknowledge for their contributions that led to this article and to the field, in general. For more on photonic devices and the physics of fiber, see the works of R. C. Alferness, A. R. Chraplyvy, E. DeSurvire, R. M. Jopson. David A. B. Biller, L. Mollenauer, M. J. O'Mahony, and Peter Smith. For more on photonic systems and switching see the works of H. S. Hinton, Alan Huang, D. K. Hunter, Harry Jordan, I. Kaminow, G. Richards, R. A. Thompson, and L. Thylen.

RICHARD A. THOMPSON

USER DOCUMENTATION

User documentation refers to printed and on-line information supplied with hardware or software that explains different aspects of using the information technology. Different in its objective from *systems documentation*, which is written to facilitate design, change, or maintenance of hardware or software, user documentation is, in general, more *function* oriented than *structure* oriented. In other words, whereas systems documentation describes *why* and *how* a system is constructed (in a manner similar to a *service manual* for a car or an appliance), user documentation describes *how to use* the software or hardware (in the same way as an *instruction manual* for a car or appliance does) so that the user may accomplish their particular objective.

In some cases, systems documentation may include proprietary information which could compromise the business interests of the vendor if other manufacturers were able to procure this documentation. Therefore, most computers or software come with various types of user documentation which will assist in the integration of the component as part of a complete information processing system. This documentation will address installation, configuration, and troubleshooting problems, but in the vast majority of instances, it will not provide architectural, maintenance, or repair information beyond that required to make the system operational.

The introduction of the personal computer has greatly expanded the availability of computer hardware and software for individual users. Furthermore, the current generation of advanced personal computers with thousands of times more computing speed, memory, and disk storage capacity have made possible network and multiuser operating systems, intuitive graphical user interfaces, and sophisticated applications that are many orders of magnitude more complex than the largest, most expensive computers of only 15 years ago.

Similarly, user documentation has undergone considerable revision and expansion in scope with the advent of personal computers and engineering workstations for the individual user, as well as the rapid growth of network-based services such as those available on the Internet. These advances in both hardware integration and software functionality have considerably broadened the target audience of user documentation to include not only end users but also people who install and maintain hardware, network and system administrators, and management personnel. All of these people may use a program or a related set of programs such as an operating system or application suite across different hardware platforms for different reasons and require documentation on specific aspects of a program's capabilities.

Application software, in particular, has become very complex over years of refinement and often embodies a great deal of functionality. The use of such complex software to its full potential has created an area of documentation research that includes the end user and related issues of usability and interface design for the nonspecialist. With the exponential increase in the use of computer power and media bandwidth, it has become practical to consider questions of ergonomics and the benefits of using the computer itself as the documentation storage device, rather than paper-based documentation. The speed and cross-referencing capability that computer-based documentation is capable of providing could significantly enhance the productivity and efficacy of the human–machine system, if it is designed effectively.

Finally, local and wide area networking has created a unique form of electronic documentation which is unique in that it resides remotely on a network such as the Internet, and as long as the user is connected to the network, this documentation is available on demand. In the fast-moving world of the Internet, this can offer one of the most cost-effective ways of maintaining current user documentation.

USER DOCUMENTATION CONTEXTS

User documentation can take many forms, varying with the level of documentation required and the experience of the computer user. A user can interact with a computer system in a large number of possible contexts, and the goal of the different documents that constitute user documentation is to provide the information required to complete the relevant tasks.

Consider Figure 1, which is an abstract diagram of a typical hardware and software system. Each of the major components of a computer system requires user documentation so that people know how to configure and use each component effectively.

USER DOCUMENTATION OF HARDWARE

The hardware of a computer consists of the electronic components, boards, peripherals, and equipment that make up the computer system. The various hardware subsystems of a computer require documentation at different levels of sophistication, taking into account the target audience, the complexity of the hardware being documented, and the ways in which the device can be used. There was a time when complete system documentation was available if a person wanted to learn the complete details of their computer (1) or to be able to isolate and replace faulty components (2).

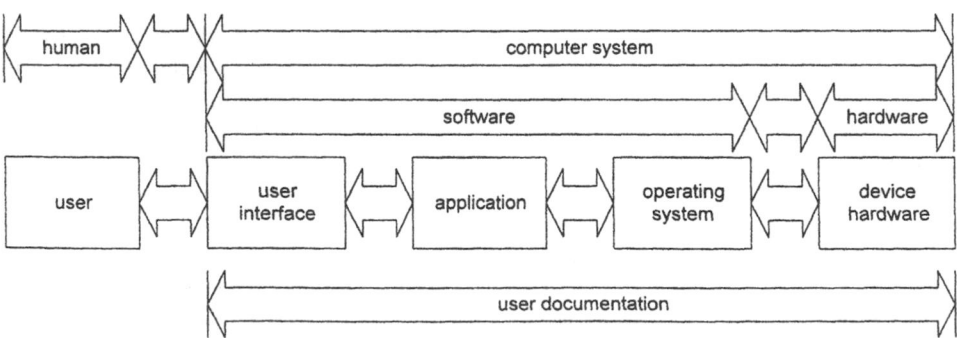

FIGURE 1   The scope of user documentation.

With greater component integration, computers consist, at least in part, of integrated circuits. Advanced production methods (3) allow lower manufacturing costs and increased performance through greater component density. Some of these are important and well-known devices such as the Intel Pentium (4) or DEC Alpha (5) processors. With most modern computers, the upgrading, maintenance or repair procedures of highly integrated chip sets or surface mount components are simply not practical or cost-effective for an end user to perform. The one exception is the microprocessor itself, which can be upgraded for higher performance because of the socket (6) used for it.

Systems documentation, which would discuss structure, maintenance, or repair, is not appropriate to include with newer hardware because it is easiest and least time-consuming to simply replace the board with the faulty component. Fortunately, if proper installation procedures, such as static discharge precautions, are followed, as would be specified in the user documentation, the probability of a defective component is remote because of stringent quality control.

For the inquisitive computer user, hardware subsystems such as the processor and expansion bus are well documented from a user standpoint and can provide some implicit information about the internals of the devices themselves.

The subsequent sections discuss various types of documentation, and the reasons for their level of detail, from the most fundamental integrated circuits and components, through to Plug and Play peripheral devices, and beyond.

CPU HARDWARE AND PINOUT DOCUMENTATION

The *central processing unit* (CPU) is an integrated circuit that performs most of the logic and information processing in a computer. A popular and well-known *microprocessor* (a CPU consisting of one chip) is the 6502, shown in Figure 2, which has found application in both general-purpose personal computers (7), such as the Apple II, and specialized control systems (8).

A CPU coupled to *random access memory* (RAM) gives a computer its programmability, where a new program can be loaded in and executed.

A hardware designer may also use a CPU in tandem with *read-only memory* (ROM) and possibly RAM in their own dedicated electronic systems to accomplish a task, rather than using discrete hardware components to implement the required logic. Such systems are called *embedded systems* (9) and are built cost-effectively using many commercially available microprocessors. Embedded systems are different from general-purpose personal computers in that they are designed to perform a small set of very specific information processing tasks as efficiently as possible (see the CPU Register Architecture and Programming Model section for a discussion of assembly language programming concepts), at a low cost, in a small form factor, and, if necessary, with low power consumption. For embedded systems, these design considerations usually curtail much of the expandability (see the I/O Channel Documentation section to understand computer expansion) and flexibility (see the Expansion Board and Peripheral Device Documentation section) that would be built into a high-performance desktop computer. Examples of microprocessor-based embedded systems are wireless radio modems, telephone answering machines, laser printers, and many battery-operated electronic toys and appliances.

Engineers who design niche systems with microprocessors need to know informa-

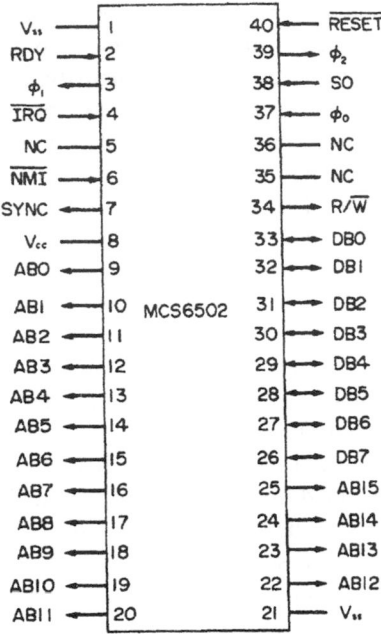

FIGURE 2   The 6502 pinout.

tion about how the processor can be interfaced to other subsystems such as memory or the peripheral devices, in order to communicate and control them with electronic signals. This information is given in the pin functionality description, also known as the *pinout*. Additional considerations are the nominal operating voltage and power dissipation of the part, as well as its clock frequency. With this knowledge, a hardware engineer can specify the support circuitry around the CPU to enable the system to acquire and process information as required, be it in a general-purpose computer or dedicated electronic system.

One special class of computing device bears mention; it encompasses the difficult design constraints of embedded systems while implementing much of the functionality of a desktop computer: the *notebook computer*. The market of this kind of computer has grown into an important area of the computer industry and has motivated the design of specialized devices, in particular *low-power versions of popular microprocessors* (10) along with design standards (refer to the I/O Channel Documentation section where PCMCIA is discussed) and small form factor peripherals (see the Expansion Board and Peripheral Device Documentation for an example of a modem used with notebook computers). These advancements make mobile computing with familiar devices, operating systems, and application software a reality.

CPU REGISTER ARCHITECTURE AND PROGRAMMING MODEL

Every processor has a *register architecture*, where program data is loaded, processed, and rewritten to memory or to a peripheral device or interface. Programming models such as that depicted in Figure 3 are the foundation for *assembly language programming* (see the CPU Instruction Set section).

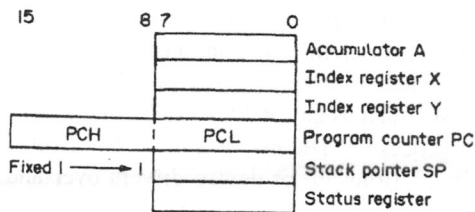

FIGURE 3   The 6502 register architecture.

Registers in a CPU, or in a *digital signal processor* (DSP) (11), are areas in these devices where data is held for processing. The machine language (the lowest-level instruction set, where information is manipulated at the *bit level*, the level of 0's and 1's) of a digital device is defined with respect to its inherent register architecture and layout.

The most important register is known as the *accumulator*. This register is so named because most machine language instructions accumulate their results in this register. Circuitry in the processor that does information manipulation, such as the *arithmetic-logic unit* (ALU) that computes Boolean AND, OR, and NOT operations, or even floating-point mathematics with some processors, presumes that the next instruction will use the same data operand and, therefore, leaves the results of their operation in the accumulator for the next assembly language instruction to being its work.

Other registers found in most microprocessors are known as *index registers*, and in combination with the accumulator and the appropriate instructions, they make operations such as looping efficient. In a typical loop, the accumulator holds the data operand to be processed. The result is stored in a memory location, which is *indexed* by an index register. This means that the index register contains a value which specifies an *offset* to determine where to store the value in the accumulator. Below is a small example of a looping routine, with accompanying inline documentation. Note how the Y index register is used both as a loop counter and a memory offset.

```
        LDY #6          LOAD Y INDEX REGISTER WITH VALUE OF 6
        LDA #0          LOAD ACCUMULATOR WITH VALUE OF 0
LOOP:   STA $5000,Y     STORE THE CONTENTS OF ACCUMULATOR IN ADDRESS
                        $5000 + Y
        DEY             DECREMENT THE VALUE IN Y REGISTER BY 1, ie 6 − 1
                        = 5
        BNE LOOP        IF Y IS NOT EQUAL TO 0, BRANCH TO LOOP
        RTS             RETURN TO OPERATING SYSTEM OR CALLING PRO-
                        GRAM
```

Common in most processors are registers for the program counter, stack pointer, and instruction pointer, although most of the assembly language instructions are for the purposes of manipulating information in the general-purpose and index registers only.

The *programming model* that the device offers in the way of register layout is of interest to both the real-time programmer and the firmware programmer who may program embedded computers or microcontrollers (see the CPU Hardware and Pinout Documentation section, where embedded systems are discussed). These applications may have very stringent timing (such as *real-time response*) or efficiency criteria and often require knowledge of a device's register architecture and instruction set to determine its applicability. This is important when a hardware engineer decides to use a more advanced version of a microprocessor such as an Intel 80386-25 where before they may have used an AMD 80286-10 (12) processor. The use of a more powerful processor brings with it additional ways to optimize firmware or device drivers over and above the processing speed gain from a faster clock rate. The richer instruction set of a more advanced processor, for example, may allow code to run more efficiently than before because the processor can operate on more data with a given instruction, or process the data in more complex ways.

CPU INSTRUCTION SET

Optimizations in low-level assembly language code depend on a sound knowledge of the processor instruction set. The instruction set defines and specifies the operations on data words within the work registers of the processor that the internal hardware logic of the processor enables it to perform.

Table 1 (13) outlines the assembly language instructions of MOS Technology's 6500 processor*, a close relative of the popular 6502. Assembly language instructions are usually given short names called *mneumonics* (i.e., memory aid) that imply what they do, and with what registers. Although they are not as intuitive as the vocabulary of a higher-level programming language such as BASIC, Fortran, C, or Java this assembly language shorthand provides a way for a programmer to order the instructions along with appropriate arguments to accomplish tasks at speeds unapproachable by any other method. The reader is advised to consult a complete CPU reference guide (14), which is usually published by the chip manufacturer. It offers greater detail regarding instruction properties such as available addressing modes, relative speeds of the instructions in different modes, and processor status flags affected.

SYSTEM BOARD DOCUMENTATION

The level of hardware documentation (15) that is familiar to most users is at the board level, such as the motherboard shown in Figure 4.

Installation information can usually be found in the user manual for the motherboard such as:

- The physical dimensions of the board for installation
- Component connector locations for power, external devices, and main processor(s)
- Jumper switch settings for configuration with different types of memory technologies and CPU speeds and voltage levels

---

*The 6500 processor was chosen rather than a comparable Intel processor because its instruction set is not unduly complicated by instructions concerning memory segmentation and offsets, added by Intel to implement greater functionality while still maintaining backward compatibility with earlier processors. The simple architecture of the 6500 makes it a better choice for discussing general aspects common to all microprocessors.

TABLE 1   The MCS 6500 Instruction Set

Mnemonic		Description
Data Move		
LDA	source	Load accumulator from source (various addressing modes)
STA	dest	Store accumulator in destination
LDX	source	Load X register from source
STX	dest	Store X in destination
LDY	source	Load Y from source
STY	dest	Store Y in destination
TAX		Move A to X
TXA		Move X to A
TAY		Move A to Y
TYA		Move Y to A
TSX		Move value in stack pointer to X
TXS		Move X to stack pointer
PHA		Push A onto stack
PLA		Pull value from stack into A
PHP		Push processor status register onto stack
PLP		Pull processor status register from stack
Data Modify		
ADC	source	Add to A with carry
AND	source	Logical AND with A
ASL		Arithmetic shift left
ASL	source	Arithmetic shift left source
BIT		Bit test with source (performs logical AND), but only affect bits in processor status register
CLC		Clear carry flag in processor status register
CLD		Clear decimal mode in processor status register
CLI		Clear interrupt masking (enables maskable interrupts)
CLV		Clear overflow flag in processor status register
CMP	source	Compare source with A
CPX	cource	Compare source with X
CPY	source	Compare source with Y
DEC	source	Decrement source memory location
DEX		Decrement X
DEY		Decrement Y
EOR	source	Exclusive OR source with A
INC	source	Increment value contained in source
INX		Increment value in X
INY		Increment value in Y
LSR		Logical shift right
LSR	source	Logical shift right value in source
ORA	source	Logical OR value in A with value in source
ROL		Rotate bits in A left, with the leftmost bit being copied to the carry flag in processor status register
ROL	source	Rotate bits in source left through carry
SBC	data	Subtract data from A with borrow (ie., carry flag goes up if value is less than zero)
SEC		Set carry flag
SED		Set decimal mode
SEI		Set maskable interrupt masking flag (to ignore maskable interrupts)
Branch/jump		(most of these depend on setting of flags in processor status register)
BCC	displacement	Branch if carry flag is clear
BCS	displacement	Branch if carry flag is set
BEQ	displacement	Branch if equal to zero
BMI	displacement	Branch if result is Minus (negative)
BNE	displacement	Branch if not equal to zero
BPL	displacement	Branch if result is Plus (positive)
BVC	displacement	Branch if overflow flag is clear
BVS	displacement	Branch if overflow flag is
JMP	address	Jump to a particular location
JSR	address	Jump to a subroutine at a particular location
RTI		Return from interrupt
RTS		Return from subroutine
Control/Miscellaneous		
BRK		Break (software interrupt vector) and transfer control to address held in FFFE & FFFF
NOP		No operation

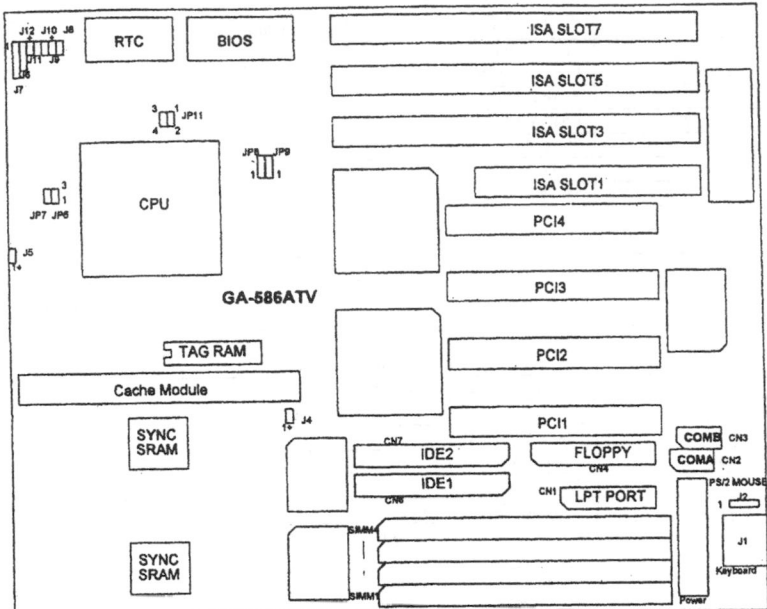

FIGURE 4   A Pentium motherboard diagram typical of that in a user manual.

- Information on BIOS and chipset configuration (see the Basic Input/Output System (BIOS) Firmware Documentation section)
- Expansion slot information such as bus type (see the I/O Channel Documentation section), bandwidth, and pinout for reference

SUPPORTING CHIPSET DOCUMENTATION FOR END USERS

The *chipset* (16) refers to the support logic that is used to reliably pass signals from one part of the computer to another, such as from the I/O bus to the CPU, or from the processor to main memory. Earlier motherboards required changing jumper settings on the board itself and used many separate chips to implement the additional circuitry that is required to connect the different subsystems (memory, clock, bus, CPU, power, etc.) of the computer into a reliable system. Modern implementations use only a few chips because industry standardization and advances in semiconductor fabrication technology have permitted greater transistor density and, hence, decreased components in the most recent motherboard designs.

For optimum performance and compatibility, most chipsets can have their operating characteristics altered to work more efficiently with other parts of the computer system. Most Intel-compatible motherboards have a setup program in firmware (ROM) which serves as the user interface to the chipset. A typical menu of choices is shown in Figure 5.

This program enables the end user to configure the integrated chipset. The software writes the settings to a nonvolatile memory and reboots the machine. During the system

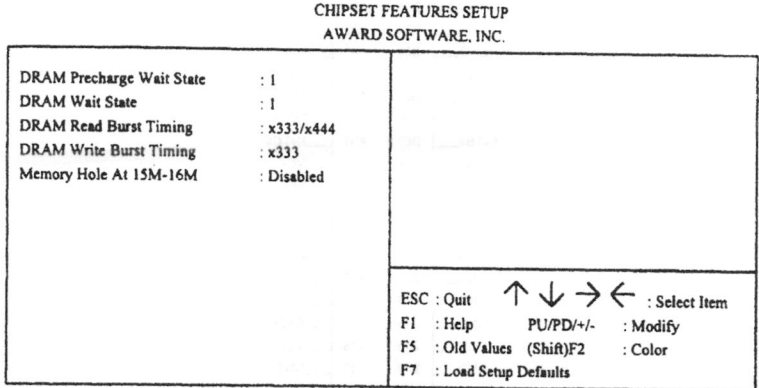

FIGURE 5   The chipset setup screen.

reset, the chipset reads the contents of the nonvolatile memory and configures itself accordingly. The chipset may need to be configured for several reasons. One of the most common reasons for an end user to manipulate the chipset values would be to adjust memory wait states or timing, as shown, to work with slower memory. Placing low-level hardware configuration routines in the BIOS makes fine-tuning of the chipset easier than manually changing hardware settings by setting jumpers or *Dual-Inline Package* (*DIP*) switches, which would require opening the computer case.

Usually, this kind of low-level configuration is done only once, when the computer system is first assembled from various components. Changes are only necessary if fundamental hardware alterations are made. Hence, this procedure is usually left to a qualified technician who is interested in compatibility and system reliability, or very advanced users who may choose to fine-tune these settings for maximum performance.

I/O CHANNEL DOCUMENTATION

The I/O channel (17) is the main hardware interface bus used to facilitate expansion of the computer system. End users are provided with this information primarily for reference purposes, but it is also to ensure compatibility with hardware they may wish to install in their system, such as *Plug and Play* (PNP) (18) cards.

Documentation of the I/O channel specifications (19) would include pinout diagrams such as Figure 6, showing the functionality of the *Peripheral Component Interconnect* (PCI) (20) bus slot.

The *Personal Computer Memory Card International Association* (PCMCIA) (21) standard allows devices such as modems and credit-card-sized hard drives to be used with PCMCIA-compatible notebook computers. As with PCI, however, technology improvements have led to variants on this standard as well, and users of notebook computers need to be aware of what types of PCMCIA slots their computer has, in order to use compatible hardware. PCMCIA Type I cards are the thinnest and are usually solid-state electronic devices such as RAM or flash memory. Type 2 PCMCIA slots are slightly

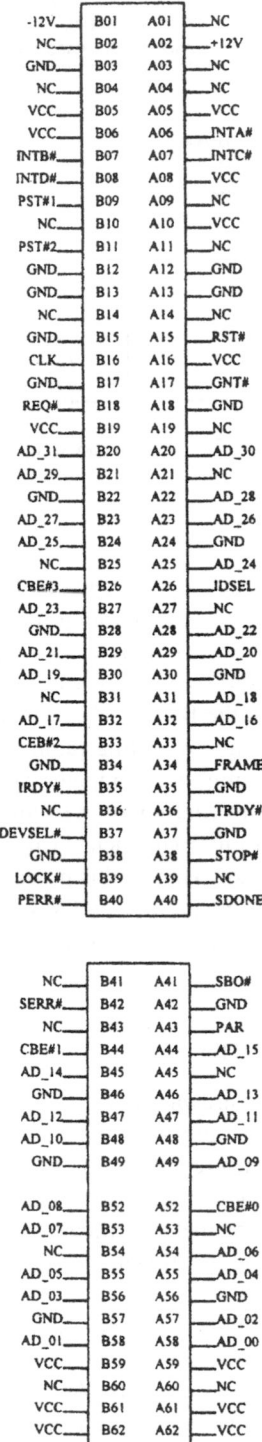

FIGURE 6   The PCI bus pin definition.

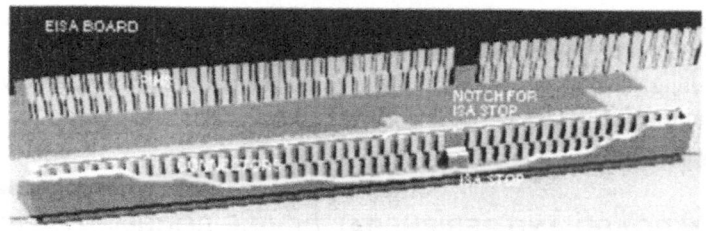

FIGURE 7   The *Extended ISA (EISA)* peripheral interface.

larger and allow for peripherals that have external interface connectors such as modems and network cards. Type 3 PCMCIA slots are the largest and are intended for small *Advanced Technology* hard drives *Attachment* (ATA) that can dramatically add to the storage capacity of portable notebook computers.

Other types of expansion buses for personal computers include the *Micro Channel Architecture* (MCA), *Extended Industry Standard Architecture* (EISA), the *VESA* Local Bus originally defined by the *Video Electronics Standards Association*, and the original 16-bit wide AT bus, referred to as ISA, Industry Standard Architecture (22). The EISA architecture and VESA Local Bus were designed to be extensions of the ISA architecture, and thus have some pinouts in common with ISA. EISA and VESA peripheral cards were designed to interface with the extra bus connector, such as that shown in Figure 7. ISA cards shown in Figure 8, would not interfere with the extra connector, as they would only require the first part of the bus for their operation.

It is important for the end user to note that small variations and revisions in electrical signaling and timing may be implemented as technology continues to improve. Although backward compatibility is always a prime consideration as these advancements are made, situations occasionally arise where the very latest cards may not work correctly with the earlier versions of an expansion slot architecture, such as PCI. The PCI local bus, in particular, has been through several revisions, as the chipset (see the Supporting Chipset Documentation for End-Users section) continues to support faster communications (with burst rates of approximately 133 megabytes per second) between the microprocessor and the PCI bus. These increasing speeds allow advanced technologies such as 100 megabit per second (100BaseT ethernet) local area networking. Even newer I/O

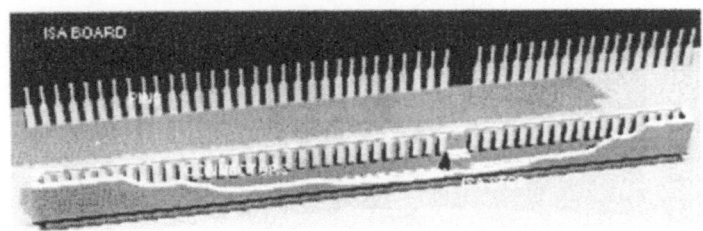

FIGURE 8   The *Industry Standard Architecture (ISA)* bus.

channels such as *Advanced Graphics Port* (AGP) found on Pentium-class motherboards make possible advanced technologies such as video boards with onboard hardware for real-time shading, texture mapping, and three dimensional graphics in hardware for unsurpassed multimedia.

EXPANSION BOARD AND PERIPHERAL DEVICE DOCUMENTATION

Most computer systems can accommodate additional hardware by making use of expansion slots (see the I/O Channel Documentation section) designed for this purpose. This allows the computer to be expanded or customized to enable to store more information, to process it faster, or to process new types of information. Exceptions to this general rule tend to be mobile and hand-held computing devices. Figure 7 shows the EISA standard, which is uncommon today, but was a response to IBM's MicroChannel Architecture, as discussed in the I/O Channel Documentation section. In contrast, the ISA bus shown in Figure 8, which EISA was intended to replace, continues to be supported, due to the prevalence of computers that use it, and availability of expansion cards that are designed for it.

Peripherals and expansion boards add extra capability to a computer system by allowing it to acquire and process digital information from new sources, and depending on the device, to send information to it as well. Examples of expansion boards are video (23) and sound cards (24), modem (25) and network cards. An example of a network interface card is shown in Figure 9.

Installed hardware can be built many different ways, as long as its interface is designed to be compatible with the specifications of the expansion bus. These specifications include many of the same design criteria detailed in the CPU Hardware and Pinout Documentation section, where engineers design hardware at the chip level. Ensuring the compliance of the expansion card with established industry standards such as PCI is the responsibility of the hardware manufacturer, but the end user would benefit from a general understanding of these principles as well, to assist with installation.

Hardware expansion usually takes several general forms:

- Expansion boards that are inserted into the computer's expansion slots and typically remain a permanent part of the computer, but do not require specialized *application* software to accompany the device. Some devices may have

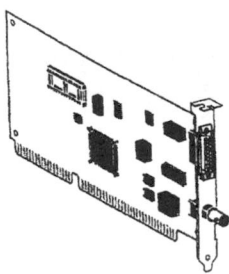

FIGURE 9   A *Network Interface Card* (*NIC*) for building a *Local Area Network* (*LAN*).

FIGURE 10   A PCMCIA modem used in notebook computers.

their own BIOS or they may include low-level device drivers. See the Basic Input/Output System Firmware Documentation and Device Drivers section. One example is the network card shown in Figure 9, which would be used by the operating system in a networked environment, after low-level *packet drivers* have been loaded into memory.

- PCMCIA cards for notebook computers, such as that shown in Figure 10, which can be *hot-swapped*, that is, changed with the power on.
- External peripheral devices, such as an external 56K or ISDN modem, tape backup system, or a printer which connects to a computer through any of several supported peripheral interfaces, and can be easily powered down or removed from the computer as necessary. Figure 11 shows an external modem.
- A combination of internal card installation, and then connecting external devices to the interface card, as in the case of installing a sound card, which allows various external devices to be interfaced to it (shown in Figure 12). In addition to low-level device drivers added for use by the operating system (see the Basic Input/Output System Firmware Documentation and Device Drivers section), these peripherals may also come with specific application software to make them immediately useful to the computer user.

As with the main board (see the System Board Documentation section), information is provided for the end user to help with installation, configuration, and use of the peripheral and/or the interface card.

- Expansion slot compatibility (see the I/O Channel Documentation section, in particular the paragraph discussing buses designed to accommodate both newer cards and older ISA cards)
- The physical dimensions of the board for installation

FIGURE 11   An external modem used for telecommunications.

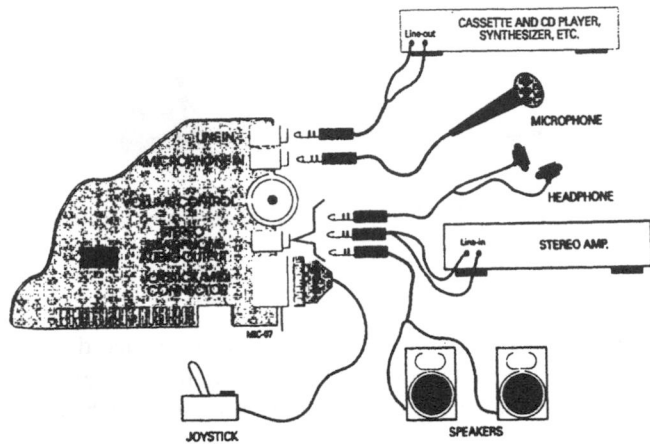

FIGURE 12   Examples of external devices for a sound card.

- Jumper switch settings for configuration of hardware *interrupt requests* (IRQ settings) and *Direct Memory Access* (DMA) channels (may also be done through software)
- Component connector locations for power and external devices
- Software documentation covering installation, configuration, and operational aspects of device drivers and user-level application software

External peripherals usually require a cable, and remain outside the computer, as they may have a control panel or other means for the user to interact with the device. This requires additional user documentation to inform the operator about how to manage and maintain the peripheral. Figure 13 shows an image scanner, which is an external peripheral device. After proper setup and configuration, as well as installation of the scanner application software, this device allows the user to scan images or text into the computer for processing.

USER DOCUMENTATION FOR SYSTEM SOFTWARE

Basic Input/Output System Firmware Documentation and Device Drivers

The *Basic Input/Output System* (BIOS) routines are the lowest level of software routines that provide hardware control and can be called by the operating system. BIOS routines provide programmers with a consistent set of basic routines to send information to and from such standard devices as the monitor, keyboard, and disk drives.

However, most end users working with the BIOS usually interact with a menu-driven interface to the BIOS, as shown in Figure 14, where they may make changes to the settings of various components. These settings are then used by the operating system to direct and control peripherals, after they have been written to a battery-powered *Complementary Metal-Oxide Semiconductor* (CMOS) memory chip.

Unlike the lower-level configuration of the chipset (see the Supporting Chipset

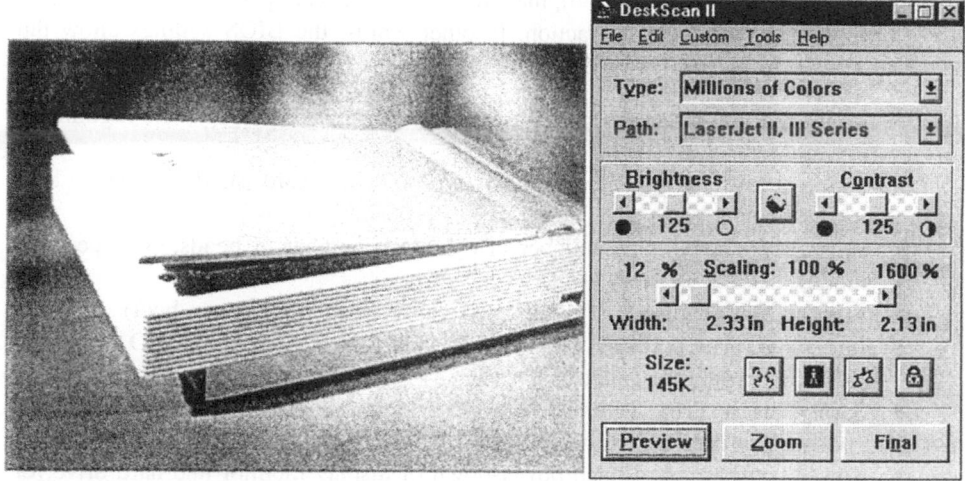

FIGURE 13   A flatbed image scanner; an external peripheral requiring both hardware and software documentation.

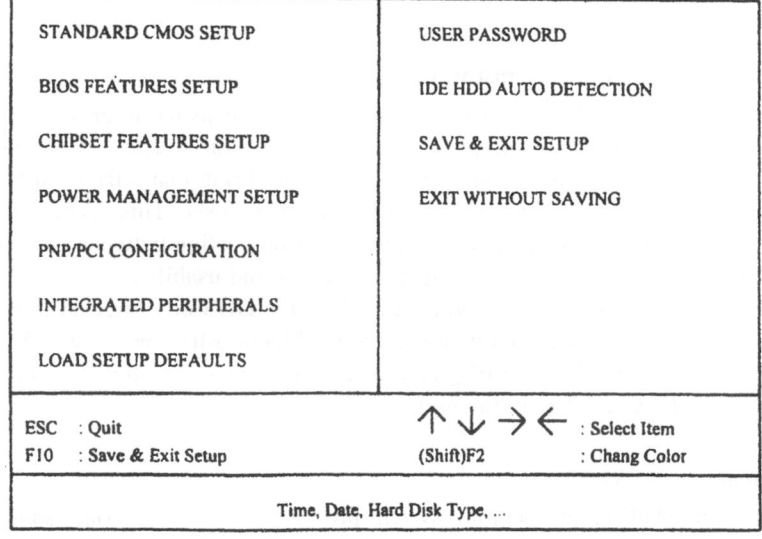

FIGURE 14   The BIOS/CMOS setup and configuration screen.

Documentation for End Users section), the BIOS settings affect operating system interaction as opposed to chip-level interaction. In other words, the BIOS settings allow the operating system to be configured for operation with the following devices:

- Memory (base memory, extended memory, expanded memory, and high memory area)
- Video subsystem and bios memory (type of video card, shadowed video bios for faster operation)
- Hard drives (type, size, number of cylinders, number of heads, and operating mode)
- Floppy drives (number of drives, disk capacity, seek at system boot)
- Integrated serial ports and parallel ports, and controllers (manage I/O addresses, IRQs, and operating modes)
- Safety and security features (password protection, virus protection of the boot sector of hard drive, hardware failure management)
- Power management (timed power-down of display monitor and hard drive for power conservation)
- Miscellaneous options (keyboard parameters, ROM shadowing)
- I/O bus configuration (IRQ and DMA channel configuration for the system bus and Plug and Play operation)

Along with the BIOS routines, low-level device driver routines installed at boot time offer additional functionality and can support add-on peripherals such as a *Small Computer Systems Interface* (SCSI) (26) driver interface such as *Advanced SCSI Programming Interface* (ASPI) (27). Drivers can add support for different ways of memory access with memory managers or allow additional modes of operation such as a *Video Electronics Standards Association* (VESA) (28) driver for video cards to operate according to this open standard.

After these drivers have been loaded into memory, the last component required before a computer becomes fully operational is a user interface, also known as a shell.

Shell and User Interface Documentation

The *shell* is the component of the operating system that acts as the interface between the user and the operating system utilities, such as moving or deleting files, and named accordingly because it metaphorically acts as a shell, ensuring that only valid commands and file operations are being carried out on behalf of the user. This crucial part of the operating system determines the nature and extent of interaction between the person and the operating system, which, in turn, affects efficiency and usability.

A shell can be a command interpreter such as the DOS or UNIX prompt or it can be designed to be user friendly and intuitive like the Macintosh or Windows 95 *graphical user interface* (GUI). In the case of graphical environments, the shell also affects how applications will *look and feel* to the user.

Command Line Shells

A command line shell is an operating system program that accepts commands typed in from a keyboard and attempts to carry out the request. UNIX is one major operating system that uses a command line shell as its default user interface. UNIX can be configured to use several different shells such as /bin/sh (the original Bourne shell), /bin/ksh (the Korne shell), and /bin/csh (the C shell). Recent versions of UNIX such as Linux (29) have even more command line shells, but they are all similar in appearance and function.

The MS-DOS shell is the best known example of a command interpreter on a personal computer, and its functionality is in large part derived from the command shells of both the CP/M and UNIX operating systems. The familiar MS-DOS prompt is shown in Figure 15, as part of the Windows 95 environment.

Documentation of command interpreters includes specifying how to customize the way the shell behaves, and its features. Most command shells have associated control files the operating system references when the shell is invoked to configure the shell's characteristics.

MS-DOS for example, uses the file AUTOEXEC.BAT to specify shell characteristics and set environment variables, some of which are shown below, such as the PATH environment variable, which lists the directories the shell will search in order to find and load a program:

```
PROMPT $p$g
PATH C: \WINDOWS;C:\DOS;C: \BIN
SET LMOUSE=C: \MOUSE
SET TEMP=C: \DOS
```

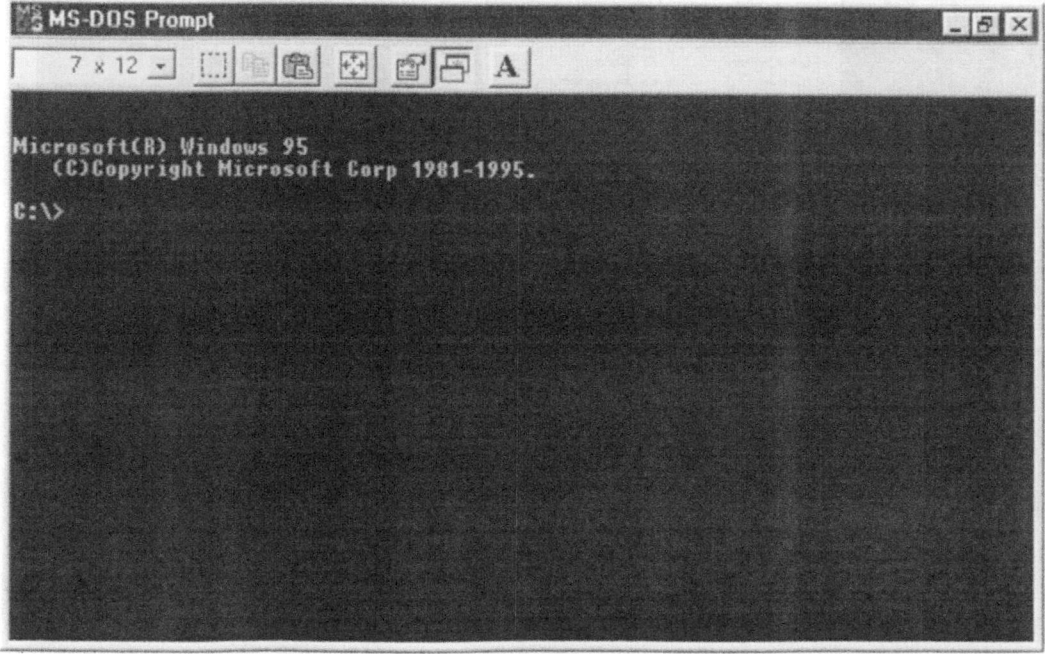

FIGURE 15   An MS-DOS session, with the DOS command line shell, in Windows 95.

Graphical User Interfaces

Since the introduction of the Motorola 68000-based Apple Macintosh in 1984, personal computers have become powerful enough to support graphically based operating systems with object-oriented features while still being able to run relatively powerful software. Subsequently, user interfaces have also become graphical, in particular window and icon based, as shown in Figure 16. In addition to providing a consistent look and feel, applications using a GUI have generalized information processing on a computer beyond text to include standardized multiplatform standards for images, sound, and music, animation, video, even three-dimensional virtual reality. The colloquial term used to describe such communicative elements is *multimedia* and implies a graphical operating environment.

A GUI is to some degree object-oriented, meaning that a particular on-screen element corresponds to an entity that the user can invoke or interact with in some way and it is *consistent throughout all applications and operating system contexts*. Usage conventions are much more stringent than in a character-based environment. For example, an application's on-line help system is accessed and used the same way whether the software is a spreadsheet, word processor, or an engineering application. This consistency facilitates reduced learning time and greater productivity for the end user.

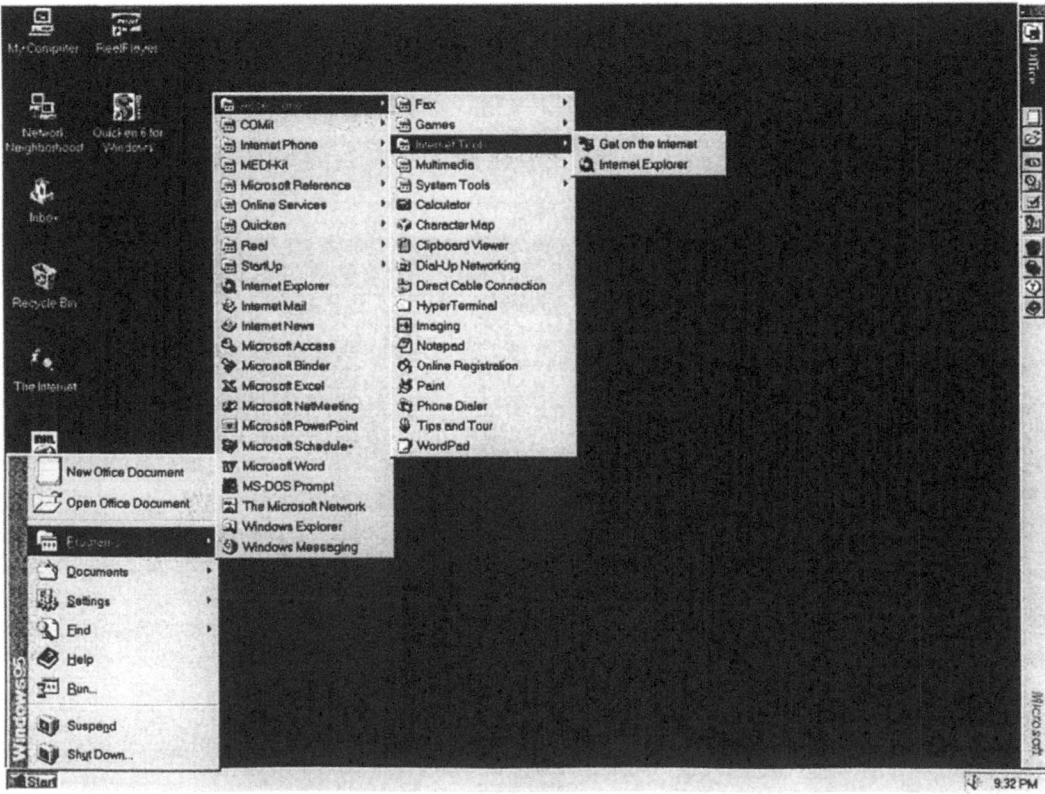

FIGURE 16   The Windows 95 operating system and GUI.

GUI Documentation: Configuration and Administration

Operating systems such as UNIX and DOS which were initially character based now offer graphical user interfaces known as X-Windows (30) and MS Windows (31), respectively. In contrast, the Apple Macintosh (32) operating system was designed (33) to run with a graphical interface from its inception. These different origins imply additional documentation issues.

Endemic to all graphical interfaces are specific nomenclatures and methods of interaction. For example, starting a program in Microsoft Windows 3.1 usually involves double-clicking a *program* icon and then opening the document, whereas on the Macintosh, double-clicking a *document* icon opens both the document and the associated application in one operation.

Windows 95 has what is referred to as a *registry*, where all critical user-oriented operating system parameters are held, including file and application associations, so a user can now double-click on a document icon to start the application and open the document, as with the Macintosh, because the association between a particular kind of file and the application that uses it is specified in the registry. An example of how a registry is examined is shown in Figure 17, using the *Registry Editor* that comes with Windows 95. It shows the registry as a tree of folders, within which are contained many hardware and software parameters that can be changed if the user wishes.

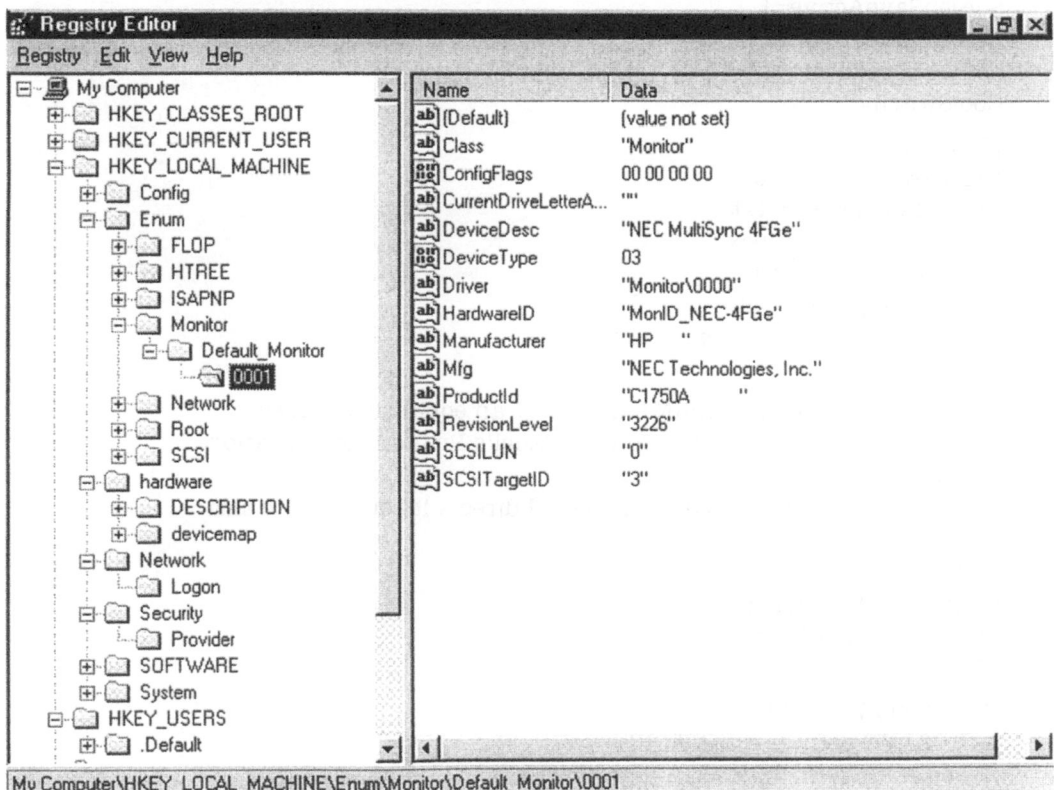

FIGURE 17   The Registry Editor of Windows 95.

However, Microsoft Windows 3.1 and X-Windows, because of the character-based origins of their host operating systems, require control files for compatibility reasons, as they also must support the execution of character-based applications, usually within the context of their graphical environment. Figure 15 illustrates how this is accomplished for the Windows 95 operating system, a window that reverts to the older character-based MS-DOS shell for command-line operations. In addition to the registry, Microsoft Windows 95 users must learn about the WIN.INI, SYSTEM.INI, and PIF files in order to tune their systems to run optimally with older software.

Below are some segments from a typical WIN.INI file, specifying file types and extensions as well as device characteristics. The text in these files is comparable to in-line *systems documentation for software*, where English explanatory comments (preceded by the ; identifier) for people are in the same file as actual control information that the computer also uses during its operation. For example, the line:

    doc=C: \WINWORD\winword.exe ^ .doc

means that files ending with the .doc extension are compatible with winword.exe, the Microsoft Word for Windows executable program.

```
[windows]
Programs=com exe bat pif
Documents=
ScreenSaveActive=1
ScreenSaveTimeOut=480
device=Panasonic KX-P4420, HPPCL, LPT1:
CoolSwitch=1

[Extensions]
crd=cardfile.exe ^ .crd
txt=notepad.exe ^ .txt
pcx=pbrush.exe ^ .pcx
wri=write.exe ^ .wri
hlp=winhelp.exe ^ .hlp
doc=C: \WINWORD\winword.exe ^ .doc

[ports]
; A line with [filename] .PRN followed by an equal sign causes
; [filename] to appear in the Control Panel's Printer Configuration
dialog
; box. A printer connected to [filename] directs its output into this
file.
LPT1:=
COM1:=9600,n,8,1,x
COM2:=9600,n,8,1,x
FILE:=

[Microsoft Word 6.0]
AUTOSAVE-path=C: \WINWORD
INI-path=C: \WINWORD
programdir=C: \WINWORD
Spelling 1033, 0=C: \WINWORD\SPELL.DLL,C; \WINWORD\SP_AM.LEX
```

Thesaurus 1033, O=C: \WINWORD\THES.DLL, C: \WINWORD\TH_AM.LEX
Grammar 1033, O=C: \WINWORD\GRAMMAR.DLL, C: \WINWORD\GR_AM.LEX
[fonts]
Arial (TrueType) =ARIAL.FOT
Arial Bold (TrueType) =ARIALBD.FOT
Courier New Bold (TrueType) =COURBD.FOT
Courier New Italic (TrueType) =COURI.FOT
Times New Roman Bold Italic (TrueType) =TIMESBI.FOT

[devices]
Panasonic KX-P4420=HPPCL, LPT1:

[Windows Help]
H_WindowPosition=[213, 160, 213, 160, 0]

The primary file for X-Windows is the Xconfig file, which specifies various operating
parameters in a manner similar to the Windows control files, but also including important
hardware details such as monitor timing and refresh rates. Below is an abbreviated Xconfig file that specifies hardware and software information in order to set up the X-Windows environment under UNIX. Note that as in the Windows control file example, both
human-readable text and machine-interpreted codes are together. The Xconfig file uses
the notational conventions of the default UNIX shell environment, the Bourne shell, in
particular the use of # as the prefix for comments. Please refer to the Command Line
Shells section for more information. This file is read by the X-Windows server program
when it starts, in order for it to know where to find fonts, the timings and refresh rates
of the monitor it will control, and so on.

```
# File generated by xf86config.
#
# Copyright (c) 1994 by The XFree86 Project, Inc.

# ************************************************************************
# Refer to the XF86Config (4/5) man page for details about the format
# of this file.
# ************************************************************************

    FontPath        "/user/X11R6/lib/X11/fonts/misc/"
#   FontPath        "/user/X11R6/lib/X11/fonts/Type1/"
#   FontPath        "/user/X11R6/lib/X11/fonts/Speedo/"
    FontPath        "/user/X11R6/lib/X11/fonts/75dpi/"
    FontPath        "/user/X11R6/lib/X11/fonts/100dpi/"
EndSection

# ************************************************************************
# Server flags section.
# ************************************************************************

Section "ServerFlags"

# Uncomment this to cause a core dump at the spot where a signal is
# received. This may leave the console in an unusable state, but may
# provide a better stack trace in the core dump to aid in debugging

#     NoTrapSignals
```

```
# Uncomment this to disable the <Crtl><Alt><BS> server abort sequence
# This allows clients to receive this key event.
# ******************************************************************************
# Pointer section
# ******************************************************************************
Section "Pointer"
#   Protocol   "MouseMan"
#   Device     "/dev/mouse"
    Protocol "PS/2"
    Device     "/dev/psaux"

# ******************************************************************************
# Monitor section
# ******************************************************************************
# Any number of monitor sections may be present
Section "Monitor"
    Identifier          "MAG DX17F"
    VendorName          "MAG"
    ModelName           "DX17F"
# Bandwidth is in MHz unless units are specified
    Bandwidth           100
# HorizSync is in kHz unless units are specified.
# HorizSync may be a comma separated list of discrete values, or a
# comma separated list of ranges of values.
    HorizSync           30-64
# VertRefresh is in Hz unless units are specified.
# VertRefresh may be a comma separated list of discrete values, or a
# comma separated list of ranges of values.
    VertRefresh 50-100
# Modes can be specified in two formats. A compact one-line format, or
# a multi-line format.
# These two are equivalent
#    ModeLine "1024x768i"  45  1024  1048  1208  1264  768  776  784  817
Interlace
#   Mode "1024x768i"
#    DotClock  45
#    HTimings  1024  1048  1208  1264
#    VTimings  768   776   784   817
#    Flags      "Interlace"
#   EndMode
# 1024x768 @ 76 Hz, 62.5 kHz hsync
Modeline "1024x768"   85   1024 1032 1152 1360   768  784  787  823
#   1280x1024 @ 60Hz, 64.0 kHz hsync
# Using 110Mhz dot clock. Should allow pixel depths to 16 bits.
#
```

dotclock/horizontalfreq = 110Mhz/64kHz = 1718.75, rounded to 1712
Horizontal sync pulse is fixed at 248 pixels (2.25us) by the X server, for
some reason. It's centered in the window from 1280 to 1712.
#
The vertical frame length should be 1024*1.05 (where does that come from,
anyway?), or 1075.
Modeline "1280x1024" 110 1280 1376 1624 1720 1024 1025 1037 1075

**
Graphics device section
**

Any number of graphics device sections may be present
Device configured by xf86config:

```
Section "Device"
        Identifier      "ATI GUP Turbo"
        VendorName   "ATI"
        BoardName     "Graphics Pro Turbo"
        VideoRam      4096
        Clocks 50.35    56.64    63.00    72.00  40.00  44.90  49.50  50.00
        Clocks  0.00   110.00   126.00   135.00   0.00  80.00  75.00  65.00
        Clocks 25.18    28.32    31.50    36.00  20.00  22.45  24.75  25.00
        Clocks  0.00    55.00    63.00    67.50   0.00  40.00  37.50  32.50
    Option        "power_saver"
EndSection
```

**
Screen sections
**

The accelerated servers (S3, Mach32, Mach8, 8514, P9000, AGX, W32, Mach64)

```
Section "Screen"
        Driver          "accel"
        Device          "ATI GUP Turbo"
        Monitor         "MAG DX17F"
        Subsection      "Display"
          Depth         8
          Modes         "1280x1024"
          ViewPort      0  0
          Virtual       1280  1024
        EndSubsection
        Subsection "Display"
          Depth         16
          Modes         "1280x1024"
          ViewPort      0  0
          Virtual       1280  1024
        EndSubsection
```

```
Subsection "Display"
        Depth           32
        Modes           "1024x768"
        ViewPort        0  0
        Virtual         1024  768
     EndSubsection
Endsection
```

ON-LINE USER DOCUMENTATION FOR OPERATING SYSTEMS

Early forms of on-line documentation such as the UNIX manual pages (also called *man pages*) were essentially on-screen versions of the printed documentation. On-line manual pages offered the increased speed of disk access to any required information, but it offered little other functionality over its paper-based counterpart. Features such as cross-referencing based on context were nonexistent, nor was there any linking of related information usually associated with on-line documentation as it is understood today. However, it was sufficient for the needs of programmers who used it primarily as a quick reference tool to learn the syntax of operating system commands and function library calls. The lack of associativity in the on-line help system was not as much a problem for them because being experts they already knew what utilities were part of the same group.

UNIX programmers knew, for example, how the utilities lex (a *lex*ical analyzer) and yacc (*yet another compiler compiler*) related to programming language specification, and therefore to each other. The UNIX operating system had as one of its original design goals the creation of a very powerful environment for software development by seasoned programmers. Its terse command names, line-oriented command shell, and counterintuitive utilities made it rather intimidating even to experienced programmers from other environments. Its design philosophy was oriented toward the expert programmer who was familiar with theoretical aspects of computer science, such as fine-state machines, computational complexity of algorithms, and abstract data structure notations, and could use this knowledge with various programs to write well-structured, high-performance software.

Subsequently, many highly disciplined software engineers have developed important and advanced software to run under the UNIX operating system, including *Transmission Control Protocol/Internet Protocol* (TCP/IP) networking, electronic mail, and Internet news software (see the Internet-Based User Documentation section for examples of these programs.) UNIX remains the operating system of choice for the majority of Internet servers because of its inherent support for wide-area networking protocols used on the Internet, its highly efficient multitasking kernel, and extensive programming facilities.

Despite its complexity, UNIX is very well documented (34) from its low-level tunable kernel parameters to its shell scripting formalisms, with both printed and on-line versions available. The on-line version is essentially identical to the printed version in terms of content and general layout.

Example: The Manual Page for the /bin/vi UNIX Command

Presented in Figure 18 is a portion of the manual page (35) for vi, a text editor that is supplied with UNIX. This program is designed to be a screen-oriented general-purpose text editor, useful for everything from simple electronic mail to the demands of software

NAME

vi — screen-oriented (visual) display editor based on ex

SYNOPSIS

vi [−t *tag*] [−r *file*] [−l] [−w*n*] [−x] [−R] [+*command*] name ...

view [-t *tag*] [−r *file*] [−l] [−w*n*] [−x] [−R] [+*command*] name ...

vedit [−t *tag*] [−r *file*] [−l] [−w*n*] [−x] [−R] [+*command*] name ...

DESCRIPTION

Vi (visual) is a display-oriented text editor based on an underlying line editor *ex*(1). It is possible to use the command mode of *ex* from within *vi* and vice-versa.

When using *vi*, changes you make to the file are reflected in what you see on your terminal screen. The position of the cursor on the screen indicates the position within the file. The *Vi Quick Reference* card, the *Introduction to Display Editing with Vi* and the *Ex Reference Manual* provide full details on using *vi*.

INVOCATION

The following invocation options are interpreted by *vi*:

−t *tag*   Edit the file containing the *tag* and position the editor at its definition.

−r*file*   Recover *file* after an editor or system crash. If *file* is not specified a list of all saved files will be printed.

−l   **LISP** mode; indents appropriately for lisp code, the () {} [[and]] commands in *vi* and *open* are modified to have meaning for *lisp* .

−w*n*   Set the default window size to *n*. This is useful when using the editor over a slow speed line.

−x   Encryption mode; a key is prompted for allowing creation or editing of an encrypted file.

−R   Read only mode; the **readonly** flag is set, preventing accidental overwriting of the file.

+*command*   The specified *ex* command is interpreted before editing begins.

The *name* argument indicates files to be edited.

The *view* invocation is the same as *vi* except that the **readonly** flag is set.

The *vedit* invocation is intended for beginners. The **report** flag is set to 1, and the **showmode** and **novice** flags are set. These defaults make it easier to get started learning the editor.

"VI MODES"

Command   Normal and initial mode. Other modes return to command mode upon completion. ESC (escape) is used to cancel a partial command.

Input·   Entered by **a i A I o O c C s S R**. Arbitrary text may then be entered. Input mode is normally terminated with ESC character, or abnormally with interrupt.

Last line   Reading input for : / ? or !; terminate with CR to execute, interrupt to cancel.

FIGURE 18   The manual page for the vi text editor.

development work. Its documentation is concise and complete, although its more advanced features depend on familiarity with both the UNIX operating system philosophy and usage conventions. Like the rest of UNIX, /bin/vi embodies a high level of functionality at the expense of user-friendliness.

HYPERTEXT AND MULTIMEDIA IN ON-LINE USER DOCUMENTATION

More recently, developments in the on-line documentation area have attempted to address usability for audiences other than computer professionals who have the deeper theoretical understanding of hardware and software. General-purpose graphical operating systems such as the Macintosh operating system and Windows 95 have been the driving force behind increasing the user-friendliness of on-line documentation for both operating systems and software applications. This section discusses in moderate detail the emergence of text, hypertext, and multimedia as initially implemented in proprietary on-line user documentation systems. Graphical environments are discussed, and finally the Internet (see the Internet-Based User Documentation section), where open standards have made possible the World Wide Web and network-centric documentation.

Hypertext: Associative Linking of Text to Enhance User Documentation

The next level in complexity from electronic versions of paper documentation are associative text documents, commonly referred to as *hypertext*. Hypertext initially meant a class of user documentation which allowed one segment of text serve as a link to other related text so that a user could very quickly navigate the document to find related information. Information that is easy to arrange in a hierarchy and relate to each other either semantically or in terms of detail lends itself best to embedding in a hypertext system.

A fine example of a text-based hypertext system is SpinInfo, shown in Figures 19 and 20. SpinInfo is an integrated program and database of knowledge that comes with SpinRite, a hard-disk maintenance program (36) for AT compatibles. Figure 19 shows the user about to select the ESDI, IDE, and SCSI Drives option. It is an excellent on-line document, providing for education, program documentation, disk drive reference, and customer support through skillful use of links to support easy navigation to find related information.

Another example to consider is a *text-based* Internet browser known as lynx (37), which runs on several operating systems. Figure 21 shows the user accessing the AltaVista (38) search engine on the Internet, through lynx. It shows how a large subset of the functionality of graphical environments can be achieved with a text-based web browser. This type of program would be used on character-based terminals, which do not have graphical abilities. Lynx extends the usefulness of such legacy hardware for activities such as web browsing. Text-based tags are included in properly written HTML code (see the Internet-Based User Documentation section) and act as a substitute for the graphics, greatly aiding intelligibility when using a character-based display device.

In this text-based example, hypertext links are enclosed in square brackets (e.g., [AltaVista]). If the user selects one of these sections of text, they are transported to another HTML document.

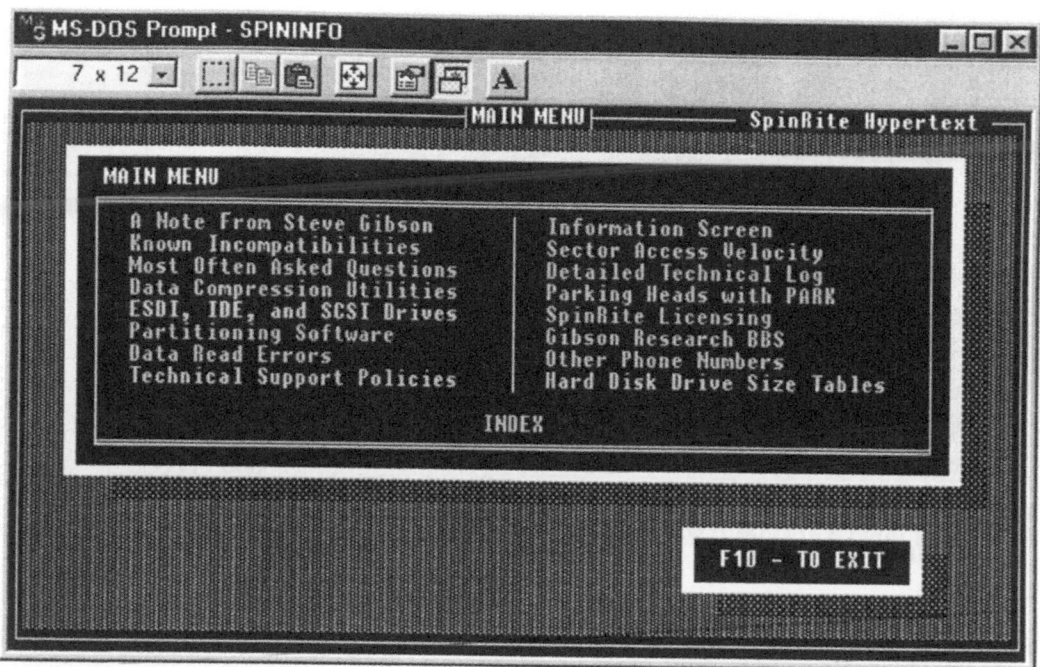

FIGURE 19   The opening screen for SpinInfo, a hypertext information system.

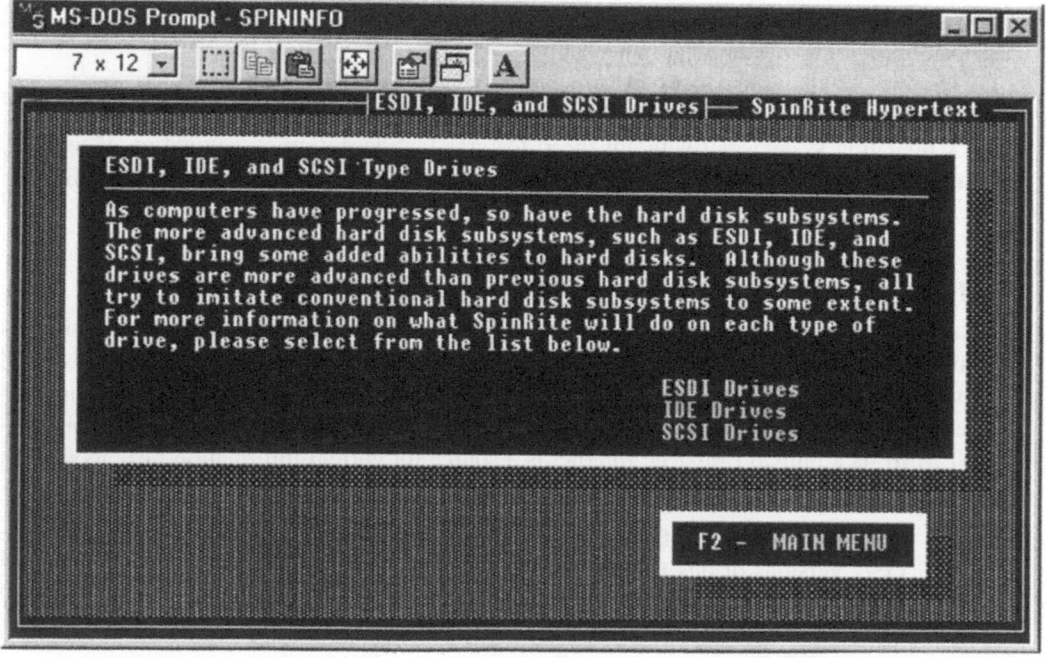

FIGURE 20   SpinInfo hypertext system giving information on hard-drive subsystems.

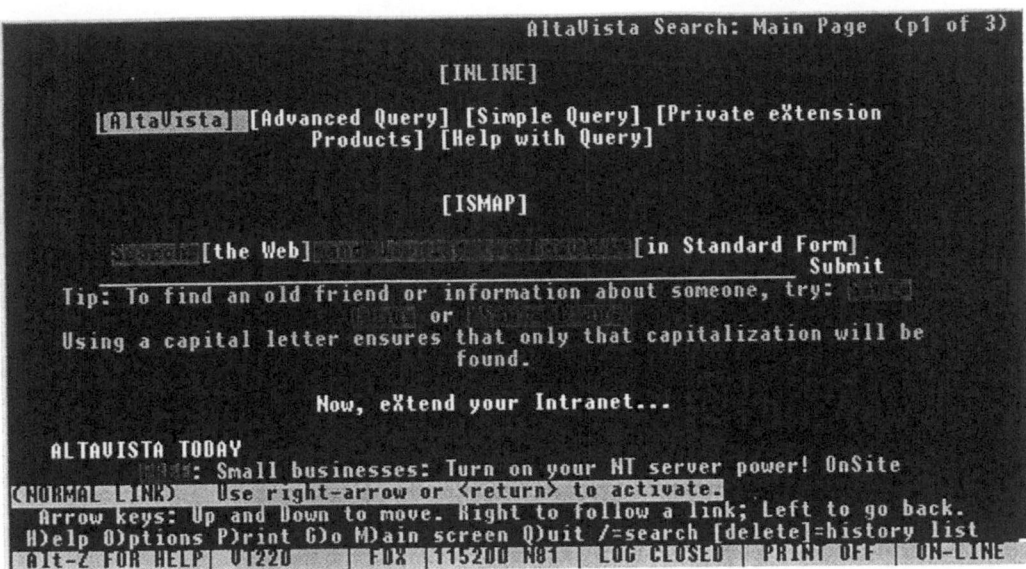

FIGURE 21   The lynx web browser, an example of character-based hypertext usage.

Graphical Interfaces and On-Line Documentation

Environments such as X-Windows and Windows 95 bring with them the ability to represent information in ways other than text. Graphical environments offer the ability to structure information with graphics and multimedia elements so that the user can quickly navigate through it to find what is needed.

Figure 22 shows the newest form of the venerable UNIX manual pages, xman. This program is a browser that permits easy access to the on-line documentation of the UNIX operating system, but with advanced features that permit quick navigation of the hierarchy of UNIX manual pages, so that it is easy to see groups of related UNIX utilities.

Unifying Hypertext and Multimedia Through Open File Standards

Today, the notion of hypertext is understood to go beyond text to include links to graphical or pictorial components. Some examples of image file formats (39) are included below, which are commonly used in image editors, desktop publishing, and on the Internet. By convention, files using these formats end with the appropriate extension (i.e., ROSE.BMP is a bitmap file). The Internet is a source for current information (40) about both open and proprietary file formats:

- BMP (BITMAP) is a file format created by Microsoft, with both Windows and OS/2 versions of this file format capable of 1-, 4-, 8-, or 24-bit images.
- EPS (Encapsulated PostScript) files are used primarily on printers capable of understanding PostScript, a page description language created by Adobe Corporation. EPS files can be 1-, 4-, 8-, 16-, 24-, and 32-bit color.
- GIF (Graphics Interchange Format) was created by Compuserve for storing and

FIGURE 22   xman, a user documentation system for X-Windows, a UNIX-based GUI.

exchanging raster images in 1-, 4-, and 8-bit images. It is one of the main standard image file formats used on the Internet-based World Wide Web. (See the Internet-Based User Documentation section.)

- JPG or JPEG (Joint Photographics Experts Group) files use a lossy image compression algorithm to discard aspects of the image through a discrete cosine transform to drastically reduce file size while maintaining subjective levels of image quality. This is the other main image format used on the World Wide Web. Refer to the Internet-Based User Documentation section for more information about how images are integrated into web pages.
- MAC (MACINTOSH) files are native to the Macintosh Paint application and are commonly used for monochrome clip art. This format allows reading and writing of 1-bit (black and white) images only.
- PCD (Photo CD) files, created by Kodak (41), are primarily for use with their high-quality stock images stored on CD-ROM, containing additional image information for use with a Color Management System (42) for maintaining color consistency across all aspects of the desktop publishing process.
- PCX is a file format created by Zsoft. This format compresses its image data with the run-length encoding (RLE) type compression. Subformats support 1-, 4-, 8-, and 24-bit color images.
- PNG (Portable Network Graphic) is a replacement for the GIF format. PNG is a full-featured (non-LZW) compressed format intended for widespread use

without the legal restraints associated with the GIF format. PNG exists in 1-, 4-, 8-, 16-, 24-, and 32-bit file subformats.

- PSD (PhotoShop Document) This is the format produced by the Adobe Photo-Shop graphics editor. Software support is widespread for 8-, 16-, and 24-bit files.
- RAS (*RASTER*) files are native to Sun Microsystems UNIX platforms. There are 1-, 4-, 8-, 24-, and 32-bit RAS files.
- TGA (Truevision Graphics Adapter) is an image file format developed by Truevision Inc. (43) for their line of Targa graphics adapters. There are various compressed and uncompressed file formats of 16-, 24-, and 32-bit TGA images. TGA (44) supports color maps, 8-bit alpha channel, gamma value, postage stamp image, textual information, and developer-definable data.
- TIF or TIFF (*Tag-based Image File Format*) is designed to promote universal interchanges of digital image data. There are many versions of TIFF files. (1-, 4-, 8-, 16-, 24-, and 32-bit files) and is a very good choice for cross-platform publishing efforts.
- WMF (*Windows MetaFile*) is a not raster-based image. WMF files consist of a collection of device independent functions that represent an image. When a program loads a metafile, these functions are executed to obtain the image. Most software supports 8- and 24-bit formats.

Multimedia (45) and hypertext have merged to emcompass additional media such as animation and sound synchronized in time; in other words, time-based media. Common file formats that support this kind of media are ones with the following file extensions:

- AVI (*Audio–Video Interleave*) is a Microsoft standard for video and sound and is compatible with web browsers used to navigate the World Wide Web (see Fig. 37).
- MOV (*Quicktime MOVIES*) files are Apple Computer's formalism for digital video with sound.
- MPG or MPEG files (*Motion Picture Experts Group*) is an open standard for animation and sound with both software and hardware support available.
- WAV (*waveform*) and AU (*audio*) files are used for playing digitized sounds and speech in applications, and on the Internet.
- MID or MIDI (*Musical Instrument Digital Interface*) files contain musical data encoded to MIDI specifications.

Following are some examples of multimedia that have been used to communicate concepts and ideas in proprietary documentation systems. Figure 23 shows a section of

flying saucers

You get 5000 points for hitting a flying saucer, or you can ignore them and concentrate on the battle at hand. Although flying saucers seem too close for comfort at times, they can't destroy your tank. When you're ready to close this box and return to the game, click on the Flying Saucer button and hear the sound of an approaching flying saucer.

FIGURE 23   Battlezone, a Windows game uses a linked sound file to instruct the user.

the Battlezone game documentation, part of the Microsoft Arcade game collection. Sound files, as demonstrated in Figures 23 and 24, can be incorporated into on-line documentation systems when they are pertinent to using the software. Figure 24 shows an example of the Missile Command game documentation, also from Microsoft Arcade.

Standards for Platform-Independent Document Creation

Open standards exist that provide special codes and rules to embed in the document for proper document design, providing all of the functionality of earlier proprietary on-line documentation systems. In addition to the text itself, extensive and powerful formatting codes can be included in the document to perform the following functions:

- Point to sections within the same document
- Point to other documents
- Run small applications programs known as *applets*
- Activate *plug-ins* to allow processing of specialized or proprietrary file formats

The following are open standards can be used during the document creation process:

- SGML (*Structured Generalized Markup Language*) is a device-independent markup language (46) where a text-based document has additional structural information embedded within it to specify textual and graphical formatting properties, as well as associative links between different segments of the document and to other documents. It is used to create device-independent documents which can be rapidly searched due to extensive tags embedded in the document.
- HTML (*HyperText Markup Language*) is a well-known subset of SGML and is the standard formalism on which the World Wide Web (WWW) is based. HTML is used when making hypertext documents for the Internet. It is the most influential markup language and will be discussed in greater detail in the HyperText Markup Language Documents section.
- PDF (*Portable Document Format*) is a third option for documents that supports easy hypertext link creation. Based on Adobe's PostScript page-description language, PDF preserves a paper-based document's original layout and can be viewed easily on screen, as well as printed with high quality. PDF has additional features for on-line use, such as text search and annotation, and multimedia links. Being easier to publish on-line than HTML, PDF documents can be generated from conventional word processing or page layout software which print to specialized software drivers provided by Adobe Acrobat (47). Also

---

defensive missiles

 The missiles you launch to protect your cities. When you're ready to close this box and return to the game, click the button and hear the sound of a defensive missile firing from one of your three missile bases.

FIGURE 24   Missile Command: another example of sound showing how to play a game.

provided by Acrobat are utilities that allow PDF documents to be *distilled* from PostScript files. PDF's popularity is the result of its ease of creation, its unique ability to bridge the gap between paper-based documentation created with a word processor, and providing the platform independence of electronic documents along with text searching, hypertext links, and multimedia elements. See Figures 38 and 39 for examples.

- VRML (*Virtual Reality Modeling Language*) (48) deserves special mention, if one wants to create a *three-dimensional* environment in the course of providing documentation. Some topics such as architectural description, aircraft routes, or mechanical engineering illustration can benefit from this Internet-centric modeling language. As personal computers and Internet speeds become greater, this particular technology will become more common and enhance future communications.

Building on these fundamentals are advanced standards for documentation. On the horizon (49) are the following:

- DHTML (*Dynamic HyperText Markup Language*) is one extension of HTML that offers dynamic styles, content, and positioning. Dynamic styles are similar to style sheets used in conventional word processing, in that it provides a template for the web page to conform to, and these can be changed on the fly. Dynamic content allows the page to respond interactively to things the user does, and dynamic positioning allows text and graphic elements to move around automatically, or in response to user behavior.

- XML (*Extensible Markup Language*) is a language specification that stands midway in complexity between HTML and SGML. XML allows the creation of entirely new tags and entirely new hierarchies of nested tags. The *Document Type Definition* (DTD) specifies the logical structure of a document and enables the definition of its grammar. This allows an XML parser to validate the tags thus declared. The DTD also defines a page's elements and its attributes as well as the relationship among those elements and attributes. For example, the DTD can specify that a list item can occur only within a list. The DTD can be used to create web pages that resemble the structure of databases rather than the relatively flat structure of HTML pages. The *Extensible Style Language* (XSL) is the language used to specify style sheets for XML. The XSL will permit new types of display modes, such as large type, document outlines, or even Braille. Also possible are "adaptive" documentation, which can adapt to the learning curve of the user, with different styles for beginning or advanced users, all from one database of knowledge. Finally, XLL (*Extensible Link Language*) will go beyond the simple links of HTML to support the following:

- Location-independent naming
- Bidirectional links
- Links that can be specified and managed outside of documents to which they apply
- *n*-ary Hyperlinks (e.g., rings, multiple windows)
- Aggregate links (multiple sources)
- Transclusion (the link target document appears to be part of the link source document)
- Attributes on links (link types)

The newest operating system versions, as well as *network-aware* and *electronic publishing* applications such as Netscape Navigator, Adobe Acrobat, and Microsoft Office, will take advantage of these and other standards to allow users to create information for the Internet and on local area networks as well (see the Internet-Based User Documentation section).

Application Documentation and Issues of Software Usability and Interface Design

Quality user documentation transcends the technological issues of creating the documents. It must also involve a proper consideration of how to structure and write about the various aspects of the computer system. It must also give due thought to the preferences of the users themselves.

Applications are programs that are used to accomplish a particular task or a group of functionally similar related tasks. Examples of popular applications are WordPerfect Office, Microsoft Excel, AutoCAD, and Adobe PhotoShop. Most applications used by the average person are modernizations of earlier methods of doing work. For this reason, applications are also the kind of software most likely used by those who have little or no previous computer experience, but may possess extensive knowledge of earlier methods and procedures. Those applications which have any historical precedent, such as typesetting, writing, mathematics, or engineering, have evolved their own nomenclature to expedite transfer of ideas, usually on the paper medium.

With regard to on-line documentation of such operations, multimedia computing systems provide random access, interactivity, and hypertext-based associativity. From a human factors standpoint, designers can use cognitive and cultural cues such as color, sound, symbols, and even animation to add unprecedented flexibility and expressive power to the previously limited scope of application software documentation. These abilities allow multimedia documentation systems to perform the roles of instructional, troubleshooting, reference, administrative, and maintenance simultaneously and as the situation demands.

The transition of earlier endeavors to the computer medium carries with it additional issues that must be considered. In order for software to be easy to learn and use, as well as allow the expert user to make full use of the capabilities of the software, programmers, user-interface designers, and documentation writers must closely collaborate in order to determine the best balance of user documentation issues. Such questions may include, but are not limited to the following.

What Are the Characteristics and Biases of the End User?

This may include users who are using the software for the first time without a deep understanding of computers; more sophisticated users who know how to use other software similar in functionality, such as earlier versions of the software, a competitor's product, software running on another operating system, or with a different interface.

How Should the User Interface Be Designed?

The problem faced by software developers in structuring their software interface is how to leverage the existing knowledge of the task with a familiar user interface while sidestepping the implicit functionality limitations of that same interface. In other words, although the computer-based application does not have many of the limitations of the earlier media and methodology, because the program presents a user interface with similar metaphors, the user may still be thinking in terms of the earlier metaphors which do not accurately carry over to the computer medium. This *analogical thinking may* limit the effectiveness of the user, because these a priori restrictions no longer apply.

In terms of marketing, it *is* sometimes possible to design an interface that will please everyone, or at least as large a number of people as possible. Designing a user interface that will be familiar to both Windows and Macintosh users, as is done with Adobe PhotoShop, to maximize product usability across the two platforms is one excellent strategy for an established cross-platform product. This strategy works even better when a family of products all work in a similar fashion, such as Adobe Illustrator (50), PageMaker (51), and PhotoShop (52) all having similar floating palettes across two different operating systems, easing the learning curve. In addition, *drag and drop* functionality among the products ensures easy interoperability for multidisciplinary projects.

How to Structure the On-Line Help System?

The on-line help system must be *scalable*, meaning that it is able to be effectively used by people of many levels of knowledge, skill, and experience to find the relevant information. The ability to create multimedia hyperlinks to related information within the help system can be a tremendous asset, provided that enough links are provided to cater to people of all skill levels. One difficulty is that different people have diverging notions of what constitutes intuitive and appropriate partitioning of the help system to best serve their needs. To this end, it must be easy for the user to discern what links to follow. To maximize effectiveness, it should be very easy for the user to find procedural or tutorial types of knowledge that refer to operations defined in the user interface. This way the user can quickly associate a given procedure with an aspect of the program's user interface, in order to become more productive. As will be discussed in the following sections, there are many ways to do this.

Software engineers should be aware that some features users desire to make the software easier to use or more powerful may simply not be programmable and attempts to do so may cause more problems than it solves. Even with the steady exponential increase in computer power and lower costs, such usability features as an expert-level assistant embedded in the software would require artificial intelligence programming and data structures that would overwhelm even the fastest computers available today, but may be possible in the future, as newer versions of software such as Microsoft Office continue to improve. See the Interactive On-Line Tutorials Within the Documentation System and the Interactive and Anticipatory User Documentation sections for advanced implementations of on-line user documentation.

In summary, evolving software will always require a consistent and intuitive design in order to maintain usability. It must also assimilate advances ranging from enhancements to existing facilities through to entirely new features that did not exist in any previous software. However, continued improvements in on-line documentation have made possible the integration of concepts such as hypertext, multimedia, and context sensitivity to gradually acclimate the user to the newer methods offered by the software.

Application Documentation in Graphical Environments

Applications can benefit from documentation which uses graphics to show how various operations in the software relate together and to present them accordingly. Figure 25 shows how this can be accomplished in a windowing environment, with hypertext links

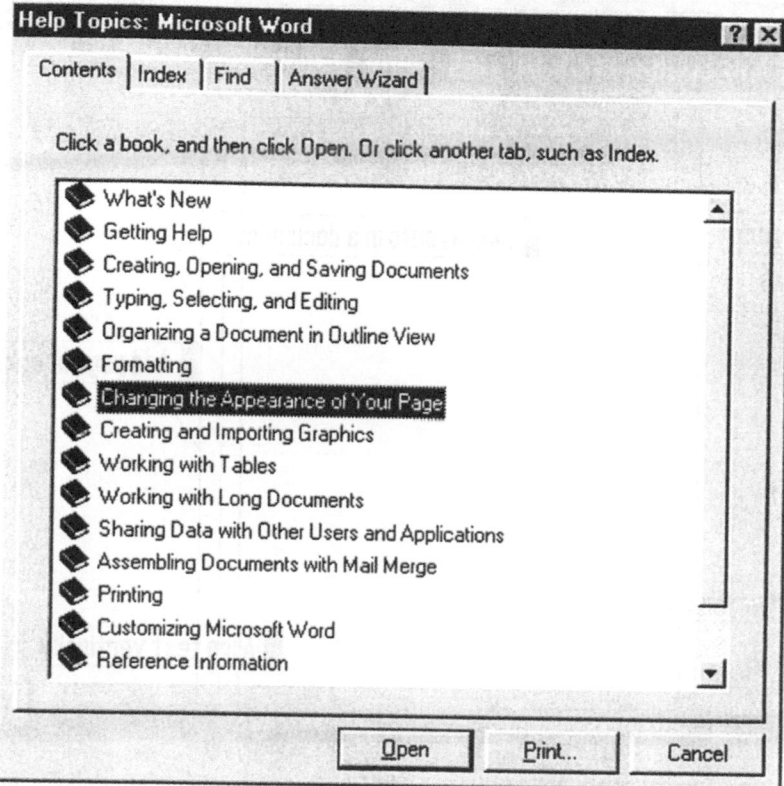

FIGURE 25   Accessing help in Microsoft Word based on the operation that the user wishes to do.

to more detailed information. Figure 26 shows the result of selecting the "Changing the Appearance of Your Page" button.

In Figure 27, specific procedural information is given for mixing layouts in the document, as mentioned in the Application Documentation and Issues of Software Usability and Interface Design section, where the on-line help system structure is discussed.

Interactive On-Line Tutorials Within the Documentation System

Some of the most advanced of these documentation systems also implement on-line tutorials, which work within the application and can help expand the knowledge of the user in a context-specific way. Microsoft Project for Windows 95 offers an interesting example of how an on-line documentation system can serve in a tutorial role (see Fig. 28).

A program with tutorials built into the system can ease the learning curve, familiarize the user with the application, and reinforce key concepts relevant to using the software effectively and efficiently.

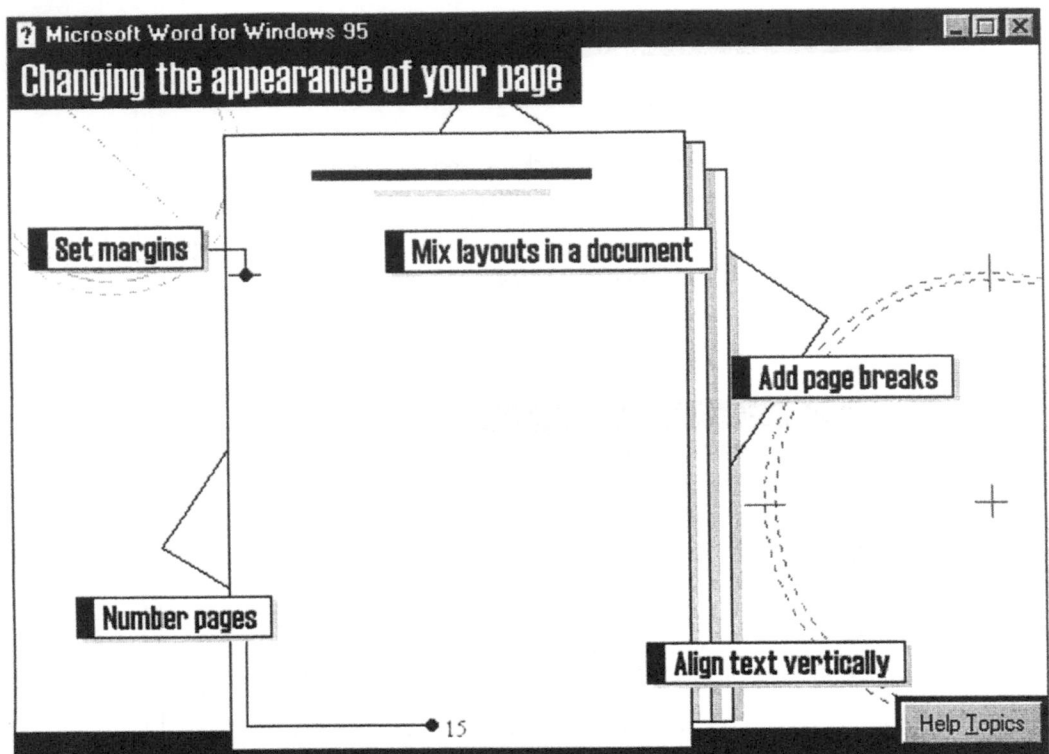

FIGURE 26   Microsoft Word for Windows 95 uses graphics to show the different options and how they relate to each other.

Interactive and Anticipatory User Documentation

A large component of a program's usability lies in how robust the on-line help of an application is, with respect to a large range of users with varying knowledge, skill, and experience. Attempts to improve the usability of on-line and end-user software documentation has led to the development of a very rudimentary form of a *conversational language interface*, which is able to parse your request for information and present a small set of further choices to select from, as well as active on-line documentation which offers assistance when appropriate. Such capabilities make possible integrated tutorial and instructional functionality within the on-line documentation.

The terminology used in the Windows 95 operating system are *wizards*. Wizards are essentially specialized routines which contain the data and procedural information to assist the user in accomplishing a task, such as installing new software or hardware or getting help. The newest wizards such as the *Answer Wizard*, shown in Figure 29, have the ability to interact with the user through a semi-intelligent conversational language interface.

The Answer Wizard is used on Windows 95 applications. Usually, one of the topics offered is the one needed to answer the question, although it is still the user's responsibility to select the right help topic. The answer wizard employs a basic natural language interface which parses the user input and tries to match it with relevant portions of the

When you want certain parts of a document to look different, divide the document into sections and format each section the way you want. Sections determine the number of columns, the size of margins, the format and sequence of page numbers, and the contents and position of headers and footers. Until you insert section breaks, Word treats a document as a single section.

To create a new section, click Break on the Insert menu, and then select where you want the next section to begin.

- Section Breaks -
☐ Next Page   ☐ Even Page
☑ Continuous   ☐ Odd Page

FIGURE 27   This text box is the result of choosing the "*Mix Layouts in a Document*" option.

on-line help database. The user is presented with the list of options, of which at least one will likely be of interest.

The most unique aspect of the on-line documentation is not merely its very rich indexing of procedures, tasks, and tutorials. Although such systems are indeed helpful, they remain *passive*, relying on the user to invoke them when the user feels it necessary.

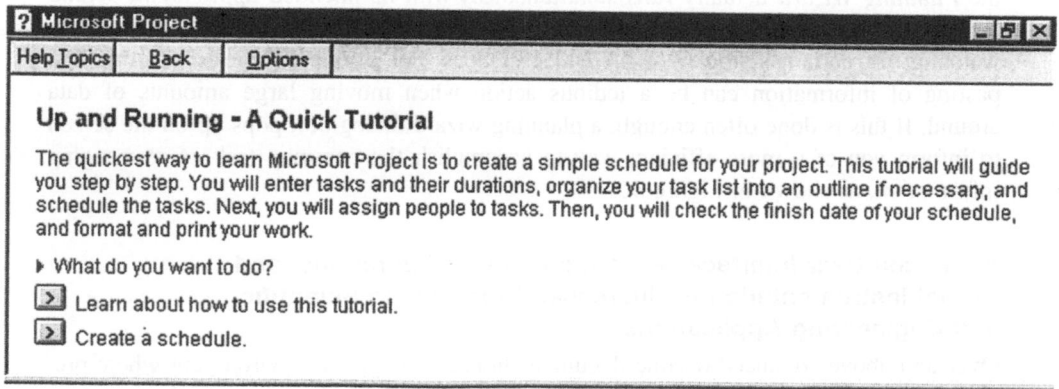

Up and Running - A Quick Tutorial

The quickest way to learn Microsoft Project is to create a simple schedule for your project. This tutorial will guide you step by step. You will enter tasks and their durations, organize your task list into an outline if necessary, and schedule the tasks. Next, you will assign people to tasks. Then, you will check the finish date of your schedule, and format and print your work.

▸ What do you want to do?

[>] Learn about how to use this tutorial.

[>] Create a schedule.

FIGURE 28   An on-line tutorial in Microsoft Project to help the user learn the software.

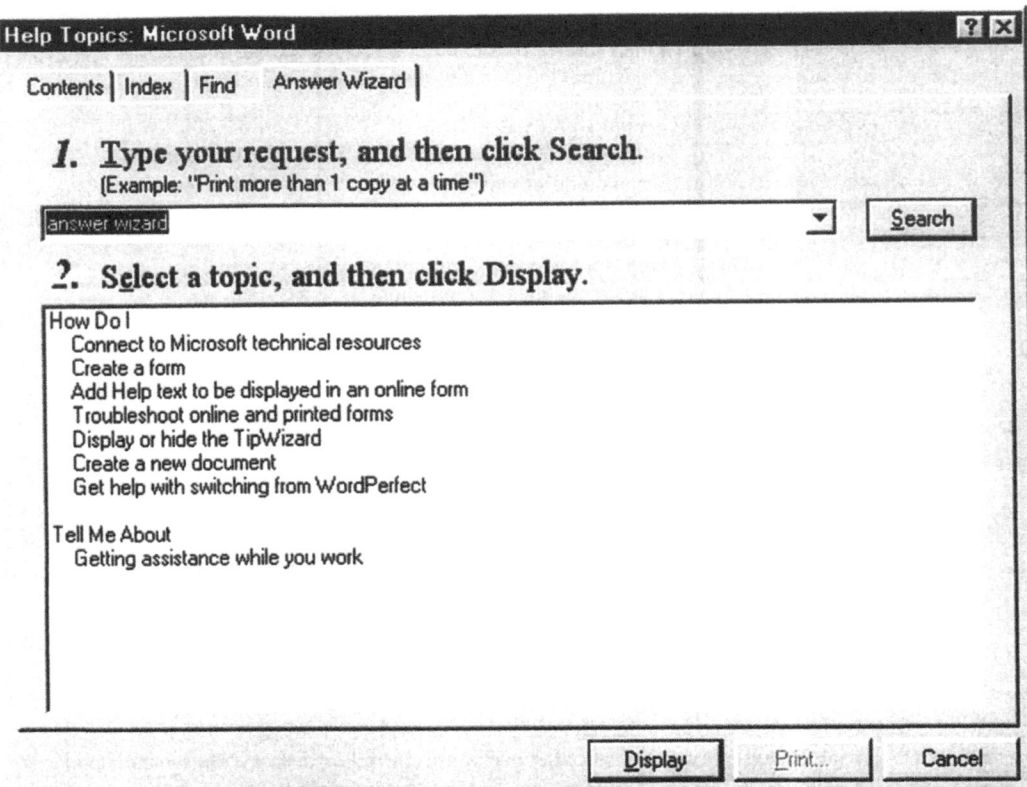

FIGURE 29   The Answer Wizard in Windows 95 helps the user find the information needed.

Given the complexity of today's software, more often than not, a user will not know when to consult the on-line documentation system for assistance, especially if they are inexperienced or new to computing. What is needed is an *active* documentation system, and this need has been acknowledged and implemented.

Whereas the Answer Wizard is passive, relying on the user to apply it effectively, the *Planning Wizard* actually *runs simultaneously with its intended application*, behind the scenes. The planning wizard is somewhat anticipatory in that it is event driven, watching for certain actions that the end user does. For example, repeated cutting and pasting of information can be a tedious action when moving large amounts of data around. If this is done often enough, a planning wizard dialog box pops up on the screen to inform you of a more efficient way to accomplish the common task of rearranging information, as shown in Figure 30.

Advanced User Interface Design, Integrated Operations, and Virtual Instrumentation for Increased Efficiency in Scientific and Engineering Applications

Over and above advanced on-line documentation, an integrated environment where previously separate operations are consolidated can dramatically improve efficiency by reducing the amount of documentation required to learn a particular application. Science

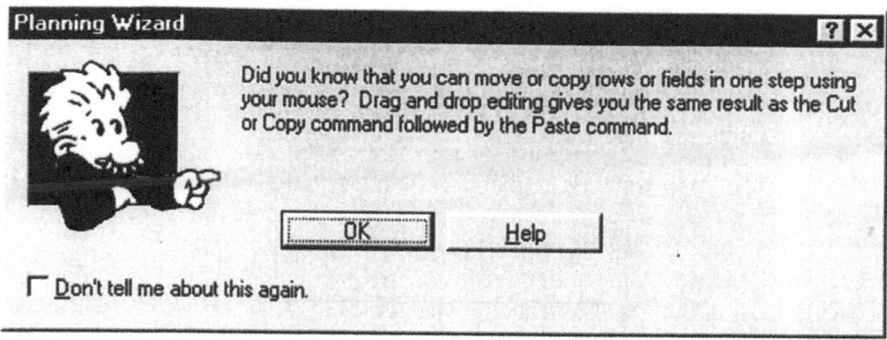

FIGURE 30   The Planning Wizard shows a better way to accomplish work.

and engineering programs are a special case of software that can bring with it particularly difficult documentation and usability issues that can span the entire range of documentation contexts, in addition to the intellectual demands of solving the problem at hand. Due consideration of these multifaceted documentation issues and judicious use of software ergonomics, also known as *user interface design*, can ease the learning curve and empower the user to be more productive and, possibly, more creative with the application software.

Software that facilitates the design and simulation of electronics can serve as a particularly clear example of how a computer application can increase functionality. Through an intuitive user interface which leverages the existing knowledge of the user (see the Application Documentation and Issues of Software Usability and Interface Design section), the software can expedite the task of accomplishing useful work.

Electrical engineering is a demanding enterprise, from learning and understanding basic concepts, through to the latest advances in system design and implementation. Using physical equipment such as digital multimeters, oscilloscopes, and logic and spectrum analyzers can be error-prone, tedious, and very expensive.

SPICE (*Simulation Program with Integrated Circuit Emphasis*), originally created from research by the University of California at Berkeley is a well-known and advanced simulation environment for modeling analog and digital circuits. This software allows engineers who understand the language of SPICE to define a circuit and observe the response of the circuit. SPICE simulation programs have existed on larger computers running UNIX for many years, but often did not have graphical front ends to aid in designing circuits.

A simple circuit as it might appear on paper is shown in Figure 31. Without a graphical user interface to create a schematic visually, a user would have enter terse SPICE netlists such as the following, which models the schematic shown in Figure 31.

```
*Spice netlist for Series.ckt
V1   7   0   DC   10V
R1   7   6   1k
R2   6   0   1k
.SAVE V(6)  V(7)  @v1[i]  @r1[p]  @r1[i]  @r2[p]  @r2[i]
*BKGND=RGB  0  0  0
*BINARY RAW FILE
```

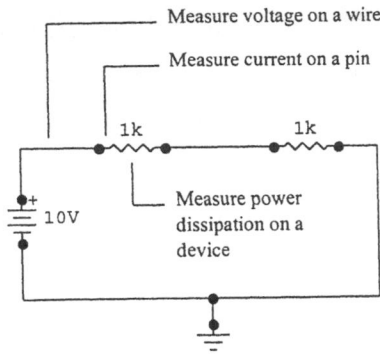

FIGURE 31   A simple circuit schematic.

```
* Selected Circuit Analyses :
.OP
.END
```

Software such as CircuitMaker from MicroCode Engineering (53) permits design with familiar electrical engineering symbols, much as one would see in a circuit schematic for the operational amplifier circuit shown in Figure 32. The graphical environment permits the use of an existing symbolic nomenclature, making it much more intuitive for both beginners and experienced users who have proficiency in electrical engineering. When the design is completed, the user can specify one of several types of analysis methods, simulate the circuit, and view the results on screen to observe the circuit response.

Graphical interfaces, as Figure 33 shows, can not only superscede conventional text-based methods, but it can also represent the analogous functionality of complex instrumentation, which ultimately eases the burden of user documentation because it is something familiar to the user.

INTERNET-BASED USER DOCUMENTATION:
ON-LINE AND GRAPHICAL

The most recent trend in user documentation has involved the Internet phenomenon. Information has never been more transient, and the Internet is the ideal place to put rapidly changing knowledge, where it can be updated quickly, as well as permitting easy access to it through a number of methods, such as browsing the web, downloading from the Internet, or electronic mail.

Established in the 1960s, originally as the ARPANET (*Advanced Research Projects Agency Network*) so that government agencies and universities could link research centers, the ARPA network joined with other networks so that information could move across international boundaries to become the Internet, or simply *the net* in colloquial terms. Thus, the Internet is a number of networks that communicate with each other

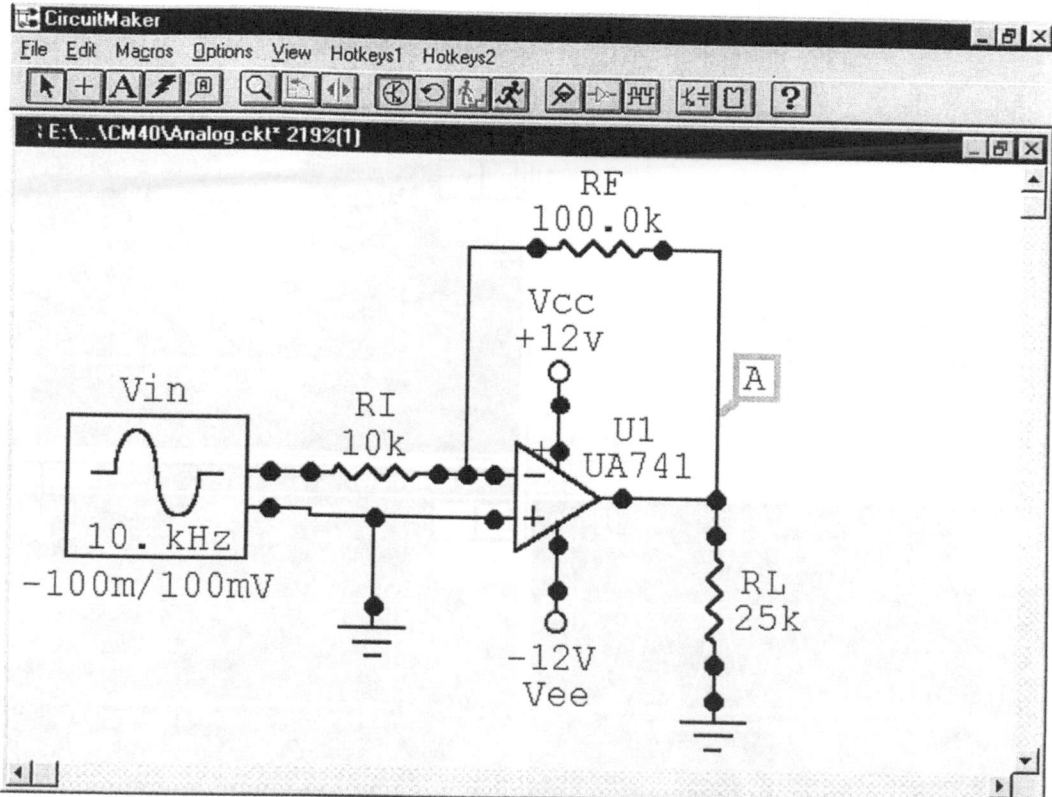

FIGURE 32   An operational amplifier circuit created with CircuitMaker.

using a common computer language, called a *protocol*. Please refer to the Online User Documentation for Operating Systems section for a brief discussion of TCP/IP, the protocol used on the Internet. Many services, originally developed on the UNIX operating system comprise the Internet, such as electronic mail and electronic mailing list servers, Usenet newsgroups, FTP remote file transfer, Telnet for logging in to remote services, and Gopher for menu-based Internet searches. The best known and fastest growing of these services is World Wide Web, or the Web.

The World Wide Web is a very popular medium for electronically publishing, distributing, and viewing information in the form of pages of text, graphics, images, movies, and other media. This section introduces the concepts, terms, and procedures used to create on-line documentation in the form of web pages and electronic documents.

The World Wide Web can be used for many things, in addition to providing information for end users: new software developments, providing patches, automated technical support, and even full software upgrades. These can be accomplished through various Internet methods and constitute the latest and one of the most powerful forms of user documentation. For specific examples, see the Common Internet URLs and the Hyper-Text Transport Protocol section.

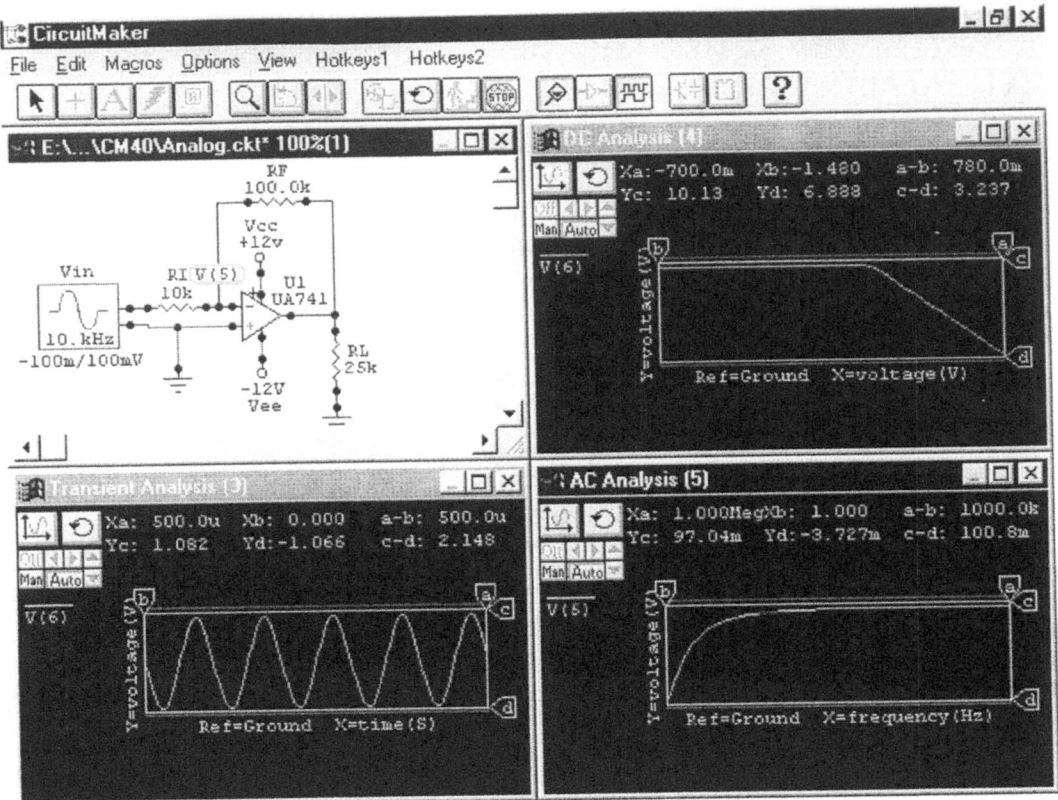

FIGURE 33   Viewing simulation results with *virtual instruments.*

INTERNET CONCEPTS IN THE CONTEXT OF THE WORLD WIDE WEB

The World Wide Web (informally called "the Web" for brevity) is essentially a vast collection of linked multimedia documents which can be accessed over the Internet using a network protocol known as the HyperText Transport Protocol (HTTP). The software that is most often used to access the Web is called a *web browser*. Examples of web browsers are Mosaic from the National Center for Supercomputing Applications (NCSA), Netscape Navigator from Netscape Communications, and Internet Explorer from Microsoft Corporation. The World Wide Web has evolved its own vocabulary to help people discuss the special nature of electronic publishing on the Internet. Understanding these common terms will help the reader to create web documents that meet their particular documentation requirements.

An overall picture of the Internet and related concepts is discussed first, so that the reader can then understand how the particulars of web page creation and publishing the web site on the Internet are accomplished. After these foundational concepts are presented, then the particulars of creating a web page for the purposes of documentation are discoursed.

Figure 34 shows a synopsis of the web page creation and distribution process.

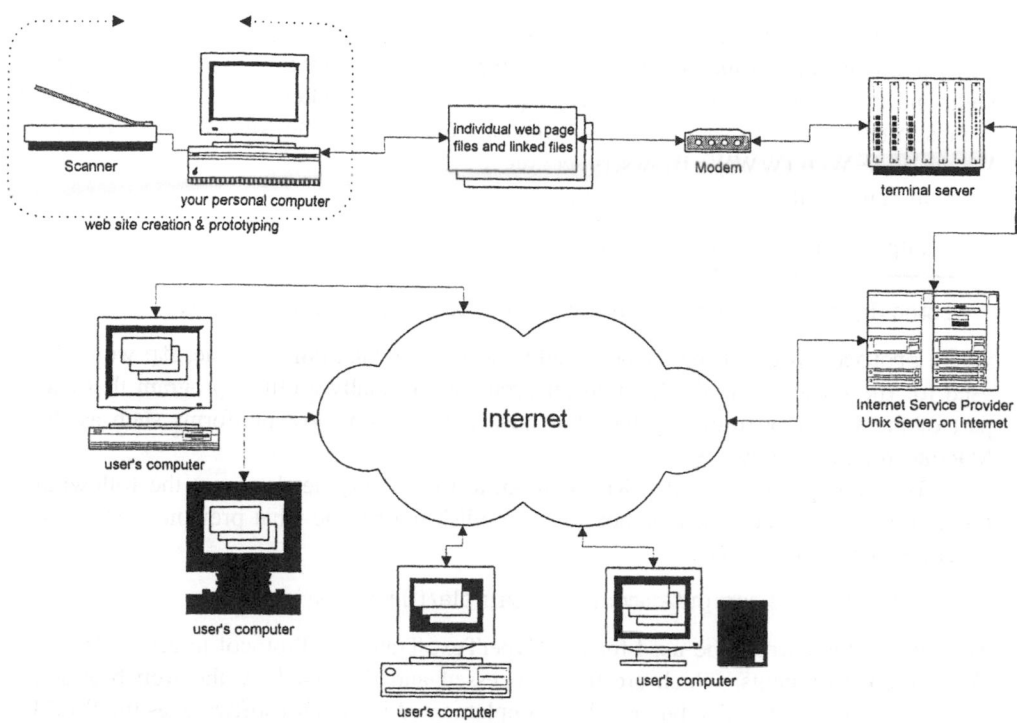

FIGURE 34   An overall picture of the Internet and web page creation.

After the web site has been created, it is uploaded to a computer on the Internet, and then other computers running web browser software can view the web site.

The Uniform Resource Locator (URL) Concept

As multiple information transfer protocols, like FTP, Gopher, Wais, Veronica, Archie, and others, were implemented on the Internet, the average user was being put under increasing demand to learn more interfaces and protocols. Each of these protocols required learning a different program.

Under UNIX with a standard shell, retrieving a file from the Internet would involve the following steps:

- Start an ftp client program, such as /usr/bin/ftp
- Open a connection to the host
- Log in as *anonymous* or *guest*
- Go to the necessary directory with the required change directory commands
- Switch to binary mode, if not already enabled
- Give the command to retrieve the file(s)
- Log out and return to your shell

To simplify the matter, the Uniform Resource Locator or URL was defined. It is a notation developed primarily to have a consistent and concise method of locating files and data objects on the Internet (as well as on local file systems, or those on a LAN) when it was becoming unwieldy to describe the access method, host machine, directory path, and the object name with different types of server and client programs. The URL is most often used with web browsers, which are discussed in the Advanced Features of World Wide Web (WWW) Browsers section.

In general, the URL is of the form

i.e. http   fully qualified hostname

protocol://machinename.domain(s)/directory/path/filename.ext,

where protocol specifies the method used to access the data. For example, ftp would be used for file retrieval via the file transfer protocol, originally a utility program that was part of the UNIX operating system, but now available on most platforms such as the Macintosh and Windows 95.

To accomplish this with URL notation, a user simply needs to put the following URL into the browser's location box to accomplish in one line what previously required several separate operations:

ftp://some.computer.com/pub/sample/file/gibberish.txt

The http method would be used for the HyperText Transport Protocol to access World Wide Web documents, which are then processed and displayed by the web browser. Many other protocols exist, but not all are implemented in modern software, as the World Wide Web itself has made some older methods of information access obsolete. See the Common Internet URLs and the *HyperText Transport Protocol* section for more examples of protocols.

The notation machinename is the name of the computer that you are trying to communicate with. This information will be checked by an Internet domain name server and matched to a specific machine on the Internet. Alternatively, the machine name can be specified with a 32-bit Internet Protocol (IP) address of the form [0-255].[0-255].[0-255].[0-255]. This means that an IP number is a set of four numbers separated by decimal points, each of which range between 0 and 255 inclusive.

The following is an example of a URL that uses the IP number rather than a hostname of a machine:

http://205.207.117.5/WATERLOOTECHJOBS/index.html

When the machinename is combined with the domain(s) in which the computer resides on the Internet, the resulting expression of machinename.domain(s) is the *fully qualified* host name of the machine that has the data. Fully qualified means that both the name of the computer and the domain in which it resides is included, making the hostname valid for the *entire Internet* rather than just that subset in the same domain as the target computer.

For instance, if a host named boxer in the somewhere.com domain were referenced, its *partially* qualified hostnames could be either boxer or boxer.somewhere. These partial names would only work from within the somewhere.com or .com domains. However, the *fully qualified domain name* (or FQDN, as it is often called) would be boxer.somewhere.com and would work from anywhere on the Internet.

The path is any *method-specific* string data used to determine which data object on that machine is being referenced. Most often, such as when using ftp and http object retrieval, the path is a directory structure and sometimes a *filename*, as discussed below. The path is similar to a traditional directory path used to navigate a normal file system, but being a generalization to the entire Internet, sometimes the first part of the path specifies a login account, such as

http://www.easynet.on.ca/~icyber/overview/products/index.html

In this example, the ~icyber a part of the path references the account where a web resides. On a UNIX system ~icyber happens to be a directory, but it is the *home directory* of a specific account, which is owned by a particular user. There may be many such home directories on multiuser computer systems, and the path allows a user to access any file, in any directory structure, on any computer on the Internet.

Finally, the filename.ext portion represents the file name and an optional extension, which specifies a particular object on the Internet. Some older file systems, such as MS-DOS, place restrictions on the length of the file name and extension, whereas other file systems are more flexible and allow spaces and capitalization, if needed. If the file that is being accessed is likely to be saved by the user, it is considerate to use file names and extensions which are compatible with as many file systems as possible. In practice, this means remaining compatible with the 8.3 limit of MS-DOS, with file names no longer than 8 characters and extensions no longer than three. Although punctuation can be used with MS-DOS, some punctuation such as ! have special significance with some UNIX shells and can cause problems when the user tries to use the file under UNIX, so the prudent person will avoid punctuation in filenames to remain as neutral as possible so that many users can download and use files without problems.

Common Internet URLs and the HyperText Transport Protocol

To reiterate the Uniform Resource Locator (URL) concept section, the URL notation generalizes the concept of the filename and directory path that has traditionally been assumed to exist on the user's local file system *to the entire Internet*. Moreover, the URL allows the specification of additional information because files, directories, and services can exist on any machine on the Internet. This information can be *served* to the user through any of several different methods, making access to a file or Internet service just as easy as when it is on a user's local hard drive.

The most common URL access methods used are as follows:

- file://   Opens a file on a mounted volume
- http://   Opens a World Wide Web page
- ftp:://   Connects to a server using the file transfer protocol
- gopher://   Connects to a Gopher server
- telnet://   Connects to a server using Telnet
- news: Connects to a Usenet newsgroup
- mailto: Sends an electronic mail message
- snews: Opens a secure newsgroup connection
- shttp://   Opens a secure World Wide Web connection

Note that URLs need not point to files. URLs may point to other objects such as the following query that references the AltaVista search engine in the cgi-bin (common gateway interface binary) directory. The cgi-bin directory holds programs or scripts that are written to receive information from the Internet, process it, and return information back to the Internet, where it will be served to the user who requested it. For example, the following query is asking the AltaVista search engine to find all web pages with the phrases *computational fluid dynamics*, *shareware*, and *source code* contained in them:

http://www.altavista.digital.com/cgi-bin/query?pg=q&what=web&
q=computati onal+fluid+dynamics+public+domain+shareware+source+code

This URL is created by the AltaVista user interface, and does not need to be manually typed. However, the URL can be stored by a web browser to be used again in the future. A URL may simply point to a directory, to access documents stored deep within databases (54):

http://popularmechanics.com/popmech/sci/tech/

URLs can even point to small applications (55) such as Java applets that are loaded into your machine from a web page on the Internet:

http://www.seds.ca/gsim/gsim.htm

Within the HTML file are references to a Java applet, which is a compiled program that ends in .class. This file can be run by the web browser's Java Virtual Machine (JVM).

HYPERTEXT MARKUP LANGUAGE DOCUMENTS

HyperText Markup Language (HTML) permits the author to create hypertext and multimedia pages which contain links to other sections within the same page, or to other HTML files on the Internet. In addition to HTML, many different file formats are used

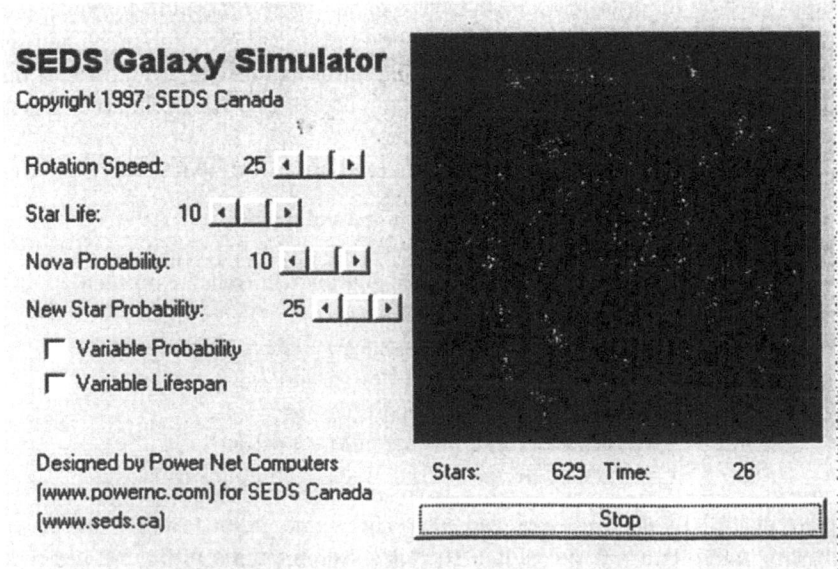

FIGURE 35   A Java applet for scientific computing.

on the World Wide Web. These files may contain images, sampled audio or music, computer-generated animation, or digital video, even three-dimensional environments. Please refer to the Unifying Hypertext and Multimedia Through Open File Standards section for a discussion about these many and varied file formats. HTML itself is the unifying concept behind the World Wide Web and, as discussed in the Standards for Platform-Independent Document Creation section, is related to SGML, but it is simpler and somewhat less flexible in terms of document layout. However, it is a constantly evolving standard, with extensions coming from market forces such as Netscape Communications offering their own enhancements, as well as committee-based evolution, such as the HTML 4.0 specification.

Another option is the use of web page design software such as Adobe PageMill or Microsoft FrontPage to create most of the site and edit HTML to add special features when needed. Refer to the final two paragraphs of An Overview of Web Site Design and Implementation section for information about this kind of Internet-centric design software. As shown in Figure 36, web site tools allow a designer to view and edit all of the tags used in HTML, in addition to the What You See Is What You Get (WYSIWYG) view. This visual approach to site design is preferred by most people because it allows them to view the site as it is evolving, making changes to the *look and feel* of the site as it is created.

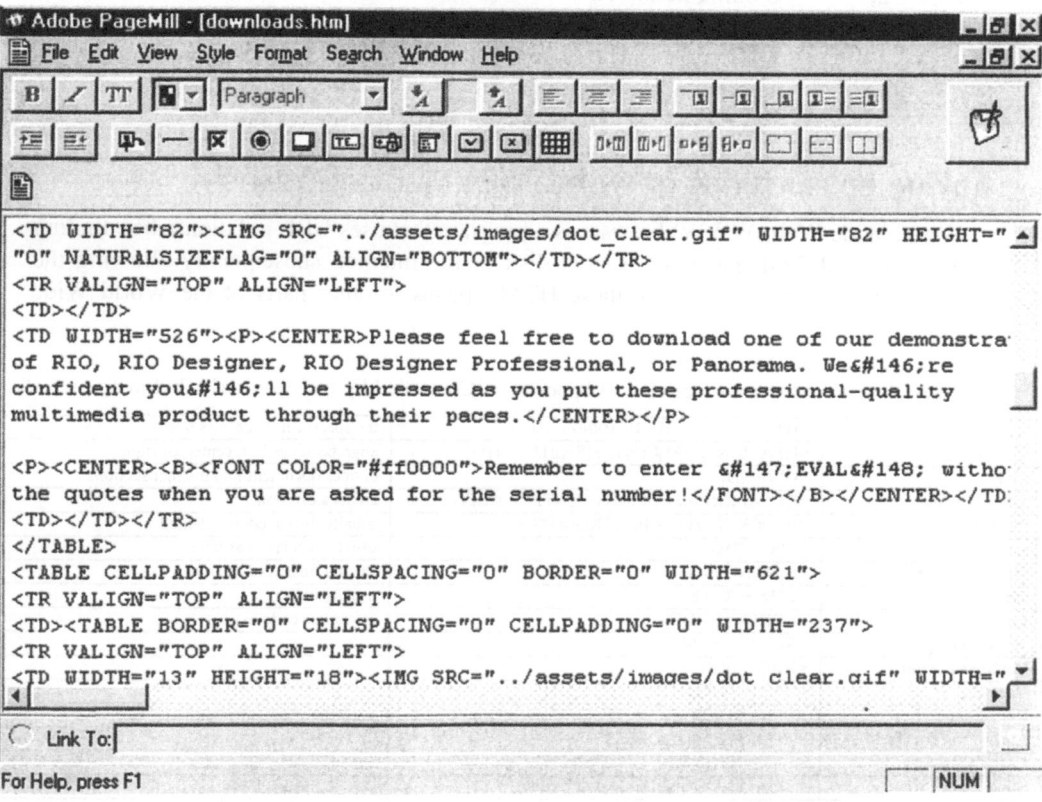

FIGURE 36   The HTML view mode of web site design software.

TABLE 2   Basic Elements

Document Type	<HTML></HTML>	beginning and end of file
Title	<TITLE></TITLE>	must be in header
Header	<HEAD></HEAD>	descriptive info, such as title
Body	<BODY></BODY>	bulk of the page

In Tables 2–14 (56), the markup tags that comprise HTML version 3.2 are presented to give an overview of the different formatting options available to HTML authors. Tutorials and information (57) on how each of these tags are used are available on the World Wide Web.

The following notation conventions apply in Tables 2–14:

- URL   URL of an external file, or just the file name if in the same directory
- ?   Arbitrary number, such as <H?> means any of the following are permissible: <H1>, <H2>, <H3>, etc.
- %   Arbitrary percentage (i.e., <hr align=left width="%"> means <hr align=left width="50%">, etc.)
- ***   Arbitrary (i.e., ALT="***" means fill in with text)
- $$$$$$ Arbitrary hexadecimal number (i.e., BGCOLOR="#$$$$$$" means BGCOLOR="#00FF1C")
- ,,,   Comma-delimited (i.e., COORDS=",,," means COORDS="0,0,50,50")
- | Alternatives such as ALIGN=LEFT|RIGHT|CENTER means to select one of these options

ADVANCED FEATURES OF WORLD WIDE WEB BROWSERS

A World Wide Web (WWW) browser is a program that uses URL notation when finding and accessing HTML pages on a local disk or the Internet, subsequently allowing the user to follow any URLs within these HTML pages to other parts of the World Wide

TABLE 3   Structural Definition (Appearance Controlled by the Browser's Preferences)

Heading	<H?></H?> IE., <H1>HEADING 1</H1>	the specification defines 6 levels
Align Heading	<H? ALIGN=LEFT|CENTER|RIGHT> </H?>	align headings left, center, or right
Division	<DIV></DIV>	divides document into distinct sections
Align Division	<DIV ALIGN=LEFT|RIGHT|CENTER> </DIV>	aligns a division
Block Quote	<BLOCKQUOTE></BLOCKQUOTE>	usually displayed as indented
Emphasis	<EM></EM>	usually displayed as italic
Strong Emphasis	<STRONG></STRONG>	usually displayed as bold
Citation	<CITE></CITE>	usually italics
Code	<CODE></CODE>	for source code listings
Sample Output	<SAMP></SAMP>	
Keyboard Input	<KBD></KBD>	
Variable	<VAR></VAR>	
Definition	<DFN></DFN>	not widely implemented
Author's Address	<ADDRESS></ADDRESS>	
Large Font Size	<BIG></BIG>	
Small Font Size	<SMALL></SMALL>	

TABLE 4   Presentation Formatting

Bold	<B></B>	
Italic	<I></I>	
Underline	<U></U>	not widely implemented yet
Strikeout	<STRIKE></STRIKE>	not widely implemented yet
Strikeout	<S></S>	not widely implemented yet
Subscript		
Superscript		
Typewriter	<TT></TT>	displays in a monospaced font
Preformatted	<PRE></PRE>	display text spacing as-is
Width	<PRE WIDTH=?></PRE>	in characters
Center	<CENTER></CENTER>	for both text and images
Blinking	<BLINK></BLINK>	the most derided tag ever
Font Size	<FONT SIZE=?></FONT>	ranges from 1-7
Change Font Size	<FONT SIZE="+|-?"></FONT>	
Base Font Size	<BASEFONT SIZE=?>	from 1-7; default is 3
Font Color	<FONT COLOR="#$$$$$$"></FONT>	
Select Font	<FONT FACE="***"></FONT>	
Multi-Column Text	<MULTICOL COLS=?></MULTICOL>	
Column Gutter	<MULTICOL GUTTER=?> </MULTICOL>	default is 10 pixels
Column Width	<MULTICOL WIDTH=?></MULTICOL>	
Spacer	<SPACER>	
Spacer Type	<SPACER TYPE=HORIZONTAL|VERTICAL|BLOCK>	
Spacer Size	<SPACER SIZE=?>	
Spacer Dimensions	<SPACER WIDTH=? HEIGHT=?>	
Spacer Alignment	<SPACER ALIGN=LEFT|RIGHT|CENTER>	

Web or to other local files. These software programs can interpret a large number of file formats, some of which are discussed in the Unifying Hypertext and Multimedia Through Open File Standards section. Multimedia files can be opened on their own with a local URL pointing directly to them, as shown in Figure 37.

Netscape Navigator can also be used to access HTML or multimedia files stored on a local hard disk, CD-ROM, or on the Internet. In Figure 37, Netscape Navigator is used to show live-action video to illustrate the capabilities of a modern fighter plane.

In addition, the Internet has also played a role in the development of new programming and scripting languages known as Java and JavaScript, respectively. These languages have specific features to support communication and information transfer over the Internet. Programming code inserted into HTML pages can be executed by the browser. This source code can either be interpreted and run as a script, or actually precompiled to a platform independent format called *bytecode*, to be run by a Java Virtual Machine. The JVM can be either a part of the web browser, or a component of the operating system. The result is a small program called a Java applet (see Fig. 35 for an example of scientific computing using Java), which can interact with the user or perform some useful function.

In terms of user documentation, HTML, Java, and most of the other multimedia formats are open standards, meaning that the software support and specifications for these file formats are publicly available. Thus, unlike multimedia elements found in, for example, Windows 95 on-line help files, *any* computer that is running a web browser program such as Netscape or Internet Explorer will be able to access the files, process them, and output the desired results through the communication channels of the computer, such as the screen, sound card, or printer.

TABLE 5   Links and Graphics

Link Something	`<A HREF="URL"></A>`	
Link to Target	`<A HREF="URL#***"></A>`	if in another document
	`<A HREF="#***"></A>`	if in current document
Target Window	`<A HREF="URL" TARGET="***|_BLANK|_SELF|_PARENT|_TOP"></A>`	
Define Target in Document	`<A NAME="***"></A>`	
Relationship	`<A REL="***"></A>`	not widely implemented
Reverse Relationship	`<A REV="***"></A>`	not widely implemented
Display Image	`<IMG SRC="URL">`	
Alignment	`<IMG SRC="URL" ALIGN=TOP	BOTTOM	MIDDLE	LEFT	RIGHT>`	
Alignment	`<IMG SRC="URL" ALIGN=TEXTTOP|ABSMIDDLE|BASELINE|ABSBOTTOM>`	
Alternate text in place of image	`<IMG SRC="URL" ALT="***">`	if image not displayed
Imagemap to define "hot" areas of image	`<IMG SRC="URL" ISMAP>`	requires a script
Client-Side Imagemap	`<IMG SRC="URL" USEMAP="URL">`	
Map Description	`<MAP NAME="***"></MAP>`	
Map Sections	`<AREA SHAPE="RECT" COORDS=",,," HREF="URL"	NOHREF>`	
Dimensions	`<IMG SRC="URL" WIDTH=? HEIGHT=?>`	in pixels
Border	`<IMG SRC="URL" BORDER=?>`	in pixels
Runaround Space	`<IMG SRC="URL" HSPACE=? VSPACE=?>`	in pixels
Low-Resolution Proxy	`<IMG SRC="URL" LOWSRC="URL">`	
Client Pull	`<META HTTP-EQUIV="REFRESH" CONTENT="?; URL=URL">`	EXAMPLE: `<META HTTP-EQUIV="REFRESH" CONTENT="7; URL=HTTP://WWW.TOTAVIA.COM /ARROW">`
Embed Object	`<EMBED SRC="URL">`	insert object into page
Object Size	`<EMBED SRC="URL" WIDTH=? HEIGHT=?>`	

Many companies and individuals use the Internet to make information available to anyone who can use a web browser. Some companies even offer *browser extensions*, known as *plug-ins*, which allow the browser to process proprietary formats, which are specific to the web, such as streaming video over the Internet. Plug-ins, PDF files, applets, shareware, demonstration software, and upgrades can be downloaded because of the generality of the URL formalism. HTML, with its ability to format information and

TABLE 6   Dividers

Paragraph	`<P></P>`	define beginning and end of paragraph
Align Text	`<P ALIGN=LEFT|CENTER|RIGHT> </P>`	
Line Break	` `	a single carriage return
Clear Textwrap	`<BR CLEAR=LEFT|RIGHT|ALL>`	
Horizontal Rule	`<HR>`	inserts a horizontal rule in document
Alignment	`<HR ALIGN=LEFT|RIGHT|CENTER>`	defines alignment of the horizontal rule
Thickness	`<HR SIZE=?>`	in pixels
Width	`<HR WIDTH=?>`	in pixels
Width Percent	`<HR WIDTH="%">`	as a percentage of page width
Solid Line	`<HR NOSHADE>`	without the 3D cutout look
No Break	`<NOBR></NOBR>`	prevents line breaks
Word Break	`<WBR>`	`<WBR>` where to break a line if needed

TABLE 7   Lists

Unordered List	<UL><LI></UL>	<LI> before each list item
Compact	<UL COMPACT></UL>	
Bullet Type	<UL TYPE=DISC|CIRCLE|SQUARE>	for the whole list
	<LI TYPE=DISC|CIRCLE|SQUARE>	this & subsequent
Ordered List	<OL><LI></OL>	<LI> before each list item
Compact	<OL COMPACT></OL>	
Numbering Type	<OL TYPE=A|a|I|i|1>	for the whole list
	<LI TYPE=A|a|I|i|1>	this & subsequent
Starting Number	<OL START=?>	for the whole list
	<LI VALUE=?>	this & subsequent
Definition List	<DL><DT><DD></DL>	<DT>=term, <DD>=definition
Compact	<DL COMPACT></DL>	
Menu List	<MENU><LI></MENU>	<LI> before each list item
Compact	<MENU COMPACT></MENU>	
Directory List	<DIR><LI></DIR>	<LI> before each list item
Compact	<DIR COMPACT></DIR>	

specify resources with URLs, has made the Internet the medium of choice for downloading patches and maintenance releases of currently used software, because of the inherently low distribution costs involved.

User documentation of various kinds may also be made available on the Internet which might not otherwise be available for perusal by interested parties, including white papers (58) (technical overviews) and other material that are beneficial for certain audiences but until recently would have been economically prohibitive to distribute to all users. An example to illustrate this would be the distribution of white papers in PDF format. Such information can be very useful to a small percentage of highly sophisticated end users, who may also perform roles pertinent to software development such as beta-testing, or to educate users in a general way about a particular technology. An example is Figure 38, which links to an electronic document for ensuring consistent color across all aspects of a publishing process. An example of an open PDF document (59) is shown in Figure 39. This document can be printed complete with graphics and equations at a high level of quality or displayed on-screen and read, making PDF an excellent choice for *dual-use* documentation.

An Overview of Web Site Design & Implementation

The basic building block of the World Wide Web is the *web document*. A web document and web page typically refer to the same thing, a single file residing on a web server, written in HTML, and accessible with a URL from a web browser. For more information

TABLE 8   Backgrounds and Colors

Tiled Bkground	<BODY BACKGROUND="URL">	
Background Color	<BODY BGCOLOR="#$$$$$$">	order is red/green/blue
Text Color	<BODY TEXT="#$$$$$$">	
Link Color	<BODY LINK="#$$$$$$">	
Visited Link	<BODY VLINK="#$$$$$$"	
Active Link	<BODY ALINK="#$$$$$$">	

TABLE 9   Special Characters

Special Character	&#?;	where ? is the ISO 8859-1 code
<	&lt;	
>	&gt;	
&	&amp;	
"	&quot;	
™	&reg;	
©	&copy;	
Non-Breaking Space		

about HTML, please refer to the HyperText Markup Language Documents section. With HTML documents, the user can move among a group of pages via hypertext links, just as they navigated through information with earlier proprietary hypertext documentation systems. For a review of the many different forms of multimedia and hypertext linking, refer to the Hypertext and Multimedia in On-Line User Documentation and the Hypertext: Associative Linking of Text to Enhance User Documentation sections.

Many pages of related material, linked with HTML tags and installed in a single location on the Web comprises a *web site*, abstractly shown in Figure 40. A site can be much more complex, with many additional sections or subsections, if needed. Any web site will contain a page known as the *home page*, which is the first page presented when a visitor accesses the web site from elsewhere on the World Wide Web, but does not specify a page in particular, such as

    http://www.gabex.com

will actually open the following URL because the browser knows to look for a file called *index.htm* or *index.html*, which is the default file to open when no file is specified in the URL. Thus, the following URL will give the same result as the previous URL:

    http://www.gabex.com/index.html

TABLE 10   Forms

Define Form	<FORM ACTION="URL" METHOD=GET|POST></FORM>	
File Upload	<FORM ENCTYPE="MULTIPART/FORM-DATA"></FORM>	
Input Field	<INPUT TYPE="TEXT|PASSWORD|CHECKBOX|RADIO| IMAGE|HIDDEN|SUBMIT|RESET">	
Field Name	<INPUT NAME="***">	
Field Value	<INPUT VALUE="***">	
Checked?	<INPUT CHECKED>	checkboxes and radio boxes
Field Size	<INPUT SIZE=?>	in characters
Max Length	<INPUT MAXLENGTH=?>	in characters
Selection List	<SELECT></SELECT>	
Name of List	<SELECT NAME="***"> </SELECT>	
# of Options	<SELECT SIZE=?> </SELECT>	
Multiple Choice	<SELECT MULTIPLE>	can select more than one
Option	<OPTION>	items that can be selected
Default Option	<OPTION SELECTED>	
Input Box Size	<TEXTAREA ROWS=? COLS=?></TEXTAREA>	
Name of Box	<TEXTAREA NAME="***"> </TEXTAREA>	
Wrap Text	<TEXTAREA WRAP= OFF |VIRTUAL|PHYSICAL> </TEXTAREA>	

TABLE 11 Tables

Define Table	<TABLE></TABLE>	
Table Border	<TABLE BORDER=?></TABLE>	
Cell Spacing	<TABLE CELLSPACING=?>	
Cell Padding	<TABLE CELLPADDING=?>	
Desired Width	<TABLE WIDTH=?>	in pixels
Width Percent	<TABLE WIDTH="%">	percentage of page
Table Row	<TR></TR>	
Alignment	<TR ALIGN= LEFT | RIGHT | CENTER | MIDDLE | BOTTOM VALIGN=TOP|BOTTOM|MIDDLE>	
Table Cell	<TD></TD>	must appear within table rows
Alignment	<TD ALIGN=LEFT|RIGHT|CENTER|MIDDLE|BOTTOM VALIGN=TOP|BOTTOM|MIDDLE>	
No linebreaks	<TD NOWRAP>	
Columns to Span	<TD COLSPAN=?>	
Rows to Span	<TD ROWSPAN=?>	
Desired Width	<TD WIDTH=?>	in pixels
Width Percent	<TD WIDTH="%">	percentage of table
Cell Color	<TD BGCOLOR="#$$$$$$">	
Table Header	<TH></TH>	same as data, except bold centered
Alignment	<TH ALIGN=LEFT|RIGHT|CENTER|MIDDLE|BOTTOM VALIGN=TOP|BOTTOM|MIDDLE>	
No Linebreaks	<TH NOWRAP>	
Columns to Span	<TH COLSPAN=?>	
Rows to Span	<TH ROWSPAN=?>	
Desired Width	<TH WIDTH=?>	in pixels
Width Percent	<TH WIDTH="%">	percentage of table
Cell Color	<TH BGCOLOR="#$$$$$$">	
Table Caption	<CAPTION></CAPTION>	
Alignment	<CAPTION ALIGN=TOP|BOTTOM>	above/below table

TABLE 12 Frames

Frame Document	<FRAMESET></FRAMESET>	instead of <BODY>
Row Heights	<FRAMESET ROWS=,,,> </FRAMESET>	pixels or %
Row Heights	<FRAMESET ROWS=*></FRAMESET>	* = relative size
Column Widths	<FRAMESET COLS=,,,></FRAMESET>	pixels or %
Column Widths	<FRAMESET COLS=*></FRAMESET>	* = relative size
Border Width	<FRAMESET BORDER=?>	
Borders	<FRAMESET FRAMEBORDER="YES|NO">	
Border Color	<FRAMESET BORDERCOLOR="#$$$$$$">	
Define Frame	<FRAME>	contents of an individual frame
Display Document	<FRAME SRC="URL">	
Frame Name	<FRAME NAME="***"|_BLANK|_SELF|_PARENT|_TOP>	
Margin Width	<FRAME MARGINWIDTH=?>	left and right margins
Margin Height	<FRAME MARGINHEIGHT=?>	top and bottom margins
Scrollbar?	<FRAME SCROLLING="YES|NO|AUTO">	
Not Resizable	<FRAME NORESIZE>	
Borders	<FRAME FRAMEBORDER="YES|NO">	
Border Color	<FRAME BORDERCOLOR="#$$$$$$">	
Unframed Content	<NOFRAMES></NOFRAMES>	for non-frames browsers

TABLE 13   Java Applets

Applet	`<APPLET></APPLET>`	
Applet File Name	`<APPLET CODE="***">`	
Parameters	`<APPLET PARAM NAME="***">`	
Applet Location	`<APPLET CODEBASE="URL">`	
Applet Identifier	`<APPLET NAME="***">`	for references elsewhere in the page
Alternative Text	`<APPLET ALT="***">`	for non-Java browsers
Alignment	`<APPLET ALIGN="LEFT|RIGHT|CENTER">`	
Size	`<APPLET WIDTH=? HEIGHT=?>`	in pixels
Spacing	`<APPLET HSPACE=? VSPACE=?>`	in pixels

However,

`http://www.gabex.com/order.html`

specifies a particular page at this web site, called *order.html*, and this is the web page that the browser will read and present to the user. On most web sites, the home page usually provides a greeting, an introductory title, and some form of index or map to the rest of the site. It is analogous to the role a title page, preface, and table of contents play in a printed literary work. The *home page* in general is usually named

`www.sitename.com/index.html`

In order for a web site to be easy to navigate and comfortable to use, the designers of the web site must give due consideration to the different roles the web site will play and the different priorities and expectations (60) of the audience who will use the web site in these contexts. Similar questions regarding on-line documentation are raised in the Application Documentation and Issues of Software Usability and Interface Design section, starting at the third paragraph, and also apply to web site creation. Designers should make allowances for the strengths and limitations of web-based documentation systems. If the functional and informational requirements are precisely defined beforehand and considered with care and deliberation, usually an overall structure of the web site will emerge, such as that in Figure 40. This site structure will serve as a guide for the following:

- Partitioning the available information comprising the web site into the appropriate subsections for purposes of site administration and future augmentation

TABLE 14   Miscellaneous

Comment	`<!-- *** -->`	not displayed by the browser
HTML 3.2 Prologue	`<!DOCTYPE HTML PUBLIC "-//W3C//DTD HTML 3.2//EN">`	
Searchable	`<ISINDEX>`	indicates a searchable index
Prompt	`<ISINDEX PROMPT="***">`	text to prompt input
Send Search	`<A HREF="URL?***"></A>`	use a real question mark
URL of This File	`<BASE HREF="URL">`	must be in header
Base Window Name	`<BASE TARGET="***">`	must be in header
Relationship	`<LINK REV="***" REL="***" HREF="URL">`	must be in header
Meta Information	`<META>`	must be in header
Style Sheets	`<STYLE></STYLE>`	not yet widely supported
Scripts	`<SCRIPT></SCRIPT>`	not yet widely supported

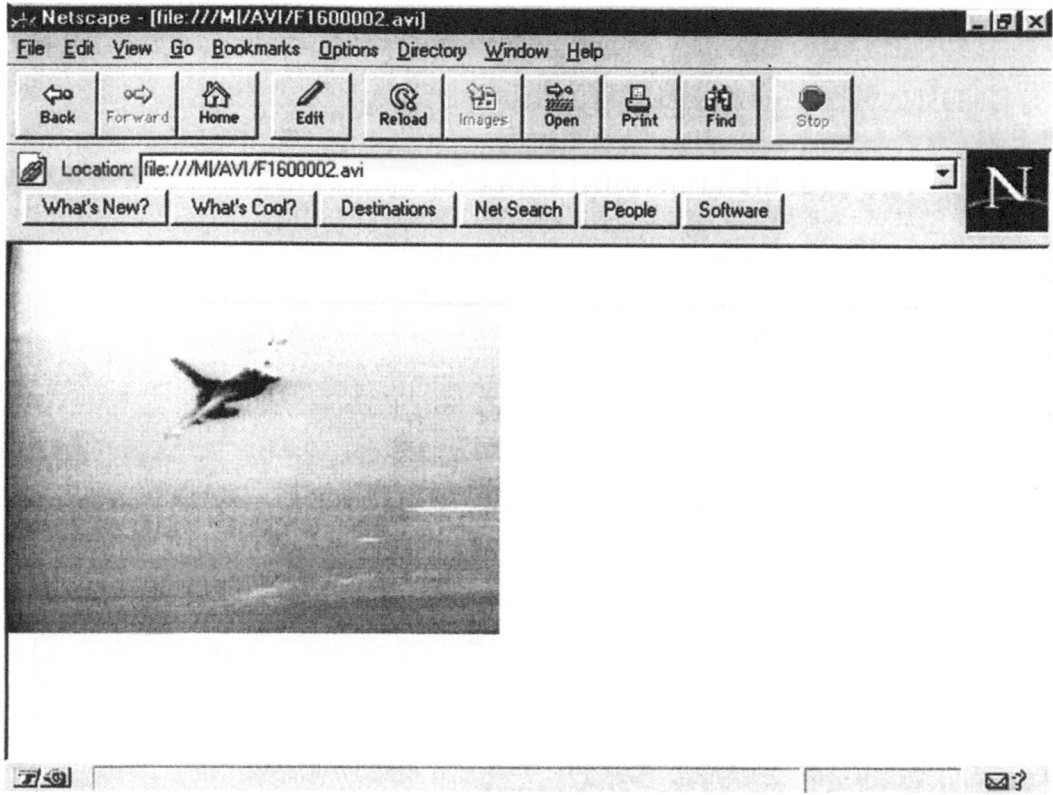

FIGURE 37   This AVI movie clip in Netscape shows the maneuverability of the F-16 fighter.

- Creating and locating the individual web pages within the site such that each page is coherent on its own while remaining consistent with the rest of the site
- Define the links between the pages so that the site affords easy navigation to related material within other pages, respecting the different agendas of the target audiences, just as properly designed on-line documentation systems are able to do

Click here for a printable White Paper about the Kodak Color Management Solutions: (235K)

FIGURE 38   An HTML link to a Portable Document Format (PDF) file.

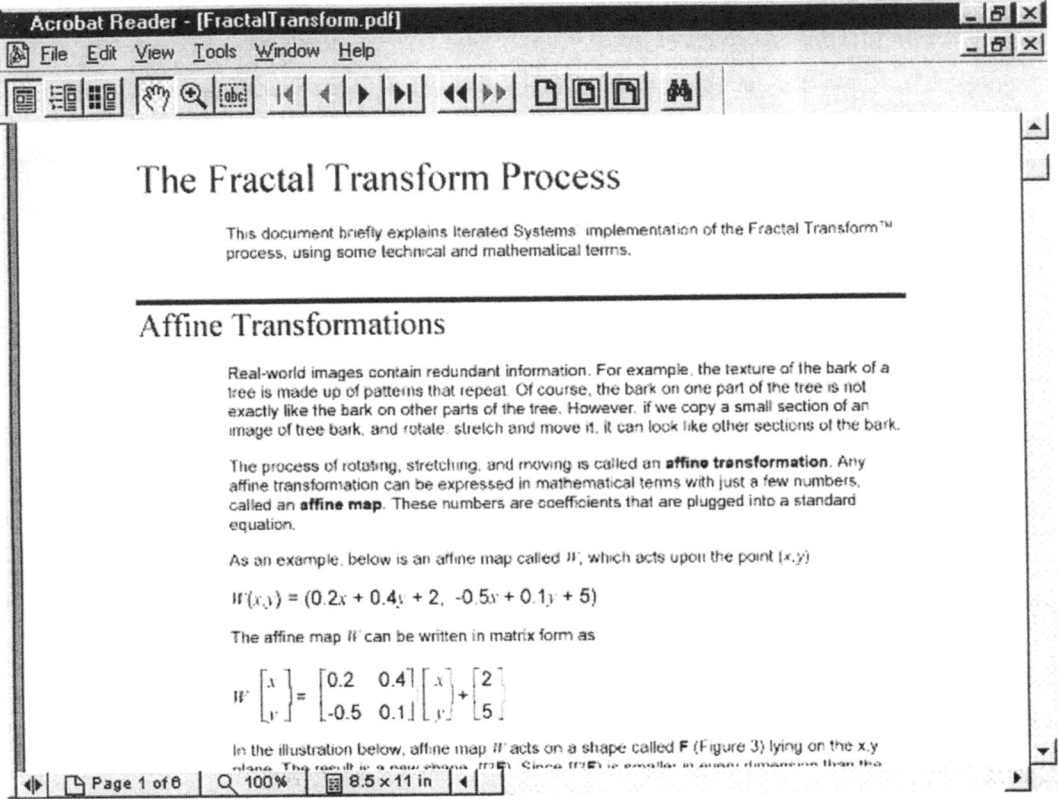

FIGURE 39   A PDF document explaining fractal image compression.

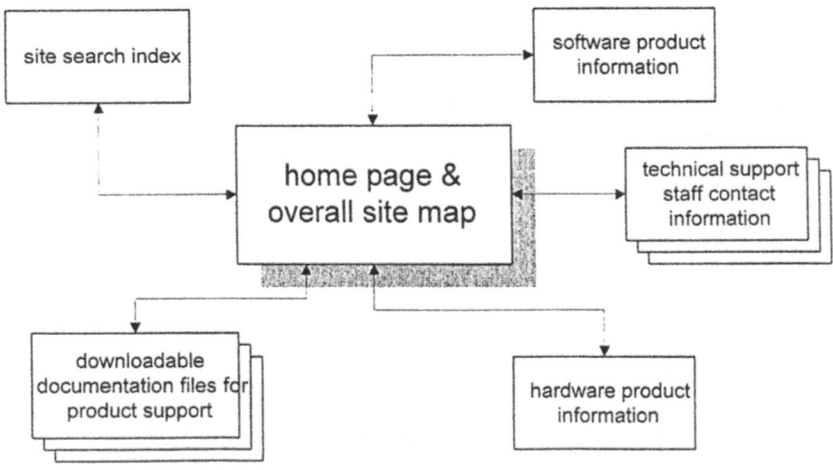

FIGURE 40   One possible document structure for a function-oriented commercial web site.

Site design is a skill similar to being a good technical writer with more traditional media. However, it is still a superset of traditional documentation methods. The hypertext, multimedia, and bidirectional information flow that can easily be designed into web sites merit time spent planning out the site.

Also, as in user interface design, functional and intelligent information layout in effect creates a user interface* for your web site. See the Advanced User Interface Design, Integrated Operations, and Virtual Instrumentation for Increased Efficiency in Scientific and Engineering Applications section for a discussion of system usability. Using text and graphics where appropriate will help to make the site easy and enjoyable† to use while keeping its bandwidth requirements down, which is still an important usability criterion when the site is being accessed over slower links such as phone line access to the Internet.

Web site designers should bear in mind that it is not necessary to use every new multimedia capability offered by advances in Internet technology to have an elegant, enjoyable web site. Indeed, overuse of these elements can be distracting and will slow navigation through the site if excessive liberties are taken with superfluous graphics, sounds, or animation files. Rather, one should match the information dissemination requirements of the site to currently available and widely used Internet software technology, respecting the modem and network connectivity speeds of the average user. Keeping the "bells and whistles" to a reasonably small proportion of the web site's content will ensure that people focus on the message rather than the medium, which is ultimately the reason for having a web site in the first place. Web page design guides should be consulted to survey current notions about how to create aesthetic and engaging web pages.

Creating a web site has become easier with the introduction of software tools, just as word processing and desktop publishing became practical with easy to use, affordable, and powerful applications running on commodity hardware. Web page implementation was originally done with a text editor and a thorough knowledge of HTML, and it still can be. However, creating a web page without visual tools will usually force the designer to focus large amounts of time on making sure the HTML document does not have errors, rather than on the usability and functionality of the document.

Software such as Adobe PageMill or Microsoft FrontPage or even NetScape's built-in editor allow the user to focus on how their web site looks to an end user as shown in Figure 41, rather than the particulars of HTML coding, as shown in Figure 36. On-screen buttons permit fast and easy modifications of web page design and allow the web designer to see the results of changes immediately. Used in conjunction with an actual web browser to permit viewing of the web pages as they are evolving, these tools permit rapid and complex web page layout while still allowing the user to modify the HTML source and add custom code when needed. JavaScript or other embedded code

---

*C. Waters, *Web Concept & Design*, New Riders Publishing, 1996, pp. 67–74, discusses the concepts of becoming a successful interface designer, logic versus reality, iconic imagery, visual metaphors, interface consistency.

†D. Siegel, *Creating Killer Web Sites*, Hayden Books, New York, 1996. This book has a companion web site: http://www.killersites.com Other books recommended by Siegel on design principles are *The Form of the Book* by Jan Tschichold, edited by Robert Bringhurst (Hartley & Marks, Vancouver, BC, 1991); *The Visual Display of Quantitative Information* by Edward R. Tufte (Graphics Press, Cheshire, CT, 1983); and *Envisioning Information* by Edward R. Tufte (Graphics Press, Cheshire, CT, 1990).

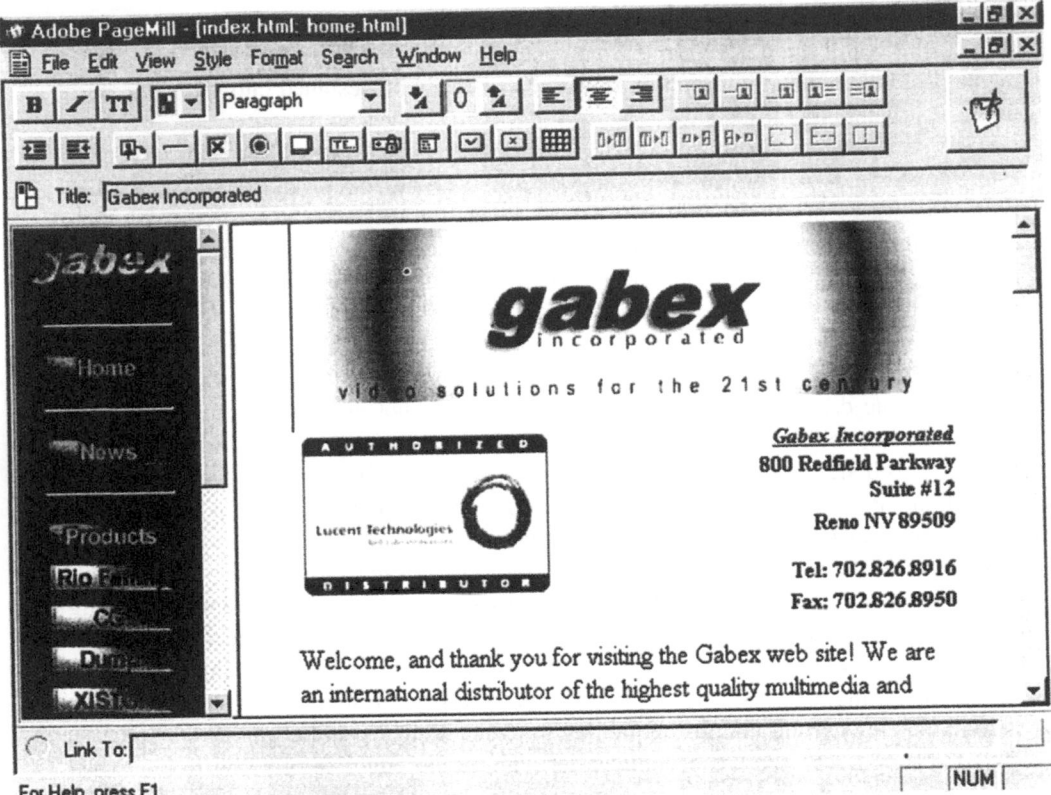

FIGURE 41   Visual design of a web site.

can be inserted to implement any special functionality needed. Then, the files that comprise the site can be electronically installed on the Internet, as shown in Figure 42.

Publishing a Web Site on the Internet

In order for others on the Internet to see your multimedia website over the World Wide Web, it must be uploaded or installed by someone onto a web server, where the rest of the world can access it. Figure 42 shows a dialog box indicating files comprising a web site are being uploaded to a web server, thus publishing it on the World Wide Web.

A web server is a computer that is usually permanently connected to the Internet with a fast link such as a T1 (1.544 megabits per second) or a T3 (45 megabits per second) connection, and runs web server software that is capable of understanding and responding to HTTP requests over a TCP/IP network. A computer functioning as a web server can run one of several network operating systems. As a general rule, multiuser/multitasking operating systems such as UNIX or Windows NT are the platforms of choice because they can run on fast, powerful computers capable of serving hundreds or thousands of requests for web pages at once.

Sometimes, individual users or very small companies may choose to have a web server running a single-user operating system such as Windows 95, but such a system

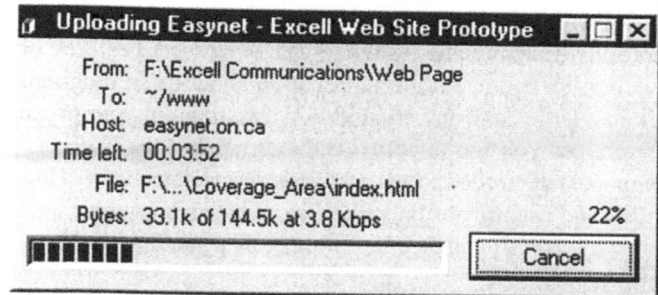

FIGURE 42   Uploading a web site to electronically "publish" it on the Web.

would not be able to respond to multiple simultaneous requests for web pages very efficiently. The reason is because operating systems originally meant for a single user do not have the kernel-level (see the last two paragraphs of the On-Line User Documentation for Operating Systems section) support for demanding enterprise computing environments such as the Internet, where dozens of people may be trying to access the computer at once. Thus, it is generally best to *create and prototype* a web site using a personal computer such as a Macintosh or Windows PC, perhaps with web design software, such as Adobe PageMill to allow you to work in a visual way, and using HTML and Java code to implement any special features you need. Then, when the page and its links have been tested and validated, it can be installed on a web server for the purposes of serving web pages to others on the World Wide Web.

Internet Service Providers and Related Issues

Running a proprietary web server involves extensive technical (system administration, network, and software maintenance, security, etc.) and administrative (managing users, helping new people, etc.) overhead. This is usually only practical or cost-effective when an organization reaches a size where the economics justify having an independent server.

Most people and small companies avoid this labor-intensive option and choose to have someone else provide them with Web access. An Internet Service Provider (ISP) is a company that maintains a web server and provides disk space for storing your web site, for individuals or businesses. An ISP may also provide dial-up, Integrated Services Digital Network (ISDN), or leased line connections for people to request web pages from the Internet, as well as take advantage of other network services such as electronic mail or Internet chat sessions. In addition, an ISP can assist with registering a unique *domain name* for an individual or organization on the Internet. Then, when a person types in a location such as www.*your_domain*.com, they will be taken immediately to your web site, which will still reside on your ISP's machine but will appear to be a unique and separate site to any Internet visitor.

The ISPs may also provide customized versions of popular Internet software. Most ISPs include a browser when a person subscribes to their service, or tell you where on the Web to download a browser, which is usually the home page of the company that created the browser, or the site of the ISP. Many browsers are available, including Netscape Navigator, Microsoft Internet Explorer, and the National Center for Supercomputing Applications (NCSA) Mosaic. There are even browsers written entirely in Java, such as HotJava from Sun Microsystems. Refer to the Advanced Features of World Wide Web Browsers section for more specific information about these programs.

If you work in a large company or educational institution, your organization probably provides the services you use to access the Internet and the Web, as they have the resources and support staff needed to maintain Internet connectivity. However, as costs continue to decrease and usability of Internet-related software improves, more companies and smaller organizations will embrace the Internet as a fundamental part of their communications infrastructure.

FUTURE INFORMATION TECHNOLOGIES AND THEIR IMPACT ON COMMUNICATIONS AND COMMERCE

Computer technology changes faster than anything else people use on a daily basis. Hence, those people serving as the intermediary between the technical community and the end user must try to anticipate and absorb new changes in the way information technology is created and used. Such proactive measures will ensure that technical writers, information designers, and software ergonomics people will be able to help shape new emerging technologies so that nonspecialists will be able to use it to improve their productivity and, possibly, their creativity.

The key to comprehending this high rate of change is to recognize that new advancements are not necessarily revolutions without precedent, but more often are incremental improvements on what already exists and is being used. Most often, leading-edge technologies are created and used by "early adopters" such as scientific or engineering groups, in response to a *sustained need*. The ARPA net arose out of the need to link government, military, and university research centers. The World Wide Web originated at CERN, the Swiss particle physics institute, and the first Web browser was Mosaic, created at the National Center for Supercomputing Applications. X-Windows was created at MIT to have a platform-independent windowing system, and UNIX was created at AT&T Bell Labs to facilitate software development. All of these aforementioned technologies are the result of the efforts of early adopters, willing to make the intellectual effort and financial commitment to create them.

Advancements such as these emerge and are absorbed into mainstream computing, which rearchitect them and define industry standards around them. Standardization makes these powerful systems easier to use, less complex, and more in line with the needs of the everyday user. Meanwhile, back in the technical circles, new ideas are always being explored, and the cycle begins again. Languages such as the Java programming language created by Sun Microsystems and VRML for creating three-dimensional scenes are just the beginning. DHTML and XML, which are a response to the limitations of HTML (see the Standards for Platform-Independent Document Creation section) will continue to transform the process of creating user documentation. Faster hardware will permit richer content, and faster communications will allow newer and qualitatively different methods of network access.

The important things to remember are as follows:

- Most new technologies can be seen to *evolve* from existing technologies, such as C++ from C, and the Internet from the ARPA net.

- An advance in one area or the creation of a new paradigm can invigorate an entirely different area.
- Understanding a range of earlier technologies creates the context necessary to understand the latest happenings and to predict future trends at any level of analysis.
- What is often perceived as a radical new technology is often a blending of two or more existing ones, which has the potential to create a *qualitative advance* in functionality, creating a new way of doing tasks, just as the graphical user interface, windows, and icons allowed new ways of computing to flourish.
- Any technology, in order to achieve long-term viability, requires standardization, acceptance by technical users, and then mass-market acceptance before it can make a societywide impact.

Many of the topics explored in this article have followed this demographic, and future methods of computing will likely do so as well. Greater integration (61) of graphical user interfaces, the Internet, and Java, which will inevitably change personal computing and the imperatives for computer documentation. In summary, new opportunities for improving computer documentation will get both its form and content from the computer technologies it seeks to clarify and on which it will reside.

REFERENCES

1. *IBM Personal Computer XT Technical Reference*, IBM Corporation, 1983.
2. R. Brenner, *IBM PC Troubleshooting & Repair Guide*, Howard W. Sams & Company, 1986.
3. "Intel Announces New Pentium OverDrive Processors," Workgroup Strategic Services Research Brief. http://www.wgss.com/briefs/overdrive.htm
4. "Intel Corporation Product Index," Intel Corporation. http://www.intel.com/intel/product/index.htm
5. "AlphaPowered: Faster than Fast." http://www.alphapowered.com/alphapowered.htm
6. "Products," FutureShop. http://www.futureshop.com/Futureshop/products/intel4.htm
7. "The 6502 Alternative—Commodore Pet." http://www.cyberstreet.com/hcs/museum/pet.htm
8. "Further Bookmarks." http://pooh.physik.uni-bremen.de/~joeken/bkzl.html
9. "Welcome to Embedded."/com" http://www.embedded.com/
10. "Mobile Pentium Processors," Intel Corporation. http://www.intel.com/mobile/mmx/index.htm
11. "Motorola DSP56301 DSP processor," BORES Signal processing. http://www.bores.com/dsp56301.htm
12. "Welcome to AMD," Advanced Micro Devices. http://www.amd.com
13. R. C. Holland, *Microprocessors and Their Operating Systems*, Pergamon Press, Elmsford, NY, 1989, pp. 56–57.
14. "Pentium® Processors—Manuals," Intel Corporation. http://www.intel.com/design/pentium/manuals/
15. *GA-586ATV User's Manual*, Gigabyte Technology, 1996.
16. "PCI chipsets list." http://warp.eecs.berkeley.edu/os2/workbench/pci_chips.html
17. "4. PCI Bus Architecture." http://2link2.com/pcibus.htm
18. "We Plugged, but They Didn't All Play," *Byte Mag.* http://www.byte.com/art/9510/sec4/art6.htm
19. "PCI Specifications," PCI Special Interest Group. http://www.pcisig.com/specs.html
20. "PCI Local Bus Highlights," PCI Special Interest Group. http://www.pcisig.com/overview.html

21. *PCMCIA System Architecture 16-Bit PC Cards*, 2nd ed., Softpro Books. http://www.viamall. com/softpro/0-201-40991-7.html
22. "Bus Systems and Interfaces, v2.5." http://www.ens.uabc.mx/cursos/bussys/astart.htm
23. "ATI Technologies, Inc. Products," ATI Technologies Corporation. http://www.atitech.ca/ products/
24. "Sound Blaster Family," Creative Labs, Inc. http://www.creativelabs.com/sound/
25. "Hayes ACCURA 56K Speakerphone Modems," Hayes Microcomputer Products, Inc. http:// www.hayes.com/products/accura/56k/voice/index.htm
26. "Why Would You Want to go SCSI?" Adaptec, Inc. http://www.adaptec.com/products/ promos/scsint/why.html
27. "ASPI Frequently Asked Questions," Adaptec, Inc. http://www.adaptec.com/support/faqs/ aspi.html
28. Video Electronics Standards Association. http://www.vesa.org/
29. "Red Hat Linux Home Page." Red Hat Software, Inc. http://www.redhat.com
30. J. Robinson, "X Windows Introduction." jlrobins@uncc.edu. http://www.cs.uncc.edu/~jlrobins/X.html
31. "Microsoft Windows 95," Microsoft Corporation. http://www.microsoft.com/windows95/
32. "Power Macintosh," Apple Computer, Inc. http://www.apple.com/powermac/
33. D. Lawson, "Macintosh as a Philosophy." http://weber.u.washington.edu/~dal/macosdef.html
34. M. Welsh, *The Linux Bible*, *The GNU Testament*, 2nd ed., Yggadrasil Computing, 1994.
35. *Unix System V User Reference Manual*, AT&T Bell Laboratories, 1984.
36. Gibson Research Corporation. http://www.spinrite.com
37. "Lynx." http://lynx.browser.org/
38. "Alta-Vista: Main Page," Digital Equipment Corporation. http://altavista.digital.com
39. *RIO Designer User's Guide*, Lucent Technologies Software Solutions Group, 1996.
40. B. Kaplan, "Image File Formats List." brian@bloomington.in.us http://www.octobernet.com/ ~brian/graphics/image.formats.html
41. "Kodak Photo CD," Eastman Kodak. http://www.kodak.com/cgi-bin/webCatalog.pl?section =&cc=US&lc=en&product=KODAK+Photo+CD
42. "KODAK Digital Science Color Management Solutions," Eastman Kodak. http://www. kodak.com/cgi-bin/webCatalog.pl?product=KODAK+Digital+Science+Color+Management+ Solutions
43. "Welcome to Truevision," Truevision, Inc. http://www.truevision.com
44. "TGA—Truevision (Targa) File Format" http://www.faqs.org/faqs/graphics/fileformats-faq/ part3/section-146.html
45. B. Kaplan, "Graphics Formats." brian@bloomington.in.us http://www.octobernet.com/ ~brian/graphics/graphics.html
46. "SGML—Your Multi-Platform Publishing and Information Management Solution," Soft-Quad International. http://www.sq.com/htmlsgml/
47. "Presenting Adobe Acrobat," Adobe Systems, Inc. http://www.adobe.com/prodindex/acrobat/
48. "VRML Consortium." http://www.vrml.org
49. "Weaving a Better Web," *Byte Mag.*, 58–68 (March 1998).
50. "Adobe Illustrator Product Information," Adobe Systems, Inc. http://www.adobe.com/ prodindex/illustrator/prodinfo.html#features
51. "Adobe PageMaker Details," Adobe Systems, Inc. http://www.adobe.com/prodinex/ pagemaker/details.html
52. "Adobe PhotoShop Details," Adobe Systems, Inc. http://www.adobe.com/prodindex/ photoshop/details.html
53. "Microcode Engineering Online Service Center," MicroCode Engineering Inc. http://www. microcode.com
54. "Index of /popmech/sci/tech/," The Hearst Corporation. http://popularmechanics.com/popmech/ sci/tech/

55. "SEDS Galaxy Simulator," Students for the Exploration and Development of Space (Canada). http://www.seds.ca/gsim/gsim.htm

56. K. Werbach, "The Bare Bones Guide to HTML." kevin@werbach.com http://www.werbach.com/barebones/barebone.html

57. K. Werbach, "WWW Help Page." kevin@werbach.com. http://werbach.com/web/wwwhelp.html

58. "JAVA White Papers," Sun Microsystems Inc. http://java.sun.com/docs/white/

59. "Fractals Q & A." http://www.iterated.com/science/fractalqna.htm. Iterated Systems, Inc. ftp://ftp.iterated.com/products/FractalTransform.pdf

60. G. Jankovic and L. Black, "Engineering a Web Site." *IEEE Spectrum*, 62–69 (November 1996.

61. T. R. Halfhill, "Hello, NUI: Network-Centric User Interfaces Are Coming to PCs as Well as to Network Computers," *Byte Mag.*, 60–72 (July 1997); An in-depth exploration of the different forms network user interfaces can take when used with different types of computing systems.

SANJAY SINGH

VIRTUAL REALITY SOFTWARE AND TECHNOLOGY

FOUNDATIONS OF VIRTUAL REALITY

Virtual reality (VR) refers to a technology capable of shifting a subject into a different environment without physically moving him/her. To this end, the inputs into the subject's sensory organs are manipulated in such a way that the perceived environment is associated with the desired virtual environment (VE) and not with the physical one. The manipulation process is controlled by a computer model based on the physical description of the VE. Consequently, the technology is able to create almost arbitrarily perceived environments.

Immersion is a key issue in VR systems, as it is central to the paradigm where the user becomes part of the simulated world, rather than the simulated world being a feature of the user's own world. The first "immersive VR systems" have been the flight simulators where the immersion is achieved by a subtle mixture of real hardware and virtual imagery.

The term "immersion" is a description of a technology, which can be achieved to varying degrees. A necessary condition is Ellis' notion (1) of a VE, maintained in at least one sensory modality (typically the visual). For example, a head-mounted display with a wide field-of-view and at least head tracking would be essential. The degree of immersion is increased by adding additional and consistent modalities, greater degree of body tracking, richer body representations, decreased lag between body movements, resulting changes in sensory data, and so on.

Astheimer et al. (2) define immersion as the feeling of a VR user that his VE is real. Analogous to Turing's definition of artificial intelligence: if the user cannot tell which reality is "real" and which one is "virtual," then the computer-generated one is immersive. A high degree of immersion is equivalent to a realistic VE. Several conditions must be met to achieve this: The most important seems to be small feedback lag; the second is a wide field-of-view. Displays should also be stereoscopic, which is usually the case with head-mounted displays. A low display resolution seems to be less significant.

According to Slater and Usoh (3), an immersive VE (IVE) may lead to a sense of presence for the participant taking part in such an experience. *Presence* is the psychological sense of "being there" in the environment based on the technologically founded immersive base. However, any given immersive system does not necessarily always lead to presence for all people. Presence is so fundamental to our everyday existence that it is difficult to define. It does make sense to consider the negation of a sense of presence as the loss of locality, such that "no presence" is equated with no locality, the sense of where self is as being always in flux.

VR DEVICES

Magnetic Position/Orientation Trackers

The primary method of recording positions and orientations is to use magnetic tracking devices such as those manufactured by Polhemus and Ascension Technology. Essentially, a source generates a low-frequency magnetic field detected by a sensor. For example, Polhemus STAR*TRAK® is a long-range-motion capture system that can operate in a wireless mode (totally free of interface cables) or with a thin interconnect cable. The system can operate in any studio space regardless of metal in the environment, directly on the studio floor. ULTRATRAK® PRO is a full-body-motion capture system; it is also the first turnkey solution developed specifically for performance animation. ULTRATRAK PRO can track a virtually unlimited number of receivers over a large area. FASTRAK, an award-winning system, is a highly accurate, low-latency three-dimensional (3D) motion tracking and digitizing system. FASTRAK can track up to four receivers at ranges of up to 10 ft. Multiple FASTRAKs can be multiplexed for applications that require more than four receivers.

Ascension Technology manufactures several different types of trackers including the MotionStar® Turn-key, the MotionStar Wireless®, and the Flock of Birds®. MotionStar Wireless was the first magnetic tracker to shed its cables and set the performer free. Motion data for each performer is now transmitted through the air to a base station for remote processing. They have combined the MotionStar DC magnetic tracker with the best wireless technology to give real-time untethered motion capture. There is absolutely no performance compromise. It can twist, flip, and pirouette freely without losing data or getting tied up in knots.

MotionStar Turn-key is a motion-capture tracker for character animation. It captures the motions of up to 120 receivers simultaneously over a long range without metallic distortion. Each receiver is tracked up to 144 times per second to capture and filter fast complex motions with instantaneous feedback. It utilizes a single rack-mounted chassis for each set of 20 receivers.

Flock of Birds® is a modular tracker with six degrees of freedom (6 DOF) for simultaneously tracking the position and orientation of one or more receivers (targets) over a specified range of ±4 ft. Motions are tracked to accuracies of 0.5° and 0.07 in. at rates of up to 144 Hz. The Flock employs pulsed DC magnetic fields to minimize the distorting effects of nearby metals. As a result simultaneous tracking, fast update rates and minimal lag occur even when multiple targets are tracked. It is designed for head and hand tracking in VR games, simulations, animations, and visualizations.

DataGloves

Hand-measurement devices must sense both the flexing angles of the fingers and the position and orientation of the wrist in real time. The first commercial hand-measurement device was the DataGlove® from VPL Research. The DataGlove (Fig. 1) consists of a lightweight nylon glove with optical sensors mounted along the fingers.

In its basic configuration, the sensors measure the bending angles of the joints of the thumb and the lower and middle knuckles of the others fingers, and it can be extended to measure abduction angles between the fingers. Each sensor is a short length of fiber-optic cable with a light-emitting diode (LED) at one end and a phototransistor at the other end. When the cable is flexed, some of the LED's light is lost, so less light is received by the phototransistor. Attached to the back is a Polhemus sensor to measure

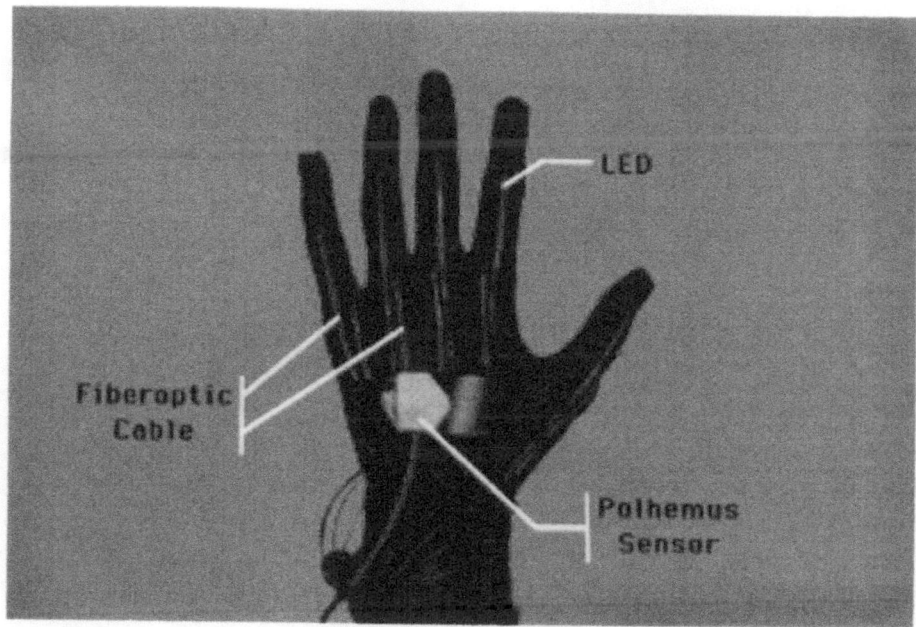

FIGURE 1   The DataGlove®.

the orientation and position of the gloved hand. This information along with the 10 flex angles for the knuckles are transmitted through a serial communication line to the host computer.

CyberGlove® of Virtual Technologies is a lightweight glove with flexible sensors which accurately and repeatably measure the position and movement of the fingers and wrist. The 18-sensor model features two bend sensors on each finger, four abduction sensors, plus sensors measuring thumb crossover, palm arch, wrist flexion, and wrist abduction. Many applications require measurement of the position and orientation of the forearm in space. To accomplish this, mounting provisions for Polhemus and Ascension 6 DOF tracking sensors are available for the glove wristband.

3D Mouse and SpaceBall®

Some people have tried to extend the concept of the mouse to three dimensions. Ware and Jessome (4) describe a six-dimensional (6D) mouse, called a bat, based on a Polhemus tracker.

The Logitech 3D mouse (Fig. 2) is based on a ultrasonic position reference array, which is a tripod consisting of three ultrasonic speakers set in a triangular position and emits ultrasonic sound signals from each of the three transmitters. These are used to track the receiver position, orientation, and movement. It provides proportional output in all six degrees of freedom: X, Y, Z, Pitch, Yaw, and Roll.

Spatial Systems designed a 6 DOF interaction input device called the SpaceBall®. This is essentially a "force"-sensitive device that relates the forces and torques applied to the ball mounted on top of the device. These force and torque vectors are sent to the computer in real time, where they are interpreted and may be composited into homoge-

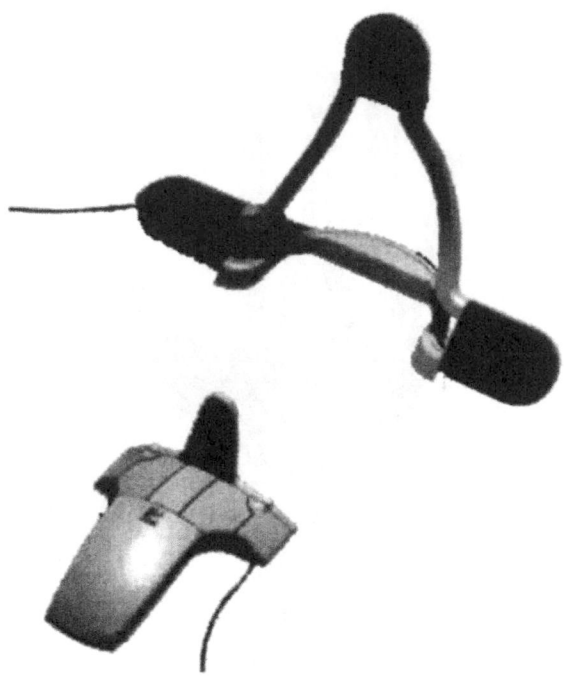

FIGURE 2   Logitech 3D mouse.

neous transformation matrices that can be applied to objects. Buttons mounted on a small panel facing the user control the sensitivity of the SpaceBall and may be adjusted according to the scale or distance of the object currently being manipulated. Other buttons are used to filter the incoming forces to restrict or stop translations or rotations of the object. Figure 3 shows a SpaceBall.

MIDI Keyboard
MIDI keyboards have been first designed for music input, but it provides a more general way of entering multidimensional data at the same time. In particular, it is a very good tool for controlling a large number of DOFs in a real-time animation system. A MIDI keyboard controller has 88 keys, any of which can be struck within a fraction of second. Each key transmits the velocity of the keystroke as well as pressure after the key is pressed.

Shutter Glasses
Binocular vision considerably enhances visual depth perception. Stereo displays like the StereoView® option on Silicon Graphics workstations may provide high-resolution stereo real-time interaction. StereoView consists of two items—specially designed eyewear and an infrared emitter. The shutters alternately open and close every 120th of a second in conjunction with the alternating display of the left and right eye view on the display, presenting each eye with an effective 60-Hz refresh. The infrared emitter transmits the

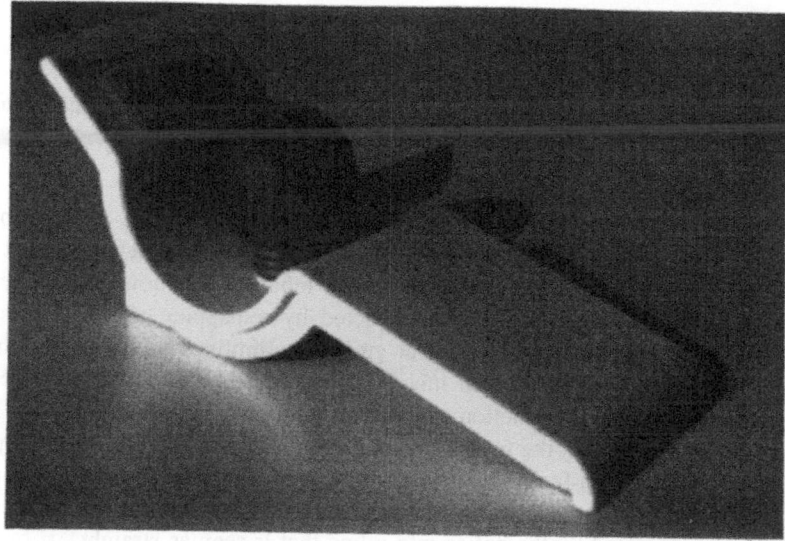

FIGURE 3   SpaceBall.

left/right signal from the workstation to the wireless eyewear so that the shuttering of the LCS is locked to the alternating left/right image display. As a result, each eye sees a unique image and the brain integrates these two views into a stereo picture.

Head-Mounted Displays

Most head-mounted display (HMD) systems present the rich 3D cues of head-motion parallax and stereopsis. They are designed to take advantage of human binocular vision capabilities and presents the general following characteristics:

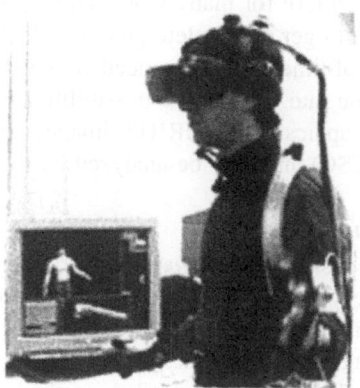

FIGURE 4   Head-mounted display.

- Headgear with two small LCD color screens, each optically channeled to one eye, for binocular vision
- Special optics in front of the screens, for a wide field-of-view
- A tracking system (Polhemus or Ascension) for precise location of the user's head in real time

Figure 4 shows the use of an HMD.

An optics model is required to specify the computation necessary to create orthostereoscopically correct images for an HMD and indicates the parameters of that system that need to be measured and incorporated into the model. To achieve orthostereoscopy, the nonlinear optical distortion must be corrected by remapping all the pixels on the screen with a predistortion function. Linear graphics primitives such as lines and polygons are written into a virtual screen image buffer, and then all the pixels are shifted according to the predistortion function and written to the screen image buffer for display. The predistortion function is the inverse of the field distortion function for the optics, so that the virtual image seen by the eye matches the image in the virtual screen buffer. A straight line in the virtual image buffer is predistorted into a curved line on the display screen, which is distorted by the optics into a line that is seen as straight.

CAVE

The CAVE™ is a multiperson, room-sized, high-resolution, 3D video and audio environment. It was developed at University of Illinois and is available commercially through Pyramid Systems Inc.

Currently, four projectors are used to throw full-color, computer-generated images onto three walls and the floor (the software could support a six-wall CAVE.) CAVE software synchronizes all the devices and calculates the correct perspective for each wall. In the current configuration, one Rack Onyx with two Infinite Reality Engine Pipes is used to create imagery for the four walls.

In the CAVE, all perspectives are calculated from the point of view of the user. A head tracker provides information about the user's position. Offset images are calculated for each eye. To experience the stereo effect, the user wears active stereo glasses which alternately block the left and right eye.

Real-Time Video Input

Input video is now a standard tool for many workstations. However, it generally takes a long time (several seconds) to get a complete picture, which makes the tool useless for real-time interaction. For real-time interaction needed in VR, images should be digitized at the traditional video frame rate. One of the possibilities for doing this is the SIRIUS® Video card from Silicon Graphics. With SIRIUS, images are digitized at a frequency of 25 Hz (PAL) or 30 Hz (NTSC) and may be analyzed by the VR program.

Real-Time Audio Input

Audio input may be also considered as a way of interacting. However, it generally implies a real-time speech recognition and natural language processing.

Speech synthesis facilities are of clear utility in a VR environment, especially for command feedback. Although speech synthesis software is available even at the personal computer level, some improvement is still needed, particularly in the quality of speech.

A considerable amount of work has also been done in the field of voice recognition systems, and now commercial systems are available. However, they are still expensive, especially systems which are person and accent independent. Moreover, systems require a training process to go through for each user. Also, the user must be careful to leave a noticeable gap between each word, which is unnatural.

Haptic Interfaces and Tactile Feedback for VE Applications

Recent developments of VE applications have enhanced the problem of user's interaction with virtual entities. Manipulation procedures consist in grasping objects and moving them among the fingers according to sequences of movements that provide a finite displacement of the grasped object with respect to the palm. Then, the realistic control of the above procedures in VE implies that the man–machine interface systems is capable of recording the movements of the human hand (finger movements and gross movements of the hand) and also of replicating, on the human hand, virtual forces and contact conditions occurring when contact is detected between the virtual hand and the virtual object. Therefore, hand-movement recording and contact-force replication represent the two main functionalities of the interface system. At present, although several examples of tracking systems and glovelike advanced interfaces are available for hand- and finger-movements recording, the design of force and tactile feedback systems still presents methodological as well as technological problems. If we consider, for example, the grasping of a cup, there are two main consequences:

- The VR user can reach out and grasp a cup but will not feel the sensation of touching the cup.
- There is nothing to prevent the grasp continuing right through the surface of the cup!

Providing a *tactile feedback* means to provide some feedback through the skin. This may be done in gloves by incorporating vibrating nodules under the surface of the glove. This is what is available in the CyberTouch® of Virtual Technologies. CyberTouch (Fig. 5) gives a tactile feedback by featuring small vibrotactile stimulators on each finger and the palm of the CyberGlove. Each stimulator can be individually programmed to vary the strength of touch sensation. The array of stimulators can generate simple sensations such as pulses or sustained vibration, and they can be used in combination to produce complex tactile feedback patterns. Software developers can design their own actuation profile to achieve the desired tactile sensation, including the perception of touching a solid object in a simulated virtual world. This is not a realistic simulation of touch, but it at least provides *some* indication of surface contact.

Exos has also incorporated a tactile feedback device (Touchmaster®) into their Dextrous Hand Master. It is based on a low-cost voice–coil oscillator. Another approach includes inflatable bubbles in the glove, materials that can change from liquid to solid state under electric charge and memory metals. The Teletact® Glove provides low-resolution tactile feedback through the use of 30 inflatable air pockets in the glove.

Providing a means to enforce physical constraints, simulating forces can occur in teleoperation environments. Some devices have been built to provide *force feedback*.

The Laparoscopic Impulse Engine is a 3-D human interface specifically designed for VR simulations of laparoscopic and endoscopic surgical procedures. It allows a user to wield actual surgical tools and manipulate them as if performing real surgical procedures. The device allows the computer to track the delicate motions of the virtual surgical

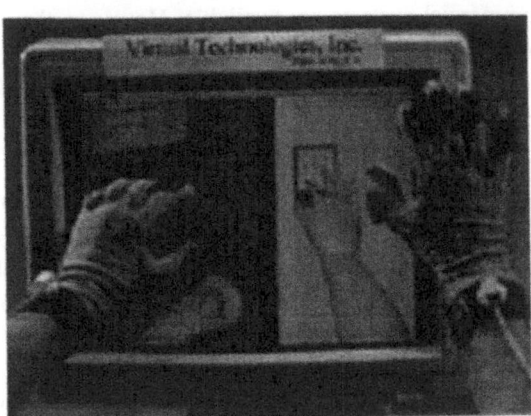

FIGURE 5   Use of CyberTouch.

instruments while also allowing the computer to command realistic virtual forces to the user's hand. The net result is a human–computer interface which can create VR simulations of medical procedures that not only look real but actually feel real!

The Impulse Engine 2000 is a force-feedback joystick which accurately tracks motion in two degrees of freedom and applies high-fidelity force-feedback sensations through the joystick handle. The Impulse Engine 2000 can realistically simulate the feel of surfaces, textures, springs, liquids, gravitational fields, bouncing balls, biological material, or any other physical sensation that can be represented mathematically. The Impulse Engine is a research-quality force-feedback interface with very low inertia, very low friction, and very high bandwidth.

The PHANToM® device's design allows the user to interact with the computer by inserting his or her finger into a thimble. For more sophisticated applications, multiple fingers may be used simultaneously or other devices such as a stylus or tool handle may be substituted for the thimble. The PHANToM device provides three degrees of freedom for force feedback and, optionally, three additional degrees of freedom for measurement.

Robotic and Magnetic Interface for VR Force Interactions made by Iowa State University is a haptic interface system that allows force interactions with computer-generated VR graphical displays. This system is based on the application of electromagnetic principles to couple the human hand with a robotic manipulator. Using this approach, the forces are transmitted between the robot exoskeleton and the human without using mechanical attachments to the robot.

The Freedom-7® by McGill University Center for Intelligent Machines has a work area sufficient to enable a user to manipulate a tool using wrist and finger motions. Primarily intended to support the simulation of a variety of basic surgical instruments, including, knives, forceps, scissors, and microscissors. The device incorporates a mechanical interface which enables the interchange of handles, for example, to emulate these four categories of instruments while providing the force feedback needed to simulate the interaction of an instrument with a tissue.

One of the extensions of the popular CyberGlove that is used to measure the position and movement of the fingers and wrist is a CyberGrasp® (Fig. 6). It is a haptic

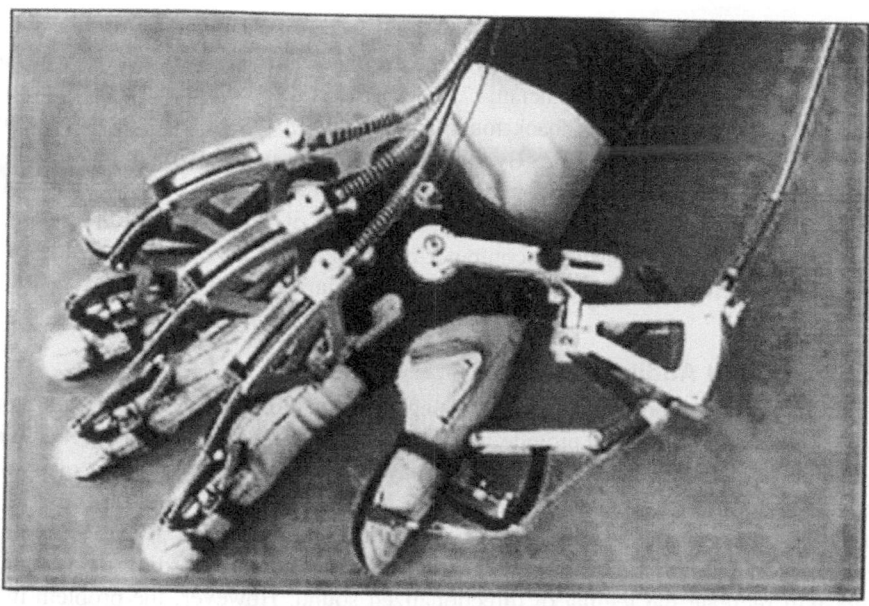

FIGURE 6 CyberGrasp.

feedback interface that enables one to actually "touch" computer-generated objects and experience force feedback via the human hand. The CyberGrasp is a lightweight, unencumbering force-reflecting exoskeleton that fits over a CyberGlove and adds resistive force feedback to each finger. With the CyberGrasp force-feedback system, users are able to explore the physical properties of computer-generated 3D objects they manipulate in a simulated "virtual world." The grasp forces are exerted via a network of tendons that are routed to the fingertips via an exoskeleton and can be programmed to prevent the user's fingers from penetrating or crushing a virtual object. The tendon sheaths are specifically designed for low compressibility and low friction. The actuators are high-quality DC motors located in a small enclosure on the desktop. There are five actuators, one for each finger. The device exerts grasp forces that are roughly perpendicular to the fingertips throughout the range of motion, and forces can be specified individually. The CyberGrasp system allows full range-of-motion of the hand and does not obstruct the wearer's movements. The device is fully adjustable and designed to fit a wide variety of hands.

A similar mechanical glove called Hand Force Feedback (HFF) was developed by Bergamasco (5) at PERCRO. He also developed a complete glove device, able to sensorize the 20 DOF of a human hand. The same laboratory developed the External Force Feedback (EFF) system, which is a design and realization of an arm exoskeleton. The arm exoskeleton is a mechanical structure wrapping up the whole arm of the user. The mechanical structure possesses 7 DOF corresponding to the joints of the human arm from shoulder to the wrist and allows natural mobility to the human arm. It allows for simulation of collisions against the objects of the VE as well as the weight of "heavy" virtual objects.

We should also mention the work of several other researchers. Robinett (6) describes how a force-feedback subsystem, the Argonne Remote Manipulator (ARM), has been introduced into the head-mounted display project at the University of North Carolina in Chapel Hill. The ARM provides force feedback through a handgrip with all 6 DOF in translation and rotation. Luciani (7) reports several force-feedback gestural transducers, including a 16-slice feedback touch and two thimbles, which is a specific morphology to manipulate flat objects. By sliding the fingers in the two rings, objects can be grasped, dragged, or compressed. Moreover, their reaction can be felt; for instance, their resistance to deformation or displacement. Minsky et al. (8) studied the theoretical problem of force feedback using a computer-controlled joystick with simulation of the dynamics of a spring–mass system, including its mechanical impedance.

Audiospace and Auditory Systems

The use of sound is reported to be a surprisingly powerful cue in VR. At the minimum, binaural sound can be used to provide additional feedback to the user for such activities as grasping objects and navigation. People may easily locate the direction of a sound source. In the horizontal plane, it is based the time between the sound arriving at one ear and the other. However, the location of sound direction is also a learned skill. We may place small microphones in each ear and make a stereo recording that, when replayed, will recreate the feeling of directionalized sound. However, the problem in VR is that we want the position of the sound source to be independent of the user's head movement! We would like to attach recorded, live, or computer-generated sound to objects in the VE.

There were several attempts to solve this problem. Foster at the NASA Ames VIEW Lab developed a device called the Convolvotron, which can process four independent point sound sources simultaneously, compensating for any head movement on the fly. Crystal River Engineering later developed the Maxitron, which can handle eight sound sources as well as simulating the acoustics including sound reflection of a moderately sized room. Focal Point produce a low-cost 3D audio card for PCs and Macintoshes.

The PSFC, or Pioneer Sound Field Control System, is a DSP-driven hemispherical 14-loudspeaker array, installed at the University of Aizu Multimedia Center. Collocated with a large-screen rear-projection stereographic display, the PSFC features real-time control of virtual-room characteristics and direction of two separate sound sources, smoothly steering them around a configurable soundscape. The PSFC controls an entire sound field, including sound direction, virtual distance, and simulated environment (reverb level, room size, and liveness) for each source.

We should also mention the work of Blauert (9) at Bochum University in Germany.

VR SYSTEMS

Architecture of a VR System

A VR application is very often composed of a group of processes communicating through interprocess communication (IPC). As in the Decoupled Simulation Model (10), each of the processes is continuously running, producing, and consuming asynchronous messages to perform its task. A central application process manages the model of the virtual world and simulates its evolution in response to events coming from the processes that are responsible for reading the input device sensors at specified frequencies. Sensory feedback to the user can be provided by several output devices. Visual feedback is provided by real-time rendering on graphics workstations, whereas audio feedback is provided by MIDI output and playback of prerecorded sounds.

The application process is, by far, the most complex component of the system. This process has to respond to asynchronous events by making the virtual world's model evolve from one coherent state to the next and by triggering appropriate visual and audio feedback. During interaction, the user is the source of a flow of information propagating from input device sensors to manipulated models. Multiple mediators can be interposed between sensors and models in order to transform the information accordingly to interaction metaphors.

Dynamics Model

In order to obtain animated and interactive behavior, the system has to update its state in response to changes initiated by sensors attached to asynchronous input devices such as timers or trackers. The application can be viewed as a network of interrelated objects whose behavior is specified by the actions taken in response to changes in the objects on which they depend.

In order to provide a maintenance mechanism that is both general enough to allow the specification of general dependencies between objects and efficient enough to be used in highly responsive interactive systems, the system's state and behavior may be modeled using different primitive elements:

- Active variables
- Hierarchical constraints
- Demons

Active variables are the primitive elements used to store the system state. An active variable maintains its value and keeps track of its state changes. Upon request, an active variable can also maintain the history of its past values. This model makes it possible to elegantly express time-dependent behavior by creating constraints or demons that refer to past values of active variables.

Multiway relations between active variables are generally specified through *hierarchical constraints*, as introduced in ThingLab II (11). To support local propagation, constraint objects are composed of a declarative part, defining the type of relation that has to be maintained and the set of constrained variables, and an imperative part, the list of possible methods that could be selected by the constraint solver to maintain the constraint.

Demons are objects which permit the definition of sequencing between system states. Demons register themselves with a set of active variables and are activated each time their value changes. The action taken by a demon can be a procedure of any complexity that may create new objects, perform input/output operations, change active variables' values, manipulate the constraint graph, or activate and deactivate other demons. The execution of a demon's action is sequential and each manipulation of the constraint graph advances the global system time.

Dynamics and Interaction

Animated and interactive behavior can be thought of together as the fundamental problem of dynamic graphics: How to modify graphical output in response to input? Time-varying behavior is obtained by mapping dynamically changing values, representing data coming from input devices or animation scripts, to variables in the virtual world's model. The definition of this mapping is crucial for interactive applications because it defines the way users communicate with the computer. Ideally, interactive 3D systems should allow users to interact with synthetic worlds in the same way they interact with the real world, thus making the interaction task more natural and reducing training.

Mapping Sensor Measurements to Actions

In most typical interactive applications, users spend a large part of their time entering information, and several types of input devices, such as 3D mouses and DataGloves, are used to let them interact with the virtual world. Using these devices, the user has to provide a complex flow of information at high speed, and a mapping has to be devised between the information coming from the sensors attached to the devices and the actions in the virtual world. Most of the time, this mapping is hard coded and directly dependent on the physical structure of the device used (e.g., by associating different actions to the various mouse buttons). This kind of behavior may be obtained by attaching constraints directly relating the sensors' active variables to variables in the dynamic model. The beginning of the direct manipulation of a model is determined by the activation of a constraint between input sensor variables and some of the active variables in the interface of the model. While the interaction constraint remains active, the user can manipulate the model through the provided metaphor. The deactivation of the interaction constraint terminates the direct manipulation.

Such a direct mapping between the device and the dynamic model is straightforward for choosing tasks where the relations between the user's motions and the desired effect in the virtual world is mostly physical, as in the example of grabbing an object and moving it, but it needs to be very carefully thought out for tasks where user's motions are intended to carry out a meaning. Adaptive pattern recognition can be used to overcome these problems, by letting the definition of the mapping between sensor measurements and actions in the virtual world be more complex and, therefore, increasing the expressive power of the devices. Furthermore, the possibility of specifying this mapping through examples makes applications easier to adapt to the preferences of new users and thus simpler to use.

Hand-Gesture Recognition

Whole-hand input is emerging as a research topic in itself, and some type of posture or gesture recognition is now being used in many VR systems (12). The gesture-recognition system has to classify movements and configurations of the hand in different categories on the basis of previously seen examples. Once the gesture is classified, parametric information for that gesture can be extracted from the way it was performed, and an action in the virtual world can be executed. In this way, with a single gesture both categorical and parametric information can be provided at the same time in a natural way. A visual and an audio feedback on the type of gesture recognized and on the actions executed are usually provided in applications to help the user understand the system's behavior.

Gesture recognition is generally subdivided into two main portions: posture recognition, and path recognition. The posture recognition subsystem is continuously running and is responsible for classifying the user's finger configurations. Once a configuration has been recognized, the hand data are accumulated as long as the hand remains in the same posture. The history mechanism of active variables is used to automatically perform this accumulation. Data are then passed to the path recognition subsystem to classify the path. A gesture is, therefore, defined as the path of the hand while the hand fingers remain stable in a recognized posture. The type of gesture chosen is compatible with Buxton's suggestion (13) of using physical tension as a natural criterion for segmenting primitive interactions: The user, starting from a relaxed state, begins a primitive interaction by tensing some muscles and raising its state of attentiveness, performs the interaction, and then relaxes the muscles. In our case, the beginning of an interaction is indicated by positioning the hand in a recognizable posture, and the end of the interaction by relaxing the fingers. One of the main advantages of this technique is that, because postures are static, the learning process can be done interactively by putting the hand in the right position and indicating when to sample to the computer. Once postures are learned, the paths can be similarly learned in an interactive way, using the posture classifier to correctly segment the input when generating the examples. Many types of classifiers could be used for the learning and recognition task. For example, in VB2 (14), feature vectors are extracted from the raw sensor data, and multilayer perceptron networks (15) are used to approximate the functions that map these vectors to their respective classes.

Body-Gesture Recognition

Most gesture-recognition systems are limited to a specific set of body parts, like hands, arms, or facial expressions. However, when projecting a real participant into a virtual world to interact with the synthetic inhabitants, it would be more convenient and intuitive to use body-oriented actions.

To date, basically two techniques exist to capture the human body posture in real time. One uses video cameras which deliver either conventional or infrared pictures. This technique has been successfully used in the ALIVE system (16) to capture the user's image. The image is used for both the projection of the participant into the VE and the extraction of Cartesian information of various body parts. If this system benefits from being wireless, it suffers from visibility constraints relative to the camera and a strong performance dependence on the vision module for information extraction.

The second technique is based on magnetic sensors attached to the user. Most common are sensors measuring the intensity of a magnetic field generated at a reference point. The motion of the different segments is tracked using magnetic sensors (Fig. 7). These sensors return raw data (e.g., positions and orientations) expressed in a single-frame system. In order to match the virtual human hierarchy, we need to compute the global position of the hierarchy and the angle values of the joints attached to the tracked segments. For this purpose, an anatomical converter (17) derives the angle values from the sensor's information to set joints of a fixed topology hierarchy (the virtual human skeleton). The converter has three important stages: skeleton calibration, sensor calibration, and real-time conversion.

Emering et al. (18) describe a hierarchical model of human actions based on fine-grained primitives. An associated recognition algorithm allows on-the-fly identification of simultaneous actions. By analyzing human actions, it is possible to detect three important characteristics which inform us about the specification granularity needed for the action model. First, an action does not necessarily involve the whole body but may be performed with a set of body parts only. Second, multiple actions can be performed in parallel if they use nonintersecting sets of body parts. Finally, a human action can already be identified by observing strategic body locations rather than skeleton joint movements. Based on these observations, a top-down refinement paradigm appears to be appropriate

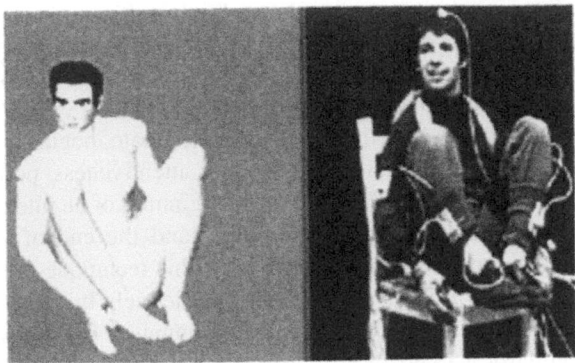

FIGURE 7   Tracking motion.

for the action model. The specification grain varies from coarse at the top level to very specialized at the lowest level. The number of levels in the hierarchy is related to the feature information used. At the lowest level, the authors use the skeleton degrees of freedom (DOF) which are the most precise feature information available (30–100 for a typical human model). At higher levels, they take advantage of strategic body locations like the center of mass and end effectors (i.e., hands, feet, the head, and the spine root).

Virtual Tools

Virtual tools are first-class objects, like the widgets of UGA (19), which encapsulate a visual appearance and a behavior to control and display information about application objects. The visual appearance of a tool must provide information about its behavior and offer visual semantic feedback to the user during manipulation. The user declares the desire to manipulate an object with a tool by binding a model to a tool. When a tool is bound, the user can manipulate the model using it, until he decides to unbind it. When binding a model to a tool, the tool must first determine if it can manipulate the given model, identifying on the model the set of public active variables requested to activate its binding constraints. Once the binding constraints are activated, the model is ready to be manipulated. The binding constraints being generally bidirectional, the tool is always forced to reflect the information present in the model even if it is modified by other objects. Unbinding a model from a tool detaches it from the object it controls. The effect is to deactivate the binding constraints in order to suppress dependencies between the tool's and the model's active variables. Once the model is unbound, further manipulation of the tool will have no effect on the model. Figure 8 shows an example of the use of a SCALE tool.

A Few VR Toolkits

WorldToolkit®

WorldToolkit®, developed by Sense8 Corporation, provides a complete VE development environment to the application developer. The structure of WorldToolKit is in an object-oriented manner. The WorldToolKit API currently consists of over 1000 high-level C

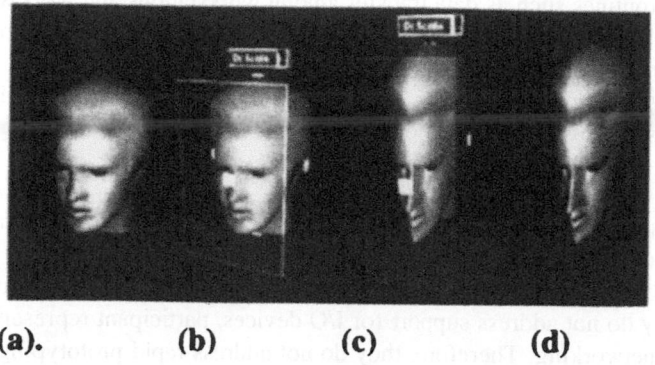

(a).   **(b)**   **(c)**   **(d)**

FIGURE 8   (a) Model before manipulation; (b) a SCALE tool is made visible and bound to the model; (c) the model is manipulated via the SCALE tool; (d) the SCALE tool is unbound and made invisible.

functions and is organized into over 20 classes, including the universe (which manages the simulation and contains all objects), geometrical objects, viewpoints, sensors, paths, lights, and others. Functions exist for device instancing, display setup, collision detection, loading object geometry from file, dynamic geometry creation, specifying object behavior, and controlling rendering.

WorldToolkit uses the single-loop simulation model, which sequentially reads sensors, updates the world model, and generates the images. Geometric objects are the basic elements of a universe. They can be organized in a hierarchical fashion and interact with each other. They may be stationary objects or exhibit dynamic behavior. WorldToolKit also provides a "level of detail" process which corresponds to a method of creating less complex objects from the detailed object.

Each universe is a separate entity and can have different rules or dynamic behavior imposed on its objects. Moving between different universes in WorldToolKit is achieved by portals, which are assigned to specific polygons. When the user's viewpoint crosses the designated polygon, the adjacent universe is entered. The idea of a portal is like walking through a door into another room. With this approach, it is possible to create several smaller universes together to make one large VE.

MR Toolkit

The MR (Minimal Reality) Toolkit was developed by researchers at the University of Alberta (20). The MR Toolkit is in the form of a subroutine library that supports the development of VR applications. The toolkit supports various tracking devices, distribution of the user interface and data to multiple workstations, real-time performance interaction, and analysis tools.

The MR Toolkit is comprised of three levels of software. At the lowest level is a set of device-dependent *packages*. Each package consists of a client–server software pair. The server is a process that continuously samples the input device and performs further processing, such as filtering; whereas the client is a set of library routines that interface with the server. The second, middle, layer consists of functions that convert the "raw" data from the devices to the format more convenient for the user interface programmer.

Additionally, routines such as data transfer among workstations and work space mapping reside in this layer. The top layer consists of high-level functions that are used for the average VE interface. For example, a single function to initialize all the devices exists in this layer. Additionally, this layer contains routines to handle synchronization of data and operations among the workstations.

Other Three-Dimensional Toolkits

Other toolkits, such as IRIS Performer from Silicon Graphics Inc., Java3D, OpenGL Optimizer, and so forth also support the development of VR applications; however, they are low-level libraries for manipulation of the environment, viewpoints, and display parameters. They do not address support for I/O devices, participant representation, motion systems, and networking. Therefore, they do not address rapid prototyping of networked virtual environments applications. Consequently, we regard these toolkits as instruments to develop VEs, rather than architectures.

VIRTUAL HUMANS IN VIRTUAL ENVIRONMENTS

The participant should animate his virtual human representation in real time; however, the human control is not straightforward: The complexity of virtual human representation needs a large number of degrees of freedom to be tracked. In addition, interaction with the environment increases this difficulty even more. Therefore, the human control should use higher-level mechanisms to be able to animate the representation with maximal facility and minimal input. We can divide the virtual humans according to the methods to control them:

- Directly controlled virtual humans
- User-guided virtual humans
- Autonomous virtual humans
- Interactive perceptive actors

Directly Controlled Virtual Humans

A complete representation of the participant's virtual body should have the same movements as the real participant body for more immersive interaction. This can be best achieved by using a large number of sensors to track every degree of freedom in the real body. Molet et al. (17) discuss that a minimum of 14 sensors are required to manage a biomechanically correct posture, and Semwal et al. (21) present a closed-form algorithm to approximate the body using up to 10 sensors. However, many of the current VE systems use head and hand tracking. Therefore, the limited tracking information should be connected with human model information and different motion generators in order to "extrapolate" the joints of the body which are not tracked. This is more than a simple inverse kinematics problem, because there are generally multiple solutions for the joint angles to reach to the same position, and the most realistic posture should be selected. In addition, the joint constraints should be considered for setting the joint angles.

Guided Virtual Humans

Guided virtual humans are those which are driven by the user but which do not correspond directly to the user motion. They are based on the concept of a real-time direct metaphor (22), a method consisting of recording input data from a VR device in real time, allowing us to produce effects of different natures but corresponding to the input data. There is no analysis of the real meaning of the input data. The participant uses the input devices to update the transformation of the eye position of the virtual human. This local control is used by computing the incremental change in the eye position and estimating the rotation and velocity of the body center. The walking motor uses the instantaneous velocity of motion to compute the walking cycle length and time, by which it computes the joint angles of the whole body. The sensor information or walking can be obtained from various types of input devices, such as a special gesture with the Data-Glove or the SpaceBall, as well as other input methods.

Autonomous Virtual Humans

Autonomous actors are able to have a behavior, which means they must have a manner of conducting themselves. The virtual human is assumed to have an internal state that is built by its goals and sensor information from the environment, and the participant modifies this state by defining high-level motivations and state changes. Typically, the actor should perceive the objects and the other actors in the environment through virtual sensors (23): visual, tactile, and auditory sensors. Based on the perceived information, the actor's behavioral mechanism will determine the actions he will perform. An actor may simply evolve in his environment or he may interact with this environment or even communicate with other actors. In this latter case, we will consider the actor as a interactive perceptive actor.

The concept of virtual vision was first introduced by Renault et al. (24) as a main information channel between the environment and the virtual actor. The synthetic actor perceives his environment from a small window in which the environment is rendered from his point of view. As he can access z-buffer values of the pixels, the color of the pixels, and his own position, he can locate visible objects in his 3D environment. To recreate the virtual audition (25), it requires a model of a sound environment in which the virtual human can directly access the positional and semantic sound source information of an audible sound event. For virtual tactile sensors, it may be (26) based on spherical multisensors attached to the articulated figure. A sensor is activated for any collision with other objects. These sensors have been integrated in a general methodology for automatic grasping.

Interactive Perceptive Actors

We define an interactive perceptive synthetic actor (27) as an actor aware of other actors and real people. Such an actor is also assumed to be autonomous, of course. Moreover, he/she is able to communicate interactively with the other actors whatever their type and the real people. For example, Emering et al. describe how a directly controlled virtual human performs fight gestures recognized by a autonomous virtual opponent (18), as shown in Figure 9. The latter responds by playing back a prerecorded keyframe sequence.

Facial Communication in Virtual Environments

For the representation of facial expressions in networked VEs, four methods are possible: video-texturing of the face, model-based coding of facial expressions, lip-movement synthesis from speech, and predefined expressions or animations.

FIGURE 9   Fight between a participant and an interactive perceptive actor.

Video-texturing of the Face

In this approach, the video sequence of the user's face is continuously texture mapped on the face of the virtual human. The user must be in front of the camera, in such a position that the camera captures his head and shoulders, possibly together with the rest of the body. A simple and fast image analysis algorithm is used to find the bounding box of the user's face within the image. The algorithm requires that the head and shoulder view be provided and that the background is static (although not necessarily uniform). Thus, the algorithm primarily consists of comparing each image with the original image of the background. Because the background is static, any change in the image is caused by the presence of the user, so it is fairly easy to detect his/her position. This allows the user a reasonably free movement in front of the camera without the facial image being lost.

Model-Based Coding of Facial Expressions

Instead of transmitting whole facial images as in the previous approach, the images are analyzed and a set of parameters describing the facial expression is extracted. As in the previous approach, the user has to be in front of the camera that digitizes the video images of head-and-shoulders type. Accurate recognition and analysis of facial expressions from the video sequence require detailed measurements of facial features. Recognition of the facial features may be primarily based on color sample identification and edge detection (28). Based on the characteristics of the human face, variations of these methods are used in order to find the optimal adaptation for the particular case of each facial feature. Figure 10 illustrates this method with a sequence of original images of the user (with overlaid recognition indicators) and the corresponding images of the synthesized face.

Lip-Movement Synthesis from Speech

It might not always be practical for the user to be in front of the camera (e.g., if he does not have one or if he wants to use an HMD). Lavagetto (29) shows that it is possible

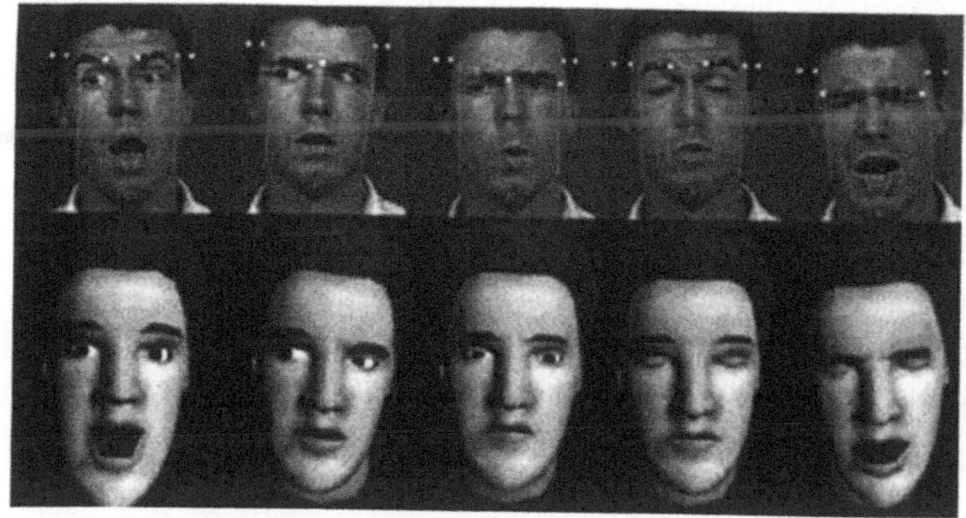

FIGURE 10   Model-based coding of the face.

to extract visual parameters of the lip movement by analyzing the audio signal of the speech.

Predefined Expressions or Animations

In this approach, the user can simply choose between a set of predefined facial expressions or movements (animations). The choice can be done from the keyboard through a set of "smileys" similar to the ones used in e-mail messages.

NETWORKED VIRTUAL ENVIRONMENTS

Introduction

Networking coupled with highly interactive technology of virtual worlds will dominate the world of computers and information technology. It will not be enough to produce slick single-users, stand-alone virtual worlds. Networked VE (NVE) systems will have to connect people, systems, information streams, and technologies with one another. The information that is currently shared through file systems or through other "static" media will have to be exchanged through the network. This information has to reside "in the net," where it is easy to get. Developing VEs that support collaboration among a group of users is a complex and time-consuming task. In order to develop such VEs, the developer has to be proficient in network programming, object management, graphics programming, device handling, and user interface design. Even after gaining expertise in such diverse specializations, developing network-based VEs takes a long time because network-based programs are inherently more difficult to program and debug than stand-alone programs.

Providing a behavioral realism is a significant requirement for systems that are based on human collaboration, such as Computer Supported Cooperative Work (CSCW) systems. Networked CSCW systems also require that the shared environment should provide a comfortable interface for gestural communication, support awareness of other users in the environment, provide mechanisms for different modes of interaction (synchronous versus asynchronous, allowing work in different times in the same environment), supply mechanisms for customized tools for data visualization, protection, and sharing. By its nature of emphasizing the presence of the users in the VE, VR can provide a powerful mechanism for networked CSCW systems.

Until recently, networked graphics applications were prototype systems, demonstrating the effectiveness of the technology. However, a current effort is to provide real applications, manifested by the 3D graphics interchange standardization efforts such as VRML 2.0 and MPEG-4. The main contributors in these standards are from the industry, which expects to diffuse their application content using these standards.

There have been an increasing interest in the area of NVEs (30–32) recently, and in the following sections, we will describe the most important systems.

State of the Art in NVEs

VEOS

Virtual Environment Operating Shell (VEOS), developed by the University of Washington, was one of the first complete NVE architectures to provide an integrated software to develop general applications. VEOS (33) uses a tightly integrated computing model for management of data, processes, and communication in the operating system level, hiding details from the applications as much as possible.

dVS

dVS, developed by Division Ltd in the United Kingdom (34), is one of the commonly used VE commercial development tools available today. The system aims to provide a modular line for creating and interacting with virtual prototypes of computer-aided design products. The architecture is based on dividing the environment into a number of autonomous entities and processing them in parallel. It is designed to suit a range of different parallel architectures. It supports loosely coupled networks, symmetric multiprocessors, and single-processor systems. An entity represents high-level 3D objects, which encapsulate all the elements of the object.

DIVE

Distributed Interactive Virtual Environment (DIVE) (35,36) was developed at the Swedish Institute of Computer Science. The DIVE system is a toolkit for building distributed VR applications in a heterogeneous network environment. The networking is based on reliable multicast communication, using the ISIS Toolkit (37). DIVE uses peer-to-peer communication to implement shared VEs. The DIVE run-time environment consists of a set of communicating processes, running on nodes distributed within a local area network (LAN) or wide area network (WAN). The processes, representing either human users or autonomous applications, have access to a number of databases, which they update concurrently. Each database contains a number of abstract descriptions of graphical objects that together constitute a VE. Associated with each world is a process group, consisting of all processes that are members of that world. Multicast protocols are used for the communication within such a process group (38).

NPSNET

NPSNET was created at the Naval Postgraduate School in Monterey by Zyda et al. (39). It uses an object- and event-based approach to distributed, interactive virtual worlds for battlefield simulation and training. Virtual worlds consist of objects that interact with each other by broadcasting a series of events. An object initiating an event does not calculate which objects might be affected by it. It is the receiving object's responsibility to determine whether the event is of its interest or not. To minimize communication processing and bandwidth requirements, objects transmit only changes in their behavior. Until an update is received, the new position of a remote object is extrapolated from the states last reported by those objects.

NPSNET can be used to simulate an air, ground, nautical (surface or submersible), or virtual vehicle, as well as human subjects. The standard user interface devices for navigation include a flight-control system (throttle and stick), a SpaceBall, and/or a keyboard. The system models movement on the surface of the Earth (land or sea), below the surface of the sea, and in the atmosphere. Other entities in the simulation are controlled by users on other workstations, who can either be human participants, rule-based autonomous entities, or entities with scripted behavior. The VE is populated not only by users' vehicles/bodies but also by other static and dynamic objects that can produce movements and audio–visual effects. NPSNET succeeds to provide an efficient large-scale networked VE using general-purpose networks and computers and the standard communication protocol, DIS.

MASSIVE

Model, Architecture and System for Spatial Interaction in Virtual Environments (MASSIVE) (40,41) was developed at the University of Nottingham. The main goals of MASSIVE are scalability and heterogeneity [i.e., supporting interaction between users whose equipment has different capabilities and who, therefore, employ radically different styles of user interface (e.g., users on text terminals interacting with users wearing head-mounted displays and magnetic trackers)].

MASSIVE supports multiple virtual worlds connected via portals. Each world may be inhabited by many concurrent users who can interact over ad hoc combinations of graphics, audio, and text interfaces. The graphics interface renders objects visible in a 3D space and allows users to navigate this space with six degrees of freedom. The audio interface allows users to hear objects and supports both real-time conversation and playback of preprogrammed sounds. The text interface provides a plan view of the world via a window (or map) that looks down onto a 2D plane across which users move (similar to Multi-User Dungeons).

SPLINE

Scaleable Platform for Interactive Environments (SPLINE), developed by Mitsubishi Electric Research Labs, is a software platform that allows one to create virtual worlds featuring multiple, simultaneous, geographically separated users, multiple computer simulations interacting with the users, spoken interaction between the users, immersion in a 3D visual and audio environment, and comprehensive run-time modifiability and extendibility. The system's main application theme is social VR, where people interact using their embodiments. An important feature of SPLINE is the support for both prerecorded and real-time audio.

The MERL group, developers of SPLINE (42), have created an application, called *Diamond Park*. The park consists of a square mile of detailed terrain with visual, audio, and physical interaction. The participants navigate around the scene through bicycling, using an exercise bike as physical input device; their embodiment moves on a virtual bicycle with speed calculated from the force exerted on the physical bicycle.

BRICKNET

BRICKNET (43), developed at ISS (Institute of System Sciences, Singapore), is designed for the creation of virtual worlds that operate on workstations connected over a network and share information with each other, forming a loosely coupled system. The BRICKNET toolkit provides functionalities geared toward enabling faster and easier creation of net-worked virtual worlds. It eliminates the need for the developer to learn about low-level graphics, device handling, and network programming by providing higher-level support for graphical, behavioral, and network modeling of virtual worlds. BRICKNET intro-duces an object-sharing strategy which sets it apart from the classic NVE mindset. In-stead of all users sharing the same virtual world, in BRICKNET each user controls his own virtual world with a set of objects of his choice. He can then expose these objects to the others and share them or choose to keep them private. The user can request to share other users' objects providing they are exposed. So, rather than a single shared environment, BRICKNET is a set of "overlapping" user-owned environments that share certain segments as negotiated between the users.

VISTEL

Ohya et al. (44) from ATR Research Lab in Japan propose VISTEL (Virtual Space Teleconferencing System). As the name indicates, the purpose of this system is to extend teleconferencing functionality into a virtual space, where the participants can not only talk to each other and see each other but also collaborate in a 3D environment, sharing 3D objects to enhance their collaboration possibilities. The current system supports only two users and does not attempt to solve problems of network topology, space structuring, or session. The human body motion is extracted using a set of magnetic sensors placed on the user's body. Thus, the limb movements can be captured and transmitted to the receiving end, where they are visualized using an articulated 3D body representation. The facial expressions are captured by tracking facial feature points in the video signal obtained from a camera.

VLNET

Virtual Life Network (VLNET) (45,46) is a general-purpose client–server NVE system using highly realistic virtual humans for user representation. VLNET achieves great ver-satility through its open architecture with a set of interfaces allowing external applica-tions to control the system functionality.

Figure 11 presents a simplified overview of the architecture of a VLNET client. The VLNET core performs all the basic system tasks: networking, rendering, visual database management, and user management including body movement and facial ex-pressions. A body deformation module is integrated in the client core. When actors are animated, each client updates the skin shapes of all visible virtual actors within the client's field-of-view. A set of simple shared-memory interfaces is provided through which external applications can control VLNET. The VLNET drivers also use these

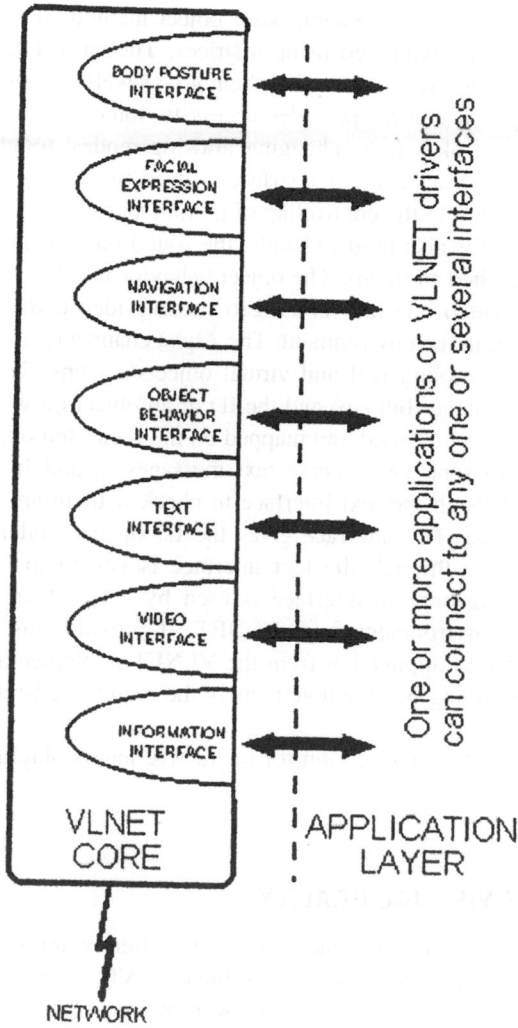

FIGURE 11   Simplified view of VLNET client architecture.

interfaces. The drivers are small service applications provided as part of VLNET system that can be used to solve some standard tasks (e.g., generate walking motion, support navigation devices like mouse, SpaceBall, etc.). The connection of drivers and external applications to VLNET is established dynamically at run time based on the VLNET command line.

The facial expression interface is used to control expressions of the user's face. The expressions are defined using the minimal perceptible actions (MPAs) (47). The MPAs provide a complete set of basic facial actions. By using them it is possible to define any facial expression. The body posture interface controls the motion of the user's body. The postures are defined using a set of joint angles corresponding to 72 degrees of freedom of the skeleton model (48) used in VLNET. The navigation interface is used for navigation, hand and head movement, basic object manipulation, and basic system control. All movements are expressed using matrices. The basic manipulation includes picking objects up, carrying them, and letting them go, as well as grouping and ungrouping of objects. The system control provides access to some system functions that are usually accessed by keystrokes (e.g., changing drawing modes, toggling texturing, displaying statistics). The object behavior interface is used to control the behavior of objects. Currently, it is limited to the controlling of motion and scaling, defined by matrices passed to the interface. It is also used to handle the sound objects (i.e., objects that have prerecorded sounds attached to them). The object behavior interface can be used to trigger these sounds. The video interface is used to stream video texture (as well as static textures) onto any object in the environment. The Alpha channel can be used for blending and achieving effects of mixing real and virtual objects/persons. The interface accepts requests containing the image (bitmap) and the ID of an object on which the image is to be mapped. The image is distributed and mapped on the requested object at all sites. The text interface is used to send and receive text messages to and from other users. An inquiry can be made through the text interface to check if there are any messages, and the messages can be read. The interface gives the ID of the sender for each received message. A message sent through the text interface is passed to all other users in a VLNET session. The information interface is used by external applications to gather information about the environment from VLNET. It provides high-level information while isolating the external application from the VLNET implementation details. It also allows two ways of obtaining information, namely the request-and-reply mechanism and the event mechanism.

Figure 12 shows a VLNET session for interactive tennis playing in a shared environment (49).

APPLICATIONS OF VIRTUAL REALITY

Virtual reality may offer enormous benefits to many different applications areas. This is one main reason why it has attracted so much interest. VR is currently used to explore and manipulate experimental data in ways that were not possible previously.

Operations in Dangerous Environments

There are still many examples of people working in dangerous or hardship environments that could benefit from the use of VR-mediated teleoperation. Workers in radioactive, space, or toxic environments could be relocated to the safety of a VR environment where they could "handle" any hazardous materials without any real danger using teleoperation or telepresence.

Moreover, the operator's display can be augmented with important sensor information, warnings, and suggested procedures. However, teleoperation will be really useful when further developments in haptic feedback is offered.

Scientific Visualization

Scientific visualization provides the researcher with immediate graphical feedback during the course of the computations and gives him the ability to "steer" the solution process. Similarly, by closely coupling the computation and visualization processes, scientific

FIGURE 12 Anyone for tennis: a VLNET session.

visualization provides an exploratory, experimentation environment that allows the investigators to concentrate their efforts on the important areas. VR could bring a lot to scientific visualization by helping to interpret the masses of data.

A typical example of scientific visualization is the NASA Virtual Wind Tunnel at the NASA Ames Research Center. In this application, the computational fluid dynamicist controls the computation of virtual smoke streams emanating from his fingertips. Another application at NASA Ames Research Center is the Virtual Planetary Exploration. It helps planetary geologists to remotely analyze the surface of a planet. They use VR techniques to roam planetary terrains using complex height fields derived from *Viking* images of Mars.

Medicine

Until now, experimental research and education in medicine was mainly based on dissection and study of plastic models. Computerized 3D human models provide a new approach to research and education in medicine. Experimenting medical research with virtual patients will be a reality. We will be able to create not only realistic looking virtual patients but also histological and bone structures. With the simulation of the entire physiology of the human body, the effects of various illnesses or organ replacement will be visible. Virtual humans associated with VR will certainly become one of the medical research tools of the next century.

One of the most promising application is surgery. The surgeon using an HMD and DataGloves may have a complete simulated view, including his hands, of the surgery. The patient should be completely reconstructed in the VE; this requires a very complete graphics human database. For medical students learning how to operate, the best way would be to start with 3D virtual patients and explore virtually all the capabilities of surgery.

By modeling deformation of human muscles and skin, we will gain fundamental insight into these mechanisms from a purely geometric point of view. This has promise of application, for example, in the pathology of skin repair after burning.

One other important medical application of virtual humans is orthopedics. Once a motion is planned for a virtual human, it should be possible to alter or modify a joint and see the impact on the motion.

Rehabilitation and Help to Disable People

It is also possible to create dialogue based on hand gestures (50) such as a dialogue between a *deaf real human* and a *deaf virtual human* using American Sign Language. The real human signs using two DataGloves, and the coordinates are transmitted to the computer. Then, a sign-language recognition program interprets these coordinates in order to recognize gestures. A dialogue coordination program then generates an answer or a new sentence. The sentences are then translated into the hand signs and given to a hand animation program, which generates the appropriate hand positions.

We may also think about using VR techniques to improve the situation of disabled patients after brain injuries. VR may play a supportive role in memory deficiencies, impaired visual–motor performance, or reduced vigilance.

Muscular dystrophy patients can learn to use a wheelchair through VR.

Psychiatry

Another aspect, addressed by Whalley (51), is the use of VR and virtual humans in psychotherapies. Whalley states that VR remains largely at the prototype stage—images are cartoonlike and carry little conviction. However, with the advent of realistic virtual humans, it will be possible to recreate situations in a virtual world, immersing the real patient into virtual scenes, for example, to reunite the patient with a deceased parent or to simulate the patient as a child, allowing him or her to relive situations with familiar surroundings and people.

With a VR-based system, it will be possible in the future to change parameters for simulating some specific behavioral troubles in psychiatry. Therapists may also use VR to treat sufferers of child abuse and people afraid of heights.

Architectural Visualization

In this area, VR allows the future customer to "live" in his a new house before it is built. He could get a feel for the space, experiment with different lighting schemes, furnishings, or even the layout of the house itself. A VR architectural environment *can* provide that feeling of space. Once improved HMDs become available, the VR design environment will offer a serious competitive advantage.

Design

Many areas of design are typically 3D such as the design of a car shape, where the designer looks for sweeping curves and good aesthetics from every possible view. Today's design tools are mouse or stylus/digitizer based and thereby force the designer to work with 2D input devices. For many designers, this is difficult because it forces them to mentally reconstruct the 3D shape from 2D sections. A VR design environment can give to designers appropriate 3D tools.

Education and Training

Virtual reality promises many applications in simulation and training. The most common example is the flight simulator. This type of simulator has shown the benefits of simulation environments for training. They have lower operating costs and are safer to use than real aircraft. They also allow the simulation of dangerous scenarios not allowable with real aircraft. The main problem of current flight simulators is that they cannot be used for another type of training such as submarine training.

Simulation and Ergonomy

Virtual reality is a very powerful tool for simulating new situations, especially to test the efficiency and the ergonomy. For example, we may produce immersive simulation of airports, train stations, metro stations, hospitals, work places, assembly lines, pilot cabins, cockpits, and access to the control panel in vehicles and machines. In this area, the use of virtual humans is essential and simulation of crowds (52) is essential. We may also mention game and sport simulation.

Computer-Supported Cooperative Work

The shared VR environment can also provide additional support for cooperative work. They allow possibly remote workers to collaborate on tasks. However, this type of system requires very high bandwidth networks like an ATM connecting locations and offices. However, it surely saves time and money for organizations. Network VR simulations could enable people in many different locations to participate together in teleconferences, virtual surgical operations, teleshopping (Fig. 13), or simulated military training exercises.

Entertainment

This is the area which starts to drive the development of VR technology. The biggest limiting factor in VR research today is the sheer expense of the technology. It is expen-

FIGURE 13   Collaborative virtual presentation application (using VLNET).

sive because the volumes are low. For entertainment, mass production is required. Another alternative is the development of virtual worlds for lunaparks/casinos.

REFERENCES

1. S. R. Ellis, "Nature and Origin of Virtual Environments: A Bibliographic Essay," *Comput. Syst. Eng.*, *2*(4), 321–347 (1991).

2. P. Astheimer, Dai, M. Göbel, R. Kruse, S. Müller, and G. Zachmann, "Realism in Virtual Reality," in *Artificial Life and Virtual Reality*, N. Magnenat Thalmann and D. Thalmann, eds., John Wiley & Sons, New York, 1994, pp. 189–209.

3. M. Slater and M. Usoh, "Body Centred Interaction in Immersive Virtual Environments," in *Artificial Life and Virtual Reality*, N. Magnenat Thalmann and D. Thalmann, eds., John Wiley & Sons, New York, 1994, pp. 125–147.

4. C. Ware and D. R. Jessome, "Using the Bat: A Six-Dimensional Mouse for Object Placement," *IEEE CGA*, *CGA-8*(6), 65–70, 1988.

5. M. Bergamasco, "Manipulation and Exploration of Virtual Objects," in *Artificial Life and Virtual Reality*, N. Magnenat Thalmann and D. Thalmann, eds., John Wiley & Sons, New York, 1994, pp 149–160.

6. W. Robinett, "Head-Mounted Display Project," in *Proc. Imagina '91*, *INA*, 1991, pp. 5.5–5.6.

7. A. Luciani, "Physical Models in Animation: Towards a Modular and Instrumental Ap-

proach," in *Proc. 2nd Eurographics Workshop on Animation and Simulation*, Swiss Federal Institute of Technology, Lausanne, 1990, pp. G1–G20.

8. M. Minsky, M Ouh-young, O. Steele, F. P. Brooks, Jr., and M. Behensky, "Feeling and Seeing: Issues in Force Display," in *Proceedings 1990 Workshop on Interactive 3-D Graphics*, ACM Press, New York, 1990, pp. 235–243.

9. J. Blauert, "Spatial Hearing, The Psychophysics of Human Sound Localization," MIT Press, Cambridge, 1983.

10. C. Shaw, J. Liang, M. Green, and Y. Sun, "The Decoupled Simulation Model for Virtual Reality Systems," in *Proc. SIGCHI*, 1992, pp. 321–328.

11. A. Borning, R. Duisberg, B. Freeman-Benson, A. Kramer, and M. Woolf, "Constraint Hierarchies," in *Proc. OOPSLA*, 1987, pp. 48–60.

12. D. J. Sturman, "Whole-Hand Input," Ph.D. thesis, MIT (1991).

13. W. A. S. Buxton, "A Three-State Model of Graphical Input," in *Human–Computer Interaction: Proceedings of the IFIP Third International Conference on Human–Computer Interaction*, D. Diaper, D. Gilmore, G. Cockton, and B. Shackel, eds., North-Holland, Oxford, 1990.

14. E. Gobbetti, J. F. Balaguer, and D. Thalmann, "VB2: An Architecture For Interaction In Synthetic Worlds," in *Proc. UIST '93*, ACM Press, New York, 1993.

15. D. E. Rumelhart, G. E. Hinton, and R. J. Williams, "Learning Internal Representations by Error Propagation," in D. E. Rumelhart, and J. L. McClelland, eds., *Parallel Distributed Processing*, Vol. 1, pp. 318–362.

16. P. Maes, T. Darrell, B. Blumberg, and A. Pentland, "The ALIVE System: Full-Body Interaction with Autonomous Agents," in *Proceedings of the Computer Animation '95 Conference, Geneva, Switzerland*, IEEE Press, New York, 1995.

17. T. Molet, R. Boulic, and D. Thalmann, "A Real-Time Anatomical Converter for Human Motion Capture," in *Proc. 7th Eurographics Workshop on Animation and Simulation*, Springer-Verlag, New York, 1996.

18. L. Emering, R. Boulic, and D. Thalmann, "Interacting with Virtual Humans Through Body Actions," *IEEE Computer Graphics Applic. CGA-18*(1), 8–11 (1998).

19. D. B. Conner, S. S. Snibbe, K. P. Herndon, D. C. Robbins, R. C. Zeleznik, and A. Van Dam, "Three-Dimensional Widgets," in *SIGGRAPH Symposium on Interactive 3D Graphics*, 1992, pp. 183–188.

20. C. Shaw and M. Green, "The MR Toolkit Peers Package and Experiment," in *Proc. IEEE Virtual Reality Annual International Symposium*, 1993, pp. 463–469.

21. S. K. Semwal, R. Hightower, and S. Stansfield, "Closed Form and Geometric Algorithms for Real-Time Control of an Avatar," in *Proc. VRAIS 96*, 1996, pp. 177–184.

22. D. Thalmann, "Using Virtual Reality Techniques in the Animation Process," in *Virtual Reality Systems*, R. Earnshaw, M. Gigante, and H. Jones, eds., Academic Press, New York, 1993, pp. 143–159.

23. D. Thalmann, "Virtual Sensors: A Key Tool for the Artificial Life of Virtual Actors," in *Proc. Pacific Graphics '95, Seoul*, 1995, pp. 22–40.

24. O. Renault, N. Magnenat Thalmann, and D. Thalmann, "A Vision-based Approach to Behavioural Animation," *J. Visualiz. Computer Animat.*, *1*(1), 18–21 (1990).

25. H. Noser and D. Thalmann, "Synthetic Vision and Audition for Digital Actors," in *Proc. Eurographics '95*, 1995, pp. 325–336.

26. Z. Huang, R. Boulic, N. Magnenat Thalmann, and D. Thalmann, "A Multi-sensor Approach for Grasping and 3D Interaction," in *Proc. CGI '95*, Academic Press, New York, 1995, pp. 235–254.

27. D. Thalmann, "A New Generation of Synthetic Actors: The Interactive Perceptive Actors," in *Proc. Pacific Graphics '96*, Taipai, 1996, pp. 200–219.

28. I. Pandzic, P. Kalra, N. Magnenat Thalmann, and D. Thalmann, "Real Time Facial Interaction," *Displays*, *15*(3), 157–163 (1994).

29. F. Lavagetto, "Converting Speech into Lip Movements: A Multimedia Telephone for Hard of Hearing People," *IEEE Trans. Rehabilit. Eng.*, *RE-3*(1), 90–102 (1995).

30. D. Zeltzer and M. Johnson, "Virtual Actors and Virtual Environments, Interacting with Virtual Environments," L. MacDonald and J. Vince, eds., 1994.

31. S. Stansfield, "A Distributed Virtual Reality Simulation System for Simulational Training," *Presence: Teleoper. Virtual Environ.*, *3*(4), (1994).

32. M. A. Gisi and C. Sacchi, "Co-CAD: A Collaborative Mechanical CAD System," *Presence: Teleoper. Virtual Environ.*, *3*(4), (1994).

33. W. Bricken and G. Coco, "The VEOS Project," Technical Report R-93-3, Human Interface Technology Laboratory, University of Washington (1993).

34. C. Grimsdale, "dVS—Distributed Virtual Environment System," in *Proc. Computer Graphics '91 Conference*, Blenheim Online, London, 1991.

35. C. Carlsson and O. Hagsand, "DIVE—A Multi-User Virtual Reality System," in *Proc. IEEE Virtual Reality Annual International Symposium* (*VRAIS '93*), Seattle, 1993, pp. 394–400.

36. L. E. Fahlen, O. Stahl, C. G. Brown, and C. Carlsson, "A Space-Based Model for User-Interaction in Shared Synthetic Environments," in *Proc. ACM InterCHI '93*, Amsterdam, 1993, pp. 43–48.

37. K. Birman, R. Cooper, and B. Gleeson, "Programming with Process Groups: Group and Multicast Semantics," Technical Report TR-91-1185, Department of Computer Science, Cornell University (1991).

38. K. Birman, "Maintaining Consistency in Distributed Systems," Technical Report TR91-1240, Department of Computer Science, Cornell University (1991).

39. M. J. Zyda, D. R. Pratt, J. G. Monahan, and K. P. Wilson, "NPSNET: Constructing a 3D Virtual World," in *Proc. 1992 Symposium on Interactive 3D Graphics*, 1992, pp. 147–156.

40. S. Benford, J. Bowers, L. E. Fahlen, C. Greenhalgh, J. Mariani, and T. Rodden, "Networked Virtual Reality and Cooperative Work," *Presence: Teleoper. Virtual Environ.*, *4*(4), 364–386 (1995).

41. C. Greenhalgh and S. Benford, "MASSIVE, A Distributed Virtual Reality System Incorporating Spatial Trading," in *Proc. the 15th International Conference on Distributed Computing Systems*, ACM, Los Alamitos, CA, 1995, pp. 27–34.

42. R. C. Waters, D. B. Anderson, J. W. Barrus, D. C. Brogan, M. C. Casey, S. G. McKeown, T. Nitta, I. B. Sterns, and W. S. Yerazunis, "Diamond Park and Spline: Social Virtual Reality with 3D Animation, Spoken Interaction, and Runtime Extendability," *Presence*, *6*(4), 461–481 (1997).

43. G. Singh, L. Serra, W. Png, A. Wong, and H. Ng, "BrickNet: Sharing Object Behaviors on the Net," *Proc. IEEE VRAIS '95*, 1995, pp. 19–27.

44. J. Ohya, Y. Kitamura, F. Kishino, and N. Terashima, "Virtual Space Teleconferencing: Real-Time Reproduction of 3D Human Images," *J. Visual Commun. Image Represent.*, *6*(1), 1–25 (1995).

45. I. Pandzic, N. Magnenat Thalmann, T. Capin, and D. Thalmann, "Virtual Life Network: A Body-Centered Networked Virtual Environment," *Presence*, *6*(6), 676–686 (1997).

46. T. Capin, I. Pandzic, N. Magnenat Thalmann, and D. Thalmann, "Virtual Human Representation and Communication in the VLNET Networked Virtual Environments," *IEEE Computer Graphics Applic.*, *CGA-17*(2), 42–53 (1997).

47. P. Kalra, A. Mangili, N. Magnenat Thalmann, and D. Thalmann, "Simulation of Facial Muscle Actions Based on Rational Free Form Deformations," in *Proc. Eurographics '92*, Cambridge, 1992, pp. 59–69.

48. R. Boulic, T. Capin, Z. Huang, L. Moccozet, T. Molet, P. Kalra, B. Lintermann, N. Magnenat-Thalmann, I. Pandzic, K. Saar, A. Schmitt, J. Shen, and D. Thalmann, "The HUMAN-OID Environment for Interactive Animation of Multiple Deformable Human Characters," in *Proc. Eurographics '95*, 1995, pp. 337–348.

49. T. Molet, A. Aubel, T. Çapin, S. Carion, E. Lee, N. Magnenat Thalmann, H. Noser, I. Pandzic, G. Sannier, and D. Thalmann, "Anyone for Tennis," *Presence*, 8(2), 1999.

50. U. Broeckl-Fox, L. Kettner, A. Klingert, and L. Kobbelt, "Using Three-Dimensional Hand-Gesture Recognition as a New 3D Input Technique," in *Artificial Life and Virtual Reality*, N. Magnenat Thalmann and D. Thalmann, eds., John Wiley & Sons, New York, 1994.

51. L. J. Whalley, "Ethical Issues in the Application of Virtual Reality to the Treatment of Mental Disorders," in *Virtual Reality Systems*, Earnshaw et al., eds., Academic Press, New York, 1993, pp. 273–288.

52. S. R. Musse and D. Thalmann, "A Model of Human Crowd Behavior," in *Computer Animation and Simulation '97, Proc. Eurographics Workshop, Budapest*, Springer-Verlag, Wien, 1997, pp. 39–51.

NADIA MAGNENAT-THALMANN

DANIEL THALMANN

Printed and bound by CPI Group (UK) Ltd, Croydon, CR0 4YY

17/10/2024

01775659-0016